The Ambiguous Legacy

This timely collection of essays offers one of the first serious efforts to assess the record of American foreign policy over the course of the twentieth century. The essays comprise the work of political scientists as well as historians, conservatives as well as liberals, foreign scholars as well as Americans. Taking off from Henry Luce's vision of an "American century," the authors discuss such important topics as the American conception of the national interest, the tension between democracy and capitalism, the U.S. role in both the developed and underdeveloped worlds, party politics and foreign policy, the significance of race in American foreign relations, and the cultural impact of American diplomacy on the world at large. The result is a lively collection of essays by authors who often disagree but who nonetheless provide the reader with keen insights about the past and provocative views of the future.

MICHAEL J. HOGAN is a professor of history at the Ohio State University and editor of *Diplomatic History*, the journal of record for specialists in American diplomatic history and national security studies. He is the editor of five volumes on aspects of American diplomatic history, including *The End of the Cold War: Its Meaning and Implications* (1992) and *Hiroshima in History and Memory* (1996). He is also the author of *Informal Entente: The Private Structure of Cooperation in Anglo-American Economic Diplomacy, 1918–1928* (1977), of *The Marshall Plan: America, Britain, and the Reconstruction of Western Europe, 1947–1952* (1987), and of *A Cross of Iron: Harry S. Truman and the Origins of the National Security State, 1945–1954* (1998). Mr. Hogan is recipient of numerous fellowships and prizes, including the Quincy Wright Prize of the International Studies Association, the George Louis Beer Prize of the American Historical Association, and the Stuart L. Bernath Prize of the Society for Historians of American Foreign Relations.

See p. 370 – Dosset material.

The Ambiguous Legacy

U.S. Foreign Relations
in the "American Century"

Edited by
MICHAEL J. HOGAN
The Ohio State University

CAMBRIDGE
UNIVERSITY PRESS

PUBLISHED BY THE PRESS SYNDICATE OF THE UNIVERSITY OF CAMBRIDGE
The Pitt Building, Trumpington Street, Cambridge, United Kingdom

CAMBRIDGE UNIVERSITY PRESS
The Edinburgh Building, Cambridge CB2 2RU, UK   http://www.cup.cam.ac.uk
40 West 20th Street, New York, NY 10011-4211, USA   http://www.cup.org
10 Stamford Road, Oakleigh, Melbourne 3166, Australia
Ruiz de Alarcón 13, 28014 Madrid, Spain

© Michael J. Hogan 1999

First published 1999

Printed in the United States of America

Typeface Sabon 11/13 pt.   *System* Adobe PageMaker® 6.5 [AU]

A catalog record for this book is available from the British Library.

Library of Congress Cataloging in Publication data

Ambiguous legacy: U.S. foreign relations in the "American Century" /
edited by Michael J. Hogan.
p. cm.
ISBN 0-521-77019-X (hb). – ISBN 0-521-77977-4 (pb.)
1. United States – Foreign relations – 1945–1989.   2. United States –
Foreign relations – 1989–   3. United States – Foreign
relations – 1945–1989 – Historiography.   4. United States – Foreign
relations – 1989– – Historiography.   I. Hogan, Michael J., 1943– .
E744.A475 1999
327.73 0072 – dc21   99–28048
CIP

ISBN 0 521 77019 X   hardback
ISBN 0 521 77977 4   paperback

For my granddaughter,
Cameron Ann Hogan

Contents

The Authors

VOLKER R. BERGHAHN teaches at Brown University. He has written widely on many subjects in German history and is currently working on the topic of philanthropy.

H. W. BRANDS is professor of history at Texas A&M University. He has written widely on many aspects of American foreign relations. His most recent book is *T.R.: The Last Romantic* (1997).

BRUCE CUMINGS is Norman and Edna Freehling Professor of History at the University of Chicago. He is the author of a two-volume study of *The Origins of the Korean War* and, most recently, of *Parallax Visions: Making Sense of American–East Asian Relations at Century's End* (1999).

GODFREY HODGSON, who has worked as a journalist and as an academic, now teaches at Oxford University. He has written dozens of books, mostly about American politics and twentieth-century history; among them are *America in Our Time* (1976) and *The Colonel* (1990), a biography of Secretary of State Henry L. Stimson. He is currently writing a biography of Daniel Patrick Moynihan.

JOAN HOFF is professor of history and director of the Contemporary History Institute at Ohio University. Harvard University Press will soon publish her *The American Way of Unilateral Internationalism in the Twentieth Century*.

MICHAEL J. HOGAN is professor of history at the Ohio State University and editor of *Diplomatic History*. In addition to editing several volumes on American foreign relations, he is the author of *A Cross of Iron: Harry S. Truman and the Origins of the National Security State, 1945–1954* (1998).

GERALD HORNE is professor and director of the Institute of African-American Research at the University of North Carolina at Chapel Hill.

MICHAEL H. HUNT is Everett H. Emerson Professor of History at the University of North Carolina at Chapel Hill. His most recent books are *The Genesis of Chinese Communist Foreign Policy* (1996), *Lyndon Johnson's War: America's Cold War Crusade in Vietnam, 1945–1968* (1996), and *Crises in U.S. Foreign Policy: An International History Reader* (1996).

AKIRA IRIYE is professor of history at Harvard University. Among his many publications are *Cultural Internationalism and World Order* (1997) and *Japan and the Wider World: From the Mid-Nineteenth Century to the Present* (1997).

ROBERT JERVIS is Adlai E. Stevenson Professor of International Politics at Columbia University. His latest book is *System Effects: Complexity in Political and Social Life* (1997).

ROB KROES, of the University of Amsterdam, is the author of numerous books on American-European cultural relations, and most recently of *If You've Seen One, You've Seen the Mall: Europeans and American Mass Culture* (1996).

WALTER LAFEBER is Noll Professor of American History at Cornell University and president of the Society for Historians of American Foreign Relations. Among his many books is *The Clash: A History of U.S.-Japan Relations* (1997), which recently won the Bancroft Prize.

GEIR LUNDESTAD is director of the Norwegian Nobel Institute and adjunct professor of history at the University of Oslo. He has published numerous books on international relations and American foreign policy, most recently *"Empire" by Integration: The United States and European Integration, 1945–1997* (1998), *No End to Alliance: The United States and Western Europe: Past, Present, Future* (1998), and *East, West, North, South: Major Developments in International Politics, 1945–1998* (4th ed., 1999).

EMILY S. ROSENBERG is DeWitt Wallace Professor of History at Macalester College and specializes in the United States's international economic and cultural interactions. She is past president of the Society for Historians of American Foreign Relations and is currently on the editorial board of the *Journal of American History*. Author of several books and many articles, her forthcoming work from Harvard University Press is titled *Financial Missionaries to the World: The Politics and Culture of Dollar Diplomacy, 1900–1930*.

TONY SMITH is chair of the Department of Political Science and Cornelia M. Jackson Professor at Tufts University. He has published books on Western imperialism, Communist ideology, and U.S. foreign policy. After serving as a fellow at the Woodrow Wilson Center and the Council on Foreign Relations in 1997–98, he is completing a book on ethnic groups and the making of U.S. foreign policy.

REINHOLD WAGNLEITNER is the author of *Coca-Colonization and Cold War: The Cultural Mission of the United States in Austria after the Second World War* (1994) and other works on cultural diplomacy. He teaches at the University of Salzburg.

Acknowledgments

All but one of the essays in this volume first appeared in *Diplomatic History*, the journal of record for historians of American foreign relations. As a new century was about to dawn, it seemed like a good idea for such a journal to evaluate the record of American foreign policy over the last one hundred years. With this goal in mind, I asked a number of leading scholars to address topics they considered significant and to trace them over as much of the twentieth century as possible. The result was a remarkable collection of essays that I decided, with the encouragement of Frank Smith, my editor at Cambridge University Press, to republish for the benefit of a larger audience. The essays have been reedited for this volume and I have also added a new introduction and a contribution of my own.

I am grateful to the authors whose essays appear in the following pages, not only for their thoughtful contributions but also for waiving any claim to the usual republication fees. Instead, these fees will be contributed as royalties from the sale of this book to the Lawrence E. Gelfand-Armin Rappaport Fund of the Society for Historians of American Foreign Relations. I am also indebted to the Ohio State University, especially the College of Humanities, for its ongoing support of my work as editor of *Diplomatic History*, and to the Mershon Center at Ohio State, which has helped to sustain my scholarship and assist my students. Thanks also to Mary Ann Heiss, the journal's associate editor, for her help in the first round of copyediting, and to Kurt Schultz, who reedited the essays and otherwise prepared the volume for publication. Finally, I owe a special debt to Bruce Khula and Nate Citino for their steady assistance with almost every aspect of this enterprise.

Columbus, Ohio   *Michael J. Hogan*
July 1999

Introduction

MICHAEL J. HOGAN

More than fifty years have elapsed since Henry Luce penned his famous editorial on the American Century. The editorial, republished in this volume, urged the American people to accept their destiny and use their influence to remake the world according to their own values. Luce lamented that isolationist attachments had kept the United States from its rightful place in world affairs, although he seemed to understand that current events, notably the wars in Europe and Asia, made continued isolation impossible. The issue was whether American involvement in these struggles would lead to permanent engagement with the world. Would the American people reshape the world in their own image, would the twentieth century be the American century, and would historians look favorably on the American contribution?

The essays that follow wrestle with these and related questions. Written by political scientists as well as historians, by area specialists as well as Americanists, by conservatives as well as liberals, some of the essays deal with the U.S. role in different parts of the world, others with the politics of foreign policy in the United States, and still others with such topics as change and continuity in American foreign policy, the Americanization of world culture, the nature of the modern American empire, American efforts to make the world safe for democracy, and the tension between democracy and capitalism, isolationism and internationalism, in the record of American diplomacy.

Certain issues run through the essays and lend coherence to the volume as a whole. All of the authors seem to agree that American foreign policy had a major influence on the twentieth-century world. They focus on different influences, however, and often reach different conclusions about whether the American contribution was to the good. To be sure, no one dissents from the view that American policy played a pivotal role in the defeat of fascism and communism, nor from the conclusion that the world is a better place without the Nazi and Soviet regimes. Perhaps this is the most that can be said of U.S. policy; perhaps it is all that needs to be said. But most of the authors go on to ask whether American policy was beneficial in other ways, whether the United States did indeed reshape the world in its own image, and to what extent was the American role contested at home and challenged abroad?

Three of the essays concentrate primarily on the thinking behind American foreign policy and on the struggle to control it. H. W. Brands focuses on the core concepts of prosperity, security, and democracy in the American definition of the national interest. Each of these concepts dominated American thinking at different points over the last one hundred years: turn-of-the-century imperialists emphasized prosperity, which they tried to promote through the acquisition of foreign markets; Wilsonians wanted to make the world safe for democracy; and Cold Warriors subordinated everything to their concern for the nation's security. For the most part Brands is critical of American foreign policy in each of these eras, arguing, in effect, that the best policies are those that achieve a reasonable balance between the three core concepts he has identified.

Like Brands, Godfrey Hodgson argues that American foreign policy has been shaped by often competing concepts or impulses. Of the two that he identifies, one stemmed from the frontier experience and looked to U.S. expansion abroad, while the other grew out of the immigrant experience and sought to isolate the United States from a world that was both corrupt and corrupting. The globalization of national economies has rendered isolationism less and less practical, or so Hodgson argues, but isolationist sentiment is still evident in the Republican party, where Luce had located it fifty years ago, and especially in the party's resistance to American interventions abroad, to foreign aid programs, and to the UN, the IMF, and other international organizations. Following a somewhat similar line, my contribution to the volume also traces the relationship between foreign policy and party politics in American history, focusing especially on the twentieth century and on the fear, articulated by American nationalists, that national security policies would undermine the country's democratic traditions and institutions.

The connection between American foreign policy and American life runs through other essays as well, although most of these essays concentrate instead on the way American policy has influenced the world. The rosiest pictures emerge from the provocative essays by Robert Jervis, Geir Lundestad, and Tony Smith. According to Jervis, an American approach to foreign policymaking – one informed by democratic norms – has spread throughout the world and is especially evident in the developed countries that now constitute the American security community. Together with nuclear deterrence, this development has produced a remarkable period of international peace, has reduced or eliminated most major threats to U.S. security, has yielded an international system in concert with American values, and has done all of this and more without serious consequences to American society.

For his part, Lundestad builds on an argument that he pioneered several years ago, and specifically on the notion that America's twentieth-century empire was an "empire by invitation." Moving from Wilsonian diplomacy through the Cold War to the new world order that followed the collapse of the Soviet Union, Lundestad argues that American hegemony was welcomed, even encouraged, by policymaking elites and ordinary people in most parts of the world. Their interests and the interests of the American people corresponded more often than not, so that "when push came to shove" they were likely to side with the United States, as they did in the struggle against communism. The United States was "the partner of choice," concludes Lundestad, who generally downplays any resistance to the American imperium as an exception to the rule, and thus as something that should not always "be taken at face value."

Smith developes a similar argument in celebrating the contribution that Wilsonianism made to the global order of the twentieth century. Luce's editorial, Smith argues, repeated Wilson's call not only for a world made safe for democracy but also for a world made safe by democracy. This was a call that Americans answered, Smith says, partly by using their military muscle to defeat fascism and contain communism but also by giving the world "a distinctively American foreign policy." This policy rested on "more than raw power and the calculations of Realpolitik." It was grounded in the American principles of liberal capitalism and democracy, which, when applied globally, helped to create a "stable," "more humane world order" organized "in a morally positive direction."

For Smith, in other words, the spread of American power led to the spread of American ideals, so that the American empire was not only an empire by invitation but also an empire of liberty. Both Smith and Lundestad see the collapse of the Soviet Union as essentially a victory for democracy over totalitarianism. As a result, the world became a more democratic place and democracy, to a large extent, was a gift of the American people. Robert Jervis advances a somewhat similar argument, as we have seen, as do other contributors to this volume, including Reinhold Wagnleitner and Rob Kroes. Like Lundestad, Wagnleitner believes that most Europeans actually welcomed American influence over the course of the century, particularly the influence of American mass culture. What is more, the spread of American popular culture, of mass markets and mass consumption, had an egalitarian effect on the European countries. It liberated them from "the strait-jackets of traditional customs and mores," argues Wagnleitner, and contributed "positively" to the "democratization" of their societies. Kroes makes a similar point in an essay that focuses on the commodification of American values in modern European advertizing. Over the course of the century, he argues, advertising tended to blend capitalist principles with democratic theory, and thus had "the effect of a civics lesson, if not of a subversive or anti-authoritarian call."

Others are more critical. Walter LaFeber, Joan Hoff, Gerald Horne, and Bruce Cumings are less inclined to draw a positive connection between American foreign policy and American democracy. LaFeber argues that American elites worked consistently to limit popular democracy in the United States. Hoff sees a parallel between the decline of participatory democracy in this country and the American failure to promote human rights around the world. Horne makes the case that democracy had little meaning for large segments of the American population, who often felt that freedom for colored people at home and abroad depended on curbing U.S. foreign policy. Cumings agrees. The major project of American diplomacy, he says, especially after the Great Depression and World War II, was the reconstruction of a global capitalist economy that turned most people of color into victims of a grossly inequitable distribution of resources.

Although Jervis celebrates the absence of superpower conflict and world war during the period of America's postwar leadership, others note the regional conflicts and the record of death and destruction that marked the era of American hegemony. For LaFeber, this record is part of a pattern of American failure, which also includes the failure to promote democratic values around the world – the kind of values that Smith sees at the heart of American foreign policy. Like Cumings, LaFeber views the twentieth century as indeed the American century, but measured only by the spread of market capitalism, not by the spread of democracy. Starting with the acquisition of Cuba and the Philippines at the turn of the century and continuing through the Vietnam War, he says, U.S. efforts to promote democracy were the exception, not the rule, which held instead that democracy had to give way whenever it hampered the spread of market capitalism.

Horne, Michael Hunt, and Joan Hoff reach similar conclusions. For Horne the twentieth century was not the century of democracy but of racial conflict and oppression, beginning with the U.S. subjugation of the Philippines and continuing through the Pacific War, the atomic bombings of Hiroshima and Nagasaki, and the postwar American efforts to bolster colonial and racist regimes in Africa and Asia. But if white supremacy captured U.S. foreign policy, it also encountered resistance, both at home and abroad. Cumings argues that people of color, especially in Asia, often resisted American hegemony. Horne notes the resistance of black nationalists in the United States, who identified with Japan's early challenge to white supremacy in Asia, with those seeking independence from U.S.-supported colonialism after World War II, and with those who opposed U.S. hegemony in the early years of the Cold War. Even at the end of the century, Horne concludes, neither the collapse of the Soviet Union nor the alliance between the United States and Japan could conceal the continuing relevance of race to global politics and diplomacy. On the contrary, the rise to power of Japan and China pointed to a resurgence not a reversal of the racial discourse that marked the American century.

Joan Hoff and Michael Hunt also develop arguments that run in a critical direction. Hoff sees the whole century as marked by the American practice of independent internationalism, by which she means the more-or-less narrow pursuit of national interests by multilateral means if possible, but unilateral means if necessary. This policy did little to promote stability or democracy, argues Hoff, who, like LaFeber, sees American leaders as more committed to market capitalism, and to a conservative version of self-determination, than to democratic principles. American leaders did little to promote social justice globally, she argues, and instead acquiesced in the erosion of national sovereignties and in the spread of an unregulated global capitalism.

For his part, Hunt, like Smith, sees in Luce's editorial an American missionary philosophy similar, no doubt, to the missionary zeal that animated Wilsonian diplomacy and that still inspires many of the non-governmental organizations (NGOs) that Akira Iryie discusses in his contribution to this volume. Like Horne and other critics, however, Hunt does not see much good coming of this philosophy. On the contrary, missionary zeal often drove Americans to the most destructive and undemocratic policies, as was the case in the Philippines and in Vietnam. It also blinded them to the limits of their power, led them to support unpopular dictators, and encouraged them to discount the vision of nationalist elites and the resilience of the Asian masses. Though less critical of the phenomenon than LaFeber and Cumings, Hunt also seems to argue that American capitalism, not American democracy, had the most enduring appeal in Asia, and that democracy took hold there less because of American policy than in spite of it.

Hunt's emphasis on the appeal of American products in Asian markets introduces another important theme that runs through several of the essays in this volume. According to this theme, the American century may not be the result of state policy and geopolitical calculations but of private influences and contributions. As noted earlier, the role of NGOs is the central focus of Akira Iryie's essay, which argues that the American century might best be understood if examined from the perspective of these private groups rather than government authorities. These groups, including education, health, human rights, environmental, and peace groups, gave the century its American character. According to Iryie, they transferred to the world stage a uniquely American experience in voluntary social organization, introduced a moral element into world affairs, and embodied America's values more reliably than its economic power and military might. They also dedicated themselves to developing an international community, and in the process, Iryie argues, kept alive the One World vision that Wilsonians had celebrated and that was threatened by the great geopolitical struggles of the century.

Volker Berghahn takes up a similar theme in his contribution to this volume. Berghahn focuses on private American philanthropical organizations, especially the Ford Foundation, and on the important role they played in breaking down resistance abroad, notably in Europe, to the spread of American technology, industrial organization, and consumer culture. In this sense, the defining aspect of the twentieth century was not the military power of the American state or the geopolitical program of American leaders but the rise of American technological and cultural hegemony, beginning with the Paris World Exhibition in 1900 and continuing through the triumph of Taylorism in the interwar period to the CIA-sponsored Congress of Cultural Freedom in the Cold War.

Berghahn's emphasis on the triumph of American mass culture, especially the culture of mass consumption, reinforces Reinhold Wagnleitner's conclusion that American popular culture, not American military power, won the hearts and minds of the Europeans after World War II and laid the basis for U.S. victory in the Cold War. Indeed, the pervasiveness of American popular culture, of blue jeans and basketball, of jazz music and rock-and-roll, of Hollywood movies and television, represented one of the most important cultural developments of the century. According to Wagnleitner, it promoted the old American vision of One World – or at least of a Pax Americana in popular culture – even though some of its greatest ambassadors, such as black jazz muscians in the 1950s, were denied the rights and privileges of citizenship in the United States.

Emily Rosenberg's essay also takes off on Luce's assertion that American mass culture had become the common currency of the world by 1941. For Rosenberg, too, the twentieth century can be defined in terms of the export of American consumer culture and of the popular images that went with it, especially the tendency in these images to equate mass production and mass consumption with modernization, including the rise of the modern woman. Rosenberg examines these images as evident in mass advertising and commercial exhibits over the course of the century, from the marketing campaign of the American automobile industry after World War I through the famous Kitchen Debate between Khruschchev and Nixon in 1959. She also notes the resistance abroad to American consumer culture and the images that went with it, especially the image of the liberated woman, so that debates about the benefits of Americanization often became debates over gender roles and the status of women.

Rosenberg's emphasis on European opposition to American popular culture is similar in some respects to Hunt's emphasis on how the people of Asia, though intrigued by American mass production, nonetheless managed to Asianize American products and thus resist the victory of American culture. Berghahn and Wagnleitner strike a similar note, as does Rob Kroes. The world has been Americanized, Kroes argues, much as Luce had envisioned, but only in the sense that non-Americans have turned American symbols and values into an international language, detached from its association with the United States, available to people everywhere, and used to suit their own purposes.

Absent in most of these essays is the kind of triumphalism that marked much American popular thought at the end of the Cold War and that we see to some extent in the essays by Smith and Lundestad. Even Smith and Lundestad, however, seem anxious to take the edge off their arguments. Smith notes that Wilsonian principles could sometimes cause problems, such as a polarization of wealth in and among nations, and he cautions against applying these principles in such places as Africa, China, and the Muslim world. Lundestad concedes that the twentieth century witnessed a good deal of uninvited American intervention and seems to admit the high price that others have sometimes paid for American imperialism, in the Philippines, for example, or in Iran, Guatemala, Indonesia, Cuba, Chile, Nicaragua, Panama, Vietnam, and elsewhere.

Although this part of Lundestad's essay sounds more like LaFeber than Smith, he closes on a positive though contentious note about the future of the invited empire. He disputes the notion, popular several years ago, that America's imperial overstretch has undermined its economic might and set the stage for its decline as a global power. On the contrary, he seems to celebrate the dawning of a unipolar age in which Soviet power has collapsed, Japan's economy is in shambles, and the United States, once counted out by its critics, is resurgent as a global economic power and as the only military superpower in the world. Given this setting at the end of the twentieth century, Lundestad apparently sees no reason why the next century should not be the second century of American hegemony. Berghahn shares a similar view, arguing at the close of his essay that the American century is still unfolding, at least in cultural, industrial, and technological terms, while Smith actually urges American leaders to continue to push for a Wilsonian liberalization of the world.

Others are not so sure. Drawing on Walter Lippmann's famous critique of American foreign policy in the early Cold War, my own essay implies that American leaders would be better off following a more realistic and less expansive diplomacy in the new century. Hunt also urges American policymakers to be more cautious, more restrained, and less arrogant in the century ahead. He will not concede that the twentieth century was the American century and even suggests that the twenty-first century could be the century of Asia – the current Asian crisis notwithstanding.

Drawing a somewhat similar conclusion, Horne notes the recent emergence of a racialist nationalism in Asia and wonders if we are already "experiencing the preliminary stages of a 'general crisis of white supremacy'" that will continue in the new century. For LaFeber and Hoff, the crisis has to do with the future of democracy in the twenty-first century. LaFeber implies that democracy faces an uncertain future unless the United States becomes more concerned with its prospects than with the spread of market capitalism, while Hoff predicts an increasingly globalized economy in which the power of democratic governments will give way to that of powerful transnational corporations.

Readers will determine for themselves which of these predictions and recommendations make sense, and which of the essays provide the best assessment of American foreign policy over the last one hundred years. The goal here is to offer a variety of voices by scholars who approach the same general subject from different backgrounds and points of view. Indeed, the different views that follow, whatever their individual shortcomings, lend a certain strength to the volume as a whole. Besides interpretative and ideological diversity, they explore a range of important issues and utilize a variety of methodological approaches. In these and other ways, they may help readers to think about the way historians conceive of their subjects and to reach their own conclusions about American foreign policy over the past century. If this is the case, our authors will have done their jobs very well.

"The American Century"

HENRY R. LUCE

We Americans are unhappy. We are not happy about America. We are not happy about ourselves in relation to America. We are nervous—or gloomy—or apathetic.

As we look out at the rest of the world we are confused; we don't know what to do. "Aid to Britain short of war" is typical of halfway hopes and halfway measures.

As we look toward the future—our own future and the future of other nations—we are filled with foreboding. The future doesn't seem to hold anything for us except conflict, disruption, war.

There is a striking contrast between our state of mind and that of the British people. On Sept. 3, 1939, the first day of the war in England, Winston Churchill had this to say: "Outside the storms of war may blow and the land may be lashed with the fury of its gales, but in our hearts this Sunday morning there is Peace."

Since Mr. Churchill spoke those words the German Luftwaffe has made havoc of British cities, driven the population underground, frightened children from their sleep, and imposed upon everyone a nervous strain as great as any that people have ever endured. Readers of LIFE have seen this havoc unfolded week by week.

Yet close observers agree that when Mr. Churchill spoke of peace in the hearts of the British people he was not indulging in idle oratory. The British people are profoundly calm. There seems to be a complete absence of nervousness. It seems as if all the neuroses of modern life had vanished from England.

In the beginning the British Government made elaborate preparations for an increase in mental breakdowns. But these have actually declined. There have been fewer than a dozen breakdowns reported in London since the air raids began.

The British are calm in their spirit not because they have nothing to worry about but because they are fighting for their lives. They have made that decision. And they have no further choice. All their mistakes of the past 20 years, all the stupidities and failures that they have shared with the rest of the democratic world, are now of the past. They can forget them because they are faced with a supreme task—defending, yard by yard, their island home.

With us it is different. We do not have to face any attack tomorrow or the next day. Yet we are faced with something almost as difficult. We are faced with great decisions.

*   *   *

We know how lucky we are compared to all the rest of mankind. At least two-thirds of us are just plain rich compared to all the rest of the human family—rich in food, rich in clothes, rich in entertainment and amusement, rich in leisure, rich.

And yet we also know that the sickness of the world is also our sickness. We, too, have miserably failed to solve the problems of our epoch. And nowhere in the world have man's failures been so little excusable as in the United States of America. Nowhere has the contrast been so great between the reasonable hopes of our age and the actual facts of failure and frustration. And so now all our failures and mistakes hover like birds of ill omen over the White House, over the Capitol dome and over this printed page. Naturally, we have no peace.

But, even beyond this necessity for living with our own misdeeds, there is another reason why there is no peace in our hearts. It is that we have not been honest with ourselves.

In this whole matter of War and Peace especially, we have been at various times and in various ways false to ourselves, false to each other, false to the facts of history and false to the future.

In this self-deceit our political leaders of all shades of opinion are deeply implicated. Yet we cannot shove the blame off on them. If our leaders have deceived us it is mainly because we ourselves have insisted on being deceived. Their deceitfulness has resulted from our own moral and intellectual confusion. In this confusion, our educators and churchmen and scientists are deeply implicated.

Journalists, too, of course, are implicated. But if Americans are confused it is not for lack of accurate and pertinent information. The American people are by far the best informed people in the history of the world.

The trouble is not with the facts. The trouble is that clear and honest inferences have not been drawn from the facts. The day-to-day present is clear. The issues of tomorrow are befogged.

There is one fundamental issue which faces America as it faces no other nation. It is an issue peculiar to America and peculiar to America in the 20th Century—now. It is deeper even than the immediate issue of War. If America meets it correctly, then, despite hosts of dangers and difficulties, we can look forward and move forward to a future worthy of men, with peace in our hearts.

If we dodge the issue, we shall flounder for ten or 20 or 30 bitter years in a chartless and meaningless series of disasters.

The purpose of this article is to state that issue, and its solution, as candidly and as completely as possible. But first of all let us be completely candid about where we are and how we got there.

AMERICA IS IN THE WAR

. . . But are we in it?

Where are we? We are in the war. All this talk about whether this or that might or might not get us into the war is wasted effort. We are, for a fact, in the war.

If there's one place we Americans did not want to be, it was in the war. We didn't want much to be in any kind of war but, if there was one kind of war we most of all didn't want to be in, it was a European war. Yet, we're in a war, as vicious and bad a war as ever struck this planet, and, along with being worldwide, a European war.

Of course, we are not technically at war, we are not painfully at war, and we may never have to experience the full hell that war can be. Nevertheless the simple statement stands: we are in the war. The irony is that Hitler knows it—and most Americans don't. It may or may not be an advantage to continue diplomatic relations with Germany. But the fact that a German embassy still flourishes in Washington beautifully illustrates the whole mass of deceits and self-deceits in which we have been living.

Perhaps the best way to show ourselves that we are in the war is to consider how we can get out of it. Practically, there's only one way to get out of it and that is by a German victory over England. If England should surrender soon, Germany and America would not start fighting the next day. So we would be out of the war. For a while. Except that Japan might then attack the South Seas and the Philippines. We could abandon the Philippines, abandon Australia and New Zealand, withdraw to Hawaii. And wait. We would be out of the war.

We say we don't want to be in the war. We also say we want England to win. We want Hitler stopped—more than we want to stay out of the war. So, at the moment, we're in.

WE GOT IN VIA DEFENSE
. . . But what are we defending?

Now that we are in this war, how did we get in? We got in on the basis of defense. Even that very word, defense, has been full of deceit and self-deceit.

To the average American the plain meaning of the word defense is defense of the American territory. Is our national policy today limited to the defense of the American homeland by whatever means may seem wise? It is not. We are not in a war to defend American territory. We are in a war to defend and even to promote, encourage and incite so-called democratic principles throughout the world. The average American begins to realize now that that's the kind of war he's in. And he's halfway for it.

But he wonders how he ever got there, since a year ago he had not the slightest intention of getting into any such thing. Well, he can see now how he got there. He got there via "defense."

Behind the doubts in the American mind there were and are two different picture-patterns. One of them stressing the appalling consequences of the fall of England leads us to a war of intervention. As a plain matter of the defense of American territory is that picture necessarily true? It is not necessarily true. For the other picture is roughly this: while it would be much better for us if Hitler were severely checked, nevertheless regardless of what happens in Europe it would be entirely possible for us to organize a defense of the northern part of the Western Hemisphere so that this country could not be successfully attacked. You are familiar with that picture. Is it true or false? No man is qualified to state categorically that it is false. If the entire rest of the world came under the organized domination of evil tyrants, it is quite possible to imagine that this country could make itself such a tough nut to crack that not all the tyrants in the world would care to come against us. And of course there would always be a better than even chance that, like the great Queen Elizabeth, we could play one tyrant off against another. Or, like an infinitely mightier Switzerland, we could live discreetly and dangerously in the midst of enemies. No man can say that that picture of America as an impregnable armed camp is false. No man can honestly say that as a pure matter of defense—defense of our homeland—it is necessary to get into or be in this war.

The question before us then is not primarily one of necessity and survival. It is a question of choice and calculation. The true questions are: Do we want to be in this war? Do we prefer to be in it? And, if so, for what?

WE OBJECT TO BEING IN IT
                            . . . Our fears have a special cause

We are in this war. We can see how we got into it in terms of defense. Now why do we object so strongly to being in it?

There are lots of reasons. First, there is the profound and almost universal aversion to all war—to killing and being killed. But the reason which needs closest inspection, since it is one peculiar to this war and never felt about any previous war, is the fear that if we get into this war, it will be the end of our constitutional democracy. We are all acquainted with the fearful forecast—that some form of dictatorship is required to fight a modern war, that we will certainly go bankrupt, that in the process of war and its aftermath our economy will be largely socialized, that the politicians now in office will seize complete power and never yield it up, and that what with the whole trend toward collectivism, we shall end up in such a total national socialism that any faint semblances of our constitutional American democracy will be totally unrecognizable.

We start into this war with huge Government debt, a vast bureaucracy and a whole generation of young people trained to look to the Government as the source of all life. The Party in power is the one which for long years has been most sympathetic to all manner of socialist doctrines and collectivist trends. The President of the United States has continually reached for more and more power, and he owes his continuation in office today largely to the coming of the war. Thus, the fear that the United States will be driven to a national socialism, as a result of cataclysmic circumstances and contrary to the free will of the American people, is an entirely justifiable fear.

BUT WE WILL WIN IT

. . . The big question is how

So there's the mess—to date. Much more could be said in amplification, in qualification, and in argument. But, however elaborately they might be stated, the sum of the facts about our present position brings us to this point—that the paramount question of this immediate moment is not whether we get into war but how do we win it?

If we are in a war, then it is no little advantage to be aware of the fact. And once we admit to ourselves we are in a war, there is no shadow of doubt that we Americans will be determined to win it—cost what it may in life or treasure.

Whether or not we declare war, whether or not we send expeditionary forces abroad, whether or not we go bankrupt in the process—all these tremendous considerations are matters of strategy and management and are secondary to the overwhelming importance of winning the war.

WHAT ARE WE FIGHTING FOR?
. . . And why we need to know

Having now, with candor, examined our position, it is time to consider, to better purpose than would have been possible before, the larger issue which confronts us. Stated most simply, and in general terms, that issue is: What are we fighting for?

Each of us stands ready to give our life, our wealth, and all our hope of personal happiness, to make sure that America shall not lose any war she is engaged in. But we would like to know what war we are trying to win—and what we are supposed to win when we win it.

This questioning reflects our truest instincts as Americans. But more than that. Our urgent desire to give this war its proper name has a desperate practical importance. If we know what we are fighting for, then we can drive confidently toward a victorious conclusion and, what's more, have at least an even chance of establishing a workable Peace.

Furthermore—and this is an extraordinary and profoundly historical fact which deserves to be examined in detail—America and only America can effectively state the war aims of this war.

Almost every expert will agree that Britain cannot win complete victory—cannot even, in the common saying, "stop Hitler"—without American help. Therefore, even if Britain should from time to time announce war aims, the American people are continually in the position of effectively approving or not approving those aims. On the contrary, if America were to announce war aims, Great Britain would almost certainly accept them. And the entire world including Adolf Hitler would accept them as the gauge of this battle.

Americans have a feeling that in any collaboration with Great Britain we are somehow playing Britain's game and not our own. Whatever sense there may have been in this notion in the past, today it is an ignorant and foolish conception of the situation. In any sort of partnership with the British Empire, Great Britain is perfectly willing that the United States of America should assume the role of senior partner. This has been true for a long time. Among serious Englishmen, the chief complaint against America (and incidentally their best alibi for themselves) has really amounted to this—that America has refused to rise to the opportunities of leadership in the world.

Consider this recent statement of the London *Economist*:

"If any permanent closer association of Britain and the United States is achieved, an island people of less than 50 millions cannot expect to be the senior partner. . . . The center of gravity and the ultimate decision must increasingly lie in America. We cannot resent this historical development. We may rather feel proud that the cycle of dependence, enmity and independence is coming full circle into a new interdependence." We Americans no longer have the alibi that we cannot have things the way we want them so far as Great Britain is concerned. With due regard for the varying problems of the members of the British Commonwealth, what we want will be okay with them.

This holds true even for that inspiring proposal called Union Now—a proposal, made by an American, that Britain and the United States should create a new and larger federal union of peoples. That may not be the right approach to our problem. But no thoughtful American has done his duty by the United States of America until he has read and pondered Clarence Streit's book presenting that proposal.

The big, important point to be made here is simply that the complete opportunity of leadership is ours. Like most great creative opportunities, it is an opportunity enveloped in stupendous difficulties and dangers. If we don't want it, if we refuse to take it, the responsibility of refusal is also ours, and ours alone.

Admittedly, the future of the world cannot be settled all in one piece. It is stupid to try to blueprint the future as you blueprint an engine or as you draw up a constitution for a sorority. But if our trouble is that we don't know what we are fighting for, then it's up to us to figure it out. Don't expect some other country to tell us. Stop this Nazi propaganda about fighting somebody else's war. We fight no wars except our wars. "Arsenal of Democracy?" We may prove to be that. But today we must be the arsenal of America and of the friends and allies of America.

Friends and allies of America? Who are they, and for what? This is for us to tell them.

DONG DANG OR DEMOCRACY
. . . But whose Dong Dang, whose Democracy?

But how can we tell them? And how can we tell ourselves for what purposes we seek allies and for what purposes we fight? Are we going to fight for dear old Danzig or dear old Dong Dang? Are we going to decide the boundaries of Uritania? Or, if we cannot state war aims in terms of vastly distant geography, shall we use some big words like Democracy and Freedom and Justice? Yes, we can use the big words. The President has already used them. And perhaps we had better get used to using them again. Maybe they do mean something—about the future as well as the past.

Some amongst us are likely to be dying for them—on the fields and in the skies of battle. Either that, or the words themselves and what they mean die with us—in our beds.

But is there nothing between the absurd sound of distant cities and the brassy trumpeting of majestic words? And if so, whose Dong Dang and whose Democracy? Is there not something a little more practically satisfying that we can get our teeth into? Is there no sort of understandable program? A program which would be clearly good for America, which would make sense for America—and which at the same time might have the blessing of the Goddess of Democracy and even help somehow to fix up this bothersome matter of Dong Dang?

Is there none such? There is. And so we now come squarely
and closely face to face with the issue which Americans hate most
to face. It is that old, old issue with those old, old battered labels—the issue of Isolationism versus Internationalism.

We detest both words. We spit them at each other with the fury
of hissing geese. We duck and dodge them.

Let us face that issue squarely now. If we face it squarely now—
and if in facing it we take full and fearless account of the realities
of our age—then we shall open the way, not necessarily to peace
in our daily lives but to peace in our hearts.

Life is made up of joy and sorrow, of satisfactions and difficulties. In this time of trouble, we speak of troubles. There are many
troubles. There are troubles in the field of philosophy, in faith
and morals. There are troubles of home and family, of personal
life. All are interrelated but we speak here especially of the troubles
of national policy.

In the field of national policy, the fundamental trouble with
America has been, and is, that whereas their nation became in the
20th Century the most powerful and the most vital nation in the
world, nevertheless Americans were unable to accommodate themselves spiritually and practically to that fact. Hence they have
failed to play their part as a world power—a failure which has
had disastrous consequences for themselves and for all mankind.
And the cure is this: to accept wholeheartedly our duty and our
opportunity as the most powerful and vital nation in the world
and in consequence to exert upon the world the full impact of our
influence, for such purposes as we see fit and by such means as
we see fit.

* * *

"For such purposes as we see fit" leaves entirely open the question of what our purposes may be or how we may appropriately
achieve them. Emphatically our only alternative to isolationism
is not to undertake to police the whole world nor to impose democratic institutions on all mankind including the Dalai Lama and
the good shepherds of Tibet.

America cannot be responsible for the good behavior of the entire world. But America is responsible, to herself as well as to history, for the world-environment in which she lives. Nothing can so vitally affect America's environment as America's own influence upon it, and therefore if America's environment is unfavorable to the growth of American life, then America has nobody to blame so deeply as she must blame herself.

In its failure to grasp this relationship between America and America's environment lies the moral and practical bankruptcy of any and all forms of isolationism. It is most unfortunate that this virus of isolationist sterility has so deeply infected an influential section of the Republican Party. For until the Republican Party can develop a vital philosophy and program for America's initiative and activity as a world power, it will continue to cut itself off from any useful participation in this hour of history. And its participation is deeply needed for the shaping of the future of America and of the world.

* * *

But politically speaking, it is an equally serious fact that for seven years Franklin Roosevelt was, for all practical purposes, a complete isolationist. He was more of an isolationist than Herbert Hoover or Calvin Coolidge. The fact that Franklin Roosevelt has recently emerged as an emergency world leader should not obscure the fact that for seven years his policies ran absolutely counter to any possibility of effective American leadership in international co-operation. There is of course a justification which can be made for the President's first two terms. It can be said, with reason, that great social reforms were necessary in order to bring democracy up-to-date in the greatest of democracies. But the fact is that Franklin Roosevelt failed to make American democracy work successfully on a narrow, materialistic and nationalistic basis. And under Franklin Roosevelt we ourselves have failed to make democracy work successfully. Our only chance now to make it work is in terms of a vital international economy and in terms of an international moral order.

This objective is Franklin Roosevelt's great opportunity to justify his first two terms and to go down in history as the greatest
rather than the last of American Presidents. Our job is to help in
every way we can, for our sakes and our children's sakes, to ensure that Franklin Roosevelt shall be justly hailed as America's
greatest President.

Without our help he cannot be our greatest President. With
our help he can and will be. Under him and with his leadership
we can make isolationism as dead an issue as slavery, and we can
make a truly American internationalism something as natural to
us in our time as the airplane or the radio.

In 1919 we had a golden opportunity, an opportunity unprecedented in all history, to assume the leadership of the world—a
golden opportunity handed to us on the proverbial silver platter.
We did not understand that opportunity. Wilson mishandled it.
We rejected it. The opportunity persisted. We bungled it in the
1920's and in the confusions of the 1930's we killed it.

To lead the world would never have been an easy task. To
revive the hope of that lost opportunity makes the task now infinitely harder than it would have been before. Nevertheless, with
the help of all of us, Roosevelt must succeed where Wilson failed.

THE 20TH CENTURY IS THE AMERICAN CENTURY
. . . Some facts about our time

Consider the 20th Century. It is ours not only in the sense that we
happen to live in it but ours also because it is America's first
century as a dominant power in the world. So far, this century of
ours has been a profound and tragic disappointment. No other
century has been so big with promise for human progress and
happiness. And in no one century have so many men and women
and children suffered such pain and anguish and bitter death.

It is a baffling and difficult and paradoxical century. No doubt
all centuries were paradoxical to those who had to cope with
them. But, like everything else, our paradoxes today are bigger
and better than ever. Yes, better as well as bigger—inherently
better. We have poverty and starvation—but only in the midst of

plenty. We have the biggest wars in the midst of the most wide-spread, the deepest and the most articulate hatred of war in all history. We have tyrannies and dictatorships—but only when democratic idealism, once regarded as the dubious eccentricity of a colonial nation, is the faith of a huge majority of the people of the world.

And ours is also a revolutionary century. The paradoxes make it inevitably revolutionary. Revolutionary, of course, in science and in industry. And also revolutionary, as a corollary in politics and the structure of society. But to say that a revolution is in progress is not to say that the men with either the craziest ideas or the angriest ideas or the most plausible ideas are going to come out on top. The Revolution of 1776 was won and established by men most of whom appear to have been both gentlemen and men of common sense.

Clearly a revolutionary epoch signifies great changes, great adjustments. And this is only one reason why it is really so foolish for people to worry about our "constitutional democracy" without worrying or, better, thinking hard about the world revolution. For only as we go out to meet and solve for our time the problems of the world revolution, can we know how to re-establish our constitutional democracy for another 50 or 100 years.

This 20th Century is baffling, difficult, paradoxical, revolutionary. But by now, at the cost of much pain and many hopes deferred, we know a good deal about it. And we ought to accommodate our outlook to this knowledge so dearly bought. For example, any true conception of our world of the 20th Century must surely include a vivid awareness of at least these four propositions.

First: our world of 2,000,000,000 human beings is for the first time in history one world, fundamentally indivisible. Second: modern man hates war and feels intuitively that, in its present scale and frequency, it may even be fatal to his species. Third: our world, again for the first time in human history, is capable of producing all the material needs of the entire human family. Fourth: the world of the 20th Century, if it is to come to life in any nobility of health and vigor, must be to a significant degree an American Century.

As to the first and second: in postulating the indivisibility of the contemporary world, one does not necessarily imagine that anything like a world state—a parliament of men—must be brought about in this century. Nor need we assume that war can be abolished. All that it is necessary to feel—and to feel deeply—is that terrific forces of magnetic attraction and repulsion will operate as between every large group of human beings on this planet. Large sections of the human family may be effectively organized into opposition to each other. Tyrannies may require a large amount of living space. But Freedom requires and will require far greater living space than Tyranny. Peace cannot endure unless it prevails over a very large part of the world. Justice will come near to losing all meaning in the minds of men unless Justice can have approximately the same fundamental meanings in many lands and among many peoples.

As to the third point—the promise of adequate production for all mankind, the "more abundant life"—be it noted that this is characteristically an American promise. It is a promise easily made, here and elsewhere, by demagogues and proponents of all manner of slick schemes and "planned economies." What we must insist on is that the abundant life is predicated on Freedom—on the Freedom which has created its possibility—on a vision of Freedom under Law. Without Freedom, there will be no abundant life. With Freedom, there can be.

And finally there is the belief—shared let us remember by most men living—that the 20th Century must be to a significant degree an American Century. This knowledge calls us to action now.

AMERICA'S VISION OF OUR WORLD
. . . How it shall be created

What can we say and foresee about an American Century? It is meaningless merely to say that we reject isolationism and accept the logic of internationalism. What internationalism? Rome had a great internationalism. So had the Vatican and Genghis Khan and the Ottoman Turks and the Chinese Emperors and 19th Century England. After the first World War, Lenin had one in mind. Today Hitler seems to have one in mind—one which appeals strongly to some American isolationists whose opinion of Europe is so low that they would gladly hand it over to anyone who would guarantee to destroy it forever. But what internationalism have we Americans to offer?

Ours cannot come out of the vision of any one man. It must be the product of the imaginations of many men. It must be a sharing with all peoples of our Bill of Rights, our Declaration of Independence, our Constitution, our magnificent industrial products, our technical skills. It must be an internationalism of the people, by the people and for the people.

In general, the issues which the American people champion revolve around their determination to make the society of men safe for the freedom, growth and increasing satisfaction of all individual men. Beside that resolve, the sneers, groans, catcalls, teeth-grinding, hisses and roars of the Nazi Propaganda Ministry are of small moment.

Once we cease to distract ourselves with lifeless arguments about isolationism, we shall be amazed to discover that there is already an immense American internationalism. American jazz, Hollywood movies, American slang, American machines and patented products, are in fact the only things that every community in the world, from Zanzibar to Hamburg, recognizes in common. Blindly, unintentionally, accidentally and really in spite of ourselves, we are already a world power in all the trivial ways—in very human ways. But there is a great deal more than that. America is already the intellectual, scientific and artistic capital of the world. Americans—Midwestern Americans—are today the least provincial people in the world. They have traveled the most and they know more about the world than the people of any other country. America's worldwide experience in commerce is also far greater than most of us realize.

Most important of all, we have that indefinable, unmistakable sign of leadership: prestige. And unlike the prestige of Rome or Genghis Khan or 19th Century England, American prestige throughout the world is faith in the good intentions as well as in the ultimate intelligence and ultimate strength of the whole American people. We have lost some of that prestige in the last few years. But most of it is still there.

* * *

No narrow definition can be given to the American internationalism of the 20th Century. It will take shape, as all civilizations take shape, by the living of it, by work and effort, by trial and error, by enterprise and adventure and experience.

And by imagination!

As America enters dynamically upon the world scene, we need most of all to seek and to bring forth a vision of America as a world power which is authentically American and which can inspire us to live and work and fight with vigor and enthusiasm. And as we come now to the great test, it may yet turn out that in all our trials and tribulations of spirit during the first part of this century we as a people have been painfully apprehending the meaning of our time and now in this moment of testing there may come clear at last the vision which will guide us to the authentic creation of the 20th Century—our Century.

* * *

Consider four areas of life and thought in which we may seek to realize such a vision:

First, the economic. It is for America and for America alone to determine whether a system of free economic enterprise—an economic order compatible with freedom and progress—shall or shall not prevail in this century. We know perfectly well that there is not the slightest chance of anything faintly resembling a free economic system prevailing in this country if it prevails nowhere else. What then does America have to decide? Some few decisions are quite simple. For example: we have to decide whether or not we shall have for ourselves and our friends freedom of the seas—the right to go with our ships and our ocean-going airplanes where we wish, when we wish and as we wish. The vision of Americas [*sic*] as the principal guarantor of the freedom of the seas, the vision of America as the dynamic leader of world trade, has within it the possibilities of such enormous human progress as to stagger the imagination. Let us not be staggered by it. Let us rise to its tremendous possibilities. Our thinking of world trade today is on ridiculously small terms. For example, we think of Asia as being worth only a few hundred millions a year to us. Actually, in the decades to come Asia will be worth to us exactly zero—or else it will be worth to us four, five, ten billions of dollars a year. And the latter are the terms we must think in, or else confess a pitiful impotence.

Closely akin to the purely economic area and yet quite different from it, there is the picture of an America which will send out through the world its technical and artistic skills. Engineers, scientists, doctors, movie men, makers of entertainment, developers of airlines, builders of roads, teachers, educators. Throughout the world, these skills, this training, this leadership is needed and will be eagerly welcomed, if only we have the imagination to see it and the sincerity and good will to create the world of the 20th Century.

But now there is a third thing which our vision must immediately be concerned with. We must undertake now to be the Good Samaritan of the entire world. It is the manifest duty of this country to undertake to feed all the people of the world who as a result of this worldwide collapse of civilization are hungry and destitute—all of them, that is, whom we can from time to time reach consistently with a very tough attitude toward all hostile governments. For every dollar we spend on armaments, we should spend at least a dime in a gigantic effort to feed the world—and all the world should know that we have dedicated ourselves to this task. Every farmer in America should be encouraged to produce all the crops he can, and all that we cannot eat—and perhaps some of us could eat less—should forthwith be dispatched to the four quarters of the globe as a free gift, administered by a humanitarian army of Americans, to every man, woman and child on this earth who is really hungry.

* * *

But all this is not enough. All this will fail and none of it will happen unless our vision of America as a world power includes a passionate devotion to great American ideals. We have some things in this country which are infinitely precious and especially American—a love of freedom, a feeling for the equality of opportunity, a tradition of self-reliance and independence and also of co-operation. In addition to ideals and notions which are especially American, we are the inheritors of all the great principles of Western civilization—above all Justice, the love of Truth, the ideal of Charity. The other day Herbert Hoover said that America was fast becoming the sanctuary of the ideals of civilization. For the moment it may be enough to be the sanctuary of these ideals. But not for long. It now becomes our time to be the powerhouse from which the ideals spread throughout the world and do their mysterious work of lifting the life of mankind from the level of the beasts to what the Psalmist called a little lower than the angels.

America as the dynamic center of ever-widening spheres of enterprise, America as the training center of the skillful servants of mankind, America as the Good Samaritan, really believing again that it is more blessed to give than to receive, and America as the powerhouse of the ideals of Freedom and Justice—out of these elements surely can be fashioned a vision of the 20th Century to which we can and will devote ourselves in joy and gladness and vigor and enthusiasm.

Other nations can survive simply because they have endured so long—sometimes with more and sometimes with less significance. But this nation, conceived in adventure and dedicated to the progress of man—this nation cannot truly endure unless there courses strongly through its veins from Maine to California the blood of purposes and enterprise and high resolve.

Throughout the 17th Century and the 18th Century and the 19th Century, this continent teemed with manifold projects and magnificent purposes. Above them all and weaving them all together into the most exciting flag of all the world and of all history was the triumphal purpose of freedom.

It is in this spirit that all of us are called, each to his own measure of capacity, and each in the widest horizon of his vision, to create the first great American Century.

1

Making the World Safe for Democracy in the American Century

TONY SMITH

How can we not be somewhat bothered today by Henry Luce's confident assertion on the eve of America's entry into World War II that the expansion of American power and the consolidation of an "American Century" were sure to contribute to the well-being of all humanity? We know the problems the United States faces domestically in race relations, income distribution, and the power of special interests in Washington. In foreign affairs, we are unsure what to do currently in the face of Islamic fundamentalism, Chinese power, or the ongoing crisis in Russia, aware that our efforts to bring peace to places as presumably open to our influence as Haiti and Cambodia have accomplished precious little. Nor should we forget Vietnam, the actions of the Central Intelligence Agency in Central America, the ease with which we abandoned large parts of Africa to their fate after they served our purposes in the Cold War. And how can we be blind to Luce's failure to recognize American self-interest, camouflaging it as a higher purpose, as if America were the servant of the international collective good – surely a disingenuous pose given the wealth, prestige, and power we now enjoy at the pinnacle of world affairs.

In a word, Luce may have had the good taste to avoid the hyperbole Woodrow Wilson demonstrated when he suggested that the United States was an instrument of the Almighty here below, but his appeal sounds very much like Abraham Lincoln's confident assertion that this country is "the last best hope of earth."

Given the continued disappointments of the American dream at home and an awareness of the mistakes we have made abroad in the past and the challenges we currently face, how can Luce's piece not be seen primarily as a tract for its times, a badly needed patriotic call to gird the loins for war by invoking freedom, justice, the promise of peace, and the American way as necessary partners in humanity's march toward a better tomorrow?

Yet however cautious we should be to avoid triumphalism in the aftermath of the Cold War – a smug self-righteousness that engenders blindness to problems at home and dangerous commitments abroad – we may still recognize that America's victory in the struggles against fascism and communism between 1939 and 1989 (the half century that stretches from the invasion of Poland to the collapse of the Berlin Wall) has resulted for much of the globe in a fundamental reorganization of political power in a morally positive direction. If for the moment democratic government is the only unchallenged form of state legitimacy virtually everywhere in the world, if social questions such as the rights of women and minorities are so widespread on almost everyone's political agenda, if economic questions concerning the relative roles of state and society everywhere have common themes, then surely it is because of the worldwide impact of a philosophical – some might prefer to say an ideological – conviction that mobilized American resolve to win the struggles against fascism and communism, not only on the battlefields but also in the framing of the organizational principles for domestic and international politics to guide world order after the defeat of fascism in 1945 and of communism in 1989. Seen from this perspective, there is much that recommends Luce's statement to us today, two generations after it was first published.

As Luce implies, the reason for America's influence in the twentieth and twenty-first centuries is best understood not simply as a degree of power relative to its competitors, but better as a style of power best summed up as liberal democratic capitalist internationalism. During Wilson's presidency (1913–21), the United States first stepped forth with a blueprint for global stability, one based on four essential principles: that states were best formed on the basis of national, democratic self-determination, that a politically plural world should be open economically, that an anti-imperialist, economically interdependent, politically plural world order needed the creation of a historically unprecedented set of international organizations with a primary responsibility to keep the peace, and that it was absolutely essential to have full-scale American involvement in world affairs in order to make these other ambitions workable.[1]

Of course, none of these ideas could have been known by Wilson at the time to lead to the kind of American-inspired world order we see today. Indeed, none of these proposals turned out to have much practical relevance to the world of the interwar years, faced as it was by the Depression and the international spread of communism and fascism as well as by an American leadership unable to define a role for the country in such circumstances.

Yet under Franklin Roosevelt and Harry Truman the Bretton Woods System and United Nations were created, Germany and Japan were democratized politically and liberalized economically, and the Marshall Plan and the North Atlantic Treaty Organization were all brought into being. Here was the sowing of liberal seeds for a harvest to be collected more than a generation later as the economic and alliance-building initiatives of the United States outstripped the Soviet competition. And in all these respects, the essential inspiration was pure Wilsonianism.

Why has an appreciation of the strength of Wilsonianism as expressed in American foreign policy since 1944, when the Bretton Woods meeting occurred, been so rare? The irrelevance of these ideas in the interwar period speaks for itself. Later, during the Cold War, observers may perhaps be excused for failing to give due attention to the liberal character of America because so often the demands of the contest with the Soviet Union seemed to make liberalism little more than a fig leaf concealing a struggle Washington was conducting on the grounds of realpolitik. Thus, the way in which the Cold War turned hot on the periphery – in

---

1   Tony Smith, *America's Mission: The United States and the Worldwide Struggle for Democracy in the Twentieth Century* (Princeton, 1994), chaps. 3–4.

Northeast and Southeast Asia, in Central America, and in parts of Africa, where power vacuums were most common – had the logic of "the great game" wherein the superpowers sparred with one another by using pawns in areas of only marginal importance to themselves to score points against each other. The willingness of Washington to work with authoritarian leaders in almost any part of the world, even if it involved abandoning constitutional (incipiently democratizing) forces to their fate, made it difficult to accept the association Henry Luce saw between the expansion of American power and the growth of freedom and justice abroad. So, too, the nuclear arms race had a logic to it quite independent of ideology, one that in key respects drove the competition regardless of the hopes of the adversaries.

As a consequence of these realities, many major American thinkers were not predisposed to look favorably on Wilsonianism as the guiding light of American foreign policy. On the left, the ruthlessness Washington could display in Guatemala, Iran, or Vietnam bred profound skepticism of the American rhetorical commitment to promoting democracy abroad as the Cold War intensified. Indeed, to the radical left, democracy promotion was transparent posturing done for nothing more than the sake of advancing the interests of international capitalism.

Meanwhile, beyond the leftist scholars, the tradition of realism as a doctrine of foreign affairs had taken hold among most of the intellectual and official elite of the country. According to the central tenets of realism as articulated by men as influential as George Kennan, Reinhold Niebuhr, and Walter Lippmann, Wilsonianism was "idealism," "moralism," or "utopianism," a faulty approach to the conduct of foreign affairs best explained by American religiosity, the country's founding based on liberal ideology, and its historical innocence as a nation never greatly threatened by powerful foes. In recent years, the major exponent of this argument has been Henry Kissinger. For these men, then, as for American leftists, the idea that aspects of Wilsonianism such as promoting democracy abroad could be in the American national interest was seen as largely nonsense, an ideological smokescreen useful to rally the public around the flag and to justify to a world audience what the United States was doing in terms of some widely accepted standard. But as an end in itself, the goal of promoting democracy abroad was not a notion to be taken seriously (indeed, if it were, grave negative consequences might flow for American interests in the world).

American leftists and realists were backed up by scholars of comparative politics. Since the late nineteenth century, this school of analysis has viewed states and peoples as largely self-contained dynamic entities. While comparativists concluded that there certainly might be defensive or imitative reactions to foreign challenges (one thinks of the work of Alexander Gerschenkron, Otto Hintze, or Barrington Moore, for example), peoples and states are like cultures and civilizations, generally best understood in their own terms. An ambition like that of Wilsonianism to reshape these peoples according to foreign design was thus likely to fail and so was not an ambition to be taken seriously.

I do not want to be understood as saying that these various criticisms of Wilsonianism are without merit. As we shall see later, liberalism still has decided limits today in how it can serve as a framework for American foreign policy. Rather, the point is that for all these wise men no particular worth at all was seen in Wilsonianism, which indeed became something of a textbook example of how American foreign policy should not be run. But with dramatic changes in the times come dramatic changes in thinking. After the Cold War, it became apparent that distinctive aspects of the character of American power had been insufficiently appreciated, aspects that insured economic strength, alliance unity, and American resolve – aspects that drew their character from the country's liberal internationalism. Much more than raw power and the calculations of realpolitik had made for American success.

The road to understanding American power in world affairs at the end of the century necessarily led back to Wilson. "To make the world safe for democracy," Wilson's war aim in 1917, was in critical ways to try to remake world order in line with distinctively American values, institutions, and interests. The United States was not simply powerful, it would not just "muddle through" the twentieth century, so much as it should be possessed of a dynamic character that gave it purpose and direction in a world filled with deadly challenge. As the century draws to a close with the preeminence not only of the United States over Germany and Russia, but especially of liberal democratic internationalism over fascism and communism, the question rightly arises of what made American power distinctive in world affairs.[2]

The Origins of American Liberal Democratic Internationalism

To take liberalism seriously is to take seriously the notion that ideas on the proper organization and use of power make history. Of course, ideas do not act by themselves; they are expressions of values and interests based on emotion, experience, and struggle that are politically operationalized. But as people live in community, and as community in turn requires organizing concepts so as to acquire stability and purpose, so ideas come to express and direct the way a people will live domestically and in their foreign relations.

In understanding the force of American liberal internationalism it must be stressed that such thinking represents not simply an ideological predisposition on the part of the United States – the country's religiosity, for example, and an elite's use of this predisposition to rally the population for involvements abroad – but much more importantly that it represents an expression of the organization of domestic American forces with respect to foreign affairs. Wilson may have been the first American president to articulate a coherent liberal vision, and FDR and Truman may have been the first presidents to give lasting institutional shape to these ideas, but most of the essential elements of such a grand design existed in more embryonic form at an earlier time.

Let us consider first the relationship between the history of American economic interests and liberal ideas for world order.

---

2   See G. John Ikenberry, "The Myth of Post-Cold War Chaos," *Foreign Affairs* 75 (May/June 1996): 75–91; Thomas Risse-Kappen, *Cooperation Among Democracies: The European Influence on U.S. Foreign Policy* (Princeton, 1995); and John Gerard Ruggie, *Winning the Peace: America and World Order in the New Era* (New York, 1996).

Twentieth-century American liberal economic internationalism reflected this country's origin in a Revolution determined to end the yoke of mercantilism on the American people. The Monroe Doctrine of 1823 and the Open Door Notes relative to China at the turn of this century confirmed the American orientation by asserting that the United States sought no special privileges in economic matters abroad; rather, it expected to be treated equally with all other states in commercial transactions. It was only under FDR and Secretary of State Cordell Hull that Washington began to attack protectionism in favor of an integrated global market such as we see trying to develop today, but the continuity with an earlier time should be readily apparent in an American attempt to depoliticize international economic relations in the expectation that in these circumstances American interests were most likely to be promoted.

To be liberal in international economic questions was implicitly to be anti-imperialist and pro-nationalist on political questions. In the late nineteenth century, imperialist powers like France or Japan looked to create spheres of influence for themselves abroad as an extension of national economic programs. Accordingly, nationalist movements in Latin America or China resisted these efforts, in the process associating themselves with an Anglo-American design for the international economic order that encouraged most-favored-nation treaties and the depoliticization of commercial intercourse among peoples.

A second ingredient in America's liberal program for world order has been its domestic political system. On the one hand, the incorporation of large numbers of foreign peoples to American ways always seemed inherently difficult. Thus, neither Mexico after 1848, nor the Philippines or Cuba after 1898, seemed attractive lands for annexation given that their inhabitants were numerous, poor, dark-skinned, and Catholic. On the other hand, democratic life, with its belief in national self-determination, has provided little justification for ruling over foreign peoples, unless it is to prepare them for democratic self-government. As a result of these various considerations, the United States showed relatively little interest in direct imperialism with its requirement of long-term domination of foreign peoples, preferring instead to take areas where population was sparse (as in Hawaii and the territories taken from Mexico) or to assure a conquered people that they would eventually be independent (as in the Philippines). In short, as a liberal democracy, the United States found direct imperial rule inherently distasteful.

A third idea basic to American liberal internationalism was that militarism was a poor way to settle conflicts. The Founding Fathers opposed the creation of a standing militia, fearful that such a force could be used by unscrupulous leaders to tyrannize the citizenry. Accordingly, at the time of the Spanish-American War, this country had fewer than forty thousand men in arms in the navy and army combined. To be sure, in the twentieth century, American democrats found that constitutional civilian control over the military was not a problem. Nevertheless, under Wilson, Washington for the first time began to look forward to schemes of collective security and peacekeeping that would dampen armed aggression by creating multilateral institutions capable of negotiating resolution even to serious conflicts among states. Of course, such measures served American interests too, for protected by mighty oceans and weak neighbors, this country had little to fear, while the partial disarmament of its potential competitors increased its own relative power. In conjunction, then, with a commitment to an open international economic system and a bias in favor of a politically plural world order, the efforts to establish multilateral peacekeeping institutions later emerged as hallmarks of American liberal internationalism.

The genius of Woodrow Wilson was that he for the first time put these various ideas into a single program to promote national security and linked them to two other liberal notions: that democratic states would be the most stable form of nationalist government likely to cooperate with the United States in its economic and organizational reworking of world affairs, and that America itself must play a leadership role in seeing that the three pillars of liberalism – economic openness, democratic government, and viable multilateral organizations – maintained themselves as dominant aspects of world order.

For economic, political, and strategic reasons, then (and not only because of religiosity and innocence as liberalism's critics would have it), Washington defined its national security in opposition to a world order based on formal imperialism. In the nineteenth century, through the Monroe Doctrine and the Open Door Notes, it worked with small-power nationalism to create politically plural regions in Latin America and Northeast Asia. At Versailles, Wilson "globalized the Monroe Doctrine" (as he put it) to dismantle the Russian, Ottoman, and Austro-Hungarian empires along lines of national self-determination. But he went beyond the Monroe Doctrine by suggesting that through democratic government and multilateral institutions a politically plural world might find stability. During World War II, FDR followed suit when he came out against the expansion of Soviet control in Eastern Europe and for the end of European empires in Africa and Asia, associating these states for stability in ways that Wilson first indicated. With the Cold War, the United States continued to champion the independence of East European peoples, and in the event saw that the principle of democratic national self-determination could lead to the disintegration of the Soviet Union itself.

In short, the function of liberal internationalism was to increase American national security by trying to organize world affairs in a way that corresponded to the needs of domestic American economic, political, and cultural interests. Its ideological base was neither innocence nor religiosity, as its critics like to allege, so much as the conceptual outcome of the play of domestic values, interests, and institutions over a long period of American national life. The result was a distinctively American foreign policy, one informed, to be sure, by concerns other than liberalism, but wherein a particular ideological construct based on deep domestic roots determined a good measure of how America acted in the world.

The Appeal of American Liberalism

America's liberal ambitions alone would have been of little moment had international forces not been receptive in many ways to the American appeal. To see the world as responding like malleable clay to the liberal democratic, capitalist vision of U.S. leadership would be quite mistaken. Indirect imperialism of the American sort can only be effective when foreign peoples lend themselves root and branch, and for their own reasons, to the design of the imperial center. For this transformation to occur suggests that a sea-change in political relations was afoot globally as the twentieth century opened.

Henry Luce correctly calls the American Century a "revolutionary century," presumably recognizing thereby that the globe had been in ferment for some two centuries by the time he wrote as new forms of government, sociocultural relations, and the ideas that expressed them all swept the world. Since the late eighteenth century, the combined forces of the American, French, and Industrial revolutions had engendered what can fairly be called "the crisis of modernity" for governmental systems the world around. The spread of Enlightenment thinking, combined with new ways of doing things economically, had intersected with the development of political forces at the local and national level in a variety of countries in northern Europe and North America in such a fashion that wholly new ideas about the proper organization of the state and its relationship with society began to gain in strength.

On the local and international level, modern nationalism appeared for the first time with its demands that an increasingly politically participatory people had a right to a government in harmony with the character of those it governed. The result was to shift ideas about the legitimacy of the state and the basis of citizenship so that the autocratic and imperial rule most of the world had known for thousands of years became progressively harder to sustain. By the early nineteenth century, nationalism as a political force had moved from northern Europe and North America to Latin America; by mid-century it had inspired "the springtime of nations" in Eastern Europe and had reached Turkey and Japan. By the end of the century, it was important in China and Russia.

In the twentieth century, nationalism was a leading factor behind the horror of World War I, and it helped to determine the shape and fate of the peace that followed. Bolshevism presented itself as a form of nationalism exceeded in militaristic ambitions only by fascism. World War II weakened the British, French, and Dutch colonial empires, encouraging nationalist forces in South and Southeast Asia and in Africa. When the Soviet empire and then the Soviet Union imploded between 1989 and 1991, a leading cause was Moscow's inability to satisfy the nationalist demands of those it governed.

Powerful as it was, nationalism proved more a solvent of traditional authority than a builder of modern states. Nationalism might undermine authoritarian monarchies and great empires, but aside from recognizing that the state needed to be in contact with the citizenry through some form of political party system, it was typically unsure how then to construct a government and to organize a people. New definitions of state legitimacy and the rights and obligations of citizenship needed to be accepted; a highly contentious ideological age was sure to be the result.

Here, then, was the historical and international basis of the appeal of Woodrow Wilson's proposition that democratic national self-determination, economic openness, and cooperation in international institutions could provide the basis for world order after 1918. The problem, of course, was that Wilson's vision appeared foreign to many and was challenged at the time by the Bolshevik Revolution and shortly thereafter by Mussolini's March on Rome. The result was a three-sided contest to overcome the crisis of modernity with a new form of government linking the state to the people in ways radically different from what had ever existed before.

Both communism and fascism were like liberal democracy in that they too could appeal to nationalist forces on the basis of having a blueprint for the proper organization of the state and the character of its relations with the people. Fascism appealed to traditional elites threatened by the rising tide of mass participation, promising to organize the populace – conceived of as a racially based nation – through a single party led by a charismatic figure. Its major focus was on combating communism, hence its appeals to that part of "the masses" who were not working class,

[handwritten marginal note:] Didn't present this conclusion well.

but instead who tended to be religious and who might find in chauvinistic appeals some relief from the strains of modern social and economic life.

It is too often assumed that fascism was essentially an irrational doctrine whose militarism was its only important characteristic. Yet because fascism exalted the traditions of the nation and because it was explicitly corporatist (that is, it claimed to respect the rights of different sectors of the population so long as they respected their obligations to the state), it could appeal to a wide range of social forces, from those that were established and traditional to those newly created by economic and social change. Whatever their differences (and they were many), fascist movements could be found not only in Italy, Germany, and Japan, but in virtually all the countries of Europe and in parts of Latin America and the Middle East as well. Its appeal is not dead even today.[3]

As another answer to the crisis of modernity, communism's blueprint for national and international order had some similarities with fascism. In each case, a charismatic leader presided over a single party that attempted to make a specific form of government and civic organization the proper expression of popular nationalism. So Lenin addressed the Soviet people, as Mao did the Chinese, exalting a particular form of "the dictatorship of the proletariat." In each case (and wherever else communism was found), there was a sustained effort to make the appeal of nationalism lead directly to a Communist form of social and state organization.[4]

In short order, communism also became an international movement embodied in a variety of national forms, although one far more tightly controlled by Moscow through the International than anything Berlin, Rome, or Tokyo was able to achieve. Communism was most unlike fascism, however, in that it opposed the traditional political establishment (including religious authorities, monarchies, the landed gentry, and the captains of industry), appealed explicitly to the most economically marginalized sectors

---

3   Walter Laqueur, *Fascism: Past, Present, Future* (New York, 1997).
4   Tony Smith, *Thinking Like a Communist: State and Legitimacy in the Soviet Union, China, and Cuba* (New York, 1987).

of the population, and (in principle at least) denounced chauvinism, racism, imperialism, and militarism as legitimate expressions of nationalist identity.

During the interwar years, the three-way contest among communism, fascism, and liberal democracy inspired little confidence that the latter would be the ultimate victor. By virtue of their dogmatic ideologies backed up by ruthless party controls over the population complemented by state economic planning, determined fascist and Communist governments and movements raised questions as to how liberal democracies, with the freedom they granted not only for diversity but also for divisiveness, could hope to survive. Democracies at the time appeared weakened by their multiple parties, divided governments, contentious class and ethnic divisions, legalistic proceduralism, and cultural permissiveness. As the Spanish Civil War demonstrated in the 1930s, fascism and communism were ready for protracted struggle; by contrast the liberal democracies were busy looking for ways to avoid war whatever the cost. It was difficult during these terrible years to believe that the future belonged to polities typified by social openness, political competition, and the rule of law.

Seen from the perspective of the struggle among ideologies to best represent interests thrown up by the demands of nationalism and the need for political modernization, the defeat of fascism in 1945 was not so much the triumph of Russia and the United States over Germany and Japan as it was the destruction of fascism as a modern state-building ideology. But the victory settled little between what continued to be two rival forms of state/society organization in an era of nationalism – communism and liberal democracy. Of course, there was some prospect of accommodation between the two forces and the states that represented them (an understanding that fortunately was reached in nuclear weaponry), and the struggle that ultimately engulfed them was, like any conflict, one in which the actual ideological character of the combatants was not always terribly apparent. Still, each side represented operational codes for the organization of state and society that in fundamental respects appeared radically incompatible with one another and that were quite likely to create serious local and international competition.

As this account suggests, given the role of ideology in international political contests, the twentieth century might well be called a time of wars of religion. For while material power, and individual and group self-interest, were obviously essential ingredients in the century's principal struggles, these forces had to be ideologically expressed in ways that gave political movements cohesion and purpose. While the role of ideas may be apparent in any epoch, in the twentieth century they had particular importance given the new basis of state power that ideology had to labor to create. In any period, the political object of struggle is to determine who rules. In this century, the question has been the far more momentous one of how rule would be structured. Can we believe that the world would be anything like the way it is today had either fascism or communism turned out to the dominant form of political organization the world around? Luce was right to answer this question without hesitation.

The Continued Importance of the Wilsonian Message

But, one may ask, why should the United States assume that the spread of the values and institutions it cherishes at home should be beneficial for this country's national security and world order in general? According to realism, for example, the dominant school of international relations theory in the United States over the last half-century, whatever the character of government, one should expect no dramatic change in the logic of world affairs so long as the essential state of nature, or anarchy, prevails. To be sure, American hegemony may make a difference to the character of this country's security. But even if we engage in humanitarian interventions to prevent famines or genocides, we should not suppose that what appears to us to be morally desirable – the spread of democratic government, for example – will necessarily have much of a practical payoff for the United States.

Yet a growing literature now suggests that this realist approach to American foreign policy is badly mistaken. As Woodrow Wilson suspected, democratic nations are indeed likely to be much more peaceful with one another than with authoritarian states; they are more likely to form enduring alliances with each other to fend off common threats; and they are likely to be better trading partners and so participate in increasing the general prosperity. Put differently, there is a strong case to be made for "national security liberalism," a term that to realists would seem an oxymoron.[5]

Hence, for example, when the United States promoted democratic government in Germany and Japan after 1945, it lay the foundations for America's eventual victory in the struggle against the Soviet Union. Without Germany as a democratic nation with a liberalized economy, how likely is it that European integration could have advanced as far as it has, providing the assistance it did for Washington during its contest with Moscow? And how reliable would this new Germany be now had it not been for the serious efforts the United States undertook after 1945 to make this country democratic and liberal, and to integrate it on these terms with its European neighbors?

As the case of Germany suggests, Wilsonianism has proved its importance to American foreign policy. It has sponsored the largest expansion of international trade and investment in history under guidelines first established by Great Britain in the nineteenth century but implemented by the United States in the twentieth. It has sponsored the longest and largest voluntary security alliance in world history. Today NATO is expanding and redefining its role from one of deterrence of a common enemy to one of collective security designed to maintain the peace among a group of allies who are alike in having democratic governments. It has proved capable of providing legitimate, stable government for those who live in democratic polities. Whatever liberal democracy's continued shortcomings, those who live under such systems feel that it has proved more capable of providing freedom and justice to its inhabitants than any other system in history.

5   Michael E. Brown et al., *Debating the Democratic Peace* (Boston, 1996); Miriam Fendius Elman, ed., *Paths to Peace: Is Democracy the Answer?* (Boston, 1997); and Zeev Maoz, "The Controversy over the Democratic Peace: Rearguard Action or Cracks in the Wall?" *International Security* 22 (Summer 1997): 162–98.

The 1990s is a postwar period, and Americans must ask themselves, as they did after 1918 and after 1945, what they must do to win the peace now that they have won the war. As in times past, the Wilsonian design rather automatically suggests itself. Perhaps the Bush administration lacked "the vision thing" (as Bush put it), but its concept of a "new world order" was essentially Wilsonian, just as was the Clinton administration's decision to replace "the containment of communism with the enlargement of democracy." In due course, Clinton and Bush found, as others had before them, that liberal democratic internationalism was far from a fully adequate set of answers as to how to defend America's interests in the world, yet it was nonetheless the vital center of America's long-term hopes for world order on its terms. As Secretary of State Madeleine Albright put it on the eve of President Clinton's departure for Africa in March 1998, "It is not only the right thing to do, it is the smart thing to do."

The Limitation of Wilsonianism

The effort to promote democracy abroad for the sake of American national security runs into two sets of problems today, much the same serious obstacles it has confronted throughout the century. One of these has to do with the irrelevance of trying to convert some parts of the world to these values and institutions when anarchy or ancient cultures resistant to this kind of evolution are firmly established political realities. The second has to do with the contradictions of liberal democratic internationalism itself, problems created by the very operation of a Wilsonian system. Liberals would be well advised to consider these limitations carefully.

In the past, certain countries and regions resisted outside efforts to change them. For example, the ruling elites of Russia, Japan, and Germany were determined in the nineteenth and early twentieth centuries that their defensive modernization not mean that they lose their national souls to Western ways. A century later, despite democracy's gains, its prospects are dim in situations of anarchy – such as typifies much of Africa, the Caucasus, and the Balkans – and also where proud and ancient civilizations stand determined that Westernization shall not be their fate. Iran (along with Islamic fundamentalists elsewhere), China (home of "Asian values"), and Africans who talk again about "African solutions to African problems" – all are possessed of powerful nationalist elements (like those of Russia, Germany, and Japan a century ago) determined to avoid incorporation into foreign ways originating in the United States.

In the face of such obstacles to democratization, Washington and its allies must know how to cooperate for the sake of mutual advantage with governments quite unlike themselves. Liberals especially need to understand what realists more readily admit: that at times one must sup with the Devil, and that at other times one must learn to respect the ways of non-democratic peoples with the realization that the democracies themselves have many problems that other peoples have learned how to avoid. One may at times applaud the efforts of the Agency for International Development or of non-governmental organizations (NGOs) like the National Endowment for Democracy, Human Rights Watch, Freedom House, or Amnesty International without for a moment assuming that what these groups want for American foreign policy would always and everywhere be prudent for Washington to endorse. What liberalism must avoid are self-righteous, quixotic crusades that further neither the interests of the world's democracies nor those of peoples in other regions.[6]

In today's world, these observations suggest that we should be bullish on promoting democracy in Latin America, Eastern Europe, and a scattering of other places (such as South Korea and South Africa) where the ground is prepared for such an evolution. But in most of Africa, the Muslim world, and China, we would be better advised to be bearish, remembering the limits of our influ-

---

6 Samuel P. Huntington, *The Third Wave: Democratization in the Late Twentieth Century* (Norman, 1991) chap. 5; Thomas Carothers, "Democracy without Illusions," *Foreign Affairs* 76 (January/February 1997): 85–99; Strobe Talbott, "Democracy and the National Interest," *Foreign Affairs* 75 (November/December 1996): 47–63; and Fareed Zakaria, "The Rise of Illiberal Democracy," *Foreign Affairs* 76 (November/December 1997): 22–43.

ence, the vulnerability of our interests, and the virtues of restraint and mutual tolerance.

Even where prospects for democratization appear to be relatively strong, it may not be evident how best to proceed – as the failure to assure democracy in countries like Haiti and Cambodia shows us today. Suggestive at times, the "democratic transition" literature nonetheless is woefully incomplete. If civil society is strengthened at the expense of the state, then there may be a war of all against all (as happened in both Rwanda and Algeria after their democratic openings), especially in the context of multiethnic societies. If the economy is privatized, a lack of rules and regulatory agency may cause a dramatic increase in corruption and the emergence of national mafias, meaning that some may gain handsomely while others lose terribly at the very moment the state as an intermediary among social forces loses in power – a situation typified today by conditions in Russia. Or again, those social forces standing to lose from increased popular political participation may seize power in the name of militaristic, nationalistic slogans reminiscent of fascism – such as now in Serbia and Croatia.

Despite these cautions, outsiders do have several levers of influence which are far more developed than they were at earlier points in the century. NGOs are one leading force for change in many parts of the world. Another is through economic mechanisms, including the International Monetary Fund (IMF), the World Bank, and the World Trade Organization, not to speak of the importance of private financial, investing, and trading agencies in the United States, Canada, the European Union, Japan, and Australia.[7]

Of course, these agencies may cause problems when they involve themselves recklessly abroad, and after the Southeast Asian crisis broke late in 1997, many voices were heard saying that political conditionality should be introduced alongside economic regulations, perhaps involving the creation of a new international

---

7   Graham T. Allison Jr., and Robert P. Beschel, Jr., "Can the United States Promote Democracy?" *Political Science Quarterly* 107, no. 1 (1992): 81–98; and Larry Diamond, *Promoting Democracy in the 1990s: Actors and Instruments, Issues and Imperatives*, Report to the Carnegie Commission on Preventing Deadly Conflict (New York, 1995).

agency for the purpose. The essential message was that despite the vastly greater means of influence Washington today possesses, it appears not to know how to proceed. In the case of Russia, for example, it is ultimately up to local political forces to ensure the transition to a modern economy. In the absence of this commitment, no new Marshall Plan aid money could reform a system whose members refuse or are unable to change their behavior.

A major restraint on the Western powers and Japan is their reluctance to use military force for the sake of democracy promotion.[8] Nevertheless, insisting on respect for the rights of minority groups and actively protecting them should genocidal threats materialize may be one form of democratic state-building. Another is an international norm punishing coups against established constitutional democracies, such as the Organization of American States inaugurated in 1991. (While the agreement failed to be effective in the aftermath of Jean-Baptiste Aristide's overthrow by the military in Haiti that same year, it may gain added strength in time to come as democracy gains in adherents in the hemisphere.) The development of an international court to adjudicate human rights violations may additionally promote the kinds of political changes that favor democracy.

Still, infatuation with power and ways to instrumentalize it should not blind liberals to the objective limits to their ambitions. If Haiti and Cambodia have proved so recalcitrant, if Russia, Mexico, and Turkey seem so unsteady, what then should we realistically expect of China, much of the Muslim world, and Africa?

Yet another, quite different set of considerations that should give pause to liberals concerns the way the workings of the liberal democratic international system itself – and not so much opposition from forces without or the strains of the transition – can breed its own undoing. One problem comes from economic globalization, the effects of which appear to be polarizing wealth not only within but also among nations. Should unregulated capitalism create rigid class hierarchies within or among states, then

---

8   Ivo H. Daalder, "The United States and Military Intervention in Internal Conflicts," in *The International Dimensions of Internal Conflict*, ed. Michael E. Brown (Boston, 1996).

democratic opposition groups may well call for limitations on unbridled market globalization.

A related problem comes from the lack of adequate international regulation of the world's economic system. In 1994, the U.S. government and the IMF were able to work together to bail out the Mexican economy and save the North American Free Trade Agreement. But it is unclear whether a larger crisis could be as effectively handled, a matter now being tested by the economic crisis in East Asia. A rise in protectionism and competitive international marketing schemes could set back the liberal world order – as a consequence, essentially, of the anarchy of this system itself – expressed in both political and economic terms.

Any such problems would be significantly aggravated if the United States began to show signs of failing in its ability or its willingness to defend the liberal international order. Surely realists are correct to stress the hegemonic role played by Washington (and New York) in assuring the viability of the current world order. The European Union remains far too embryonic, and the Japanese too weak politically and economically, for either to take up a leadership role from the United States. Should a protectionist economic coalition join with a unilateralist security movement within the United States, then this country's drift toward neo-isolationism might become difficult to stem. By its very momentum, such a development could create a disintegrating environment for multilateral trade and security and so feed an American withdrawal from world leadership. A "vicious cycle" of neo-isolationism (disguised as unilateralism) could then replace the "virtuous cycle" of liberal multilateralism. Those who doubt that such a turn of events could occur might consider the positions taken in recent years by Patrick Buchanan in the Republican party, by Richard Gephardt in the Democratic party, and by Ross Perot as a popular independent candidate.

Nor should liberals assume that democracy is some kind of panacea for whatever ails relations among democratic states. As a hegemonic power, the United States has constantly had to deal with a range of problems caused by other democratic capitals. So, the French and the Indians have repeatedly demonstrated their ability to act independently of Washington in world affairs, thumbing their nose at what America felt was necessary. Or again, the Israelis have shown that small power can have a big influence in a region, in the process often contravening what Washington would like to see it doing. Or consider the free-riding of the Japanese and the Scandinavians, peoples willing to accept the benefits of a world order run by America but unwilling to share equitably the burden of maintaining that system.

These considerations notwithstanding, from the current perspective, a melt-down of the American-sponsored world liberal order does not seem likely. The degree of preeminence that the United States today enjoys by most measures of power, combined with the consensus in elite circles at home and abroad on what is needed to maintain it, suggests that whatever the reverses and retrenchements called for, they will be steps backward preparing for greater steps forward.

Eventually some combination of circumstances that today cannot be well appreciated may bring an end to Luce's forecast of an American Century. But for the present we may note that American liberal internationalism has surprised many who were not only its critics but also those who were its advocates by successfully promoting the essential elements of a grand design for world order whose character has taken shape only slowly over the three generations since this country entered World War I. Then Woodrow Wilson was ahead of his times, but confident nonetheless, declaring that he would rather be defeated in the short term for a cause destined eventually to triumph than to win a victory in a struggle destined eventually to be lost. Like many other great leaders, Wilson had serious faults – of which religious sanctimoniousness and racial prejudice are today the most glaring. But in many ways the history of American foreign policy has confirmed his essential genius (and the convictions of Henry Luce as well) – his understanding that the expansion of American power worldwide might indeed be of benefit not only to this country but to the cause of humanity in general so long as it was dedicated to the promotion of democratic government worldwide. As Wilson had put it in 1889, writing on "Leaders of Men,"

Great reformers do not, indeed, observe time and circumstance. Theirs is not a service of opportunity. They have no thought for occasion, no capacity for compromise. They are early vehicles of the Spirit of the Age. They are born of the very times that oppose them . . . Theirs to hear the inarticulate voices that stir in the night-watches, apprising the lonely sentinel of what the day will bring forth.[9]

9   Wilson cited in Charles Seymour, "Wilson and His Contributions," in *Woodrow Wilson: A Profile*, ed. Arthur S. Link (New York, 1968), 162.

2

"Empire by Invitation" in the American Century

GEIR LUNDESTAD

Henry Luce, the American Century, and "Empire by Invitation"

In his famous article in *Life* of 17 February 1941, Henry R. Luce referred to "the belief – shared let us remember by most men living – that the 20th Century must be to a significant degree an American Century." Although Luce celebrated internationalism in a rather nationalistic vein, he did, however briefly, put the rise of the United States in a comparative context. All previous dominant powers had operated on the basis of some sort of internationalist ideology. "Rome had a great internationalism. So had the Vatican and Genghis Khan and the Ottoman Turks and the Chinese Emperors and 19th Century England. After the first World War, Lenin had one in mind. Today Hitler seems to have one in mind."

Luce recognized that America's role would in great measure depend on the response it received from the rest of the world. On this point he was relatively optimistic, because "most important of all, we have that indefinable, unmistakable sign of leadership: prestige. And unlike the prestige of Rome or Genghis Khan or 19th Century England, American prestige throughout the world

I want to thank Heidi Storeheier for her invaluable research assistance. She did a particularly fine job in not just bringing to my attention, but even writing short reports on relevant literature on many different issues. She also located most of the opinion polls referred to in the text.

is faith in the good intentions as well as the ultimate intelligence and ultimate strength of the whole American people."[1]

While Luce was wrong in some remarkable ways, he was surprisingly correct in some big ways. First, it was rather weird to announce that the twentieth century would be the American Century when four decades of that century had already elapsed without the United States assuming the mantle of leadership. Still, the twentieth century was in many respects the American Century, particularly the latter half.[2]

Second, although Luce tended to neglect the economic and military elements in the great-power base of the United States, he was right that the United States had "prestige" and that the world had faith in "the good intentions as well as in the ultimate intelligence and ultimate strength of the American people." So much so, in fact, that the United States, much more than any of the other powers Luce mentioned, was frequently *invited* to play the kind of great-power role it did after the Second World War.

The purpose of this essay, then, is to use Luce's famous article as the starting point for a discussion of the extent to which my own argument about "empire by invitation" can be applied to the entire American Century.[3] With the limited space available, in this context the emphasis will be on the invitational, not on the imperial part of my argument.

1 See Henry R. Luce, "The American Century," in this volume.
2 Luce refers several times to the twentieth century as the American Century. Still, it is obvious that he thought this label applied only to a limited extent to the first four decades since the United States had then failed to assume its leadership role. Thus, he wrote that as to the "golden opportunity handed to us on the proverbial silver platter . . . we bungled it in the 1920's and in the confusions of the 1930's we killed it." Obviously, Luce's article was primarily a plea that the United States now finally to assume its global leadership role, not an analysis of what had already taken place. Luce's "American Century" has often been compared with Henry Wallace's "Century of the Common Man" presented in 1942–43. For a recent account using these two concepts as organizing principles for much of the analysis see Donald W. White, *The American Century: The Rise & Decline of the United States as a World Power* (New Haven, 1996), esp. 8–12.
3 Geir Lundestad, "Empire by Invitation? The United States and Western Europe, 1945–1952," *SHAFR Newsletter* 15 (September 1984): 1–21. A revised and improved version with the same title was published in *Journal of Peace Research* 23 (September 1986): 263–77. Then, the argument was further revised in "The American 'Empire' 1945–1990," in my *The American "Empire" and Other Studies of US Foreign Policy in a Comparative Perspective* (Oxford-Oslo, 1990), 31–115, esp. 54–70.

It goes without saying that no single concept can encompass American foreign policy toward all major parts of the world in an entire century. My original concept dealt only with Western Europe from 1945 to 1952, and this is undoubtedly the period when "empire by invitation" makes the most sense. Yet, with obvious limitations, I intend to show that toward Europe, particularly Western Europe, the invitational side of the argument can be extended both backward and forward in time, that is, at least back to the First World War and up to the present. The geographical limitations of the invitational argument are more evident than the chronological ones, but it may nevertheless be relevant to certain other parts of the world, most obviously North East Asia and Australia, for much of the period from the Second World War until the present day.

West European Invitations to the United States, 1918–20

The Spanish-American War of 1898 made the United States a prominent power outside the North American mainland, primarily in the Caribbean and the Pacific. In Europe the American Century began to emerge with the First World War. This was also when the first European military-political invitations were issued to the United States, not to dominate, but to play an important role even in the Old World.

In the early phase of the war the European Great Powers, and Britain and Germany in particular, actively tried to influence the position of the United States. Britain hoped to bring the United States in on its side; Germany hoped to keep it neutral. In 1915–16 the two sides listened politely to various American peace ideas so as not to antagonize Washington. On 1 February 1917 the Germans abruptly ended this policy by resuming their unrestricted submarine warfare.[4]

In October 1918, when the Germans were losing the war, they appealed to President Woodrow Wilson personally "to negotiate

---

4   Akira Iriye, *The Globalizing of America, 1913–1945*, vol. 3, *The Cambridge History of American Foreign Relations* (Cambridge, England, 1993), 23–30.

an armistice which could lead in turn to a peace treaty based on Wilson's Fourteen Points." The appeal was in part an effort to play the United States against Great Britain and France, but on the German left there was also "a sense of ideological solidarity with Wilson's vision of a liberal peace settlement." According to German historian Klaus Schwabe, "it was Germany's peace initiative, of all things, which had cast the United States in the role of arbiter between the warring parties, a role which Wilson had been seeking for a long time."[5]

The most striking example of a European invitation to Washington came after the war, with the guarantee against Germany that the French wanted from Britain and the United States. The idea of an Anglo-American guarantee was originally presented in March 1919 by British Prime Minister David Lloyd George and was intended to soften the harsh French attitude toward Germany. Wilson agreed to the idea and French Prime Minister Georges Clemenceau quickly adopted it too, not as a substitute for the harsh French desires, but as a supplement.

So, from March 1919 on the French strongly favored a guarantee from the United States that the latter would come to their assistance in case of German aggression against France. In the end Lloyd George came to make the British guarantee contingent on the United States standing by its guarantee, as became clear when he inserted the word "only" into the treaties so that only when the American treaty was ratified would the British treaty come into force. "In this sense, the American commitment was as much a guarantee to Britain as to France." Should the United States reject the treaty, Britain would also be rid of its responsibility.[6]

5   Klaus Schwabe, *Woodrow Wilson, Revolutionary Germany, and Peacemaking, 1918–1919* (Chapel Hill, 1985), 11, 30–39, esp. 32-34.
6   The quotation is from Anthony Lentin, "The Treaty That Never Was: Lloyd George and the Abortive Anglo-French Alliance of 1919," in *The Life and Times of David Lloyd George*, ed. Judith Loades (Bangor, 1991), 124. For other good accounts of the American guarantee to France see Lloyd Ambrosius, *Woodrow Wilson and the American Diplomatic Tradition: The Treaty Fight in Perspective* (Cambridge, England, 1987), esp. 108–13; Melvyn P. Leffler, *The Elusive Quest: America's Pursuit of European Stability and French Security, 1919–1933* (Chapel Hill, 1979), 3–18; P. M. H. Bell, *France and Britain, 1900–1940: Entente and Estrangement* (London, 1996), 117–26; A. Lentin, "Several Types of Ambiguity: Lloyd George

On the American side the guarantee was very much the work of Wilson. Yet, despite their negative attitude to the League of Nations, most Senate Republicans supported the French treaty. The treaty was to act as a deterrent against German revanchism; it did not require the United States to furnish either men or money to back it up. In the end, however, the treaty was not ratified by the Senate. Wilson lost interest in it after the Senate defeated his much-cherished League; the Republicans did not bring it up when the president showed no interest. French appeals for U.S. ratification were in vain. The French responded with "panic" and the British with "dismay" after the Senate had let the treaty suffer a somewhat mysterious death. After Warren Harding took over as president, the French again tried to bring the treaty to a vote in the Senate, but the new president was not prepared to take on the "irreconcilables" in his own Republican party. That was the end of the American commitment to France.[7]

The question of the French guarantee revealed that not only France but also Britain had a strong interest in keeping the United States committed to Europe. This could be seen even on the economic side. In October 1918 the United States finally accepted membership on the many wartime inter-Allied councils that regulated the supplies of armaments, raw materials, shipping, and the like. As Michael J. Hogan has argued, the British wanted to "transform the economic agencies of the wartime coalition into semipermanent reconstruction and relief councils." These councils were to have administrative control over American and other Allied resources, regulate neutral and enemy competition, control enemy shipping, and organize commercial and raw material arrangements among the victors, including "the joint develop-

and the Paris Peace Conference," *Diplomacy & Statecraft* 6 (March 1995): 223–51, esp. 242–43; and Jean-Baptiste Duroselle, *France and the United States: From the Beginnings to the Present* (Chicago, 1976), 102–20. For an older account see Louis A. R. Yates, *United States and French Security, 1917–1921* (New York, 1957).

7   Ambrosius, *Woodrow Wilson and the American Diplomatic Tradition*, 215; William R. Keylor, "The Rise and Demise of the Franco-American Guarantee Pact, 1919–1921," *Proceedings of the Annual Meeting of the Western Society for French History* 15 (1988): 367–77; Leffler, *The Elusive Quest*, 3–39, esp. 30–33.

ment of underdeveloped regions."[8] Hogan states that the British had the "support" of the French government when they pressed for the continuation of the wartime councils. It actually seems, however, that the French, led by trade minister Etienne Clémentel, himself inspired by his young representative in London, Jean Monnet, pushed this course even harder than the British.[9]

Again, the European invitations were to be rejected. Virtually all of America's big businesses wanted to return to free enterprise and therefore favored the rapid dissolution of the inter-Allied councils. The director of the Food Administration, Herbert Hoover, who had been given a key role in determining U.S. aid policies to Europe, strongly favored such a policy, and in the end Wilson pushed aside all proposals for the continuation of the councils.[10]

Thus, the United States turned down the most explicit European invitations to play an active military-political and even economic role in Europe. After the French treaty had been rejected, the Harding administration started down the road of greater isolation from Europe, and in the 1930s the various Neutrality Acts considerably quickened the isolationist pace.

As so many historians have stressed, this did not really mean that the United States isolated itself from Europe. On other economic matters, involving anything from the Dawes and Young reparation settlements for Germany to investment, trade, and tourism, the United States became an important actor. Thus, American investment in Europe almost doubled, from $700 million in 1919 to $1.3 billion in 1929.[11]

On the cultural side, as early as 1901 British journalist William Stead had published his book *The Americanization of the World.*

---

8   Michael J. Hogan, *Informal Entente: The Private Structure of Cooperation in Anglo-American Economic Diplomacy, 1918–1928* (Columbia, MO, 1977), 20–37, esp. 20–22.
9   Ibid., 20; Duroselle, *France and the United States*, 110–13.
10   Duroselle, *France and the United States*, 111–12.
11   Frank Costigliola, *Awkward Dominion: American Political, Economic, and Cultural Relations with Europe, 1919–1933* (Ithaca, 1984), 139, 149–50, 154–55. In the 1920s American exports to Europe were higher than they had been before the First World War, but, not very surprisingly, smaller than they had been in 1916–20. Although the United States maintained a favorable balance of trade, in the 1920s imports from Europe increased more than U.S. exports, also compared with the years during the war. For this see U.S. Department of Commerce, Bureau of the Census, *Historical Statistics of the United States. Colonial Times to 1970. Part 2* (Washington, 1975), 903, 906.

In his article Luce himself mentioned some examples of America's global cultural reach: "American jazz, Hollywood movies, American slang, American machines and patented products." These were "in fact the only things that every community in the world, from Zanzibar to Hamburg, recognizes in common."[12]

The Americanization of Europe really started in the interwar years. Between 60 and 95 percent of the movies shown in the 1920s and 1930s in Britain, France, Italy, the Netherlands, and Germany (before 1933) were made in America. American jazz and literature became quite popular in Europe. As Paul Claudel, French ambassador to the United States and himself a man of letters, told the Americans in 1930:

Your movies and talkies have soaked the French mind in American life, methods, and manners. American gasoline and American ideas have circulated throughout France, bringing a new vision of power and a new tempo of life. The place in French life and culture formerly held by Spain and Italy, in the nineteenth century by England, now belongs to America. More and more we follow the Americans.[13]

While America's cultural influence in Europe increased after the First World War and, more dramatically still, after the Second, it is of course true that the French basically remained French, the Norwegians Norwegian, and so on.[14] Thus, after the First World War, most Europeans still had their reservations about the role and influence of the United States. In London, "Atlanticists" argued with "imperial isolationists" who stressed Britain's imperial role and who responded negatively to anything that indicated that the United States might be replacing Britain as the world's leading power. They were particularly concerned about Anglo-

---

12 Luce, "The American Century," in this volume.
13 Quoted from Costigliola, *Awkward Dominion*, 20. See also Richard Pells, *Not Like Us: How Europeans Have Loved, Hated, and Transformed American Culture since World War II* (New York, 1997), 7–22; and Iriye, *The Globalizing of America, 1913–1945*, 112–15. For the growing American impact on Norway see Sigmund Skard, *The United States in Norwegian History* (Westport, 1976), 145–72.
14 This is the rather basic point in Pells's *Not Like Us*, a point not very surprising to most Europeans. Yet, the definition of what exactly it meant to be French, Norwegian, and so on, kept changing over time, and American influence was one of many factors in this development.

American naval rivalry and economic competition.[15] In France the difficult question of French war debts to the United States dominated Franco-American relations in the 1920s.[16] In Germany too the image of America was ambiguous. On the one hand there was the German admiration for U.S. technical and economic achievements, on the other the contempt for what the Germans called *Amerikanismus*, the American preoccupation with materialism over finer and nobler things.[17]

Still, as we have seen, in 1918–20 there was no lack of European invitations on the most important security and economic issues. The invitations continued in the 1920s on everyday matters of economics and culture. Invitations were one thing; the American response was something entirely different. Invitations alone could not determine America's actions.

"Empire by Invitation" and Western Europe, 1945–52

In my original article about "empire by invitation," the focus was almost exclusively on Western Europe from 1945 to 1952. There is no need here to repeat all the arguments from that article or from my later writings. Nor is there space to repeat my comparisons of the American, British, and Soviet empires from my *The American "Empire"*. Let me just emphasize that while all empires have elements both of imposition and of invitation, the invitational side was clearly much stronger with the American than with the British and the Soviet empires.[18]

It also bears repetition that the position of the United States in 1945 was really unique in history. The comparisons with earlier Great Powers, such as for instance Britain after 1815, are really

15 These terms have been taken from B. J. C. McKercher, "The Deep and Latent Distrust: The British Official Mind and the United States, 1919–1929," in McKercher, *Anglo-American Relations in the 1920s: The Struggle for Supremacy* (London, 1991), 209–38. For a study of dramatic tension between the United States and Britain see Christopher M. Bell, "Thinking the Unthinkable: British and American Naval Strategies for an Anglo-American War, 1918–1931," *International History Review* 19, no. 4 (1997): 789–808.

16 Duroselle, *France and the United States*, 121–46.

17 Hans W. Gatzke, *Germany and the United States: A "Special Relationship"?* (Cambridge, MA, 1980), 75–102.

18 Lundestad, *The American "Empire"*, esp. 54–56.

misleading. In the overwhelming size of its economy, in its superior military strength, and in its popular message to the world, its
soft power, the United States was in a league of its own. The
economic basis was probably the single most important element
and provided much of the underpinning for the other factors mentioned.

My argument about "empire by invitation" has on the whole
been favorably received.[19] Most of the critical comments have
concerned my use of the term "empire" and the imperial part of
my argument, which is not of primary concern here.[20] In my new
book, *"Empire" by Integration: The United States and European
Integration, 1945–1997*, I have further explained my use of the
term. The United States was by far the strongest power the world
had ever seen. It, like other Great Powers, protected its interests
vigorously, most often with success. It generally did this, however, in more indirect ways than traditional imperial powers had
done. The countries within the U.S. sphere of influence were also

19   See, for instance, John Lewis Gaddis, "The Emerging Post-Revisionist Synthesis on the
Origins of the Cold War," *Diplomatic History* 7 (Summer 1983): 171–90, esp. 177, 181–83;
Bruce K. Kuniholm, "Response," ibid., 201–4; Arthur M. Schlesinger, Jr., *The Cycles of
American History* (Boston, 1986), 161; Michael J. Hogan, *The Marshall Plan: America, Britain, and the Reconstruction of Western Europe, 1947–1952* (New York, 1987), 444; Thomas
G. Paterson and Robert J. McMahon, *The Origins of the Cold War* (Lexington, MA, 1991),
110–18; Thomas Alan Schwartz, *America's Germany: John J. McCloy and the Federal Re-
public of Germany* (Cambridge, MA, 1991), 299–300; Robert Keohane, "The United States
and the Postwar Order: Empire or Hegemony," *Journal of Peace Research* 28, no. 4 (1991):
435–39; the contributions by David Reynolds and Anders Stephanson in Reynolds, ed., *The
Origins of the Cold War in Europe: International Perspectives* (New Haven, 1994), 7, 36–37;
Steven Hugh Lee, *Outposts of Empire: Korea, Vietnam, and the Origins of the Cold War in
Asia, 1949–1954* (Montreal, 1995), 4–5; Douglas J. Macdonald, "Communist Bloc Expansion in the Early Cold War," *International Security* 20 (Winter 1995/96): 159–60; David
Reynolds, "America's Europe, Europe's America: Image, Influence, and Interaction, 1933–
1958," *Diplomatic History* 20 (Fall 1996): 653; and John Lewis Gaddis, *We Now Know:
Rethinking Cold War History* (Oxford, 1997), 26–53, esp. 26–28, 51–53, 284–86, 304–5n.4,
312n.120. There are also many references to "empire by invitation," both critical and less
so, in discussions on the Internet website H-DIPLO. A particularly valuable contribution was
made on 12 December 1997 by Piers Ludlow under the subject heading "France, the Western
Alliance, and the Origins of the Schuman Plan." See also contributions under the subject
heading "The Legitimacy of the American Empire."
20   Keohane, "The United States and the Postwar Order: Empire or Hegemony," 435–39;
Jasmine Aimaq, *For Europe or Empire? French Colonial Ambitions and the European Army
Plan* (Lund, 1996), esp. 32–46; Thomas D. Lairson, "Revising Postrevisionism: Credibility
and Hegemony in the Early Cold War," in *Re-Thinking the Cold War*, ed. Allen Hunter (Philadelphia, 1998), 63–90.

largely independent. That is why I have chosen to put "empire" in quotation marks. American policy was based on American values, in the same way British policy had been based on British values, Soviet policy on Soviet values, and so on.[21]

On the invitation side, where the emphasis is in this essay, the main argument against my view seems to be that the invitations did not really *determine* U.S. foreign policy.[22] American foreign policy was determined primarily by America's own interests, not by invitations from the outside.

This point is obviously true, so true, in fact, that it was made explicitly clear in my *Journal of Peace Research* article: "I just take it for granted that the United States had important strategic, political, and economic motives of its own for taking on such a comprehensive world role."[23] Indeed, the invitations had to be combined with America's own interests. After 1945 the European invitations were extended to a United States disposed to respond in a much more affirmative way than it had in 1918–20.

At the same time, however, it should be stressed that the invitations after the Second World War were clearly more insistent, lasted longer, and came from many more countries than on the earlier occasion. And while little is really known about the state of public opinion in Europe after the First World War, if we are to generalize about public opinion after the Second World War the invitations extended to the United States by most Western European governments came to receive the basic support of the populations involved.[24]

---

21   Geir Lundestad, *"Empire" by Integration: The United States and European Integration, 1945–1997* (Oxford, 1998), 2–4. For a suitable definition of "empire" in this wider sense see Gaddis, *We Now Know*, 27 ("I mean, by this term, a situation in which a single state shapes the behavior of others, whether directly or indirectly, partially or completely, by means that can range from the outright use of force through intimidation, dependency, inducements, and even inspiration").

22   I have discussed this point with many historians and political scientists, particularly with John Gaddis and Melvyn Leffler.

23   Lundestad, "Empire by Invitation?" 268. In American "Empire" I strengthened this formulation further and wrote that "neither the Europeans nor any other foreigners could determine US foreign policy. This was done in Washington largely on the basis of America's own interests" (p. 56).

24   Lundestad, "Empire by Invitation?" 272–73.

At first the European invitations were primarily economic in nature. While the United States emerged as the world's main creditor even after the First World War, both Britain and France were after all still creditor states.[25] After the Second World War the United States was virtually the only major source of credit. Practically every Western European country, certainly including Britain and France, wanted fresh economic assistance from the U.S. government. (The American credits extended after the First World War came largely from private banks.)

In 1945–47 the Europeans received $8.3 billion from the United States in bilateral form – from 1948 to 1952, $14.1 billion through the multilateral Marshall Plan. The Western Europeans thus invited the Americans into Europe, despite the conditions set by Washington, whether in the form of currency convertibility or special shipping clauses.[26] It is another matter that particularly under the Marshall Plan the Europeans were able to soften such conditions considerably. Most Central and Eastern European countries also wanted economic assistance from the United States, but Soviet influence and disputes with Washington about free elections and other conditions for such assistance stopped most loans to these countries. The Soviet Union then prevented them from taking part in the Marshall Plan.[27]

Even politically the Western Europeans wanted to involve the United States from the very end of the Second World War. As far as the combined boards were concerned, the strong British desire to continue many of these also after the Second World War underlined the remarkable continuity between the periods after the two world wars. The major differences were that these boards had become much more important during the Second than during the

25   Derek H. Aldcroft, *From Versailles to Wall Street, 1919–1929* (Harmondsworth, 1987), 239–67.
26   U.S. Department of Commerce, *Historical Statistics of the United States* pt. 2:874. The best analysis of the conditions set by Washington is still found in Hadley Arkes, *Bureaucracy, the Marshall Plan, and the National Interest* (Princeton, 1972), esp. 153–72.
27   Geir Lundestad, *The American Non-Policy towards Eastern Europe, 1943–1947: Universalism in an Area Not of Essential Interest to the United States* (Oslo, 1975), esp. 384–408.

First World War and that the British desire to continue this form of cooperation was even more strongly expressed now.

Again the British invitations went beyond what Washington could accept. The Anglo-American Combined Chiefs of Staff system was ended, as was cooperation on atomic energy. On the more secret level of the military and intelligence services Anglo-American cooperation did indeed continue, although in diluted form. Soon the British also worked hard to transfer some of their burden in Germany onto the United States—leading to the establishment of the Bizone in January 1947 – and to involve the United States in Greece and Turkey – leading to the announcement of the Truman Doctrine in March 1947.[28]

On the European continent, from the wartime years to the signing of the North Atlantic Treaty the Dutch in particular followed a consistently Atlanticist policy emphasizing the role of the United States, and they did so despite the American-Dutch feud over Indonesia.[29] Even on the French side, the desire to involve the United States was made explicit even before the Second World War ended. In an internal note of April 1945, General Charles de Gaulle insisted that the continued presence of the United States in European affairs was necessary: one should "link in the future the United States with the security of the European continent and establish through their presence the conditions of a necessary balance of power in Europe."[30]

On the military side, in late 1947–early 1948 British Foreign Secretary Ernest Bevin conducted a virtual campaign to involve the United States in an Atlantic security system. Again he was supported by the Dutch and, to an increasing extent, by the Belgians. Even the French came to follow a similar course. After some delicate French efforts in 1946–47 at establishing contacts between the French and the American military, in December 1947 Atlanticist Foreign Minister Georges Bidault asked the Americans to conclude a secret military agreement with France for the

---

28 Robert M. Hathaway, *Ambiguous Partnership: Britain and America, 1944–1947* (New York, 1981) is still the best book on this important topic.
29 Cees Wiebes & Bert Zeeman, "Benelux," in Reynolds, ed., *The Origins of the Cold War in Europe*, 172–86.
30 Quoted from Georges-Henri Soutou, "France" in ibid., 100.

defense of Western Europe. On 4 March 1948, Bidault requested Washington "to strengthen in the political field, and as soon as possible in the military one, the collaboration between the old and the new worlds, both so jointly responsible for the preservation of the only valuable civilization."[31]

The British and the French perspectives were somewhat at variance, with London emphasizing the wider Atlantic structure and Paris primarily military assistance directly to France, but the effect was the same: strong invitations to the United States to become more involved in Europe even militarily.

In the negotiations to set up NATO virtually every European country wanted to make the American military commitment to Europe as automatic as possible. After NATO had been formed, all the Europeans wanted to have the United States participate in their regional groups. Following the outbreak of the Korean War the European pressure on Washington to reinforce the American troops in Europe was strong, as was the insistence on creating an integrated command structure under an American commander. Even Norway, which did not permit the stationing of foreign troops on its soil, worked hard to "nail" the United States to Northern Europe and particularly to get "a hook in the nose of the US Air Force."[32]

In my opinion it would have been most interesting to study the European response to the new role for the United States after 1945 even had the European response had no effect on America's actions. Yet the invitations clearly did have an effect. Obviously there would not have been any economic assistance had the Europeans not wanted it. Considering Washington's initially luke-

---

31 The quotation is from Georgette Elgey, *La republique des illusions 1945–1951* [The republic of illusions 1945–1951] (Paris, 1965), 382. See also Charles G. Cogan, *Forced to Choose: France, the Atlantic Alliance, and NATO—Then and Now* (Westport, 1997), 26–45; Soutou, "France" in Reynolds, ed., *The Origins of the Cold War in Europe*, 100–106; and Wiebes & Zeeman, "Benelux," in ibid., 178–86. The French efforts at military contacts in 1946–48 are associated with the name of Deputy Chief of the Army Pierre Billotte. For this see particularly Cogan, *Forced to Choose*, 26–31.

32 For Norway see Rolf Tamnes, "Norway's Struggle for the Northern Flank, 1950–1952," in *Western Security: The Formative Years. European and Atlantic Defence, 1947–1953*, ed. Olav Riste (Oslo, 1985), 225–34. For a more general account see S. F. Wells, Jr., "The First Cold War Buildup: Europe in United States Strategy and Policy, 1950-1953" in ibid., 181–97.

warm response to Bevin's pleas for an Atlantic security system, it seems likely that the setting up of NATO would at least have been substantially delayed had it not been for the European invitations. The heart of NATO, Article 5, would probably not have had even its semiautomatic nature had the Europeans not pushed as hard as they did for a more-or-less automatic American response to Soviet aggression. Thomas G. Paterson and Robert J. McMahon's suggestion that the United States "would have had to force its will on other peoples if it had not been for the 'invitation'"[33] is not only unhistorical; it also seems rather unlikely.

The experience after the First World War indicates that European invitations alone were not enough to change America's attitude, although it is impossible to tell what would have happened had the invitations then been as insistent, lasted as long, and come from as many countries as they did after the Second World War. After 1945, with the United States prepared to play a much more active role, the invitations did not force the Americans to do anything they did not really want to do, but they certainly influenced at least the timing and scope of America's actions vis-à-vis Europe.

West European Invitations, 1952–89

The American-European structure set up in 1947–51 remained remarkably stable throughout the Cold War years. The Europeans definitely wanted the Americans to remain involved in Europe economically, politically, and militarily. NATO was the key link between the two sides of the Atlantic. In writings on NATO the crisis aspect has frequently been emphasized. If the standard of comparison is a state of harmony, then there were almost always crises in NATO.

If, however, the standard is other alliances in history, then one is bound to emphasize the closeness of the American-European relationship. This is true whether one goes back in history and compares NATO with the Holy Alliance and the ententes and

33   Paterson and McMahon, *The Origins of the Cold War*, 110.

alliances before the First World War or one compares it with contemporary alliances such as the Sino-Soviet treaty, the Warsaw Pact, or the American-inspired alliance system in Asia. Not only has NATO lasted longer than any of the other alliances mentioned, but membership is also much broader. No country has left NATO while Greece and Turkey (1952), West Germany (1955), and Spain (1982) have joined.[34]

Despite France's withdrawal from NATO's military command in 1966 and despite its frequent criticism of the United States, so evident in references to the "double threats" and "twofold imperialisms" facing France, in times of crisis France generally remained as loyal as other NATO allies to the alliance and to the United States. And to substitute for the military withdrawal, agreements were worked out between the American supreme commanders of NATO and the French chiefs of staff to bring about the necessary cooperation in times of war.[35]

With the United States in place economically, politically, and militarily, the temptation must have been great to take the American presence for granted and then to complain about the many ways in which the Americans influenced various national priorities. In a way this was what happened in France under Charles de Gaulle. Although the French president wanted NATO as such to continue and definitely favored both the American nuclear guarantee to Western Europe and American troops in Europe, but not in France, he took strong exception to Washington's views on many different foreign policy issues. The German *Ostpolitik* could be seen in the same perspective. With the United States so securely in place, West Germany was freer to explore its own policies toward East Germany, Eastern Europe, and the Soviet Union.

On the invitational side, except for the French, the European governments also wanted to keep the American troops in their respective countries. In fact, in some countries, Italy being the best example, there was a strong interest in increasing the num-

34 See my "Introduction" in Geir Lundestad, ed., *No End to Alliance: The United States and Western Europe: Past, Present, and Future* (London, 1998).
35 Pierre Melandri, "The Troubled Partnership: France and the United States, 1945–1989," in ibid.

ber of U.S. troops.[36] Whenever the American Congress threatened to legislate reductions in U.S. troop levels in Europe, the administration would receive the strong support of European governments to beat back these efforts.[37]

On the economic side, while American economic assistance tapered off in the 1950s, the $16.7 billion that Western Europe received in military assistance from 1950 to 1970 was most welcome.[38] U.S. investment in Western Europe increased rapidly. In 1950 such investment stood at $1.7 billion, only slightly higher than in 1929 ($1.3 billion). This was about one seventh of total U.S. investment abroad. By 1970 investment in Western Europe had grown to $24.5 billion – about one-third of total U.S. investment abroad. In 1990 investment in Europe (the Eastern half was now included) had skyrocketed to $215 billion – which was half of all U.S. investment abroad. Investment in Britain alone totaled $73 billion. European governments virtually competed to attract American capital. Efforts, particularly in France in the 1960s, to limit American investment were rather short-lived.[39]

On the cultural side, as Richard Pells has argued, what struck Europeans as new about American mass culture "was not its presence – they had been going to American movies and hearing American music since the 1920s – but its pervasiveness."[40] New generations of Europeans were inviting American mass culture in at an ever growing pace.

As far as public opinion was concerned, the pattern from 1945 to 1952 was reinforced. American-European cooperation was not limited to the elites, as is at least implied by corporatist historians.[41] While of course no identity of interest was perceived

36 See Simon W. Duke and Wolfgang Krieger, eds., *U.S. Military Forces in Europe: The Early Years, 1945–1970* (Boulder, 1993). For Italy in particular see Leopoldo Nuti, "U.S. Forces in Italy, 1945–1963," ibid., 269–72.
37 Henry Kissinger, *White House Years* (Boston, 1979), 938–49.
38 U.S. Department of Commerce, *Historical Statistics of the United States* pt. 2:872–74.
39 The numbers are from ibid., 870; U.S. Department of Commerce, Bureau of the Census, *Statistical Abstract of the United States, 1995* (Washington, 1995), 809. See also Pells, *Not Like Us*, 190. For French policies on American investment see Richard F. Kuisel, *Seducing the French: The Dilemma of Americanization* (Berkeley, 1993), 176–84.
40 Pells, *Not Like Us*, 204–62 (quotation is from 205).
41 The best known of these historians are Michael J. Hogan and Charles S. Maier. In his celebrated article "The Two Postwar Eras and the Conditions for Stability in Twentieth-

between the home country and the United States, public opinion in Britain, West Germany, and Italy on the whole remained quite friendly to the United States while French opinion was clearly more ambivalent. Thus, in polls from 1956 to 1963 more than 70 percent in Britain consistently answered that "the basic interests of Britain and those of the United States" were either very much in agreement or fairly much in agreement as opposed to rather different, very different, or no answer. In West Germany the corresponding percentage varied more but the average was about 70. The percentage for Italy also varied, with a somewhat lower average of about 55 percent. In France the percentage fluctuated from a high of 53 to a low of 27, with an average of about 40 percent.[42]

In the late 1960s the Vietnam War considerably strengthened anti-American sentiment in Europe. In the late 1970s–early 1980s the furious debate in many European countries about the deployment of U.S. intermediate nuclear forces (INF) and Ronald Reagan's strong anticommunism had a similar effect. Criticism of many aspects of American foreign policy increased. So, now the publics were indeed becoming more ambivalent to the United States than were their governments.

The most striking fact concerning Britain in this later period was that in 1981–82 public confidence in the United States declined much more dramatically than in other major European countries. In fact, in these years more people disapproved than approved of the American bases in Britain. Yet the basic sympathy for NATO and for the American role in Europe remained. A study of attitudes even in the late 1970s and early 1980s revealed that in Britain "one reason for the high level of support for NATO

Century Western Europe," *American Historical Review* 86, no. 2 (1981): 333–34, Maier referred to "the elites superintending Western society" over half a century. I have discussed their corporatist views in "The United States, the Marshall Plan and Corporatism," in *Maktpolitik och Husfrid. Studier i internationell och svensk historia tilägnade Gøran Rystad* [Power politics and domestic peace: Studies in international and Swedish history dedicated to Gøran Rystad] (Lund, Sweden, 1991).

42   Richard L. Merrit and Donald J. Puchala, eds., *Western European Perspectives on International Affairs* (New York, 1968), 254–55.

is that both it and the United States are, according to a variety of polls, regarded as staunchly dependable."[43]

In West Germany there might be occasional outbursts of sympathy for a united and neutral Germany, but on the whole confidence in the United States and in NATO remained strong. While in 1956–57 a majority would actually have welcomed the withdrawal of American troops from Europe, in the 1960s, 1970s, and early 1980s strong majorities tended to favor American troops in Europe.[44] In Italy, too, confidence in the United States and in NATO largely endured, although from a two-thirds majority of favorable opinion in the 1950s and 1960s, the U.S. image declined to a low of 41 percent during the mid-1970s.[45]

In Holland, Denmark, and Norway, support for membership in NATO and for the American security guarantee remained stable at a high level from decade to decade. In the 1980s, however,

43　Ivor Crewe, "Britain: Two and a Half Cheers for the Atlantic Alliance," in *The Public and Atlantic Defense*, ed. Gregory Flynn and Hans Rattinger (Totowa, NJ, 1985), esp. 39–47 (quotation is from p. 45). See also Ivor Crewe, "Why the British Don't Like US Anymore," *Public Opinion* (March/April 1987): 51–56; "West European Views about the United States and Various International Relations," *World Opinion Update* 3 (1982): 70–72; and Peter Fotheringham, "Great Britain: Generational Continuity," in *The Successor Generation: International Perspectives of Postwar Europeans*, ed. Stephen F. Szabo (London, 1983), esp. 97–98. For the negative attitude to Reagan see particularly Ivor Crewe, "Britain Evaluates Ronald Reagan," *Public Opinion* (October/November 1984): 46–49. For the rapid decline in British confidence in the United States see Bruce Russett and Donald R. Deluca, "Theater Nuclear Forces: Public Opinion in Western Europe," *Political Science Quarterly* 98 (Summer 1983): 179–96, esp. 183–84; and Philip Sabin, "British Perceptions of the USA and the USSR: The Limits of Comparative Opinion Polls," in *Debating National Security: The Public Dimension*, ed. Hans Rattinger and Don Munton (Frankfurt, 1991), 73–100.

44　Hans Rattinger, "The Federal Republic of Germany: Much Ado About (Almost) Nothing," in Flynn and Rattinger, eds., *The Public and Atlantic Defense*, esp. 138–47; Elisabeth Noelle-Neumann, ed., *The Germans: Public Opinion Polls, 1967–1980* (Westport, 1981), 408–9, 415–27, 434–37; Russett and Deluca, "Theater Nuclear Forces: Public Opinion in Western Europe," 185–86. See also Stephen F. Szabo, "West Germany: Generations and Changing Security Perspectives" in Szabo, *The Sucessor Generation*, esp. 59–66; Peter Schmidt, "Public Opinion and Security Policy in the Federal Republic of Germany," *ORBIS* 28 (Winter 1985): 719–42; Elisabeth Noelle-Neumann, "The Missile Gap: The German Press and Public Opinion," *Public Opinion* (October-November 1983): 45–49; Wolfgang Donsbach, Hans Mathias Kepplinger, and Elisabeth Noelle-Neumann, "West Germans' Perceptions of NATO and the Warsaw Pact: Long-Term Content Analysis of Der Spiegel and Trends in Public Opinion," in Rattinger and Munton, eds., *Debating National Security*, 250–66; and *World Opinion Update* 4 (1980): 33.

45　Sergio A. Rossi, "Public Opinion and Atlantic Defense in Italy," in Flynn and Rattinger, eds., *The Public and Atlantic Defense*, 196-218 (quotation is from p. 216).

even here the skepticism about Reagan's policies led to a decline in confidence in the United States in other respects.[46]

As far as France was concerned, strong neutralist leanings were combined with a conviction that the United States would defend Western Europe in case of a Soviet attack. In 1985, 69 percent of the French believed that in a war they could "count on" the United States, actually a higher percentage than in either West Germany (67) or Britain (56).[47] While the percentage of the population who thought NATO essential was clearly smaller in France than in other NATO countries, there was "net support" for NATO even in France.[48]

Two additional observations should be made about France. First, there are strong indications that the "national security elite" had a rather sophisticated and more positive attitude to the United States than the rest of French opinion.[49] Second, while in most countries confidence in the United States declined, in France there appears to have been some rehabilitation of the American image

46   For a collection of essays on anti-Americanism in Europe see Rob Kroes and Maarten Van Rossem, eds., *Anti-Americanism in Europe* (Amsterdam, 1986). For studies of polls in various Western European countries in these years see Philip Everts, "NATO, the European Community, and the United Nations," in *Public Opinion and Internationalized Governance*, ed. Oskar Niedermayer and Richard Sinnott (Oxford, 1995), 402–19; Philip P. Everts, "Public Opinion on Nuclear Weapons, Defense, and Security: The Case of the Netherlands," in Flynn and Rattinger, eds., *The Public and Atlantic Defense*, 262–67; Koen Koch, "Anti-Americanism and the Dutch Peace Movement," in Kroes and Van Rossem, eds., *Anti-Americanism in Europe*, 108–9; Ragnar Waldahl, "Norwegian Attitudes toward Defense and Foreign Policy Issues," in Flynn and Rattinger, eds., *The Public and Atlantic Defense*, 308–10; Bjørn Alstad, ed., *Norske Meninger, 1946–93: 1: Norge og verden* [Norwegian opinions, 1946–93. 1: Norway and the world] (Oslo, 1993), esp. 82–84; and "West European Views about the United States and Various International Issues," *World Opinion Update* 3 (1982): 70–72.

47   Renata Fritsch-Bournazel, "France: Attachment to a Nonbinding Relationship," in Flynn and Rattinger, eds., *The Public and Atlantic Defense*, esp. 88–99. For the poll mentioned see *World Opinion Update* 9 (1985): 2. For a study of anti-Americanism in France in general see Denis Lacorne, Jacques Rupnik, and Marie-France Toinet, eds., *The Rise and Fall of Anti-Americanism: A Century of French Perception* (London, 1990).

48   Richard C. Eichenberg, *Public Opinion and National Security in Western Europe* (Ithaca, 1989), 123–27. Net support was defined as the percentage who thought NATO essential minus those who responded that NATO was not essential.

49   Thus, at the "national security elite level" in the early 1980s "the desire for a close alliance with the United States is shared in France by 81 percent, in Great Britain by 69 percent, and in the Netherlands by 81 percent." The 81 percent in France and Holland was in fact the highest percentage in the five countries studied: France, Holland, Britain, West Germany, and Norway. For this see Asmus, "Public Opinion and Security Policy in the Federal Republic of Germany," 737–38. See also Russett and Deluca, "Theater Nuclear Forces: Public Opinion in Western Europe," 187.

in the late 1970s–early 1980s. This was probably due to the French discovery of the gulag and the Soviet threat in general at a time when most other Europeans felt that with detente the Soviet threat had receded a great deal.[50]

European Invitations, 1989–98

With the end of the Cold War the American presence in Europe could no longer be taken for granted. The number of U.S. troops in Western Europe was reduced to one hundred thousand, compared to a high of more than four hundred thousand in the late 1950s;[51] in relative terms American trade was continuing to shift away from the Atlantic to the Pacific (in 1979 trade across the Pacific for the first time exceeded trade across the Atlantic; in 1996 U.S. trade with Asia stood at $570 billion, compared to $270 billion with Europe);[52] America's interest in European affairs was obviously declining compared to what it had been during the Cold War, and particularly in the early Clinton years the administration almost seemed to take delight in pointing out its limited interest in Europe. The implication seemed to be that now the Europeans would have to handle their own affairs.

With this kind of attitude in Washington, it was rather obvious that if the Europeans really wanted the Americans to remain closely involved in European affairs, they had better tell them so. The old invitations had to be reissued.

This is also what happened. In country after country the invitations to the United States were in fact renewed. The motives for the new invitations varied: lingering fear of Russia, concern about the position of united Germany or about the effects of regional

---

50　Stephen F. Szabo, "European Opinion after the Missiles," *Survival* 27 (November/December 1985): 265–73, esp. 270; "West European Views about the United States and Various International Issues," 70–71.

51　Zbigniew Brzezinski, *Game Plan: How to Conduct the U.S.-Soviet Contest* (New York, 1986), 207.

52　In fact, the United States apparently exported more to Singapore than to France or Italy. For this see Kishore Mahbubani, "An Asia-Pacific Consensus," *Foreign Affairs* 76 (September/October 1997): 151.

crises in Bosnia and elsewhere, economic interest, the need to have the United States as Europe's ultimate arbiter.

No European government really wanted the Americans to leave. To start with the smallest countries: In Iceland, where since the Second World War the Americans had had an important, but controversial air base, and the U.S. Air Force now suggested it might pull out all the fighter jets, the Icelandic government persuaded the Americans to retain a small presence. In Norway, where the United States had a comprehensive system of co-located bases (really prepositioning of equipment) and now wanted to dismantle most of them, the Norwegian government convinced Washington to keep more than the United States had initially wanted.[53] In Germany, where fears had been expressed that even the American troops might have to leave since the Russians had left, the emphasis was now on the Americans staying.

The most paradoxical change took place in France. When de Gaulle's vision had triumphed – when Europe had in some ways been united from the Atlantic to the Urals – President Jacques Chirac announced that France would rejoin NATO's integrated military structure. Many factors contributed to this remarkable change: the appraisal that a European defense identity could best be promoted within, not outside NATO, the French experiences in the Gulf War and in Bosnia, reduced defense spending in France, Germany's unification, and so on.[54]

In the end, since the United States and France could not reach agreement on the conditions under which France would rejoin the military structure – the disagreement as to whether a European or an American should be heading NATO's Southern Command was particularly important – France only joined NATO's Military Committee and certain other bodies, not the integrated command as such. Yet it was symptomatic that when push came

53 David Oddsson, *Icelandic Foreign Policy and Atlantic Issues* (Oslo, 1997), 6–7; Dr. Valur Ingimundarson to Geir Lundestad, 24 March 1998; Jørgen Kosmo, *Norwegian Security and Defence Policy – Future Challenges* (Oslo, 1997), 4–5; Rolf Tamnes, *Oljealder, 1965–1995* [Oil Age, 1965–1995] (vol. 6 in *History of Norwegian Foreign Policy*) (Oslo, 1997), 142–44.

54 For my discussion of America's role as the ultimate arbiter in Europe see *"Empire" by Integration*, 132–33, 137–46. For recent developments in France see Frédéric Bozo, "France," in *NATO and Collective Security*, ed. Michael Brenner (London, 1998), 39–80.

to shove in the dispute over the Southern Command even France's closest ally, Germany, abandoned the French. Nothing was to be done that could lead to a reduced American interest in Europe. And Spain now became fully integrated into NATO's military command.

In relations between the United States and the European Union (EU) interesting developments took place. In earlier years it was the Americans who had taken the initiative to deepen the American-European relationship. This had been seen in Kennedy's famous interdependence speech in 1962 and in Kissinger's Year of Europe initiative in 1973. The November 1990 Transatlantic Declaration was a more balanced effort with the Germans taking the initiative, but in close cooperation with Washington. The initiative behind the New Transatlantic Agenda and the Joint Action Plan between the United States and the EU signed in Madrid in December 1995, however, was clearly European. As early as November 1992, Chancellor Helmut Kohl had felt the need to commit the Americans more strongly to Europe. He was quickly supported by other Europeans, certainly including the Spanish, and even the French. Under the New Transatlantic Agenda the United States and the EU were to work together in about one hundred different policy areas. A very elaborate system of consultation was set up between the two sides of the Atlantic.[55]

The attitudes of the European publics toward the United States and NATO were strikingly friendly after the end of the Cold War. By 1991, NATO had recovered most of the support it had lost in the early 1980s.[56] In Britain favorable attitudes to NATO remained at about 70 percent. German attitudes fluctuated more, but support for NATO never fell below 60 percent. In Britain and Germany the public looked to NATO rather than to such organizations as the OSCE, WEU, or EU to deal with European security problems. Italy, while still strongly favoring NATO, was becoming somewhat more European in its security orientation. In France the public looked more to the EU, but the remarkable

55   The last paragraphs are in great part based on my *"Empire" by Integration*, esp. 114–25, 143–46.
56   Everts, "NATO, the European Community, and the United Nations," 406–10.

swing toward a more positive attitude to NATO and the United States continued into the 1990s. In 1993–95, French support for NATO stood at about 60 percent. In Spain, a relatively new member of NATO, support was at a lower level, around 40 percent. Among the smaller countries, Denmark, Norway, and the Netherlands continued to fully back NATO, while Greece in particular, with its strained relations with Turkey, was rather skeptical of NATO.[57]

In the 1990s Europe remained culturally as attached to the United States as it had ever been, as measured in everything from the popularity of American movies and television programs to the increase in sales of Coke in Central and Eastern Europe.[58]

The American leadership role in Europe remained quite striking even after the end of the Cold War. The unification of Germany in 1989–90 was in many ways George Bush's finest hour, and the American president was able to secure his primary objective – a unified Germany staying within NATO – in the face even of German doubts. On the unification issue the cooperation between Washington and Bonn was telling, as was the fact that London and Paris were left largely on the sidelines.[59]

After the Clinton administration had resolved its initial doubts about what role it would actually play in Europe, the United States again took charge of basic security matters in Europe. This was clearly seen on the issue of NATO expansion, where Washington first proposed the Partnership for Peace scheme, then switched to membership directly in NATO for some Central and Eastern European countries, and finally decided that only Poland, Hungary, and the Czech Republic would join in the first round. With Germany as its close ally on this matter, and with the support also of

---

57   Richard Sinnott, *European Public Opinion and Security Policy*, Chaillot Paper no. 28 (Paris, 1997), 19–24, 43, 53; Everts, "NATO, the European Community, and the United Nations," 410–19; Philippe Manigart and Eric Marlier, "Public Opinion and Security Matters in Europe," in *European Security*, ed. Wilfried von Bredow, Thomas Jäger, and Gerhard Kümmel (London, 1997), 3–21.
58   Pells, *Not Like Us*, 201, 211, 219, 221, 231–32.
59   The story of Germany's unification is superbly told in Philip Zelikow and Condoleezza Rice, *Germany Unified and Europe Transformed: A Study in Statecraft* (Cambridge, MA, 1995).

Britain, France could not do much. In Bosnia, after a great deal of hesitation and confusion, Washington finally took military and political command in the fall of 1995. This led to the Dayton agreement in November–December. On the military side, it was evident that if the Americans pulled out of Bosnia, so would the Europeans. Both on NATO expansion and on Bosnia the Europeans clearly expected the United States to take the lead, although complaints could occasionally be heard about the unilateral way in which Washington sometimes acted.[60]

Virtually all the Central and Eastern European countries wanted to become members of NATO. For most of them the reason was quite obvious, although it was rarely stated in public: NATO membership was really a concerted invitation from the Central and Eastern Europeans to the United States to protect them against a renewed threat from Russia. Membership in the EU could then help in solving their economic problems. The more general emphasis on American involvement could be openly expressed. The foreign ministers of former "neutrals" – the term was now clearly out of favor – Finland and Sweden thus wrote that "we wish to emphasize the value of continued strong U.S. involvement" in the Nordic and Baltic areas.[61]

Some of the Central and Eastern European publics had somewhat larger problems than their governments in going directly from the Warsaw Pact to NATO. Among the ten countries of Poland, Romania, Slovenia, Estonia, Latvia, Lithuania, Hungary, the Czech Republic, Bulgaria, and Slovakia an average of 53 percent supported membership in NATO for their respective countries, while 17 percent had not made up their minds and 10 percent were against joining NATO. For rather obvious historical reasons, Romania and Poland were at the high end with 76 and 65 percent, respectively. For almost equally obvious historical

---

60   David Calleo, "Western Transformation after the Cold War," in Lundestad, ed., *No End to Alliance*. For a good, short account of the NATO enlargement issue see Jonathan Eyal, "NATO's Enlargement: Anatomy of a Decision," *International Affairs* 73, no. 4 (1997): 695–719.
61   Tarja Halonen and Lena Hjelm-Wallen, "Working for European Security Outside the NATO Structure," *International Herald Tribune*, 15 March 1997.

reasons, Bulgaria and Slovakia were at the low end, both with 27 percent.[62]

While during the Cold War the Soviet Union had been strongly opposed to NATO's existence and wanted the United States to withdraw its troops from Western Europe, Moscow's policy in connection with Germany's unification in 1989–90 seemed to reveal that at least in this new situation even Moscow saw American troops as a stabilizing force.[63] It may well be that this interest continues with the new Russia, despite its opposition to NATO's expansion into the territory of the former Warsaw Pact.

Alliances and Invitations outside Europe

While my invitational perspective undoubtedly suits American-European relations the best, it may still be useful in analyzing U.S. relations even with certain other parts of the world.

If we take the setting up of alliances as a concrete example, the ANZUS treaty of 1951 between Australia, New Zealand, and the United States comes very close indeed to the NATO pattern. The ANZUS treaty was "made in Australia." In 1946–47 Foreign Minister H. V. Evatt tried hard to get the United States to give a formal security guarantee to Australia, preferably in the form of a Pacific pact. He failed, in great part because Washington simply was not interested in taking on such a commitment in these distant areas. In 1949 the new Menzies government, with Percy Spender as foreign secretary, renewed Australia's quest for a Pacific alliance (but excluding Japan). Again the Aussies met with a rebuff in Washington.

---

62   George Cunningham, "EU and NATO Enlargement: How Public Opinion is Shaping up in Some Candidate Countries," *NATO Review* (May–June 1997): 16–18. See also Sinnott, *European Public Opinion and Security Policy*, 21–25. In the referendum in Hungary on NATO membership in November 1997, 85 percent voted in favor, a far higher percentage than earlier polls had indicated. (The turnout was only 49 percent, however.) The sharp increase is primarily explained by the Hungarian government's vigorous campaign in favor of Hungary's NATO membership.

63   Zelikow and Rice, *Germany Unified and Europe Transformed*, 170–71, 205–7, 236–38, 276–78, 300.

With the outbreak of war in Korea and Washington's interest in rapidly concluding a peace treaty with Japan, Spender gained the necessary leverage vis-à-vis the Truman administration. Yet, as late as October 1950 the State Department still hesitated. Then New Zealand too changed, from supporting a U.S. presidential declaration to defend Australia and New Zealand to favoring a tripartite alliance. In July 1951, Spender finally achieved his treaty.[64] Australia and New Zealand continued to have close relations with the United States, also during the Vietnam War. In 1986, however, the United States suspended its security obligation to New Zealand, due to the latter's antinuclear policy.

Not only Australia and, to a lesser extent, New Zealand, but several countries in Asia also conducted a virtual campaign to involve the United States on their side. Naturally, those most threatened by communism were the most eager to get Washington's backing; on the whole they got it, particularly after the outbreak of the Korean War. South Korea and Taiwan were the most striking examples. The pull on Washington from local autocrats Syngman Rhee and Chiang Kai-shek became increasingly strong. South Korea got its security treaty with the United States in 1953, Taiwan in 1954. But as Nancy Bernkopf Tucker writes with reference to Taiwan, in words that in modified form applied also to South Korea, "Faced in 1950 with abandonment by the Truman administration, Taipei, by 1954, had woven a web of political, economic, and military ties that made the mutual defense treaty signed that year almost superfluous."[65]

---

64 For a short account of the origins of ANZUS see R. J. O'Neill, "The Korean War and the Origins of ANZUS," in *Munich to Vietnam: Australia's Relations with Britain and the United States since the 1930s*, ed. Carl Bridge (Melbourne, 1991), 99–113. For longer accounts see J. G. Starke, *The ANZUS Treaty Alliance* (Melbourne, 1965); and W. David McIntyre, *Background to the ANZUS Pact: Policy-Making, Strategy, and Diplomacy, 1945–55* (Basingstoke, 1995). For Spender's own version see Sir Percy Spender, *Exercises in Diplomacy: The ANZUS Treaty and the Colombo Plan* (Sydney, 1969). Melvyn Leffler writes about the situation in the Asia-Pacific region at this time that "in Asia (as in Europe) a successful strategy aimed at co-opting Japanese (or German) power compelled the United States to incur commitments that would otherwise have been eschewed." See Melvyn P. Leffler, *A Preponderance of Power: National Security, the Truman Administration, and the Cold War* (Stanford: 1992), 394. See also ibid., 346–47, 428–29, 482.

65 Nancy Bernkopf Tucker, *Taiwan, Hong Kong, and the United States, 1945–1992* (New York, 1994), 35. For an account stressing the U.S. imperial side more than the invitations see

With South Korea feeling threatened by North Korea and Taiwan by China, support in these two countries for the American defense guarantee remained solid, also after the end of the Cold War and the introduction of democracy.[66]

Japan was occupied by the United States from 1945 to 1951, and in an occupied country it makes little sense to talk about invitations. At the same time, it is striking how Japan has kept the system introduced during the American occupation. Thus, no changes have yet been made in the American-sponsored constitution of 1947. Polls in Japan have generally indicated that not only has the United States been far and away the most popular outside country, but support for the American security treaty of 1951 has remained strong, with the particular exception of the Vietnam years. From the 1970s onward two-thirds of Japanese have consistently supported the treaty. For the Japanese it was a nice arrangement indeed to have the United States take care of most of their defense needs while they could concentrate on their country's economic growth. With the U.S.-Japanese defense guidelines of September 1997, the relationship somewhat more resembles a traditional alliance than a unilateral American guarantee.[67]

In the process leading to the setting up of the South-East Asia Treaty Organization (SEATO) in September 1954, it was evident that the locals – the Philippines, Pakistan, and Thailand – wanted a much stronger and more NATO-like organization than did the

Lee, *Outposts of Empire.* ("'Invitation' was an important aspect of this empire but not its predominant element. On the perimeter of the communist empire, Korea and Vietnam were to act as local Western proxies," p. 254). As I have tried to show, "empire" does not necessarily exclude invitation.

66   This impression was strongly reinforced in conversations I had with South Korean high officials and intellectuals during my visit there 5–13 September 1997.

67   Akira Iriye, *Japan and the Wider World: From the Mid-nineteenth Century to the Present* (London, 1997), 88–119, esp. 118–19, 128–31, 151–52, 179–80; Glenn D. Hook, *Militarization and Demilitarization in Contemporary Japan* (London, 1996), esp. 119–22; Michael Richardson, "U.S. Calms Asians on Troop Levels," *International Herald Tribune*, 17 March 1997. See also Lundestad, *American "Empire"*, 60–62. The conclusion is also based on my conversations with Japanese high officials and intellectuals during a visit to Japan 20–27 September 1997. On small Okinawa, where most of the American troops in Japan are actually based, the American presence is quite controversial. See Robert D. Eldridge, "The 1996 Okinawa Referendum on U.S. Base Reductions", *Asian Survey* 37 (October 1997): 879–904.

United States. In fact, the first two countries in particular had long been working hard, and with increasing success, to achieve security guarantees from the United States. Their motives were mixed: hopes of getting both economic and military assistance and support against their neighbors or rebel groups. The SEATO structure became as loose as the United States wanted it to be, but the basic fact in this context remained that the locals definitely encouraged the United States to play an active role in the region both economically and militarily.[68]

It was another matter that these countries had a rather spotty record as far as democracy was concerned and that by signing up with them the United States antagonized other, even more important states in the region, such as India and Indonesia. The Vietnam War meant the end of SEATO. In 1975 it was agreed "to phase out" the organization due to "changed conditions."[69]

The relationship of the ASEAN countries with the United States has been rather complex in recent years. On the one hand, Malaysia, as well as Indonesia under General Suharto, condemned U.S. policies on human rights, democracy, and other questions. In 1991 the United States even had to give up its traditional bases in the Philippines. On the other hand, most of the ASEAN countries want the United States to maintain some form of military presence in the region, in particular to act as the balancer of a rising China. To make this easier, several of them, including even Malaysia, have quietly sought military cooperation with the United States and even permitted certain facilities short of bases.[70]

---

68   SEATO consisted of the United States, Britain, France, Australia, New Zealand, Pakistan, Thailand, and the Philippines. For accounts of its formation see Gary R. Hess, "The American Search for Stability in Southeast Asia: The SEATO Structure of Containment," in *The Great Powers in East Asia, 1953–1960*, ed. Warren I. Cohen and Akira Iriye (New York, 1990), 272–95; Nick Cullather, *Illusions of Influence: The Political Economy of United States-Philippines Relations, 1942–1960* (Stanford, 1994), 141–52; and Robert J. McMahon, *The Cold War on the Periphery: The United States, India, and Pakistan* (New York, 1994), 154–88.

69   Peter Teed, *Dictionary of Twentieth-Century History, 1914–1990* (Oxford, 1992), 435.

70   M. L. Smith and D. M. Jones, "ASEAN, Asian Values and Southeast Asian Security in the New World Order," *Contemporary Security Policy* 18 (December 1997): 126–56; Gerald Segal, "How Insecure is Pacific Asia?" *International Affairs* 73, no. 2 (1997): 235–49, esp. 245-48; Allen S. Whiting, "ASEAN Eyes China: The Security Dimension," *Asian Survey* 37 (April 1997): 299–322; Jose T. Almonte, "Ensuring Security the 'ASEAN Way'," *Survival* 39

Thus, all opposition to America's role should not be taken at face value. Today, for instance, while Chinese authorities are officially against all U.S. bases in East Asia, in practice they understand that the American troops in South Korea and in Japan actually serve to stabilize the situations there. Withdrawals would increase chances both of conflict on the Korean peninsula and of Japan building up its military forces dramatically.[71]

Since the United States did not formally join, but only supported in other ways the Baghdad Pact of 1955 between Britain, Turkey, Iraq, Iran, and Pakistan, it is not so easy to use that pact to study invitational roles vis-à-vis the United States. Views on the origins of the pact have also differed. One school maintains that the Western powers initiated the pact, another that the initiative came more from regional actors. In the only book-length study of the pact so far, Elie Podeh concludes that "while the notion of establishing a Middle Eastern defense organization originated in the West, the Turco-Iraqi Pact – the nucleus of the Baghdad Pact – clearly derived from a regional response." Turkey, Iraq, Iran, and Pakistan all had their own reasons for involving the United States in their affairs, reasons that sometimes had to do with the Cold War, but often even more with economic needs and regional rivalries. The main reason the United States did not join the Baghdad Pact was that by entering into close relations with the four countries mentioned, it would jeopardize relations with other crucial partners, Israel, Egypt, Saudi Arabia, and Jordan.[72] With Iraq leaving after the revolution of 1958, the Baghdad Pact

---

(Winter 1997–98): 80–92; Mahbubani, "An Asia-Pacific Consensus," 149–58; Richardson, "U.S. Calms Asians on Troop Levels," 4; "Asia-Pacific Opinions Mixed on New Defense Guide," *The Japan Times*, 25 September 1997.

71   Author's conversations in Beijing with Vice Foreign Minister Wang Yingfan, 16 September 1997.

72   The preceding is based primarily on Elie Podeh, *The Quest for Hegemony in the Arab World: The Struggle over the Baghdad Pact* (Leiden, 1995), esp. 1–5, 243–52 (quotation is from p. 247). See also Nigel John Ashton, *Eisenhower, Macmillan, and the Problem of Nasser: Anglo-American Relations and Arab Nationalism, 1955–59* (London, 1996), 41–60; Mark J. Gasiorowski, *U.S. Foreign Policy and the Shah: Building a Client State in Iran* (Ithaca, 1991), 121–26; James A. Bill, *The Eagle and the Lion: The Tragedy of American-Iranian Relations* (New Haven, 1988), 113–20; George McGhee, *The US-Turkish-NATO Middle East Connection: How the Truman Doctrine and Turkey's NATO Entry Contained the Soviets* (London, 1990), 156–65.

became the Central Treaty Organization (CENTO). CENTO in turn was dissolved after the Iranian revolution of 1979.

American-Israeli relations were unique. After a somewhat slow start, beginning in the 1960s the relationship became increasingly close, although occasionally quite tense. Israel was in many ways extremely dependent on the United States; at the same time, no small country had the same kind of leverage with Washington as the Israelis and their supporters in America.[73]

Finally, in Latin America the U.S. role was clearly different from what it was in other parts of the world. Here the United States took its supremacy more or less for granted. Washington frequently intervened in the matters of especially Central American and Caribbean states (something to which I shall return). As a result, coercion and denunciation of the "Yankee gringo" were more widespread than invitations to Uncle Sam to provide leadership.

Nevertheless, even many Latin Americans willingly agreed to take part in various U.S.-sponsored arrangements. The inter-American movement began in earnest in 1889 under Washington's leadership, and it quickly grew to include most of the countries in the Western Hemisphere. In the spring of 1945, when the Latin Americans felt that the emerging United Nations could threaten solidarity in the hemisphere, they put forward a joint statement proclaiming that if the Security Council was permitted to manage even American affairs, this "would mean the end of the Monroe Doctrine." The March 1945 Act of Chapultepec on hemispheric ✗ defense "meant the perfection of the American system without interference from outside powers. The inter-American system disappears if the Security Council rules." This was a truly remarkable statement in view of the frequent Latin attacks on Washington's unilaterally proclaimed Monroe Doctrine and was

---

73 For recent studies of the American-Israeli relationship see Yaacov Bar-Siman-Tov, "The United States and Israel since 1948: 'A Special Relationship'?" *Diplomatic History* 22 (Spring 1998): 231–62 and the commentaries to that article by Peter L. Hahn (pp. 263–72) and David Schoenbaum (pp. 273–83) in the same issue; George Wildman Ball, *The Passionate Attachment: America's Involvement with Israel, 1947 to the Present* (New York, 1992); David Schoenbaum, *The United States and the State of Israel* (Oxford, 1993); and Abraham Ben-Zvi, *The United States and Israel: The Limits of the Special Relationship* (New York, 1993).

probably in great part meant to attract U.S. support on the question of the UN structure. The hemispheric approach also formed the basis for the Rio treaty of 1947 and the Organization of American states of 1948.[74] On really crucial occasions, such as the Cuban missile crisis of 1962, Washington was generally able to attract the support of its Latin neighbors.

Interventions and Invitations outside Europe

While the United States was in most respects clearly the strongest power in the world for most of the twentieth century, only after 1945 did it develop the interests and capabilities to intervene more regularly outside the Western Hemisphere and the Pacific. Thus, from 1 January 1946 through 31 December 1975, the United States used its armed forces as a political instrument 215 times, most often in the Third World. The corresponding number for the Soviet Union was 190, but Moscow applied force most frequently *within* its empire, something that Washington, with certain exceptions, had less need for.[75]

Since the definition of "political use of armed force" was rather broad, these numbers do not by themselves tell us whether these interventions were invited or not.[76] Interventions, whether on the small scale of most of the 215 or on the grand scale of the American interventions in the two world wars, can also be invited. The

---

74   The quotation is from Thomas M. Campbell, *Masquerade Peace: America's UN Policy, 1944–45* (Tallahasee, 1973), 168. See also O. Carlos Stoetzer, *The Organization of American States* (Westport, 1993), 13–30; Lester D. Langley, *America and the Americas: The United States in the Western Hemisphere* (Athens, GA, 1989), 162–68; Lundestad, *American "Empire"*, 59–60; and Leffler, *A Preponderance of Power*, 172–73.

75   Barry M. Blechman and Stephen S. Kaplan, *Force without War: U.S. Armed Forces as a Political Instrument* (Washington, 1978), 14, 23–28, 547–53; Stephen S. Kaplan, *Diplomacy of Power: Soviet Armed Forces as a Political Instrument* (Washington, 1981), 42, 689–93. For other lists of interventions see William Blum, *The CIA: A Forgotten History. US Global Interventions* (London, 1986), esp. 412–21; and James Cable, *Gunboat Diplomacy, 1919–1991: Political Applications of Limited Naval Force* (London, 1994), 158–213.

76   The definition used was the following: "A political use of armed forces occurs when physical actions are taken by one or more components of the uniformed military services as part of a deliberate attempt by the national authorities to influence, or to be prepared to influence, specific behavior of individuals in another nation without engaging in a continuing contest of violence" (Blechman and Kaplan, eds., *Force without War*, 12).

American response exactly in the world wars and, after 1945, to the many crises over Berlin underlines this fact.

On the whole, in Western Europe the United States was able to cooperate with governments that were both democratically elected and friendly to the United States. Here it is therefore difficult to come up with clear-cut examples of the United States intervening in internal matters directly against the wishes of the national governments involved. Even in Western Europe, however, not all the invitations were issued by democratic governments. Greece, Turkey, Spain, and Portugal were largely authoritarian until the 1970s. Thus, in the events in Greece in 1947 the Americans in fact wrote both the Greek application for aid and the thank-you notes for the Truman Doctrine.[77] What role Washington – that is, the Central Intelligence Agency (CIA) and the Pentagon – played in bringing the Greek colonels to power in 1967 is fiercely debated.[78] Also in Europe, the abrupt withdrawal of financial support from Czechoslovakia in the fall of 1946 provided an example of the United States withdrawing support from a democratically elected government when this government was seen as too dependent on Moscow.[79]

In other parts of the world democracies were relatively few. Washington's choice then frequently seemed to be between left- and right-wing dictatorships. The restraints on the United States not intervening in explicitly domestic matters were also much weaker here than in Western Europe. As President Kennedy's statement went: "There are three possibilities in descending order of preference: a decent democratic regime, a continuation of the Trujillo regime or a Castro regime. We ought to aim at the first, but we really can't renounce the second until we are sure that we can avoid the third."[80] Although Kennedy was referring specifi-

---

77 For a further discussion of this point see my American *"Empire"*, 65–67.
78 See, for instance, the differing accounts in Blum, *The CIA: A Forgotten History*, 243–50; and Stephen G. Xydis, "Coups and Countercoups in Greece, 1967–73 (with postscript)," *Political Science Quarterly* 89 (Fall 1974): 507–38.
79 This event is analyzed in detail in my *American Non-Policy towards Eastern Europe, 1943–1947*, 167–73.
80 Arthur M. Schlesinger, Jr., *A Thousand Days: John F. Kennedy in the White House* (Boston, 1965), 769.

cally to the situation in the Dominican Republic, his lesson really applied to most of the Third World.

Particularly in vast and complex Asia it is virtually impossible to generalize about intervention by invitation or by imposition. While in many countries there was often a great deal of skepticism about the United States, in times of crisis the United States could still act with considerable local support. This point was perhaps best illustrated in the Middle East. During the Cold War the requests in 1958 from the Lebanese president and the Jordanian king to the United States to intervene provided examples of an invitational kind, although the invitations were undoubtedly issued in part to undercut domestic rivals. The United States did intervene in Lebanon while the British handled Jordan.[81]

After the end of the Cold War the Gulf War of 1990–91 illustrated the support for American intervention even more clearly. After Saddam Hussein's Iraq in August 1990 had invaded Kuwait, the United States was able to organize a very wide coalition indeed to undo this action. The United Nations Security Council strongly condemned Iraq, with even Cuba and Yemen eventually voting in favor. Within eight days of the Iraqi move a majority in the Arab League consisting of the smaller Gulf states, Egypt, Saudi Arabia, Syria, Lebanon, and Morocco – this was the first time a division had taken place in the league on a substantive matter – voted to permit the Arab states to join the emerging American-led coalition. True, most of these countries would have preferred that the Iraqis be forced to leave without American intervention. Even the Saudis hesitated before they agreed to call in the Americans. Yet when push came to shove Syria, Egypt, and Saudi Arabia contributed significant forces to the Multinational Coali-

---

81 For accounts of these interventions see William B. Quandt, "Lebanon, 1958, and Jordan, 1970," in Blechman and Kaplan, eds., *Force without War*, 225–57; Ritchie Ovendale, "Great Britain and the Anglo-American Invasion of Jordan and Lebanon in 1958," *International History Review* 16 (May 1994): 284–303; and Douglas Little, "His Finest Hour? Eisenhower, Lebanon, and the 1958 Middle East Crisis," *Diplomatic History* 20 (Winter 1996): 27–54.

tion that in early 1991 so successfully threw the Iraqis out of Kuwait.[82]

On the other hand, the many examples of imposed interventions provide a clear warning against taking the invitational aspect too far. The earliest such example in Asia in this century occurred in the Philippines in the immediate aftermath of the Spanish-American War of 1898. Most Filipinos supported the United States over Spain in that war, but when they then demanded their independence a war broke out with the United States. This war cost at least two hundred thousand Filipinos and nearly two thousand Americans their lives. It was considerably reduced in scope in 1901–2 only on Washington's promise that the American occupation would end when the Filipinos had been "trained for self-government." Thus, the United States entered the American Century fighting what indeed looked very much like a traditional imperial war.[83]

The first example after 1945 of Washington, in this case the incoming Eisenhower administration, covertly trying to overthrow a government in Asia probably took place in Iran in 1953. The CIA operation to remove Mohammad Mossaddeq and his National Front government would not have succeeded without some Iranian participation (the shah, important military leaders) and without Mossaddeq's position already having deteriorated even economically, but this was still imposition rather than invitation. And, as James Bill has argued, the American intervention "was the first fundamental step in the eventual rupture of Iranian-Ameri-

---

82 For a good review article of the already vast literature on the Gulf War see L. Carl Brown, "Review Article: Shield and Storm in the Desert," *International History Review* 16 (February 1994): 92–113. The best account of the Gulf War is probably Lawrence Freedman and Efraim Karsh, *The Gulf Conflict, 1990–1991: Diplomacy and War in the New World Order* (Princeton, 1993). For a short account see George Joffe, "Middle Eastern Views of the Gulf Conflict and its Aftermath," *Review of International Studies* 19, no. 2 (1993): 177–99. For an interesting Arab view see Mohamed Heikal, *Illusions of Triumph: An Arab View of the Gulf War* (London, 1992).

83 For a short account of the events in the Philippines see Walter LaFeber, *The American Search for Opportunity, 1865–1913*, vol. 2, *Cambridge History of American Foreign Relations* (Cambridge, England, 1993), 156–68. For a longer account see Glenn Anthony May, *A Past Recovered* (Quezon City, Philippines, 1987).

can relations in the revolution of 1978–79."[84] In Indonesia in 1958 the lack of support was the basic reason why the CIA's operation to topple Achmad Sukarno failed so dismally. The administration even had to bypass its own embassy in Djakarta.[85]

Similarly, it would be difficult to argue that the United States fought the Vietnam War by invitation. About the situation in Vietnam in 1954 President Eisenhower himself wrote in his memoirs that he had never talked with a person knowledgeable about Indochinese affairs who did not agree that "had elections been held at the time of the fighting, possibly 80 per cent of the population would have voted for the Communist Ho Chi Minh as their leader rather than Chief of State Bao Dai."[86]

This realization did not stop the Eisenhower administration from building up the separate state of South Vietnam under Ngo Dinh Diem's leadership. When even Diem's limited support eroded and his firm loyalty to the United States came to be doubted – he appears to have opposed the introduction of American combat troops and rumors existed about a possible approach to Hanoi – more and more top policymakers in Washington wanted him deposed. President Kennedy himself vacillated, but with U.S. Ambassador Henry Cabot Lodge clearly favoring the Vietnamese military plotters, Diem was overthrown and, to Kennedy's consternation, murdered on 2 November 1963. After the death of Diem, the changes of government in Saigon were so frequent and the dependence of these governments on the United States so obvious that again the invitational perspective makes little sense. Rather, this was imposition.[87]

---

84   The best account of the situation in Iran is probably Bill, *The Eagle and the Lion*, 51–97 (quotation is from p. 94). See also Gasiorowski, *U.S. Foreign Policy and the Shah*, 57–84.
85   The best account of Eisenhower's policy toward Indonesia is Audrey R. & George McT. Kahin, *Subversion as Foreign Policy: The Secret Eisenhower and Dulles Debacle in Indonesia* (New York, 1995).
86   Dwight D. Eisenhower, *Mandate for Change* (New York, 1965), 449.
87   See, for instance, Henry Cabot Lodge's comment: "I don't think we ought to take this government seriously. There is no one who can do anything. We have to do what we think we ought to do regardless of what the Saigon government does." U.S. Department of State, *Foreign Relations of the United States, 1964–1965* (Washington, 1998), 3:193. Among the many accounts of the American role in Vietnam in general and the fall of Diem in particular I prefer George C. Herring, *America's Longest War: The United States and Vietnam, 1950–1975* (New York, 1979), 73–107; George McT. Kahin, *Intervention: How America Became*

In Latin America, the Monroe Doctrine of 1823 was hardly in voked in the nineteenth century and was originally intended to protect Latin American revolutions against European intervention. After the Spanish-American War of 1898 the United States actually supported the independence of Cuba, as opposed to that of the Philippines, but under the restrictions imposed by the Platt Amendment this Cuban independence was substantially curtailed. When the United States landed troops in Cuba in 1906, this was done with the approval both of the government and the rebels trying to overthrow it. In 1903–4 Washington helped establish Panama's independence from Colombia in return for very extensive U.S. rights, particularly in the Canal Zone.[88]

Yet, in traditionally imperialist ways the United States did not particularly seem to care whether its interventions in Central America and the Caribbean were invited or not. In 1905 Theodore Roosevelt, through the Roosevelt Corollary to the Monroe Doctrine, reinterpreted the doctrine to give the United States protection against revolutionaries in Latin America.[89] While Roosevelt justified intervention in the name of the Monroe Doctrine and Robert Taft in the name of dollar diplomacy, Woodrow Wilson, on this as on most other points, preferred the language of political reform and general principles.[90] After more than thirty mili-

Involved in Vietnam (New York, 1986), 146–81; and Robert D. Schulzinger, *A Time for War: The United States and Vietnam, 1941–1975* (Oxford, 1997), 97–123. Joseph G. Morgan, *The Vietnam Lobby: The American Friends of Vietnam, 1955–1975* (Chapel Hill, 1997) shows that the ties between Diem and the Vietnam Lobby in the United States may well have been weaker than we had earlier thought. For an official study of the American role in the planned assassination not only of Diem but also of Fidel Castro, Patrice Lumumba, Chilean Gen. René Schneider, and Rafael Trujillo see U.S. Senate, Select Committee to Study Governmental Operations, *An Interim Report, Alleged Assassination Plots Involving Foreign Leaders* (New York, 1976). The report concluded that although various U.S. agencies had indeed drawn up plans of one sort or another for the assassination of these leaders, with the possible exception of General Schneider the United States was probably not involved in any of the actual killings.

88   For analyses of these events in Cuba and Panama see LaFeber, *The American Search for Opportunity, 1865–1913*, 139–55, 193–96; David Healy, *Drive to Hegemony: The United States in the Caribbean, 1898–1917* (Madison, 1988), 77–94, 126–33; Allan Reed Millett, *The Politics of Intervention: The Military Occupation of Cuba, 1906–09* (Columbus, 1968), 59–112; and John Major, *Prize Possession: The United States and the Panama Canal, 1903–1979* (Cambridge, England, 1993), 34–77.

89   See, for instance, LaFeber, *The American Search for Opportunity, 1865–1913*, 198–201.

90   This point is taken from Iriye, *The Globalizing of America, 1913–1945*, 35.

tary interventions, Herbert Hoover abandoned the traditional interventionist attitude. In 1933 Secretary of State Cordell Hull
formally proclaimed that "no state has the right to intervene in
the internal or external affairs of another." The troops in the
Canal Zone in Panama now remained the only U.S. troops in the
Western Hemisphere outside of U.S. territory.[91]

As we know, this was not the end of U.S. interventionism in the
Western Hemisphere. After the Second World War, the United
States intervened against democratically elected governments in
Guatemala in 1954 and, more indirectly, in Chile in 1970 and
1973, and against internationally recognized, although formally
less democratic governments in Cuba in 1961, in Nicaragua in
1980–85, in Grenada in 1983, and in Panama in 1989. All these
interventions were roundly condemned internationally. The intervention in the Dominican Republic in 1965 was at the invitation of the country's rulers, although the invitation was issued
under rather complex local circumstances.[92]

In this perspective the U.S. intervention in Haiti in 1995 was
most untraditional in that it was meant to restore democratic rule
and as such was authorized by the UN Security Council. Even
the local military rulers ended up cooperating with the U.S. forces.
Similarly, in the 1990s, with the military dictators gone and the
radical left in eclipse, not only democracy but also free-market
economics and American mass culture became almost popular in
Latin America.[93]

---

91   Ibid., 82–83, 147–48.
92   For an overview of U.S. interventions from a legal point of view see Max Hilaire, *International Law and United States Military Intervention in the Western Hemisphere* (The Hague,
1997). For some comparative comments on U.S. interventions see H. W. Brands, Jr., "Decisions on American Armed Intervention: Lebanon, Dominican Republic, and Grenada," *Political Science Quarterly* 102, no. 4 (1987): 607–24. For the most recent interventions see
Richard N. Haass, *Intervention: The Use of American Military Force in the Post-Cold War
World* (Washington, 1994), esp. 19–48. For an account of American interventions in Central
America see Walter LaFeber, *Inevitable Revolutions: The United States in Central America*
(New York, 1993). For the interventions in Guatemala and Chile I prefer Piero Gleijeses,
Shattered Hope: The Guatemalan Revolution and the United States, 1944–54 (Princeton,
1991) and Paul E. Sigmund, *The United States and Democracy in Chile* (Baltimore, 1993).
93   Anthony Faiola, "'Yankee' Is Cool in Latin America," *International Herald Tribune*, 22
January 1998.

The First American Century?

Today, and for the foreseeable future, the United States clearly remains Number One, a power significantly stronger than not just any other single power but even than any likely combination of powers. Despite considerable reductions in U.S. defense spending, with the collapse of the Soviet Union and of much of Russia's military might as well, and with even larger reductions in the defense spending of most other Great Powers, America's military lead appears more pronounced now than in decades. Economically, since the 1970s America's share of the world's gross national product has stabilized at around 25 percent. With the U.S. budget deficit finally largely under control and with the economic woes of Japan and much of East Asia, America's relative economic position looks considerably stronger today than it did only a decade ago. America's vast and, it seems, once again increasing lead in information technology will probably have economic and military consequences that we do not fully foresee at present.[94] America's message to the world – in the form of democracy, the market economy, freer trade, and American mass culture – has rarely, if ever, affected the world more than today.

Today the predictions made ten years and less ago by Paul Kennedy and others about the decline of the United States appear oddly dated. In his *The Rise and Fall of the Great Powers*, Kennedy predicted the decline of the United States. No sooner was the book out than that other superpower, the Soviet Union, collapsed. Then, in *Preparing for the Twenty-First Century*, Kennedy forecast that the twenty-first century would belong to Japan. Again, no sooner was the book out than Japan entered into its first period of serious economic and political stagnation since the early 1950s.[95]

---

94 Joseph S. Nye, Jr., and William A. Owens, "America's Information Edge," *Foreign Affairs* 75 (March-April 1996): 20–36.
95 Paul Kennedy, *The Rise and Fall of the Great Powers: Economic Change and Military Conflict from 1500 to 2000* (New York, 1987); idem, *Preparing for the Twenty-First Century* (London, 1993). Today my own *American "Empire"*, which criticized Kennedy for his declinist views, seems rather mild in its criticism.

Thus, it can indeed be argued that we are still in Luce's American Century. Compared to the Cold War, especially the pre-Vietnam years, at least one major difference exists, however: Washington's somewhat reduced interest in much of the outside world, most clearly seen in its relative reluctance to risk lives and spend money on its global role. Although Washington orchestrated Desert Storm to drive the Iraqis out of Kuwait and although the United States initially committed twenty thousand troops to the implementation of the Dayton accords in Bosnia, America's fear of "foreign entanglements" is striking. When eighteen U.S. soldiers were killed in Somalia, the American troops left. Most forms of foreign assistance are out. In relative terms the official development assistance of the United States is the smallest of all the OECD countries (with the exception of Turkey and South Korea).[96]

Dominance easily breeds American arrogance and foreign irritation. So also with the American role in the world today. In the United Nations, Washington is roundly condemned for trying to dictate the UN's actions while at the same time refusing to pay its membership dues; in NATO, grumbling is heard about the peremptory manner in which the United States decided the question of new members; Russia's Boris Yeltsin and China's Jiang Zemin proclaim a "strategic partnership" directed against those who would "push the world toward a unipolar order." In Canada, in France, in South Africa, virtually everywhere, complaints are heard about the various ways in which the U.S. Congress in particular is trying to make American laws apply to the rest of the world, in the form of sanctions against Cuba, Libya, and Iran. Charges are even heard about the return of "the ugly American."[97]

"Realists" have argued that no alliance survives the disappearance of the threat against which it was directed. When the enemy

---

96   For a short account of the intervention in Somalia see Haass, *Intervention*, 43–46. For development assistance see The OECD Observer, *OECD in Figures: Statistics on the Member Countries* (Paris, 1997), 68–69.
97   See, for instance, David E. Sanger, "Ugly American Returns," *International Herald Tribune*, 6 October 1997; and William Drozdiak, "U.S. Dominance Breeds Irritation," ibid., 5 November 1997.

holding the alliance together disappears, realignment follows; a ganging up against a new leader soon takes place.[98]

This time it seems to be different. Not only is there no end to NATO;[99] many new countries even want to join. Despite the occasional denunciation of "a unipolar order," there is no real ganging up against the United States. In fact, the United States appears to be the partner of choice for all the major powers.[100] This is probably in part because its power is so overwhelming and so multifaceted, but in part also because its power is of a somewhat different nature than that of traditional superpowers. Rarely does the United States conquer; it rules in more indirect, more American ways, so indirect, in fact, that frequently, but far from always, it is still invited to play the preeminent role it does toward the end of the (first?) American Century.

---

98   For a good realist analysis see Kenneth N. Waltz, *Theory of International Relations* (Reading, MA, 1979). For NATO predictions see, for instance, John J. Mearsheimer, "Back to the Future: Instability in Europe after the Cold War," *International Security* 15 (Summer 1990) 5–56. See also Mearsheimer, "The Future of America's Continental Commitment," in Lundestad, ed., *No End to Alliance*.

99   *No End to Alliance* is the title of my edited book on American-Western European relations. See note 34.

100   This paragraph is based in part on Josef Joffe, "How America Does It," *Foreign Affairs* 76 (September/October 1997): 13–27.

3

America and the Twentieth Century: Continuity and Change

ROBERT JERVIS

At the end of the century, the United States finds itself in a place that is surprising in many respects, but that is surprisingly familiar in others. Indeed, much more than anyone had reason to expect during the Cold War, the American security position resembles what it was at the start of the century while the world has become more compatible with American values. Of course this does not guarantee that the next century will turn out well. Henry Luce said of the twentieth century: "No other century has been so big with promise . . . and in no one century have so many men and women and children suffered such pain and anguish and bitter death."[1] The first part of the statement clearly applies to the century we are entering; while appreciating the frequency of overoptimistic predictions, I doubt if the second part will.

It is a commonplace that "in the twentieth century, scientific and technological innovation increased at an exponential rate. . . . The Industrial Revolution extended over generations and allowed time for human and institutional adjustment. The Computer Revolution is far swifter, more concentrated, and more drastic in its impact."[2] Almost everyone agrees that change has been proceeding at an accelerated rate. Furthermore, it is usually argued that change is greater and more rapid in domestic than in international affairs. Our everyday lives and societies have been

1   See Henry R. Luce, "The American Century," in this volume.
2   Arthur Schlesinger, Jr., "Has Democracy a Future?" *Foreign Affairs* 76 (September/October 1997): 5–6.

revolutionized by technological change and economic growth while international politics maintains its basic consistency, in large part because it remains a system of self-help and anarchy in the sense of absence of government.[3] I believe this position is not merely exaggerated but incorrect. Domestic life in the United States changed much more in the first half of this century than the second, while international politics has seen three true revolutions in the last fifty years. The United States is much the same country that it was in 1950; international politics has been altered in its fundamentals. In this article I will briefly discuss the first part of this proposition and then elaborate in greater detail the second part, with special attention to the ways in which the international changes were linked to and supported the American domestic system.

Measuring change is notoriously difficult. But perhaps because I am not an historian I feel comfortable arguing that a Rip Van Winkle who went to sleep in 1900 and awoke in 1950 would be much more disoriented than his counterpart who napped from 1950 to 2000. Most of our cities look more or less as they did fifty years ago; the changes in the first half of the century were much more dramatic and extensive. The earlier era also saw the transition from rural to urban life, a greater change than the subsequent outflow to the suburbs. The American state was also transformed more in the earlier era, with the limited growth of the welfare state in the War on Poverty and associated programs under Lyndon B. Johnson and Richard M. Nixon and the later withdrawal under Ronald Reagan being minor compared to the growth of the reach of government produced by two world wars and a depression. I suspect that if public opinion polls had existed early in the century we would find parallel evidence for a greater change in public beliefs and values in the first half of the century as well, although this is not to deny the importance of the recent changes in actual and, perhaps even more, desired race

3   For recent statements of this position from different perspectives see Kenneth Waltz, *Theory of International Politics* (Reading, MA, 1979); and Paul Kennedy, *The Rise and Fall of the Great Powers: Economic Change and Military Conflict from 1500 to 2000* (New York, 1987).

relations, an acceleration of the trend toward equality for women, and, partly linked to this, the alteration of sexual mores. The prevalence of television and computers, the two leading technical changes in the second half of the century, seem to me not only less transforming than these social changes but to have had less impact than radio, the telephone, movies, and automobiles had in the earlier era.

It goes without saying that the United States has had an enormous influence on the world throughout the twentieth century. Its intervention in World War I tipped the balance; its refusal to join the League of Nations or to provide political and economic leadership deepened the Depression and facilitated the rise of the Axis; its intervention in World War II made victory possible (although the Soviet Union did the bulk of the fighting against Germany); no point on the globe was untouched by American military, political, and economic policy after World War II; for the indefinite future, no country will come close to rivaling America's world-wide influence.[4] What is harder to gauge is the influence of the world and America's foreign relations on the American society, economy, and polity. Judgments are particularly hard because we must ask ourselves not only about the changes within the United States that accompanied or followed interaction with the rest of the world but what the United States would have looked like under different circumstances. This counterfactual is even more difficult than usual because so many hypothetical paths for the United States can be imagined.[5]

To argue that the United States would look much as it does today had its foreign involvement been less or different is to imply a sort of teleology that is now understandably out of fashion. More common are arguments like those of Michael Sherry: "Militarization reshaped every realm of American life – politics and foreign policy, economics and technology, culture and social rela-

---

4   It is frequently argued that the influence of all countries, including the United States, is diminishing in comparison to that of global economic forces. See, for example, Robert Keohane and Helen Milner, eds., *Internationalization and Domestic Politics* (New York, 1996).

5   For a good discussion of the uses of counterfactuals see Philip Tetlock and Aaron Belkin, eds., *Counterfactual Thought Experiments in World Politics* (Princeton, 1996).

tions – making America a profoundly different nation."[6] But it is devilishly hard to say what the United States was different from or what it would have been otherwise. Indeed, common sense would indicate that foreign affairs have had much less impact on the United States than on any other country in the world. All the major European countries were partly occupied if not conquered by foreign invaders, with the exception of Great Britain, which suffered enormous casualties in World War I, heavy bombardment in World War II, and the loss of its empire after the war. Furthermore, the United States has extensively intervened in the domestic affairs of every country in the world through overt and covert instruments; the reciprocal flow has been tiny in comparison, the recent uproar over Chinese contributions to Clinton's 1996 campaign and a few gestures of friends and enemies to influence American elections in the Cold War notwithstanding.

Nevertheless, the two world wars and the Cold War helped build a powerful state, especially in its ability to tax and its connections with most forms of social life.[7] Specifics are easy to tick off, especially since 1945. Higher education was drastically altered by the GI Bill, the National Defense Education Act, and extensive support for scientific research. The transportation system was shaped by the implicit subsidy of the aircraft industry through the procurement of military airplanes, and by the development of the interstate highways, justified on the grounds of national defense. Computers were originally developed for military purposes and would have progressed much more slowly were it not for heavy military investments; the internet, far from being the product solely of individual inventors and entrepreneurs, was built around the ideas and network developed by the Department of Defense to facilitate communication after a Soviet nuclear attack.

6   Michael Sherry, *In the Shadow of War: The United States Since the 1930s* (New Haven, 1995), x.
7   See, for example, Ronald Schaffer, *America in the Great War* (New York, 1991); Bartholomew Sparrow, *From the Outside In: World War II and the American State* (Princeton, 1996); John Morton Blum, *V was for Victory* (New York, 1976); Sherry, *In the Shadow of War*; John Kenneth White, *Still Seeing Red: How the Cold War Shapes the New American Politics* (Boulder, CO, 1997).

The civil rights movement owed much to the sense that the United States was claiming to be the champion of liberty and equality abroad and the feeling that, as Eleanor Roosevelt put it, civil rights "isn't any longer a domestic question – it's an international question," one that "may decide whether democracy or communism wins out in the world."[8]

Indeed, almost every social and political development in the United States has been explained as a reaction to or a function of Cold War imperatives, from heightened homophobia, to social conformity, to lack of faith in the future, to the loosening of social bonds and norms, to the shape of the political parties. Influence no doubt there was, but establishing its degree is much more difficult. Without a Cold War would the United States really have failed to invest in science, abstained from building superhighways, and maintained official racial discrimination? Were the links between all sorts of social phenomena and American foreign policy really present, let alone strong? It is easy to posit almost any connection, as when it is argued that the popularity of Henry Dryfuss's famous design for a circular room thermostat reflected the need to sooth fears of war in the 1950s.[9] Had a square won popular approval, I am sure that an equally plausible argument could have been produced.

More interesting and important was the speculation Louis Hartz voiced in 1955 that America's involvement with the world would lead it to understand that its political traditions and view of a "fixed, dogmatic liberalism of a liberal way of life" were not natural and inevitable, let alone superior, but were the product of a unique social structure that sprung from the founding of America as bourgeois fragment that skipped "the feudal stage of history" and was "born equal," to take the phrase Hartz borrows from Tocqueville.[10] Lacking robust strands of both reactionary and

---

8 Quoted in Sherry, *Shadow of War*, 146.
9 Herbert Muschamp, "Form Follows Function into Ideal Circles." *New York Times*, 28 March 1997.
10 Louis Hartz, *The Liberal Tradition in America* (New York, 1955) (the quotations are from 9, 3, 5). Hartz's thesis has been subject to vigorous dispute, but I believe his essential point remains valid. For a parallel argument about the deficiencies of liberal thought see Hans Morgenthau, *Scientific Man Versus Power Politics* (Chicago, 1946).

revolutionary thought, the United States found it difficult to understand the rest of the world which had evolved quite differently. For Hartz, this went a long way to explaining red scares at home and the failure to appreciate indigenous nationalisms and revolutions abroad. Given its self-replicating beliefs, basic change could never come from within the United States: "The larger forces working toward a shattering of American provincialism abroad as well as at home lie . . . in the world scene itself."[11] Having to deal with, persuade, and lead countries with very different social structures and understandings of the world could produce radical intellectual, and therefore political, change in the United States. "What is at stake is nothing less than a new level of consciousness, a transcending of irrational Lockianism, in which an understanding of self and an understanding of others go hand in hand."[12] But Hartz was not sure this would happen, and so he ended his book with these questions: "Can a people 'born equal' ever understand peoples elsewhere that have to become so? Can it ever understand itself?"[13] Even now, at the end of the century, these questions remain perhaps the most important ones, and among the most difficult to answer.

Although it remains unclear how much America has changed, especially in the last half-century, and how great the influence of world politics on the United States has been, it is noteworthy that the beginning and the end of the century resemble each other much more than they do the long era between in the extent to which the United States initially was, and now is, free from security threats. Lincoln's 1836 boast remained true seventy-five years later:

Shall we expect some transatlantic military giant to step the Ocean and crush us at a blow? Never! All the armies of Europe, Asia, and Africa combined, with all the treasure of the earth (our own excepted) in their

11 Hartz, *Liberal Tradition*, 308.
12 Ibid.
13 Ibid, 309.

military chest; with a Buonaparte for a commander, could not by force take a drink from the Ohio or make a track on the Blue Ridge, in a trial of a thousand years.[14]

The United States could choose foreign involvement, of course, and did so to pursue a variety of goals. The absence of any pressing need to fight did not mean that the country would not go to war. Thus we can still debate the motives that impelled American entry into World War I, but fear that America otherwise would be at Germany's mercy is not high on the list on the list of candidate motives.

This changed with the appearance of Hitler and a militaristic Japan, and, even more, with the rise of Soviet power and the unstable situations in Europe and Asia following World War II.[15] When the Soviet Union disintegrated, however, the United States was returned to something like its earlier degree of security.[16] This does not mean that it faces no external threats. Proliferation of weapons of mass destruction (WMD) could not only threaten American allies and inhibit the United States from using force to support them[17] but could also menace the United States itself. But American foreign policy activism would probably increase the latter danger. That is, American troops would be in danger from

---

14   Quoted in Walter McDougall, *Promised Land, Crusader State: The American Encounter with the World Since 1776* (Boston, 1997), 52.
15   For a dissent from the consensus view that American security was deeply menaced before World War II see Bruce Russett, *No Clear and Present Danger: A Skeptical View of the United States Entry into World War II* (New York, 1972). Revisionists argue that American power was so overwhelming and Soviet goals so limited that there was no major threat to American security after the war. But if the more Marxist-oriented of the revisionists are correct that the USSR and instability did indeed threaten the ability of American capitalism to expand overseas, and if such expansion was necessary for the maintenance of the American domestic system, then the American ruling class indeed did face a threat so severe as to compel a strong and active foreign policy.
16   See Eric Nordlinger, *Isolationism Reconfigured: American Foreign Policy for a New Century* (Princeton, 1995); and the literature cited in footnote 53 below.
17   But for a well-developed argument that the U.S. willingness to use force to oppose Iraq in 1990–91 would not have been different had that state possessed nuclear weapons see Barry Posen, "United States Security Policy in a Nuclear-Armed World, Or: What if Iraq Had Had Nuclear Weapons?" *Security Studies* 6 (Spring 1977): 1–31. For a general discussion of the threat from WMD see Richard Betts, "The New Threat of Mass Destruction," *Foreign Affairs* 77 (January/February 1998): 26–41.

WMD only if they fought countries that had them. It also seems likely that actively opposing governments and groups which seek to upset the status quo throughout the world will increase the chance of terrorism in the United States, with or without WMD.

This does not mean that the United States should not or will not be heavily engaged politically and even militarily throughout the world. It is just that such policies are not required by narrow security interests, just as they were not in 1900. American policy is of course likely to be very different from a hundred years ago because American power and the environment in which it operates are very different. But both periods are ones of a relatively high degree of freedom of choice (and this makes them troublesome from the standpoint of realist accounts of international politics that see state behavior as a response to a compelling external environment).

America's freedom of action is no longer unique, however, as it was in earlier eras when only the United States was made secure by its large size, its geographic removal from other great powers, and the continuing feuds among the latter. International politics has changed enormously, at least among the developed countries. All of them are now more secure than they have ever been. In other words, this century has turned out to be America's in the sense that at its end almost all the states the United States cares most about have gained many of the advantages that belonged to the United States alone at its start.

This is true, I believe, because international politics has seen three major changes – revolutions may not be too strong a term – in the past fifty or fifty-five years.

Although the causes can be debated, the fact is striking: we are experiencing the longest period of peace among the great powers in history.[18] The last fifty years have been filled with wars within

18 Paul Schroeder, "Does Murphy's Law Apply to History?" *Wilson Quarterly* 9 (New Year's 1985): 88; Joseph Nye, Jr., "The Long-Term Future of Nuclear Deterrence," in *The Logic of Nuclear Terror*, ed. Roman Kolkowicz (Boston, 1987), 283; Robert Jervis, *The Meaning of the Nuclear Revolution* (Ithaca, NY, 1989), 23–38. Of course, one can argue about exactly what constitutes a great power war: Soviet and American pilots shot each other down during the Korean War, and if we count China as a great power, the United States and the People's Republic fought in Korea and, less directly, in Vietnam.

and between less developed countries, many of which were fueled by rivalries among the major states, but for the great powers, the phrase "postwar years" means not only that this is the period that came after World War II, but that it is an era – and one of unlimited duration – in which they do not fight each other. This is a breathtaking change in world politics, which previously consisted of the state of war among the major powers. To say this of course does not mean that they were always fighting, but that for all but the United States their diplomacy – and much of their domestic politics – was conducted in the shadow of war. Indeed, rarely did more than a generation go by without at least some of them fighting each other.

Most people expected this pattern to continue after 1945. Stalin told his Yugoslav comrades that "we shall recover in fifteen or twenty years, and then we'll have another go at it."[19] While the remark should not be overinterpreted, there is little reason to believe that he expected an unprecedented era of peace. Although American decision-makers doubted that Stalin wanted war, they thought that miscalculation could produce this result, a worry that blended into concern that war would arise from the escalation of limited Soviet military actions as the USSR gained first nuclear parity and then, arguably, some form of superiority. But these fears were misplaced, or at least were not realized, in part because statesmen took steps to see that they would not be. The result was that the years from 1945 to 1990 were unprecedented in being without a great-power war, but not in lacking the expectation of one.

I believe that two interrelated factors were at work and produced many other major changes in international politics as well: bipolarity and the development of nuclear weapons. While it would be a digression to analyze the vigorous disputes about the causes and the effects of both of them, I should note the consensus, at least among American scholars, that bipolarity is less warprone than the more familiar multipolar system. Important here is that bipolarity is conceived not as the world being divided into

19   Quoted in Milovan Djilas, *Conversations with Stalin* (New York, 1962), 114–15.

two hostile camps, as it was before World War I, but rather as a world in which two superpowers are in a class by themselves and so each could counteract the other by generating resources internally rather than having to rely on allies. This meant that the superpowers were neither likely to be dragged into war because of allies' interests nor would fail to meet pressing threats in the hope that allies would pick up this burden.[20]

Three aspects of international politics under bipolarity fitted well with American political traditions. First, the fact of a permanent enemy meant that American public opinion did not have to face the uncomfortable notion that the United States might have to shift its allegiance and even its affections in phase with the vagaries of world politics. American foreign policy could then be infused with morality and self-righteousness, as so often had been the case in the past.[21] Second, the United States could maintain its habit of unilateralism. Throughout its history, the United States rarely had to deal with allies as equals, a pattern that could continue under bipolarity. While it could not command their support, in most cases this was not required. Thus there was some basis for the constant stream of complaints by American allies, not to speak of the neutrals, that they were not fully consulted or their interests taken to heart. Bipolarity allowed the United States to be more cavalier than great powers had been in the past. Many American commentators stressed that the United States had risen to the demands of world politics by shedding its traditions and assuming a leadership role, as Luce had said was necessary for this to be the American Century.[22] But without implying what the United States did was easy or foreordained by the requirements of international politics, one may question how well

---

20   The classic statement of this position is Waltz, *Theory of International Politics*. Also see Glenn Snyder and Paul Diesing, *Conflict Among Nations* (Princeton, 1977); Robert Jervis, *System Effects: Complexity in Political and Social Life* (Princeton, 1997), 110–24; and Dale Copeland, "Neo-Realism and the Myth of Bipolar Stability," *Security Studies* 5 (Spring 1996): 29–47.
21   George Kennan, *American Diplomacy, 1900–1950* (Chicago, 1951); Arnold Wolfers, *Discord and Collaboration* (Baltimore, 1962), chap. 15.
22   Luce, "The American Century."

the United States would have done had power been distributed more equally among the Western countries.

Contrary to the pure logic of bipolarity, however, the United States did pay significant heed to the values and preferences of its allies, especially in Western Europe. This brings up the third link between bipolarity and American behavior. As Thomas Risse-Kappen shows, the United States was strongly influenced by the habits and norms of democracy which stressed consultation, responsiveness, and compromise.[23] To a significant extent, allies were treated as though they were part of the American polity, with a legitimate voice in what the United States would do. Allies then gained influence not only from the American expectation that they would fail to cooperate if the United States did not adjust its policy, but also from the American sense that this was the appropriate way to do business. The United States was then not being forced to cede authority by the demands of a hostile world, but was incorporating like-minded states into its sphere.

It is difficult to determine how much of this pattern is to be explained by the fact that the United States was a democracy – which implies that any democracy in America's place would have behaved in this way – and how much was related to particularly American characteristics, such as its being highly pluralistic with power diffused both within the government and between the government and the wider society. In part because of the separation of powers, the American system is distinguished by multiple points of access and multiple levers of influence. This makes American policy more subject to the pulls and tugs of domestic interests; it also makes it easier for allies to get a full hearing and to gain more influence than their physical resources could provide.

Throughout the Cold War, analysts saw the weakness of the American state as a major liability, and they were right to see that it reduced the consistency and subtlety of American foreign policy. It was also often believed that the open alliance system made it particularly vulnerable. Even when it did not seem likely that the

---

23   Thomas Risse-Kappen, *Cooperation Among Democracies: The European Influence on United States Foreign Policy* (Princeton, 1995).

alliance would fly apart through internal discord, the Soviets were provided with a plethora of entry points through which to divide it. In the end this did not happen. Part of the reason was maladroit Soviet diplomacy which consistently missed opportunities to make offers on issues like the SS–20 deployment that were attractive enough to garner European support but did not go far enough to meet American desires. But part of the reason why the alliance held together was that the American openness and responsiveness lent it great resilience.

In retrospect, the difference between NATO and the Warsaw Pact not only epitomized the differences between the social and political systems of the two camps but also heavily contributed to the victory of the former and the disintegration of the latter. It is not that the Soviet Union never made concessions to its allies, either because it feared the results of having to use armed force, as was the case in its dealings with Poland in 1956, or because of the fear that without assistance its partner would collapse, as was frequently the case with East Germany, but rather that the regimes the Soviet Union established were never able to come to peace with their own societies and so true give-and-take was impossible. The Warsaw Pact then often appeared to be a solid front, but it did not rest on secure foundations and would crumble without the threat of force to maintain it. NATO often buckled and twisted in response to external and internal pressures, but could adjust and maintain its essential features because it was based on consent and mutual interest. Thus John Gaddis notes the importance of the differences in the two alliance systems for how the Cold War came out the way it did and points to the reciprocal causation within each alliance: "The difficulty of managing any empire is bound to vary [according to whether its subjects collaborate or resist]; but it is the *occupied*, not the occupiers, that make this choice."[24]

Accompanying bipolarity was the second new element in the mid-twentieth century: nuclear weapons and, more specifically,

---

24 John Lewis Gaddis, *We Now Know: Rethinking Cold War History* (New York, 1997), 285. See also Ole Holsti, P. Terrence Hopmann, and John Sullivan, *Unity and Disintegration in International Alliances* (New York, 1973).

their possession in suitable numbers and configurations by the two superpowers to give each of them second-strike capability. By some time in the 1960s, the United States and USSR possessed stockpiles sufficiently large and invulnerable that neither could expect to survive an all-out nuclear war without utter devastation, and this truly constituted a "nuclear revolution" because it made winning an all-out war impossible. What was new was not "overkill" in the sense of one side being able to destroy the other many times over, but rather "mutual kill" in the sense that gaining a military advantage in an exchange would not allow the state to protect itself.[25] Thus Ronald Reagan and Mikhail Gorbachev could announce after their first summit meeting that "a nuclear war cannot be won and must never be fought."[26] In previous eras, hostile leaders could declare that they would never fight each other, as Chamberlain and Hitler did at Munich and Stalin and Hitler did less than a year later. But they never said that a war could not be won, because they knew that it could be. Perhaps the level of destructiveness of modern non-nuclear weapons would have produced the same result had nuclear weapons never been invented,[27] but I doubt it is a coincidence that the existence of nuclear weapons coincided with unprecedented peace among the major powers and that there were no serious military crises between the superpowers after the development of mutual second-strike capability.[28]

Although many states benefitted from "the long peace,"[29] nuclear weapons had particular advantages for the United States, especially by privileging technology. Despite the fact that American

25   The literature of course is voluminous: the first statement, which anticipated much later thought, was Bernard Brodie, et al., *The Absolute Weapon* (New York, 1946). Also central are Glenn Snyder, *Deterrence and Defense* (Princeton, 1961) and Thomas Schelling, *Arms and Influence* (New Haven, 1966).
26   Quoted in Don Oberdorfer, *The Turn: From the Cold War to a New Era* (New York, 1991), 153.
27   John Mueller, "The Essential Irrelevance of Nuclear Weapons: Stability in the Postwar World," *International Security* 13 (Fall 1988): 55–79. For a rebuttal see Robert Jervis, "The Political Effects of Nuclear Weapons," ibid., 80–90.
28   For further discussion see Robert Jervis, *The Meaning of the Nuclear Revolution* (Ithaca, NY, 1989).
29   John Lewis Gaddis, *The Long Peace* (New York, 1987), chap. 8.

weapons had not been as sophisticated as those of Germany in World War II, the American self-image was of a country with "know how" and technological proficiency and so nuclear weapons played into what Americans perceived was their strength. Even more important, these weapons could substitute for manpower, which was of particular importance for a country in which large standing armies were not valued for socializing young men, encouraging their patriotism, or developing a potent arm of the state. Relatedly, nuclear weapons allowed the American defense budget to be kept to roughly 6–8 percent of GNP, which, while large by previous standards, was still small enough to limit government control of the economy. The fear that higher defense spending would not only ruin the economy but tip the balance between society and the state and produce a "garrison state" was most strongly expressed by President Eisenhower, but was widely shared.[30]

Nuclear weapons may have been particularly important at the start of the Cold War, when no one else had them. Although American decision-makers did not believe that atomic bombs could win World War III and the United States refrained from using atomic threats to try to roll back Soviet influence where it had become established, the nuclear monopoly did help give American elites and the general public the confidence to remain in Europe. This unprecedented source of power may have eased the United States into a role that was unprecedented for it. Indeed, although the idea of the nuclear revolution with its claim that war could be avoided indefinitely was never fully accepted, for many it did help sustain the feeling that the Cold War competition could be continued because it would lead, not to war, but to peace.[31]

---

30   Harold Lasswell, "The Garrison State and Specialists on Violence," *American Journal of Sociology* 46 (January 1941): 455–68. For an excellent discussion of how the United States avoided this feared outcome see Aaron Friedberg, "Why Didn't the United States Become a Garrison State?" *International Security* 16 (Spring 1992): 109–42.

31   Ronald Reagan was perhaps the president with the least faith in deterrence, and this helps explain both his commitment to missile defense and his interest in Gorbachev's Reykjavik proposal to abolish nuclear weapons, which would have overturned American defense policy in Europe.

There is also a converse side to George Kennan's opposition to nuclear weapons on the grounds that "the peculiar psychological overtones by which these weapons will always be accompanied will tend to give them a certain top-heaviness as instruments of our national policy."[32] This concern came naturally to a professional diplomat who had faith in the efficacy of his trade. But Kennan also found American diplomacy badly designed, awkwardly executed, and excessively influence by emotion and public opinion. A policy that relied on nuclear weapons and that sought stability by means of unambiguous threats then may have been more appropriate for the United States as it was as compared to Kennan's preferred approach, which would have suited the United States as Kennan wished it to be. Nuclear threats required credibility which, although creating difficulties, also gave the United States a clear objective and an unchanging orientation that could keep American policy steadfast and reduce the demands on its diplomacy.

Even if nuclear weapons deserve some of the credit for preventing World War III without ruining the American economy or permitting the Soviet Union to dominate Western Europe, at a number of points they were less than supportive of American values and the American domestic political system. To begin with, they accelerated the gravitation of power toward the executive branch. The Founding Fathers worried about the reciprocal relationships between an activist foreign policy and the aggrandizement of the executive, which they saw as the most energetic and potentially dangerous branch of government. They were therefore careful to put the power to declare war firmly in the hands of Congress. Nuclear weapons, with their danger of surprise attack and the requirement for readiness to retaliate instantly, if not to strike preemptively, meant that Congress could play little role in the

---

32   George Kennan, "International Control of Atomic Energy," 20 January 1950, in U.S. Department of State, *Foreign Relations of the United States, 1950* (Washington, 1977), 1:37. Kennan later called this "one of the most important, if not the most important, of all the documents I ever wrote in government" (Kennan, *Memoirs, 1925–1950* [Boston, 1967], 472). Kennan's prophecy may well have been accurate. See Alexander George and Richard Smoke, *Deterrence in American Foreign Policy: Theory and Practice* (New York, 1974).

ultimate decision. The need – or at least the claim – for secrecy also removed power from Congress. Related considerations meant that Congress could do very little in the event of a serious crisis. Even its ability to criticize, kibitz, and second-guess were undercut because if the president handled the crisis well, the carping would be forgotten and if he handled it badly the disastrous external consequences would dwarf any punishment that Congress or public opinion would levy. Of course any militarized diplomacy provided incentives and pressures for centralized and secretive decision-making, as Roosevelt's actions in the North Atlantic in 1940–41 illustrate. But in the absence of nuclear weapons Congress might have learned how to oversee and constrain this kind of behavior.

As many scholars have noted, nuclear weapons accelerated the development of the "imperial presidency" with increased power over domestic as well as foreign policy.[33] At least up to a point, power begets power and the president's control of nuclear policy both required and facilitated greater influence in other areas. But checks and balances were not entirely absent: even as trusted a president as Eisenhower found that legislation and the vigilance of the Joint Committee on Atomic Energy limited his ability to share atomic secrets and material with allies and prevented him from sponsoring European nuclear forces that would allow American troops to be withdrawn from Europe.[34]

My discussion so far has treated the president as synonymous with the executive branch. But the Cold War in general and nuclear weapons in particular shifted some power away from the president to the military. To the extent that foreign policy opportunities were defined in military terms, the military grew in power and prestige. As experts in the primary mechanisms for American defense they were entitled to a large say in policy formation. It was difficult for any president to support a foreign policy in the face of strong military opposition; when the military could not be readily persuaded of the merits of an arms control proposal, for

---

33 The classic study is Arthur Schlesinger, Jr., *The Imperial Presidency* (Boston, 1973).
34 Marc Trachtenberg, *History and Strategy* (Princeton, 1991), chap. 5.

example, it had to be bought off by additional programs. While many intellectuals found this process abhorrent and felt that the military had too large a role, the process still was essentially democratic: the military's influence grew out of the widespread belief that the views expressed by its leaders had merit.

Nuclear weapons drew power away from the president and toward the military in another and potentially more troublesome way, however. The same requirement for a rapid response that undercut Congress's role in any decision to go to war could also reduce the president's power. If the United States were under nuclear attack, there might not be time to gain presidential authorization for retaliation; if the Soviets destroyed Washington, there might not be a president around to order an American response. So it made sense for the president to authorize what was called "pre-delegation" and permit the military to fire nuclear weapons under specified circumstances.[35] Indeed, even before the Soviets had a potent nuclear force the definition of "civilian control of atomic bombs" shifted from the bombs being in the physical possession of the civilian Atomic Energy Commission to their being on air bases and airplanes with civilian control exercised through the ultimate authority of the secretary of defense and the president.[36] In the moment of highest danger, then, not only Congress but the president might have proven irrelevant. Little of America's democratic system or values could play a role.[37]

Events never reached this point, of course. So perhaps we should look elsewhere for more important tensions between nuclear weapons and democracy. The prevailing theories of deterrence argued that what was central was the credibility of each side's threats. In

35   This practice was begun under Eisenhower, and its exact extent, the degree to which his successors altered the authority, and the ability of the president to keep control if it ever became clear that an attack was imminent or under way all are unclear. For a good discussion see Bruce Blair, *Strategic Command and Control* (Washington, 1985). Recently released documents are available on the National Security Archive website (http://www.seas.gwu.edu/nsarchive/news/19980319.htm).
36   Peter Feaver, *Guarding the Guardians: Civilian Control of Nuclear Weapons in the United States* (Ithaca, 1992).
37   For a general discussion of the relationships between nuclear weapons and democracy see Robert Dahl, *Controlling Nuclear Weapons: Democracy versus Guardianship* (Syracuse, 1985).

the situation of mutual second-strike capability, military advantage could not enable the state to stand firm in the game of chicken if it believed that its adversary would not back down. Each side therefore had to read the other's resolve and project an image of high resolve itself. Doing so successfully would deter a crisis – because the other would not dare take risky actions – or compel its termination on favorable terms if one should arise. But how was resolve to be judged and projected? Because few signs of high resolve cannot be objectively specified, statesmen had to make subjective judgments, and had to guess how their opposite numbers were making them as well. Thus, Secretary of State Rogers justified the measured American response to the North Korean shooting down of an American surveillance airplane in neutral waters by saying: "The weak can be rash. The powerful must be more restrained."[38]

Richard Nixon's views about how the Soviets were reading American resolve were perhaps more common and certainly more disturbing. He believed that the protests against the war in Vietnam not only were leading North Vietnam and the USSR to expect the United States to make additional concessions, but also might lead the Soviets to doubt America's general resolve, which could tempt them to step up pressures on Western Europe and follow dangerously assertive policies. The antiwar movement was then endangering the nation, Nixon believed; curbing dissent was necessary and violations of civil liberties were a small price to pay. For Nixon, the whole of set of "dirty tricks" leading up to Watergate were indeed seen as in the national security interest.[39] Perhaps he was either rationalizing his intolerance for domestic dissent or displaying his paranoia, but there was a disturbing logic behind his behavior.

This is not the end of the potential conflicts between deterrence and democracy. According to deterrence theory, there is a limit to how effectively a sensible state could project an image of high

---

38 Quoted in Seymour Hersh, *The Price of Power: Kissinger in the Nixon White House* (New York, 1983), 72.
39 The best discussion, albeit somewhat exaggerated, is Jonathan Schell, *The Time of Illusion* (New York, 1975).

resolve. In the last analysis, after all, an all-out war would be far more costly than even the worst imaginable political defeat: in a game of chicken, it is irrational to refuse to swerve if you think the other side may well continue to drive straight ahead. So state' are – or should be – led to the "rationality of irrationality," as Thomas Schelling brilliantly sho.ved.[40] That is, because the other side is likely to back down if it believes that the state cannot control its behavior or is unable to appreciate the dangers of stand-ing firm, it can be rational for the state to make the other side think that it is irrational, and this often involves actually being irrational.

This is not merely a ҳrick of game theory: as Daniel Ellsberg pointed out, Hitler employed this tactic to good effect in bargain-ing with Benes and Chamberlain.[41] Nixon probably had not read the literature on the subject, but he instinctively realized that the North Vietnamese might back down if he could convince them that he was unpredictable and could not be counted on to con-form to normal restraints – the "madman theory" as he called it.[42] If Nixon was extreme in both his appreciation of the uses of irrationality and his fear that domestic dissent could undermine perceptions of American resolve, other presidents were not en-tirely immune from these thoughts which, after all, were implicit in common conceptions of how influence could be gained when war was no longer a rational tool of statecraft.

Perhaps more useable than irrationality is the tactic of commit-ment. That is, one state can deter the other or force it to back down by convincing it that, if it does not do so, the state will have

40   Schelling, *Arms and Influence*, 36–43.
41   Daniel Ellsberg, "The Theory and Practice of Blackmail," in *Bargaining: Formal Theo-ries of Negotiation*, ed. Oran Young (Urbana, IL, 1975), 343–63 (reprint of RAND memo P-3883, 1959).
42   H. Robert Haldeman, *The Ends of Power* (New York, 1968), 82–83, 98. Llewellyn Thompson, United States ambassador to Moscow, reports a conversation over Berlin in 1961 in which Khrushchev sought to neutralize this kind of tactic: "I told him . . . that if he signed a separate treaty [with East Germany] and force was used to interfere with our communica-tions it would be met with force. He replied that if we wanted war we would get it but he was convinced only madmen would want war and western leaders [were] not mad." Quoted in Richard Reeves, *President Kennedy: Profile of Power* (New York, 1993), 136. See also ibid., 169.

no choice but to act in a way that will precipitate a crisis if not a war.[43] States should then seek the counterintuitive goal of *reducing* their options; if they cannot tie their own hands and make it impossible for them to alter their policy, then they should at least greatly increase the cost they will pay if they do so, which will give them greater incentives to maintain the policy. Occasionally, states can physically commit themselves to a course of action, for example by delegating the decision to use nuclear weapons to front-line commanders, as noted earlier. More often, commitment works through statements and symbolic actions that pledge the state's honor and reputation on living up to its promises and threats. To a large extent, this was NATO's purpose. Although a degree of physical commitment was involved in that a Soviet attack on Western Europe would have automatically killed American soldiers (and dependents),[44] the treaty, the troops, and rhetoric were most important for making it much more costly for the United States to do anything other than fight, with nuclear weapons if need be. American tactics during the Cuban missile crisis largely worked through commitment as well. Although the naval blockade could prevent additional missiles from reaching Cuba, it could not physically remove those that were in place. Rather it exerted great pressure on the Soviet Union to back down by committing the United States to seeing that they were removed.

Recently, scholars have argued that commitment is easier for democracies than for dictatorships because of the importance of public opinion in the former.[45] There are problems here, how-

---

43 The seminal statement is Schelling, *The Strategy of Conflict* (Cambridge, MA, 1960). Commitment has always played a role in world politics, but is particularly important with nuclear weapons because the threat to use them is both crucial and inherently incredible. John Lewis Gaddis, *Strategies of Containment* (New York, 1982), shows that one important determinant of the extent to which an administration was willing to rely on threats of nuclear war to protect American interests around the world was the degree of faith it put in the deterrent power of commitment and reputation.

44 At the start of Anglo-French conversations before World War I, General Wilson asked his French counterpart what would be the smallest British force that would be of any practical use. "One single private soldier," General Foch replied, "and we would take good care that he was killed." Charles Callwell, *Field Marshall Sir Henry Wilson: His Life and Diaries* (New York, 1927), 1:78.

45 The most well-developed analysis is James Fearon, "Domestic Political Audiences and the Escalation of International Disputes," *American Political Science Review* 88 (September 1994): 577–92.

ever. To start with, commitment is in some tension with our basic notions of democracy, which imply a degree of popular control of foreign policy that limits the extent to which one administration can bind its successors. Commitment is particularly troublesome for the United States, which has more of a tradition of popular influence over foreign policy than is the case for most European democracies. Indeed, for this very reason in the early years of the Cold War many commentators doubted the American ability to follow a protracted and consistent policy.

It remains to be determined whether democracies in general or the United States in particular in fact do find it easier to make credible threats and live up to their commitments than do more authoritarian regimes. But it is clear that at least occasionally changes in leadership did lead the United States to go back on its word during the Cold War. Interestingly enough, this may have been the case more frequently with promises than with threats. Of course the United States never had to face the question of whether it would live up to its major military commitments to its closest allies; the Soviets were deterred or had no hostile intentions in the first place. But changes in administrations and, perhaps, in underlying public opinion did make it inconvenient for the government to follow previous promises to the Soviet Union, and in at least two important cases one can interpret the historical record as indicating that it did not do so. The first occurred at the start of the Carter administration, which Soviet leaders expected to carry out what they believed was the binding promise of its predecessor to conclude a SALT II treaty along the lines of the Vladivostok agreement. This Carter and his colleagues declined to do, pushing instead for deeper reductions and adopting an interpretation of the contentious issues of American cruise missiles and the Soviet Backfire bomber that Soviet leaders believed – or professed to believe – were contrary to informal promises made by Kissinger. According to Ambassador Dobrynin, Secretary of State Vance explained that

the new administration does not consider itself completely committed to the approach of the former administration and that the Carter government strive toward a real, and not just a superficial reduction in strategic arms.

> I [Dobrynin] noted . . . [that] in conducting such important negotiations we start from the fact that we are dealing with the government of the USA, and that the reevaluation by every new administration of agreements reached by its predecessor does not strengthen the basis for international agreements.[46]

The second case occurred six years later when Ronald Reagan called for the Strategic Defense Initiative (SDI). The Soviets and many American experts argued that this violated the Anti-Ballistic Missile (ABM) treaty. Reagan and his colleagues countered that it did not because it would rely on space-based systems. But the administration does not appear to have reached this conclusion on the basis of careful study; what carried more weight than the wording of previous agreements was the belief that SDI would strengthen Western security and save lives if war were to occur. This was true despite the fact that scholars – if not decision-makers – understood that deterrence rested on the credibility of promises as well as threats in that the threat to act in undesired ways if the adversary should take unacceptable actions had to be paired with the promise to refrain from doing so as long as the adversary cooperated. (Interestingly enough, while the Soviets rejected the American interpretation of the ABM agreement, they were willing to buy the same horse twice and offered many concessions in an unsuccessful effort to get Reagan to re-commit the United States not to develop ABMs.)

To show that democracies are uniquely unwilling to keep their promises would require careful comparisons with the behavior of dictatorships. During the Cold War, it was often argued that the Soviet Union broke its treaty commitments with impunity. Although the record is still ambiguous, there were some clear violations, most obviously the building of an ABM radar at Krasnoyarsk

---

46 A. F. Dobrynin, "Record of the Conversation with the Secretary of State of the USA C. Vance," 21 March 1977, *Cold War International History Project Bulletin* 5 (Spring 1995): 154.

and the illegal production of biological weapons. But these were not cases in which a new leader disputed the wisdom of a treaty signed by his predecessor. It was simply believed that the advantages of surreptitiously breaking the treaty outweighed the risks and costs (which, at least in the former case, were badly underestimated). So it is at least possible that the analysts who argued at the start of the Cold War that American administrations would find it particularly difficult to maintain established policies were correct, at least as far as promises were concerned. An international environment that called for this kind of consistency was then uncongenial for the United States.

The logic of commitment works largely through the perceived importance of reputation. If a state fails to live up to its commitment in one instance, the argument goes, then others will be less likely to heed its word in the future. This was one of the fundamental premises supporting the Domino Theory, articulated in slightly different ways by American statesmen throughout the Cold War. Relatedly, the importance of reputation is a linchpin of American academic theories of international politics, some espoused by people like Kissinger who went on to positions of power. It is noteworthy, however, that for all the theoretical importance and elegance of these arguments, there have been remarkably few studies of how reputations are formed, maintained, damaged, and affect others' behavior. A generation ago Glenn Snyder and Paul Diesing observed that while states do seem preoccupied by their own reputations, when they come to estimate how others will behave, this factor is not given serious consideration.[47] More recent studies have similarly found that deterrence theory's simple picture of reputation is misleading in its neglect of the multitude of ways in which various audiences perceive and interpret the state's behavior.[48]

---

47 Snyder and Diesing, *Conflict Among Nations*, 187–89.
48 Ted Hopf, *Peripheral Visions: Deterrence Theory and Soviet Foreign Policy in the Third World, 1965–1990* (Ann Arbor, 1994); Jonathan Mercer, *Reputation and International Politics* (Ithaca, 1996). For a discussion of the latter see the symposium, "What's in a Name? Debating Jonathan Mercer's Reputation and International Politics," *Security Studies* 7 (Autumn 1997): 31–113. Also see Glenn Snyder, *Deterrence and Defense* (Princeton, 1961), chap. 1; John Orme, *Deterrence, Reputation, and Cold-War Cycles* (London, 1992); Elli

It may not be entirely accidental that the American academic community did not examine the reputational premise that supported much Cold War policy. Not only was the theory elegant, allowing the construction of sophisticated theories that gave much intellectual satisfaction,[49] but the notion may have fitted particularly well with American political and psychological needs. If reputation did not matter, then commitment would be difficult, perhaps insurmountably so, calling into question the credibility of threats whose implementation would involve costs greater than the immediate benefits. If threats could not be bolstered by being tied to reputation and the Communist states were strongly motivated to expand, then it might be beyond American power to offer security guarantees.

There is also some evidence that the United States stressed the importance of reputation more than did other countries. In a stimulating essay, Patrick Morgan suggests that what amounted to close to an obsession with reputation sprang at least in part from American statesmen's

persistent fear that the public would not sustain a resolute, responsible posture . . . in world affairs . . . [and] a consistent lack of confidence on the part of the United States in friends and allies, a feeling that they were fair-weather supporters, that any sign of U.S. weakness would cause them to suffer domestic political disarray and to adjust their foreign policies toward accommodation with the Soviet Union. . . . It would seem that underlying this worry about the inconstancy of friends is a deeper doubt about ourselves. . . . Is not the Munich analogy so compelling, because, deep down, one can never escape feeling that in the nuclear age the same thing could easily happen again?[50]

Lieberman, "What Makes Deterrence Work: Lessons from the Egyptian-Israeli Enduring Rivalry," *Security Studies* 4 (Summer 1995): 833–92; Paul Huth, *Extended Deterrence and the Prevention of War* (New Haven, 1988); and Robert Jervis, "Domino Beliefs and Strategic Behavior," in *Dominoes and Bandwagons: Strategic Beliefs and Great Power Competition in the Eurasian Rimland*, ed. Robert Jervis and Jack Snyder (New York, 1991), 20–50.

49   See, for example, Robert Jervis, *The Logic of Images in International Relations*, 2d ed. (New York, 1989).

50   Patrick Morgan, "Saving Face for the Sake of Deterrence," in *Psychology and Deterrence*, ed. Robert Jervis, Richard Ned Lebow, and Janice Gross Stein (Baltimore, 1985), 148–51.

Americans could hardly have been unaware of the fact that throughout its history the United States was not known as a country that could be counted on in world affairs. Furthermore, it had difficulty relying on the concept of honor which in socially stratified societies served some of the functions of reputation. Issuing threats and promises whose fulfillment would lead to the devastation of one's homeland would have been a terrible burden for any country; it was particularly stressful for a state that had previously shunned leadership. Believing in the importance of reputation and its ability to render as rational the undertaking of commitments that otherwise would have been foolish may have been comforting and fit well with the new American self-image as a country that could be relied on to keep its word.[51]

In summary, while the nuclear revolution conflicted with or restricted some democratic practices, it may also have allowed the United States to keep the peace and maintain the status quo in the areas of the world that mattered most to it without undue cost. In 1945, few would have predicted that high conflict, strenuous arms competition, and limited wars could occur for two generations without leading to general war, American isolation, or the undermining of the American domestic system. In fact, it was perhaps this revolutionary change in world politics that allowed the domestic changes to be relatively limited.

The third enormous change in world politics reverses the first and may be built on the second. But it is even more far-reaching than either of them and allows – and perhaps was partly caused by – an even closer fit between American values and world politics. With the end of bipolarity and the Cold War it is not the United States but the other developed countries (Western Europe, Canada, Australia, New Zealand, and Japan) are without major security threats. Earlier I noted that one could conjure up dangers to the United States, mostly from terrorism. A parallel analysis

---

51 Secretary of State Albright's defense of the American threats to attack Iraq in early 1998 unless it allowed a resumption of UN inspection is interesting in this regard: "If we have to use force, it is because we are America. We are the indispensable nation. We stand tall. We see further into the future." (Quoted in Bob Herbert, "War Games," *New York Times*, 22 February 1998, Section 4, 17).

could apply to other developed countries. But what is more important and totally unprecedented is that these countries do not menace each other. I would be amazed if the safes in these country's ministries of defense would yield relevant war plans. Since such documents are drawn up for the most unlikely contingencies, their absence is significant. Indeed, it is hard to find a serious analyst who would claim that there is any significant chance that these countries would go to war with each other for the foreseeable future, which means they form what Karl Deutsch called a "security community,"[52] one that is the largest and most important that the world has ever seen.

This is not to say that war, let alone violence, is now banished from the international system: there is little reason to expect it to abate between and within less-developed countries, although it is possible that over time either the example or the influence of the developed countries could pacify the rest of the world. It is also possible that, perhaps in a shorter period of time, Russia or the People's Republic of China could develop sufficient strength and hostile intentions to menace countries in the security community. And this community itself could perhaps be disrupted by a severe shock, presumably of an economic nature, that would heighten rivalries and lead some countries to abandon democracy. But unless and until any of these events occur, politics among the developed states will be peaceful.

Since the history of international politics has been shaped by – indeed has largely consisted of – war among the most powerful units, the widespread security community constitutes a truly radical change. This means that world politics will be very different from what it has been in the past.[53] Even if it is true that the

---

52 Karl Deutsch, et al., *Political Community and the North Atlantic Area: International Organization in the Light of Historical Experience* (Princeton, 1957).
53 For further discussion see John Mueller, *Retreat from Doomsday: The Obsolescence of Major War* (New York, 1989); Stephen Van Evera, "Primed for Peace: Europe after the Cold War," *International Security* 15 (Winter 1990/91): 7–57; Robert Jervis, "The Future of World Politics: Will It Resemble the Past?" ibid. 16 (Winter 1991/92): 39–73; James Goldgeier and Michael McFaul, "A Tale of Two Worlds: Core and Periphery in the Post-Cold War Era," *International Organization* 46 (Spring 1992): 467–91; and Max Singer and Aaron Wildavsky, *The Real World Order: Zones of Peace/Zones of Turmoil* (Chatham, NJ, 1993). For gloomier

nuclear revolution kept the peace between the superpowers, it only did so by the constant threat of war, thus leading international politics to retain many of its traditional features, albeit in modified form. Widespread uncoerced peace such as has existed in more limited spheres in the past (forr example, Canadian-American relations) is quite different and we should not expect its implications to be narrow or restricted to what we can see today.

It will be a challenge for scholars to understand politics in a world in which threats of force and military balance play such a diminished role; even more, it will be a challenge – and an opportunity – for statesmen and societies to develop new ways of dealing with each other, since conflicts of interest will not disappear along with the threat of great-power war.[54] What is most relevant here is that this world both conforms to and challenges the American domestic system and values. Most obviously, peace among the great powers has been the profoundest wish of those who valued the rule of law. Indeed, most citizens of developed states now take for granted a degree of security and freedom from fear that had been almost unimaginable to all but Americans previously. That others are now so benefitted fulfills the aspiration of most Americans. But it is far from clear how American policy will or should be constructed in a world of reduced threats. Multiple interests and values will contend and the weak American state and pluralistic political system make coherence unlikely. With security no longer the primary goal, choices between economic and ideological goals will be necessary, but exactly how they are made is likely to vary according to specific circumstances and a changeable national mood. Policy will have to draw on Ameri-

---

views see John Mearsheimer, "Back to the Future: Instability in Europe after the Cold War," *International Security* 15 (Summer 1990): 5–56; Christopher Layne, "The Unipolar Illusion: Why New Great Powers Will Rise," ibid. 17 (Spring 1993): 5–51; Kenneth Waltz, "The Emerging Structure of International Politics," ibid. 18 (Fall 1993): 44–79; and idem, "Evaluating Theories," *American Political Science Review* 91 (December 1997): 915–16. For discussion of why people do not feel as reassured as this analysis indicates that they should see John Mueller, "The Catastrophe Quota: Trouble after the Cold War," *Journal of Conflict Resolution* 38 (September 1994): 355–75.

54   For an interesting discussion see Joseph Joffe, "How America Does It," *Foreign Affairs* 76 (September/October 1997): 13–27.

can values and aspirations at the very time when the idea of shared national values is questionable.

What is also interesting is the extent to which the developed world has come to resemble the United States, for better and for worse. All the rich countries appear to be quite stable. Economically, they also have become more similar to the United States in the reduction of central direction of the economy and, with the possible exception of Japan, the endorsement of a high degree of individualism. While it is premature to proclaim the end of history, the degree of convergence is noteworthy. In a real sense, this is now an American Century even if these developments do not lead to increased American power. Power is desired for purpose – for shaping the world – and the domestic societies throughout the developed world are very consistent with American values. Whether this world will turn out entirely to America's liking is, of course, another matter. We should remember the well-known saying: "Be careful what you wish for, you may get it."

4

The Idea of the National Interest

H. W. BRANDS

Prior to diplomacy is policy, which guides the diplomats in their actions; prior to policy are the ideas that inhabit the heads of the policymakers, shaping their perceptions of the world and informing their responses to those perceptions. Monarchs and dictators may manage to determine policy on the basis of narrow notions of personal self-interest, although most even of the autocratic sort persuade or delude themselves of a coincidence between self-interest and national interest. Democracies are hardly spared selfishness in their leaders, but democratic politics demand that policies be defended, even when they do not originate, in terms of national interest – of a conception of an overriding common good transcending the specific interests of parties, factions, and other entities smaller than the nation as a whole.

In American politics and diplomacy, the search for the national interest has been constant, from the founding of the Republic to the present. The first enunciation of national interest coincided with the proclamation of the existence of the United States of America, and indeed the coincidence was as much conceptual as chronological, for until the Treaty of Paris of 1783, national existence – that is, independence – was the essential national interest. National existence remained an issue through the War of 1812, as the British invasion of Washington demonstrated; it was contested in another, more deadly form in the sectional crisis that culminated in the Civil War. Americans in the late eighteenth and nineteenth centuries were not so preoccupied with the existential issue as to ignore other elements of national interest (Did republicanism in America require republicanism elsewhere, as in France in the 1790s or Latin America in the 1820s? Could American commerce be sacrificed, as by Jefferson in 1807, without fatal loss of profit and prestige? Was the Western Hemisphere actually an American bailiwick, as intimated by James Monroe in 1823 and amplified by assorted successors? Was territorial expansion, whether by purchase, coercion, or outright war, vital to the American future?) but not until the memories faded from Antietam and Gettysburg was the existential question sufficiently settled that Americans could take it for granted, and define national interest in predominantly external terms on a consistent basis.

This is precisely what they did starting in the late 1890s and continuing throughout the twentieth century. During that period they subsumed a number of notions under the rubric of national interest; these included the pursuit of prosperity, identified diplomatically with the acquisition and retention of foreign markets for trade and investment; the defense and promotion of democracy and associated American values and institutions (not least among them, capitalism); and national security, a catch-all that took up where the original existential issue left off but expanded after 1945 until it nearly swallowed every other consideration of national interest. The end of the Cold War, the disintegration of the Soviet Union, and the concomitant reduction of the threat of nuclear Armageddon restored much of the balance among the elements of national interest, allowing Americans at the end of the twentieth century to remember just what it was their security apparatus was designed to defend.

Prosperity was on the minds of Americans in the 1890s; democracy and security less so. This followed the simple rule of human nature that people value most what they have least. The country was as secure from external assault as anyone could reasonably expect; democracy, having been vindicated in the Civil War, appeared equally unchallenged. Prosperity, however, was problematic. The Panic of 1893 presaged the worst depression in American history to date, a depression that eventually eased but left vivid marks and memories across the land.

One proposed solution to the prosperity problem was the acquisition of foreign markets. Actually, this solution was not simply *proposed*; it was almost universally endorsed. Foreign markets were good; the more the better. The only real question was whether the markets should be acquired with or without the territory they encompassed.

The territorial acquisitionists adduced a variety of reasons in arguing that additional real estate would further the national interest. Navalists like Alfred Thayer Mahan coveted coaling stations and bases for the fleet they thought America deserved (and which, after lobbying by Mahan and allies, it was in the process of building). There was a security angle to this argument, although it followed from the prosperity argument, rather than standing alone. The fleet would safeguard the markets America acquired, and ensure access thereto. Preemptive imperialists and others afflicted with Europe-envy remarked about the rapidity with which Britain, France, and Germany were snatching colonies in Africa and Asia, and fretted that if the United States did not act forthwith, all the promising places on the planet would be taken.

The territorial acquisitionists failed to achieve critical mass until another argument augmented their numbers and amplified their voices. The nationalist revolt in Cuba that began in 1895 produced a bloody stalemate, with attendant atrocities that stirred the sympathies of the American people (after arousing the cupidity of the American press). By 1898 even the reluctant William McKinley was coming to believe that American intervention might be necessary to end the suffering of the Cubans. Side effects of intervention would include, certainly, the expansion of American influence in the Caribbean; probably, the enlargement of American markets; possibly, the multiplication of American territory; conceivably, the extension of democracy.

Thoughtful discussion of the national interest rarely takes place with war looming ahead; it is more commonly encountered in the cooler aftermath of conflict. So it was with the Spanish-American War. Americans took up arms against Spain almost rashly, to terminate an intolerable situation in Cuba; only amid the peace negotiations did they consider carefully what the war meant for their country. The framing question was whether the country should annex the Philippines and Puerto Rico, seized as spoils in the fighting. Put most bluntly: Was empire in the national interest?

A curious collection of progressives and reactionaries, farmers and industrialists, philanthropists and racists, said no. Far from extending democracy, they warned, empire would extinguish it – in the United States. Empire would spit on the graves of the founders and impugn the wisdom of the God Who put two oceans between American shores and the broils of the Old World. Empire would raise taxes. It would threaten civilian control of the military and foster the growth of a garrison state. It would saddle Americans with responsibility for lesser breeds beyond the pale – and probably beyond the possibility – of civilization.

The pro-annexationists matched the antis progressive for progressive, reactionary for reactionary, and so on, down to racist for racist. They decried the pessimism of their opponents in projecting doom for a country that was the model of strength and resilience. They puffed the prosperity argument, plumping the Philippines as the entrepôt to the China market. They turned the democracy argument against the antis: far from endangering democracy, annexation would enable Americans to carry it across the Pacific and into the Caribbean. Albert Beveridge, the most eloquent (or egregious) of the annexationists, asserted that the annexation question turned on one more fundamental: What was America for? What was Americans' purpose in the world? Boldly essaying to speak for the Deity, Beveridge declared, "He has made us the master organizers of the world to establish system where chaos reigns. He has given us the spirit of progress to overwhelm the forces of reaction throughout the earth."[1]

The imperialists – to use the name the annexationists eschewed but that accurately described them – won the battle but lost the war. They convinced the Senate to approve the treaty transferring

---

1   Quoted in H. W. Brands, *Bound to Empire: The United States and the Philippines* (New York, 1992), 33.

the Philippines and Puerto Rico to the United States, but they ultimately failed to convince the American people that colonialism was consonant with the American national interest. Annexation sparked a revolt by Filipino nationalists that quickly dimmed the luster of the late splendid little tiff against Spain; soon Americans found themselves in the thuggish role the Spanish had played in Cuba. The Philippine war proved long and utterly demoralizing; although the American side won, even Theodore Roosevelt, who generally judged hoisting the white man's burden bully prebreakfast exercise, had to admit in the aftermath of the Philippine war that Americans lacked the stomach for empire. Rather than forming a strong point for American expansion in East Asia, Roosevelt said, the Philippines had become "our heel of Achilles."[2]

Cured of the colonial temptation (although unsure how to divest themselves of their current colonial commitments) Americans pursued prosperity – more precisely, foreign markets – by nonterritorial means. The trouble with this approach was that it left American commerce vulnerable to depredation by other countries. John Adams, Thomas Jefferson, and James Madison had encountered the problem a century earlier; fortunately for American merchants and merchantmen, the hundred-years' peace that followed the fall of Napoleon minimized, to the point of provoking amnesia, the exposure of Americans to collateral damage in conflicts among their principal customers.

After August 1914 the memories came flooding back. As Europe went to war, Americans reflected on where lay the national interest in the present crisis. By a stretch of only the most fevered imagination was American security, in the normal sense of national sovereignty and territorial integrity, at risk in the fight over there. Yet American prosperity probably depended on continued access to European markets, if not immediately then in the long term. To suffer the interdiction of American trade was to jeopardize American prosperity.

2   Ibid., 84.

To parse the issue so finely, however, was to miss the point. Not for the last time (or the first: it happened during the Napoleonic wars as well) did a threat to American trade trigger larger concerns. "We wrap ourselves around our money-making, and transfigure it," Walter Lippmann wrote in 1917. "It is then identified with all that is most precious. The export of bicycles or steel rails is no longer the cold-blooded thing it looks like in statistical reports of commerce. It is integrated with our passion. It is wife and children being respected. So when trade is attacked, we are attacked."[3]

Thus, between 1914 and 1917, attacks on American neutral rights – attacks that might have been obviated by a Jeffersonesque embargo – came to be seen as an assault on America itself. "We will not choose the path of submission and suffer the most sacred rights of our nation and our people to be ignored or violated," Woodrow Wilson asserted in requesting a war declaration in April 1917.

Besides, the German challenge was not simply a challenge by one foreign country to America; it was autocracy's affront to the principle of democracy. As currently ruled, Wilson said, Germany was the "natural foe to liberty"; if it remained so ruled, it would remain freedom's foe. "A steadfast concert for peace can never be maintained except by a partnership of democratic nations." Consequently, in taking up the gage the German emperor had thrown down, the United States was assuming democracy's defense. "The world must be made safe for democracy. Its peace must be planted upon the tested foundations of political liberty."[4]

Conflation of causes is a chronic hazard of American (and probably democratic) war-making; in lining up support for belligerence, the bellicose cast their net as widely as feasible, hoping to catch anyone with half a mind for war. Such had happened in the run-up to the war with Spain; such happened in the approach to war with Germany. The war was about neutral rights; it was about American security; it was about democracy.

3 Walter Lippmann, *The Stakes of Diplomacy* (New York, 1915, 1917), 75–76.
4 Arthur S. Link, ed., *The Papers of Woodrow Wilson* (Princeton, 1983), 41:519–27.

But if conflation is the rule on going to war, parsimony guides peacemaking. The divergent objectives among the war party are masked, once war is declared, by the overriding objective of winning the war; let peace approach, however, and the coalition begins to crumble. Put otherwise, while definitions of the national interest may differ going into a war, these differences are suppressed in the immediate interest of victory. Once that immediate interest has been achieved, the divergence among the larger definitions reappears.

Such had been Wilson's convenience in 1917; such was his undoing in 1919. The deliberate pace of the peace negotiations left Americans to ponder at their leisure the national interest of the United States in the international structure their president proposed. Recognizing the tendency of wartime coalitions to break up (not just in the United States, but between the United States and the Allies), Wilson offered something for everyone: Fourteen Points' worth. His blueprint proved too ambitious; after the Allies demurred at Paris, Americans objected when Wilson brought the Versailles treaty home.

The sticker for the Senate (admittedly for a minority there, but a vetoing minority) was the League of Nations. In asserting the necessity of the League and the primacy of the principle of collective security, Wilson made the revolutionary claim that the American national interest was inseparable from the larger international interest. Americans as a group were not ready to accept this idea. Their version of the national interest was considerably narrower. He would save America by saving the world; they would save America and let the world fend for itself.

Wilson, in the end, reluctantly acknowledged that the nation knew its national interest better than he did. "I think it was best after all that the United States did not join the League of Nations," he said in 1924. "Now, when the American people join the League it will be because they are convinced it is the right thing to do, and then will be the only right time for them to do it."[5]

---

5   Thomas J. Knock, *To End All Wars: Woodrow Wilson and the Quest for a New World Order* (Princeton, 1995), 272.

The right time took more time than Wilson imagined. Disillusionment with the internationalist interpretation of the national interest only grew with increasing distance from Versailles. During the 1920s Americans revised not simply their interpretation of what the American national interest *should be*, but what it *had been*. The most influential commentators on American foreign policy during that Republican decade stripped away the layers of Wilsonian idealism that had colored American intervention in the Great War; what remained was economic self-interest, and cynical self-interest at that. "The World War is on all fours with every other war in having an economic foundation," said C. Hartley Grattan.[6] Harry Elmer Barnes concurred, calling Wilson's pre-intervention neutrality a sham and moaning, "We have been played for a bunch of suckers."[7]

This feeling grew as a fresh crop of leaders in Europe emerged, apparently intent on proving that all the carnage had been for nothing. Japan's simultaneous evolution into an East Asian nemesis gave Americans cause for judging war – recent and incipient – to be the ground state of world affairs, and for concluding that whatever the American national interest might be, it had little to do with the interests of other countries.

Charles Beard put this attitude most persuasively. Beard had shocked respectable American opinion in 1913 by questioning the motives of the Founders with his *Economic Interpretation of the Constitution*; now he spied similar motivations – rather more easily and more convincingly – behind American foreign policy. In *The Idea of the National Interest* Beard identified two historical strains in American interpretations of the national interest. The first he associated with Thomas Jefferson; agriculturally based, it put primary importance on domestic markets and the development of America's resources at home. Let Americans cultivate their own garden, said Beard's Jeffersonians, and what the rest of the world did would not much matter. The second strain, linked to Alexander Hamilton, promoted manufactures and overseas

---

6   C. Hartley Grattan, *Why We Fought* (New York, 1929), 127.
7   Harry Elmer Barnes, *The Genesis of the World War* (New York, 1926), 646.

trade. Beard's Hamiltonians held that Americans could ignore the world only at peril to their prosperity, if not their safety.

Beard – a successful part-time farmer – much preferred the Jeffersonian version, and he was encouraged to note that the current administration showed signs of heeding the counsel of the patron saint of the Democratic party. "Fragments of a new conception of national interest appeared in the policies and measures of President Franklin D. Roosevelt," Beard wrote in 1934. "Amid them was the central idea: by domestic planning and control the American economic machine may be kept running at a high tempo supplying the *intra*national market [emphasis added], without relying primarily upon foreign outlets for 'surpluses' of goods and capital."[8]

This kind of thinking, combined with a visceral revulsion to war that, while powerful, did not really qualify as thinking, gave rise to the neutrality legislation of the mid-1930s. Echoing the embargo of Jefferson, the neutrality laws represented a rejection of Hamilton and a repudiation of Wilson. In 1917 the United States had gone to war to defend Americans' right to trade and travel during wartime; now Congress was effectively surrendering that right even before the war began.

Yet the new neutralists of the 1930s ran into the same problem as the old neutralists of the 1910s (including originally Wilson himself, despite what Harry Elmer Barnes alleged). Diplomatic neutrality need not imply moral neutrality, but moral unneutrality makes diplomatic neutrality difficult, especially in a democracy. As the unmitigated evil of Nazism and the unabashed aggression of Japan became undeniable, neutrality became untenable to a growing number of Americans. Those, like Beard, who clung to a narrowly nationalist view of the national interest – "Anyone who feels hot with morals and is affected with delicate sensibilities can find enough to do at home, considering the misery of the 10,000,000 unemployed, the tramps, the beggars, the sharecroppers, tenants and field hands right here at our door," he wrote –

---

8   Charles A. Beard, *The Idea of National Interest: An Analytical Study in American Foreign Policy* (New York, 1934), 1, 552.

found themselves attacked as closet Nazis and fascist fellow-travelers.[9]

The discomfort this caused might not have been enough to push America to war, but as the experience of the Spanish war and the Great War demonstrated (and as Lippmann had observed in 1917), the distinctions among issues become blurred once the guns start going off. From a recognition of Hitler's malevolence to a belief that he somehow threatened the United States was a logical step, albeit one the cautious Roosevelt took carefully. After the summer of 1940, there was little lingering disagreement in America that Hitler had to be halted; the debate between the America Firsters and the Committee to Defend America by Aiding the Allies was mostly over where the halting would occur, and who would do it. It was harder to make the case that the Japanese threatened essential American interests – so Roosevelt, who was convinced they did, backed them into a corner from which the only escape, as Tokyo surveyed the scene, crossed American territory. The attack on Hawaii, and to a lesser extent on the Philippines, foreclosed further discussion.

From December 1941 until mid-1945 the overriding and universally agreed upon national interest was the defeat of Germany and Japan; as that defeat drew near, debate resumed, much as it had after the two previous wars.

Strikingly, the starting point for the debate after World War II was the ending point for the debate after World War I – the point on which Wilson's version of the national interest had foundered. For the first time, a working majority of Americans accepted the Wilsonian argument that the national interest was inextricable from the international interest. Unilateralism, isolationism even, had been conceivable after the Great War; it was inconceivable after the Greater War. American prosperity rested on the prosperity of other countries. American democracy depended on the survival of democracy elsewhere. American security could not be achieved separate from the security of Europe and Asia.

---

9   Charles A. Beard, "A Reply to Mr. Browder," *New Republic*, 2 February 1938.

These views were not universally held, nor were they immune to differences of interpretation. But it quickly became clear that they formed the basis for American policy in the postwar period. The Truman Doctrine, the Marshall Plan, the Berlin airlift, NATO, the American defense of South Korea – all were based on a fundamental understanding of the national interest that was decidedly international in orientation.

International, however, was not the same as internationalist; nor was collective security in the Cold War quite what Wilson had envisioned. For a time the true heirs to Wilson had their say, although the fact that Henry Wallace became their leading voice revealed the decreasing seriousness with which they were taken. Wallace decried the confrontational approach of the Truman administration, which, he said, needlessly antagonized the Russians, polarized the world, and jeopardized the mission of the United Nations. The way to peace was through peace, informed by a spirit of cooperation, not through the hostility of a Cold War.

Countering Wallace were those who contended that an international outlook was best informed by nationalist attitudes. No, the United States must not turn its back on the world; but neither should it place its fate in the hands of those who, by the evidence of hundreds of statements since 1917, wished ill to American values and institutions. The Soviets had been indispensable allies against Hitler, but Hitler died in his bunker. Stalin still lived. And while he did, Americans had better keep their powder dry. Twenty years earlier, ten years even, it would have been entirely unnecessary to emphasize what this group now stressed: the national in national interest.

The nationalists in the post-1945 period developed a theoretical justification for their position; the most influential of the theorists was Hans Morgenthau. A refugee from Nazi Germany who wound up in the political science department at the University of Chicago, Morgenthau explained that internationalism was a will-o'-the-wisp chased after by wooly-minded Wilsonians who failed to understand how the world worked. He proceeded to provide a primer:

International politics, like all politics, is a struggle for power. Whatever the ultimate aims of international politics, power is always the immediate aim. Statesmen and peoples may ultimately seek freedom, security, prosperity, or power itself. They may define their goals in terms of a religious, philosophic, economic, or social ideal. They may hope that this ideal will materialize through its own inner force, through divine intervention, or through the natural development of human affairs. But whenever they strive to realize their goal by means of international politics, they do so by striving for power.[10]

Careful readers of this text noted that it did not deny the existence of idealism, nor even contend that idealism – of the Wilsonian or any other sort – had no role in international affairs. But for Morgenthau, idealism lay beyond the portfolio of the practicing policymaker, who needed to inquire into ultimate causes no more than the ordinary policeman needed to know the root causes of urban poverty.

In this book, the quickly classic *Politics among Nations*, and several others, Morgenthau propounded, expounded, and just plain pounded on the idea that power constituted the coin of the international realm (of the domestic realm too, but such was for others to argue). Peace would come not through the good offices of the United Nations but through careful attention to the balance of international power.

Others joined Morgenthau in the cleverly christened (by themselves) school of Cold War "realism." George Kennan cabled at length from Moscow warning of Stalin's designs on the West; he sequeled with a catchy piece in *Foreign Affairs* prescribing a policy of political and ideological encirclement of the Soviet Union. Deeper than Kennan and almost as catchy was theologian Reinhold Niebuhr, whose previous *Moral Man and Immoral Society* and *The Children of Light and the Children of Darkness* prepped readers for *Christian Realism and Political Problems*. The difference between Christian realism and the infidel brand was what gave America its moral edge in the contest with the Communists. Yet

---

10   Hans J. Morgenthau, *Politics among Nations: The Struggle for Power and Peace* (New York, 1948), 13.

Niebuhr, tempering his realism with realism, cautioned Americans against assuming that the mere fact of their semi-institutionalized Christianity would afford them victory over the atheists of the Kremlin. "The final victory over man's disorder is God's and not ours," Niebuhr homilized.[11]

Niebuhr had reason to warn against facile assumptions of Providential partisanship. By the early 1950s Americans had come to interpret the national interest in almost religious terms. Not since the imperialist moment at the turn of the century – and, considering the substantial dissent of the anti-imperialists, perhaps not even then – had Americans as a nation been so convinced of the divine, or at least divinely guided, righteousness of their country's foreign policy. Harry Truman took the first step on the path of righteousness in the speech that announced the Truman Doctrine. "At the present moment in world history nearly every nation must choose between alternative ways of life," Truman said, and he proceeded to delineate the difference between those alternatives.

One way of life is based upon the will of the majority, and is distinguished by free institutions, representative government, free elections, guarantees of individual liberty, freedom of speech and religion, and freedom from political oppression.

The second way of life is based upon the will of a minority forcibly imposed upon the majority. It relies upon terror and oppression, a controlled press and radio, fixed elections, and the suppression of personal freedoms.

It went without saying that the United States headed the first camp; what *did* require saying was that the United States would be taking upon itself responsibility for defending the first camp against the second. "It must be the policy of the United States to support free peoples who are resisting attempted subjugation by armed minorities or by outside pressures." Although the context of this speech was an aid request for Greece and Turkey, the principle apparently applied to other countries, perhaps all countries. "The

11   Reinhold Niebuhr, *Christian Realism and Political Problems* (New York, 1953), 116.

free peoples of the world look to us for support in maintaining their freedoms," Truman asserted. "If we falter in our leadership, we may endanger the peace of the world – and we shall surely endanger the welfare of our own Nation."[12]

The Manichaeism that informed Truman's statement grew only more marked during the next few years. It probably peaked, institutionally, in NSC–68, that over-the-top manifesto of American Cold War thinking. To an even greater degree than Truman in his Greek-aid speech, the NSC–68 authors hammered upon the conflict of values between West and East, and they did so in explicitly religious terms. Freedom of religion characterized the democratically tolerant West; just the opposite motivated the dictatorially intolerant East, where a "perverted faith" bent all to its evil will. "It is the first article of this faith that he [the ordinary individual] finds and can only find the meaning of his existence in serving the end of the system. The system becomes God, and submission to the will of God becomes submission to the will of the system."[13]

Officially, of course, the United States could not wage war, even Cold War, in the name of religion. The First Amendment forbade it, and prudence cautioned against gratuitous insults to potential allies in Islamic, Hindu, or Buddhist countries. (Since the Christian God was frequently spoken of as the "Judeo-Christian" God, Israel presumably would be less sensitive. It was, but only *less* sensitive.)

Unofficially, however, the contest against communism was commonly construed religiously, as a struggle against "Godless communism." Americans who knew nothing else of communism knew that it was atheistic, and therefore a threat to every God-fearing nation and person on the planet. Americans of the Cold War were hardly original in dragooning God into service on their side; other zealots had done it in other countries for centuries, and in America the ranks of the religiously inspired ran from Puritans through abolitionists and imperialists to prohibitionists. Yet never

---

12   *Department of State Bulletin*, 23 March 1947.
13   U.S. Department of State, *Foreign Relations of the United States, 1950* (Washington, 1977), 1:235–92.

had the national interest assumed such pervasively religious overtones. The ideological struggle with the Communists became almost theological; a naive observer of Cold War America could
have been forgiven for thinking that the fate not merely of the
world, but of heaven and earth, hung on the outcome of the contest with the Kremlin.

Such enthusiasm had policy consequences – or would have if certain groups had had their way. If communism was fundamentally evil, then mere containment of communism was a pact with
the devil, either figuratively or literally. During the early 1950s
conservatives within the Republican party advocated a more forceful method of dealing with the Communists. "Liberation" or
"rollback" would lift the Communist yoke from the necks of the
millions upon whom it now weighed. This would certainly benefit those millions, by replacing totalitarianism with democracy;
it would benefit Americans, by eradicating the primary threat to
American security.

   Actually, whether the liberationists were conservatives or something else – perhaps radicals – was a fair question. It was also an
indication that, regardless of whether politics stopped at the water's
edge, any meaningful nomenclature of foreign policy preference
according to accepted categories of left and right did.

   Robert A. Taft made precisely this point in opposing most Cold
War initiatives of the Truman administration. The Ohio Republican considered himself a conservative, and he may well have
been the last true conservative of the Cold War. Taft opposed the
Cold War on the same grounds that he had opposed the New
Deal: that it would increase the size of government. Taft had not
learned nothing from World War II; he recognized that American
welfare depended to some degree on the welfare of other countries. "It does not follow, however," he said, during the 1951
Senate debate over the dispatch of American troops to Europe,
"that because we desire the freedom of every country in the world
we must send an American land army to that country to defend
it." To Taft's way of thinking – which echoed the anti-imperialists of 1898 and Charles Beard during the interwar years – an

overly ambitious formulation of the national interest would actually undermine the genuine national interest. "If we commit ourselves to more than we can carry out, we weaken the whole nation."[14]

Hans Morgenthau, no conservative, nonetheless counseled caution as well. Morgenthau worried that American policymakers would get carried away with the anti-Communist ideology that was sweeping the land. Ideology, however satisfying to the national ego, was no guide to the national interest. The matter moved Morgenthau to capitals and exclamation points:

FORGET AND REMEMBER!

FORGET the sentimental notion that foreign policy is a struggle between virtue and vice, with virtue bound to win.

FORGET the utopian notion that a brave new world without power politics will follow the unconditional surrender of wicked nations.

FORGET the crusading notion that any state, however virtuous and powerful, can have the mission to make the world over in its own image.

REMEMBER that the golden age of isolated normalcy is gone forever and that no effort, however great, and no action, however radical, will bring it back.

REMEMBER that diplomacy without power is feeble, and power without diplomacy is destructive and blind.

REMEMBER that no nation's power is without limits, and hence that its policies must respect the power and interests of others . . .

And, above all, remember always that it is not only a political necessity but also a moral duty for a nation to follow in its dealings with other nations but one guiding star, one standard for thought, one rule for action:

THE NATIONAL INTEREST.[15]

If Americans seemed obsessed with the apocalyptic struggle of good and evil, it was at least partly because after 1945, and espe-

---

14   *Congressional Record*, 8 February 1951, 1117–21.
15   Hans J. Morgenthau, *In Defense of the National Interest: A Critical Examination of American Foreign Policy* (New York, 1951), 241–42.

cially after 1949, the apocalypse appeared nearer than in recent millennia. The invention of nuclear weapons raised the grim possibility that six thousand years of human development, by the reckoning of Bishop Ussher, or six million years, by Charles Darwin, might be canceled in a flash. It was enough to make anyone think in apocalyptic terms.

It also led to a dramatic reconfiguration of the elements of national interest. Security, in the sense of physical protection against external attack, had always been part of the mix, but not since 1814 had the home territory of the United States been seriously at risk. (Hawaii in 1941 was a territory, and therefore not quite home.) Nuclear weapons in the hands of the Soviets changed the situation entirely. A Soviet takeover – invasion followed by occupation – remained the stuff of better-dead-than-red fantasy, but a Soviet attack of devastating proportions, by aircraft-borne bombs or missile-delivered warheads, was not at all out of the question. And precisely because Americans had for so long been immune from physical attack, the knowledge that they were no longer so was all the more traumatic.

From the trauma arose an inordinate concern with security, a concept and term that trumped every other aspect of the national interest for nearly two generations starting in the late 1940s. The concept took institutional shape in the National Security Act of 1947, which created the National Security Council, as well as such other security mainstays as the Department of Defense and the Central Intelligence Agency. The conversion of the War Department to the Defense Department fairly well captured the new thinking of the nuclear era. Heretofore war had been clearly distinguishable from peace; now the nation's security was at risk, and needed defending, full-time.

Likewise with spying. Henry Stimson had closed the State Department's "Black Chamber" during the Hoover era on grounds that gentlemen did not read each other's mail. As war secretary under Franklin Roosevelt, Stimson evinced no compunctions about running spies, presumably on the reasoning that war suspended gentlemanly obligations. The establishment of the CIA suggested that the suspension was permanent – or at least for the duration of the Cold War. Gentlemen or no, the cost of ignorance of the intentions and capabilities of one's enemies escalated enormously once nuclear weapons entered the arsenals of the great powers.

What patriotism was in Samuel Johnson's day, security became in the Cold War. Security sanctioned disregard for civil liberties during the McCarthy era; it justified an enormous enlargement of the defense budget and the creation of what Dwight Eisenhower ruefully called the "military-industrial complex"; it led to an extension of American military alliances, formal and informal, until they girdled the globe; it afforded a rationale for American support of regimes in Latin America, Asia, and Africa that would not have passed muster under the most latitudinarian definition of democracy, or even decency; it provided cover for activities that would have been rejected out of hand by an earlier generation of Americans.

General James Doolittle explained this last point to Dwight Eisenhower in the context of a 1954 review of American intelligence and covert operations. The rationale applied, *mutatis mutandis*, to many of the other activities undertaken in the name of security.

It is now clear that we are facing an implacable enemy whose avowed objective is world domination by whatever means and at whatever cost. . . . If the United States is to survive, long-standing American concepts of "fair play" must be reconsidered. We must develop effective espionage and counter-espionage services and must learn to subvert, sabotage and destroy our enemies by more clever, more sophisticated, and more effective methods than those used against us.[16]

Nor was the security card playable only in foreign and defense policy. Or, to put the matter more suggestively, under the aggrandized concept of security, *everything* was part of foreign or defense policy. When Eisenhower wanted to complete the St. Lawrence Seaway, he trotted out the security argument, saying

16 United States Senate, Select Committee to Study Government Operations with respect to Intelligence Activities, 94th Cong., 2d sess., *Supplementary Detailed Staff Reports on Foreign and Military Intelligence* (Washington, 1976), 4:52–53.

that the steel mills of the Great Lakes would be starved of ore if the ships could not get up the big river of the north. When he sought support for the interstate highway system, he pointed out how useful the thruways would be in the evacuation of cities in the event of Soviet atomic attack. When John Kennedy started the countdown to America's mission to the moon, he (and many others) couched the challenge in terms of a race against the Russians; to lose would be to damage American prestige and thereby undermine American security. Lyndon Johnson justified the War on Poverty with the argument, among others, that how America treated its least favored would go far toward winning or losing the allegiance of that large majority of the human race for whom poverty was a fact of everyday life.

The security argument was highly elastic, as evidenced by its employment on both sides of many policy debates. Perhaps most striking in this regard was the connection made between national security and race relations, by both the advocates of integration and their opponents. Since the publication of the *Communist Manifesto* in 1848, agitators for change have been branded Communists; consequently it was to no one's surprise that opponents of the Jim Crow system of segregation in the American South were so labeled during the 1950s and 1960s. Yet by elevating communism to the major threat to American security, the Cold War lent a bite to the red-baiting slanders they had previously lacked. Moreover, the security angle brought the big guns of the federal government to bear, and, with disgraceful frequency, those guns targeted reformers whose only crime was to demand that America live up to its promises. Martin Luther King, Jr., to cite the most conspicuous example, faced a concerted campaign of surveillance, disinformation, and sabotage by J. Edgar Hoover's Federal Bureau of Investigation – a campaign that included an ominous anonymous letter warning King to quit the civil rights movement or perhaps even kill himself (this part of the letter was suggestive rather than explicit) lest "your filthy, abnormal fraudulent self is bared to the nation."[17]

17   David J. Garrow, *The FBI and Martin Luther King, Jr.* (New York, 1981), 126.

Yet the connection between race and security could cut the other way as well. Dwight Eisenhower was hardly a progressive on race; he regretted as social engineering the 1954 *Brown v. Board of Education* decision banning school segregation (almost as much as he regretted appointing Chief Justice Earl Warren, who orchestrated the unanimous decision). But once civil rights became an issue that drew worldwide attention – as it was bound to do in the age of decolonization in Asia and Africa – Eisenhower recognized that America could not afford to be backward thereon. To Orval Faubus's Arkansas challenge in 1957, Eisenhower responded by explaining the stakes:

At a time when we face grave situations abroad because of the hatred that Communism bears toward a system of government based on human rights, it would be difficult to exaggerate the harm that is being done to the prestige and influence, and indeed to the safety, of our nation and the world.

Our enemies are gloating over this incident and using it everywhere to misrepresent our whole nation. We are portrayed as a violator of those standards of conduct which the peoples of the world united to proclaim in the Charter of the United Nations. There they affirmed "faith in fundamental human rights" and "in the dignity and worth of the human person" and they did so "without distinction as to race, sex, language or religion."[18]

Much as it galled Eisenhower to be Earl Warren's enforcer, the security of the nation required it. The general sent in the troops to force open the schoolhouse doors.

Conceptions of security may have grown like kudzu during the Cold War, covering every other element of national interest, but they didn't quite choke out those other elements. Prosperity and democracy continued to exist as items worth worrying about, although in an age of obsession with security, they were frequently redefined in terms of security.

---

18 *Public Papers of the Presidents*, 24 September 1957 (Washington, 1958), 694.

The prosperity issue, which had indirectly elicited American intervention in World War I, before being abandoned during the neutralist thirties, staged a comeback during the Cold War. In fact, the comeback commenced while World War II was still under way. At Bretton Woods in 1944, American negotiators insisted on the establishment of an international financial regime designed to prevent a recurrence of the Great Depression, which seemed as good an explanation of World War II as any – and one more amenable to the kind of governmental activism favored by the New Dealers who directed American postwar planning than such alternatives as original sin. The means to the end of depression-prevention was the familiar one of opening of foreign markets to American commerce. Dean Acheson, at that time assistant secretary of state for economic affairs, sounded like any number of expansionists from the 1890s when he told a congressional committee, "We cannot have full employment and prosperity in the United States without the foreign markets."[19]

Once the Cold War started, the prosperity brief was folded into the security argument. Unless the United States remained economically strong, ran the reasoning, it could not defend itself militarily or ideologically against the Communists. This argument informed most discussions of economic issues during the Cold War, and was codified in such official documents as NSC–162/2, which in 1953 asserted that a vital interest of America was to "maintain a sound economy based on free enterprise as a basis both for high defense productivity and for the maintenance of its living standards and free institutions."[20]

The prosperity argument infused domestic as well as foreign policy; for the first time the federal government undertook on a regular basis to manage the economy. Whether, in political terms, this could have been accomplished without the Cold War and the security rationale it provided, is an intriguing question; memories of the Great Depression might have sufficed.

19 United States Congress, House of Representatives, 78th Cong., 2d sess., *Hearings before the Special Committee on Post-war Economic Policy and Planning* (Washington, 1945), 1083.
20 *Foreign Relations of the United States, 1952–1954* (Washington, 1984), 2:577–97.

But the prosperity argument, as translated into terms of free trade and the opening of foreign markets, certainly formed a reliable element of American foreign policy from 1945 through the end of the 1990s. Beginning at Bretton Woods, continuing past the 1948 inauguration of the General Agreement on Tariffs and Trade, to the subsequent "rounds" of negotiations that extended the GATT, and ultimately to the transformation of the GATT into the World Trade Organization, one presidential administration after another defended the opening of markets as essential to the prosperity of America and what, until the 1990s, most presidents were happy to call the "Free World."

The prosperity argument had a couple of corollaries, each directly related to national security. The first was that prosperity per se was an antidote to the unrest that provoked revolutions and other disturbances of the international peace. This corollary provided the basis, and many of the votes, for the Marshall Plan and subsequent programs of American economic aid to other countries. The second corollary applied specifically to the GATT and associated ventures in economic integration; this held that where goods crossed borders, armies didn't. If France and Germany learned to trade with each other, they would forget to fight with each other.

Critics of American policy saw the apparently inexorable expansion of the American trading and investment system as a form of imperialism. Indeed, it was worse than imperialism, the critics contended, in that *real* imperialists at least recognized that responsibility accompanied power, and felt some obligation, however paternalistic, to the peoples under their sway. The new imperialists – multinational corporations and their power-elite lackeys – exercised power but acknowledged no responsibility to anyone but their stockholders.

It probably would not have appeased these critics to hear the market-expanding policies of the United States described as a kind of economic Wilsonianism. Where Wilson contended that democracy could not be safe in one country, the free traders contended that capitalism could not be safe in one country. (In fact, Wilson himself had made freer, if not *free*, trade point three of his famous fourteen.) In enunciating the elements of the national interest, American leaders much preferred promoting democracy to touting capitalism; but it was almost an article of faith in post-war America that the two went together.

This had not always been so. As late as the 1930s, at a time when capitalism was covering itself in neither glory nor dividends, alternatives to capitalism exerted a strong appeal upon the American intelligentsia, a not inconsequential number of whom joined the Communist party. But the Cold War changed things in two ways. First, it placed communism so far beyond the realm of respectability in America that democratic socialism, though practiced by some of America's closest allies, came to seem oxymoronic. Second, the economic Wilsonians delivered the goods, quite literally. The Cold War years were the most prosperous in American history. Hair-splitters could debate whether this was due to the growing globalization or to the military Keynesianism of the Cold War, but there it was. Conflating democracy and capitalism in defining the national interest might have made lousy logic, but it made potent political economy.

Historically minded students of the national interest perhaps wondered what had happened to that other aspect of the prosperity argument, the one that provoked American intervention in World War I (a century after fueling a quasi-war with France and a real one with Britain), and that in a reactive form had furnished much of the reason for the neutrality legislation of the 1930s: namely, the defense of neutral rights in wartime. The short answer was that after 1945 the issue of wartime neutrality essentially ceased to exist for the United States. Few Americans, either leaders or public, could conceive of a meaningful war – one that would threaten any important American interest, economic or otherwise – that the United States would not join at the outset. Neutral rights had always been a worry of the weak or diffident; after 1945 the United States was neither weak nor diffident.

As the dueling applications of the security mantra to such issues as race demonstrated, citing security as the overriding national interest hardly ended discussions of the subject. The hard question was what constituted security. Did the security of the United States require, for example, the defense of every non-Communist government that appealed to Washington for help? Harry Truman had implied that it did, and for a decade and a half after the enunciation of Truman's doctrine, Americans tended to take him at his implication. The exceptions – China being the most spectacular – simply proved the rule, or perhaps the corollary that while the "fall" of a non-Communist country might or might not gravely endanger the United States, it inflicted unacceptable damage on the party in power at the time.

Yet the question would not go away, and it reemerged with a vengeance in Vietnam in the 1960s. Here the question became: How much must the United States invest, by way of blood and treasure, in preserving the government of South Vietnam? Actually, phrased that way, it was a trick question, for as American involvement in the overthrow of the Diem government in 1963 demonstrated, the United States was not defending a *government* in South Vietnam. Nor was it clearly defending a people, considering how grievously the war wounded the South Vietnamese and their society.

What the United States was defending, by the time the serious chips were being pushed onto the table, was American credibility. In this regard the Vietnam War made sense (for the United States, if not for the Vietnamese), at least according to what passed for sense in an era beguiled by the security argument. For all of America's nuclear might, the safety of the Free World depended on the confidence of America's allies that the United States would do what it promised to do. Washington had said it would defend Saigon; therefore Washington must defend Saigon. By this means was credibility converted into a vital national interest.

Yet the credibility argument, like most subspecies of the security argument, was two-edged. The allies surely worried about America's credibility, its resolve for fulfilling commitments; but they also worried about America's judgment. By the mid-1960s, the Europeans – the allies that really mattered – were seriously concerned that American leaders had become so obsessed with Vietnam that they might forget what the Cold War was really about. With half-a-million men in Vietnam, and half-a-hundred-thousand dead, could the Americans respond, either militarily or emotionally, to a crisis on the central Cold War front in Europe?

The judgment issue arose in another context as well, and not only among America's allies. And it arose on a point that perhaps better than any other demonstrated that security as a national interest meant nothing in the absence of an accepted definition of what security entailed.

From that Alamagordo dawn in 1945, nuclear weapons held the dual promise of securing America's future or eliminating it. Opinions split, with the pro-nuclearists seizing the high ground of government and the anti-nuclearists occupying the lowlands at the fringes of the Cold War consensus. During the 1950s and early 1960s the direct threat of nuclear war escalated with the introduction by both superpowers of hydrogen weapons and intercontinental bombers and missiles; meanwhile an indirect threat – of nuclear poisoning via radiation-exuding fallout – emerged with the testing of nuclear warheads in the atmosphere. Consequently, even as the official national security apparatus of the United States built more and bigger bombs, claiming that the national interest required it, a growing group of dissenters held that the national interest required just the opposite.

"A sober nation can become drunk with victory," Albert Einstein had said in 1946, by way of calling for a reconsideration of the role of nuclear weapons in American security planning.[21] Linus Pauling, another Nobelist (once already, for chemistry; he would garner a second, for peace), reached the same conclusion. Referring to strategies for the use of nuclear weapons, Pauling declared, "We cannot accept the idea of such monstrous immorality. The time has now come for morality to take its proper place in the conduct of world affairs. The time has now come for the nations of the world to submit to the just regulation of their conduct by international law."[22]

21　*New York Times Magazine*, 23 June 1946.
22　Linus Pauling, *No More War!* (New York, 1958), 209.

If the free traders were economic Wilsonians, Einstein and Pauling and such other advocates of disarmament as Norman Cousins were nuclear Wilsonians—although in this case they weren't making the world safe *for* something, but safe *from* something, namely nuclear weapons. (Here again Wilson had actually anticipated them. Point four of his fourteen called for disarmament.) But the principle was the same: the national interest of the United States was so tied up in a larger international interest that the former could not be achieved, or even credibly addressed, without fundamental consideration of the latter.

Until the late 1970s the nuclear Wilsonians had better luck than original Wilsonians, although worse than the economic Wilsonians. The last group got GATT, the first the Partial Test Ban of 1963 and the SALT I Treaty of 1972. The test ban essentially terminated the production of atmospheric fallout, while SALT I made a beginning on arms control without materially mitigating the threat of nuclear war.

It was only one of the many ironies of Richard Nixon's remarkable career that he turned out to be the answer to the antinuclearists' prayers (admittedly, an unsatisfactory answer, but better than anything else available). A larger irony was that after doing so much to ratchet up the Cold War, Nixon did his best to end it. And he essentially succeeded, although his success was subsequently forgotten.

Nixon's insight was that ideology had become obsolete – worse than obsolete, downright counterproductive. Anti-Communist ideology prevented the United States from exploiting the most important development in international affairs since 1945: the bitter and ever-bitterer rivalry between the Soviet Union and China. And the failure to exploit this rivalry prevented a graceful exit from Vietnam, which grew more imperative with each passing month after the Tet offensive of 1968.

Nixon cut the Gordian knot by announcing plans to visit China. At a blow the charter Cold Warrior signaled that geopolitics had supplanted ideology in American diplomacy. The Truman Doctrine was already a dead letter, killed on the ground in Vietnam, with its *Nunc Dimittis* contained in the Nixon Doctrine, which warned small nations not to count on the United States to fight their wars. Now, by jaunting to Beijing – on his way to Moscow, to no one's surprise – Nixon declared that it was diplomatic business as usual with foreign governments regardless of their ideological hue. For twenty-five years, the fundamental national interest had been the containment of communism; with Nixon embracing Communists in both the Forbidden City and the Kremlin, the national interest quite obviously was being redefined.

Had Nixon survived in office, detente would have been recognized for what it was – the peace settlement of the Cold War – and the redefinition of the national interest could have proceeded in an orderly and sensible fashion. But Watergate sank Nixon and left detente to his far less experienced and less deviously capable successors, Gerald Ford and Jimmy Carter.

Following the Ford interregnum, Carter strove manfully to refashion the national interest to suit the new post-Cold War era. "For too many years we've been willing to adopt the flawed and erroneous principles and tactics of our adversaries, sometimes abandoning our own values for theirs," he said. "We've fought fire with fire, never thinking that fire is better quenched with water." Vietnam was the best, or worst, example of the intellectual and moral poverty of this approach. But the nation had learned from that tragic experience. "Through failure we have now found our way back to our own principles and values." These principles and values pointed to a foreign policy freed from an "inordinate fear of communism" and inspired instead by genuine respect for democracy, including basic human rights, and a desire to promote the prosperity not only of the United States but of the less-developed countries. "Our policy is rooted in our values," Carter concluded. "Our policy is designed to serve mankind."[23]

For a time, Carter made progress in his effort to to release the national interest from the security straightjacket that had encased

23   *Public Papers*, 22 May 1977 (Washington, 1977), 954–62.

it since the start of the Cold War. His emphasis on democracy and human rights raised the visibility of those subjects in international forums even as it raised the cost to American clients of undemocratic behavior and human rights violations. His ambassador to the United Nations, Andrew Young, announced a reorientation of American thinking from the East-West security axis of the Cold War to a North-South economic dialogue.

Unfortunately for Carter, influential groups within America loved the Cold War too much to let it go. Whatever it did for American national security, the end of the Cold War challenged the psychological security of the many people who had grown up with the Cold War and learned to accept it as the basis of international affairs; it simultaneously undermined the economic security of the defense industry and others that had made a good living from the Cold War.

The Cold War-revivalists found their voice among the "neoconservatives," refugees, in many cases, from the prewar left who found renewed certitude at the opposite end of the ideological spectrum. Led by the likes of Norman Podhoretz and Jeanne Kirkpatrick, the neoconservatives decried detente as the contemporary equivalent of appeasement, derided Carter's emphasis on democratic rights and economic egalitarianism, and demanded that security be restored as the touchstone of the national interest.

Carter got no help from events. While he was arranging the return of the Panama Canal to Panama, a move the neoconservatives (and some others) castigated as a giveaway of an asset vital to American security, revolutions in Nicaragua and Iran unseated regimes friendly to the United States and installed groups unfriendly – in the case of Iran, actively hostile. Iranian radicals proceeded to seize several dozen American diplomats and hold them hostage for more than a year, causing Carter's foreign policy plausibility to plunge further. Moscow delivered the coup de grace to detente by invading Afghanistan at the end of 1979. Whether this signaled a reversion to totalitarian form, as the neoconservatives said, or principally a response to instability among the Afghans, it cut the last of the ground from under Carter's (and Nixon's) efforts to push America past the Cold War.

Ronald Reagan was the darling of the neoconservatives, partly because he gave them jobs and partly because he restored security, defined in traditional Cold War terms, to primacy among American national interests. Reagan's big arms buildup allowed America to "stand tall" again, in the Republican phraseology of the day, and to slam shut what the neoconservatives styled the "window of vulnerability" to Soviet nuclear attack. Meanwhile the Reagan Doctrine of aid to anti-Communist insurgencies in Central America and elsewhere institutionalized the "liberationist" philosophy of the early 1950s – and of which little has been heard since then. Combined with rhetoric that made the Soviet Union out to be an "evil empire" and "the focus of evil in the modern world," the Reagan approach represented a concerted effort to rev up the Cold War once more.[24]

Yet the effort never really took hold. Rearmament was applauded in the expected places – associations of defense contractors, metal-workers' union halls, chambers of commerce of Sunbelt cities surrounded by military bases – but the provocative rhetoric sent shudders through millions of Americans who worried that all the new weapons might actually be used. Indeed, the Reagan restoration provoked a resurgence of the antinuclear movement, with demands ranging from no-first-use to a freeze on deployment to total abolition. At the same time, the American public yawned in the face of administration demands for anti-Communist action in Central America. Congress did more than yawn; it repeatedly passed legislation to cut off aid to the Nicaraguan contras – legislation the Reagan administration just as repeatedly, if secretly, defied.

Consequently, it came as a relief to all but the most zealous neoconservatives (and single-minded arms makers) when Mikhail Gorbachev inherited power in the Kremlin and intimated a desire

---

24 *Public Papers*, 29 January 1981 (Washington, 1982), 55–62; *Public Papers*, 8 March 1983 (Washington, 1984), 359–64.

to be done with the Cold War once and for all. He did not indicate a desire to be done with the Soviet system, but before the changes he set in motion ran their course, that was precisely what he accomplished.

Whether the Cold War ended in 1971, with Nixon's opening to China, or 1985, with Gorbachev's accession to power, or 1989, with the collapse of the Berlin Wall, or 1991, with the breakup of the Soviet Union, by the early 1990s none could doubt that the American national interest would have to be retooled for a world without another superpower.

And so it was, with the other elements of the national interest triumvirate – prosperity and democracy – regaining much of the ground they had lost to security during the Cold War. When George Bush responded to the Iraqi invasion of Kuwait by organizing for war to oust the invaders, Bush administration spokespersons adduced various explanations as to what was at risk in the Gulf. They were hard pressed to say that the defense of Kuwait and Saudi Arabia would benefit democracy directly – neither country being remotely democratic – but democracy and its necessary precondition, self-determination, were clearly behind the "new world order" of which Bush spoke so frequently. The late 1980s and early 1990s witnessed an unprecedented sprouting of democracy around the globe; only if the new democracies, many of them weak and tentative, felt safe from external attack, would that blessed institution blossom.

For those who found the "new world order" unlikely, administration officials fell back on the prosperity argument. Should Saddam Hussein control the oil of the Gulf, they explained, there was no telling what havoc he could wreak on the economies of the West. Secretary of State James Baker was blunt about the crux of the matter: "If you want to sum it up in one word: it's jobs."[25]

---

25 Lawrence Freedman and Efraim Karsh, *The Gulf Conflict 1990–1991: Diplomacy and War in the New World Order* (Princeton, 1993), 224.

Security didn't disappear as a concern of Americans, but it took a decidedly different form than in the harrowing days of the Berlin blockade and the Cuban missile crisis. Terrorist attacks – on the World Trade Center in New York, on American airliners, on American embassies – demonstrated that security was never absolute. Although the Soviet Union had disappeared, many of Moscow's missiles remained, and they remained a worry to those who made a living worrying about American security.

Yet the case of Russia perhaps best indicated the approaching balance among the various elements of the national interest. The United States orchestrated international aid to Russia; the aid had three aims: to promote democracy in the former homeland of communism, thereby reinforcing the general democratic trend in international affairs; to put Russia on a path to prosperity, which would benefit not only the Russian people (with positive effects on democracy there) but foreign merchants and investors, including Americans, as well; and to prevent a reversion to the authoritarianism (nuclearly armed) that had endangered American security for half of the twentieth century.

The restoration of balance was not irreversible. With the nuclear genie out of the bottle, security could never be assumed, the way it often had been before World War II. But as the twentieth century drew to a close, Americans remembered that there was more to the national interest than security. Two decades earlier, after the Cold War ended the first time, Jimmy Carter interpreted the connections among the three central elements of the national interest. Carter said: "The great democracies are not free because we are strong and prosperous. We are strong and influential and prosperous because we are free."[26] Carter's critics took issue with this, or at least with the implications he drew from it. Security came first, they said; prosperity and democracy would follow.

Whether or not either side to this debate realized it, their argument was as old as the century. Since 1898 Americans had agreed that the national interest encompassed prosperity, democracy, and security; but which of the three counted most in the national in-

26 *Public Papers*, 22 May 1977 (Washington, 1977), 954–62.

terest depended on who was counting and when. The imperialists of 1898 pushed prosperity, demanding access to foreign markets. Woodrow Wilson sought to make the world safe for democracy. American Cold Warriors turned security into the touchstone of foreign policy.

If the century taught anything, it was that none of the three elements could stand alone – or even stand out too far, without risk of damage to itself or the others. The pursuit of prosperity via annexation of the Philippines rendered the United States less secure in Asia without doing much for Asian democracy (or, for that matter, American prosperity); Wilson's crusade for democracy provoked an isolationist backlash that undermined both American prosperity and American security; the security obsession of the Cold War led to anti-democratic dirty tricks in the Third World, a terrifying arms race, and a war in Vietnam that tore America apart and cracked the consensus on which notions of Cold War security rested.

During the Cold War, American strategists constructed a nuclear "triad," a three-legged stool of ground-, sea-, and air-launched weapons. The reasoning was that stable deterrence required strength in each leg; should any one leg atrophy, deterrence might topple. The American national interest – with democracy, prosperity, and security as the three legs – was like that. If events of the twentieth century are any guide, it still is.

① How?

② How? —? I guess WW II

5

The Tension between Democracy and Capitalism during the American Century

WALTER LaFEBER

The American Century's early years were marked by Woodrow Wilson's proclamation that the world must be made safe for democracy. At the close of the twentieth century, the need to spread American-style democracy throughout much of the world (and, in the view of many, the success of having done so during the 1980s and the 1990s) has supposedly shaped U.S. foreign policy and, as well, the way Americans perceive that world. Thus, it seems that the successes of the American Century and the U.S. determination to expand a democratic system are unusually one and the same. Indeed, it has even been argued that the spread of democracy is a most important theme and dynamic in the American Century's evolution.[1]

---

1 Joshua Muravchik, *Exporting Democracy; Fulfilling America's Destiny* (Washington, 1991), esp. 1–18. A workable definition of democracy is given by Daniel Bell in *The Cultural Contradictions of Capitalism* (New York, 1996), 14: "Democracy is a socio-political system in which legitimacy lies in the consent of the governed, where the political arena is available to various contending groups, and where fundamental liberties are safeguarded." Fareed Zakaria's "The Rise of Illiberal Democracy," *Foreign Affairs* 76 (November/December 1997): 22–43, is especially valuable for pointing out how viable democracy rests on what he calls "constitutional liberalism." Without such "liberalism," which includes a tradition of the rule of law and protection of human rights, the processes of democracy – such as elections – can become meaningless and indeed dangerous. This is a distinction that many U.S. officials have in the past accepted and used to justify both American exceptionalism (that is, the Americans have such "constitutional liberalism" but others as yet do not) and the loose, if not cynical, use of democracy to justify certain foreign policies.

The historical record, however, shows no such consistent theme or dynamic. The leading U.S. diplomat in Asia at the start of the American Century, Willard Straight, was closer to the truth when he observed that "Japan and Russia [make] money out of politics," while Americans make "politics out of money." Instead of spreading democracy abroad, most Progressive Era (1900–1933) officials thought many foreign peoples, especially in Latin America, Asia, and Africa, were incapable of developing and maintaining democratic systems, at least for the foreseeable future. Far from making the world safe for democracy, Woodrow Wilson and the U.S. Congress so compromised the principle during 1918–20 that informed observers (and leading Wilsonians) such as Walter Lippmann developed a realist worldview to demonstrate why democratic systems were dangerous as either the originators or objectives of foreign policy. The realists who held sway over policymaking in the early Cold War considered the advancing of democracy to be of distinctly secondary interest as they built up political, military, and economic systems to contain and roll back communism.[2]

The turning point came in the 1970s and 1980s. Led by the realpolitik of Richard Nixon and Henry Kissinger and the economic needs of the Trilateral Commission, the belief spread that the excessively democratic counterculture of the 1960s was a major reason why the post-Vietnam American Century was stalling into decline. A much-discussed part of this turn was Jeanne Kirkpatrick's argument that U.S. policy should work with authoritarian regimes because, while they were not democratic, they, unlike totalitarian governments, shared American beliefs in open economic systems.

The Trilateral Commission's and Kirkpatrick's rationales were pivotal because they highlighted the importance of valuing access and protection for capital over the expansion of democracy. The most durable and productive key for unlocking the motivations of U.S. foreign policy since the 1890s has been Washington offi-

2 Straight to Knox, 12 February 1911, Willard Straight Papers, Cornell University, Ithaca, New York.

cials' belief that a global system based on the needs of private capital, including the protection of private property and open access to markets, could best protect the burgeoning American system and its values, including its own version of democracy at home.[3]

In the mid-1980s an emphasis on democracy again claimed prominence in U.S. overseas policies. It marked the first time since Woodrow Wilson's presidency that democratic rhetoric gained such attention. In the hands of the Reagan administration and some of its allies, especially the quasi-governmental National Endowment for Democracy (NED), this rhetoric aimed at undermining Communist, especially Soviet (much less so Chinese), power. Thus, after a sixty-year hiatus, the argument for spreading democratic systems was again heard, and again, as with Wilson, the argument targeted the Soviet Union and its empire.[4]

The American push for expanding liberal democracy has thus been an on-and-mostly-off policy during the American Century. It has been mostly off because of racism, exceptionalism, a fear at times of results from truly democratic elections, a dislike if not hatred for the kind of participatory democracy spawned by the events of the 1960s, and, of particular importance, the consistent demonstration in actual policy that the expansion of capitalist systems is more important than the expansion of liberal democratic systems. As the president of the European Bank for Reconstruction and Development, Jacques Attali, phrased it in the mid-1990s, "The main mission of American diplomacy seems to be the 'export' of western values, including democracy – at least as long as doing so serves American interests."[5]

3 Two pioneering works that in rather different ways elaborate on this thesis are Martin Sklar, "The Open Door, Imperialism, and Post-Imperialism," unpublished, in author's possession; and Thomas J. McCormick, *America's Half-Century: United States Foreign Policy in the Cold War and After* (Baltimore, 1995).
4 Two quite different views of this process, and especially of the National Endowment for Democracy, are Muravchik, *Exporting Democracy*, esp. 204–26; and William I. Robinson, *Promoting Polyarchy: Globalization, U.S. Intervention, and Hegemony* (New York, 1996), which argues that the NED and the other Reagan approaches aimed at "low-intensity democracies" whose purposes were to give off the effect of democracy while actually retaining class inequalities and access for capital and trade.
5 Jacques Attali, "The Crash of Western Civilization: The Limits of the Market and Democracy," *Foreign Policy* 107 (Summer 1997): 54.

From the 1890s through Luce to the 1990s

When the first glimmerings of the American Century appeared in the 1890s to 1914 era, little was heard from U.S. officials about expanding democracy. President William McKinley seemed to be little concerned about teaching his new conquests, the Cubans and Filipinos, how to build democratic societies. In any case, regardless of such possible concerns, he and his immediate successors failed miserably in both countries. One reason for the failure was a blatant racism that, for example, allowed McKinley's running mate in the 1900 election, war hero Theodore Roosevelt, to argue that the treatment accorded Native Americans provided adequate precedent and justification for treating Cubans and Filipinos (and Puerto Ricans) any way that suited U.S. interests. To ensure that Cuba respected those interests, McKinley and Roosevelt imposed the Platt Amendment, which severely restricted self-government on the island but provided protection and encouragement for private capital. The growing gap between the Cubans' ability to govern themselves and the effects of that capital led to such polarization that President Franklin D. Roosevelt finally terminated the Platt Amendment in 1934. But it was too late. As Cuba divided between the very rich (which included many U.S. investors involved in the all-important sugar industry), and the poor, Cubans understandably, if not always accurately, blamed Washington or their problems. Given this past, if the 1959 Cuban Revolution had not been anti-American, it would not only have been surprising, it would not have been a revolution.[6]

U.S. policy in the Philippines focused, even more than in Cuba, on the need to carry out educational, political, and religious reforms so the society could become more like the American. The islands could thus serve the purpose for which the United States had acquired them in 1898–99: to serve as a stable base for the

---

6 Theodore Roosevelt, *The Letters of Theodore Roosevelt*, 8 vols, ed. Elting E. Morison et al. (Cambridge, MA, 1951–54), 2:1385, 5:1404. Emily Rosenberg identifies five features of U.S. "liberal-developmentalism" in overseas activities at the start of the American Century. They stress the importance of "private free enterprise" and "free or open access for trade and investment." None mentions democracy. Emily Rosenberg, *Spreading the American Dream: American Economic and Cultural Expansion, 1890–1945* (New York, 1982), 7.

projection of U.S. power on the Asian mainland. The Philippines served exactly that purpose in mid-1900 when McKinley dispatched five thousand troops from Manila to intervene in Peking for the protection of U.S. citizens and property interests under siege by the violently anti-foreign Boxers. By 1907, however, Theodore Roosevelt – in one of the more revealing and significant reassessments in the American Century's diplomacy – decided that, given new developments, most notably the threat posed by Japan's rising power, the Philippines now formed "our heel of Achilles." But Roosevelt went further. He understood that U.S. efforts to transform Filipino society had resoundingly failed. The president concluded that Americans lacked the "character" to create the bases for democratic institutions in faraway, unfamiliar places. He came to realize that Progressive Era racism (which he exemplified) ironically helped prevent Americans from expanding their own political beliefs into their western Pacific empire. Roosevelt pulled the U.S. Navy's Pacific base back from Manila to Hawaii. He instructed his successor, William Howard Taft, not to interfere from such a weak position in Asian affairs for the sake of an open door for American capital – advice Taft and his successors did not accept. Roosevelt preferred to work with Japan, rather than with China (or against Japan), so American capital could have some protection. By 1907–10, Roosevelt was at least becoming consistent.[7]

It was a consistency Woodrow Wilson never grasped. Wilson better resembled Thomas Jefferson: his principles, not his practices, were best emulated. It became Wilson's tragedy that he brought to the White House the practice of a Progressive Era racism, gut faith in an American exceptionalist democracy, a deep devotion to competitive capitalism, and the confidence that a more intelligent use of governmental (especially executive) powers could best realize the expansion of that democracy and capitalism – at the same time the globe burst into world war and revolution.

---

7 James Chace and Caleb Carr, *America Invulnerable: The Quest for Absolute Security from 1812 to Star Wars* (New York, 1988), 138–40; John Milton Cooper, Jr., *The Warrior and the Priest: Woodrow Wilson and Theodore Roosevelt* (Cambridge, MA, 1983), 112.

In his first test in the foreign policy arena, Wilson, facing from his perspective a choice of evils in revolutionary China, recognized the monarchical regime of Yuan Shih-k'ai in the hope that Yuan would better protect U.S. interests than would his more radical rival, Sun Yat-sen. Wilson also believed he could better protect those interests, and work with Yuan, by going it alone in China rather than (as Roosevelt advised), working with Japan and the other foreign powers. The policy turned out to be a disaster. As war in Europe gave the Japanese a free hand, they made demands on China that Wilson could not moderate (although the British finally did to some extent). As Yuan's regime was swept aside by growing revolution, and Japan cut deals with its European allies to take over Germany's strategic holdings in China, Wilson had to deal with Tokyo from a position of weakness at the 1919 Paris Peace Conference. In his speech to Congress he had vowed to use U.S. power to "make the world safe for democracy." But at Paris he subordinated democratic principles and self-determination so Japan could keep its newly gained strategic positions in China. The most the president could realize was a set of agreements in which Japan promised to respect the open door for U.S. interests outside the Japanese holdings, and a new consortium arrangement with other foreign powers to promote U.S. capital investments in China.[8]

Wilson's failure to reconcile his democratic dogma with capitalist demands in China was minor compared with what awaited him in Europe. When the Russian Provisional Government replaced the tsar in March 1917, Americans could go to war with some belief that all the allies were presumably democracies. When the Provisional regime was pushed aside by V. I. Lenin and Leon Trotsky's Bolsheviks, however, Russia was no longer seen as a democracy and, much worse, threatened other European nations with revolution. It was this Leninist threat that Wilson tried to meet head-on in 1918 with his Fourteen Points speech. He outlined a liberal democratic, capitalist (open-door, freedom-of-the-

8   Thomas J. Knock, *To End All Wars: Woodrow Wilson and the Quest for a New World Order* (New York, 1992), 249–50; Harold Nicolson, *Peacemaking, 1919* (London, 1939), 146.

seas) alternative to the Bolsheviks' revolutionary doctrine. But a danger lurked at the core of the president's liberal program: what if open elections brought Bolsheviks to power in central Europe? Or what if honoring the democratic wishes of particular ethnic groups (say, Germans in parts of Czechoslovakia or Poland), weakened the *cordon sanitaire* (as young Wilsonian adviser, Walter Lippmann, phrased it) constructed to contain the Bolsheviks to the east?[9]

The president, with agony, remorse, and full realization that he was again choosing from bad alternatives, made his choices. He went along with the European right wing, the "forces of the past," in one historian's words, and surrendered democratic self-government for the sake of security (and allied cooperation). When elections in Austria and elsewhere threatened to bring revolutionaries to power, he allowed his overseer of food supplies, Herbert Hoover, to threaten to shut off such help if the elections went the wrong way. The voters understood, some ethnic groups were placed under disliked governments, and many American liberals who took democratic practices seriously (especially since they believed such practices were the best hope for undercutting Lenin's appeal) were alienated. Perceived with some reason as having sold out to antidemocratic forces of the past in eastern Europe, central Europe, and China, Wilson was deserted by liberals for being too conservative and by many conservatives for trusting his new League of Nations to make everything right over time. The reaction went much further. A "Red Scare" of 1919 infected even the United States. Scapegoats, especially recent immigrants, were imprisoned or rounded up and sent back to the old country.[10]

Germany and Austria-Hungary lost World War I, but another loser during the war and immediately after was democracy. The acerbic, eloquent, antiwar Progressive Randolph Bourne had

9 Walter Lippmann, "The Political Scene," in *New Republic*, "Supplement," 22 March 1919.
10 Arno Mayer, *Politics and Diplomacy of Peacemaking; Containment and Counterrevolution at Versailles, 1918–1919* (New York, 1967), for the context and characterization; Herbert C. Hoover, *The Ordeal of Woodrow Wilson* (New York, 1958), esp. 134–41; Lloyd Gardner, *Safe for Democracy: Anglo-American Response to Revolution, 1913–1923* (New York, 1984), 186–191, 258–62.

prophesied much of this in 1917–18. If Wilson could not stop the divided forces for war between 1914 and 1917, Bourne asked, how could he ever hope to defeat the much stronger, more united, and victorious conservative forces at a peace conference? Another Progressive, Walter Lippmann, became similarly disillusioned after 1918 – less because of Wilson's actions than because he concluded that the failures of war and the peace conference were larger failures of the democratic peoples. These peoples had little interest in, and less aptitude for, the intricacies of a new diplomacy, Lippmann argued, but they nevertheless insisted on meddling in that policy, especially through their equally parochial representatives in Congress.[11]

Out of Lippmann's and other work in the 1920s came a "realist" foreign policy school that, while relatively small at the time, established principles on which the post-1945 realists in Washington rebuilt a war-devastated world and fought a Cold War. These principles included an emphasis on military force (an emphasis that did not gain much support in the interwar years), and on a monolithic decision-making process in which diplomatic experts (such as Lippmann or, later, George Kennan and Dean Acheson) were to be supreme and not beholden to the mushy, multiple voices of an unruly, inconsistent democracy. Ironically, American liberals who believed more strongly in democracy contributed inadvertently to Lippmann's thesis. Led by John Dewey, Horace Kallen, and Bourne, and inspired by William James's work in philosophy, these liberals stressed the growing presence and importance of cultural pluralism in the United States. As Alexis de Tocqueville had argued a century earlier, a feverishly pluralist democracy was the natural obstacle of every foreign policy official whose work demanded unity at home, not pluralism; and who had to be assured, along with those the official dealt with abroad, that the ever-stewing melting pot would retain a consis-

11   Ronald Steel, "Revolting Times," *Reviews in American History* 13 (December 1985): 588; David Green, *Shaping Political Consciousness: The Language of Politics in America from McKinley to Reagan* (Ithaca, 1987), 83.

tency and an even temperature so U.S. policies would be predictable over the long term.[12]

Between the perceived threats of Bolsheviks abroad and the dangers supposedly posed by a pluralistic American society at home, U.S. foreign policy officials did all they could to inoculate themselves against the germs of democracy. The New York Council on Foreign Relations, created in 1921–22 as a direct reaction to Wilson's failure to harness democracy properly during the war and after, was one such vaccination. A self-selected elite made up largely of corporate leaders, top government officials, and influential journalists (such as Lippmann) and academics, the council provided a quiet retreat for those of mostly similar minds to discuss and create foreign policy principles far from the maddening crowds on Capitol Hill.[13]

Political scientist Walter Dean Burnham argued much later that the election of 1896, won by William McKinley against Populist-Democrat William Jennings Bryan with overpowering financial support from the frightened business community, introduced a new political system that lasted down through much of the twentieth century. This system included the growing disenfranchisement of African Americans in the South, while a virtual one-party Democratic South and Republican Northeast and Midwest evolved. Because of these changes, Americans grew less interested in national politic, voter participation steadily declined, and, as Burnham emphasized, corporate business leaders and elite party officials increasingly ruled with fewer worries about an overactive democracy (as those leaders had to worry when more than 80 percent of qualified voters turned out in the elections of the 1870s and 1880s). The New York Council on Foreign Relations became one product of this post-1896 system, at once a reaction to Congress's repudiation of the League of Nations in 1919 and,

---

12   Walter Lippmann, *Public Opinion* (New York, 1922) esp. pts. 3-5; Ronald Steel, *Walter Lippmann and the American Century* (New York, 1981), provides the context; Louis Menand, "The Return of Pragmatism," *American Heritage* 48 (October 1997): esp. 56–60.
13   Robert D. Schulzinger, *The Wise Men of Foreign Affairs: The History of the Council on Foreign Relations* (New York, 1984), is superb on the origins and results of the council.

as well, a determination to strengthen those currents Burnham identified as radiating out of the 1896 political transformation.[14]

Another product of this post-1896 system and the post-1920 attempt to find insulation against the demands of a pluralistic democracy was an enhanced executive branch. Charles Evans Hughs, Frank B. Kellogg, and Henry Stimson followed in the post-1896 tradition of strong executive power in foreign affairs (a power much less seen between 1867 and 1896). With help from other powerful members of the executive, such as Herbert Hoover, they kept diplomatic initiatives in their own hands. When Congress and the public tried to interfere (as in the effort to outlaw war during 1927–28), the elite officials shrewdly blunted, then detoured the interference onto paths that followed their own policies.

Above all, U.S. officials kept democracy at bay simply by defining foreign policy less in political terms (which could attract attention and debate from Congress and the public) than in terms of private economic relationships. Tough executive leaders stood on the bridge of the ship of state in Washington, but the vessel's engine room was New York City's financial district. Arrangements between private bankers in New York, especially the diplomatically talented Thomas Lamont of the powerful J. P. Morgan banking house, and their counterparts in Tokyo, London, Paris, and Berlin, provided the fuel that propelled the diplomacy of the 1920s. That fuel was especially the dollar, for the United States emerged from the world war as the globe's greatest economic center. By manipulating dollars, New York private and central bankers, often but not always working with Washington officials, moved to rebuild Europe on American terms, control Japan's development of the Asian mainland, and spread the blessings and principles of U.S.-style capitalism. These financial arrangements seldom were scrutinized by debates in Congress or other public places.[15]

---

14   Walter Dean Burnham, "The Changing Shape of the American Political Universe," in *Walter Dean Burnham, The Current Crisis in American Politics* (New York, 1982).
15   Robert Freeman Smith, "Thomas W. Lamont," in *Behind the Throne: Servants of Power to Imperial Presidents, 1898–1968*, ed. Thomas McCormick and Walter LaFeber (Madison,

Having little interest in expanding democratic influences on foreign policy debates at home, it was not surprising that U.S. officials demonstrated even less interest in expanding democratic principles abroad. In certain pivotal areas, of course, hopes for democracy had apparently been driven out by the realities of revolution. Mexico, China, and the Soviet Union provided major examples. As did Nicaragua, which became an especially instructive case because U.S. officials had controlled it through military occupation since 1912. In 1925 the American troops finally left, but the political situation – apparently not yet properly fixed for self-government by thirteen years of U.S. rule – quickly deteriorated. The Marines reentered, only to be met by the forces of Nicaraguan revolutionary leader Augusto Sandino. Washington officials believed that Sandino had been radicalized by a stay in Mexico. In truth, he seemed to care less about radical change than about simply getting U.S. troops out of his country. A bloody seven-year war ensued until, in 1933, the foreign troops withdrew and left the country to a U.S.-trained Nicaraguan police force led by Anastasio Somoza. When Sandino offered to negotiate a political settlement, Somoza executed him, then set up a dictatorship enforced by his U.S.-trained troops. Few North Americans cared.[16]

After all, by 1933 they had major problems at home. The dollar, poised to perform miracles in the 1920s, had self-destructed between 1929 and 1931. With the falling dollar fell as well the power of the failed private bankers, sometimes from window ledges of tall buildings. The bankers had paid too little attention to warnings from Washington officials about bad investments abroad and overheated speculation in the stock market at home, although, to be fair, many of those warnings had been little more than whispers.

After 1933, and especially after 1945, U.S. officials derived particular lessons from this 1920 to 1933 experience: the international financial arrangements that necessarily undergirded politi-

WI, 1993); Frank Costigliola, *Awkward Dominion: American Political, Economic, and Cultural Relations with Europe, 1919–1933* (Ithaca, 1985).
16   Neill Macauley, *The Sandino Affair* (Chicago, 1967), esp. 211–12.

cal and other types of diplomacy (as cultural) were far too important to leave to private business people who were captives of the short-term bottom line and, consequently, made politically myopic by their financial interests. An example of such myopia occurred in Germany, where U.S. business continued to invest money in the 1920s far longer than the economy could absorb it, then necessarily pulled back in the early 1930s when the economy needed an infusion of dollars. In some instances, U.S. business leaders then insisted on working with the Nazi-controlled economy in the later 1930s, far past the time that prudence recommended against such a course. After World War II, the role the bankers played in the 1920s was to be filled by strong government-created and controlled institutions, such as the Bretton Woods arrangements (including the World Bank and International Monetary Fund), and an open commerce based on reciprocal trade agreement legislation of 1934 and after. Democratic controls thus began to creep back in, in some measure, but they did not creep too far. The World Bank and IMF depended heavily on support from the private sector, and the trade legislation was passed by Congress to cover long periods of time. There were few regular debates on Capitol Hill about these subjects. The international counterparts of reciprocal trade measures, such as the post-1947 World Trade Organization, were, after they got up and running, controlled by bureaucratic elites. In other words, the lessons learned from the 1920s did not include the conclusion that the inclusion of more democracy was necessary in the building of an effective international economic system.

Many of those who did argue after 1945 for more democratic debates over foreign policy faced the unenviable task of trying to defend the Neutrality Acts. These laws, the most important of which passed Congress between 1935 and 1937, attempted to keep the country from becoming economically, and then militarily, involved with either side of any war in Europe and, to a lesser extent, Asia. In the end (that is, with the Japanese attack on Pearl Harbor in December 1941) the Neutrality Acts failed. Many of their congressional and public supporters were reviled, especially for their supposed naiveté in believing the expanding U.S. overseas economic and security systems could somehow be suited with a war-proof vest and left untouched by the distending evils of Nazism and Japanese militarism.

Such blame is incomplete. While the New Deal did much to preserve democracy domestically, it did too little to help democracy play a constructive role in foreign policy. The public leadership of President Franklin D. Roosevelt and Secretary of State Cordell Hull until 1941 was weak, contradictory, and at times (as during the Spanish Civil War's outbreak in 1936, the Brussels Conference of 1937 called to deal with Japan's invasion of China, and the Munich crisis of 1938) disastrous. During 1940–41, Roosevelt lied to Americans as he tried to rectify the earlier failures of his leadership and take the country into war. The anti-Semitism of important State Department policymakers and the Pollyanna-like simplemindedness of others prevented Americans from learning about the extent of Nazi evil. Ignorance about Asian peoples and the belief in the early 1930s that Japan should be let loose to destroy Bolshevik and other revolutionary dangers in the Far East led to the appeasement of Japan. It was not the finest moment for the leaders of American democracy.[17]

As the leaders of that democracy failed after 1919, so did many of them fail to care about democracy abroad, especially during the 1930s. The Good Neighbor policy toward Latin America had little rhetoric about the importance of democracy, and the rhetoric that did exist disappeared as security concerns became uppermost by the late 1930s. A particularly stunning example of how much the concern about making the world safe for democracy had dissipated came when Americans and their leaders refused to respond as the Nazis destroyed the Czechoslovak democracy in 1938–39, then laid siege to France and Great Britain during 1939–40. During 1940–41, Roosevelt tried to portray the British as fellow democrats, and he received powerful help from Edward R. Murrow's dramatic radio broadcasts from London as

---

17   Richard W. Steele, "The Great Debate: Roosevelt, the Media, and the Coming of the War, 1940–1941," *Journal of American History* 71 (June 1984): esp. 69; David S. Wyman, *The Abandonment of the Jews* (New York, 1984), x–xi, 180-98, 311–47.

German bombs fell. But neither the president nor anyone else could figure out how to use Americans' supposed allegiance to democracy to persuade them to help defend democracy elsewhere.

The reason for that failure is not difficult to see in hindsight: since becoming a global power in 1898–1900, Americans and their leaders had shown little interest in expanding democracy abroad except possibly in 1917–19 – and that sour experience only confirmed their earlier judgment. Americans saw their system as perhaps too exceptional for easy export; those who had naively tried to take it abroad, such as missionaries in China or Woodrow Wilson in Mexico, had come to bitter ends. U.S. officials and the public meanwhile assumed that the political virtues as well as profits of their capitalism could be enjoyed without having to lose any significant political freedom of action and, in the interwar years, without undesirable expenses for creating military power.

After December 1941, the rhetoric of freedom (such as Roosevelt's "Four Freedoms") and democracy picked up markedly. But it was also compromised in at least two respects: the most powerful American ally, the Soviet Union, was not a democracy and not interested in the expansion of democratic processes; and Roosevelt had far too vivid memories of serving as assistant secretary of the navy under Woodrow Wilson and watching close-up the tragic presidential effort to make the world safe for democracy. Roosevelt planned to make the world safe for American power. If that effort translated into democracy, the president would happily accept it. But in such areas as French Indochina, Japan, Germany, and even France itself, he believed democracy would require considerable time for any viable growth. Roosevelt's suggested division of postwar responsibilities (China with U.S. help to be the policeman in Asia, Great Britain and the Soviet Union to walk the beat in Europe, and the United States to take care of the Western Hemisphere) did not indicate he was overly concerned about creating democratic systems in large portions of the globe.[18]

---

18 Fraser Harbutt, "Churchill, Hopkins, and the 'Other' Americans," *International History Review* 8 (May 1986): 261; for the FDR view of postwar alignment and the context,

The central problem, however, was how to handle postwar Germany and Japan. Within that problem lay a contradiction that plagued the American Century in the late 1940s. The German and Japanese economies had to be restored quickly because they had been the industrial hubs of Europe and Asia respectively. Without their restoration, U.S. officials assumed, those regions would collapse economically and then probably turn leftward politically. Then American capitalism – which, as Henry Luce preached in his 1941 editorials, had no choice but to become an international system – would collapse. Here was the contradiction: the services of experts and politicians who had worked in Berlin and Tokyo during the 1930s would be required to rebuild Germany and Japan quickly.

For a moment in late 1944, Roosevelt was prepared to strip the German economy and purge totally these agents and accomplices of the 1930s. In weeks, however, different, if not cooler, views prevailed. These were conveyed by Hull and Secretary of War Henry Stimson, who warned that disemboweling Germany's economy might make Americans and British feel better, but in the long run it would create a highly dangerous vacuum at Europe's center. Roosevelt backed down, and after his death in April 1945, U.S. policy moved to rebuild the Western occupation zones while purging the worst of the Nazi officials. In some ways, Japan posed an even greater challenge. In Europe, a rapidly rebuilt British or French industrial complex might possibly have partially replaced German economic power. In Asia, however, no alternative to Japan was in sight, especially after Chiang Kai-shek's China noticeably turned more fascistic, anti-American, and chaotic after late 1943. During the first eighteen months of the Japanese occupation, General Douglas MacArthur carried out a purge of the nation's militarists, while building a democratic base by allowing unions to gain strength and granting historic rights to women. But Japan's economy floundered.[19]

Walter LaFeber, "Roosevelt, Churchill, and Indochina, 1942-1945," *American Historical Review* 80 (December 1975): 1277-95, outlines FDR's views of the policemen.
19   Howard B. Schonberger, *Aftermath of War: Americans and the Remaking of Japan, 1945–1952* (Kent, OH, 1989), is pioneering on the reversal of U.S. policy.

In 1947, the Truman administration, through special emissary George Kennan, ordered MacArthur to reverse course. As the United States began fully to engage the Soviet Union in Cold War, it was imperative to rebuild a capitalist Japan, Southeast Asia, and Western Europe rapidly. The purges in Japan stopped, former wartime administrators regained power, unions were attacked (especially when suspected of having Communist members), and, overall MacArthur's political drive was sacrificed to quick economic recovery. The bases for Japan's politically insensitive bureaucratic controls, political party corruption, a virtual one-party political system, and the ready sacrifice of democratic processes and protection to the need for a rapidly growing export economy, as well as the determination after 1947 that Southeast Asia must remain open for Japanese exploitation of markets and raw materials – all of these basic policies were laid down during the U.S. occupation between 1947 and 1951.[20]

Washington's dilemma of having to choose between an emphasis on rebuilding democracy or an emphasis on multilateral capitalism could be seen in its micro version in Japan. The larger, encompassing version was the global strategy for containing and, if possible, rolling back the Soviet empire. Harry Truman revealed how U.S. leaders would deal with that dilemma when he made the single most important public announcement of his foreign policy plans on 12 March 1947. The Truman Doctrine, as the speech came to be known, committed the United States "to support free peoples who are resisting attempted subjugation by armed minorities or by outside pressures." The president did not explicitly identify the Soviet Union as the villain. He did not have to, especially after he declared there existed only two "ways of life" from which Americans should choose: "the will of the majority" and "free institutions, representative government, free elections . . . freedom from political oppression," or "the will of a minority forcibly imposed upon the majority," with that minority relying "upon terror and oppression . . . fixed elections, and the

20 Schonberger, *Aftermath of War*, and William S. Borden, *The Pacific Alliance: United States Foreign Economic Policy and Japanese Trade Recovery, 1947–1955* (Madison, WI, 1984), link the reversal and the role of Japan in Southeast Asia.

suppression of individual freedoms." His formulation of the alternatives gave Americans little choice but to choose the first,
even if it meant spending billions of tax dollars – even if it meant
confronting communism wherever U.S. officials believed it appeared.[21]

The president thus accomplished what no other American leader
has been able to do without an all-out declaration of war: forge
out of a parochial, diverse American society a long-term (in this
case, forty-four years) consensus to support the executive branch's
foreign policies. Truman accomplished this by emphasizing the
need to support democracies that were under pressure from minorities who fixed elections and suppressed "individual freedoms."

In reality, however, whether a nation was ruled by "the will of
the majority" and enjoyed "freedom from political oppression"
turned out to be much less important to U.S. officials (and the
public) than whether that nation supported Washington in conflicts with the Soviets – and whether that nation integrated its
economy into the postwar multilateral capitalist trading system
that U.S. leaders so carefully and painfully constructed. Truman
revealed this priority at the same moment he demanded that
Americans support "free peoples." The president's specific task
in the speech was to a create consensus for Congress to send $400
million to Greece and Turkey, both of which were facing Communist pressures. His problem was that neither nation was known
in the 1940s for "free institutions," "free elections," and "freedom from political oppression." British occupation authorities
had fixed elections so disreputable right-wing monarchial factions could come to power in Greece between 1944 and 1947.
Truman granted that "the Government of Greece is not perfect,"
but argued that it had come to power "in an election" (he omitted
the circumstances of the balloting). Turkey also presented problems, not least because during World War I it supported Germany
and during World War II – caught between demands from Germany and the Soviet Union – it remained neutral until early 1945,

21 *Public Papers of the Presidents . . . Harry S. Truman . . . 1947* (Washington, 1963), 176–
80.

when Ankara finally declared war on the Nazis. Truman wisely chose not to discuss this past.

The president's dilemma reappeared often over the next four decades of Cold War. An easier choice did appear in 1947–48 when the Truman administration initiated the Marshall Plan to rebuild Western Europe's economies. These nations were overwhelmingly democratic, although, again, Greece and Turkey were debatable. There could be no debate about the $50 million sent to the Portuguese dictatorship of Antonio de Oliveira Salazar, but Salazar had been helpful during the war (although neutral), and was certainly anti-Communist. Most important, Portugal occupied a highly strategic location. Nor could there be debate about the authoritarian rule of Marshal Tito in Yugoslavia, which received a special Marshall Plan grant of $61 million. Tito's new hatred for the Soviets after early 1948 was sufficient qualification.[22]

The same year that Truman built a foreign policy consensus around support of governments placed in power by "free elections," he signed into existence the Central Intelligence Agency. The CIA's work had antidemocratic consequences abroad and at home. Its first known covert activity aimed to ensure that the large Italian Communist Party would not win national elections in 1948. The Communists did lose; the CIA claimed it had proven the value of secretly helping to fix another nation's political processes. In reality, the Communists probably lost for reasons having little to do with the CIA. Most Italians were anti-Communist and learned from extensive propaganda that badly needed Marshall fund money might not flow to a Communist government in Rome. But the CIA successfully took credit. As one Agency official later bragged, "In an election in such-and-such a country the KGB backs a candidate, the CIA backs a candidate,

---

22   Michael J. Hogan, *The Marshall Plan: America, Britain, and the Reconstruction of Western Europe, 1947–1952* (Cambridge, England, 1987), is instructive for the absence of officials' discussions about political democracy and the emphasis on economic essentials, for example, 119, 169; Imanuel Wexler, "Marshall Plan," in *Encyclopedia of U.S. Foreign Relations*, 4 vols., ed. Bruce Jentleson and Thomas G. Paterson (New York, 1997), 3:113–17.

and the CIA candidate wins." Many Americans who valued democracy did not measure themselves by KGB standards.[23]

The CIA's better-known successes occurred in the 1950s when President Dwight D. Eisenhower, who as a military officer had long been a master of spy operations, provided guidance, and the domestic anti-Communist consensus provided leeway. In 1953, a CIA-directed operation in Iran helped overthrow the government of Prime Minister Mohammad Mossaddeq, a populist-type politician, so the rule of Shah Mohammed Reza Pahlavi could be restored. Mossaddeq's sin was demanding more money for Iran from the Anglo-Iranian Oil Company, which had long been paying more in taxes to the British government than in shared profits to the Iranians whose oil was being exploited. The British condemnation of Mossaddeq had not been sufficient for the Truman administration; it refused to threaten the Iranians. Eisenhower had different views. After the CIA returned the shah to power, the young ruler agreeably renegotiated his country's oil arrangements so that for the first time U.S. companies were cut in for 40 percent of the production. Enjoying strong American protection, the shah remained in power for twenty-five years until he was overthrown by a revolution that turned out to be anti-American as well as anti-Shah.[24]

In 1954, the CIA overthrew the elected government of Guatemala's President Jacobo Arbenz. Eisenhower had concluded that Arbenz was coming under Communist and Soviet influence. The primary evidence for such a belief was Arbenz's demand that the American-owned United Fruit Company give up mostly unused land to needy peasants. Washington officials viewed the demand as a dangerous precedent for U.S. investors and thus to American security. The reality about Guatemalan politics and economic needs was considerably more complex and, in any case, Communists were a long way from being able to seize power.

23 Rhodri Jeffreys-Jones, *The CIA and American Democracy* (New Haven, 1989), esp. 50–52.
24 Mark Hamilton Lytle, *The Origins of the Iranian-American Alliance, 1941–1953* (New York, 1987), esp. 203–18.

But the outcome was clear: Arbenz's reform-minded government was replaced by a military dictatorship in 1954. Over the next forty years the military built the worst human-rights record in the Western Hemisphere.[25]

President John F. Kennedy's Alliance for Progress tried a different approach to Latin America after 1961. The alliance pledged to devote $100 billion to create conditions so Latin America could develop both democratic processes and new middle classes so the processes would work properly. Kennedy's approach was shaped not only by his concern for Latin American democracy, but more immediately by his determination that no other revolution like Fidel Castro's would succeed. Two years before, Castro had overthrown the U.S.-supported Cuban dictatorship.

Planned as a ten-year program, the alliance's plans lay in shambles within four. Force-fed capitalism, U.S. officials discovered, did not work without prior democratic reforms. Indeed, such capitalist infusion undercut the Alliance's objectives: aid money and foreign investments enriched the elites and their military allies who controlled many Latin American nations. As the rich grew richer and the poor poorer, and as reformers grew more radical in demanding economic and political justice, a half-dozen revolutions and military coups erupted.[26]

Kennedy unsuccessfully tried to discourage some of the military takeovers. His successor, Lyndon B. Johnson, was more direct. In 1964, the Brazilian military overthrew an elected government whose economic policies were unacceptable to Washington and to Brazil's military. The United States quietly encouraged the generals who planned to take power. The new regime imposed military rule on Brazil for the next twenty years. During those two decades, the United States was the regime's best trading partner, while Brazil attracted more U.S. investment than any other Latin American country. In 1965, President Johnson, with Latin

25 Richard H. Immerman, *The CIA in Guatemala: The Foreign Policy of Intervention* (Austin, 1982), esp. 190–201.
26 *Public Papers of the Presidents . . . John F. Kennedy . . . 1961* (Washington, 1962), 175; Arthur Schlesinger, Jr. "The Alliance for Progress," in *Latin America, The Search for a New International Role*, ed. R. C. Hellman and H. J. Rosenblum (New York, 1975), esp. 74–75, but entire essay for why the Alliance failed.

American support led by the Brazilian generals, landed troops in the Dominican Republic to prevent, as Johnson saw it, a possible Communist takeover. Such a danger was actually highly remote. The Johnson administration's manipulation of the facts (such as wildly overestimating the number of Communists on the scene, an error quickly and easily discovered by American journalists), eroded the president's credibility, especially among congressional leaders such as Senator J. William Fulbright (D–AR). The invasion had been preceded by well-founded newspaper stories that Johnson and his top advisers cared less about the faltering (if not increasingly dangerous) alliance, and more about Latin American stability – regardless of whether or not military rulers imposed such stability – that would be attractive to private investors.[27]

American rhetoric about promoting democracy in the good neighbor of Latin America proved to be only rhetoric. For a quarter-century, with few exceptions, any quest for democracy in the region was distinctly secondary to the U.S. quest for private economic opportunity and public support for military-dominated regimes that would maintain order. These priorities notably appeared in Richard Nixon's policies toward Chile between 1970 and 1973. In a landmark speech at Kansas City in 1971, President Nixon predicted that the future of world power would be predicated on economic (not political democratic) power: in the coming decades and the new century, "economic power" would "be the key to other kinds of power." If Americans hoped to continue their century, he warned, they would have to wage a disciplined economic war against the other four "great economic superpowers," two of whom (the Soviet Union and China) were not democracies. (The other two superpowers, he said, were Japan and Western Europe.)[28]

To maintain a cooperative Western Hemisphere, Nixon and his National Security Council adviser, Henry Kissinger, ruthlessly

27 Phyllis Parker, *Brazil and the Quiet Intervention, 1964* (Austin, 1979), 58–81, 92–103.
28 *Public Papers of the Presidents ... Richard Nixon ... 1971* (Washington, 1972), 806–12 for Kansas City speech; *New York Times*, 6 March 1975.

undermined the elected Chilean government of Salvador Allende. They helped destroy Allende in part because U.S. corporations, whose properties he moved to nationalize, demanded they do so, but in larger part because Nixon and Kissinger did not tolerate what they believed to be a democratically elected version of Fidel Castro. Allende died as he was overthrown by the military. When the U.S. ambassador asked the generals to stop torturing Allende's followers and to observe human rights, Kissinger ordered the ambassador "to cut out the political science lectures."[29]

Nixon and Kissinger were well positioned ideologically to cut U.S. losses in Vietnam and end the nation's longest and most tragic war. No serious observer believed the United States had entered that conflict to make Vietnam safe for democracy. When the story began in 1945, Franklin D. Roosevelt subordinated his anticolonial principles to allow French (and British) troops to reoccupy France's Southeast Asian colonies precisely because he believed the Vietnamese, Laotians, and Cambodians would not be ready for generations to govern themselves. When the first major U.S. military commitment occurred in 1949–50, it resulted from the Truman administration's determination to keep Southeast Asia open for Japanese economic exploitation and also to save the embattled French position so Paris officials would be politically able to join NATO. After Ho Chi Minh's forces drove out the French in 1954, the United States brought in Ngo Dinh Diem to save South Vietnam. Diem was a Roman Catholic who ruled over a country that was 90 percent Buddhist. By 1963, as Diem's floundering rule came under fire from Buddhists, U.S. Ambassador Henry Cabot Lodge admitted that Diem and his powerful brother "are essentially a medieval, Oriental despotism of the classic family type." That year, Lodge and the Kennedy administration were deeply involved in the South Vietnamese military coup that overthrew and executed Diem and his brother. Succeeding governments were run by military officers whose only

---

29 Walter Isaacson, *Kissinger, A Biography* (New York, 1992), 311–12; Seymour Hersh, *The Price of Power: Kissinger in the Nixon White House* (New York, 1983), 260, 267–69.

legitimacy derived from fixed elections and hundreds of thousands of U.S. troops.[30]

In 1967–68, Washington officials were concerned not about making South Vietnam safe for democracy, but about somehow ending the war quickly to protect the U.S. democratic system itself. As antiwar protesters filled Washington's streets, and, more ominously, increasingly frustrated Main Street and Wall Street Americans who demanded an end to the conflict either through withdrawal or, as many wanted, all-out military victory, U.S. officials understood that their credibility both at home and abroad was in grave danger. They concluded that many more troops could not be spared for Vietnam because the soldiers were required to maintain order at home. President Lyndon Johnson was warned by a close adviser that continued losses could lead to "national self-doubt and timidity" that could spawn "real danger from the demagogue." When Nixon and Kissinger finally began pulling out U.S. troops while publicly hoping that somehow South Vietnam could fill the growing void, they more realistically hoped for a "decent interval" between the time the last Americans left and South Vietnam collapsed. Preferably the interval would end after Nixon left the presidency and he was safe from a feared political backlash at home and the shattering of U.S. credibility abroad.[31]

Neither happened when South Vietnam fell to the Communists in 1975. Because of, not despite, the rampaging debates of 1964 and 1975, American democracy was in better shape than Johnson's advisers, Nixon, and Kissinger (or later critics of the 1960s) believed. The theme of those protests, especially after Martin Luther King and the growing civil rights movement joined them in 1966–68, was that Americans had little business going abroad to search out societies to save when their own society needed immediate and expensive attention. American democratic processes notably worked when Nixon had to be the first president to resign from

---

30 Lloyd Gardner, *Pay Any Price: Lyndon Johnson and the Wars for Vietnam* (Chicago, 1995), 444–45 on LBJ's policies; LaFeber, "Roosevelt, Churchill, and Indochina," on FDR's anticolonial policies and his reversal in 1945.
31 Isaacson, *Kissinger*, 313.

office. He ostensibly left because he was caught committing the criminal act of trying to cover up the illegal burglary of Democratic party offices in Washington during mid-1972. Nixon's crime, however, was not the single coverup, but a range of actions that demeaned the presidency and corrupted democratic processes, including placing phone taps on reporters, challenging Congress's constitutional right to spend monies, setting up covert "plumbers" units to discover leaks about the president's plans to act against political opponents, making secret commitments to defend South Vietnam with U.S. bombing (and without congressional consultation) after the 1973 peace was signed. Nixon argued that since 1945 U.S. presidents had held the power to commit such acts for the defense of the nation's security in the Cold War.

By the 1970s, both American democracy and capitalism were caught in these crosscurrents. The props of the American Century seemed to buckle. The American Century had reached a turning point as it tried to deal with the humiliation of Vietnam, massive protests on American streets, the rise of fierce competition from Europe and Japan as an inflation-plagued U.S. economy suffered relative decline, a polarizing Latin America, and a once imperial, now disgraced, presidency.

It was nothing less than *A Crisis of Democracy*, to use the title of a widely noted book from the Trilateral Commission. This group, made up of elite business, governmental, and academic figures from Western Europe, Japan, and the United States, had been formed in 1972–73 so private discussions could be held to discuss the growing dangers to Western- and Japanese-style capitalism. In 1975, the commission's analysts argued that the West, and especially the United States, suffered from an "excess of democracy." The "democratic surge of the 1960s" was condemned for having become so democratic that it was nearly out of hand: "In the United States," one author, Samuel P. Huntington of Harvard, feared, "the strength of democracy poses a problem for the governability of democracy in a way which is not the case elsewhere." The problem, in other words, was not the series of policies since 1945 that had too often been antidemocratic overseas and at home – and had finally climaxed with the disaster in

Vietnam and the first resignation of an American president – but the resurgence of democracy that had begun, if only temporarily, to curb these Cold War foreign policies and presidencies.[32]

Presidents Jimmy Carter and Ronald Reagan tried to navigate this turn in the American Century differently. Carter sought to restore Americans' confidence in their overseas policies by stressing the importance of human rights in foreign affairs. He played down the overriding influence of Cold War against the Soviet Union and played up the importance of helping newly emerging nations. Carter stressed covert action and military power less, and mediated diplomatic settlements more. He achieved historic breakthroughs in helping to broker a peace agreement between Israel and Egypt, and working out the long-sought settlement that returned the Panama Canal area to Panama. In the end, however, Carter failed. His human rights policies were not well thought through and encountered resistance when applied to such nations as Iran, a pivotal U.S. security outpost since 1953. Carter's policies were blamed for helping to destabilize the shah's regime and also for upheavals in Central America (where the Somoza dictatorship in Nicaragua was toppled by Sandinista revolutionaries). After the Red Army invaded Afghanistan to prop up a Marxist regime in late 1979, Carter launched a new set of Cold War policies, including massive military spending increases. At home, the economy and Carter's popularity sank in tandem as the Iranian upheaval disrupted oil supplies and then set off an inflationary spiral that drove interest rates to historic high levels.

After defeating Carter in the 1980 election, Ronald Reagan vowed to follow a different agenda. He moved to save the endangered American Century by rallying the nation around an anti-Communist crusade abroad. This approach required reinvigorating confidence in governmental power and acts – that is, it meant reinvigorating the Truman Doctrine. There was irony here, for while expanded government powers were necessary to fight the new Cold War, Reagan gained popularity by promising to fight

32   Michel Crozier, Samuel P. Huntington, Joji Watanuki, *The Crisis of Democracy: Report on the Governability of Democracies to the Trilateral Commission* (New York, 1975), esp. 3–9, 59–115.

big government. In reality, he was condemning the 1960s and Lyndon Johnson's Great Society that had pumped life into American democracy by passing unprecedented laws to protect civil rights, the elderly, the poor, and the nation's educational and cultural systems. By its nature, however, the Great Society brought new forces into the political arena that by their nature produced more chaotic politics, economic demands, and a focus on domestic problems that required governmental attention. Reagan rejected the democratic demands of the Great Society programs in order to fight, as he saw it, for the defeat of communism abroad.

Again – as with Wilson's dilemmas in 1917–20, the advent of McCarthyism and the CIA activities in the 1950s, and the realpolitik of Nixon in the 1970s – attempts to expand the American Century abroad had inevitable consequences for the American Century's democratic principles at home. And again in the choice between democracy and capitalism abroad, capitalism won – until it was discovered how expanding capitalism could be rationalized by advocating the expansion of democracy.

One insight into the Reagan administration's approach could be found in Jeanne Kirkpatrick's 1979 essay "Dictatorships and Double Standards," which the former Hollywood actor and California governor read during his 1980 presidential campaign. He was so taken with Kirkpatrick's thesis that he appointed her ambassador to the United Nations. Her ideas were appealing because they were simple and played directly to Reagan's own beliefs. They especially provided a tool to attack Jimmy Carter's human rights policies. Kirkpatrick argued that in order to fight "totalitarian" regimes, Americans were justified in supporting "authoritarian" governments. Totalitarians included Hitler and especially Stalin and other Communist dictators. Their systems were evil because they controlled every part of society, especially the economy, which was closed to private enterprise and foreign access. Authoritarians included Latin American dictators and the shah of Iran. They violently oppressed their people and presided over corrupt, undemocratic regimes, but Kirkpatrick preferred them because they sought to maintain "traditional" societies that could evolve and – most important – kept their economies more accessible so outsiders could enjoy opportunities for exploiting markets and raw materials.[33]

Kirkpatrick's theory was deeply flawed. Authoritarians such as Somoza in Nicaragua (or the tsar in Russia during 1917) had so ransacked their countries that the people had rebelled to create revolutionary regimes hated by Kirkpatrick and Reagan. This exploitation had been furthered, moreover, by foreign investors who, by taking advantage of the authoritarians' political cronyism and more open society, transferred wealth abroad and made revolution more likely at home. Of special importance, her theory allowed Reagan to stand aside while the authoritarians smashed human rights and corrupted democratic processes.

By the late 1980s, Kirkpatrick's theory collapsed when the totalitarian Communist systems, which she argued could not change for the better, evolved with little bloodshed into governments (many even elected) that then broke up the seventy-year-old Soviet empire. The undoing of her theory, however, came too late to dissuade the Reagan administration from supporting authoritarians and opposing more democratic forces. In Central America the president waged relentless overt and secret wars against nationalist, often Marxist, groups that aimed to redistribute more equitably their nation's wealth and to limit the military-backed political elites in Nicaragua, El Salvador, and Guatemala. When one of the world's most democratic nations, Costa Rica, opposed Reagan's military approach, the United States moved vigorously to belittle and block Costa Rica's efforts. In the Philippines, the president supported the highly corrupt dictator, Ferdinand Marcos, until nearly the bitter end in 1986 when more astute U.S. officials convinced Reagan that Marcos was both a lost and a highly dangerous cause. In South Africa, the Reagan administration supported the brutal apartheid policy of the minority all-white government that suppressed the majority black population. It was congressional action during 1985 to 1987, not presidential, that began to

---

33   Jeane J. Kirkpatrick, *Dictatorships and Double Standards: Rationalism and Reason in Politics* (New York, 1982), esp. 2–52.

pressure U.S. economic and political supporters of apartheid to pull back.[34]

Particularly after 1982, Reagan and his advisers increasingly emphasized the importance of advancing democratic principles. They focused, however, on Communist and Marxist regimes, not on the non-democratic governments, for example in Central America, the Philippines, Indonesia, or South Africa. The purpose of emphasizing democracy was to fight the Cold War with different weapons. The Soviet empire did collapse between 1989 and 1991. The role played in this collapse by the Reagan administration will long be debated. A strong argument can be made that the Soviets disappeared much less because of the American rhetoric and military buildup than because of the Communist system's inability to adjust and exploit the revolution in information technology – computers, copiers, faxes, earth satellites, cable – that transformed the globe in the 1970s and after. Western-style capitalism not only adjusted to these changes but rapidly grew richer and more powerful from them. An international capitalist system, rather than nation-bound democratic processes or military forces, played the major part in winning the Cold War at the end of the first American Century.[35]

The other major Communist power, China, drew appropriate conclusions: the Soviet system badly lagged in the 1970s and collapsed in the 1980s because Moscow officials waited too long to make economic adjustments, then tried to catch up by reforming political institutions that could not withstand both the economic and the political demands. After the late 1970s, China opened its economy to the new technologies and the foreign capital that best knew how to develop and exploit them. Political opening, however, was unacceptable. When dissent turned into mass rallies

---

34   James Chace, "The End of the Affair?" *The New York Review of Books*, 8 October 1987; Julia Preston, "Oscar Arias," *Washington Post*, 30 October 1987; Kenneth A. Rodman, "'Think Globally, Punish Locally': Nonstate Actors, Multinational Corporations, and Human Rights Sanctions," *Ethics & International Affairs* 12 (1998): esp. 25–27 on South Africa.
35   Matthew Evangelista, *Taming the Bear: Transnational Relations and the Demise of the Soviet Threat* (forthcoming, 1999) argues persuasively about the inability of the Soviet system to adapt; also the succinct argument and context in Thomas J. McCormick, "Troubled Triumphalism," *Diplomatic History* 21 (Summer 1997): esp. 488.

during the spring of 1989, Chinese officials ruthlessly cracked down. The high number of killed and imprisoned might never be known. President George Bush condemned the bloody suppression and cut back U.S. programs in China. Within months, however, Bush dispatched top aides to reopen exchanges and relations. The 1.5 billion Chinese offered mind-boggling economic potential to investors, while China's military forces – judged by experts to be the most rapidly growing in the world – were too important to be ignored simply because of the crackdown on democratic-minded dissenters.

President Bill Clinton's administration continued to hold Bush's priorities. Although he promised in his 1992 election campaign to place human rights in China above economic access, by 1994–95 Clinton reversed course. While protesting human-rights violations, the president no longer made an improving Chinese record on human rights the prerequisite for continued U.S. economic cooperation. Access to the burgeoning China market was too important, especially as Americans raced to keep up with competitors from Hong Kong, Japan, and Western Europe. These competitors by and large cared little about how China handled human rights. The justification for such a calculation was that an accessible, more pluralistic, increasingly capitalistic economy would lead gradually and peacefully to a more open, pluralist, and democratic political system. Logic and hope led to this conclusion.

The history of the American Century offered less evidence for such a conclusion. Democratic traditions and processes have to be present before economic and technological transformations if those political institutions are to mediate and moderate the resulting tensions. The major political victories for democracy in the American Century occurred in post-1945 Germany and, to a lesser degree, Japan, as well as in parts of Eastern Europe that broke free of Soviet domination. All these areas had some tradition of democratic processes: in Germany and Japan there were also occupation-instituted reforms. Even prior democratic transformation could sometimes be insufficient to stop the eruption of civil war from socioeconomic upheavals resulting from the application of new technologies. The Trilateral Commission's *Crisis of Democracy* even argued in 1975 that an "excess of democracy" could help lead to civil war – as in the United States itself when, according to Huntington, Jacksonian America was a cause of the Civil War and a kind of preview of how such "excess" could undermine the American Century.[36]

Throughout the past century, great tension has thus existed between the American hope of making the world safe for democracy and Americans' determination to make the world open for their particular types of economic enterprise. They have repeatedly resolved the tension by ignoring or rationalizing away their Wilsonian urges so they could maximize the reach of an economic system that, as Henry Luce candidly phrased it in 1941, must, for example, make Asia worth many billions of dollars of profit each year, "or else confess a pitiful impotence." For, Luce argued, "America is responsible, to herself as well as to history, for the world environment in which she lives." Since Americans have a system that is dependent on that "environment," it followed that Franklin D. "Roosevelt must succeed where Wilson has failed."

If Roosevelt and his successors indeed succeeded, in Luce's terms, it was because they figured out how to create a government-private sector coalition to support the indispensable internationalization of the nation's economic system, while controlling democratic and isolationist impulses at home (especially with the Truman Doctrine), and not giving priority to spreading potentially destabilizing democratic reforms abroad. Democracy and attempts to expand democracy are by nature expensive, wasteful, and, as John Kennedy found with the Alliance for Progress, most disorderly. The Great Society's programs of the 1960s were rolled back not only by the Reagan agenda of the 1980s and 1990s but by the discipline thought to be necessary to balance budgets, free up capital, and open trade so Americans could better compete in the globalization process triggered by the new information technology. The nation's wealth soared as the system became more

36 Crozier et al., *The Crisis of Democracy*, 113–15.

internationalized – and as voter participation continued its post-1896 decline, public faith in the world's leading democratic government dropped, and for the first time since the 1930s the gap between the well off and the poor dangerously widened.[37]

The success of capital has been the reason why the twentieth and probably twenty-first centuries can be characterized as American. The gravest danger to the American Century occurred in the 1930s when that capital self-destructed. The New Deal and the Truman Cold War policies put the U.S. capital system back together in new forms. The system's post-1970s globalization phase has not been a warm friend of democracy in terms of either its effects on Americans whose incomes have dropped relative to those of the wealthiest Americans, or its weakening of local cultures at home and overseas. The market has worked its wonders, as Henry Luce hoped, but the prerequisites of democracy have not then automatically advanced.

Policies shaped by the desire to create democratic systems in foreign lands formed the exception rather than the rule in post-1900 U.S. diplomacy. When explicitly pro-democratic policies were advanced, the cost involved was usually perceived to be slight. When the cost promised to be high, as in Latin America during the 1960s or China in the 1980–1990s, the push stopped. The American Century was and is many things, but it has especially been a century shaped by U.S. policies demanding that the world be made safe and accessible for the American economic system.

---

37 Many observers have warned that globalization threatens democracy. A good brief analysis is David Held, "Democracy," in *The Oxford Companion to the Politics of the World*, ed. Joel Krieger (New York, 1993), esp. 224, which also has a good bibliography; Uri Bronfenbrenner et al., *The State of Americans; This Generation and the Next* (New York, 1996), esp. chaps. 3 and 5, is excellent on the social and economic effects of post-1970s changes.

6

The American Century:
From Sarajevo to Sarajevo

JOAN HOFF

Independent Internationalism Revisited

When Gertrude Stein dogmatically asserted that the twentieth century began in 1920, she did not know that it also marked the beginning of modern U.S. foreign policy. The First World War and its aftermath set in motion on its bloodthirsty course what would become the American Century. The century proclaimed American in 1941 by publisher Henry R. Luce commenced in the 1920s because the nineteenth century did not end until 1914 with the events following the assassination of Archduke Franz Ferdinand in Sarajevo, which led to World War I. The century ended in 1991 with acts of destructive ethnic cleansing that began in the same historic city. In both 1914 and 1991, the killings in Sarajevo were inextricably associated with violent national self-determination. Given the horrors of this century it is conceivable that we should not want to remember it as American.

The worldwide ramifications of occurrences in Sarajevo at the beginning and end of what Eric Hobsbawm has called the "short twentieth century" (with the American portion of this century being even shorter) are sobering rather than uplifting and say more about the irrational human conditions leading to self-determined nation-states than the rational practice of democracy so prominent in the rhetoric of American diplomats during these same time periods. Moreover, there is little reason to believe, other than on the grounds of ethnocentrism, that democracy as a political base for nation-states was divinely intended to triumph in any enduring sense at the end of the American Century. In the globalized economy of the next century, oligarchic city-states, regional states within national borders sometimes referred to as regional fiefdoms, or nomadic, one-dimensional, anarchistic communities without territory and only spasmodic political power, rather than democratic nations, could become the norm as the New World Order develops along the paradoxical lines of globalism and tribalism. Neither development is promising in terms of democratic practice or theory. It may well be that the common end result of globalism and tribalism will be international anarchy rather than "common will and that conscious and collective human control under the guidance of law [which] we call democracy." According to Robert Kaplan, "democracy may not be the system that will best serve the world – or even the one that will prevail in places that now consider themselves bastions of freedom." Not only are contemporary democracies of relatively recent origin, most having emerged after 1914, but there are probably more anarchistic anti-democratic forces at work undermining the nation-state in the 1990s than there are reinforcing ones, despite the insistence of the United States to the contrary.[1]

At the end of the twentieth century it is time for the United States to take stock and shoulder responsibility not only for the future but for some of the less than savory aspects of the last fifty years of American domination. U.S. diplomacy for most of this century has been characterized by a mercurial assortment of unilateral and collective actions that I first described in the 1970s as "independent internationalism." This term refers, not to the ide-

---

1   Mathew Horsman and Andrew Marshall, *After the Nation-State: Citizens, Tribalism, and the New World Disorder* (New York, 1994), x, 260–61; Jean-Marie Guéhenno, *The END of the NATION STATE*, trans. Victoria Elliott (Minneapolis, 1995), 43–45; Robert Kaplan, "Was Democracy Just a Moment?" *The Atlantic Monthly*, December 1997, 55–56; Benjamin R. Barber, *Jihad vs. McWorld* (New York, 1995), 3–8 (first quotation, 5); Kenichi Ohmae, *The End of the Nation State: The Rise of Regional Economies* (New York, 1995), 5, 79–100, 141–49.

ology that imbued U.S. diplomacy by 1900, but to the modus operandi of the country's foreign affairs. Most simply it means that when the United States cannot, or does not, want to solve a particular diplomatic problem through unilateral action, it seeks cooperative methods for pursuing its goals. It is in these short-lived and usually opportunistic times of cooperation that the dual shibboleths of self-determination or self-government wrapped in the rhetoric of democracy prevail in American foreign policy discourse. But the country's first inclination for most of this century has been to act unilaterally whenever possible and to cooperate with other nations only when absolutely necessary. A presidential commission first noticed this trend in 1933, reporting to Herbert Hoover that the postwar diplomacy of the United States in the 1920s had alternated "between isolation and independence, between sharply marked economic nationalism and notable international initiative in cooperation moving in a highly unstable zigzag course."[2] The United States continued to follow this "unstable zigzag course" of independent internationalism in the 1930s, after the Second World War when its power was unprecedented, and again in the post-Cold War era, with its latest nominal cooperative effort having taken place during the Gulf War.

Understanding that U.S. diplomacy in the American Century has been characterized by independent internationalism places in proper perspective many old dualistic foreign policy debates over moralism or idealism versus realism, nationalism/isolationism versus internationalism, protectionism versus free trade, spheres of influence versus balance of power, nuclear deterrence versus rule by central coalition, collective security versus hemisphere defense, and even capitalism versus communism. Acknowledging the practice of independent internationalism also allows for a more realistic assessment of such familiar U.S. diplomatic slogans as Manifest Destiny, the Open Door, the Good Neighbor policy, Pan Americanism, Pax Americana, liberal international

---

2   Joan Hoff Wilson, *American Business and Foreign Policy, 1920–1933* (Lexington, KY, 1971), xiv–xvii, 26, 241.

capitalism, containment, national self-determination, democracy and, most recently, New World Order.[3]

Yet, most members of the foreign policy elite have not explicitly examined this variable pattern of U.S. diplomacy since it was first identified in the early 1930s, preferring to debate ad nauseam the binary oppositions or simplistic slogans just mentioned. Such an examination could not have been made during the Cold War for obvious ideological reasons. With that bipolar conflict over, it should be possible for American foreign affairs experts and scholars to reassess traditional strategies for controlling nation-state anarchy between (and sometimes inside the poorest) nation-states and to devise a less erratic and arbitrary way of implementing them, other than independent internationalism, to serve the best interests of the United States and the world now that it is the only hegemon on the block. But to do so realistically, they must now factor in the "irreversible effects" of modern information technology not only on capitalism but on the nation-state system.[4]

---

3   Ronald Steel, *Temptations of a Superpower* (Cambridge, MA, 1995), 47; Eugene R. Wittkopf, ed., *The Future of American Foreign Policy*, 2d ed. (New York, 1994), 10, 61, 77. Debates over these dichotomies and terms reached a point of saturation in academic arguments over the origins of the Cold War and Vietnam War in the 1960s and 1970s and seem about to do the same in the next decade over why the Cold War ended. While some historians have argued that Woodrow Wilson sought a New World Order as a result of World War I, he did not use the phrase. Unfortunately, the words bring to mind the Pan-German foreign policy of the 1930s promoting the idea of a European New Order, and the Japanese employed the term, New Order, after proclaiming their East Asia Co-Prosperity Sphere in 1938. In both instances the United States protested these "new order" proclamations, specifically denying in a note to the Japanese on 31 December 1938 that "there was need or warrant for any one Power to take upon itself to prescribe what shall be the terms and conditions of a 'new order' in areas not under its sovereignty and to constitute itself the repository of authority and the agent of destiny in regard thereto." See Thomas J. Knock, *To End All Wars: Woodrow Wilson and the Quest for a New World Order* (New York, 1992); Lloyd E. Ambrosius, *Wilsonian Statecraft: Theory and Practice of Liberal Internationalism* (Wilmington, DE, 1991); Howard Jablon, "Cordell Hull, his 'Associates,' and Relations with Japan, 1933–1936," *Mid-America* 56 (July 1974): 160–75; and Noam Chomsky, *Ramparts* 5 (April 1967): 48. President George Bush revived the phrase New World Order in connection with the fall of communism in 1989, particularly during the celebrations over the Gulf War in 1991. Now New World Economic Order is being used to describe free-trade globalism, or what used to be described by Wilsonians as the liberal (capitalist) internationalism.
4   Richard Rosecrance, "A New Concert of Powers and U.S. Foreign Policy," in Wittkopf, ed., *Future of American Foreign Policy*, 61; *Daedalus* 124 (Spring, 1995): xiv; Susan Strange, "The Defective State," in Wittkopf, ed., Future of American Foreign Policy, 72; Horsman and Marshall, *After the Nation-State*, 236; Ohmae, *End of the Nation State*, vii, passim.

Those who make it their business to assess the three most common ways nations have attempted since the nineteenth century to control the "formal state of anarchy" in which Thomas Hobbes insisted they exist, namely, rule by a central coalition, balance of power, and most recently, nuclear deterrence, now commonly agree, with varying degrees of cynicism, that the longest period of relative tranquility was from 1945 to 1989 when bipolar nuclear deterrence prevailed despite, or because of, its obvious risk to humanity and economic costs. The hundreds of thousands of lives lost during this time in civil conflicts and surrogate wars conducted by the two superpowers make the term "long peace" less than an accurate one for describing those forty-four years. The type of deterrence practiced in this period prevented nuclear disaster because the world was dominated by two competing superpowers. Diffusion of nuclear power in the post-Cold War world translates into terror, not deterrence. Recognition of this accounted for the horror and dismay with which major powers responded to the nuclear tests by India and Pakistan in May 1998.[5]

In contrast to the "long peace" since 1945, balance-of-power arrangements first misleadingly symbolized by the Congress of Vienna in 1815 seldom worked effectively in the nineteenth century because the major European nations waited for each other to initiate action against disruptive states. By 1914 balance-of-power agreements actually fomented rather than prevented war. Rule by a concert of great powers, also set in motion by the 1815 Vienna Congress, succeeded for only fifteen years and when reconstituted through the Council of the League of Nations it failed

5 Wittkopf, ed., *Future of American Foreign Policy*, 10–11; Horsman and Marshall, *After the Nation-State*, 263. For the "long peace" theory see John Lewis Gaddis, *The Long Peace: Inquiries into the History of the Cold War* (New York, 1987); idem, "The Cold War, the Long Peace, and the Future," *Diplomatic History* 16 (Spring 1992): 234–46; and Charles W. Kegley, Jr., ed., *The Long Postwar Peace* (New York, 1991). *New York Times*, 5 June 1998, reporting that the United States, Russia, China, Britain, and France – the five permanent members of the UN Security Council and all nuclear powers themselves – asked India and Pakistan to freeze their nuclear weapons development in return for help in reducing their tension over the disputed territory of Kashmir, but disagreed over whether to enforce economic sanctions. While the United States was first to impose economic sanctions on both countries, Germany and Japan suspended nonhumanitarian aid to India and these two countries, plus the United States, Canada, and Italy have pressed India and Pakistan to sign the 1996 nuclear test-ban treaty.

even more quickly. In both previous periods when such concerts were attempted, ideological and economic differences undermined the collective efforts of major nations, and these divisive forces are apt to do so again in the post-Cold War period, especially if the global economy does not continue to prosper.[6] The leader in any new coalition of remaining regional powers (Russia, the European Community, Japan, and China) has to be the United States, albeit devoid of the hegemonic freedom it enjoyed in the West during its bipolar struggle with the Soviet Union when it practiced independent internationalism with virtual impunity.

Even with such purposeful and cooperative American leadership, the long-term success of such a concert is not likely should the predicted decline in power of nation-states, and the concomitant decline in authority of such multilateral organizations as the UN, NATO, OECD, EU, GATT, IMF, WTO, NAFTA, and OPEC, actually take place. Most of these organizations were formed before post-World War II economic interdependence began to be replaced with globalization. Their functions and effectiveness will have to be critically reassessed by any new concert of nations led by the United States. Without such concerted action, unstable balances of power or unworkable multiple deterrence systems will emerge to undermine further an already unstable global economy.[7] Whether the United States is ready to give up its selfish, but relatively successful and instinctual, practice of independent internationalism to lead a new concert of possibly weakened nation-states is another matter. Ten years (and two presidential administrations) after the end of communism it has yet to take up this difficult mantle of finding systematic ways to regulate the global economy and practice reliable world leadership.

6   Rosecrance, "A New Concert of Powers," 61–75; Wittkopf, ed., *Future of American Foreign Policy*, 10–11; Terry L. Deibel, "Strategies before Containment: Patterns for the Future," in Wittkopf, ed., *Future of American Foreign Policy*, 76–90. See also Edward Vose Gulick, *Europe's Classical Balance of Power* (Ithaca, 1955); and Marc Tractenberg, "The Meaning of Mobilization in 1914," *International Security* 15 (Winter 1990/91): 120–50.
7   Alfred E. Eckes, "Cowboy Capitalism: Lessons from the Asian Meltdown," *Chronicles*, July 1998, 26–28; idem, "'The End of Globalization': Will the Dinosaurs Return?" 30 September 1998, unpublished paper; "Globalization in Crisis," *Multinational Monitor* 19 (January/February 1998): 5–6, 10–27; and William Greider, "The Global Crisis Deepens," *The Nation*, 19 October 1998, 11–16.

This combination of unilateral and cooperative actions began to emerge as a pattern of U.S. foreign policy in the 1920s when, contrary to conventional wisdom, Republican administrations did not retreat to an isolationist stance as the country emerged from World War I a leading industrial and creditor nation for the first time in its history. While internationalism did not prevail in all American diplomatic encounters in the 1920s, it did become a basic consideration of leading businessmen, bankers, and certain government officials such as Herbert Hoover, Charles Evans Hughes, Frank Kellogg, and Henry Stimson. True, the United States did not fulfill Woodrow Wilson's dream of joining his creation, the League of Nations; nonetheless, multilateral disarmament and bilateral debt agreements constituted the major practical international actions on the part of the United States during the 1920s and early 1930s. The Kellogg-Briand Pact stands as the most idealistic (and impractical) collective attempt to ensure peace during those years. At the same time, however, Congress passed xenophobic immigration and protectionist tariff legislation. Realizing that imposing American-style elections did not produce democratic governments, Hoover, Hughes, and Stimson unilaterally initiated the removal of troops from Central America, which, in time, gave rise to the full-blown, cooperative Good Neighbor policy of Franklin Roosevelt's administration before 1940. The Great Depression prompted FDR to back out of any more economic cooperation over debts and reparations at the London Economic Conference in 1933, and with passage of the Neutrality Acts later in that decade American diplomacy assumed a more isolationist posture than it had in the 1920s. Even the various collective nonintervention pledges that the United States made at Latin American conferences were quickly reinterpreted just before and after the Second World War to reassert the unilateral interventionist rights of the United States in Latin America implicit in the original Monroe Doctrine and its various corollaries. Unfortunately, however, no systematic coordination of economic and political foreign policy was achieved as the country pursued independent internationalism for the first time as a world power in the interwar years.

Even though the United States did not become a member of either the League of Nations or the World Court in the 1920s and 1930s, it began to participate in a greater number of international conferences on disarmament, peace, and international economic matters than ever before and, of course, became a major force behind the creation of the United Nations in 1945. So its nineteenth-century commitment to international arbitration (which had been particularly noticeable in the late nineteenth and early twentieth centuries with its participation in the Hague Peace Conferences of 1899 and 1907) continued until the outbreak of the Cold War. In fighting what was portrayed as a battle to the death with communism after 1945, the United States adopted a unilaterally interventionist foreign policy known as liberal internationalism based "on the assumption that the security and prosperity of every place on earth is vital to America's own." At first, post-World War II leaders hoped that U.S. economic interdependence would be approved by non-Communist countries under the auspices of the United Nations. When that support did not materialize, successive American presidents moved to negotiate regional collective security alliances such as the North Atlantic Treaty Organization (NATO, 1949), the military agreement with Australia and New Zealand (ANZUS Pact, 1951), the Southeast Asia Treaty (SEATO, 1954), the Central Treaty Organization (CENTO, 1959) whereby the United States, along with Britain, agreed to aid Pakistan and Iran, and bilateral treaties of mutual defense with the Philippines, Japan, South Korea, and Nationalist China and to proclaim a number of unilateral presidential doctrines on foreign policy beginning with the Truman Doctrine in 1947 and continuing through the Reagan Doctrine in 1984.[8]

---

8   Alan Tonelson, "What Is the National Interest?" *The Atlantic Monthly*, July 1991, 35. **The Truman Doctrine** (1947), proclaimed initially in reference to Greece and Turkey, but later applied to other parts of the world, stated that "it must be the policy of the United States to support free peoples who are resisting subjugation by armed minorities or by outside pressures." **The Eisenhower Doctrine** (1957) gave unilateral notice that the United States would intervene in the Middle East if any government threatened by a Communist takeover requested aid. **The Johnson Doctrine** (1965) stated that the president could use military force whenever he thought communism threatened the Western Hemisphere and was first issued when LBJ sent troops into the Dominican Republic. **The Nixon Doctrine** (1969), originally aimed at "southern tier" Third World countries in East Asia, came to represent the formal

Consequently, when the United Nations did not provide reliable support for America's efforts to combat communism all over the world in the 1950s and 1960s, opposition to this international organization increased in government and popular circles in the United States. This lack of UN support stemmed from the fact that since the 1950s two-thirds of the votes in the UN General Assembly have been controlled by nonaligned, developing nations from the Third World who believed that the bipolar conflict between the United States and the Soviet Union made them mere pawns in a bipolar Cold War game, especially when "hot wars" broke out between the two superpowers or their surrogates as in Korea, Vietnam, and Angola. (The UN has only recently begun to return to favor in the United States as a result of its support for allied action in the Gulf War, made possible by a significant break in the unity of nonaligned nations on the question of outside interference in the Middle East.)

Finally, as one of the two most powerful nations of the Cold War period, the United States tried independently to enforce the Monroe Doctrine in Latin America and to exercise influence in other parts of the world unilaterally through foreign aid or military intervention whenever it decided that its economic or security interests were threatened. The Monroe Doctrine was perverted, according to Gaddis Smith, not only by the ideological nature of that bipolar conflict but also by the covert and overt U.S. military actions of all Cold War presidents in Latin America and by their partisan use of the doctrine for domestic purposes. Increasingly, through the unilateral proclamation of other presidential doctrines and secret executive orders, the United States honored the territorial integrity of undemocratic nations if they were non-Communist and interfered with or disapproved of self-

---

institutionalization of the policy of Vietnamization; that is, it noted that while the United States continued to support regional security and national self-sufficiency for nations in the Far East, it would no longer commit American troops to this effort. **The Carter Doctrine** (1980) maintained that any attempt by the Soviet Union "to gain control of the Persian Gulf will be regarded as an assault on the vital interests of the United States." **The Reagan Doctrine** (1986) announced that American foreign policy would actively promote democracy throughout the world by giving humanitarian and military aid to "democratic revolutions" wherever they occurred.

determination if it resulted (or threatened to result) in the establishment of Communist or even Socialist governments. This included at least two documented cases of governmental attempts to assassinate foreign leaders.[9] In the process, the power of the presidents of the United States to wage undeclared overt and covert wars increased significantly as the Cold War was hurriedly militarized in the late 1940s.

While the Korean War received accidental sanction from the UN Security Council, Harry Truman never bothered to obtain congressional approval for this first "limited" Cold War. And it came as no particular surprise when the United States refused to endorse the 1954 Geneva Accords calling for elections to reunite Vietnam and Dwight Eisenhower blocked that nationwide vote in 1956 because Ho Chi Minh was certain to win. He also allowed the CIA to help overthrow the nationalist government of Iran in 1953, sent marines into Lebanon in 1958, and approved the organizing of indigenous military units to invade both Guatemala and Cuba. As a result, historians began in the 1980s to question the wisdom of Ike's "hidden hand" diplomacy, especially in the Third World. Likewise, John Kennedy approved the invasion of Cuba by CIA-trained commandos in the now infamous Bay of Pigs operation and initiated the introduction of American forces in Vietnam, both in 1961. JFK also tried unsuccessfully to make the Dominican Republic a "showcase for democracy" through economic and military aid under the ten-year program known as the Alliance for Progress.[10] Under Lyndon Johnson 25,000 U.S.

---

9 Gaddis Smith, *The Last Years of the Monroe Doctrine, 1945–1993* (New York, 1994), 7; William M. LeoGrande, *Our Own Backyard: The United States in Central America, 1977–1992* (Chapel Hill, 1998); Glenn Hastedt, *American Foreign Policy: Past, Present, Future*, 2d. ed. (Englewoods Cliffs, NJ, 1991), 217–37. Of the six cases of alleged U.S. attempts to assassinate foreign leaders (Fidel Castro, Cuba; Patrice Lumumba, Congo [Zaire]; Rafael Trujillo, Dominican Republic; General Rene Schneider and Salvador Allende, Chile; and Ngo Dinh Diem, Vietnam) only two were found to be substantiated by evidence: Castro and Lumumba.

10 Melanie Billings-Yun, *Decision against War: Eisenhower and Dien Bien Phu, 1954* (New York, 1988); George Herring, *America's Longest War: The United States and Vietnam, 1950–1975* (New York, 1986), 25–72; Richard H. Immerman, "The United States and the Geneva Conference of 1954," *Diplomatic History* 14 (Winter 1990): 43–66; idem, "Confessions of an Eisenhower Revisionist: An Agonizing Reappraisal," *Diplomatic History* 14 (Summer 1990): 319–42; Robert F. Burk, "Eisenhower Revisionism Revisited: Reflections on the

and Organization of American States (OAS) troops were sent into the Dominican Republic to establish order and a conservative regime, while U.S. soldiers in Vietnam reached a peak level of 542,000 in 1969 without any congressional declaration of war. After secretly and then openly widening the Vietnam War into Laos and Cambodia, in the early 1970s Richard Nixon used the CIA to contribute to the downfall of the democratically elected socialist government of Salvador Allende Gossens in Chile, and under Gerald Ford in 1975 the United States unsuccessfully engaged the CIA in an attempt to defeat the Soviet-backed Popular Movement for the Liberation of Angola (MPLA). In the 1980s U.S. troops went into Lebanon and bombed Libya, and Presidents Ronald Reagan and George Bush successfully presided over the invasions of both Grenada and Panama in the late 1980s. And then there was UN approval of the Gulf War, which some regarded as "the use of a multilateral instrument to carry out a unilateral war" by the Bush administration. There have also been the fitful military actions of the Clinton administration in Somalia (initiated under Bush and then the UN), Bosnia, Haiti, Iraq, Sudan, and Afghanistan. All of these unilateral actions were undertaken in the name of U.S. economic or national security and sometimes on behalf of self-determination (now called nation building). To say the least, these unilateral or pseudo-collective activities, largely undertaken without congressional consultation, resulted in quite a few unintended consequences and in one instance – the Iran/contra affair under Reagan – contained unconstitutional overtones more ominous than those involved in Watergate. Having won the Cold War, unless the United States can now magnanimously admit that its goals and means in that conflict have not always contributed to world stability, let alone

Eisenhower Scholarship," *Historian* 50 (February 1988): 196–209; Stephen G. Rabe, *Eisenhower and Latin America: The Foreign Policy of Anti-Communism* (Chapel Hill, 1988); Robert McMahon, "Eisenhower and Third World Nationalism: A Critique of the Revisionists," *Political Science Quarterly* 101 (Fall 1986): 453–73; Stephen Rabe, "The Caribbean Triangle: Betancourt, Castro, and Trujillo and US Foreign Policy," *Diplomatic History* 20 (Winter 1996): 55–78; Piero Gleijeses, *The Dominican Crisis: The 1965 Constitutional Revolt and American Intervention* (Baltimore, 1978).

democracy, it may end up wondering early in the next century: Who lost the post-Cold War world?[11]

Most importantly, in the course of carrying out these covert and overt Cold War interventions based on an ever-widening perception of threats to its ubiquitous security interests, the United States began to lose its moral and democratic compass using a similar rationale to that in the novel, *The Spy Who Came in From the Cold*, when author John le Carré has Control [head of British Intelligence] say to agent Alec Leamas:

Thus we do disagreeable things, but we are defensive. That I think is still fair. We do disagreeable things so that ordinary people here and elsewhere can sleep safely in their beds at night. Is that too romantic? Of course, we occasionally do very wicked things . . . And in weighting up the moralities, we rather go in for dishonest comparisons; after all, you can't compare the ideals of one side with the methods of the other, can you now? . . . I mean, you've got to compare method with method, and ideal with ideal. I would say that since the war, our methods – ours and those of the opposition – have become much the same. I mean you can't be less ruthless than the opposition simply because your government's policy is benevolent, can you? That would never do . . . I mean in our world we pass so quickly out of the register of hate or love-like certain sounds a dog can't hear. All that's left in the end is a kind of nausea (pp. 23–24, 26).

Thus, during the Cold War the practice of independent internationalism reached an apex with unilateral actions prevailing over ostensible collective actions through the United Nations or those carried out in conjunction with former World War II allies. Even before nonaligned nations began to dominate the UN General Assembly in the 1950s, the United States had all but abandoned collective UN actions in favor of the independent economic arrangements coming out of the 1944 Bretton Woods meeting, such

---

11   Hastedt, *American Foreign Policy*, 1–8; Phyllis Bennis, *Calling the Shots: How Washington Dominates Today's UN* (New York, 1996), 25; LeoGrande, *Our Own Backyard*; Thomas J. McCormick, *America's Half-Century: United States Foreign Policy in the Cold War* (Baltimore, 1989); Thomas G. Paterson, *On Every Front: The Making and Unmaking of the Cold War*, rev. ed. (New York, 1992).

as the World Bank, the International Monetary Fund (IMF), and the various rounds of the General Agreement on Tariffs and Trade (GATT). While these institutions were supposed to be subjected to UN oversight and function as multilateral UN agencies, voting rights were weighted according to financial shares held by member states and they functioned largely at the behest of the United States until the excessive expense of the Cold War, highlighted by the Vietnam War, began to wreak havoc on the guns-and-butter American economy.[12]

Even the much-touted Marshall Plan was not only less unilateral in nature than it appeared on the surface but also less motivated as much by faith in the ultimate triumph of democracy and capitalism as it was by fear that the American system would not take hold in postwar Europe in the face of the popularity of communism in some early elections and the widespread belief that liberal capitalism had failed in the interwar years. Nowhere was U.S. fear of failure more evident than in postwar Czechoslovakia, where opposition to the economic revitalization of Western Germany under the Marshall Plan temporarily united Communist and non-Communist parties in the Czech National Front, in which each tried unsuccessfully to carve out greater social and economic democracy for itself through its own brand of state socialism. By insisting on international economic plans based on a strong German economy and expanding markets, the United States compromised the position of the non-Communist Czechs, thereby contributing to the success of the Communist coup in 1948.[13] This

---

12 Horsman and Marshall, *After the Nation-State*, 33; Bennis, *Calling the Shots*, 11–12. Diane Kunz is one of the few economic historians to argue that the American economy successfully provided both guns and butter throughout the Cold War, but her argument is less persuasive for the period after 1970, as is her insistence that GATT produced a free-trade system, ignoring the many postwar concessions the United States made to its economic allies at the expense of some of its own industries and workers. See Kunz, *Butter and Guns: America's Cold War Economic Diplomacy* (New York, 1997).

13 Michael J. Hogan, *The Marshall Plan: America, Britain, and the Reconstruction of Western Europe, 1947–1952* (Cambridge, 1987), 427–45; Geir Lundestad, "Empire by Invitation? The United States and Western Europe, 1945–52," *SHAFR Newsletter* 15 (September 1954): 1–21; Melvyn P. Leffler, "National Security and US Foreign Policy," Michael McGwire, "National Security and Soviet Foreign Policy," Charles S. Maier, "Hegemony and Autonomy within the Western Alliance," and Charles Gati, "Hegemony and Repression in the Eastern Alliance," all in *Origins of the Cold War: An International History*, ed. Leffler and David S.

was not the first opportunity America had to insist in a heavy-handed way on its version of democracy and capitalism abroad in this century. Nor was it the first time that democracy would take a back seat to American-defined self-determination and capitalism. In fact, all three times the United States undertook such action on a global scale, it was motivated by reaction to developments in one country officially known by three different names in this century: Russia/Union of Soviet Socialist Republics/Commonwealth of Independent States.

The first occurred immediately following the First World War when Woodrow Wilson in July 1918 decided to intervene in the Siberian front of the Russian civil war. Some historians even argue that in "ideologically holding out for an entirely democratic, capitalistic Russia, the United States pursued a policy that resulted in the loss of the entire nation to Western political and economic traditions."[14] This first unsuccessful attempt to counter a hostile foreign ideology with military intervention in the name of Wilsonian self-determination set a pattern of insisting on the exportation of democracy and capitalism, which the United States would fine-tune with practice for the rest of the American century. The second time the United States tried this tactic the stakes were higher because all of post-World War II Europe appeared to be vulnerable to views that were Communist at worst and socialist at best. While the Marshall Plan was money originally administered in Europe through the Economic Cooperation Administration (ECA), it soon became worldwide and merged with the Mutual Security Program (MSP) in 1952. The third opportunity for the United States to impose its brand of democracy and capitalism came at the end of the Cold War. Although in the 1990s its

---

Painter (New York, 1994), 15, 76, 154–98; Sonia L. Nelson, "The Impact of U.S. International Economic Plans on Czechoslovakia's Postwar Development, 1943–1948" (Ph.D. diss., Northern Illinois University, 1994).

14 Georg Schild, *Between Ideology and Realpolitik: Woodrow Wilson and the Russian Revolution, 1917–1921* (Westport, 1995), 126; Lloyd C. Gardner, *Safe for Democracy: The Anglo-American Response to Revolution, 1913–1923* (New York, 1984), 125–202. For a more favorable view of Wilson's decision to intervene militarily in Russia see Betty Unterberger, *The United States, Revolutionary Russia, and the Rise of Czechoslovakia* (Chapel Hill, 1989), 196–318.

economic position was not as dominant as in 1947, when it represented 50 percent of the world's combined gross product, the U.S. proportion still hovers around 25 percent at the end of the American Century.[15]

Despite recovery in the United States from the global economic turndown of the first half of the 1990s, slow growth continues to characterize the new world economy, especially as contagion spread from the recession in Japan, to the collapse of the economies of certain Pacific Rim countries, to financial chaos in Russia, and to the dangerous weakening of major Latin American financial and commercial structures during the summer and fall of 1997.[16] This worldwide slowdown has fostered nationalist, ethnic, and religious hatred all over the globe, but especially in Africa and the former Soviet republics – a situation for which U.S. foreign policy has developed no clear strategy except to insist, as it did throughout the Cold War, that the world and especially the remaining developing nations, will benefit from what has become an endless capitalist pursuit of export markets abroad and what I call the practice of Ferengi democracy at home.[17]

Therefore, the end of the Cold War has fortuitously provided as yet a largely ignored opportunity for the United States to reflect about whether the practice of independent internationalism behind the rhetoric of anticommunism caused it to lose its soul when it adopted the methods of the enemy to win the Cold War.

15 Hogan, *The Marshall Plan*, 54–87, 187–88, 427–45; idem, "The Search for a 'Creative Peace': The United States, European Unity, and the Origins of the Marshall Plan," *Diplomatic History* 6 (Summer 1982): 267–85; Alan S. Milward, "Was the Marshall Plan Necessary?" ibid. 13 (Spring 1989): 231–53; Melvyn P. Leffler, "The United States and the Strategic Dimensions of the Marshall Plan," ibid. 12 (Summer 1988): 277–306; Robert E. Wood, "From the Marshall Plan to the Third World," in Leffler and Painter, eds., *Origins of the Cold War*, 201–14; Wittkopf, ed., *Future of American Foreign Policy*, 282.
16 Wittkopf, ed., *Future of American Foreign Policy*, 282–83; and Leonard Silk, "Dangers of Slow Growth," in ibid., 329–36.
17 The Ferengi are an ugly *Star Trek* race of "perfect" capitalists driven only by their quest for profit and governed by numerous rules of commerce. Thanks to the Supreme Court, money is free speech in the United States and without campaign finance reform, political offices, especially at the national level, appear to be for sale to the largest contributors. For copious documentation of the obvious, namely that "the richest among us . . . have the greatest influence over political power," see Charles Lewis and the Center for Public Integrity, *The Buying of Congress: How Special Interests Have Stolen Your Right to Life, Liberty, and the Pursuit of Happiness* (New York, 1998).

George Kennan warned against just such a possibility at the beginning of the American Century when, in his famous 1946 "long telegram," he said: "Finally, we must have courage and self-confidence to cling to our own methods and conceptions of human society. After all, the greatest danger that can befall us in coping with the problem of Soviet communism is that we shall allow ourselves to become like those with whom we are coping."[18]

Over a half-century later, it is also time to have the courage and self-confidence to ask whether the terms democracy, liberal capitalism, and self-determination should be bandied about with such arrogance so evident in the current atmosphere of American "triumphalism."[19] Most importantly, the end of the Cold War affords the United States time to improve the practice of democracy and social justice at home, to reassess the impact of the spread of the heretofore unregulated global capitalism on the American worker, and to redefine sovereignty other than in Wilsonian terms of inviolate self-determined nationhood. In short, the relationships between democracy and capitalism and between democracy and national self-determination can be more realistically reassessed now that the ideological frenzy known as Cold War is over. Unfortunately, such a reevaluation has not progressed very far within the Washington beltway because it requires facing the fact that the American score card on democracy is long on rhetoric and short on results, primarily because the practice of independent internationalism has more often than not sacrificed democracy on the twin altars of self-determination and capitalism as this century has "progressed" from one Sarajevo tragedy to another.

Reassessing Self-Determination

Reassessment of self-determination will be especially difficult because the United States was born in a fit of self-determination

---

18   U.S. Department of State, *Foreign Relations of the United States, 1946* (Washington, 1972), 6:709; Kennan, *Memoirs: 1925–1950* (Boston, 1967), 559.
19   *Daedalus* 124 (Spring 1995): xxi.

during the American Revolution. The country quietly nourished and groomed this autonomous brand of nationhood for itself and, for most of the nineteenth century, touted it to other nascent nations finding themselves in civil turmoil. Self-determined self-government was the hallmark of the origins of the United States and at the heart of its drive to become the example for how the rest of world should operate, long before Woodrow Wilson made it an international code word for national sovereignty during the First World War.

The right of peoples in the name of self-determination to decide their own national destinies, as demonstrated in the actions of American revolutionaries, had little to do with the evolution of domestic democracy in the United States later in the nineteenth century. Self-determination initially provided the country's leaders with a domestic and foreign policy self-image long before it became a bona fide guiding diplomatic principle in the second decade of the twentieth century. Several other foreign policy principles also emerged from the American Revolution and found more practical application following the War for Independence than did self-determination. These included neutrality, freedom of the seas, and political (but not economic) isolationism, continental expansion, better known by the term coined in 1845, Manifest Destiny, and international cooperation in the form of arbitration of boundary and fishing disputes. While powerful components of U.S. foreign policy in the nineteenth century, they became virtually extinct by 1920 with the exception of international cooperation, while self-determination finally came into its own. It should be noted that even these now defunct aspects of postrevolutionary foreign policy contained no inherent democratic overtones. As the United States became a major military and economic nation following the First World War, only its commitment to international cooperation, along with self-determination, survived. Neither – until World War I – was associated with democracy until both were internationally revived due to President Wilson's complex redefinition of, and personal adherence to, these concepts during the war, at the Versailles peace negotiations, and his unsuccessful attempt to bring the United States into the League of Nations in 1919.

Of these two left-over, nineteenth-century concepts, however, U.S. promotion of self-determination in the interwar years tugged more fervently at politicians' heart strings because it could much more easily be packaged in the mystique of the American Revolution than could international cooperation through the League of Nations. Self-determination also resonated with the struggles of the new nations in keeping with Wilson's naively idealistic belief that the war had turned the international political tide in the direction of democracy. Even Woodrow Wilson's much-quoted desire "to make the world safe for democracy" during World War I came only after he unsuccessfully deployed U.S. military force "to teach the South American republics to elect good men."[20]

Self-determination, however, should not be confused with either the wholesale exportation or even consistent promotion of democracy by the United States in this century, despite official rhetoric to the contrary. This is especially true in those areas of Central and South America where the United States has exercised the most direct and indirect influence since 1900. The Cold War exacerbated this disjunction between self-determination and democracy in American foreign policy, especially as this bipolar struggle between the United States and the Soviet Union expanded into the Third World countries in Africa and Asia. Unfortunately, government manipulation of traditional confusion among average American citizens over the relationship between self-determination and democracy has increased exponentially since the Cold War ended.

At the same time, both terms have come under closer scrutiny by international lawyers than ever before because of the outburst of ethnic, religious, and gender cleansing *within* old and new national boundaries after the Soviet Union imploded during the Bush administration. While not all these atrocities have occurred in Eastern Europe in the 1990s, the incidents in Bosnia and the threat-

---

20   Wilson quoted in Arthur Link, *Woodrow Wilson and the Progressive Era, 1910–1917* (New York, 1954), 119, 281.

ening situation in Kosovo have convinced some within Western jurisprudence circles and committees of the UN that traditional national self-determination and its corollary, inviolate sovereignty, may need to be redefined. Increasingly they are questioning whether such slaughter within self-determined borders can any longer be honored as the right of nation-states and whether the UN's (and earlier the League of Nations') commitment to noninterference in the internal affairs of member states should be reexamined. In particular, following the Gulf War and UN attempts to obtain relief for the Kurds and verify the existence of weapons of mass destruction in Iraq, French diplomats openly questioned whether the UN Charter's prohibition against interfering in the internal affairs of member states (Article II, section 7) should be amended to reflect the need to intervene on humanitarian grounds.[21]

In the best of all possible worlds, one could hope that the American Century, during which national self-determination was celebrated and promoted after both world wars through international organizations, will close with an attempt to delineate sovereignty more in keeping with universal human rights than with sacrosanct nationhood. But that would require a more candid discussion of the evolution of the purpose and mission of the United Nations over the last fifty years and of the meaning of democracy, sovereignty, and citizenship at the end of the American Century.

While it can be argued that democracy was successfully forced through massive occupation and economic reorganization on Japan and Germany after World War II, historically, "American diplomacy has not made promoting democracy a major goal" in this century, either in terms of money spent annually to aid democratic institutions or as the result of covert and overt military interventions. Even Japan, if truth be told, "with the same party in power for decades, [has only] a charade of democracy." Japan's success, until the late 1980s has not been political or even exclusively capitalistic, except to American eyes. Instead, Japan's postwar achievements have been based on a common cultural memory

21 Bennis, *Calling the Shots*, 39–40, 246.

and ritual that poses as domestic democratic confrontation from time to time, especially in highly staged economic conflicts with the United States. Not until 1993 did the Liberal-Democratic party, which had practiced rural socialism for years, fall from power due to the country's economic difficulties. Not until the late 1990s have these same difficulties finally made it possible for the public to become interested in politics and for a Western concept of the nation-state to "begin to take form in the Japanese consciousness." A constitutional design exists for popular sovereignty that has only begun to develop.[22]

The spotty American record in promoting democracy in this century does not mean the United States should ignore taking advantage of the unprecedented opportunity to promote democracy presented by the end of the Cold War. It should be doing so, however, with more realism and less hyperbolic rhetoric than President Bill Clinton did on his trips to Eastern Europe and Russia in 1994 and to Africa, Latin America, and China in 1998. In particular, one would never know from the president's remarks during these visits that worldwide half of the "democratizing" countries that he so indiscriminately praised either conduct questionable elections or are what have been called "illiberal democracies," that is, democracies that do not accord the freedom of constitutional liberalism to their peoples, especially their female citizens. The question of how many contemporary democracies constitute civic or constitutional communities is important because

---

22 Larry Diamond, "Promoting Democracy," in Wittkopf, ed., *Future of American Foreign Policy*, 101–16 (quotation at 105); Guéhenno, *The END of the NATION STATE*, 31–32. I disagree with Tony Smith's conclusion that "the American impact was greater on democratization in Japan than in West Germany" for all of the reasons he goes on to cite about Japan not "play[ing] by the rules." See Smith, *America's Mission: The United States and the Worldwide Struggle for Democracy in the Twentieth Century* (Princeton, 1994), 146–76 (quotations, 173–74). Part of the reason Japan has developed at best its own distinctive brand of cultural democracy and capitalism lies in the fact that even MacArthur had to exercise his unlimited authority in Japan through the symbol of the Emperor and such prewar institutions as the Diet and an entrenched bureaucratic structure. For more on the distinctive and questionable democratic nature of Japanese policies see Masuru Tamamoto, "Reflections on Japan's Postwar State," Daedalus 124 (Spring 1995): 1–22; Kenichi Ohmae, *The Mind of the Strategist: The Art of Japanese Business* (New York, 1982); Guéhenno, *The END of the NATION STATE*, 10–16, 50–51, 107–10; and articles in *International Security* 17 (Spring 1993) by Samuel Huntington, Nobuo Okawara, and Thomas U. Berger.

political scientists Jack Snyder and Edward Mansfield have statistically indicated that emerging nations practicing pseudo-democracy "not grounded in constitutional liberalism" are more often than not "hypernationalistic and war-mongering" compared to established autocracies or liberal democracies.[23] In other words, the axiom emanating from Washington that all so-called democracies do not go to war with one another is simply not true.

The Washington diplomatic elite is also so reluctant to discuss publicly other sensitive foreign policy subjects in an age of political correctness, such as the declining state power as capitalist markets explode internationally, that it is being said that the end of the Cold War has caused a "conceptual vacuum" compared to the energy thrown into formulating innovative U.S. foreign policy following the Second World War. Whether going back to the time in which the Cold War came into existence is good advice remains to be seen. In many ways the decade of 1920s may have more in common with the 1990s than do the 1940s. Still another important question that also has its roots in the 1920s and 1930s concerns the foreign policy implications of the switch from the quantitative trend of economic interdependence to the qualitative change in the international economic system, known as globalization – not simply on the power of individual states but on established multinational organizations. In any case, there can be no new ideas about national security or citizenship or international cooperation until U.S. foreign policy experts and politicians address such questions and begin to reconceptualize and rescue some remnant of democratic state sovereignty from the anti-state tentacles of global capitalism. Instead, with leaders governing by polls instead of educating and guiding an apathetic public, "foreign policy is increasingly made by narrow interest

---

23   Fareed Zakaria, "Democracies That Take Liberties," *New York Times*, 2 November 1997; idem, "The Rise of Illiberal Democracy," *Foreign Affairs* 76 (November-December 1997): 22–43; Oscar Schacter, "The Decline of the Nation-State and its Implications for International Law," *Columbia Journal of Transitional Law* 36 (1997): 12; Barber, *Jihad vs. McWorld*, 11, 13; Wolfgang H. Reinicke, "Global Public Policy," *Foreign Affairs* 76 (November/December 1997): 127. To speak of China as aiding the worldwide cause of nuclear nonproliferation, especially in relation to the "vibrant democracy" of Pakistan, as Clinton has, is to insult common sense, to say nothing of the intelligence of many non-governmental foreign policy experts (*New York Times*, June 1998).

groups," and so the country is practicing a "hollow hegemony" with the "rhetoric of transformation but the reality of accommodation."[24]

Even before the United States won the Cold War, American scholars and foreign policy formulators avoided tackling the real, as opposed to rhetorical, meaning of such terms as self-determination, self-government, and even democracy as practiced in this country at the end of the twentieth century. Partly this was because, as Tony Smith has pointed out, there was little attempt to undertake comparative analyses of the impact abroad of democratic ideas that have not necessarily originated in or with the United States.[25] The American Republic was not founded in the name of the democracy; the term was not on the lips of most political leaders when they spoke of self-determination until the first quarter of the twentieth century; and American efforts to promote democracy in this century failed more than they succeeded, especially during the Cold War years. For all these reasons, national self-determination has been a more successful guiding principle of U.S. foreign policy in this, the American Century, than democracy. It also dovetailed better with the country's practice of independent internationalism because it could be pursued through either unilateral or collective actions and be used in support of dictatorial, as well as democratic, leaders, depending on who best served the ideological and economic interests of the United States.

In Pursuit of Self-Determination

Following the American Revolution, therefore, there were more explicit theorizing and practical attempts at national self-determination in Europe than in the Western Hemisphere. The fate of both Corsica and Poland gave rise to issues of national identity in the 1760s to the 1790s as the first was swallowed up by the French

---

24 *Daedalus* 124 (Spring 1995): xix (first quotation), xxiii; Zakaria, "The Rise of Illiberal Democracy," 38; idem, "Our Hollow Hegemony: Why Foreign Policy Can't Be Left to the Market," *New York Times Magazine*, November 1, 1998, 44ff, quotations at 74.
25 Smith, *America's Mission*, 4.

and the latter partitioned by Russia, Prussia, and Austria. Edmund Burke and Jean-Jacques Rousseau commented quite pointedly on the violation of national self-determination in the case of Corsica, comparing the transfer of a nation without its consent to "trees on an estate" or like "herds of cattle, without consulting [the people's] interests or their wishes." These and other theorists outside the United States came to define national self-determination as the right of people to be consulted about how and by whom they should be governed. What was meant by "people" remained very ambiguous, except for the fact that until this century "women have never been viewed as a 'people' for the purposes of right to self-determination."[26] Whether self-determination could be possible without national identity remained unclear. In other words, initially nationalism and self-determination were not necessarily synonymous and neither had an intrinsic connection to the practice of democracy.

The French Revolution, rather than the American, set in motion the temporary establishment of free republics in Europe and Latin America, raising questions about the complex relationships between people as a nation, popular sovereignty, and national will. Male plebiscites became one method for determining popular national will from the 1820s through the 1860s as Serbs, Greeks, Romanians, Czechs, Croats, and Italians all tried to unite with varying degrees of failure. None of their nationalizing efforts received anything but superficial support from the United States, which remained more involved in domestic matters having to do with internal improvements and continental expansion, which meant denying self-determination to Native Americans and, ultimately, to the South when it finally tried to secede.[27]

The Civil War abruptly ended what little presidential and congressional support for the self-determination legacy was inherent in both the American Revolution, the Monroe Doctrine, and

---

26 Derek Heater, *National Self-Determination: Woodrow Wilson and His Legacy* (New York, 1994), 1–2; Hilary Charlesworth, Christine Chinkin, and Shelley Wright, "Feminist Approaches to International Law," *American Journal of International Law* 85 (October 1991): 643.
27 Dankwart A. Rustow, "Democracy: A Global Revolution?" *Foreign Affairs* 69 (Fall 1990): 74.

Manifest Destiny. As a result, President Abraham Lincoln and his secretary of state, William H. Seward, found it necessary to disavow groups continuing to support the perennially popular Hungarian revolution and the Polish revolution of 1863. And, of course, the Union took precedence over Southern demands for self-determination. Thus, federal policy during and immediately following the Civil War contradicted the previous, albeit largely rhetorical U.S. commitment to self-determination for other nations, Secretary Seward's attempts to reassert it during the Andrew Johnson administration against both Austria and France in Mexico notwithstanding.[28] This contradiction appeared to be reversed when the country fought to free Cuba from Spanish rule in 1898, only then to put it under the 1901 Platt Amendment, which left the Cubans with "little or no independence," according to General Leonard Wood, the American-appointed governor of the island. In anticipation of the practice of independent internationalism that the United States later adopted in the 1920s, where the United States lacked power, as in the Far East, it continued to advocate a cooperative Open Door economic policy; where it dominated, as in Latin America, it practiced a unilateral Closed Door diplomacy.

At the time of the "splendid little" Spanish-American-Cuban-Filipino War, the United States not only acquired an overseas empire and tried to assert itself into the affairs of the world for economic gain with "dollar diplomacy" under Theodore Roosevelt and William Howard Taft but by 1900 it had also developed a foreign policy ideology – all the while refusing to use the leftist-tainted term "ideology." Since America's inception, four very general and intertwined phenomena slowly coalesced in the course of the nineteenth century that would influence the way in which decision makers have formulated U.S. foreign policy and the way in which diplomatic scholars have interpreted it for the entire twentieth century. They were: 1) a maddeningly unself-conscious ideology, which by the beginning of the twentieth century had

---

28   Steven J. Valone, "Seward and the Reassertion of the Monroe Doctrine," *Diplomatic History* 19 (Fall 1995): 583–600.

conflated national greatness with the promotion of liberty abroad (the word liberty usually meaning the American model of democ racy and capitalism), 2) a racist, sexist, and often religiously grounded suspicion of revolutions in the rest of the world, waiting to be exacerbated by the Cold War, 3) sea changes that occurred in the economy of the United States (gradually up to 1890s and then dramatically after World War I and II and again at the end of the Cold War), and 4) traumatic generational events (usually major wars and/or sociocultural dislocations) that have temporarily shaped both popular and elite thinking about how the nation should conduct itself on the international scene.[29]   This last component of the American foreign policy ideology has meant that we usually overlearn the lessons of the previous war or other national trauma. For example, Congress passed a series of Neutrality Acts in the last half of the 1930s placing various limitations on trading with nations at war that were perfectly designed to keep the United States out of the First World War, but not the one the country was then facing – the Second World War. And of course, after Vietnam the United States viewed every conflict as though it might become another Vietnam, including Bill Clinton's belated decision to commit NATO troops in Bosnia in 1995.

With this ideology at least subconsciously in place by 1900, the stage was set for American diplomacy to become overtly aggressive against other indigenous peoples with Roosevelt's "taking" of Panama from Colombia and Wilson's war against Mexican rebels. In fact, until the Cold War, the first two decades of the twentieth century marked the most willful exercise of U.S. power outside its own boundaries, as it ruthlessly subdued Filipinos and bluffed its way into the spheres of influence of major world powers with Secretary of State John Hay's "Open Door Notes" demanding both the territorial and political integrity of China along

---

29   Michael H. Hunt, *Ideology and U.S. Foreign Policy* (New Haven, 1987), 17, 171, passim; Jerald A. Combs, *American Diplomatic History: Two Centuries of Changing Interpretations* (Berkeley, 1983), x, passim; Smith, *America's Mission*, 19–27; Jeffrey Kimball, "The Influence of Ideology on Interpretive Disagreement: A Report on a Survey of Diplomatic, Military and Peace Historians on the Causes of 20th-Century U.S. Wars," *The History Teacher* 17 (May 1984): 355–81.

with equal commercial opportunity for the United States in Asia. At the same time the country began to practice a "Closed Door Policy" in the Western Hemisphere with Roosevelt's transformation of the Monroe Doctrine from one of nonintervention by European powers to one of intervention in Central and South America by the United States.

U.S. violations of its own founding principle of self-determination in the first twenty years of this century were accompanied by abandonment of other long-held American diplomatic concepts following the First World War. As noted above, from 1776 until 1900 American foreign policy adhered to several principles based entirely on its position as a relatively powerless, developing nation in a world dominated by England and France. From the late eighteenth century until World War I, the United States did not yet have sufficient economic or military power to enforce most of its diplomatic principles except in Latin America.

By 1920 the United States had established protectorates in the form of financial supervision and/or militarily intervened into eight Caribbean and Central American countries, all in the name of establishing stability to protect U.S. property or citizens – at the expense of the sovereignty of these nations. Thus, the first systematic attempts of the United States to become a hegemonic power took place in the Western Hemisphere as it turned its back on self-determination in that part of the world, mirroring the way it had turned its back on self-determination for Native Americans and Southern secessionists in the nineteenth century. This is not surprising when it is remembered that although the Monroe Doctrine endorsed the concept of self-determination, it implicitly asserted a "soft" U.S. sphere of influence over Latin America, to use John Vloyantes's term. Given the weakness of the United States as an international power in 1823 it could not enforce any of the principles of the Monroe Doctrine, but by making a unilateral statement, American leaders reserved for themselves the sole right to determine which principles would be implemented in accordance with national interest. In this sense the doctrine can be said to have been a realistic unilateral assertion of national interest subject to the changing power status of the country until

Woodrow Wilson unsuccessfully tried "to purge all taint of an exclusive United States sphere of influence from the doctrine by transforming it into a universal sphere of influence for democracy and self-determination – an interesting piece of intellectual gymnastics bound to cause confusion." In doing so, according to Gaddis Smith, Wilson succeeded in compromising the realistic strain of the original Monroe Doctrine. Consequently, the United States would sporadically try to exert "hard" influence over Central American nations in the first half of the twentieth century and both "hard" and "soft" influence over most of South America during the Cold War – all in the name of democratic self-determination, when in fact it was simply shoring up its sphere of influence in the Western Hemisphere.[30]

This confusion and denial of the relationship between self-determination and spheres of influence must be blamed on President Wilson. While he reintroduced self-determination as the basis for national sovereignty in the post-World War I era, he himself ultimately acceded when the Allies took exception to his principle and acted in ways that were more in keeping with his own earlier violations of self-determination for Haiti, Nicaragua, and Mexico. He even tried to insert in the 1916 treaty with Nicaragua a clause similar to the Platt Amendment denying the independence of Cuba, and his statements about self-government for the Philippines made it clear that it could not be granted until "our work there is done and they are ready." For Wilson, the act of self-determination depended upon the amalgamation of nationalism and self-government rooted in some form of democracy. Nationality, as Wilson defined it at the beginning of the American Century, consisted of a vague state of consciousness, a "community of thought," rather than rigid geographical or ethnoreligious characteristics as it is more commonly thought of now. He thus blurred the fact that manifestations of nationalism

---

30   John Vloyantes, *Spheres of Influence: A Framework for Analysis* (Tucson, AZ, 1970); Walter LaFeber, "The Evolution of the Monroe Doctrine from Monroe to Reagan," in *Redefining the Past: Essays in Diplomatic History in Honor of William Appleman Williams*, ed. Lloyd C. Gardner (Corvallis, OR, 1986), 121–41; Smith, *The Last Years of the Monroe Doctrine*, 8–9, 28–29.

have no intrinsic relationship to democratic government by insisting that the "peace should rest upon the right of peoples, not the rights of Government – the rights of people great or small, weak or powerful – their equal rights to freedom and security and self-government."[31]

This conflation of democracy and nationalism into the single concept of self-determination became embodied in Wilson's Fourteen Points and League of Nations Covenant, only to be found wanting in practical terms when trying to protect rights of minorities within national boundaries determined by majority and in the League's mandate system – both of which represented "the principle of national self-determination deferred."[32] Wilson's legacy of liberal internationalism, however flawed in theory and practice, became the basis of the Charter of the United Nations and for the emphasis the United States placed on self-determination during the Cold War. This allowed foreign policy formulators to pay little attention to democracy or legitimate nationalist claims of newly emerging nations as long as they sided with the United States in the Cold War against the Soviet Union. As noted, the United States emerged from World War II at the height of its economic and military power; thus, it was in a perfect position to practice independent internationalism disguised in the rhetoric of liberal capitalist internationalism. Now that it has won the Cold War, what kind of democracy is the United States currently practicing, and is the self-determination it has long supported for itself and others relevant to the projected global economic conditions of the twenty-first century?

---

31 Heater, *National Self-Determination*, 25, 32 (last quotation, Wilson replying to Pope Benedict XV's appeal for peace after the United States entered World War I). See also *To End All Wars*, 34–35, 42–43, 56–57, 249–50; Arthur Walworth, *America's Moment, 1918: American Diplomacy at the End of World War I* (New York, 1977), 172–94; and Lloyd E. Ambrosius, "Wilsonian Self-Determination," *Diplomatic History* 16 (Winter 1992): 141–48. For a more positive view of Wilson's definition and practice of self- determination see Betty Unterberger, "The United States and National Self-Determination: A Wilsonian Perspective," *Presidential Studies Quarterly* 26 (Fall 1996): 926–41.
32 Heater, *National Self-Determination*, 93.

Limitations of Liberal Democracy

In the Western, industrialized world we all think we know what democracy means in very general terms. At the end of the twentieth century it usually refers to freely contested elections by two or more organized parties conducted on the basis of universal adult suffrage resulting in direct or representative governmental institutions that adhere to the rule of law so that property and civil liberties can be protected and peaceful transitions of power ensured. Often, however, ballot box governments created through the self-initiation or outside imposition of elections have been viewed as ends in and of themselves during the American Century when, in fact, much more is required for a functional and constitutionally liberal democracy, especially when post-industrial capitalism is beginning to undermine certain time-honored democratic beliefs and principles.

Since the United States has trusted its past and future to free elections longer than any other nation in history, its rather singular political features (not all of which are democratic) should be noted. First, there is the ambiguous commitment to individual liberty, which, well into the twentieth century, focused more on political freedom and property rights for white men than universal suffrage, civil rights, or equality as far as women and racial minorities were concerned. Second, there is the belief that democratic government in the United States was (and is) owned and operated by a secure middle class of informed voting citizens with a highly developed sense of civic responsibility that took most of the nineteenth century to develop.[33] Third, it is usually assumed that our unique system of checks and balances, along with our two-party system (largely preserved through the distinctly undemocratic function of the electoral college), makes us impervious to the plutocratic, oligarchic, or autocratic pitfalls that have plagued other democracies because they ensure the enactment of just laws

33 Zakaria, "The Rise of Illiberal Democracy," 38, 40–41; *Daedalus*, vi; Rustow, "Democracy: A Global Revolution?" 85–89; Smith, *America's Mission*, 13–19; Steel, T*emptations of a Superpower*, 110; Kaplan, "Was Democracy Just a Moment?" 58, 61.

and policies that have been vigorously debated by an informed and involved citizenry.

But this is not the only view of how liberal capitalist democracy functions in the United States. For example, as Lewis H. Lapham pointed out during the 1996 presidential election, two governments – one permanent, one provisional – exist in contemporary capitalist America: the first hidden from view and the second touted in public. The permanent government consists of

a secular oligarchy . . . comprise[d of] the Fortune 500 companies and their attendant lobbyists, the big media and entertainment syndicates, the civil and military services, the larger research universities and law firms. It is this government that hires the country's politicians and sets the terms and conditions under which the country's citizens can exercise their right . . . to life, liberty, and the pursuit of happiness. Obedient to the rule of men, not laws, the permanent government oversees the production of wealth, builds cities, manufactures goods, raises capital, fixes prices, shapes the landscape, and reserves the right to assume debt, poison rivers, cheat customers, receive the gifts of the federal subsidy, and speak to the American people in the language of low motive and base emotion.

The provisional government is the spiritual democracy that comes and goes on the trend of a political season and oversees the production of pageants. . . . Positing a rule of laws instead of men, the provisional government must live within the cage of high-minded principle, addressing its remarks to the imaginary figure known as the informed citizen or the thinking man. . . . But let the words threaten to result in actions that will disturb the comfort of the permanent government and the speaker quickly becomes seen as a dangerous and irresponsible demagogue.[34]

Whether one agrees with Lapham or with the more traditionally positive view of contemporary American democracy cited above, given its complex specifics at the end of the American Century, it would not seem particularly well suited for those recently liberated countries of Eastern Europe and Russia, or most Third World nations since World War II.

---

34 Lapham, "Lights, Camera, Democracy!" *Harper's Magazine* (August 1996): 33–38 (quotations, 35–36).

First, Western democracies have always been based on a strong, middle-class, educated base, usually accompanied by low birth rates – conditions that most nations of the world simply do not enjoy. Until a developing nation establishes a middle class and civil institutions, its chances of becoming a stable democracy are slight. Often this middle class is created not by democratic procedures but by authoritarian ones and only then can this bourgeois element claim democratic rights for itself against the very dictators who helped create its prosperity.

One can see this pattern of middle-class turn toward democracy in the Pacific Rim nations (which the popular revolt against Suharto in May 1998 demonstrated very dramatically) in the southern tip of Latin America, but not in most of the rest of Central or South America, or southern Asia, or sub-Saharan Africa. Even when countries in these areas have changed from dictatorships to democracies, the change has not been accompanied by the adoption of constitutional liberalism. A perfect example of this can be found in Pinochet's Chile. Moreover, the collapse of some economies in the Pacific Rim, while leading to the overthrow of a dictator in Indonesia, may, at the same time, undermine the newly formed and fragile beginnings of limited democratic governments in South Korea, Thailand, Singapore, and Malaysia. And to talk of democracy in the "failed states" of Haiti, Rwanda, Somalia, Liberia, Afghanistan, the Democratic Republic of Congo (Zaire), Angola, and Sudan, where anarchy, poverty, and disease are rampant, is delusional. Even in Venezuela, Colombia, Argentina, Brazil, and Peru the democratic record is turbid, to say the least. Russia, Albania, Bulgaria, Romania, Bangladesh, Slovakia, Ghana, Armenia, Kazakhstan, Belarus, and Azerbaijan, unlike Hungary, Poland, and the Czech Republic, have no established bourgeois or democratic traditions on which to base their newly created democracies. And, of course, such rogue nations as Iran, Iraq, and Libya remain beyond even the pretense of democratic influence.[35]

35 Jon Lee Anderson, "The Dictator [Pinochet], *The New Yorker*, 19 October 1998, 44–57; Schacter, "The Decline of the Nation-State," 18; Kaplan, "Was Democracy Just a Moment?" 58, 60.

The second and even less mentioned assumed component part of democracy not only in the United States but also in most Western industrialized nations calling themselves democratic, is that women have never been granted the same employment, educational, reproductive, and sexual rights as men. While most of the unique features of American democracy are well known, this last point is almost never mentioned, yet it is extremely important in terms of U.S. foreign policy, which has seldom made women's rights a priority, especially in Third World countries. While one could cite many AID programs that ignored the agricultural function of women by giving modern agricultural equipment to men in developing nations, one of the worst examples of the sexism of U.S. foreign policy occurred in 1979 when the United States decided to back the Afghan mujahedin insurgents against the invading Soviet forces, despite their oppressive, patriarchal, Islamic fundamentalist discrimination against women. In fact, the mullahs' revolt against the puppet government established by the USSR in Kabul resulted in part from the fact that the Soviets improved economic and educational opportunities for Afghanistan's women. Now, with the Taliban in control of most of Afghanistan, it is only a matter of time before the United States and the UN recognize this extremist regime which is currently denying women the right to work, education, and even medical treatment.[36]

As practiced by newly established countries since the fall of communism in 1989, democracy has proven less than beneficial for women when combined with nascent nationalism. This is why a feminist approach to international law is needed as the United States rethinks its foreign policy in the post-Cold War world – to make sure that human rights includes women's rights, which means rethinking the definition of national and global citizenship based on equality rights so that they include equitable rights that correspond to women's experiences and needs, as they are reflected in different countries all over the world. In other words, a common inferior or second-class citizenship has been

---

36   Charlesworth, et al., "Feminist Approaches to International Law," 642; Cynthia Enloe, *Bananas, Beaches, and Bases: Making Feminist Sense of International Politics* (New York, 1989), 57.

imposed on women throughout the world going back to Athenian Greece and is at the end of the American Century more evident than ever.[37]

The history of citizenship for women in the United States and under United Nations' covenants proves that equal rights alone, while a necessary starting point for obtaining first-class citizenship for women, is not enough because such equality is typically based on male standards, and women do not exist on an equal footing with men in either post-industrial or less-developed nations. Unless women simply want to aspire to act as, and be treated as, men, despite the odds against achieving this privileged status, equitable, not simply equal, treatment of women must be included in any future definition of national or global citizenship. As feminist attorneys have said: "The rhetoric of human rights, on both the national and international levels, regards women as equal citizens [when they are not], as 'individuals' subject to the same level of treatment and the same protection as men. But the discourse of 'traditional values' may prevent women from enjoying any human rights, however they may be described [because male standards are still the norm]."[38] Despite the self-evident

---

37   Nicole Loraux, *Citizenship and Women: The Children of Athena: Athenian Ideas about Citizenship and the Division of Labor between the Sexes*, trans. Caroline Levine (Princeton, 1993), 6–21, passim. While teaching in Dublin in 1993–94, I reconsidered what citizenship means for women outside the United States. But more importantly, the disintegration of Yugoslavia (and later the peace in Northern Ireland) also made me think about the meaning of nationalism for women and the connection between citizenship and nationalism. Neither subject has been given enough consideration by historians of women in the last thirty years, despite their other often dramatic reinterpretations of history. I have argued for a number of years that women in the United States and most other Western democracies remain second-class citizens because they lack three basic freedoms enjoyed by men under most constitutional or other forms of government. These three basic freedoms usually denied to women citizens are: 1) freedom from inferior legislative, constitutional, or juridical status (usually meaning the denial of economic and legal privileges enjoyed by mainstream men), 2) freedom from fertility and family discrimination (denial of reproductive rights, including restricted access to abortion and an inferior position within traditional family hierarchies, otherwise known today as the return to family values), 3) freedom from fear (denial of protections from the uncontrolled and often ignored violence against women throughout the world). For details see Joan Hoff, *Gender, Law, and Injustice: A Legal History of U.S. Women* (New York, 1994), ix–xvii, passim; and idem, "The Impact & Implications of Women's History," in *Women & Irish History*, eds Maryann Gialanella Valiulis and Mary O'Dowd (Dublin, 1997), 15–24.
38   Charlesworth, et al., "Feminist Approaches to International Law," 637–38; Hilary Charlesworth, "Alienating Oscar? Feminist Analysis of International Law," in *Reconceiving*

nature of this critique of contemporary human rights, male definitions of democratic citizenship continue to prevail, as so well
demonstrated in an article by Fareed Zakaria, managing editor
of Foreign Affairs. In praising constitutional liberalism he makes
no mention of how insufficient this concept, based on male standards of equality, remains for most women throughout the world,
or that the United States has yet to ratify four UN human rights
treaties affecting the legal status of women worldwide.[39]

Democratization may be an inexorable trend (or end) of history, according to writers on both the left and the right, but they
usually do not stress that this "relentless progress" has always
been at either the expense or the neglect of women. Not surprisingly, the end of the Cold War has allowed more critics of U.S.
foreign policy to point out what has long been obvious: political
liberties necessary for free elections do not always result in civil
liberties, particularly in semiliterate, poverty-stricken nations lacking the basic prerequisites for democracy. The emergence of such
illiberal democratic nationalism after the end of the Cold War is
but one example of the return of patriarchy at the end of the
twentieth century, contrary to the claims of postmodern feminists
who either deny the existence of patriarchy in the past, or predict
that postmodern society has (or shortly will) eliminate all vestiges of patriarchy in the future. Only postmodernists, along with
mainstream global economists, can deny statistics documenting
that "capital markets have widened the gap between rich and
poor" worldwide in the last twenty years, including in the United
States, and promoted patriarchy from within the structure of multinational corporations down to the poorest families within nation-states – all the while praising family values, self-determination, and capitalism.[40] Even more sobering is the fact that during

Reality: Women and International Law, ed. Dorinda G. Dallmeyer, Studies in Transnational
Legal Policy, no. 25 (The American Society of International Law, 1993), 1–18.
39   Zakaria, "Democracies That Take Liberties," 15; idem, "The Rise of Illiberal Democ-
racy," *Foreign Affairs* 76 (November–December, 1997): 22–43. The four treaties are: The
Elimination of all Forms of Discrimination Against Women, the American Convention on
Human Rights, the International Covenant on Economic, Social and Cultural Rights, and the
International Convention on the Elimination of All Forms of Racial Discrimination.
40   Lawrence Osborne, "The Women Warriors," and Eyal Press, "The Free Trade Faith,"

the American Century the United States through the practice of independent internationalism has privileged both self-determination and capitalism over democracy, giving rise to the disturbing notion that capitalist growth, at least the latest version based on globalization, may be inimitable to democratic principles.

Disconnection between Capitalism and Democracy

There is about as much causal connection between democracy and free-market capitalism as there is between moon cycles and business cycles. "Neither history nor philosophy link[s] free markets and free men," according to John Ralston Saul. "They have nothing more to do with each other than the accidents of time and place." In fact, it can be historically documented that capitalism has usually taken off when there was less, not more, democracy in most Western countries.

One need only look at both England and the United States in the different centuries when these countries industrialized to realize that it was before universal suffrage, child labor laws, and health regulations existed. Likewise, capitalism began to thrive in the undemocratic times of Louis Philippe, and again under Emperor Napoleon III, Kaiser Wilhelm II, and Czar Nicholas II. Benjamin R. Barber has argued that in the last fifty years

market economies have shown a remarkable adaptability and have flourished in many tyrannical states from Chile to South Korea, from Panama to Singapore. . . . Capitalism requires consumers with access to markets and a stable political climate in order to succeed: such conditions may or may not be fostered by democracy, which can be disorderly and even

---

Lingua Franca 7 (December 1997/January 1998): 56, 39; William Finnegan, *Cold New World: Growing Up in a Harder Country* (New York, 1998); James K. Galbraith, *Created Unequal: The Crisis in American Pay* (New York, 1998). In the United States, for example, the "great American middle class is, by any measure, shrinking," with a smaller percentage of homeowners than in 1973, a 28 percent decline in entry-level wages in real dollars for male high school graduates, and a decline in wages and benefits for all unskilled labor (*New York Times*, 12 and 14 June 1998, and 19 July 1998). See also *New York Times*, 11 June 1998, for the negative impact of shrinking Asian economies on the educational and economic status of women.

anarchic, especially in its early stages, and which often pursues public goods costly to or at odds with private-market imperatives-environmentalism or full employment for example. On the level of the individual, capitalism seeks consumers susceptible to the shaping of their needs and the manipulation of their wants while democracy needs citizens autonomous in their thoughts and independent in their deliberative judgments. . . . [B]ut capitalism wishes to tame anarchic democracy and appears to have little problem tolerating tyranny as long as it secures stability."[41]

Most recently growth capitalism of the 1980s and 1990s, in the form of maximization of profits based on the service sector and financial speculation, has functioned best under deregulation with fewer democratic or environmental controls. One of the best recent examples is Algeria whose economy boomed between 1989 and 1997, while its "social and political history has all been downhill." Islamic fundamentalism emerged in 1988 to counter the corruption and mismanagement of twenty-five years of independence by the state's one and only party, the National Liberation Front (FLN). After the Islamic Salvation Front (FIS) was banned, elections canceled, and military rule openly established in 1992, violence spread and "secular writers, teachers, and other professionals have been assassinated. Women who refused to cover their heads have been harassed and some of them killed."[42] Most vestiges of democracy have disappeared, but until world oil prices crashed in 1997, Algeria's capitalist economy flourished because of forced privatization, debt rescheduling, and exacting foreign loans – emanating from the disciplined jurisdiction of the World Bank and IMF, and implemented by the military.

I stress the disconnection between capitalism and democracy because of the overexpectations currently being created by the United States and by other Western nations in Eastern Europe

41   John Ralston Saul, *Voltaire's Bastards: The Dictatorship of Reason in the West* (London: 1992), 359–61; Barber, *Jihad vs. McWorld*, 14–15 (quotation); Joan Hoff, "The City on the Hill: America's Role in the World," in *The Humanities and the Art of Public Discussion* (Washington, DC, 1991), 16–26.
42   *New York Review of Books*, 23 April 1998, 27–30 (quotation, 28); Martin Stone, *The Agony of Algeria* (New York, 1997).

and the former republics of the Soviet Union on the implicitly ideological assumption that capitalism guarantees democracy and that democracy is functioning well in postindustrial nations despite declining voter participation and shrinking middle classes. This presumed marriage of markets and democracy has been turned into the mantra of "democratic markets" by the Clinton administration and is rooted in the illusory idea promoted by the Democratic Leadership Council (and mainstream Republicans) that state governments and markets continue to serve one another in the post-Cold War world in the same ways they did before technology transformed economic globalism from rhetoric into a reality in the last twenty years. Beginning with the speech of Clinton's first national security adviser, Anthony Lake, at Johns Hopkins University in September 1993 and continuing with the president himself and all his other foreign policy advisers, there has been the persistent insistence that business contacts will inevitably lead to the liberalization of politics.[43] This conflation of democracy with free-trade capitalism may have rhetoric on its side, but not history.

Although many U.S. leaders in the 1940s and 1950s believed that economic nationalism had been a cause of World War II, their professed public faith in trade liberalization soon succumbed to maintaining Cold War alliances as the United States began to practice "unilateral free trade." This meant that the United States initially revived the postwar economies of Europe, Japan, Korea, Taiwan, Mexico, and Brazil, not by adhering to its proclaimed free-trade principles, but by privately accepting the protectionist policies of these nations, making "some big tariff cuts" without insisting on reciprocity, often at the expense of its own domestic industries – steel being the most obvious example. Privately, the Bureau of the Budget admitted that "[domestic] economic objectives . . . must be subordinated to our politico-security objectives," and Truman's assistant secretary of state for economic affairs said that "the great question is whether the country is

---

43   Barber, *Jihad vs. McWorld*, 14, 305 n. 22; Zakaria, "The Rise of Illiberal Democracy," 34.

willing to decide in the broader national self-interest to reduce tariffs and increase United States imports even though some domestic industry may suffer serious injury."[44]

Economic historians have noted that the result of weaning political allies from the postwar temptation of state socialism or even state capitalism marked the "deindustrializating [of] the United States" because decision makers were "prepared to allow discrimination against [American] exports to alleviate the strain of involvement in international trade for its allies." According to Stephen Krasner, the "United States used its power . . . to promote general political goals rather than specific economic interests. . . . It was prepared to allow discrimination against its own exports to alleviate the strain of involvement in international trade for its allies." Thus, postwar trade liberalization actually did not result in free-trade reciprocity. Instead, it benefitted U.S. trading partners more than the American domestic economy through the 1960s, as the nation became the prime consumer of the world's goods. Since then, expansionist commerce, based on the American model of products and consumption habits, has become the definition of economic growth for the rest of the world.[45]

Even without the Vietnam War the unwillingness of the United States to bring its international economic policies in line with the need of its domestic industries would have resulted in unemployment, inflation, balance-of-payments problems, and mounting trade deficits, although the latter was initially masked by lower defense budgets beginning with Nixon through the first two years of the Carter administration. Blinded by the presumed impera-

---

44   Zakaria, "Our Hollow Hegemony," 44; Melvyn P. Leffler, *Preponderance of Power: National Security, the Truman Administration, and the Cold War* (Stanford 1992), 317, quoting the Bureau of the Budget for 14 April 1950; Steve Dreyer, *Trade Warriors: STR and the American Crusade for Free Trade* (New York, 1995), 38; Alfred Eckes, "Trading American Interests," *Foreign Affairs* 71 (Fall 1992): 133–54.
45   Paul A. Tiffany, *The Decline of American Steel: How Management, Labor, and Government Went Wrong* (New York, 1988), 77 (quoting Eugene Grace of Bethlehem Steel); Stephen D. Krasner, "The Tokyo Round: Paticularistic Interests and Prospects for Stability in the Global Trading System," *International Studies Quarterly* 23 (December 1979): 494. See also Victoria and Gerard Curzon, "The Management of Trade Relations in the GATT," in *International Economic Relations of the Western World, 1959–1971*, ed. Andrew Shonfield (London, 1976), 1:200.

tives of the Cold War, the ideology of an affluent society, economic stimulus through tax cuts under the Kennedy and Johnson administrations, and the funding of both the Great Society and the war in Vietnam, however, U.S. foreign policy experts ignored the country's serious domestic industrial problems until the late 1960s. Consequently, the United States chalked up its first merchandise trade deficit in 1971 as efforts by the AFL and CIO failed to alter American trade and investment policies. As in the interwar years, the United Stated failed to balance its economic and political foreign policies.[46]

The prolonged Vietnam conflict finally forced the Nixon administration to abandon the Bretton Woods system established in 1944 to set up a stable postwar system of multilateral international payments based on fixed exchange rates, pegged to the gold-backed U.S. dollar. Faced with a gold drain, "rising prices, a weakened dollar, and chronic trade and payment imbalances," the United States in 1971, in one of its most blatantly unilateral acts, allowed the dollar "to float" on international markets to increase American market share abroad and to stop any more speculative pressures against the dollar by the country's Asian and European allies. This amounted to the deregulation of international currencies which ultimately led to deregulation of businesses within national boundaries. It also led to the creation of three rival regional trading blocs based on the yen, the mark, and the dollar, and to international exchange-rate instability and currency speculation. Most importantly, unstable, floating exchange rates did not automatically result in freer trade, lower inflation rates, and domestic prosperity as macroeconomic managers predicted for the remainder of the Cold War. Instead, the profligate military spending policies of both superpowers continued to divert "considerable capital from civilian investment – particularly in education, social services, public health, and infrastructure projects such as mass transportation; it also promoted inflation

46   Judith Goldstein, *Ideas, Interests, and American Trade Policy* (Ithaca, 1993), 163–68; Dreyer, *Trade Warriors*, 146; Robert Pastor, *Congress and the Politics of Foreign Economic Policies, 1929–1976* (Berkeley, 1980), 128–34; Susan Strange, *States and Markets* (New York, 1988), 45–78, 161–85.

(which the Soviets were better able to hide) and contributed to the deterioration of nonmilitary domestic industries, [to] lowered productivity, and ultimately . . . to the decline of public life in general."[47]

Global recessions triggered by rising oil prices in 1974 and again in 1978 only reinforced the American drive to macromanage the world economy through increasing its own imports while simultaneously trying to persuade its allies to stimulate their economies in order to buy more American-manufactured goods. Since the United States had not forced compliance with free trade on such nations when this might have been possible immediately following World War II, it had less leverage after their economies had recovered.

Largely unnoticed in the battle over trade policy was the fact that in dismantling the postwar international financial system, the United States had set in motion a "change in the relationship among nation, state and economy" primarily due to raging inflation at home and abroad. So began a shift away from state control and national economic management and thus away from democratic supervision of corporations in the West. Instead, "privatization, a market-driven approach to currency management, and dismantling of the welfare systems which had been erected in previous decades became the new orthodoxy," with the United Kingdom under Margaret Thatcher leading the way. Multinational corporations increasingly escaped national control as they became transnational (TNC). The name of the game became foreign direct investment (FDI) flows, which the United States dominated until the 1980s. By 1989 the European Union had caught up with American FDI flows and Japan was not far behind. Although this profound change in the function of the world economy affected primarily developed Western nations, it spread to Third World countries, forcing them to compete for investment and to adopt market-driven policies. The Soviet bloc's "autarkic industrializing process," which had never paid much attention to

---

47 Carole Fink, "1968: An International Perspective," Occasional Paper Series, Contemporary History Institute, Ohio University, May 1998, 8 (quotations); Joan Hoff, *Nixon Reconsidered* (New York, 1994), 140, 143–44.

foreign trade, except to obtain vital imports, found itself locked out of this world trade race. Finally, facing declining growth rates similar to those in the West, Mikhail Gorbachev was forced to launch the economic reform known as perestroika, and the rest, as they say, is history.[48]

The phrase "democratic markets" has become a euphemism in the 1990s for deregulation, privatization, and free trade. But when one considers that fifty-one of world's one hundred largest economies are corporations that are not organized along democratic lines, the connection between democratic nation-states and capitalism becomes even more tenuous. Instead of nations amassing economic power and becoming democratic, multinational corporations are engaging in massive mergers with the blessings of the very states whose power is declining and with it democratic supervision over decisions affecting the material condition of average citizens all over the world. While the reasons for this decline in nation-state power are complex, all are related to unregulated global capitalism made possible through advances in information technology. Greater economic interdependence has been developing for most of this century, but the 1990s mark the first time that international markets have actually begun to create a borderless world. This is because technology in the form of global communications networks has become the driving force behind the global economy. When capital transfers can exceed a trillion dollars per day, national exchange controls cannot be applied effectively.[49]

By the 1990s massive mobility of capital under this post-Bretton Woods system had replaced mercantilist concern over trade restrictions. Instead of being preoccupied with fending off populist or nationalist protectionist sentiment, more and more governments were becoming obsessed with encouraging investment and finance

---

48 Horsman and Marshall, *After the Nation-State*, 32–40; Daniel Yergin and Joseph Stanislaw, *The Commanding Heights: The Battle between Government and the Marketplace That Is Remaking the World* (New York, 1998).
49 Vincent Cable, "The Diminished Nation-State: A Study in the Loss of Economic Power," *Daedalus* 124 (Spring 1995): 23-54; Kaplan, "Was Democracy Just a Moment?" 71; Schacter, "Decline of the Nation State," 7–8n.2.

capital. To encourage such capital flow postindustrial nations have not only deregulated their domestic economies but also are now bringing pressure to bear on developing nations "to compete with each other by offering cheaper labor and lower health and environmental standards in order to attract private investors." For such countries, the competition for the ephemeral corporate favors "may be a race to the bottom." No wonder such debt-ridden countries are beginning to think about a moratorium on their debts. Instead of "gargantuan oligopolistic transnational corporations" competing with each other, the competition has devolved to poorer governments competing with each other to borrow money to repay loans needed to offer "the cheapest and most compliant labour; the weakest environmental, health, and safety standards; the lowest taxes; most fully developed infrastructure." This is primitive, global capitalism at its worst and, as noted above, perfectly in keeping with the brand of Ferengi democracy the United States is currently practicing and presumably promoting abroad.[50] Such disembodied globalization cannot help but undermine the functioning of democratic nation-states in the next century.

As transnational corporations take over the role of direct foreign investment formerly played by capital exporting nation-states and as profits accrue primarily from expanding foreign markets, the ties these corporations and the business class running them have to the economic or political goals of their governments of origin become problematic, except when companies need to be rescued by state intervention. It is not simply that TNCs withdraw from national constraints and from global civic responsibilities. Their CEOs and other "privileged information/communication workers increasingly withdraw public support from the larger society" by retreating to live only with other affluent transnational executives, investment bankers, financiers, lawyers, and media personalities in suburban enclaves with security guards.

50   Schacter, "Decline of the Nation-State," 9; Ohmae, *End of the Nation State*, vii-viii, 4–5; Jeffrey Goldberg, "The Crude Face of Global Capitalism," *The New York Times Magazine*, 4 October 1998, 51–56; George Soros, "The Capitalist Threat," *Atlantic Monthly* (February 1997): 45–58.

As of 1992, the most affluent eighth of the U.S. population lived in these guarded communities, which symbolize the increasing class chasm and fragmentation of U.S. society. So the elites within the most elite nations are setting their own pattern of affluent isolationism from not simply the poor but also from average middle-class workers, at home and abroad.[51] Thus, the gap between capitalism and democracy is not only reinforced, as is the disconnect between the permanent and provisional governments in the United States, discussed above.

Yet it is difficult to find Western government leaders at home or abroad who are willing publicly to admit to their citizens that the post-Cold War world they are overseeing requires an honest reassessment of what is happening to both democracy and capitalism at the end of the American Century. Hollow slogans and policies based on the uninhibited self-interest of the traditional "middleman" will not do. There is the distinct possibility that the pursuit of perpetual economic expansion based the illusion of permanently enhanced, low wage-productivity growth will inevitably undermine democratic principles.

The New Sovereignty

Who governs in a world driven by an anonymous, impersonal, globalized market? Enter the world of international lawyers who draft commercial business rules and regulations for arbitration of transnational economic disputes. A study of policymaking within the European Enterprise Group, the European Round Table of Industrialists, and the European Community Committee of the American Chamber of Commerce reveals that attorneys for transnational corporations have shaped the rules, institutions, and

---

51 Barber, *Jihad vs. McWorld*, 271; Robert Reich, *Work of Nations* (New York. 1991), chap. 23. Instead of a "melting pot," the United States has become a "salad," whose demographic ingredients mixed, but did not merge. The difference between a "melting pot" and a "salad" assumes postmodern overtones when it is remembered that "E pluribus unum" dates back to a recipe in an early poem by Virgil in which he said that the "ingredients do not merge; the union is simply the sum of its parts" ("Nation-State," *The Economist*, 5 September 1992, 23).

norms of the regulatory of framework of the European Union, constraining the autonomy of member states. Such legal arrangements reflect pure techno-economic power and private interests with little restraint by national politics or community values, thus rendering useless for all practical purposes the slogan of non-governmental groups advocating a political role for civil society: think globally; act locally. While there are a few radical economic alternatives to consumerist capitalism on the horizon, such as the Green movement, neo-fascism, and neo-progressive-mixed economy ideas, none will have had significant impact at the end of the American Century. At the moment, only international organized crime and their often accompanying terrorist activities are in a position to restrain or compete with technology-driven global market forces protected by their own legion of international lawyers.[52]

This transfer of state power to these legal and quasilegal global arrangements and technocrats is curious for three reasons. First, the most industrially advanced and presumably most democratic states seem destined to play a major role in diminishing their own sovereignty, witness the transnational legal regime known as the European Monetary Union on the eve of the issuance of the Euro.[53] Second, many of the anti-democratic forces currently undermining the nation-state are supported by supposedly liberal domestic groups and individuals inside Western countries such as: the minimal state seemingly required by a free market, communitarian anarchistic societies, identity politics based on parochial cultures, ethnicity, or religion, antimigration sentiments, and non-governmental associations that reach down to the local level and are indifferent to national boundaries. Third, the degree to which liberal capitalist internationalism pays even lip service to the will of the people puts it in opposition to the internal practices of

---

52   Maria Green Cowles, "The Politics of Big Business in the European Community: Setting the Agenda for a New Europe" (Ph.D. diss., The American University, 1994); Schacter "Decline of the Nation-State," 13–17; Guéhenno, *The END of the NATION STATE*, 133; Horsman and Marshall, *After the Nation-State*, 249–55.
53   Roger J. Goebel, "European Economic and Monetary Union: Will the EMU Ever Fly?" *Columbia Journal of European Law* 4 (Spring 1998): 250–320; Martin Feldstein, "EMU and International Conflict," *Foreign Affairs* 76 (November-December 1997): 60–73.

many traditional nation-states as the cautious and confused reaction of the United States, the UN, and NATO to the 1998 crisis in Kosovo so clearly demonstrated.[54]

Recently, a usually ignored aspect of liberal capitalist internationalism set in motion by Woodrow Wilson has reemerged, namely, the idea as expressed in Article 21 of the Universal Declaration of Human Rights: "The will of the people shall be the basis of authority of government." In legal terms this phrase has come to mean that the will of the people can only be expressed "through periodic and genuine elections by equal and universal suffrage."[55] Yet most recognized nations do not in practice meet this electoral standard or the related one that duly elected governments cannot be overthrown. And if the international community ever tried to systematically prevent or retaliate for the overthrow of democratically elected governments, such action would, ironically, also further weaken the traditional national sovereignty. This is not to say that the nation-state is on its way out anytime soon. It does mean, however, that all traditional nation-states will have to adjust to the combination of undemocratic forces set in motion by the techno-economic revolution and the resurgence of tribal nationalism currently under way in the wake of the end of the Cold War.

Thus, sovereignty cries out to be redefined, but to date mainly international lawyers, rather than government officials or political scientists or historians, have led the way. But can their commercial and technocratic legalese alone save the humanitarian features of democracy at the end of the American Century? All indications are that the more contractual society becomes, the more fragmented, atomized, and impersonal it becomes. Even the efforts of international lawyers in connection with war crimes tribunals and truth and reconciliation commissions, as important

---

54 Horsman and Marshall, *After the Nation-State*, ix–xx; Tamamoto, "Reflections on Japan's Postwar State," 15–21.

55 Schacter, "The Decline of the Nation-State," 19–20. The most recent controversial case occurred when the Security Council demanded the ouster of the military regime in Haiti in 1993. So many governments expressed reservations about this action that the council had to make clear this was a "unique and exceptional" case.

as they are, do not address the question of justice or sovereignty in relation to global economics.

Since the Cold War ended, few American leaders have reexamined traditional Wilsonian views of nation-state sovereignty based on self-determination or questioned the type of democracy and capitalism the country is espousing for the rest of the world. Self-determination remains bogged down in a traditional corpus of international legal rules stressing anti-colonialism, forbidding foreign occupation, and requiring very vague consultation with the aspirations and rights of minorities within newly established national borders. Unlike American espousal of self-determination in the nineteenth century, which often took place in the name of "freedom," in the twentieth century American self-determination has championed "independence" from colonization, and since 1989 from Communist- or lingering colonial-imposed multicultural national unity. The difference with respect to these three types of self-determination is one of kind and not simply degree. The last type represented in the breakup of the USSR and Czechoslovakia and Yugoslavia took place not exclusively out of some abstract passion for freedom, or social justice, or civic virtues, but in the name of ethnic or religious nationalism accompanied by ravenous consumer demand for pornographic magazines and videos, American pop music, fast foods, and Western designer clothes and cosmetics. If one judges by initial exports to these newly emerging nations, works on the social contract, civil society, and rights of minorities were not high on the list.[56]

Since it is likely that many of the rash post-Cold War experiments in establishing nation states of questionable economic viability on the basis of nationalist and ethnic or religious fervor will fail to make the transition to either capitalism or democracy, there is the distinct possibility that the New World Order will be characterized by numerous failed or disintegral nation states not anticipated by Western nations when they first celebrated the death

---

56   Guéhenno, *The END of the NATION STATE*, 1–3; Antonio Casese, "Self-Determination of Peoples and the recent Break-Up of USSR and Yugoslavia," and Rein Mullerson, "Self-Determination of Peoples and the Dissolution of the USSR," both in *Essays in Honor of Wang Tieya*, ed. Ronald St. John MacDonald (Dordrecht, The Netherlands, 1994), 131–44, 567–86; Barber, *Jihad vs. McWorld*, 303n.6.

of communism. If this proves to be the case, then it will necessitate giving more serious consideration to what Ronald Reagan's secretary of state, George Shultz, has called "the new sovereignty" on the part of the United States rather than more military planning, on the "Invincible Force" doctrine that has led many Americans to believe that surgical bombing will prevent soldiers from being committed and dying on the ground. This inane idea gained such political favor at home following the Gulf War that it is continuing to dominate military planning under Clinton.

Under Shultz's new sovereignty, post Cold War world "responsible powers" would have to make multinational and long-term military decisions about when to violate previously impenetrable sovereignty on the part of "irresponsible powers" that violate human rights within their borders. In 1991 the Bush administration attempted to push the idea of new sovereignty even further when it recognized six former Soviet nations as states but refused to establish diplomatic ties with them until "we are satisfied they have made commitments to responsible security policies and democratic principles." Subsequently, Secretary of State James Baker submitted criteria for obtaining diplomatic recognition, including strong pro-democratic, pro-human rights, and anti-internal violence causes. The European Union accepted these criteria at an extraordinary European Political Council meeting on 16 December 1991 in a joint declaration titled "Guidelines on the Recognition of New States in Eastern Europe in the Soviet Union."[57] But the Clinton administration has not seen fit to implement or improve upon these attempts by its Republican predecessor to redefine sovereignty and humanitarian military commitments in the post-Cold War world.

It is not that time has run out for redefining sovereignty along the lines of humanitarian considerations or to reassess the current inhuman practices of primitive global capitalism. But the need to do so is urgent because globalization is creating the very condi-

---

57 Testimony of Ralph Johnson, deputy assistant secretary of state for European and Canadian affairs, 17 October 1991, *Foreign Policy Bulletin* 2 (November–December 1991): 39, 42 (quotation); John Mattras and Marjorie Lightman, "Clinton's Second Term: Making Women's Rights a Foreign Policy Issue," *Presidential Studies Quarterly* 27 (Winter 1997): 122–26.

tions that could foment anarchistic resistance to a world based on the grand Wilsonian design for the American Century. Ironically, the United States finds itself promoting democracy as never before even though it is practicing it less at home and honoring it only selectively abroad. When pushed on this issue, as with China, the country's leaders continue to privilege economics over human rights, but not when it comes to Cuba or North Korea. It may well be that the American Century will ultimately be judged as the one in which the United States contributed as much to the decline of democracy as to its preservation through its independently internationalist pursuit of self-determination and capitalism for itself and others.

The world has not seen such territorial and demographic changes since the Napoleonic era. While the bloodless fall of communism has not turned the universe as upside down as much as conventional wisdom would have us believe, the New World Order is looking "increasingly disordered and dangerous-not only for liberal capitalism (the putative 'winner' of the Cold War) but for democracy too." It is not that democracy, any more than Christianity before it, will make the "world peaceful, or in practice, more moral but only more complex." It is just this complexity that the United States must confront. Citizenship rights may have to be defined in terms of global legal personalities rather than by traditional national standards; sovereignty for nation-states will also have be redefined at the end of the American Century. Instead of more New World Order rhetoric about the glories of free-market capitalism, inconsistent economic sanctions and military interventions, and cheap misleading privatization solutions to expensive problems such as stabilizing the Russian economy, the United States has to realize that the volatility of electronic capital transfers has put unregulated global free trade on the defensive. Innovative ideas for new governance of the world economy are in the air everywhere except in Washington, ranging from taxing currency speculation to establishing another United Nations Security Council to monitor world economic affairs. On- and off-again economic sanctions and air power strikes are no substitute for abandoning the righteous Wilsonianism of the American Century and thinking hard about new ways for the United States to share the world's responsibilities and privileges of global leadership.[58]

Global citizenship that includes human rights for women as well as men, authentic, instead of opportunistic, consistent cooperation with a strengthened United Nations, assuming unequivocal leadership, not of an expanded NATO, but of a concert of regional powers, and genuine reform of American democracy at home are a few of the strategies the United States could adopt. Its role as a future world leader must be tempered by the recognition that it is leaving behind a short American Century bounded forever by events set in motion by tragedies in Sarajevo. The success of its role as a humble hegemon in the next century will be determined in large measure by how gracefully and equitably it can preside over the impermanence of its current preeminence.

---

58   John Mueller, "Quiet Cataclysm: Some Afterthoughts about World War III," *Diplomatic History* 16 (1992): 66; Horsman and Marshall, *After the Nation-State*, 40; Kaplan, "Was Democracy Just a Moment?" 55; Zakaria, "Our Hollow Hegemony," 80; "Redrawing the Free Market," *New York Times*, 14 November 1998.

7

East Asia in Henry Luce's "American Century"

MICHAEL H. HUNT

Though most often remembered as a catch phrase, "The American Century" stands as one of the purest distillations of that twentieth-century vision of the world transformed in the American image. The notion of an American Century articulated by Henry Robinson Luce in a February 1941 *Life* editorial offers an inviting point of departure to reflect on a turbulent century of U.S. engagement in East Asia and to sketch some of the defining features of U.S.-East Asian relations over the past century. This essay begins with a brief treatment of the ideological impulse that shaped Luce's – and arguably the dominant American – approach to the region. It continues by tracing the travails that his crusade encountered there and by identifying the main sources of those travails. It concludes by suggesting alternatives to Luce as the prophet of the American project in Asia.

The Luce vision

When Luce addressed his countrymen in 1941, he did so as a therapist disturbed by national malaise. He found them "unhappy," "nervous," "gloomy," and "apathetic." To calm their "foreboding" about the future, he prescribed emulation of the moral certitude and commitment displayed by the British. Their decision to stand up to Hitler, Luce announced, had banished national "nervousness" and even "all the neuroses of modern life."

Luce traced his own country's malaise back to the rejection of the internationalist path on which Woodrow Wilson had embarked in 1919. To redeem the resulting isolationist errors of the interwar years and escape their current emotional slough, Americans had only to assert themselves self-confidently in world affairs. Struggle would bring peace to the troubled heart.[1]

Luce was eager to give a push to a president edging perceptibly toward deeper involvement in the global conflict and to a public that still hesitated on the brink of war with Germany, and so he laid down as the most immediate national challenge stopping Germany. But Luce was already looking ahead to the even greater, long-term task of harnessing American policy to "the triumphal purpose of freedom." This was an enterprise attended, Luce conceded, by "stupendous difficulties and dangers." But "as the most powerful and vital nation in the world," the United States had an obligation to advance freedom through "a sharing with all peoples of our Bill of Rights, our Declaration of Independence, our Constitution, our magnificent industrial products, our technical skills." A failure to rise to the challenge of greatness would put the United States at risk, Luce warned. "This nation cannot truly endure unless there courses through its veins from Maine to California the blood of purposes and enterprise and high resolve." On the other hand, by playing their proper role in the world, Americans could not only save their collective soul but also make an epochal contribution to human redemption. Now shifting into the voice of the preacher, he identified that contribution as nothing less than "lifting the Life of mankind from the level of the beasts to what the Psalmists called a little lower than the angels."

Thanks to Miles Fletcher and Lawrence Kessler, for their critical comments on a draft of this essay and to Christopher Endy for his research assistance.

1   The quotes that appear in this and the following paragraph come from Henry Luce, "The American Century," in this volume. *Life* then had a weekly circulation around three million. Time Inc. added to Luce's national audience by distributing free reprints and placing advertisements in the *New York Times*. Republication quickly followed in the *Readers Digest* and the *Washington Post*. Robert E. Herzstein, *Henry R. Luce: A Political Portrait of the Man Who Created the American Century* (New York, 1994), 180. My understanding of Luce rests primarily on the Herzstein biography, which runs only to the mid-1940s, and on W. A. Swanberg's spirited, sharply critical full-scale study *Luce and His Empire* (New York, 1972).

While Luce's call for Americans doing some heavy lifting around the world had nothing sustained to say about East Asia or for that matter any other region, the 1941 essay left no doubt that the world was "fundamentally indivisible." Freedom, peace, and justice would not prosper in one place unless they prevailed in most places. An activist foreign policy would thus have to advance on a broad front – in Asia no less than in Europe – with equal urgency. This sweeping globalism was sustained by two fundamental truths to which Luce clung throughout his public career. One was the simple belief that "we live in a moral universe." The other, closely related to the first and far reaching in its practical implications, was that "the laws of this country and of any country are invalid and will be in fact inoperative except as they conform to a moral order which is universal in time and space."[2] Confident in his knowledge of that divinely sanctioned order, Luce was, not surprisingly, insistent that Americans act decisively in accord with its dictates. "A nation that is formed out of a belief in liberty under law – for others as well as for itself – need not be timorous about asserting its Authority. It need not be laggard in backing its Authority, as necessary, with power."[3]

The accident of birth had done much to shape Luce's thinking on the American Century while also assuring East Asia a prominent place in his conception of it. "Harry" had been born in 1898, the first child of a Presbyterian missionary couple just arrived in Shandong. His father, Henry Winters Luce, had reached China in 1897 after training at Yale and Princeton and marriage to Elizabeth Middleton Root, the daughter of a Utica, New York, lawyer. In 1900, with attacks against missionaries turning deadly, the Luce family (including the two-year-old Harry) fled to the safety of a U.S. navy vessel and then to Korea. They returned behind American and other foreign troops sent to restore order and punish Chinese wrongdoing. Calmer, more productive times for missionaries followed with the senior Luce playing a leading role in promoting Christian education. His gifts as a fundraiser

2   Quotes from Luce speech in Dallas, 19 April 1951, in Swanberg, *Luce*, 307–08.
3   Luce speech before the New York University Club, 28 January 1961, quoted in Swanberg, *Luce*, 418.

helped sustain American schools, most notably Yenching University in Beijing. These were golden years for the missionary educational enterprise while also promising a much-expanded American role in Chinese affairs through the Open Door policy.

The scene unfolding before Harry Luce of Americans, not least his father, taking a prominent place in China's education and defense nourished patriotic and humanitarian impulses that would shape Luce's career in a striking variety of ways. (That these initiatives were entangled with the unequal treaty system, the bane of Chinese nationalists, seems never to have dawned on the younger Luce.) Out of Luce's special experience came an impulse to sermonize (already evident in childhood) and a commitment to service that would take secular form. As a publisher, he would think of himself as an preacher-educator, imparting to his readers information but, even more important, moral direction. It left him with a deep and abiding conviction that China was a fit, indeed prime target for American uplift. The Chinese hungered for what the United States had to offer—whether models of political and economic development, religious faith, or diplomatic and military support – and Americans had a categorical obligation to satisfy that hunger.

Finally, out of the China missionary milieu came a paradoxical personality. The boy who became the hard-driving, chain-smoking media mogul was intellectually intense, emotionally introspective, and obsessively curious about the world around him. Yet his intellectual and emotional equipment somehow locked him into an ethnocentric, self-righteous, almost cartoonish conception of China. Luce would come to regard himself as a China expert by virtue of his having grown up there and made return visits in 1932, 1941, and 1945. But in fact his childhood was spent in physical isolation from Chinese – in a walled-off mission compound that afforded regular contact only with household servants. His visits were hurried affairs during which Luce largely limited himself to the company of political luminaries and carefully kept inconvenient details about China as it was from clouding or confusing his strong vision of what he wanted China to become. He appears to have known little about the very people with whom he would come to closely identify, and he would never learn the language of the country for which he claimed to speak. Unfortunately for Americans and Asians alike, the resulting simple, superficial conception of China would prove impervious to challenge by those far better informed, and it would carry over to shape Luce's general approach to Cold War Asia.

Travails of a vision, 1898–1998

Had Luce in 1941 been able to set aside his morally charged, highly selective sense of the past and look back at the U.S. conquest of the Philippines at the outset of that century, he would have at least been forewarned of the travails that his vision for an American Century in Asia would suffer. The dreams of American ascendance and freedom's advance proclaimed by President William McKinley in late 1898 and early 1899 as he moved to take the Philippines nicely anticipated what Luce also would want in Asia. McKinley told Americans that they were launched on "a holy cause" to advance "the banner of liberty" across the Pacific, that they fought in the name "of liberty and law, of peace and progress," and that they should adopt a policy of "benevolent assimilation" so that that Filipinos "shall for ages hence bless the American republic because it emancipated and redeemed their fatherland, and set them in the pathway of the world's best civilization."[4] These high ideals did not, however, ensure success in the Philippines any more than they would later in Luce's Asia.

The occupation project quickly went bad as American claims to control in early 1899 provoked organized military resistance. Not to be thwarted, the U.S. Army embarked on a campaign of pacification. It led to atrocities, made easier by the dehumanizing language of "nigger" and "goo-goo" quickly adopted by troops frustrated by a stealthy foe who operated with civilian support over familiar home terrain. This unexpected resistance raised the costs of empire. Washington had to commit 70,000 troops to the

---

4 McKinley quotes from Lewis L. Gould, *The Spanish-American War and President McKinley* (Lawrence, 1982), 104, 111, 119.

islands at the height of the war and ultimately pay out $600 million. Of the 126,500 Americans who saw service there, 4,234 soldiers would die (perhaps the highest ratio for any U.S. war). Filipinos paid a higher price. The killed in action came to at least 20,000. More striking, war-related famine and disease produced among the general population between 1899 and 1903 deaths over normal mortality of 775,000 (out of a population of about 7.5 million in 1900). In other words, about a tenth of the archipelago's population perished in the name of benevolent assimilation.[5]

The brutality of pacification, combined with charges that Americans were betraying their own ideals, began to erode support at home and resulted in a basic redirection of the American colonial project. A diverse coalition of critics – Southern Democrats, fiscal conservatives, hide-bound defenders of simple republican government, and women's organizations – attacked the McKinley administration and forced expansionists to scale back their goals. American proconsuls in the Philippines struck a compromise with regional elites themselves unhappy with the immediate costs and doubtful about the long-term viability of resistance. To secure immediate acceptance of American control, the occupiers had to promise well-to-do, landed Filipino leaders ultimate independence for their country and an increasing role in governance for those leaders. Able at last to turn to uplift, the U.S. colonial administration left a record that fell far short of the initial U.S. commitment to making the islands a flourishing example of free men and free markets. American tutors failed to develop the economy, upgrade basic education, or democratize the political system in preparation for independence. As benevolent assimilation turned into benevolent neglect, a peculiarly Filipino model of economic and political development ("cacique democracy") took hold, marked by economic stagnation and one of the widest gaps between the privileged and the poor anywhere in the world. Even as Luce's notions of an American Century gained currency in the

---

5 The new, higher estimate of overall mortality emerges from Ken De Bevoise, *Agents of Apocalypse: Epidemic Disease in the Colonial Philippines* (Princeton, 1995).

1940s and 1950s, Washington made no effort to resuscitate the old liberal project for the islands. Cold War concerns with securing military bases there reinforced long-standing accommodation of the Filipino elite to perpetuate the pattern of neglect.[6]

A man oblivious to what events in the Philippines said about the obstacles to freedom's advance was even less open to doubts when in his late thirties and early forties he himself first stepped forward as an advocate of an active East Asian policy. Luce had left China in 1912 to occupy himself first with his education – a year in Britain followed by Hotchkiss, then Yale, then back to Britain for a year at Oxford. In 1922 he embarked full time on creating the innovative *Time* magazine. Only in the early 1930s, his fortunes made, did he begin to look back to China, forced to focus by the specter of Japanese aggression. That the country of his birth came to serve as the touchstone of his thinking about the region made him almost constitutionally incapable of grasping limits of the sort first suggested by the Philippines.

Luce, who generally imagined great men in control of the world's destiny, turned Chiang Kai-shek, leader of the Nationalist party and head of the Nanjing government, into the embodiment of his hopes for the rise of a liberal, American-oriented China. Chiang first figured as the strongman indispensable to stopping Japan. That he had an attractive, American-trained wife (Soong Meiling) whose family had converted him to Christianity added to his appeal. Luce's infatuation with his "Generalissimo" can be traced through the famous string of *Time* covers devoted to the Chinese leader. The first three – in 1927, 1931, and 1933 – treated Chiang cautiously. Signs of enthusiasm were apparent in the fourth cover story in 1936 followed by an even more appreciative treatment in January 1938 when the Chiangs graced the front of *Time* as the

---

6 See Benedict Anderson's deft development of "Cacique Democracy in the Philippines: Origins and Dreams," in *Discrepant Histories: Translocal Essays on Filipino Culture*, ed. Vicente L. Rafael (Philadelphia, 1995), 3–47; Alfred W. McCoy, ed., *An Anarchy of Families: State and Family in the Philippines* (Madison, 1993), esp. McCoy's introductory essay; John T. Sidel, "Philippine Politics in Town, District, and Province: Bossism in Cavite and Cebu," *Journal of Asian Studies* 56 (November 1997): 947–66, ostensibly a challenge to conventional wisdom that manages in fact to sound variations on a familiar theme; and Nick Cullather, *Illusions of Influence: The Political Economy of the United States-Philippines Relations, 1942–1960* (Stanford, 1994).

man and woman of the year. The apotheosis came in 1942 when Chiang got his seventh cover story and Luce personally proclaimed him "the greatest soldier in Asia, the greatest statesman in Asia, America's best friend."[7] Time Inc.'s media outlets – its magazines, films, and radio programs – dutifully retailed Luce's conception of a China advancing under Chiang's leadership and American patronage, while the powerful publisher turned his personal hand as organizer, lobbyist, and pundit to ensuring that China got the generous humanitarian, economic, and military aid that he thought it deserved.

Throughout the Pacific War Luce's hero-worship led him to exaggerate any successes scored by Chiang and to shift the blame for any of his shortcomings to the dire conditions facing China or the inadequacy of U.S. support. Critics of Luce's fairy-tale view of China, no matter how well informed, ran up against the bodyguard of protecting rationalizations. Luce seemed to listen attentively to the doubts expressed by his own reporters – none more carefully than Theodore White. Just out of Harvard, he had become *Time*'s wartime China correspondent. But when White and other bright young recruits threatened the simple certitudes of the American Century, Luce dismissed them as missing the big picture and overlooking the simple, fundamental fact that the American Century carried obligations, foremost to set matters right in China. So even though White sent back reports that Chiang was a dictator, militarily ineffectual, in deepening political trouble, and surrounded by corruption, the idealized Chinese leader lived on between the pages of Luce publications. White found other, more reliable outlets for his views, and a once close relationship with Luce turned to estrangement.

In the 1930s, as Luce focused on the fate of the Pacific, he gave Japan only peripheral attention. Tokyo's villainy required little study. Like most other Americans, Luce underestimated Japan's political determination to pursue an imperial course or the military skill it would bring to bear on that enterprise. Instead, Luce

---

7   Luce quoted in T. Christopher Jesperson, *American Images of China, 1931–1949* (Stanford, 1996), 37.

assumed that a weaker Japan would recognize superior American strength and retreat in the face of American resolve. Luce had good company in thinking that a show of U.S. economic muscle alone might force the Japanese into line. Pearl Harbor and the sudden surge of Japanese forces across the western Pacific came as a stunning surprise. But what followed gave credence to his idea that the American Century was indeed taking hold in Asia. After American forces battered Japan into submission in 1945, the occupation that they initiated seemed to follow the Luce script. Guided by a sense of righteousness and a determination to cleanse Japan of its past sins, the occupation set that reformed country on a fresh path. Japan would now march alongside China, buoyed by its wartime triumph, toward a liberal future, and East Asia would assume a proud place of prominence in the unfolding American Century.

In 1944, with victory in the global war all but assured, Luce began scanning for some new external threat that would give urgency to the pursuit of the global American project. During his college years he had watched the Kaiser's Germany and then the Red Scare of 1919–20 galvanize Americans (himself included). Communism remained a Luce bugaboo, made more acute by a visit he paid to the Soviet Union in 1932. By 1939 Hitler's Germany had combined with Japan to overshadow the Bolshevik menace. With the defeat of those two most recent foes of freedom in sight, Luce returned his suspicious gaze to the Soviet Union. Moscow's territorial ambitions alarmed him, but even more dangerous was the challenge its militant faith posed to free peoples and institutions. *Time*'s foreign news editor, Whittaker Chambers, reinforced Luce's own revived anti-Communist animus. A disillusioned Communist, Chambers turned on his old faith with an intensity only an apostate can muster. Luce was also influenced by the right-wing opinions of his outspoken, politically active wife, Claire Booth Luce. His sharpening suspicion of the Soviets made him an influential harbinger of the Cold War. And those concerns, combining with his dreams of an American-influenced China, led him into a loose association of pro-Chiang advocates (dubbed the China Lobby) who were convinced that the looming Communist threat would make Asia a battlefront every bit as important as Europe.

In the fluid period immediately following the end of the war, Luce continued his energetic support of Chiang Kai-shek as an anti-Communist bulwark. When Chiang proved as ineffectual against the Chinese Communists as he had been against the Japanese, Luce once more called for a redoubling of American support in the name of preserving a friendly, democratic, Christian China. U.S. policymakers shared Luce's alarm but refused to jump China ahead of Europe on the strategic priority list at a time of sharply limited resources to contain the Communist menace. Dismayed by the misuse of several billion dollars in aid lavished earlier on Chiang's government, they resisted entreaties by Luce and others for a major, last-minute salvage effort. *Life* damned this defeatist policy. The magazine's severe editorial judgment handed down in April 1948 was that "American behavior in and toward China has been the most completely disastrous failure of U.S. foreign policy since the war."[8] A strongly partisan Republican, Luce readily blamed Democrats for depriving Chiang essential aid and prayed for Harry Truman's defeat in the November election. In December, with Truman reelected and with Chiang in retreat before Mao Zedong's Communist forces, Luce put his favorite strongman on *Time*'s cover for the eighth time. The tag for the accompanying story read, "Asia's howitzers could now be heard in Kansas City."[9] The reverberations from a collapsing China would carry – or at least so Luce hoped – all the way to the American heartland and awaken the country from its slumber.

China's Communists now loomed as the prime regional threat magnified by their ties to an expansionist Soviet Union. Their battlefield successes acutely posed the sort of "stupendous difficulties and dangers" that Luce had anticipated for American crusaders in 1941. The fall of China to those Communists in 1949

8 *Life*, 5 April 1948, quoted in Patricia Neils, *China Images in the Life and Times of Henry Luce* (Savage, MD, 1990), 203.
9 Jesperson, *American Images*, 164.

while the U.S. government looked on impassively constituted the most blatant, shocking denial imaginable of Luce's dreams of Americanization in the land of his birth. *Life* pronounced the outcome "a victory for the Soviet Union and a moral disaster for the U.S."[10] Luce would now help turn this betrayal into a prime article of indictment against Democratic appeasement.

The Korean War, the fourth American conflict in Asia during Luce's lifetime, did nothing to redeem China's loss or assuage his frustration. President Truman acted promptly in June 1950 to stop the North Korean invasion of the south and then allowed General Douglas MacArthur's forces to advance the frontiers of freedom all the way to the Chinese border. Luce was pleased. When Mao responded by sending his troops across the Yalu River into battle against the Americans, Luce turned militant. In early January 1951, with American forces still struggling to regain their footing, a *Life* editorial accused Mao's China of wanting "to seize and dominate all Asia" and called on Americans "to acknowledge the existence of war with Red China and to set about its defeat, in full awareness that this course will probably involve war with the Soviet Union as well."[11] The recommendation with its apocalyptic overtones reflected Luce's impatience with Cold War obstacles to the advance of his century. But rather than a groundswell of support for taking the offensive, he got instead public disaffection with the Korean commitment and a refusal by the Truman administration to take another military gamble on the peninsula. The Korean War would remain limited; Truman would fire MacArthur (to Luce's immense regret) to keep it that way; and the war would end in mid-1953 with Mao's forces bloodied but still standing along the thirty-eighth parallel where the fighting had begun. The accumulated costs were high. Nearly 34,000 Americans had died and another 100,000 had been wounded. The Chinese had suffered at least 360,000 killed or wounded. Some 3 to 4 million Koreans had fallen victim to fighting that had ravaged the peninsula.

---

10 *Life*, in March 1949, quoted in Neils, *China Images*, 250.
11 *Life*, 8 January 1951, quoted in Swanberg, *Luce*, 309.

Against the backdrop of this pair of setbacks – outright defeat in China and then a costly, mismanaged standoff in Korea – Luce joined the chorus calling for a resolute stand elsewhere in East Asia. Chiang Kai-shek, who got his tenth and last *Time* cover story in April 1955, was still accorded full honors for keeping China's aspirations for freedom alive on Taiwan. Like Chiang, Luce still imagined Nationalist forces making a triumphant return someday to the mainland (though it became harder and harder for either of them to sustain this fantasy). But Chiang now had to make room for new heroes – Syngman Rhee, Ngo Dinh Diem, and Ramon Magsaysay – in the Luce pantheon of great Asian leaders. In each case their installation was announced by a *Time* cover story. And once installed, these additional deputies of the American Century remained, like Chiang, firm fixtures in Luce's plans to save and then remake Asia.

No position along the redrawn and now reinforced containment line proved more important to Luce than Vietnam. He paid that country several of his patented rush tours conducted in VIP fashion and yielding simple, crystal-clear solutions to intractable local problems. Already in 1950 *Life* had put up a wanted poster for "Ho Chi Minh's gangsters" and argued that the heavy-handed power grab by this disreputable group justified American support for the opposing French forces and for France's hand-picked ruler, the "respected" Bao Dai. If Indochina fell, the magazine warned in terms that would become cliché in U.S. policy discourse, then so too would Burma, Thailand, and Indonesia, and that in turn would expose India to Communist penetration.[12] The French and Bao Dai did no better than Chiang at holding the line, and so in 1954, with the Eisenhower administration constructing a new line of defense in South Vietnam, Luce searched for another anti-Communist standard bearer. Diem seemed to fit the bill. His visage first graced the front of *Time* in April 1955. The accompanying story presented him as "a resilient, deeply religious Vietnamese nationalist," who had shown that he could lead the people of South Vietnam "from the brink of Communism into their long-

---

12   *Life*, 28 August 1950, quoted in Swanberg, *Luce*, 310.

sought state of sovereign independence." A Diem visit to the United States in May 1957 evoked another *Time* celebration of the "proud, doughty little Ngo Dinh Diem" and the "peace and stability" that he had brought to his country.[13]

Luce's investment in Vietnam created predictable problems with his reporters. He called *Life*'s Douglas Duncan on the carpet in 1953 for his "defeatist" photo essay on the French war effort. Later, frustration with Luce's editorial policy drove his chief correspondent in Southeast Asia, Stanley Karnow, to resign in favor of a job with the competition. When Diem began to lose his luster in the early 1960s among American observers, Luce denied that his hero might have serious faults and was soon on a collision course with Karnow's successors. They insisted that Diem's war for the countryside was failing and that Diem's urban power base was dissolving. Time-Life headquarters in New York either ignored these negative appraisals or slapped down their authors if they became too insistent. In September 1963 Luce lent his backing to one of these attempts to put reporters in their place – a public salvo by *Time*'s managing editor, the conservative Otto Fuerbringer, against the Saigon press corps. He charged that the reporters' closed community acted as an echo chamber for pessimism and that their naiveté made them an easy mark for wily Buddhist activists determined to bring Diem down. The *Time* staffers in Saigon, Charles Mohr and Merton Perry, resigned in protest.[14]

Luce stood his ground even as troubles swept Saigon. Diem, who had proven tentative and testy earlier in his dealings with occupying French and Japanese authorities, stayed true to form in his dealings with the increasingly assertive Americans. With the war in trouble and frictions with Diem mounting, President John Kennedy gave muffled approval for a coup. The generals who took charge in Saigon after assassinating Diem had learned

13　*Time* comments on Diem from Clarence R. Wyatt, *Paper Soldiers: The American Press and the Vietnam War* (New York, 1993), 64, 65.
14　Swanberg, *Luce*, 348–50, 439–41; Wyatt, *Paper Soldiers*, 121–22. *Time*'s difficulties with its Vietnam reporters outlived Luce to judge from Robert Sam Anson, *War News: A Young Reporter in Indochina* (New York, 1989), 39–40, 68–73.

the art and rewards of collaboration under the French and had no difficulty taking American direction. When they proved both politically and militarily inept, Luce drew the predictable conclusion: the South Vietnamese, like other embattled Asians, needed a strong show of American support if freedom were to survive and ultimately prosper in their land. The greater the problems facing local leaders, he reasoned, the greater the American obligation to help. When help in this case finally assumed the form of U.S. combat forces in 1965, *Time* cheered with a cover proclaiming "The Turning Point in Vietnam." The arrival of American troops and equipment conveyed a welcome message of resolve. The embattled country now throbbed, so the magazine told its readers with forced optimism, "with a pride and a power, above all an esprit," and Saigon showed signs of gaining "a spring in the step and a sparkle in the eye missing for years."[15] What generous American economic and military aid and American military advisers (up to sixteen thousand by the end of the Kennedy presidency) could not achieve, then surely a large American combat presence would.

By the time of his death Luce had good grounds to suspect that this limited Cold War conflict in Asia would develop along lines no better than the previous one in Korea. Once more, Washington would not wage all-out war. Defense of Europe still had top priority, and in any case an expanded conflict carried the risk of bringing the Chinese in and provoking nuclear confrontation with the Soviets. Once more both Congress and the public, after accepting a unilateral presidential decision to fight, began to tire. As in Korea, three years of inconclusive combat were enough to undercut support for the president and wound his party electorally. But unlike Korea, Vietnam dragged on beyond that third year (1968), further deepening public disaffection and divisions. The Luce of 1941 had prescribed foreign crusading to raise national morale. Vietnam was dramatically confirming what Korea and the Philippines had already suggested – that foreign activism might instead spawn bitter domestic recrimination.

15 Swanberg, *Luce*, 460.

The Vietnam War concluded with a defeat of Luce's ideals as dramatic and complete as the American Century would witness. As in Korea, the people whom the Americans sought to protect suffered most dearly. An estimated 1.4 million Vietnamese – civilians as well as combatants on one side or the other – died during the U.S. combat phase of the war (1965 through 1972), and another 300,000 fell before the war finally ended in April 1975. Those numbers only begin to suggest the devastation done to the people of Indochina and their lands. But Americans had paid as well – some 58,000 dead, a price tag conservatively estimated at $141 billion, and an enduring sense of national dishonor and shame.

Even before the Vietnam drama had fully played out, President Richard Nixon began to redirect American Asian policy in ways at odds with the fundamentals of the American Century. A man who had earlier joined Luce in capitalizing on Democratic appeasement in China and Korea and in taking a stand on Vietnam had by the time of his resignation in 1974 grounded U.S. policy on an acceptance of regional diversity and diminished U.S. responsibility.[16]

Extrication from the war in Vietnam served as Nixon's point of departure. When he entered the White House in 1969, Nixon was ready to cut his losses. He pressed relentlessly forward on Vietnamization – shifting responsibility for the fighting back to the South Vietnamese military where it had been before 1965. He continued generous aid, and added for good measure fresh blows at the enemy delivered by American bombers all across Indochina and by American and South Vietnamese units marching into the enemy's Cambodian and Laotian sanctuaries. But the war was ultimately for the South Vietnamese to win or lose. Nixon's retreat to a secondary role in Vietnam was accompanied by a lowering of expectations about U.S. regional commitments.

16 Crediting Nixon with foreign policy achievements, whether in Asia or elsewhere, remains distinctly distasteful to some, most recently William Bundy in *A Tangled Web: The Making of Foreign Policy in the Nixon Presidency* (New York, 1998). A compelling assessment awaits the opening of official and personal papers not just in the United States but abroad as well.

What came to be known as the Nixon Doctrine placed on Asian rather than American boys the primary burden of defending non-Communist regimes, backed by preexisting U.S. defense arrangements, notably for South Korea, Taiwan, and Japan. This decision to step away from the frontline was consistent with the experience of a president who had twice in his political career seen the electorate make clear its distaste for seeing Americans killed on the Asian mainland.

An accommodation with Mao's China, consummated in the course of 1971 and 1972, emerged as the centerpiece of the new approach to Asia. It finally brought the United States to terms with China's revolution. The proponents of diplomatic recognition had become more vocal during the 1960s, and Nixon himself had gingerly endorsed that position in public in 1967 and then after his 1968 election translated talk of contact into a working policy. He hoped his China initiative would create a new relationship helpful in bringing Moscow to heel in arms control talks and extracting from Hanoi concessions in the peace talks. But behind the opening were also long-term considerations quite contrary to those that had guided Luce. Nixon had concluded that the United States would have to learn to live with rather than convert or destroy Communist China. A close aide recalled Nixon explaining in July 1971 as his opening to Beijing gathered momentum: "In 25 years you can't have a quarter of the people of the world isolated and have any chance of peace."[17] The unavoidable price of the new relationship was to leave Taiwan an unresolved bone of contention – a part of China (as Beijing claimed) but not to be regained by force (as Washington insisted) – and thus to make the relationship hostage to sudden crises in the Taiwan Strait.

Finally, Nixon's acquiescent policy toward an economically resurgent Japan reinforced the trend toward a more modest American role in Asia. The Japanese competitive edge was sharpening just as the U.S. economy was beginning to show the effects of the

17 H. R. Haldeman, *The Haldeman Diaries: Inside the Nixon White House* (New York, 1994), 322.

relentless pursuit of the good life. Low savings rates harmful to capital formation and economic productivity were the inevitable concomitants of high levels of consumption, while a runaway preference for foreign goods among American consumers led to persistent trade deficits, not least with Japan. With mounting pressure on the dollar, Nixon succumbed in 1971 and broke the dollar's fixed link to gold that had made the U.S. currency the single point of reference for international trade and investment since the end of the war. The dollar now floated ingloriously, subject like any currency to the tides of the market and sharing with the yen as well as the mark a place of prominence in international currency markets. The erosion of U.S. economic dominance had only begun.

Nixon's successors – whether Republican or Democrat – sustained his modest, accommodating approach to the region through the close of what was to have been the American Century in Asia. Nowhere was that approach more evident than in the continuing engagement with China under the frustratingly durable Communists. The country that had begun the century as the sick man of Asia would in the 1980s and 1990s solidify its claim as a major regional power. No matter what critics might say about this "rogue state" with its troubling authoritarian politics, China's diplomatic influence and economic success made it impossible for Washington to ignore and dangerous to challenge. President Jimmy Carter dawdled for a time on China policy and then at the end of 1978 completed the process of diplomatic normalization begun by Nixon. While Ronald Reagan had made a political career by talking of freedom's advance and the evil of communism, his administration kept the lines to Beijing open. George Bush, who put considerable stock in China ties that he himself had helped create as the first permanent U.S. representative in Beijing in 1974– 75, shielded the relationship from heavy sanctions following the repression of the 1989 democracy demonstrations. The Bush administration reminded the public of China's international importance, the difficulty of imposing political change, the wisdom of supporting a development policy bringing prosperity and ineluctably in time greater freedom to China, and the harm sanctions would inflict on American business. The Clinton administration would closely follow the same line backed by corporations with a stake in friendly relations.

Nixon's successors also continued through the 1970s and 1980s to backpedal before the advancing Japanese economy as pundits began to ask the heart-burning question whether Japan was really "number one" in a sphere where Americans had long prided themselves on primacy. Made-in-Japan consumer goods flooded the American market, turning once prosperous industrial areas into rust belts. At the same time Japanese investors poured money into the American stock market and took control of American properties, including such national icons as Rockefeller Center and Columbia Pictures. The 1990s brought some balm to raw American sensibilities. The Japanese economy entered a prolonged rough patch, while the United States enjoyed a remarkable run of prosperity. But the fact still remained that the economically insurgent countries of the western Pacific, with Japan in the lead, had irrevocably altered the economic landscape. Their extraordinary growth had dramatically boosted the regional share of global GNP from somewhere around 4 percent in 1960 to well over 25 percent by the end of the century. Reconfigured international trade and investment patterns reflected this surge, with U.S. trans-Pacific trade – to take one example – surpassing U.S. trade with the Atlantic world by the mid-1980s.

The American retreat before an assertive East Asia brought from Luce's ideological heirs outspoken criticism and persistent calls for moral revitalization of U.S. foreign policy. During the closing years of the Cold War, neo-conservatives railed against consorting with Chinese totalitarians and abandoning old allies on Taiwan. More recently, proponents of human rights, including vocal members of Congress, have called for pressuring the Chinese Communists to grant greater political freedom to their people. These Luce legatees carefully scrutinized the transition of Hong Kong from British colonial to Chinese Communist rule, lamented China's control over Tibet, decried forced abortions under Beijing's population control policy, and demanded freedom of religious practice. Their greatest success in casting China's leadership as the foremost foes of freedom in Asia came after the repression of the 1989 protests. Americans had glimpsed in television images an imminent end to Communist control in the world's most populous country. Nowhere else around the world was the revulsion against the repression more strongly felt, setting off a drum-beat of public condemnation of "the butchers of Beijing" and calls for stiff sanctions. American leaders dutifully signaled displeasure.[18] Later, as normalizing relations with Vietnam became a subject of public discussion, opponents attacked that country's equally repressive political system and Washington's dismaying tendency to make deals with totalitarians.

These preoccupations carried over in less strident terms into relations with Japan. Influential American commentators criticized the "unnatural" constraints under which nominally free Japanese lived. They were swallowed up as employees by their companies, forced as consumers to operate within a closed domestic market, and acquiescent as voters to control by a single party through much of the postwar period. Japanese needed to spend more and work and save less. A fundamental restructuring of domestic economic arrangements – not least breaking up the clubby internal market created by large industrial banking combines cooperating with Liberal Democratic politicians and powerful bureaucrats – was critical. It would level the competitive playing field but also create an environment of freer choice on which the development of Japanese individualism depended. Japanese commentators responded that naked market forces and rampant individualism would stir conflict and harm social cohesion, perhaps even undermine the gains achieved by the country's fragile, resource-poor economy. By the early 1990s three-fourths of Japanese polled thought Americans were looking for a scapegoat

---

18 Richard Madsen, *China and the American Dream: A Moral Inquiry* (Berkeley, 1995); and Randall E. Stross, *Bulls in the China Shop and Other Sino-American Encounters* (New York, 1990), are telling treatments of how hopes for a politically and economically transformed China flourished in the 1970s and 1980s only to be destroyed in 1989. These two accounts are also inadvertently revealing on the emergence of the "Tiananmen massacre" as a prism through which disillusioned American scholars came to organize their assessment of China and Sino-American relations. It thus turns out that even those highlighting American ethnocentrism can be themselves deeply tinctured by it.

for their own economic and social problems.[19] Almost half of all Japanese and Americans by then saw their two countries locked in a competition to determine who would be the number-one economic power in the new century. Talk of war, nominally confined to trade, began to revive on each side negative images quiescent since the end of the Pacific War.

Though often rebuffed, advocates of freedom could still point to substantial progress by the closing decades of the American Century. In Japan the Liberal Democratic party's hammerlock on power extending over nearly four decades was finally broken in 1993 elections, though it remained the dominant political force and soon regained effective control of the cabinet. South Korea made a successful transition from military government to elected civilian leadership in 1992, the climax of a five-year program of political reform. On Taiwan the iron grip of the Nationalist party gradually loosened through the 1980s as it ended the decades-old state of emergency, opened the political system to rival parties (even those calling for Taiwan's independence), and held the first democratic elections. Legislative and local races became sharply competitive even while the presidency remained in Nationalist hands. Even in China and Vietnam the prospects for democracy and dissent seemed brighter than ever. That Chinese students were able to mount a month-long challenge to the one-party state in 1989 indicated that basic political changes were under way. Party leaders could slow or channel these changes but not halt them. Vietnam's party-state was broadening the parameters for legitimate discussion, conceding more oversight by the national legislature, and tolerating the existence of some public interest groups. North Korea stood out as the only recalcitrant.

What freedom's champions may have overlooked is that these democratic sprouts began to appear only after Cold War winds had given way to the warmer, softer breezes of regional détente. A case can be made that these sprouts were not the product of American crusading (as Luce would have liked to think) but rather that crusading had gotten in the way. Only after the crusaders

---

19 *New York Times*, 29 December 1992.

had decamped did conditions become conducive to political change. The end of the Cold War in Asia during the 1970s, combined with sustained and spreading regional prosperity, helped to loosen the grip of authoritarian military governments and party-states alike.

What freedom's champions may also have missed is how Asians were following their own distinct path of "illiberal" democratic development. It built on indigenous values. It was preoccupied with the effective use of state power to promote societal and national goods. It was suspicious of unbridled individualism and aggressive pluralism. It valued order and consensus. It viewed Western prescriptions for political change as paternalistic at best and at worst as a strategy for destabilization of an increasingly successful and self-confident region.[20] American hectoring on political issues combined with economic and strategic irritants to inspire a popular literary genre urging Asians to "say no" and defiantly follow a course true to their own values and interests. Ishihara Shintaro and Morita Akio originated the "say no" genre in 1989, and it has since found imitators elsewhere in the region, most notably the 1996 best-selling *Zhongguo keyi shuo bu* (The China that can say no) by Song Qiang et al.[21]

Finally, what champions of freedom may have missed is that American consumer products and values were leaving a deeper mark on the region than the American political model. This is not how the American Century was supposed to work. In 1941 Luce had identified the spread of American goods and technology as an incidental feature of that century, advancing alongside or behind but not in advance of freedom. East Asians seemed to defy Luce's expectations, taking aggressively to the market place while approaching political freedom with greater caution.

U.S. dominance during the regional Cold War had helped plant a diffuse but pervasive consumer culture. The United States made

20   Daniel A. Bell et al., *Towards Illiberal Democracy in Pacific Asia* (New York, 1995), offers a thought-provoking development of these points.
21   Ishihara's views alone appear in translation as *The Japan That Can Say No* (New York, 1991). To my knowledge neither the Song Qiang volume nor any of its contemporaneous kin has yet to appear in English despite the importance of this popular expression of Chinese nationalism.

mass markets possible in the first place by sponsoring a relatively open international trading system and by opening its large, affluent, product-hungry market to Asian imports. The Japanese exploited this opportunity, and their success drew imitators first on the American side of the Cold War lines (in Taiwan, South Korea, Hong Kong, and Singapore) and then as the Cold War waned in the 1970s on the part of China. American aid programs during the height of the Cold War and American outlays for wars in Korea and Vietnam were an important additional stimulus to economic growth in the region.

As prosperity reached into authoritarian no less than more open societies, East Asians became enthusiastic consumers of a wide range of mass-market American products ranging from casual clothes and fast food to TV programming and popular music. Walt Disney enterprises offers a striking example of how these goods easily jumped the Pacific at the very time that the politically freighted products that Luce promoted endured a slow, difficult crossing. Japan learned to love the Mouse during the American occupation and emerged an avid market for Disney products. Adults who grew up in the 1950s and 1960s recall raptly watching the Mickey Mouse Club or Disney films with their simple, vivid stories of good triumphing over evil. Since 1984 those adults have been able to evoke their own childhood memories and entertain their own children at Japan's stunningly successful version of the Disney theme park. Located in Tokyo, it opened a window on an exotic, purportedly American world, but allowed visitors to view that world in a comfortable, familiar environment. Reassurance ranged from the kind of food served and the way it was served to the messages conveyed about Japan's own national character and history.[22] The Disney phenomenon also took root in

---

22   Mary Yoko Brannen, "'Bwana Mickey': Constructing Cultural Consumption at Tokyo Disneyland," in *Re-Made in Japan: Everyday Life and Consumer Taste in a Changing Society*, ed. Joseph J. Tobin (New Haven, 1992), 216–34. Feature-length Hollywood films offer another striking example. Already in the interwar period they claimed 30 percent of the Japanese market and they still held that share in the late 1940s. By the early seventies the figure had risen to nearly half in a country that represented the fourth most important foreign source of Hollywood film revenue. Jeremy Tunstall, *The Media Are American: Anglo-American Media in the World* (New York, 1977), 282, 284, 289–92, 299.

China in the wake of Deng Xiaoping's open-door economic reforms. Amid the strife of spring 1989 Chinese coeds walked around campus sporting outfits that mixed nicely tailored skirts and jackets with Mickey Mouse T-shirts. Children at Beijing birthday parties squealing in delight at adults wearing elaborate mouse costumes and the success of *The Lion King* speak to the widening Disney appeal and the likelihood for the success of yet another theme park, this one planned for China's prosperous southern coast.

While the prominence of American consumer products in East Asia is indubitable, their cultural significance is tough to measure. Does wearing Levi's, eating at McDonald's, or watching an episode of *Dallas* transform individual psyches or alter broad patterns of social interaction to such an extent that it leaves an identifiable and significant American imprint? We cannot take at face value the claims of those who see made-in-America dreams taking root in ground prepared by made-in-America products. Any persuasive argument for Americanization (or "Coca-colonization") generated by mass-market exports must think of it not as a free-standing, independent process but as a subset of Westernizing influences. Those influences in turn need to be seen as nested within the broader patterns of modernization (a global trend conventionally associated with urbanization, industrial development and consolidation, the shift to a nuclear family, rising levels of literacy and technological skills, and increasing personal mobility at the expense of community).

And here we come to the complexities of distinguishing specifically American influences and reaching an overall verdict on the significance of those influences.[23] In much of East Asia both Westernization and modernization go back at least to the late nine-

---

23 I found particularly helpful in composing the assessment that follows Joseph J. Tobin's "Introduction: Domesticating the West," and Millie R. Creighton's "The *Depato*: Merchandising the West While Selling Japaneseness," in Tobin, ed., *Re-Made in Japan*, 1–76, as well as the nuanced collection edited by James L. Watson, *Golden Arches East: McDonald's in East Asia* (Stanford, 1997). Mark Schilling, *The Encyclopedia of Japanese Pop Culture* (New York, 1997), drives home the point that such cultural products as movies, films, television programs, and toys need to be understood in terms of a complex interplay of international and domestic influences. Schilling's engaging entries repeatedly indicate that whatever the mix of influences, the outcomes are distinctly Japanese.

teenth century and thus were already well begun before the United
States began to emerge as a major player on the scene. It might,
moreover, be fair to say that the United States was less an agent of
modernization in East Asia than a parallel case. Changes occur-
ring in Tokyo, Shanghai, Manila, Saigon, and Singapore were
carrying East Asians toward mass-market destinations by routes
arguably distinct from the track followed by New York, Chicago,
and Atlanta. Further complicating matters, East Asian borrowing of American goods and practices was but a part of a complex
and changing mix of borrowing from abroad, notably but by no
means exclusively from the West. Thus, any effort to gauge the
American impact has to take account of changing consumer tastes
and the diluting effect of other outside influences. A Japanese
seeking the cachet of a foreign car might once have turned to a
big Detroit model but might more recently look instead to a powerful, well-engineered German make or to a flashy Italian design.
A jacket bearing the Calvin Klein label might well jostle for attention from the fashion-conscious shopper against something
bearing Yves Saint Laurent's name – and both may well have
been designed and made in Japan, not the United States or France.

The final complication facing any assessment of Americanization is "domestication."[24] Imported products and practices do
not simply drive out or negate older indigenous practices or goods
on a one-for-one basis (as some stark versions of Americanization
would have it). Rather, imports are subject themselves to transformation in order to become assimilated to daily life in a new
cultural context with its own distinct internal dynamics. Foreign
and native may exist side by side, or they may meld into something altogether new. Japan can again provide helpful examples.
Behind the American practice of giving an engagement ring is a
deeply personal statement of an emotional commitment between
two people. Taken up by Japanese, this practice has become part
of the marriage contract worked out between the families of the
bride and the groom. To take another borrowing, department
stores have, since making their appearance in the late nineteenth

---

24 Other terms invoked by anthropologists and sociologists include "localization,"
"indigenization," and "hybridization."

century, come to serve a variety of roles without analogue outside Japan. They can be a site for working out the details of socially prescribed, ritualized gift giving, a center for information on how to consume foreign products, and even a place to cultivate an appreciation of foreign art. American English, yet a third example, may dominate Japanese foreign language borrowing, but rather than carrying over in some pristine fashion, words and phrases take on new meaning as they become embedded in Japanese usage. At what point does the import get so fundamentally transformed in the way it is used or regarded that it loses its original significance?

If perspective on recent developments is difficult, gauging their implications for the future is even harder.[25] The defining development of this century in East Asia would appear to be not just the rapid mid-century rise of the United States to prominence but also Japan's recovery from defeat in the Pacific War and China's revival after a century and a half decline. China and Japan (even with the latter's economy mired in crisis) have come to constitute a new, culturally distinct regional power center standing in the global configuration roughly on a par with North America and Europe. This tripartite division of the globe at century's end, so different from the situation at the outset, may well define the framework for twenty-first century international relations.

How Asians adjust to their much-transformed position will do much to set a regional agenda to which Americans will have to react. The direction that national identity takes within each of the major states in the region, above all China and Japan, should

---

25   The following exercise in futurology was abetted by Eric Jones et al., *Coming Full Circle: An Economic History of the Pacific Rim* (Boulder, 1993), esp. chaps. 10–11; Yu Bin, " East Asia: Geopolitique into the Twenty-first Century – A Chinese View," Discussion Paper, Asia/ Pacific Research Center, Stanford University, June 1997; Harumi Befu, "Nationalism and *Nihonjinron*," in *Cultural Nationalism in East Asia: Representation and Identity*, ed. Befu (Berkeley, 1993), 107–35; and Gerritt W. Gong, ed., *Remembering and Forgetting: The Legacy of War and Peace in East Asia* (Washington, 1996). For a critical examination of the idea of global economic convergence with obvious implications for the future of the Pacific see Suzanne Berger and Ronald Dore, eds., *National Diversity and Global Capitalism* (Ithaca, 1996). For critical discussion of the fashionable but amorphous idea of an "Asia-Pacific region" or a "Pacific Rim" see Alexander Woodside, "The Asia-Pacific Idea as a Mobilization Myth," in *What Is in a Rim? Critical Perspectives on the Pacific Region Idea*, ed. Arif Dirlik (Boulder, 1993), 13–28.

prove of fundamental importance. So too the persistence of stubborn historical animosities and bitter memories of suffering and loss inflicted in the course of an often bruising twentieth century. These and other domestic constraints on leaders will in turn affect their handling of major regional issues, including a wide range of tough territorial disputes and the potential for a dangerous and costly arms race. The uncertain fate of a Russia with one large foot in Asia, political and religious ferment along inner Asian frontiers, and tensions on the Indian subcontinent all add fresh imponderables. Taken together, these considerations can give a considerable headache to anyone trying to estimate whether relations within the region and with the broader world will develop in a cooperative or conflictual direction. Almost certainly an interesting time lies ahead as the United States works to accommodate its shaken but still sturdy globalist pretensions to a new regional arrival whose cultural distance from the American experience will pose a challenge to understanding and cooperation without equal in U.S. relations with either Europe or Latin America.

Obstacles in Luce's Path

In trying to explain the difficulties encountered by Luce's dream of an American age, the obvious place to begin is with Asian elites. Those who accepted collaborative arrangements with the United States, such as Filipino leaders at the turn of the century as well as Chiang and Diem, might seem pliable tools to advance the cause of freedom, but they in fact put their own interests first. Even more troublesome were the elites who chose the path of resistance. By raising the cost of the American crusade, they repeatedly frustrated American crusaders.

Of these elites none proved more direct and deadly a threat to American goals than the Chinese and Vietnamese Communists. What above all else set them at odds with Luce and led to bloody collisions with formidable American power in the Pacific was their faith in the necessity of a strong state. For those who created the Chinese party in 1921 and the Vietnamese party in 1930 and went on to lead those parties to power, the state occupied the center of a constellation of vital concerns. They regarded the state as a prerequisite to creating an ordered and moral society, essential to achieving territorial security, and the indispensable tool for saving their poor, imperiled nations. It was also for them a structure of power whose fate was intimately tied to that of their own class. The intellectually and morally cultivated had a duty to turn their talents to the care of the body politic; a legitimate government had an obligation to recruit and carefully attend the views of such men of talent. This obsession with the state would carry some of the best and brightest of China and Vietnam into a lifelong career of revolutionary politics dedicated to realizing their dreams of national transformation. In the name of state-building they would search for an effective political vehicle and the cadre to steer it. They would construct an ideology to give their political enterprise direction and legitimacy. And they would seek popular support essential in the first place to winning power and over the long term to sustaining the state-directed development program.[26]

Luce's hostility to the Communist cause found its analogue in the unsavory associations East Asian leaders entertained about freedom. Those who took their Marxism seriously associated Luce's freedom with the false democracy of a doomed capitalism. That system's nominal liberty was but a screen for a class dictatorship's exploitation and repression of the majority. An East Asian preoccupation with group solidarity prompted another criticism – of freedom, especially the American version of it, as an expression of selfish individualism. When Mao labeled as "democratic individualists" those Chinese political figures seeking to steer clear of party commitments, his use of the term conveyed a pejorative meaning that even today attaches to self-regarding behavior in the eyes of an older generation. Individual political

---

26 This treatment of elites guided by strong-state preoccupations draws on my *The Genesis of Chinese Communist Foreign Policy* (New York, 1996), esp. chap. 3. See also Theodore Huters et al., eds., *Culture and State in Chinese History: Conventions, Accommodations, and Critiques* (Stanford, 1997), esp. the introduction by R. Bin Wong et al. and chap. 12 by Wong.

rights that Americans made so much about seemed from the other side of the Pacific to ignore more basic economic rights and, no less serious, to threaten to dissolve social solidarity and even to sow destructive anarchy that might lead to fearful political paralysis and national division.

It is hard to imagine a gulf wider than the one that separated Luce from Mao. They met once and only briefly – in October 1945 in Chongqing, while Mao was engaged in a long, tiring, and inconclusive round of negotiations with Chiang at a difficult time for the Communist party. Luce recalled Mao reacting to their encounter with "polite grunts" and "an intense but not unfriendly curiosity."[27] Beyond the personally gratifying impression that the Communist leader already knew about the American publisher, Luce spotted nothing that put Mao in the same league as Chiang or hinted at his potency as a foe of the American Century. Had Luce's usually insatiable curiosity not deserted him on this occasion, he might at least have turned to Edgar Snow's biography of Mao, published in *Red Star Over China* in 1938. There he would have gotten some sense of the man who would topple Chiang and carry China beyond the reach of Luce's dreams of American influence and patronage.

Luce would have glimpsed in that account a young man whose preoccupation with China's vulnerability and weakness had set off a feverish search for a vision to guide a regenerated China toward "wealth and power." From the outset Mao's politics had been powerfully conditioned by an anxiety over the foreign peril facing China. His earliest years had coincided with the loss of Korea and Taiwan, the occupation of Beijing, the repeated payment of indemnities to the powers, and the informal partition of the northeast territory. Sometime around 1910–11, Mao, then in his late teens, had picked up an 1896 pamphlet on China's imminent dismemberment. It so impressed him that years later he could still recall its opening line – "Alas, China will be subjugated" – and his own feeling of depression "about the future of

---

27   Quoted in Herzstein, *Henry R. Luce*, 407.

my country" and the dawning realization "that it was the duty of all people to help save it."[28]

Between 1917 and 1921 Mao made the transition from student to full-time politico with contacts that extended beyond his native Hunan to the more cosmopolitan Beijing and Shanghai. Out of this period, the culmination of a decade of intellectual searching, emerged a complex and unstable amalgam of revolutionary values. At the core remained a patriotic concern with remaking the Chinese nation. "The first and foremost need," he then asserted, "is for a strong and powerful government!"[29] The Bolshevik revolution and the Soviet state captured his imagination as the models for building a strong new China that could rescue a people sunk deep in darkness and oppression. With his embrace of Leninism went a rejection of others "isms" that Mao had for a time at least contemplated favorably, including liberalism and democracy as well as anarchism. They might be good in the abstract, but they would not serve China well.

Through a tumultuous revolutionary career spanning over a half century, Mao would remain attached to the party-state model borrowed from the Soviet Union and tinctured with influences from China's own imperial system. He made it a tool of revolution as he developed bases of Communist political control and military power in the late 1930s and 1940s. The creation of the People's Republic in 1949 put in Mao's hands a more fully realized version of that model. By the time of his death in 1976 Mao had made good use of the Chinese state (whatever his recurrent doubts about its revolutionary credentials). He had regained much of the territory lost in the waning decades of the last empire and established China as a force in Asia. He had also lifted China into the ranks of the major industrial countries (in the top half dozen) and achieved an annual average GDP growth rate of around 5 percent despite the reverses of the Great Leap and the disruption of the Cultural Revolution.[30]

28   Mao quoted in Hunt, *Genesis*, 75.
29   Mao quoted in ibid., 76.
30   Angus Maddison, *Monitoring the World Economy, 1820–1992* (Paris, 1995), 83.

Rejected as model, the United States still figured prominently as a practical problem during Mao's entire tenure as party leader. How was this country that was, just as Luce asserted, a rising global force to be factored into the party's revolutionary strategy and later China's foreign policy? Mao's answers went through some fascinating gyrations. During the late 1930s he vacillated between thinking the United States was an attractive ally against reactionary forces in China and abroad, on the one hand, and a dangerous bully bent on dominating the Pacific and making China a colony, on the other. In the latter part of 1941 Mao watched the United States move toward full participation in the war and began to see taking shape a great-power alignment that signified nothing less than "the opening of a new stage in the history of the world."[31] Josef Stalin and Franklin Roosevelt would work together not only to win the war but afterward to create an international environment favorable to progressive causes. Mao anticipated that the United States would use its considerable influence over the Nationalists to guarantee peace and reform in China and that his party would as a result enjoy a postwar breathing space in which it might openly organize and compete for power. These hopes, nurtured and translated into party policy during the war, did not survive long into the peace. By the late 1940s Mao saw the Truman administration swinging in a reactionary direction, throwing its unconditional support to Nationalist hard-liners and even contemplating a direct military intervention.

As Sino-American estrangement deepened in the 1950s, Mao's worries about his adversary persisted but were tempered by his conviction that the United States was not so fearsome as it might on the surface seem. Like other Marxists, he saw the United States always on the brink of economic crisis and locked into a deadly rivalry with other capitalist states. Yet he was also impressed that American capitalists "believe in studying the facts" (a comment offered as praise in 1961),[32] and so he expected them

---

31 Mao in August 1944, quoted in Hunt, *Genesis*, 150.
32 Quote from He Di, "The Most Respected Enemy: Mao Zedong's Perception of the United States," in *Toward a History of Chinese Communist Foreign Relations, 1920s–1960s*, ed. Michael H. Hunt and Niu Jun (Washington, [1995]), 50.

to act rationally in order to prolong the life of their declining system and to avoid international crises that might precipitate a vulnerable capitalism's sudden collapse. The accommodation with Nixon in Mao's last years seems like less of a surprise if viewed against the backdrop of his shifting assessments of formidable yet fragile American power managed by ultimately rational elites.

Even more than Mao, Ho Chi Minh was a mystery to Henry Luce. The latter's obtuseness on matters of Asian politics was compounded by the lack of information on the former's secretive, underground career. Had Luce had one of his correspondents interrogate American diplomats serving in Indochina in the late 1940s, he might at least have gained some notion of the blend of nationalist and Communist elements that inspired Ho's opposition to continued French colonial control. Though a combination puzzling to most Cold War Americans, nationalism and communism formed the central strands of Ho's own vision and made sustained, broad-based resistance possible.

A predictable preoccupation with national weakness and vulnerability strongly gripped Ho early in life and led him and other Vietnamese patriots to take as their overriding task ending foreign control and uniting a country whose inherent diversity had been accentuated by the impact of French colonial rule in the south. Ho's personal search for answers to Vietnam's problems took him to Europe in 1911 and culminated with the discovery of Leninism in Paris in 1920 and the acceptance of patronage from the USSR as the only active anticolonialist power. As a Communist, Ho devoted the rest of his life to creating a party-state strong enough to win his country's liberation and then promote its unity, security, and prosperity. Between 1941 and 1945 an embryonic version of Ho's state came into existence behind the façade of the shrewdly constructed if initially puny united-front organization, the Viet Minh. It gradually extended its base of operations from the remote northernmost part of the country and fielded the rudiments of an army. In August 1945 the Vietnamese state took on more formal dimensions with the seizure of Hanoi and the declaration of the Democratic Republic of Vietnam. The capacity of this party-state to achieve the formidable goals of its creators – to defeat the French, wear down Diem, and successfully confront the Americans – validated Ho's faith in his own lifetime. After his death in 1969 his lieutenants would battle on with the resources that only the strong state could deliver. They too would score impressive achievements, driving out the Americans, imposing political and economic integration at the end of the war, and even superintending the transition toward a market-oriented, export-driven development policy.

Like Mao, Ho accorded postwar American power respectful attention. His dominant concern was at first to turn the wartime American sponsorship of the principle of self-determination into postwar fact for Vietnam. He shared the belief that the Soviet-American coalition would survive beyond the war and give impetus to a period of international peace and decolonization. Ho's work with the Office of Strategic Services (OSS) during the closing phase of the Pacific War and his August 1945 declaration of independence quoting from the American founding document were expressions of his desire to use U.S. anticolonialism to impede the returning French. Though Washington ignored Ho, he remained interested in winning American sympathy or at least neutrality in the armed conflict that he was soon waging against the French. And to that end during the spring and summer of 1947 Ho's representatives made behind-the-scenes overtures to U.S. diplomats in Bangkok (though with no more success than earlier). Through the 1950s, with the United States assuming a formal anti-Communist stance in Indochina and backing it with money and advisers, Ho gave priority to avoiding provocations that might draw the United States more deeply into the region, either to save the French or after 1954 to shore up Diem.

Even into the early 1960s Ho remained hopeful of avoiding a costly direct collision with the preeminent Pacific power. He trusted, he remarked in a revealing comment in fall 1963, the essential rationalism of American elites. While conceding that he did not know the Americans well, what he did know suggested that "they are more practical and clear-sighted than other capitalist nations." Since they must know that their system was crisis prone and ill suited to wage distant and unpopular wars, then surely "they will not pour their resources into Vietnam endlessly. One day they will take pencil in hand and begin figuring. Once they really begin to analyze our ideas seriously, they will come to the conclusion that it is possible and even worthwhile to live in peace with us. Weariness, disappointment, the knowledge that they cannot achieve the goal which the French pursued to their own discredit will lead to a new sobriety, new feelings and new emotions."[33] Ho's conviction on this point, conditioned by strong Marxist assumptions, led him to a misreading of the United States (think of Luce straining at this very time to deepen the American commitment) and to another war of attrition to settle the fate of his country. But he also assumed, correctly as it turned out, that such a war would wear down the will of the Americans as it had the French. The more deeply the United States got mired in the fighting, the more American leaders would encounter, as the French had, opposition by the "working masses." That opposition would in time either reverse the war policy (as it had in France in 1953–54) or exacerbate internal pressure that would end in a social upheaval and complete collapse of the war effort.

A second, less obvious source of Luce's travail is to be found in the "good" common folks of Asia whom these "bad" leaders regularly led astray. Like most Americans who gave the matter any thought, Luce had a simple, off-handed conception of the mass of Asians perhaps most influenced by growing up with household servants and exposure to Pearl Buck's popular *The Good Earth*. Trapped by ignorance and poverty into political passivity, Asians seemed to be waiting for enlightened leaders, blessed by American backing, to point them toward a better life. Luce's conception of simplicity, passivity, and latent longings for the American way created a yawning gulf between his notions of the Asian landscape and the peasant majority who inhabited it. This profound misunderstanding would help bring the American crusade in Asia to grief. Peasants did engage in politics. That the terms might seem distant from American practice and hence hard for Ameri-

---

33 Ho remarks reported in Meiczyslaw Maneli, *War of the Vanquished*, trans. Maria de Görgey (New York, 1971), 154–55.

can observers to grasp did not make the politics any less consequential. Making the task of bridging the gulf even more difficult
was the complex political patterns that prevailed across rural East
Asia reflecting the inherent diversity of conditions and outlooks
within the region.

The Philippines offers one early example of peasant politics in
action. American pacifiers arriving at the turn of the century
encountered a peasantry guided not by a sense of nationalism or
by the lure of sweeping socioeconomic changes. Left to their own
devices, most peasants would have given top priority to tending
their fields and avoiding the loss of valuable time and limited
property, not to mention the risk of death entailed in warfare.
But in areas where the leaders of their community called them to
service, they responded out of a sense of obligation as clients dependent on their particular patrons for land and protection against
life's vicissitudes. One careful study of an embattled province
(Batangas) in southern Luzon during the Philippine-American War
shows peasants taking up arms at the behest of their patrons first
against Spanish colonial authority and then against the Americans. Those not called to arms were generous enough in meeting
levies of money and food to ensure adequate supplies for the troops
during the first phase of the anti-American war in that province
(January 1900 to April 1901). Not surprisingly, a few months of
hard fighting or the arrival of planting or harvesting season could
undermine the sense of obligation, and suddenly units in the field
could find their ranks dramatically thinned. When elite enthusiasm for resistance also began to erode, the local commander was
forced to make an unusually populist appeal to give his troops
fresh incentive to fight. Even this appeal had only a short-term
effect, and by the year's end all classes wanted an end to the conflict that had done such damage to the province.[34]

---

34   I draw here on Glenn A. May's finely crafted *Battle for Batangas: A Philippine Province
at War* (New Haven, 1991). See Benedict J. Kerkvliet, *The Huk Rebellion: A Study of Peasant
Revolt in the Philippines* (Berkeley, 1977), on how in the Philippines case peasants operating
in a different time and place (1920s–1940s in northern Luzon) could become an important
source of rural insurgency and shake the national political system as well as its guarantors in
Washington.

Though rural issues proved if anything more critical for Americans in Vietnam, the dynamics of the village war remained as much mysteries to commanders on the scene and to policymakers in Washington as they had in the Philippines half a century earlier. A sense of national superiority over a small, poor, backward country and a paternalistic commitment to saving it once more made American ethnocentrism not just easy but inevitable. In the conventional view that prevailed among policymakers and Americans in-country, peasants played a part in the conflict only under "Viet Cong" compulsion – if not verbal intimidation and psychological manipulation then outright terror. CIA and Rand analysts learned enough in the 1960s to question the accuracy of this picture. They were particularly acute in seeing that the politics of the countryside often turned on land questions and that the National Liberation Front, like the Viet Minh before it, was led by politicians skilled at reading constituent interests (largely landless peasantry) and mobilizing their support by taking a stand four square behind rent reduction and land redistribution. The difficulties Americans encountered in the countryside were the result of peasants understanding the difference between the insurgent program and the status quo supported by landlords and by distant political authorities, whether the French, the Diem family, Vietnamese generals, or the Americans. Peasants took sides because they judged the risks of supporting change were more than balanced by immediate and likely long-term economic and social gains to their families and villages.[35] These insights did not, however, penetrate the thinking of U.S. leaders. The view of the peas-

---

35 For an excellent example of intelligence insight that foreshadows later scholarly findings see the 1963 CIA report from Saigon, in U.S. Department of State, *Foreign Relations of the United States, 1961–1963* (Washington, 1991), 4: 642–45. Pierre Brocheux's excellent *The Mekong Delta: Ecology, Economy, and Revolution, 1860–1960* (Madison, 1995), is the most recent addition to the literature on the countryside over which much of the American war was fought. See also the case studies by Jeffrey Race, *War Comes to Long An: Revolutionary Conflict in a Vietnamese Province* (Berkeley, 1972); David Hunt, "Villagers at War: The National Liberation Front in My Tho Province, 1965–1967," *Radical America* 8 (January–April 1974): 3–184; James W. Trullinger, Jr., *Village at War: An Account of Revolution in Vietnam* (New York, 1980); and Eric M. Bergerud, *The Dynamics of Defeat: The Vietnam War in Hau Nghia Province* (Boulder, 1991). David Hunt, "U.S. Scholarship and the National Liberation Front," in *The American War in Vietnam*, ed. Jayne Werner and David Hunt (Ithaca, 1993), 93–108, is a helpful survey of the literature.

ant as passive victim was as influential among dissenters in the U.S. policy establishment, such as George Ball, as it was among interventionists, such as Robert McNamara. It also influenced the ultimate arbiter on the issue, Lyndon Johnson, who thought of successful rural politics in South Vietnam in terms of pressing the flesh and spreading the pork.

This gap between what historical actors thought they knew and the rural reality, so consequential for the course of the war, persists afterward in American popular memory and even to some degree in the historiography. Peasants – that is to say, the majority of Vietnamese who fought and were fought over – are all too often treated as incidental to the real story dominated by Americans and especially Americans in combat. Still carrying notions about the Vietnamese countryside that predominated among Americans during the war, those interested in the war today usually steer clear of considering the political legitimacy built up by an enemy still most often referred to not by its proper name but by the vague, pejorative term, "Viet Cong." That legitimacy is an important part of the story because it left American soldiers facing widespread, irregular resistance enjoying broad popular support. The predictable results were American reprisals against individual civilians and profligate use of firepower against civilian communities. Anyone seeking Vietnam's lessons has to confront these consequences made inevitable by the successful National Liberation Front program of enlisting peasants in the politics of war.

The proposition that land was central to the rural conflict needs qualifying by taking account of Vietnam's diverse countryside. The precise conditions prevailing within a particular locale influenced the particular form that the politics of land would take. The Mekong Delta in the south supported a fluid, frontier society. Its peasantry was entrepreneurial and mobile. With an eye on getting ahead, peasants were quick to relocate to places where the land was available on more promising terms; yet the highly commercialized land system that took shape in the delta through the nineteenth and twentieth centuries thwarted them. It was marked by high concentrations of ownership and consequently high levels of tenancy. Peasants hungering for their own land, on which they could produce for the market, understood that land-lords living in Saigon or perhaps some provincial capital and staunchly supporting the Saigon government stood in their way. The tight, closed villages of the Red River Delta in the north, the product of two thousand years of continuous agricultural settle-ment, offer a contrast. The incidence of land ownership was far greater than in the south, but high population density meant that most plots were small, and most peasant owners suffered from such large debts that their claim to ownership was only nominal. Reduction of debts had an appeal in the north as enormous as the programs of rent reduction and land redistribution did in the south. But even this broad generalization about two agricultural pat-terns to which Vietnamese Communists had to adjust their politi-cal program needs further refining as one looks more closely within each of these regions. Take for example one subregion, the westernmost part of the Mekong Delta. Along with the many land-hungry peasants who threw in their lot with the Communist front organizations to create bastions of resistance to the French, to Diem, and to the Americans, there were also areas where peas-ants with Cao Dai, Hoa Hao, or Catholic loyalties stood apart from the insurgency.

The third serious obstacle to the realization of Luce's dream of influence in East Asia is to be found closer to home and took a form that Luce himself was intimately familiar with. Consumer culture had made his media empire possible. A wealth of adver-tisements luring readers to indulge their hedonism through an endless array of goods and services paid the bills for Time Inc. and made Luce a wealthy and influential public figure. Those advertisements spanning decades and speaking in a rich and ap-pealing variety of marketing voices instructed readers (in the words of someone who knew the Luce empire from the inside) in "how to dress, what to buy, and what to value in life."[36] Luce believed that global ambitions and consumerism could coexist as long as the latter functioned not as an end in itself but as a demonstration

---

36　Andrew Kopkind quoted in Jesperson, American Images, 22.

of the superiority of the American way of life. He did not antici-
pate that as consumer culture came to engage the imagination of
his readers, they might put their own immediate satisfaction ahead
of national destiny. By so prominently encouraging the pursuit of
material goods and pleasures as a way of life, Luce helped undermine popular support for crusading in East Asia and subvert an
American Century whose gratifications were (as he saw it) to be
deferred and measured largely in terms of enlightened national
self-sacrifice.

The very issue of *Life* in which Luce published "The American
Century" foreshadowed the ultimate conflict between two definitions of that century – one harnessed to meeting the claims of
providential mission around the globe and the other striving to
realize the promise of abundance at home. While his own piece
of editorializing in this issue asked of his readers discipline and
courage to remake the world, the surrounding advertisements told
them of the pleasures of daily life – unprecedented convenience
and mobility, freedom from physical discomfort, and the cultiva-
tion of good looks – that were within reach of all. Placed just
before "The American Century" was a call from Texaco to use
Havoline Motor Oil in order to avoid costly automobile repairs.
With thoughts of preventive maintenance in mind, the reader clam-
bered over Luce's hard moral abstractions to reach gentler, more
gratifying terrain, beginning with a pitch for California prunes.
With "their regulative effect" they promised to keep constipa-
tion-induced headaches at bay. Just beyond the prunes lay a spread
for girdles. Slim, leggy young women sprawled across this advertisement in a way that could be construed as either glamorous or
tastefully erotic. The arresting banner announcing the undergar-
ments read, "Where It Goes, Nobody Knows."

Americans reading Luce's 1941 essay had already had their
dreams of abundance denied by the Great Depression. Soon formal participation in a global war would further defer those dreams
by creating demands for military service and restrictions on production of civilian goods. Within a decade after the war those
same Americans would at last have the chance to indulge an abundance that would come to surpass anything in the imagination of

an older generation. When policymakers now asked the citizenry to set aside comforts and pleasures – to pay higher taxes and even serve, perhaps die, in foreign lands – in the name of preserving freedom, they would find little enthusiasm. In the late 1940s an electorate and Congress eager for a full dose of domestic normalcy intimidated Truman. His inability to raise taxes or levy the manpower to fill out a shrinking army left him with a toothless Cold War policy. With available military resources far short of multiplying commitments, China fell uncontested in 1949. When Washington did intervene to save South Korea and South Vietnam, the public dutifully followed, at least at first. But when wars there continued inconclusively, it turned querulous and eventually hostile. Good consumers were, as it turned out, impatient crusaders.

Polls taken during the American war in Vietnam highlight how popular aspirations for economic self-betterment, reinforced by moral and strategic critiques, helped plant doubts about the sacrifices demanded by foreign commitments. By late 1967 a majority of Americans for the first time characterized that war as a mistake. When asked then about the most urgent problem that they personally or their families faced, the high cost of living was the runaway top choice (mentioned by 60 percent of respondents). Only 5 percent pointed to Vietnam. When the question was then rephrased in terms of problems facing not individuals or families but rather the nation, Vietnam for the moment at least figured more prominently – as the top problem for 50 percent. The high cost of living came in third with 16 percent. By March 1971 Vietnam and the economy were running neck and neck (28 to 24 percent) even when the question was posed in terms of national rather than personal problems. And by the end of the year the economy had pulled far out ahead of Vietnam (41 to 15 percent).[37]

The grip of consumerism was even more evident among American soldiers sent in the late 1960s and early 1970s to wage war in a strange, distant country. They spoke of home as "the land of

---

37   George H. Gallup, *The Gallup Poll: Public Opinion, 1935–1971*, 3 vols. (New York, 1972), 3:2086, 2090, 2292, 2311, 2338.

the big PX," and those on major, rear-echelon bases lived in conditions that sought to reproduce the comforts of home. They were well fed, and on occasion even units in the field received hot meals, cold drinks, and ice cream. Mail was regular. Alcohol and drugs were readily available at cut-rate prices. Hot showers and air conditioners pampered the body. Hired Vietnamese did the cleaning and polishing. Entertainment included regular movies, television, performances by touring Hollywood stars as well as lesser lights, clubs for officers and NCOs, and sports facilities (sometimes even swimming pools). An elaborate system of post exchanges made goods available at subsidized prices. Brothels flourished outside large installations under the watchful eyes of U.S. medical teams. Everyone in country was entitled to a five-day vacation (R&R) usually midway through the tour of duty and usually in a major Asian city where the soldier could indulge his appetite for consumption and entertainment even more fully than in Vietnam. This way of war waged by a people of plenty necessitated an enormous logistical effort that might have been better directed to more obvious military objectives. But so potent was the call of consumerism that politicians, the Pentagon brass, and the commanders in the field had to answer it to maintain morale.[38]

Alternative Visions

Henry Luce championed a crusade that failed worst where it may have counted the most to him – in East Asia. Within a region struggling to recover from the privations of international conflict and civil war, assertive Americans spawned fresh devastation, often prolonged or even created instability, and in the final analysis may have done more to obstruct and delay than to advance the cause of freedom that Luce so prized. Rather than producing national unity and élan at home (also a source of pride),

38 Ronald H. Spector, *After Tet: The Bloodiest Year in Vietnam* (New York, 1993), 262–78; Christian G. Appy, *Working-Class War: American Combat Soldiers and Vietnam* (Chapel Hill, 1993), 237–39.

the effort first sowed political dissension in the late 1940s and 1950s and then engendered a sour disillusionment in the 1960s and after.

To capture the dark side of an American Century project that proved morally complicated in a way that Henry Luce would never be able to grasp, we need another prophet. Had Mark Twain had the chance to read Luce's 1941 essay, he would have found there little that would have surprised him. Already at the turn of the century he had confronted quite similar nationalist fervor in the McKinley administration and its supporters in Congress and the press. At first acquiescent as they pressed their overseas projects, Twain had by the fall of 1900 turned skeptical after reading about atrocities and looting associated with the "pacification" of the Philippines and the American role in the international occupation of North China.

Twain's mounting gloom carried him to conclusions strikingly at odds with those Luce would later champion. In an interview in October 1900 he contemplated Americans "spreading themselves over the face of the globe" and concluded mildly, "I don't think that it is wise or a necessary development." The United States had "no more business in China than in any other country that is not ours." In the Philippines, by insisting on the imposition of American ideas rather than accepting whatever ideas a majority of the Filipinos wanted, "we have got into a mess, a quagmire from which each fresh step renders the difficulty of extrication immensely greater." Early in 1901 Twain published his first sustained reflections, the sardonic "To the Person Sitting in Darkness." There he asked: "Shall we go on conferring our Civilization upon the peoples that sit in darkness, or shall we give those poor things a rest?" Widely circulated, Twain's piece of corrosive humor proved a smashing success for the Anti-Imperialist League.[39]

39 William M. Gibson, "Mark Twain and Howells: Anti-Imperialists," *New England Quarterly* 15 (December 1947): 444–45; Twain, "To the Person Sitting in Darkness," *North American Review* 172 (February 1901): 161–76.

The debate over the Philippines and China faded, but Twain continued to brood over how crusading by a chosen people could turn so nasty and brutal that it betrayed their fundamental values. The death of loved ones along with his own failing health, fading literary powers, and financial woes accentuated his somber mood in this, the last decade of his life. His troubled reflections took as its most obvious target the inhumanity that lurked within the high-sounding appeals of nationalism. That "the holy fire of patriotism" could burn out of control was the message of "The War Prayer," a parable from 1905 (not published until 1923 and rediscovered by protestors against the Vietnam War). As though with Luce in mind, Twain conjured up "a time of great and exalting excitement" as the country prepared for the clash of arms. Into this scene he introduced "an aged stranger" to serve as his alter ego. Standing before a church congregation gathered to ask "the God of Battle" to bless their young patriots about to march off to war, the stranger cautioned, "When you have prayed for victory you have prayed for many unmentioned results which follow victory – which *must* follow it, cannot help but follow it." He proceeded to make the point graphically in a long prayer that is hard to read today without thinking of images of destruction associated with Luce's century – of dead Filipino irregulars lying jumbled in a trench, of refugees clogging Korean roads, and of peasants fleeing burning South Vietnamese villages:

O Lord, our God, help us to tear their soldiers to bloody shreds with our shells; help us to cover their smiling fields with the pale forms of their patriot dead; help us to drown the thunder of the guns with the shrieks of their wounded, writhing in pain; help us to lay waste their humble homes with a hurricane of fire; help us to wring the hearts of their unoffending widows with unavailing grief; help us to turn them out roofless with their little children to wander unfriended the wastes of their desolated land in rags and hunger and thirst, sport of the sun-flames of summer and the icy winds of winter, broken in spirit, worn with travail, imploring Thee for the refuge of the grave and denied it – for our sakes who adore Thee, Lord, blast their hopes, blight their lives, protract their bitter pilgrimage, make heavy their steps, water their way with their ears, stain the white snow with the blood of their wounded feet! We ask it, in the spirit of love, of Him Who is the Source of Love, and Who is the ever-faithful refuge and friend of all that are sore beset and seek His aid with humble and contrite hearts. Amen.

In quickly closing the tale, a pessimistic Twain conceded that the stranger's ironic shafts would bounce harmlessly off the armor of self-righteous nationalism. "It was believed afterwards, that the man was a lunatic, because there was no sense in what he said."[40]

Twain's private questioning carried him beyond this warning against the destructive potential of nationalism to a sweeping rejection of simple, clear notions of human progress so fundamental to McKinley's contemporary justification for action in the Philippines and to Luce's later, still bolder summons to the nation. Twain rested his case on the iron law of unintended consequences governing even those who thought of themselves as a special people. In a dialogue between "The Dervish and the Offensive Stranger" dating from 1902 (but also not published until 1923) he again introduced an outsider ("The Offensive Stranger"), this time to argue for a universe without discernible order or meaning. The Stranger began by conceding to the Dervish that in human affairs it was possible to distinguish between good and evil impulses. But the consequences of those impulses were beyond human control or understanding as they played out down the corridors of time in an infinitely complex pattern. Thus, the Stranger argued, the effects "from any act, even the smallest, breed on and on, century after century, forever and ever, creeping by inches around the globe, affecting coming and going populations until the end of time, until the final cataclysm."[41]

As we look back on a century in which the tide of American ambitions rose and then receded and foward to a new century

---

40 Jim Zwick, ed., *Mark Twain's Weapons of Satire: Anti-Imperialist Writings on the Philippines-American War* (Syracuse, 1992), 156–60; Everett Emerson, *The Authentic Mark Twain: A Literary Biography of Samuel L. Clemens* (Philadelphia, 1984), chaps. 10–11.
41 Zwick, *Mark Twain's Weapons*, 147-48.

filled with uncertainty, Twain's musings deserve attention. They would have us recall the inevitable barbarity that attends all crusading, and they caution against the unexpected turns that even the best intentioned of enterprises are bound to take. But the public and publishers in Twain's day were not ready for his iconoclastic assault on the arrogance that marked the American Century at its outset. Luce at mid-century would have recoiled before a world so bereft of moral meaning and so devoid of hope for national destiny and control. And even today with our nationalist spirit slack, we are more comfortable with Luce's summons to do good in the world than with Twain's searching assault on meaning and morality.

Whose vision would guide the United States if in decades ahead relations with Asia were to turn ugly? This is an eventuality that cannot be ruled out. The continuing presence of some hundred thousand American troops in Northeast Asia (down only fifty thousand from late Cold War levels) and the continuing commitment under the security treaty with Japan virtually guarantee for the foreseeable future U.S. entanglement in case of troubles on the Korean peninsula or in the Taiwan Strait. Even if the United States were to call the troops home, leave Japan to manage its own security, and withdraw to the far shore of the Pacific, Washington might still find it difficult to stay on the sidelines in case of serious regional instability. With calls in the air for the United States to take up the role of policeman, makeweight, or peacemaker, would Twain's dark fears or Luce's grandiose hopes prevail?

Even taken together, Twain and Luce fail to capture important dimensions of the century past and possibilities for the century to come. Here we might use a third prophet, Walt Disney, to speak for the growing American impact on regional patterns of consumption over the past four decades and for the promise of continued influence for the American cultural industry. Though Disney shared with Luce a faith in freedom that found expression from the early 1940s in a staunchly right-wing anticommunism, his animating vision was quite distinct – of the world as a profitable mass market. Disney summed up his unabashedly commercial philosophy in comments to some French cartoonists whose artsy approach left him cold: "Don't go for the *avant garde* stuff. Be commercial. What is art, anyway? It's what people like. So give them what they like. There's nothing wrong with being commercial." To that end he assiduously sought to learn the tastes of foreigners as well as Americans so that he could "give them what they like."[42]

Disney's pursuit of foreign markets dated back to the 1930s when he began to fully grasp their sales potential. One early feature-length animation, *Snow White* from 1937, earned from its initial overseas release together with reissues something on the order of $30 million, perhaps twice the domestic take.[43] Foreign markets remained important to Disney's growing entertainment empire after World War II as cartoons made way for more and more feature-length films (including Westerns, historical romances, and broad comedies for a juvenile audience), television, and finally in Disney's last years the famous theme parks. Already wildly successful in Europe before the war, Disney products made inroads after the war in an increasingly prosperous Asia (as noted above). Supplying escapist fantasy, not political exhortation, enabled Disney and others in the American entertainment industry to bridge the Pacific and leave a mark that surpassed anything that Luce dreamed of.

From the start Disney recognized that his commercial success depended on him doing all the things that other successful international business did – staying ahead technologically, holding production costs down, and offering a quality, standardized product. But above all his success depended on what might be called the strategy of producing for the lowest common cultural denominator if products were to cross borders and reach into the minds and open the pocketbooks of diverse peoples around the globe. The large but heterogeneous home market had already taught him how to speak across lines of region, class, ethnicity, and gen-

---

42 Bob Thomas, *Walt Disney: An American Original* (New York, 1976), 277 (quote); Steven Watts, "Walt Disney: Art and Politics in the American Century," *Journal of American History* 82 (June 1995): 84–110.
43 Estimates in Leonard Maltin, *The Disney Films* (New York, 1973), 32.

der in order to attract a truly mass audience. What had been produced for the home market – chiefly action and escapist stories – traveled well abroad and had, like other Hollywood products, an especially strong appeal to youth, women, and workers.

No better example of Disney's ability to create characters that could appeal to a wide audience and cross national boundaries can be found than Mickey Mouse. Born in 1928 and almost named Mortimer, he carried the personality and voice of Walt Disney and the cartooning skills of Disney's associate, Ubbe Iwerks. Already in 1929 with five shorts out, this mouse had created a craze, filling theaters, creating fan clubs, and selling merchandise (such as watches, toys, and clothes bearing his image). That Mickey Mouse was a universally appealing character quickly became apparent as adulation spread from the United States through Europe's already large audience of moviegoers. The secret to the mouse's wide appeal was ambiguous identity. His age and nationality were, for example, anyone's guess. Only his gender was clear – and that from his name. That Mickey Mouse and others in the Disney stable of cartoon characters did little talking helped as well. By letting the picture tell the story, Disney could limit the dialogue and the distraction of subtitles or voice-overs. The lighter the baggage that Mickey carried, the more easily he crossed borders.

Disney's presence in this triptych of American Century prophets would have made Luce uneasy. The spread of political and economic freedom was a serious matter with heroic, epochal overtones. Such notable American exports as jazz, slang, and Hollywood movies could establish the country's standing as a world power only in "trivial ways" (as Luce put it in his seminal 1941 essay).[44] He would have seen nothing heroic about a trans-Pacific consumer culture symbolized by a mouse and nothing gratifying in Asian enthusiasm for American-supplied diversions outracing an interest in American-style freedom. Even so, the relevance of Disney's vision seems assured well into the next century as the appeal of American culture continues to command

---

44 See Luce, "American Century," in this volume.

vast audiences. As the exponent of a U.S. relationship with Asia in which the common goal of promoting prosperity has increasingly taken precedence over the divisive cause of promoting freedom, Disney may prove a better prophet of the American Century than either a frustrated Luce or a problematic Twain.

8

The American Century
and the Third World

BRUCE CUMINGS

To begin thinking about this subject, it seemed appropriate to retrieve the 17 February 1941 issue of *Life* that carried Henry Luce's original essay, "The American Century." My faith in college students' probity and tender concern for their peers was requited when I found the speech ripped out of the University of Chicago library's lone copy. So I contented myself with perusing what remained of the magazine. This single issue displayed, by quick count, 447 white people, 46 blacks, 1 Hispanic, and no Asians (not counting the evanescent pages 61 to 66, where Henry Luce once held forth). Nineteen of the blacks come from a scene in *Cabin in the Sky*, a Broadway musical with an all-black cast; the majority of these are very light skinned and some appear to be white. A single black face also inhabits a photo of the Art Students League of New York. The remaining blacks are residents of Whale Cay in the Bahamas, a private island owned by Betty Carstair, an heiress of the Standard Oil Bostwick family.

Photos show Ms. Carstair guiding the Duke and Duchess of Windsor around the island, directing a construction gang of blacks engaged in building roads, and leading the rank-and-file members of the 87th Bahamas Regiment, her private army made up mostly of current and former Boy Scouts. *Life* said that Ms. Carstair runs the island with "a firm and feudal hand" and has done wonders for the natives, all of whom work for her: "She makes them eat more vegetables, forbids them anything stronger than beer, prohibits voodoo practices, and takes holidays away from the whole island if there is any mass bad behavior." Such bad behavior might include eating white rice, since the owner had directed that only brown rice should be served on Whale Cay.

The lone Hispanic is Fulgencio Batista, recovering from yet another coup attempt in Cuba. This time the plot included the Army and Navy Chiefs of Staff and the national police chief, not an insubstantial coalition. But *El Jefe* got wind of it and shipped the three of them off to Miami before things got out of hand: "Within 48 hours Batista had restored the constitutional guarantees, received the congratulations of the United States Ambassador, been kissed by his friends, became a father for the third time and proudly announced: 'Democracy has been saved.'"

All of the advertisements in this issue feature whites, except for a white in blackface who recommends California prunes as an aid to health. One ad promotes the Paramount film *Virginia* ("The Magnificent Love Story of a Beautiful Rebel") starring Madeleine Carroll and Fred MacMurray, replete with drawings of "the stately mansions" and "galloping red-coated fox hunters" of "the new North and the modern South." Most of the whites in the multitude of ads in any issue of *Life* in 1941 appear to be WASPs, with a typical blonde-hair, blue-eyed, fresh-scrubbed look to them.

What does all this mean? That the "Third World" of people of color, most of them in internal or external colonies in 1941, did not exist for *Life Magazine*, and did not exist for the white majority of Americans. They were invisible, people without history, people with a future only through the civilizing appurtenance of white leadership. Few above the age of forty would need to be told this, but that underlines how recent the colonial era was – alive at the end of World War II, but soon to disappear in a broad wave of independence movements and struggles for basic rights over the next three decades.

When we turn to the blonde-haired, blue-eyed, fresh-scrubbed publisher himself and his celebrated essay (a pristine copy of which I found in a local public library), the dominant impression is what a good salesman Henry Luce was, and what a poor thinker: the truly original coinage that he struck in 1941 does not last past his memorable title. The American Century was a wonderful logo for this eternal optimist to merchandise the American dream, but his ideas did not go beyond vexation about creeping "national socialism" in America (read New Deal), the bankruptcy of an isolationism that still could not grasp why Americans should fight and die for "dear old Danzig or dear old Dong Dang," and the recommendation that the consumer paradise that had arisen in the 1920s, when American industry perfected both mass production and the means to digest the same goods en masse ("the abundant life," as Luce called it), is or should be available "for all mankind" once they wake up to "America's vision." This program, of course, should not march forward just with an overflow of consumer durables, but under the banner of American idealism: "It must be a sharing with all peoples of our Bill of Rights, our Declaration of Independence, our Constitution, our magnificent industrial products, our technical skills. It must be an internationalism of the people, by the people and for the people."

Amid much frothy rhetoric like this ("We must undertake now to be the Good Samaritan of the entire world," etc.), Luce held out to underdeveloped peoples the chance to escape their problems by becoming American – an absurd proposition in 1941. But he put his finger on a truth, the same one an American officer in Stanley Kubrick's *Full Metal Jacket* fingered when he answered Private Joker's weighty question – "Why are we in Vietnam?" – with this: "Inside every Vietcong is an American trying to get out." Or as Luce put it, "Once we cease to distract ourselves with lifeless arguments about isolationism, we shall be amazed to discover that there is already an immense American internationalism. American jazz, Hollywood movies, American slang, American machines and patented products, are in fact the only things that every community in the world, from Zanzibar to Hamburg, recognizes in common."

I often take North Korea to be the vanguard of the Third World, anti-American rejectionist front. Some years ago I knew a North Korean staffer in that country's United Nations observer group in New York. I asked him what he and his colleagues did for recreation in the improbable penthouse atop a building in Manhattan that the staff inhabited, and he said they watched television. Their favorite show? "Charlie's Angels," he replied, a show with three girls playing detective, their jiggling breasts being the main attraction. And with this, I grasped the truth of Baudrillard's observation: "Whatever happens, and whatever one thinks of the arrogance of the dollar or the multinationals, it is this culture which, the world over, fascinates those very people who suffer most at its hands, and it does so through the deep, insane conviction that it has made all their dreams come true."[1]

If Henry Luce both understood and epitomized this "insane conviction," Third World peoples did not provide much evidence of a thirst for the American way in 1941 or during thirty years of anti-imperial wars after World War II. Henry Luce's concern, however, was not with "worlds" but with directions: toward Europe, or away from it. He preferred the latter as the most prominent of the "Asia-firsters" (dear-old-Dong-Dang again). But his Asia was Ms. Carstair's Whale Cay writ large, a place to be led by whites and ultimately to be dissolved not in anti-imperial revolt, but in the solvent of Americanism. The formative Third World experience for him was the United States's relationship to Latin America, a region in which both Washington and American firms felt confident that no power worthy of respect could possibly stand in the way of the realization of American interests. Thus, the pattern of intervention here long predated either Luce's American Century or the Cold War (with the exception of Castro's Cuba), and has been relatively unaffected by the collapse of the Soviet Union.[2] It was the Asian Third World, as we will see, that gave real definition to the American Century.

At the same time another influential body of opinion, the Council on Foreign Relations in New York, was moving away from Europe – but in a different sense. Germany dominated continental Europe in 1941, with Britain blocking its way to the rest of the

1   Jean Baudrillard, *America* (New York, 1989), 77.
2   Readers interested in recent American foreign policy with regard to Central America should consult William M. LeoGrande's excellent new book, *Our Own Backyard: The United States in Central America, 1977–1992* (Chapel Hill, 1998).

world. The council therefore envisioned "a great residual area potentially available to us and upon the basis of which American foreign policy may be framed." Later termed "the Grand Area," this space became the council's metaphor for American expansion into various corners of the globe hitherto off limits, especially the British, French, and Dutch colonies but also China and Japan, a vast expanse now undermined or made "open" by the effects of the ongoing European war.

This was not simply a reflection of the council's accustomed Atlanticism, but a Pacific strategy aimed at expansion into a domain marred only by ongoing Japanese aggression. One month before the appearance of Luce's essay the council issued "American Far Eastern Policy," which recommended all-out aid to China to keep Japan pinned down on the continent, and the embargo of war materials to Japan – policies that Franklin Roosevelt implemented within months.[3] Obviously the Grand Area included what later came to be called the Third World: but what should be the mechanism of American operation within this global realm? Did the council propose to colonize it like Whale Cay, to police it as Batista did Cuba, or to Americanize it à la Henry Luce? The answer is that the Grand Area was the world economy and it was to be open for trade, not necessarily human uplift, and the mechanisms of operation would be those later established at Bretton Woods. The American who, in my view, did the most to bring this about had already sketched this future when the European war began, almost two years earlier.

Henry Luce was a publisher, and a most successful one. But his world view was narrow, particularly in its either/or attitude to Europe and Asia. The true captains of the American Century were those who thought in both/and terms: Europe and Asia, the open door and partnership with imperial Britain, intervention in both Latin America and Europe,[4] a world economy with no ulti-

---

3 Council on Foreign Relations, aide-memoire E–B26, "American Far Eastern Policy," 15 January 1941, cited in Laurence H. Shoup and William Minter, *Imperial Brain Trust: The Council on Foreign Relations and United States Foreign Policy* (New York, 1977), 129–36.
4 Time has not dimmed the impact of a stunning phone conversation between John J. McCloy and Henry Stimson in May 1945: McCloy remarked that "we ought to have our cake and eat

mate limit. Dean Acheson embodied the fullness of American
ambition and expressed it concisely in a speech delivered shortly
after Germany invaded Poland, entitled "An American Attitude
Toward Foreign Affairs," a text truly pregnant with ideas that
built the American Century. As he later put it in reflecting back
on this speech, he had really sought at the time to "begin work on
a new postwar world system."[5]

"Our vital interests," Acheson said in this speech delivered at
Yale, "do not permit us to be indifferent to the outcome" of the
wars in Europe and Asia; nor was it possible for Americans to
remain isolated from them – unless they wished a kind of eternal
"internment on this continent" (only an Anglophile like Acheson
would liken North America to a concentration camp). He located the causes of the war and the global depression that preceded it in "the failure of some mechanisms of the Nineteenth
Century world economy" that had led to "this break-up of the
world into exclusive areas for armed exploitation administered
along oriental [*sic*] lines." In its time, "the economic and political system of the Nineteenth Century . . . produced an amazing
increase in the production of wealth," but for many years it had
been in an "obvious process of decline." Reconstruction of the
foundations of peace would require new mechanisms: ways to
make capital available for industrial production, the removal of
tariffs, "a broader market for goods made under decent standards,"
"a stable international monetary system," and the removal of
"exclusive or preferential trade arrangements." The world
economy was his main emphasis, but in good Achesonian
realpolitik fashion he also called for the immediate creation of "a
navy and air force adequate to secure us in both oceans simultaneously and with striking power sufficient to reach to the other
side of each of them."

---

it too; that we ought to be free to operate under this regional arrangement in South America,
at the same time intervene promptly in Europe," to which Stimson replied, "I think that it's
not asking too much to have our little region over here which never bothered anybody." I first
read this colloquy in Gabriel Kolko, *The Politics of War* (New York, 1968), 470–71.
5   Dean Acheson, "An American Attitude Toward Foreign Affairs," 28 November 1939, in
Morning and Noon (Boston, 1965), 267–75. See also Acheson's reflections on the speech
(ibid., 216–17). I am indebted to Heajeong Lee for bringing this text to my attention.

Dean Acheson later had the opportunity to implement these ideas, first at Bretton Woods, then with the Marshall Plan and the Truman Doctrine, and finally with NSC–68; he is the person who comes closest to being the singular architect of American strategy from 1944 to 1953. A short few years after he gave this prescient speech and Henry Luce claimed the century for Americans, the United States accounted for half of the industrial production of all the world, emerging from the war as the single unscathed and emboldened superpower – thus making both men look like visionaries. Yet by the turn of the last century the United States was the most productive industrial economy in the world, and everyone knew this by the early 1920s as American firms pioneered mass production and consumption and its banks became the effective center of global commerce. But it had a laughably small military, and neither the political will nor the domestic political base for global hegemony. The years from 1914 to 1941 were thus not part of an American century, but years of hegemonic interregnum in which England could no longer lead and the United States was not yet ready to do so. The German invasion of Poland changed all that, culminating in the Pearl Harbor attack, which finally committed the United States to global leadership at a time when economic collapse, global war, and the resultant chaos required the construction of the new world system that Acheson envisioned in 1939.

The Third World as the Fulcrum of Postwar American Foreign Policy

In memoirs written thirty years after his Yale address, Acheson began again with a fond reprise of the "century of international peace" after Waterloo and the Congress of Vienna in 1815:

Economically, the globe was indeed 'one world.' The great empires of Europe, through their colonies and spheres of influence, spread authority, order, and respect for the obligation of contract almost everywhere;

and where their writs did not run, their frigates and gunboats navigated.[6]

He proceeded in the rest of this fine book to recount the emergence of an American-led world system after 1945.

The moment when the baton of world leadership finally and definitively passed from London to Washington came on 21 February 1947, when a British Embassy official informed Acheson that England could not give Greece and Turkey $250 million in military and economic aid. Acheson walked off to lunch with a friend, remarking that "there are only two powers in the world now," the United States and the Soviet Union.[7] Acheson did not mean that an era of bipolarity had dawned, although he meant that as well; he meant something much deeper – the substitution of American for British leadership. Acheson was present at this creation and unabashedly "hegemonic," and did not mistake the opportunities and perils of America's new position in the world. His problem was to be pregnant with an idea that he could not articulate, lest Harry Truman lose the next election (for example, by announcing that the United States had now replaced England as the power with all the burdens-of-last-resort in the world economy). To put it differently, the internationalist forces in American politics lacked a strong domestic base, particularly in the Congress. George Kennan provided the solution to this dilemma with an elegant metaphor: containment. Imagine, America marches outward, inherits Britain's role, and you mark it up for the defense. Imagine, a doctrine defining hegemony by what it opposes, obviating the necessity to explain to the American people what it is, and what its consequences will be for them. It is only today, after the fall of the Berlin Wall and the collapse of the Soviet Union, that Americans can see this obscured, underlying

---

6 Dean Acheson, *Present at the Creation: My Years in the State Department* (New York, 1969), 7.
7 Thomas J. McCormick, *America's Half-Century: United States Foreign Policy in the Cold War* (Baltimore, 1989), 72.

system that keeps going in spite of the disappearance of its ostensible raison d'être.

Paradoxically, it was not in 1941 but in 1947 that Henry Luce found himself in tune with world events. No one expressed the synthesis between the overt containment policy and the more important world economy concerns better than Luce. In his June 1947 *Fortune* editorial called "The U.S. Opportunity," he wrote that Americans must become "missionaries of capitalism and democracy" and used as his "classic current example" the archetypal multinational corporation – the American oil firm. Aramco, he wrote, not only developed Middle Eastern oil but built schools, water works, even whole cities where there had only been desert. His next example was Nelson Rockefeller, whose family ran the various branches of Standard Oil and whose far-flung activities in Latin America exemplified "the traditional internationalism of the oil business." Nelson was "fired with a great idea": the transformation of Latin America by American capital.

In the past American business had been content to exploit "the world's greatest free trade area," that is, the national market at home; now, however, big corporations constituted the "front-line soldiers and batallions in the battle of freedom." Among these "great corporations," Luce listed exclusively high-technology, competitive firms with large international markets: Standard Oil, General Motors, General Electric, ITT, Pan American Airlines, Westinghouse, IBM, and Coca Cola, which (Luce said later) was "pursuing the 'Coca-colonization' of the world." Here "at the top," American business was "already international." And so, it was "no longer the case that we can lie in the sun without having to worry about the Koreans and the Azerbaijanis."[8]

The main arena of expansion for Henry Luce, of course, was Asia. His argument had a particular appeal in the American domestic context, linking multinational corporations to traditional expansionism, that is, linking internationalism and nationalism, Europe and Asia, in a way that former isolationist constituencies

8 Henry Luce editorial, *Fortune* (June 1947); for the "Coca-colonization" statement see *Fortune* (February 1950), where Luce defended Truman's Point Four program for the Third World. See also W. A. Swanberg, *Luce and His Empire* (New York, 1972), 183.

could understand. Although widely ridiculed for his effervescent rhetoric and his diehard support of the Chinese Nationalists, Luce symbolized better than anyone else the interventionist compromise that grew out of the domestic clash of the old isolationist and the new internationalist forces.

The struggle with communism was thus but one part, and the secondary part, of a project to revive the world economy from the devastation of the global depression and World War II – just as Acheson had originally suggested in 1939. At first the problem seemed to be solved with the Bretton Woods mechanisms elaborated in 1944, but when by 1947 these had not worked to revive the advanced industrial economies, along came the Marshall Plan for Europe and the "reverse course" in Japan that removed controls on its heavy industries. When by 1950 the allied economies were still not growing sufficiently, NSC–68 (a document mostly written by Paul Nitze but guided by the thinking of Acheson – by then Truman's secretary of state) hit upon military Keynesianism as a device that did, finally, prime the pump of the advanced industrial economies.[9]

The Korean War, seen by the North Koreans as a war of national liberation in the face of American attempts to re-stitch South Korea's economic linkages with Japan, turned into the crisis that built the American national security state and pushed through the money to pay for it: the vast procurements for this war constituted a "Marshall Plan" that worked for Western Europe and especially Japan (whose industrial takeoff began in the early 1950s). From June to December 1950 the defense budget quadrupled (from roughly $13 to $56 billion in 1950 dollars), but it did so in the midst of a massive crisis over China's intervention in the Korean peninsula: only with the opening of Sino-American war did Congress finally begin to fund the national security state at the levels to which it has since become accustomed.

---

9 William Borden, *Pacific Alliance: United States Foreign Economic Policy and Japan's Trade Recovery, 1947–1955* (Madison, 1984), 12–14. Here I also rely on Borden's "Military Keynesianism in the Early 1950s," a paper presented to my International History Workshop (University of Chicago, 14 February 1994).

George Kennan was famously unhappy with the implementation of his containment doctrine, but in 1994 he was also less sure of what the end of the Cold War meant than most analysts:

I viewed [containment] as primarily a diplomatic and political task, though not wholly without military implications. I considered that if and when we had succeeded in persuading the Soviet leadership that the continuation of the[ir] expansionist pressures . . . would be, in many respects, to their disadvantage, then the moment would have come for serious talks with them about the future of Europe. But when, some three years later [1950], this moment had arrived – when we had made our point with the Marshall Plan, with . . . the Berlin blockade and other measures – when the lesson I wanted to see us convey to Moscow had been successfully conveyed, then it was one of the great disappointments of my life to discover that neither our Government nor our Western European allies had any interest in entering into such discussions at all. What they and the others wanted from Moscow, with respect to the future of Europe, was essentially "unconditional surrender." They were prepared to wait for it. And this was the beginning of the 40 years of Cold War.[10]

What does this mean? How can we interpret this rendering of history? The estrangement between Acheson and Kennan holds the key to unlocking the rapidly unfolding events from the autumn of 1949 (the Soviet atomic bomb, the devaluation of the British pound, the victory of the Chinese revolution) to the winter of 1950 (Sino-American war, defeat in northern Korea, and the quadrupling of defense spending).[11] The war in Korea was the lever ("Korea came along and saved us," in Acheson's famous words) through which Washington finally found a reliable method that would pay the bills for cold and hot wars on a global scale.

---

10 *New York Times*, Op-Ed Page, 14 March 1994. Kennan added, "Those of my opponents of that day who have survived [read Paul Nitze] would say, I am sure, 'You see. We were right. The collapse of the Soviet Union amounted to the unconditional surrender we envisaged. . . . And we paid nothing for it.' To which I should have to reply: 'But we did pay a great deal for it. We paid with 40 years of enormous and otherwise unnecessary military expenditure."
11 Cumings, *The Origins of the Korean War*, vol. 2, *The Roaring of the Cataract, 1947–1950* (Princeton, 1990), 35–61, 408–38.

It also committed American leaders to containment, rather than liberation or rollback.

The Chinese intervened not to boost the American defense budget but to block a "rollback" into North Korea, and the devastating impact of that intervention took any serious attempt at "liberating" the peoples of Communist countries off the American strategic agenda thereafter, thus limiting strategy in the Vietnam War to one of containing communism in South Vietnam (which ultimately proved impossible). The failure of Korean rollback put decisive outer limits on "positive action" for the next several decades. Containment was the real Eisenhower policy, vastly preferable to the centrist elites then in control of foreign policy. John Foster Dulles, putative architect of liberation and rollback, was instrumental in placing these same limits: well before the 1956 Hungarian rebellion (usually thought to spell the end of his rollback fantasies), he had criticized "preventive war" doctrines and liberation schemes: trying to "detach" satellites from the USSR, he said, "would involve the United States in general war." Later on Dulles searched for a place where a "mini-rollback" might be accomplished, its feasibility defined by getting in and out unscathed and not provoking the Chinese or the Russians. The paltry place of choice, which Dulles brought up frequently in NSC meetings in the 1950s, was Hainan Island off the Sino-Vietnamese coast. Like another rollbacker, Ronald Reagan at Grenada in 1983, Dulles was reduced to an "island" strategy, a "quick in, quick out" chimera. But of course Dulles never tried this.[12]

The Korean War thus fathered a virtual "stalemate machine" in Washington that governed one intervention after another, producing rapid entry but no effective exit – except in the "quick in, quick out" ideal scenario possible only with places the size of Martha's Vineyard, like Grenada. These boundaries on containment explain the bipartisan stalemate between conservatives and liberals over the Bay of Pigs in 1961, the unwillingness to invade the North during the Vietnam War, and the compromise on whether to contain or invade and destroy the Nicaraguan revolution

12   See my extended discussion in ibid., chap. 22.

throughout the 1980s. Here was the crucible that produced American anti-Communist strategy, a containment policy that would work politically at home and strategically abroad and that explains the relative peace-and-quiet of the "North" during the Cold War. Meanwhile, both superpowers saw the non-Communist Third World as an arena of proxy conflict.

The containment stalemate machine ended in the 1990s as the object of its desire disappeared with the collapse of Western communism. But the domestic interests that formed around the containment system are still dominant and still find utility in Third World interventions, now directed against assorted "renegade states." In 1991 we were again at war, to "contain" Iraq's invasion of Kuwait – but, as it happened, not to "roll it back." The tanks screeched their brakes in the sand well short of Baghdad, thus to avoid another Korea (according to President Bush's national security advisor, Brent Skowcroft). Today the military-industrial complex still finds a breath of life in the presumed dangers of rogue Third World nations: Iran, Iraq, Sudan, Libya, and the ever-necessary North Korea.

East Asia thus had a violent and bloody history that taught a lesson Kennan had already understood in 1947: only his limited conception of containment would work; to plunge into civil conflicts in the Third World would only spill American blood and treasure to no good end. The repositioning of Japan as a major industrial producer in the context of a raging anti-imperial revolution on the Asian mainland explains most of East and Southeast Asian history for the next three decades (until the Indochina War finally ended in 1975). And here we encounter a human agency the Achesons and the Kennans never imagined: the fierce energy of aroused peoples in the 1940s, collectivities for whom imperialism and a recent feudal past were hated realities, and the promises of the American vision an utter chimera. Korea was the unexpected and unpredicted Third World fulcrum of American Cold War strategy, touching off an American struggle with successive anti-imperial revolutions: the Korean, the Chinese, and the Vietnamese. But each of these conflicts would have flabbergasted an American statesman, should a mystic have conjured them in a crystal ball in 1945. The Asian orientation of American policy would not have surprised Henry Luce, perhaps, but the cumulative popular resistance to his "American vision" would have astonished him. Only in the 1970s would he find evidence that East Asia wanted to join the American Century on his terms: actually, on terms rather close to those he enunciated in 1947, as American firms in declining industries like textiles began to move offshore and to organize production in places like South Korea, Taiwan, and Malaysia. A new trope signified this extraordinary shift: "Pacific Rim."

The Rise of the Pacific

Rather suddenly in the 1970s, especially up and down the American West coast, a hue and cry emerged about a new Pacific era: "Pacific Rim" became the code word for all card-carrying internationalists and multinational corporation executives (and it was a short step from there to "Pacific Century"). This "Rimspeak" provided constructs that instantly revalued East and Southeast Asia, as Westerners (mostly Americans) recognized and defined it, in ways that highlighted some parts and excluded (or occluded) others. When East Asia was "painted Red," it held an apparent outward-moving dynamic whose core was Beijing: "400 million Chinese armed with nuclear weapons," in Dean Rusk's 1960s scenario, threatened nations along China's rim with oblivion: South Korea, South Vietnam, Taiwan, Indonesia, Thailand, and the big enchilada, Japan. (Dean Acheson's "defense perimeter" through island Asia pointed to the same problem in 1950.) China and North Korea were among the most rapidly growing industrial economies in the world in the 1950s and early 1960s, "success stories" sadly to be contrasted with basket-case South Korea (as AID people always called it up through the mid-1960s), incompetent South Vietnam, mendicant Philippines, running sore Indonesia (with a formidable internal Communist movement until 1965), and hopelessly obtuse and retarded Burma.

"Pacific Rim" revalued all that. Suddenly the rim was the locus of dynamism, bringing pressure on the mainland of Asia. The "success stories" were any countries that sought export-led capitalist development, and the "basket cases" (also known as "failed states") were any countries still committed to self-reliant or socialist development, from Burma to North Korea. This new discourse was also deeply solicitous of the benighted and laggard socialist economies, however, and therefore sought a formal end of ideology: "Pacific Rim" invoked a new-born community that anyone, socialist or not, could join – as long as they began to go capitalist. Here the great victory, accomplished in the two decades since Deng Xiaoping's 1978 reforms, was China: a China increasingly integrated with the world economy, possessing a China market of such obsessive concern to American business as to warm the cockles of Henry Luce's heart. As China waxed and Japan waned on American horizons in the 1990s,[13] perhaps the breadth of this American victory can be appreciated in China's beleaguered efforts to polish its application to the World Trade Organization (WTO), while Washington continues to demand more reform before approving Beijing's entry.

Was there an indigenous path toward the postwar reconstitution of the Asian region? The people of the rim have tried two ways before: the imperial pan-Asianism of Japan in the late 1930s and early 1940s, full of opprobrium toward the "white" nations and colonizers, but never very successful in gaining non-Japanese adherents; and the Communist pan-Asianism of the 1950s, when Mao's China deeply influenced Korea, Vietnam, and various socialist movements in Asia. This had a brief heyday after North Korea and China fought the United States and its allies to a standstill in Korea, with the high point at Bandung in 1954, which we can take as the beginning of the three-decade-long run of a different Third World force, the non-aligned movement. With victories here and there – perhaps above all, the OPEC cartel's success in breaking the oil regime run by American and European multi-

---

13 An important nationwide poll of American attitudes on foreign affairs found in 1995 that while the mass of Americans (62 percent) continued to worry about economic competition from Japan, far fewer among the American elite (21 percent) still did so. Five years earlier the figures for both groups were 60 percent for the public, 63 percent for the "leaders." See John E. Reilly, ed., *American Public Opinion and United States Foreign Policy 1995* (Chicago, 1995), 25.

nationals – this attempt at an independent, third path nonetheless fizzled in the late 1970s (its last gasp was the New International Economic Order or NIEO), and it is as dead as dead can be today. The Third World may have had a host of common developmental problems, but the First World was eminently more united on ways of maintaining its predominance.

The "Abundant Life" Today

Henry Luce's American Century did not begin in 1900, but in 1941. He spoke in the future tense about the creation of "the first great American century" with the United States as "the dynamic center of ever-widening spheres of enterprise." What can we say today about his "American vision" of uplift for all mankind, articulated so bluntly? In the past half-century, average human well-being around the globe unquestionably has improved. Life expectancy rose from 46.4 years in 1950–55 to 64.4 in 1990–95, and the absolute number of people who were chronically undernourished fell from 941 million circa 1970 to 786 million circa 1990, in spite of rapid population growth. But if the world's poor still hanker after American mass culture, the rich have gotten much richer in the same period. The ratio of per-capita income between the top fifth and the bottom fifth of the globe's population was 30 to 1 in 1960, 45 to 1 in 1980, and 60 to 1 by the 1990s.[14]

A new *Human Development Report* compiled by the United Nations showed that some 358 global billionaires have wealth equal to the combined incomes of the world's 2.3 billion poor people, that is, nearly half of the global population. Eighty percent of the world's people live in Third World countries, but they have just 22 percent of the world's wealth. The lowest fifth of the nations held 2.3 percent of the world's wealth thirty years ago; now they possess exactly 1.4 percent. In more concrete terms, the

14   Joel E. Cohen, "How Many People Can the Earth Support?" *New York Review of Books*, 8 October 1998.

assets of the three richest people in the world exceed the combined GDP of the 48 least developed countries; the richest fifth of the world's people consume 86 percent of all goods and services, 45 percent of all meat and fish, 74 percent of all telephone traffic, and 87 percent of all vehicles. Of some 4.4 billion people in the Third World (still connoted as "developing countries" by the UN), three fifths lack access to safe sewers, two thirds lack toilets, one third have no access to clean water, and a fifth lack any kind of modern health care. About one quarter of Third World peoples are illiterate, and of these, two thirds are women. This report estimates that it would cost $13 billion to provide basic health and nutrition to everyone in the world and $6 billion to give every human being a basic education; meanwhile, Americans spend $17 billion annually on pet food and $8 billion on cosmetics.[15]

The frontier technology of the past twenty years, symbolized by the microchip, appears ready to homogenize the world in Luce's image: billions of Third World peoples are now exposed to McDonald's hamburgers and "Coca-Colonization." President Clinton visited a remote village in Africa in 1998 and urged that the local school connect up to the World Wide Web (he did not appear to notice that the school had no electricity). Is Luce's vision of Americanization soon to be realized? I don't think so. Using the Web I can find satellite photos of this village, learn the ethnicity of its inhabitants, and count the number of homes with running water. But the villagers cannot see me or the World Bank employees who catalog such information. They are less free than before the advent of the computer, because knowledge is power. Instead of homogenizing these Africans, turning them into the Americans they no doubt would like to be (given the alternatives), "the technological annulment of temporal/spatial distances," in Zygmunt Bauman's words, tends to polarize us and them.[16]

Today the pot of gold at the end of the developmental rainbow seems everywhere to recede into the future, even for the "miracle"

---

15 United Nations, Human Development Report, 1998, as cited in "The News of the Week in Review," *New York Times*, 27 September 1998. See also Cohen, "How Many People?"
16 Zygmunt Bauman, *Globalization: The Human Consequences* (New York, 1998), 18.

economies of the Pacific Rim. When the Second World of Communist countries, blocs, and iron and bamboo curtains unexpectedly disappeared a decade ago, so did American indulgence for the neomercantilism of its East Asian allies, which was always a function of the Cold War struggle with their opposites. Since 1993 the "Clinton Doctrine" has been one of aggressive foreign economic policy designed to promote exports, to open targeted economies to American goods and investment (especially in the service industries that now dominate the American economy – accounting for 85 percent of GDP – and in which it has a barely challenged global lead), while maintaining the Cold War positions that give Washington a diffuse leverage over its allies like Japan and Germany and that pose a subtle but distinct threat to potential adversaries like China. All this goes on under the neoliberal legitimation of Smithean free markets and Lockean democracy and civil society – that is, Luce's "American vision."

As one would predict of a mature hegemonic power, the United States now prefers the virtues of a multilateral economism to the vices of direct coercion and intervention, and thus the IMF and the World Bank have vastly enhanced their utility in Washington's eye, and even the abandoned Bretton Woods mechanism – an international trade organization – has materialized in the form of the WTO. From the standpoint of the IMF, the best state is that state weak enough so that it cannot resist IMF ministrations, but strong enough to maintain order and impose these ministrations. This is perilously close to the status of the Qing Dynasty in the late nineteenth century, when the British came to understand that China's central government needed to have enough strength to keep the country intact, but not enough to keep it from being exploited.[17] The deep meaning and intent of the American and IMF response to the global financial crisis is to close the historical chapter in which the United States-sheltered "developmental states" have prospered.

---

17   A point made forcefully in Walter LaFeber, *The Clash: A History of United States-Japan Relations* (New York, 1997).

After the 1997 bailouts of Thailand and South Korea, influential analysts inveighed against a model of development that had been the apple of Washington's eye since the 1960s. Deputy IMF Director Stanley Fischer said true reform would not be possible "within the Korean model or the Japan Inc. model." "Korean leaders are wedded to economic ideals born in a 1960s dictatorship," an editorial in *The Wall Street Journal* said, leading to "hands-on government regulation, ceaseless corporate expansion, distrust of foreign capital and competition"; the thirty largest firms, accounting for a third of the country's wealth, were now said to be "big monsters" who "gobbled up available credit" and relied on "outdated notions of vertical integration for strength." The chief economist at Deutsche Morgan Grenfell, Ed Yardeni, perhaps trumped all the pundits in heaping scorn on the Korean "miracle": "The truth of the matter is that Korea, Inc. is already bankrupt. . . . All that's left is to file the papers. This is a zombie economy."[18] In this way, apparently autonomous "Asian tigers," prospering within an indulgent hegemonic net for thirty years, find themselves rendered bewildered and dependent by a dimly understood hegemonic mechanism that now places their entire society and economy under global jurisdiction.

Today we are left with the daunting reality that among the claimants to comprehensive, advanced industrial status a century ago (England, France, Germany, Italy, the United States, Russia, Japan), there have been no new entrants and only six of the original group remain (with Russia now having an economy smaller than South Korea's).[19] The Third World is dominated by the advanced countries in a way unprecedented since the colonial era, and with most of it outside the loop of the prosperity of recent years, it therefore is the prime source of war, instability, and class conflict – but with no convincing antisystemic model to follow. All the systemic alternatives to the Grand Area, to the One World

---

18   Editorial by Joseph Kahn and Michael Schuman, *Wall Street Journal*, 24 November 1997; Fischer quoted in ibid., 8 December 1997. Yardeni's "zombie" remark was broadcast widely on CNN Television News; see the full quotation in *Washington Post*, 11 December 1997.

19   For a cogent and prescient analysis of the end of Third World development see Immanuel Wallerstein, *Historical Capitalism* (London, 1983), 95–98.

of multinational capital, have collapsed: above all the East bloc
and the Soviet Union in 1989–91, but also the neomercantile model
of East Asian development. But the least noticed collapse of our
time is that of the Third World, the site of revolutionary nationalism and anti-imperial wars for three decades after 1945, the self-
constituted alternative to both blocs in the Cold War that lasted
from Bandung through the Non-Aligned Movement and into the
late-1970s demands for a New International Economic Order.
Twenty years later we have a collection of failed states running
from Zambia to North Korea, an enormous if amorphous population of stateless people from Kosovo to Sudan, and the recurrent television spectacle of millions of people starving to death,
from Sudan again to North Korea. The Third World moves not
up the developmental ladder, but from statehood to catastrophe.

From the Third World if not the American perspective, the case
of North Korea is particularly poignant. No postcolonial nation
so rigorously and so obstinately chose an alternative path than
North Korea, founded in a deep desire, reinforced by a half-century of Japanese imperialism and a devastating clash with the
United States, for independence and self-reliance – to the point
not merely of diminishing returns (those come in the mid-1970s)
but of near national annihilation. Now North Korea inhabits
perhaps the most photographed territory in the world, as American satellites surveil every inch of its surface and demand en-
trance to any facility that these eyes-in-the-sky cannot see.[20] The
ultimate resting point of North Korean obstinacy is a regimen of
American remote-control proctology. Pyongyang's residual power
resides only in the imagined space of what cannot be seen, just as
Washington redoubles its efforts to monitor a world simultaneously
unruly and more available than ever to eavesdropping, thus to
discipline and punish Third World miscreants.

---

20   The most recent example being an intelligence leak to reporter David Sanger about a
huge underground facility being constructed by "swarms" of people in North Korea, which
might well be a subterranean complex for reprocessing plutonium, as the Israelis did in their
Dimona complex (*New York Times*, 17 August 1998). Subsequently in high-level talks with
an American delegation the North Koreans offered a guided tour of this facility, described as
for civilian uses, if at the end the Americans would compensate them for the expenses of the
tour, and for slander (*Korean Central News Agency*, 5 September 1998).

Conclusion: Still the American Century

If England's century began with the Congress of Vienna and ended in 1914, and if America's began in 1941 as Luce thought (and assuming that we get a century as the British did), this means that we should only begin to wring our hands and fill ourselves with the proper fin-de-siècle angst around the year 2040. At the turn of the new century, Americans can perhaps revel in the robust middle age of United States's global leadership. But just a few short years ago they could not, because the scholars and popular pundits who are supposed to know the occult science of international affairs were full of dread about American decline and Japanese and German advance. The American century looked like an unaccountably short one.

The prematurely reported demise of the American Century was surrounded in the public and the academic sphere by a great deal of nonsense in the 1980s and early 1990s. Today it is disconcerting to recall the towering influence of work by "declinists" like Paul Kennedy (*The Rise and Fall of the Great Powers*), Robert Keohane (*After Hegemony*), Thomas McCormick (*America's Half-Century*), and Clyde Prestowitz (*Trading Places*); and it is positively embarrassing to read recent accounts like Samuel Huntington's *Clash of Civilizations* and Donald White's *The American Century* that still seem to assume an America on the road to ruin.[21] These authors cover the American political spectrum: Huntington identifies himself with conservative politics, Keohane and White with moderate (or neo-) liberalism, Prestowitz with neoconservatism and a new American nationalism, and McCormick with a liberal/left position long identified with the work of historian William Appleman Williams.

---

21 Samuel Huntington, *The Clash of Civilizations and the Remaking of World Order* (New York, 1996); Paul M. Kennedy, *The Rise and Fall of the Great Powers: Economic Change and Military Conflict from 1500 to 2000* (New York, 1989); Robert Keohane, *After Hegemony: Cooperation and Discord in the World Political Economy* (Princeton, 1984); Clyde V. Prestowitz, Jr., *Trading Places: How We Are Giving Our Future to Japan and How to Reclaim It* (New York, 1993); Donald W. White, *The American Century: The Rise and Decline of the United States as a World Power* (New Haven, 1996).

The "key question" of Keohane's book, for example, was "how international cooperation can be maintained among the advanced capitalist states in the absence of American hegemony."[22] Samuel Huntington had a Realpolitik conception of hegemony that mistook maturity for decline: "European globalism is no more, and American hegemony is receding, if only because it is no longer needed to protect the United States against a Cold War Soviet threat."[23] This presumed conclusion to American preeminence is also metaphorical, a vehicle for the passions: Huntington wraps the end of the Cold War into a coming "clash of civilizations," through a nostalgic reprise of 1950s modernization theory and a disillusioned lament on the passing of the Eastern establishment and its Anglo-Saxon counterparts in Europe, thus yielding a plea for a renewed Atlanticism (precisely at a time when American trade with Asia towers over Atlantic exchange). From a very different perspective Thomas McCormick, in an otherwise fine book on the postwar period, deployed an understanding of hegemony that propelled him toward a final chapter of deep pessimism: "American hegemony was dead," he wrote, but that decline might also "be ushering in frightening developments that would make Lenin a prophet twice in this century."[24]

All of these books were wrong about American decline. Often, they were wrong not because of the evidence they brought to bear, but because of a flawed understanding of America's role in the world in the first place: primarily, a failure to understand that the main task of American statesmen after World War II was the reconstruction of the world economy. Instead of a premature end to the American Century or a coming clash of civilizations, today there appears to be one dominant global civilization, the American, and several atavisms masquerading as civilizational challenges – Islamic fundamentalism, Balkan mayhem, the (not-very) Confucian East, the obsolescent economic nationalism of Japan

22   Keohane, *After Hegemony*, 43.
23   Huntington, "The West: Unique, not Universal," *Foreign Affairs* 75 (November/December 1996): 28–46. See idem, *Clash of Civilizations*.
24   McCormick, *America's Half-Century*, 240–41.

and South Korea, the declining Chinese Communist grip on a rapidly growing capitalist China, and a Russia that does not clearly appear to have an economy in 1998, let alone a competing civilization. So in this sense, if perhaps only in this sense, Henry Luce was truly a visionary in 1941.

9

Race from Power:
U.S. Foreign Policy and the
General Crisis of "White Supremacy"

GERALD HORNE

Explicit doctrines of racial supremacy are in bad odor nowadays, particularly among foreign policy elites; such retrograde ideas are viewed widely as the justly neglected relic of a long-forgotten era. Suggestive of this trend are the critical studies of the "construction of whiteness" that have proliferated of late.[1] Among other things, these studies have asked a quite profound question: How was it that those who had warred on the shores of Europe – English versus Irish, French versus German, Russian versus Pole, Serb versus Croat, even Jew versus Gentile – all of a sudden on

---

1   Richard Delgado and Jean Stefancic, eds., *Critical White Studies: Looking Behind the Mirror* (Philadelphia, 1997); Michelle Fine, Lois Weis, Linda C. Powell, and L. Mun Wong, eds., *Off White: Readings on Race, Power and Society* (New York, 1997); Susan Gubar, *Racechanges: White Skin, Black Face in American Culture* (New York, 1997); Toni Morrison, *Playing in the Dark: Whiteness and the Literary Imagination* (Cambridge, 1992); Ruth Frankenberg, *White Women, Race Matters: The Social Construction of Whiteness* (Minneapolis, 1993); Joe L. Kincheloe, Shirley R. Steinberg, Nelson M. Rodriguez, and Ronald E. Chennault, eds., *White Reign: Deploying Whiteness in America* (New York, 1998); Mike Hill, ed., *Whiteness: A Critical Reader* (New York, 1997); Ian F. Hancy Lopez, *White By Law: The Legal Construction of Race* (New York, 1996); Eric Lott, *Love and Theft: Blackface Minstrelsy and the American Working Class* (New York, 1993); David Roediger, *The Wages of Whiteness: Race and the Making of the American Working Class* (New York, 1991); Noel Ignatiev, *How the Irish Became White* (New York, 1996); Grace Elizabeth Hale, *Making Whiteness: The Culture of Segregation in the South, 1890–1940* (New York, 1998); Theodore Allen, *The Invention of the White Race: Volume One: Racial Oppression and Social Control* (New York, 1994); Elvi Whittaker, *The Mainland Haole: The White Experience in Hawaii* (New York, 1986).

arriving on these shores were reconstructed as "white" and provided real or imagined privileges based on "white supremacy"?

Some of these studies have noted that in addition to providing a cohesive identity for disparate European immigrants, "whiteness" and "white supremacy" had the added advantage of providing a convenient rationale for seizing the resources and labor of those of a darker hue who were presumed to be "inferior": that is "race" ("whiteness") was derived from "power" and, yes, "power" was derived from "race."

Still, despite the richness of this plethora of studies, few have sought to place the construction of whiteness in the context of U.S. foreign policy – although this global context was highly relevant in this process: minimally, preventing the proliferation of ethnic tensions that had helped to plunge Europe into war so often encouraged the construction of "whiteness" and "white supremacy." For the most part these studies have not sought to include Africans – as opposed to African-Americans – in its comprehension of the construction of "whiteness"; nor have they contemplated that the closing of the frontier in North America and the final defeat of Native Americans led directly to an assault on the "frontier" in Africa. Nor have these studies, broadly speaking, posited Asia – and notably Japan's rise after its 1905 defeat of Russia – as a central factor in the evolution of "white supremacy."

Above all, one cannot begin to understand U.S. foreign policy during this century without contemplating race and racism, just as one cannot begin to understand the ebb and flow of race and racism in this nation without contemplating the global context. Indeed, just as some have suggested that "class struggle" is the motive force of history, this insight should be complemented with the idea that relations – or "struggles" – between and among nations is the locomotive of history and, most definitely, is the leading factor determining the advance and retreat of "white supremacy."

Racial construction has not been a static process. The discrediting of fascism as a result of the Holocaust, the civil rights movement in the United States, and the anti-apartheid movement in

South Africa were among the epochal events that caused a basic reconsideration of notions of racial supremacy; moreover, the ability of nations as various as Japan and the Soviet Union to transform U.S. tacit or explicit backing for "white supremacy" into a liability for Washington also helped to inspire less overtly racialist thinking on these shores.

Nevertheless, during the Cold War era it was often said that U.S. "wars in the Third World were a substitute for a Third World War": despite the bluster and tension in the Moscow-Washington relationship, the United States did not go to war with the Soviet Union, but instead wreaked havoc on Korea, Vietnam, Grenada, Panama and Iraq, among other nations. This reality, perhaps, should alert us to the fact that despite official nostrums, disarticulated notions of "white supremacy" did not disappear during the American Century.[2] Likewise, it is significant that atomic bombs were detonated by the United States in Asia, not Europe.

Yet "white supremacy" – this conception of the virtual divine right of some of European heritage to dominate all others and all else[3] – has been far from immutable. It is generally thought to have emerged as a justification for slavery and the slave trade[4] or

2   Of course, "white supremacy" is far from being an exclusively U.S. phenomenon. See, for example, Alice L. Conklin, *A Mission to Civilize: The Republican Idea of Empire in France and West Africa, 1895–1930* (Stanford, 1997); Allison Blakely, *Blacks in the Dutch World: The Evolution of Racial Imagery in a Modern Society* (Bloomington, 1993); Frances Twine Winddance, *Racism in a Racial Democracy: The Maintenance of White Supremacy in Brazil* (New Brunswick, 1998); Gretchen Fitzgerald, *Repulsing Racism: Reflections on Racism and the Irish* (Dublin, 1992); Panikos Panayi, ed., *Racial Violence in Britain, 1840–1950* (Leicester, 1993); and Jay Kinsbrunner, *Not of Pure Blood: The Free People of Color and Racial Prejudice in Nineteenth-Century Puerto Rico* (Durham, 1996).

3   See, for example, George Fredrickson, *White Supremacy: A Comparative Study in American and South African History* (New York, 1981); John Cell, *The Highest Stage of White Supremacy: The Origins of Segregation in South Africa and the American South* (New York, 1982); and Clifton C. Crais, *White Supremacy and Black Resistance in Pre-Industrial South Africa: The Making of the Colonial Order in the Eastern Cape, 1770–1865* (New York, 1992).

4   Winthrop Jordan, *White over Black: American Attitudes toward the Negro, 1550–1812* (Chapel Hill, 1968); Audrey Smedley, *Race in North America: Origin and Evolution of a Worldview* (Boulder, 1993); Vron Ware, *Beyond the Pale: White Women, Racism, and History* (New York, 1992); Milford Wolpoff and Rachel Caspari, *Race and Human Evolution* (New York, 1997); Pat Shipman, *The Evolution of Racism: Human Differences and the Use and Abuse of Science* (New York, 1994); Michael N. Pearson, *Port Cities and Intruders: The*

as a distorted extension of the Enlightenment,[5] though stirrings in this direction can be detected as early as the thirteenth century in response to the invasions spearheaded by Genghis Khan and his progeny – which left a deep "psychological impact" on Europe; "gargoyles" were devised to portray images of these "inhabitants of the East" as "monsters and fantastic beings . . . The arrival of the Mongols in medieval Europe was akin to an invasion of extra-terrestrials."[6] The process of creating an "other" was essential to the origins and evolution of "white supremacy."

Unfortunately, part of the problem with some of the recent writings on "whiteness" and "white supremacy" is their dual fixation on African-Americans as the virtual exclusive antipode to "whiteness" – while slighting Asia – and a reluctance to examine the period before the African slave trade in explicating this phenomenon.[7]

Swahili Coast, India and Portugal in the Early Modern Era (Baltimore, 1997); Gert Oostindie, ed., *Fifty Years Later: Antislavery, Capitalism and Modernity in the Dutch Orbit* (Pittsburgh, 1996).

5   Charles Mills, *The Racial Contract* (Ithaca, 1997); Emmanuel Chukwudi Eze, *Race and the Enlightenment* (Cambridge, 1997); William B. Cohen, *The French Encounter with Africans: White Response to Blacks, 1530–1880* (Bloomington, 1980); David Goldberg, *Racist Culture: Philosophy and the Politics of Meaning* (Cambridge, 1993).

6   Robert Marshall, *Storm from the East: From Genghis Khan to Khubilai Khan* (Berkeley, 1993), 118, 133, 134; See also Leo de Hartog, *Genghis Khan: Conqueror of the World* (New York, 1989); Roxann Prazniak, *Dialogues across Civilizations: Sketches in World History from the Chinese and European Experiences* (Boulder, 1996); and Jack Goody, *The East in the West* (New York, 1996). More than half a millenium later, Genghis Khan was still roiling relations between Asia and Europe. When Deng Xiaoping of China met with Ho Chi Minh in 1960, the Vietnamese leader informed him that the USSR's Nikita Khrushchev was concerned about the campaign in China to restore the gravesite of Genghis Khan; this "smelled of 'yellow peril,'" it was said. One Soviet comrade was reported to have said, "Why do they celebrate him as a progressive figure? Many nations had to suffer under his attack." More work needs to be done to ascertain the extent to which "white supremacy" – and fear of the "yellow peril" – impacted the central development that extended the continuation of the American Century, that is the so-called Sino-Soviet dispute. See "The Short Version of the Negotiations Between CPSU and CCP Delegations (September 1960)," *Cold War International History Project Bulletin* 10 (March 1998): 172–73. See also Gordon Chang, *Friends and Enemies: The U.S., China and the Soviet Union, 1948–1972* (Stanford, 1990); and David Allan Mayers, *Cracking the Monolith: U.S. Policy against the Sino-Soviet Alliance, 1949–1955* (Baton Rouge, 1986).

7   Josep Fontana, *The Distorted Past: A Reinterpretation of Europe* (Cambridge, 1995); Bryce Harland, *Collision Course: America and East Asia in the Past and the Future* (New York, 1996).

W. E. B. Du Bois announced almost one hundred years ago that "the problem of the twentieth century is the problem of the color line." Yet, this founder of the NAACP pointedly did not limit this formulation to "black-white" relations; in fact, he went on to state forcefully what he did mean in words that too often have been forgotten: this "problem" included "the relation of the darker to the lighter races of men [*sic*] in Asia and Africa, in America and the islands of the sea."[8] In some ways today's era has seen a retreat from the more expansive racial discourse of a century ago, which not only refused to view race as bipolar but also insisted on its global nature. This more expansive approach inherently is more appropriate when considering U.S. foreign policy and the question of "white supremacy."

During the Cold War, Soviet social scientists often referred to what they termed the "general crisis of capitalism." This phrase was intended to suggest that with the Bolshevik Revolution of 1917, a fatal breach in the capitalist system had been made and, ineluctably, this system was undergoing an inevitable decline. As one Soviet textbook from that era put it, "under conditions of the general crisis of capitalism, this system is no longer able to keep peoples in subjugation, and one after another they throw off the yoke of capital."[9] Implicit in these words was the idea that capitalism's "general crisis" would impact the fate of the colonies, which were mostly in Africa and Asia. In other words, capitalism's general crisis also signified a crisis for a system of economic exploitation that was heavily racialized.

Of course, the events of 1989 and the subsequent collapse of the Soviet Union have raised serious questions about the viability of this theory of capitalism's "general decline." What has gone largely unnoticed in the wake of the decline of Communist parties, however, is the concomitant "general crisis of white su-

---

8   W. E. B. Du Bois, *The Souls of Black Folk* (Boston, 1997), 45.
9   Clemens Dutt, ed., *Fundamentals of Marxism-Leninism* (Moscow, n.d.), 317. See also Fenner Brockway, *The Colonial Revolution* (New York, 1973); Fedor Mikhailovich Leonidov, *Racism—An Ideological Weapon of Imperialism* (Moscow, 1965); and H.R. Cowie, ed., *Imperialism and Race Relations* (Melbourne, 1986).

premacy," that is, the decline of the system that has meant global domination of those of Euorpean descent and – despite the currency crisis across the Pacific – the return of Asia to a preemiment position in the global economy.

Recently in the journal *Foreign Affairs*, Jeffrey Sachs and Steve Radelet spoke to this question:

Beginning in the early 1500s, for more than four centuries now, the West has been ascendant in the world economy. With but 14 percent of the world's population in 1820, Western Europe and four colonial offshoots of Great Britain (Australia, Canada, New Zealand, and the United States) had already achieved around 25 percent of world income. By 1950, after a century and a half of Western industrialization, their income share had soared to 56 percent, while their population share hovered around 17 percent. Asia, with 66 percent of the world's population, had a meager 19 percent of world income, compared with 58 percent in 1820. In 1950, however, one of the great changes of modern history began, with the growth of many Asian economies. By 1992, fueled by high growth rates, Asia's share of world income had risen to 33 percent. This tidal shift is likely to continue, with Asia reemerging by the early twenty-first century as the world's center of economic activity.[10]

The authors dimiss the impact of the "Southeast Asian currency crises of 1997" as "not a sign of the end of Asian growth but rather a recurring – if difficult to predict – pattern of financial instability that often accompanies economic growth."

Even if one does not accept every aspect of these analysts' bold predictions, it is apparent that the rise of Asia means that something fundamental has happened in the global economy and, without fail, that development will have corresponding impact on diplomatic relations. Unintentionally these analysts' words return us to the days of yore when race was seen – unlike today – not as a solely domestic issue but as a global question of monumental proportions.

---

10   Steven Radelet and Jeffrey Sachs, "Asia's Reemergence," *Foreign Affairs* 76 (November/December 1997): 44–59. See also Janet Abu-Lughod, *Before European Hegemony: The World System, A.D. 1250–1350* (New York, 1989).

The prognostication of these analysts may come as a shock at the end of this century, though it may not have surprised those around at the end of the nineteenth century. The war of 1898 with Spain, which can fairly be said to have marked the beginning of the "American Century," led to a robust debate in the United States about the theory and praxis of "white supremacy." Likewise, the U.S. decision to interfere in the internal affairs of Hawaii near this same time led to a similar exchange of views: Should the United States risk polluting "whiteness" by gobbling up this island kingdom[11] or should it intervene on behalf of the settlers precisely to preserve "white supremacy"? These earthshaking events – the annexation of Hawaii and the war of 1898 – were heavily infected with race; and, of course, the development that signaled "white supremacy's" general crisis – Tokyo's victory over Moscow in 1905 – also implicated race.

Such racial dilemmas were to vex the United States for a good deal of the "American Century," if not before.[12] Of course, after the discrediting of notions of racial supremacy in the wake of the defeat of fascism,[13] U.S. foreign policy shifted to anticommunism as its motive force; but even here, since the challenges to private property that anticommunism was designed to blunt emerged most dramatically in the "Third World," anticommunism itself – which was a broad church that could embrace believers of all colors – often appeared to some as no more than an updated mechanism to protect racial privilege.[14]

11   Thomas Osborne, *"Empire Can Wait": American Opposition to Hawaiian Annexation, 1893–1898* (Kent, 1981); Joseph A. Fry, *John Tyler Morgan and the Search for Southern Autonomy* (Knoxville, 1992); Richard H. Miller, ed., *American Imperialism in 1898: The Quest for National Fulfillment* (New York, 1970); Christopher Lasch, "The Anti-Imperialists, the Philippines and the Inequality of Man," *Journal of Southern History* 24 (August 1954): 319–31; David Healy, *U.S. Expansionism: The Imperialist Urge in the 1890s* (Madison, 1970); Julius Pratt, *Expansionists of 1898: The Acquisition of Hawaii and the Spanish Islands* (Baltimore, 1936); Sylvester K. Stevens, *American Expansion in Hawaii, 1842–1898* (Harrisburg, 1945). I am grateful to Eric Love for helping to shape my thinking on this period.
12   Marie-Jeanne Rossignol, *Nationalist Ferment: Origins of the Foreign Policy of the United States, 1789–1812* (Paris, 1994).
13   Stanley G. Payne, *A History of Fascism, 1914–1945* (Madison, 1995); Michael Burleigh and Wolfgang Wippermann, *The Racial State: Germany, 1933–1945* (New York, 1991).
14   Gerald Horne, *Black and Red: W. E. B. Du Bois and the Afro-American Response to the*

Theodore Roosevelt, the man who led this nation into the American Century, was an admirer of some of the most notorious white supremacists of his era. He was among those who were obsessed with notions of race and, particularly, what was called "race suicide," that is, the idea that those of European descent were a global minority whose birth rates portended even steeper declines. Men and women – who were "white" – should be "eager lovers," he thought, in order to arrest this development; these conceptions of race, which implicated gender, were also intended to undergird class privilege.[15] An indication of Roosevelt's beliefs was his friendship with Madison Grant, one of the leading racial theorists of that era.[16]

Another leading racial theorist was Lothrop Stoddard, who in turn was quite friendly with Madison Grant. Unlike many today who speak of race solely in the domestic context, Stoddard saw race as a global phenomenon. "The first real challenge to white world supremacy," he thought, "was the Russo-Japanese War of 1904." As a result of an Asian nation's victory over a European power, this holder of a Harvard doctorate argued that "throughout Asia and even in Africa, races hitherto resigned or sullenly submissive began to dream of throwing off white control." The United States as one of Europe's "white outposts" was viewed as central to reversing this "rising tide of color."[17] Instead, Moscow's

Cold War, 1944–1963 (Albany, 1986); Gerald Horne, *Black Liberation/Red Scare: Ben Davis and the Communist Party* (London, 1994).

15 Thomas G. Dyer, *Theodore Roosevelt and the Idea of Race* (Baton Rouge, 1980), 165, 17. See also George Sinkler, *The Racial Attitudes of American Presidents from Abraham Lincoln to Theodore Roosevelt* (Garden City, 1972); Fritz Hirschfield, *George Washington and Slavery: A Documentary Record* (Columbia, 1997); The connection between race and gender supremacy has not gone unexplored. See, for example, Jessie Daniels, *White Lies: Race, Class, Gender and Sexuality in White Supremacist Discourse* (New York, 1997); Gail Bederman, *Manliness and Civilization: A Cultural History of Gender and Race in the United States, 1880–1917* (Chicago, 1995); Glenda Gilmore, *Gender and Jim Crow: Women and the Politics of White Supremacy in North Carolina, 1896–1920* (Chapel Hill, 1996); Ann Laura Stoler, *Race and the Education of Desire: Foucault's History of Sexuality and the Colonial Order of Things* (Durham, 1995); Zillah R. Eisenstein, *Hatreds: Racialized and Sexualized Conflicts in the 21st Century* (New York, 1996); and Jacinth Samuels, *The Sound of Silence: Racism in Contemporary Feminist Theory* (Ottawa, 1991).

16 See Madison Grant, *The Passing of the Great White Race or the Racial Basis of European History* (New York, 1916).

17 Lothrop Stoddard, *Clashing Tides of Color* (New York, 1935), 9, 54.

defeat at the hands of Tokyo marked a crucial turning point in the general crisis of "white supremacy," just as it accelerated the crisis of Czarist Russia.

Mimicking Du Bois, Stoddard proclaimed that the "'conflict of color' bids fair to be the fundamental problem of the twentieth century." Also like Du Bois, he did not see this conflict as merely a "black-white" issue. Instead, writing in the aftermath of World War I, he went so far as to say that "there is no immediate danger of the world being swamped by black blood. But there is a very imminent danger that the white stocks may be swamped by Asiatic blood." Grant, who wrote the introduction to his friend's text, confessed that he was riveted by the "conflict between the East and the West – Europe and Asia," which had "lasted for centuries, in fact, it goes back to the Persian Wars." For his part, Stoddard was deeply worried that World War I, which was "from the first the White Civil War," would "gravely complicate the course of race relations" and weaken the ability of Europe and Euro-America to resist the advance of the darker peoples.[18]

Still, what was particularly upsetting to these influential racial theorists was Russia's defeat at the hands of Japan; in retrospect they probably would agree with the assertion that this development served to inaugurate the "general crisis of white supremacy," not only because it signaled the rise of a legitimate Asian power but, as well, it signaled monumental changes in Russia that were to shake the very foundations of colonialism in Africa and Asia.

Stoddard argued that "1900 was, indeed, the high-water mark of the white tide which had been flooding for four hundred years," but Tokyo's triumph marked the "beginning of the ebb." Sadly, he recalled, "the legend of white invincibility was shattered, the veil of prestige that draped white civilization was torn aside, and the white world's manifold ills were laid bare for candid examination."[19]

Ironically, W. E. B. Du Bois agreed in some ways with these racial theorists. The defeat of Russia at the hands of Japan, he

18   Lothrop Stoddard, *The Rising Tide of Color against White Supremacy* (New York, 1920), v, vi, xxiii, 301.
19   Ibid., 153.

thought, awakened among Euro-Americans a "fear of colored revolt against white exploitation." Just as Tokyo's victory fomented an enduring "Japan-phobia" and "Japanic" among many Euro-Americans, it made Du Bois an enduring "Japan-phile."[20]

From the point of view of "white supremacy," there was justifiable concern about Russia's defeat. Japan's victory "electrified the atmosphere in India. It shattered the illusion of European invincibility." India as well as other colonized nations learned another lesson that did not augur well for the hegemony of European colonialism; for Tokyo's victory revealed that the "state played an indispensable and large part in the development of a nation . . . and therefore that good government by a foreign nation was no substitute for self-government."[21]

It should not be thought that Grant, Stoddard, and their ilk viewed all "whites" as similarly qualified to take advantage of the racialized division of the world. As the Holocaust was to reveal, racialist thinking also carried deadly implications for those "whites" not viewed as being at the top of the racial pyramid – those of the "Mediterranean race," for example. Another problem that was to vex "white supremacy" during the American Century was convincing the subalterns of Europe that a system of racial oppression was of no significance – and in fact was beneficial – to them.[22]

But this takes race out of the equation.

Inevitably, doctrines of "white supremacy" helped to spawn competing – defensive and less bigoted – philosophies, such as Pan-Africanism[23] and Pan-Asianism. Speaking to Japanese

---

20   W. E. B. Du Bois, *Dusk of Dawn: An Essay toward An Autobiography of a Race Concept* (New York, 1968), 232.
21   R. P. Dua, *The Impact of the Russo-Japanese (1905) War on Indian Politics* (New Dehli, 1966), vii, viii.
22   Lothrop Stoddard, *Racial Realities in Europe* (New York, 1924), 5.
23   American Society of African Culture, ed., *Pan Africanism Reconsidered* (Berkeley, 1962); Abdul Aziz Said, ed., *Ethnicity and U.S. Foreign Policy* (New York, 1981); Tony Martin, *The Pan-African Connection: From Slavery to Garvey and Beyond* (Dover, 1983); Immanuel Geiss, *The Pan-African Movement: A History of Pan-Africanism in America, Europe and Africa* (New York, 1974); Adelaide Cromwell Hill and Martin Kilson, eds., *Apropos of Africa: Sentiments of Negro American Leaders on Africa from the 1800s to the 1950s* (London, 1969); Sylvia M. Jacobs, *The African Nexus: Black American Perspectives on the European Partitioning of Africa, 1880–1920* (Westport, 1981); Owen Charles Mathurin, *Henry Sylvester Williams and the Origins of the Pan-African Movement, 1869–1911* (Westport, 1976); Floyd

merchants in Kobe months before his death on the subject of
"'Great Asianism'," Sun Yat-sen "narrated a personal testimony
to the impact" of Tokyo's victory over Moscow. The Chinese
leader "was in a ship crossing the Suez Canal soon after the victory when some locals enthusiastically mistook him for a Japanese. Even after discovering their mistake, however, they continued to celebrate their solidarity with him against the imperialist
powers. In [his] speech, Sun developed the theme of a racial or
color war against the white race, for whom (he cites in English)
"'blood is thicker than water,' which is why the British were sad-
dened by Russia's defeat despite their political alliance with the
Japanese."[24] Such rumblings eventually obligated the more sober
"white" elites – particularly in the United States where conceptions of racial identity were more developed – to move away from
overt articulations of racial supremacy to conceptions like anticommunism, which were on the surface "race neutral."

Lothrop Stoddard's concern about the impact of Japan's rise on
what could be called the "racial correlation of forces globally,"
was mirrored by key U.S. strategists. Alfred Thayer Mahan took
to the pages of the *New York Times* to argue that Hawaii should
be annexed as a counterweight against Japan and other looming
Asian powers, for example, China. "Shall [Hawaii] in the future
be an outpost of European civilization," he asked plaintively, "or
of the comparative barbarism of China[?]"[25]

Concern about the implications of Japan's rise for "white supremacy" was not just a preoccupation of Washington. It was
Japan that was crucial in the evolution of alliance systems in international affairs after 1895, just as Russo-Japanese relations
became a key determinant of events in Europe.[26]

J. Miller, *The Search for a Black Nationality: Black Emigration and Colonization, 1787–1863* (Urbana, 1975); Sterling Stuckey, *The Ideological Origins of Black Nationalism* (Boston, 1972); Elliott P. Skinner, *African-Americans and U.S. Foreign Policy toward Africa, 1850–1924* (Washington, 1992).

24   Prasenjit Duara, "Transnationalism and the Predicament of Sovereignty: China, 1900–1945," *American Historical Review* 102 (October 1997): 1030–51. See also Marius Jansen, *The Japanese and Sun Yat-Sen* (Cambridge, 1954).

25   *New York Times*, 31 January 1893.

26   John Albert White, *Transition to Global Rivalry: Alliance Diplomacy and the Quadruple Entente, 1895–1907* (New York, 1995).

Despite these ritual invocations of "white supremacy," contradictorily the United States often had to rely on African-American troops to impose its diktat in the Philippines, Cuba, Puerto Rico, and the other "fruits" of empire. Of course, these soldiers of color took on this mission with grave ambivalence; indeed, the tensions created by this process ultimately helped to undermine "white supremacy" itself as it became more and more difficult to launch wars with soldiers of color in the vanguard. The war with Spain, for example, "rather than creating a sense of brotherhood between black and white Americans," led to "increased racial tensions in the United States."²⁷ This was the era of the acceleration of lynching and the forcible ouster of African-Americans from positions of political power throughout the South.²⁸

The 1890s – March 1896, to be precise – also marked the time when an Italian invasion was soundly rebuffed by Ethiopia; at the time there was "no parallel case in modern history" of a "European army . . . annihilated by a native African race."²⁹ Ironically, as "white supremacy" was becoming ever more prominent in U.S. foreign policy, forces already were at play that were serving to undermine it. Inspiration from abroad and setbacks at home led African-Americans and their allies to escalate their assault against "white supremacy" as they founded the National Association for the Advancement of Colored People (NAACP), with W. E. B.

27   Piero Gleijeses, "African-Americans and the War against Spain," *North Carolina Historical Review* 23 (April 1996): 184–214; See also Willard B. Gatewood, Jr., *Black Americans and the White Man's Burden, 1898–1903* (Urbana, 1975); idem, *"Smoked Yankees" and the Struggle for Empire: Letters from Negro Soldiers, 1898–1902* (Fayetteville, 1987); George P. Marks, ed., *The Black Press Views American Imperialism* (New York, 1971); Igor Dementyev, *USA: Imperialists and Anti-Imperialists: The Great Foreign Policy Debate at the Turn of the Century* (Moscow, 1979); Hazel M. McFerson, *The Racial Dimensions of American Overseas Colonial Policy* (Westport, 1997); Alexander De Conde, *Ethnicity, Race and American Foreign Policy: A History* (Boston, 1992); and Melvin Small, *Democracy and Diplomacy: The Impact of Domestic Politics on U.S. Foreign Policy, 1789–1994* (Baltimore, 1996).
28   Ida B. Wells-Barnett, *Crusader for Justice: The Autobiography of Ida B. Wells* (Chicago, 1970); Ida B. Wells, *Southern Horrors and Other Writings: The Anti-Lynching Campaign of Ida B. Wells, 1892–1900* (Boston, 1997); Nell Irvin Painter, *Standing at Armageddon: United States, 1877–1919* (New York, 1987).
29   George Berkeley, *The Campaign of Adowa and the Rise of Menelik* (New York, 1969), vii. See also Boake Carter, *Black Shirt, Black Skin* (Harrisburg, 1935); Teshale Tiberu, *The Making of Modern Ethiopia, 1896–1974* (Lawrenceville, 1995); and Harold Marcus, *The Life and Times of Menelik II: Ethiopia, 1844–1913* (New York, 1975).

Du Bois in a principal post.[30] Hence, though it would be a mistake to view "white supremacy" exclusively through the prism of "black-white" relations, it would be similarly mistaken to deem this dyad irrelevant.

U.S. writers as diverse as Ernest Hemingway, Saul Bellow, and John Updike have incorporated African themes in their work; as one scholar has put it, for a number of writers from the United States the "main, global role of Africa seems to be the replacement of the vanished American frontier as a quarry of natural, spiritual values."[31] Of course, the American Century dawned as the frontier was receding in North America. Thus, it was not just writers who saw Africa as a virtual replacement for the "vanished American frontier."

The nation that was to become Zimbabwe provides an apt example of how U.S. nationals propelled "white supremacy" in Africa at a time when Washington's – official – foreign policy was thought to be focused elsewhere.

Frederick Russell Burnham was born on an Indian reservation in Minnesota and later followed the frontier west as it was closing in Arizona and California while gaining a well-deserved reputation as an "Indian fighter." He sailed for Southern Africa in 1893, in search of a new frontier: he joined Cecil Rhodes's war against King Lobengula in the land that eventually was called Rhodesia. Burnham, an avowed advocate of what he called "white supremacy," was quick to draw comparisons between the wars that led to the expropriation of Native Americans and the war that led to the dispossession of the Africans.[32]

---

30   Charles Flint Kellogg, *NAACP, A History of the National Association for the Advancement of Colored People* (Baltimore, 1967); Robert Zangrando, *The NAACP Crusade against Lynching, 1909–1950* (Philadelphia, 1980).
31   Daniel Kanyandekwe, "Dreaming of Africa: American Writers and Africa in the Twentieth Century" (Ph.D. diss., State University of New York-Buffalo, 1996), 187.
32   Frederick Russell Burnham, *Scouting on Two Continents* (Bulawayo, 1975), 218; idem, *Taking Chances* (Prescott, 1994); See also Mary and Richard Bradford, eds., *An American Family on the African Frontier: The Burnham Family Letters, 1893–1896* (Niwot, CO, 1993); Arthur Keppel-Jones, *Rhodes and Rhodesia: The White Conquest of Zimbabwe, 1884–1902* (Montreal, 1983); and Dane Kennedy, *Islands of White: Settler Society and Culture in Kenya and Southern Rhodesia, 1890–1939* (Durham, 1987).

For Burnham and others of his ilk, the sweeping aside of darker peoples—be they in North America or Africa – was an inevitable process; similarly, this encounter with Africa as the American Century commenced served to reinforce rudimentary notions of "white supremacy."

As early as June 1893, Burnham felt sufficiently confident to proclaim that "the American element is growing and bids fair to be [a] controlling one here inside 5 years." He envisioned a re-play of what had occurred in the the the U.S. West – dispossession of the indigenous and stocking the land with immigrants from the Pan-European world. In words that would have resonated in the U.S. South, Burnham confided that the "one great stumbling block" in this African colony was "the presence of the nigger." His spouse had the wish that there would be "no blacks in Africa," though she spared the squeamish by not revealing how this feat could be accomplished. Burnham's brother-in-law didn't "blame the whites for wanting to kill the nigs."[33]

Burnham was one among many U.S. citizens who were instrumental in bolstering the imperial project of Cecil Rhodes. For many of these North Americans, subjugating Africa under the banner of "white supremacy" was more palatable than doing the same thing under the aegis of the United States's former colonial master in London: racial identity prevailed over national identity. Arguably, Rhodes would not have been as successful but for the timely assistance of his brethren from the United States.[34] Britain had tried to burn down Washington, DC, during the War of 1812,

33 Frederick Russell Burnham to Madge Blick, June 1893, Frederick Russell Burnham to Josiah Russell, circa 1894, Blanche Blick Burnham to Blick family, 6 February 1894, and John Blick to parents, 16 October 1894, in Bradford and Bradford, eds., *An American Family on the African Frontier*, 65, 133, 121, 176, 268.
34 Maurice Heany, one of the biggest businessmen in "Rhodesia" and a cousin of Edgar Allen Poe, also fought Native Americans in the West before crossing the Atlantic. Coleman Joseph, born in Philadelphia, built Bulawayo's first synagogue. See Eric Rosenthal, *Stars and Stripes in Africa* (Cape Town, 1968), 7, 15, 37, 176. Mining engineers from the United States, like John Hays Hammond and Gardner Williams, pioneered in the development of gold mines in the region (Bradford and Bradford, eds., *An American Family on the African Frontier*, xi). See also R. W. S. Turner, "American Links with Early Days of Rhodesia," *Rhodesia Calls* 55 (May–June 1969): 4–13.

and tensions between the two states were not easy to extinguish.[35] Just as "whiteness" served in the United States to calm preexisting tensions between those of English and Irish descent or Serb and Croat descent, this construction played a similar role on the international scene by helping to reconcile John Bull and Uncle Sam; and just as "whiteness" was substantially defined in the United States as being the antipode of a negative "blackness," it played a similar role in Africa.

But "white supremacy" in the United States was never solely targeted at African-Americans: Native Americans were the first victims. Thus, not surprisingly, when Frederick Russell Burnham met Winston Churchill, as the American Century was beginning, the future prime minister "questioned me sharply and minutely on my early life among the Indians and made me recount almost step-by-step every contact I had ever had with any enemy along the wide frontier from Texas to California."[36]

Burnham, who eventually returned to the United States and became a wealthy oil baron, was friendly with Theodore Roosevelt, who also traveled extensively in Africa. The U.S. president acknowledged that Cecil Rhodes's "work" in "Matabeleland represented a great and striking conquest for civilization."[37]

The "Pioneer Column," which was in the vanguard of Rhodes's colonizing project, was reminiscent of earlier "pioneer" efforts in North America. Perhaps this is why so many from the United States were part of this crusade. Typical of this group was William Harvey Brown, born in Des Moines; he came to Africa in 1890 on behalf of the Smithsonian but stayed on and became a

35 Richard Norton Smith, *The Colonel: The Life and Legend of Robert R. McCormick, 1880–1955* (Boston, 1997): this famed publisher was typical of those among the U.S. elite who maintained staunch anti-British views. See also Anne Orde, *The Eclipse of Great Britain: The United States and British Imperial Decline, 1895–1956* (New York, 1996); Mark Curtis, *The Ambiguities of Power: British Foreign Policy since 1945* (London, 1995); and Anita Inder Singh, *The Limits of British Influence: South Asia and the Anglo-American Relationship, 1947–1956* (New York, 1993); Alternatively, see Giora Goodman, "'Who is Anti-American?' The British Left and the United States, 1945–1956" (Ph.D. diss., University of London, 1996).
36 Burnham, *Taking Chances*, 266.
37 William N. Tilchin, *Theodore Roosevelt and the British Empire: A Study in Presidential Statecraft* (New York, 1997), 24.

"prominent Rhodesian and a member of the Legislative Council."[38] Brown's ideas reflected "white supremacy." He considered Africans to be "savages and barbarians" and felt that "forced servitude" was good for them. He hinted at genocide against Africans, whom he compared to Native Americans, and contrasted both negatively with the "Anglo-Saxon race." He saw Africa as an extension of the rapidly closing frontier in the United States and as an "outlet for the overcrowded countries of Europe"; Africans, he concluded, were "more likely to vanish than remain."[39]

Thus, the United States entered the twentieth century with two contradictory impulses: on the one hand, there was the clearcut rise of "white supremacy"; on the other hand were forces, particularly among African-Americans, that were opposed to its ascension. But since African-Americans were in the process of being ousted from what little influence they held, those opposed to "white supremacy" found it difficult to resist this juggernaut.

Within the global context, Japan played a pivotal and contradictory role in this process; just as the United States sought to utilize chauvinism to justify its domination of its recent colonial appendages, Japan did the same in Korea. Yet, Japan was not "white," and thus its ascension was viewed with no small trepidation among those who held "white supremacy" dear.

This paradoxical situation came clear in the aftermath of World War I, when Japan clamored at Versailles for the establishment of principles of international discourse favoring racial equality. Needless to say, this development was viewed with more than mild concern by the Southerner – Woodrow Wilson – who occupied the White House, not to mention his Dixiecrat comrades. There was a fierce debate on this Japanese resolution on the "equality of nations"; the U.S. delegation feared what this might mean con-

---

38 Adrian Carter, *The Pioneers of Mashonaland* (Bulawayo, 1977), 101.
39 William Harvey Brown, *On the South African Frontier: The Adventures and Observations of an American in Mashonaland and Matabeland* (New York, 1899), x, 391, 400, 418, 420.

cerning immigration, particularly to California.[40] The United
States viewed itself not just as an Atlantic nation but as a Pacific
one as well; a key difference between the two, of course, was that
racial tensions were more prominent in the latter region. Reputedly, "the President said that he did not trust the Japanese."[41]

The very existence of Japan – a modern capitalist nation in
Asia – called into question the essential premises of "white supremacy" and, as a partial consequence, was viewed as a dire
threat to the United States. Japan's existence also hindered the
execution of U.S. foreign policy during this era, as Tokyo established friendly relations with the leaders of a sector of the U.S.
body politic that was not necessarily favorable to "white supremacy" – African-Americans. After World War I, A. Philip
Randolph, the legendary black labor leader, "concluded that Japan, plus the power of other free nations 'combined with an international league of workingmen' could effectively pressure the
Western powers."[42] Randolph backed up his rhetoric by joining
in 1919 with Marcus Garvey and others at the home of the one of
the nation's few black women millionaires, C. J. Walker, to form
the International League of Darker Peoples. The league was short-
lived, but one thing it did do was to arrange a meeting with a
visiting Japanese publisher and editor at the Waldorf-Astoria in
New York City in order to seek Tokyo's assistance in raising the
question of racial equality at Versailles. Tellingly, the league not
only encompassed those of African descent but those of Asian –
particularly Japanese – descent as well.[43]

Increasingly, a growing sector of those in the African disapora
felt that they could play upon the contradictions between Wash-

40   Arthur Link, ed., *The Papers of Woodrow Wilson*, vol. 57, *April 5–22, 1919* (Princeton,
1987), 570–71. See also Henry P. Frei, *Japan's Southward Advance and Australia: From the
Sixteenth Century to World War II* (Honolulu, 1991).
41   Arthur Link, ed., *The Papers of Woodrow Wilson*, vol. 54, *January 11–February 7,
1919* (Princeton, 1986), 379. See also Phil Hammond, ed., *Cultural Difference, Media Memories: Anglo-American Images of Japan* (London, 1997); and Robert Lansing, *The Peace Negotiations: A Personal Narrative* (Boston, 1921), 243–56.
42   Judith Stein, *The World of Marcus Garvey: Race and Class in Modern Society* (Baton
Rouge, 1986) 50.
43   Robert Hill, ed., *The Marcus Garvey and Universal Negro Improvement Association
Papers*, vol. 1, *1826–August 1919* (Berkeley, 1983), 345.

ington and London on the one hand and Tokyo on the other to their own advantage. Both British and U.S. military intelligence took careful note of an editorial in Garvey's newspaper, *Negro World*, which said as much: "With the rising militarism of Asia and the standing militarism of Europe one can foresee nothing else but an armed clash between the white and yellow races. When this clash of millions comes, an opportunity will have presented itself to the Negro people of the world to free themselves. The next war will be between the Negroes and the whites, unless our demands for justice are recognized. With Japan to fight with us we can win such a war."[44] Eliminating the more egregious aspects of "white supremacy" was increasingly seen in Washington as a question of national security, though this forced march away from the power of race was often cloaked in the disguise of morality.

Japanese newspapers carried editorials condemning lynchings of African-Americans in the Deep South. When African-Americans were outraged by the production of the film *Birth of a Nation*, a visiting delegation of Japanese filmmakers praised their efforts to counter this racialist propaganda. Tokyo, in short, was being looked to by many African-Americans as a savior.[45] Hence, as U.S. relations with Japan soured after World War I, some were beginning to view African-Americans as a potential "fifth column" in future conflicts between these two giants.

Japan's relations with African-Americans were a reflection of its dealings with the continent of Africa itself; rather quickly, Tokyo recognized that the aching Achilles' heel of the European powers – and their cousins in Washington – was their praxis of "white supremacy" in Africa and elsewhere, which allowed Japan to more readily portray itself as a viable alternative to these nations. Indeed, competition in Africa was a salient factor in the rapid deterioration of relations between Tokyo and London dur-

---

44   Ibid., 404.
45   Reginald Kearney, "Afro-American Views of the Japanese, 1900-1945" (Ph.D. diss., Kent State University, 1991); Claude Clegg, *An Original Man: The Life and Times of Elijah Muhammad* (New York, 1997). See also George W. Shepherd, Jr., *Racial Influences on American Foreign Policy* (New York, 1970); and Arnold Shankman, *Ambivalent Friends: Afro-Americans View the Immigrant* (Westport, 1982.)

ing the first half of the twentieth century. During the late 1920s particularly, the expansion of Japanese economic interests began to threaten European interests, most notably in Africa.[46]

The developing relationship between Ethiopia and Japan captured the attention of many in the African diaspora. When discussion was bruited about a merger – via marriage – of the royal families in both nations, African-Americans especially, who were forbidden by law in most jurisdictions to marry Euro-Americans, were conspicuously moved.[47] Contrarily, in South Africa – where the "highest stage of white supremacy" had been reached – it was slowly being recognized that this system was facing external pressure from Tokyo and elsewhere that could only buttress a preexisting internal pressure.[48]

Similarly, World War I led directly to another development that can be said to have contributed to the general crisis of "white supremacy": the Bolshevik Revolution. And, like Tokyo, this new "threat" was linked with the staunchest domestic opponent of "white supremacy": African-Americans. Reportedly, Woodrow Wilson felt that the "American Negro" troops "returning from abroad would be our greatest medium in conveying bolshevism to America." In addition to the question of "reds," the president was also deathly concerned with the question of "whites." Thus, he added, the "French people have placed the Negro soldier in France on [a level of] equality with the white man, and 'it has gone to their heads.'"[49]

"White supremacy" was producing ever more complex complications for U.S. foreign policy. Early in 1919 one harried U.S.

---

46   Richard Albert Bradshaw, "Japan and European Colonialism in Africa, 1800–1937" (Ph.D. diss., Ohio University, 1992), 15. See also Shinya Sugiyama, *Japan's Industrialization in the World Economy, 1859–1899: Export Trade and Overseas Competition* (London, 1988); Kweku Ampiah, "British Commerical Policies against Japanese Expansionism in East and West Africa, 1931–1935," *International Journal of African Historical Studies* 23 (1990): 619–41; and Peter Lowe, *Great Britain and the Origins of the Pacific War: A Study of British Policy in East Asia, 1937–1941* (New York, 1977).
47   *Chicago Defender*, 13 July 1935.
48   Hedley A. Chilvers, *The Yellow Man Looks On: Being the Story of the Anglo-Dutch Conflict in Southern Africa and Its Interest for the Peoples of Asia* (London, 1933).
49   Arthur Link, ed., *The Papers of Woodrow Wilson*, vol. 55, *February 8–March 16, 1919* (Princeton, 1986) 471. See also Theodore Kornweibel, Jr., *"Seeing Red": Federal Campaigns against Black Militancy, 1919–1925* (Bloomington, 1998).

intelligence agent argued that increasingly African-American radi-
calism was aiming at a "combination of the other colored races
of the world. As a colored movement it looks to Japan for leadership; as a radical movement it follows Bolshevism and has intimate relations with various socialistic groups throughout the
United States."[50] The "combination" of this "Colored Scare"
and "Red Scare" was taken quite seriously by Washington.

As ever, U.S. elites had to worry that "white supremacy" at
home had a noticeable downside: those not sharing in its bounty
might feel obligated to align with the real and imagined enemies
of Washington, thereby jeopardizing national security.[51] Even
France of all nations, whose exploitation of Africans was noticeably egregious, often took a different tack toward African-Americans, which provided it with leverage in Washington.[52]

Still – Japan and France notwithstanding – it was the advent of
the Soviet Union that stirred the most concern, not only because
this nation quickly attracted a number of leading African-American intellectuals but, in addition, it also made inroads in Africa
itself by pledging to assist those nations struggling to throw off
the yoke of colonialism.[53] Yet even here Japanese played a pivotal role. Sen Katayama helped to organize Communist parties
in Japan, Mexico, Canada, and the United States. Eventually he
was elected to the leading body of the Communist International,
based in Moscow, where in 1928 he helped to formulate the official position of the Reds on the "Negro Question," which included the "right of Negroes to self-determination in the Southern States." The "Comintern" pledged to assist African-Ameri-

50   Kornweibel, *"Seeing Red"*, 81.
51   Merton Dillon, *Slavery Attacked: Southern Slaves and Their Allies, 1619–1865* (Baton
Rouge, 1990); Benjamin Quarles, *The Negro in the American Revolution* (Chapel Hill, 1961).
52   John D. Hargreaves, ed., *France and West Africa: An Anthology of Historical Documents* (New York, 1969); Arthur Helps, ed., *Letters of Oswald Spengler, 1913–1936* (New
York, 1966), 159; Tyler Stovall, *Paris Noir: African-Americans in the City of Light* (Boston,
1996); Michel Fabre, *From Harlem to Paris: Black Writers in France, 1840–1980* (Urbana,
1991).
53   Philip S. Foner, *The Bolshevik Revolution: Its Impact on American Radicals, Liberals
and Labor* (New York, 1967); Allison Blakeley, *Russia and the Negro: Blacks in Russian
History and Thought* (Washington, DC, 1986); Daniel Mason and Jessica Smith, eds., *Lenin's
Impact on the United States* (New York, 1970).

cans in their effort to discard the yoke of Jim Crow and third-class citizenship – a promise that could not be easily disregarded. Katayama was also a close friend of the Jamaican-American poet, Claude McKay, during this writer's sojourn with the organized left.[54] McKay was just one of a host of leading black intellectuals – a list that was to include W.E.B. Du Bois, Shirley Graham Du Bois, Paul Robeson, Langston Hughes, and Claudia Jones, among others – who were to align with the forces of socialism: the pestilence of "white supremacy" was no small factor in helping to explicate this crucial decision.

As Tokyo, then Moscow, in jujitsu fashion began to turn "white supremacy" back against those in the United States who benefited from it, it was beginning to dawn that racialist thinking could carry the seeds of its own destruction. Just as capitalism itself inexorably spawned its own gravediggers, the same could be said for "white supremacy." This realization helped to guarantee that ultimately Washington could gain an advantage over its erstwhile allies in Paris and Brussels and Lisbon by taking positions on colonialism in Africa that were not in total accord with those of Western Europe; this realization also helped to insure that Jim Crow itself would not survive the "American Century."

The implications of the Bolshevik Revolution for "white supremacy" were glimpsed early on by Lothrop Stoddard, Madison Grant, and other theorists of "white supremacy." The latter saw "Asia in the guise of Bolshevism with Semitic leadership and Chinese executioners . . . organizing an assault upon western Europe." The former saw Lenin as "a modern Jenghiz Khan plotting the plunder of a world"; Bolshevism, he exclaimed, was "in fact, as anti-racial as it is anti-social" and "thus reveals itself as the arch-enemy of civilization and the race. Bolshevism is the renegade, the traitor within the gates, who would betray the cita-

54 Karl G. Yoneda, "The Heritage of Sen Katayma," *Political Affairs* 14 (March 1975): 38–57. See also Hyman Kublin, *Asian Revolutionary: The Life of Sen Katayama* (Princeton, 1964); See also Wayne Cooper, *Claude McKay: Rebel Sojourner in the Harlem Renaissance: A Biography* (Baton Rouge, 1987); and Tyrone Tillery, *Claude McKay: A Black Poet's Struggle for Identity* (Amherst, MA, 1992).

del . . . Therefore, Bolshevism must be crushed out with iron heels, no matter what the cost."[55]

Japan did not live up to the promise bestowed upon it by many African-Americans, particularly after Italy's invasion of Ethiopia.[56] Then again, Washington's own tepid response to this international crisis did not inspire confidence either.[57] Nevertheless, an influential sector of Black Nationalists continued to be drawn to Tokyo – even as tensions with Washington accelerated: particularly ominous was their uniting on a common platform of "anti-whiteness."[58]

These viewpoints were not borne by a sliver of opinion among African-Americans. Though Gunnar Myrdal confirmed the general anti-fascist outlook of African-Americans he did not miss the fact that some took "vicarious satisfaction in imagining a Japanese . . . invasion of the Southern states;" the Swedish social scientist warned that if black demands were neglected after the war, no one could guarantee their reaction "if later a new war were to be fought more definitely along color lines."[59]

In 1942 a number of African-American nationalists – including Elijah Muhammad, later to be deified by both the early Malcolm X and Louis Farrakhan – were arrested because of their pro-Japanese sympathies. Even Roy Wilkins, the moderate leader of the NAACP, had to concede that the catastrophe at Pearl Harbor was caused in part by the tendency among many Euro-Americans to

55 Stoddard, *Rising Tide of Color*, xxxi, 219, 221.
56 James Dugan and Laurence Lafore, *Days of Emperor and Clown: The Italo-Ethiopian War, 1935–1936* (Garden City, 1973). See also William R. Scott, *The Sons of Sheba's Race: African-Americans and the Italo-Ethiopian War, 1935–1941* (Bloomington, 1993); Joseph E. Harris, *African-American Reaction to War in Ethiopia, 1936–1941* (Baton Rouge, 1994); Thomas M. Coffey, *Lion By the Tail: The Story of the Italian-Ethiopian War* (New York, 1974); S. K. B. Asante, *Pan-African Protest: West Africa and the Italo-Ethiopian Crisis, 1934–1941* (London, 1977); and Harold G. Marcus, *Ethiopia, Great Britain and the United States, 1941–1974* (Berkeley, 1983).
57 Brice Harris, Jr., *The United States and the Italo-Ethiopian Crisis* (Westport, 1981).
58 Ernest Allen, Jr., "When Japan was 'Champion of the Darker Races': Satokata Takahashi and the Flowering of Black Messianic Nationalism," *Black Scholar: Journal of Black Studies and Research* 24, no. 1 (1994): 23–46.
59 Gunnar Myrdal, *An American Dilemma: The Negro Problem and Modern Democracy* (New York, 1944), 815, 1016, 1400.

despise any not regarded as "white." Folklore emerged about a black sharecropper who told his white boss during the war, "By the way, Captain, I hear the Japs done declared war on you white folks."[60] U.S. elites had to be concerned that African-Americans not only might be less than enthusiastic about going to war against Japan but – perhaps worse – this minority might harbor a burgeoning "fifth column" that could undermine the war effort.

With an intense sobriety Herbert Hoover viewed the military landscape in 1942 through the lens of "white supremacy": "When the Japanese take Burma, China and organize the forces of the discontent in India," he warned,

we are looking in the face of something new . . . The white man has kept control of Asiatics by dividing parts of them against the other . . . and generally establishing an arrogant superiority. Universally, the white man is hated by the Chinese, Malayan, Indian and Japanese alike . . . Unless [Japanese] leadership is destroyed, the Western Hemisphere is going to confront this mass across the Pacific. Unless they are defeated, they will demand entry and equality in emigration . . . and there will be in twenty-five years an Asiatic flood into South America that will make the Nazis look like pikers . . . And we will have to go through with it until we have destroyed [Japan]. That may take a million American lives and eight or ten years, but it will have to be done.[61]

A considerable percentage of those "million American lives" to be sacrificed would be of African descent, and many of them were beginning to wonder why they should give their lives simply to

60   John Dower, *War Without Mercy: Race and Power in the Pacific War* (New York, 1986), 175–76. See also Robert O. Ballou, *Shinto, the Unconquered Enemy: Japan's Doctrine of Racial Superiority and World Conquest* (New York, 1945); Russell Braddon, *Japan Against the World, 1941–2041: The 100-Year War for Supremacy* (New York, 1983); Willard H. Elsbree, *Japan's Role in South-East Asian Nationalist Movements* (Cambridge, 1953); Akira Iriye, *Power and Culture: The Japanese-American War, 1941–1945* (Cambridge, 1981); V. G. Kiernan, *The Lords of Humankind: Black Man, Yellow Man and White Man in an Age of Empire* (Boston, 1969); John J. Stephan, *Hawaii Under the Rising Sun: Japan's Plan for Conquest after Pearl Harbor* (Honolulu, 1984); Hugh Tinker, *Race, Conflict and International Order: From Empire to United Nations* (New York, 1977); Rubin Francis Weston, *Racism in U.S. Imperialism: The Influence of Racial Assumptions on American Foreign Policy, 1893–1946* (Columbia, 1972).
61   Walter LaFeber, *The Clash: A History of U.S.-Japanese Relations* (New York, 1997), 217.

protect and preserve "white supremacy." The same question was being asked in different ways across the globe. When Sir Stafford Cripps was dispatched by London to an Indian National Congress gathering in Delhi in an attempt to enlist support for the British war against Japan in return for a form of independence, Mahatma Gandhi reputedly said in reply, "This is a postdated cheque on a crashing bank."[62]

World War II, inter alia, represented a true crisis of "white supremacy." It was becoming evident that Washington – and London particularly – were finding it ever more difficult to explain why lives must be sacrificed so that they would not be dominated by Tokyo and Berlin, while the United States and United Kingdom continued to maintain racialized systems of oppression at home and abroad. Ineluctably, World War II compelled these great powers to endure a "race" away from the "power" that the more outlandish versions of "white supremacy" represented. Even though powerful forces in the United States had significant influence on Nazi ideology, there was a sobering realization in Washington that doctrines of racial and ethnic supremacy – if left unchecked – could lead to a holocaust of unimaginable proportions.[63] Still, like the cowboys of old, the United States began to exit the saloon of "white supremacy" with their guns blazing, dropping atomic bombs in a final flourish on Japan as a concluding reminder of what would befall those so bold as to challenge the existing racial order. Then they turned their attention to Moscow, which too had been seeking to take advantage of "white supremacy" – the once proud system of racial privilege that now was being seen as a major liability threatening the continued existence of the "American Century."

---

62   Richard Storry, *Japan and the Decline of the West in Asia, 1894–1943* (London, 1979), 4. See also Bradford A. Lee, *Britain and the Sino-Japanese War, 1937–1939* (Stanford, 1973); and Gunter Bischof and Robert L. Dupont, eds., *The Pacific War Revisited* (Baton Rouge, 1997).
63   Stefan Kuhl, *The Nazi Connection: Eugenics, American Racism and German National Socialism* (New York, 1994); Lawrence Le Blanc, *The United States and the Genocide Convention* (Durham, 1991); Frank Chalk and Kurt Jonassohn, *The History and Sociology of Genocide: Analyses and Case Studies* (New Haven, 1990).

Though the praxis of "white supremacy" was castigated officially and eroded substantially during the Cold War, it was not
extinguished altogether. Instead, it was buttressed by an aggressive anticommunism that had the advantage of being – at least
formally – non-racial. However, the anticolonial upsurge was
designed to overturn the racialized system of oppression – and
underdevelopment – that colonialism represented.[64] In turn, the
unjust – and racialized – enrichment that colonialism represented
could be better defended in this new era by terming anti-colonial
opponents as "Communist."[65] The tagging of anticolonialists as
"red" slowed down the movement against colonialism and – perhaps not coincidentally – gave "white supremacy" a new lease
on life.

In the United States this battle against "white supremacy" had
a certain uniqueness. Mary Dudziak is largely correct in asserting that "desegregation" was a "Cold War imperative."[66] Without slighting at all the heroic contribution of those who participated in the "civil rights movement," it is long past time to recognize that – just like the anti-apartheid movement – the international community played a substantial role in compelling the
United States to move away from the more outrageous aspects of
"white supremacy." How could Washington credibly charge
Moscow with human rights violations when minorites in this nation were treated so horribly? The pressure from the interna-

64   Walter Rodney, *How Europe Underdeveloped Africa* (Washington, 1981); Amilcar Cabral,
Return to the Source: Selected Speeches (New York, 1974); Samora Machel, *Samora Machel,
An African Revolutionary: Selected Speeches and Writings* (London, 1985); Kenneth Kaunda,
Zambia Shall Be Free: An Autobiography (New York, 1963); and Kwame Nkrumah, *Neo-
Colonialism: The Last Stage of Imperialism* (London, 1968).
65   Robert J. McMahon, *Colonialism and Cold War: The United States and the Struggle for
Indonesian Independence, 1945–1949* (Ithaca, 1981); Sean Kelly, *America's Tyrant: The CIA
and Mobutu of Zaire* (Washington, 1993); William Roger Louis, *Imperialism at Bay, 1941–
1945: The United States and the Decolonization of the British Empire* (Oxford, 1977); H.W.
Brands, *The Specter of Neutralism: The United States and the Emergence of the Third World,
1947–1960* (New York, 1989); David N. Gibbs, *The Political Economy of Third World Intervention: Mines, Money and U.S. Foreign Policy in the Congo Crisis* (Chicago, 1991); Richard
D. Mahoney, *JFK: Ordeal in Africa* (New York, 1983); Kwame Nkrumah, *The Challenge of
the Congo* (New York, 1967); Stephen Weisman, *American Foreign Policy in the Congo,
1960–1964* (Ithaca, 1974).
66   Mary L. Dudziak, "Desegregation as a Cold War Imperative," *Stanford Law Review* 41
(November 1988): 61–120.

tional community was felt most directly – and powerfully – during the 1957 school desegregation crisis in Little Rock. It is clear in retrospect that President Dwight Eisenhower's decision to commit troops to this racial tinderbox in Arkansas was motivated substantially by his sensitivity to the damage this crisis was having on the global image of the United States.[67] Simultaneously, these domestic maneuvers affected U.S. foreign policy as Washington found it more difficult to align with erstwhile allies in South Africa and Rhodesia as recently enfranchised African-Americans and a newly energized anticolonial movement began to object.[68]

The importance of the international community in the battle against segregation can be detected by examining the travails of those in the vanguard of this struggle on this side of the Atlantic. The attack on Paul Robeson accelerated when he was reported to have cast doubt on the desire of African-Americans to participate in a war against the Soviet Union, thus reminding U.S. rulers of the unease they had felt about waging war against Japan a few years earlier.[69] Martin Luther King's difficulties accelerated after he began to denounce the war in Vietnam more forcefully.[70] African-Americans – and their opponents – implicitly recognized that a formidable weapon in the conflict with domestic racism was international leverage.

---

67 Azza Salama Layton, "International Pressure and the U.S. Government's Response to Little Rock," *Arkansas Historical Quarterly* 56 (Autumn 1997): 257–72. See also the forthcoming definitive article on this subject by Mary L. Dudziak, "The Little Rock Crisis and Foreign Affairs: Race, Resistance and the Image of American Democracy," *Southern California Law Review*.
68 Penny M. Von Eschen, *Race Against Empire: Black Americans and Anticolonialism, 1937–1957* (Ithaca, 1997); Brenda Gayle Plummer, *Rising Wind: Black Americans and U.S. Foreign Affairs, 1935–1960* (Chapel Hill, 1996); Robert Weisbord, *Ebony Kinship: Africa, Africans and the Afro-Americans* (Westport, 1973); Jake C. Miller, *The Black Presence in American Foreign Affairs* (Washington, 1978); Lewis V. Baldwin, *Toward the Beloved Community: Martin Luther King, Jr., and South Africa* (Cleveland, 1995); Gerald R. Gill, "Afro-American Opposition to the United States' Wars of the Twentieth Century: Dissent, Discontent and Disinterest" (Ph.D. diss., Howard University, 1985); Austin M. Chakaodza, *International Diplomacy in Southern Africa: From Reagan to Mandela* (London, 1990); Patrick J. Furlong, *Between Crown and Swastika: The Impact of the Radical Right on the Afrikaner Nationalist Movement in the Fascist Era* (Hanover, 1991).
69 Jeffrey Stewart, ed., *Paul Robeson: Artist and Citizen* (New Brunswick, 1998).
70 Kenneth O'Reilly, *"Racial Matters": The FBI's Secret File on Black America, 1960–1972* (New York, 1989), 242–45, 286–90.

Still, Robeson, King, and others persevered and helped to keep global issues on the front burner at a time when the domestic struggle against Jim Crow was preoccupying most. Africa generally and Southern Africa particularly became the epicenter of the struggle against "white supremacy" during the Cold War. Moscow – the much reviled "evil empire" of U.S. propaganda – actually provided diplomatic and material assistance to the Africans, much to the consternation of Washington: the United States had to be concerned that African-Americans particularly would be moved by this development, which could present a ticklish domestic and international problem for Washington. Thus, during the decisive stages of the Algerian Revolution, Moscow, according to Soviet leader Boris Ponomarev,

supplied free to the People's Liberation Army . . . 25 thousand rifles, 21 thousand machine guns and sub-machine guns, 1300 howitzers, cannons and mortars, many tens of thousands of pistols and other weapons. Over 5 million rubles' worth of clothes, provisions and medical supplies were supplied to Algeria by Soviet social organizatons alone. Hundreds of wounded from the Algerian Liberation Army were saved and treated in the Soviet Union. Soviet wheat, sugar, butter, conserves, condensed milk, etc., streamed into Algeria.[71]

Moscow provided similar assistance to those fighting colonialism and other forms of exploitation in Indo-China, Southern Africa and Cuba, which too had a substantial population of African descent. Indeed, this assistance to those fighting racialized systems of oppression was no small factor in sparking an economic and political crisis that led to the collapse of the USSR.

Many in the United States felt such aid violated the basic norms of "peaceful coexistence" and "detente," though without this Soviet aid, Asians and Africans – and Cubans – would have faced more difficulty in confronting their opponents. These opponents – particularly those in Washington – continually asserted that their

---

71 "Stenogram: Meeting of the Communist Party of the Soviet Union and the Chinese Communist Party, Moscow, 5–20 July 1963," *Cold War International History Project* 10 (March 1998): 180.

Anti-communism a smokescreen for
white supremacy?

opposition to this Third World-Moscow alliance was based not on some outdated devotion to "white supremacy" but the Cold War creed of anticommunism.

Southern Rhodesia, the colony that Frederick Russell Burnham had helped to found decades earlier, provides an illustrative case study of the fate of "white supremacy" during a Cold War era when this doctrine was officially denounced. The fact is that despite these official bromides, racialist thinking continued to exert a powerful influence on U.S. foreign policy, even when it was not disguised in the finery of the newer philosophy of anticommunism.

Dean Acheson, by his own admission, was "present at the creation" of the Cold War confrontation. His anti-Communist credentials were impeccable and he was a member in good standing of the U.S. ruling class. However, in his private communications – and at times those in public as well – he conceded that "white supremacy" was no negligible factor in explaining his support for the minority regimes in Southern Africa. Often that support was expressed directly to Sir Roy Welensky, a prominent member of the Rhodesian elite.

In 1965 this colony had refused to accede to the "winds of change" blowing through the continent and declared a "unilateral declaration of independence" in defiance of the movement toward decolonization. Though denounced by many in the international community, Acheson – and many other influential U.S. leaders – adamantly backed the rebel regime in Rhodesia. Why? Sir Roy hinted at one reason in 1971 when Richard Nixon was cozying up to China, a maneuver that was decisive in creating a bloc that ultimately brought down the Soviet Union. One would have thought that the usually far-sighted Rhodesian leader would have sensed the obvious geopolitical implications of this stratagem, but he had other important issues on his mind – namely the impact the Nixon maneuver had on "white supremacy" – as he informed Acheson:

We Whites seldom appreciate the extent to which the Black and the Brown man order their thinking on how strong or weak they think one is, and it is, therefore always unwise to start off on a basis they think one is afraid of them. This may sound childish to you Dean, but I've lived all my life where the Whites have been outnumbered many times. I don't know the Yellow man, but I'm told that he is even more concerned about his dignity and face-saving than the Black man and will always interpret our casual ways as being weak.[72]

Acheson fed and reflected this racialist thinking, telling his inter-locutor, "I still cling to Bret Harte's aphorism, 'That for ways that are dark And for tricks that are vain The Heathen Chinese is peculiar.' But no more so than the heathen Japanese."[73]

Welensky, Acheson, and many other leaders from the Pan-Eu-ropean world were not simply driven by anticommunism during the Cold War – they were driven by "white supremacy" as well. It did appear that as the Pan-African ideal took hold in the midst of the Cold War, a revived "Pan-Europeanism" arose to counter it. This was particularly the case in the United States. However, what has been ignored in explaining why so many in the United States would seek to thwart the newly proclaimed anti-racist con-sensus of the Cold War era is the simple fact that the "personal was political." In other words, it was not only the case that U.S. investors perceived that they had a material stake in maintaining the bounty of cheap labor and minerals that "white supremacy" had delivered;[74] in addition, quite a few in the United States had "kith and kin" in Southern Africa whom they backed avidly in

---

72   Sir Roy Welensky to Dean Acheson, 30 July 1971, Dean Acheson Papers, box 34, Ster-ling Memorial Library, Yale University, New Haven, CT. For a fuller exploration of the U.S.-Rhodesian axis see Gerald Horne, "Gangsters, 'Whiteness,' Reactionary Politics and the U.S.-Rhodesian Connection," *Southern Africa Political and Economic Monthly* 9 (November 1995): 31–34. See also Gerald Horne, *From the Barrel of a Gun: The U.S. and the War Against Zimbabwe, 1965–1980,* forthcoming.
73   Dean Acheson to Sir Roy Welensky, 7 October 1971, Acheson Papers. Sir Roy had a virtual obsession with China: "I heard the announcement that China had put her first satellite into orbit. I noticed our newspapers this morning treated it as almost a minor event – I consider it one of the most serious bits of news I have listened to for a long time!" (Sir Roy Welensky to Dean Acheson, 27 April 1970, Acheson Papers).
74   Robert Kinloch Massie, *Loosing the Bonds: The United States and South Africa in the Apartheid Years* (New York, 1993); Thomas Borstelman, *Apartheid's Reluctant Uncle: The United States and Southern Africa in the Early Cold War* (New York, 1993); Janice Love, *The U.S. Anti-Apartheid Movement: Local Activism in Global Politics* (New York, 1985).

their attempt to establish minority rule: racial fears were a primary motive for this support, specifically fears of Europeans being overrrun by African "hordes."

Ian Smith, the leader of the illegal regime in Rhodesia, had an uncle that was "well established in the United States." When he met then Secretary of State Henry Kissinger, Smith noted that "like me," the diplomat's wife was "conservative by nature, had Scottish blood through ancestry and believed that we had much in common."[75] President Lyndon Baines Johnson was "very interested" in the Baines School in Bulawayo and wondered if it was part of a familial relationship. He could only trace this branch of his family back to 1741 and did not know if this meant that he too had relatives in Rhodesia.[76] A. R. W. Stumbles, a former Speaker of the Rhodesian Parliament, like many leading Rhodesians was born in South Africa but "his father . . . Robert's great-grandmother was first cousin to American President George Washington." The "W" in his name stood for Washington.[77] Angus Graham, who served as Rhodesia's minister of external affairs and one of that nation's leading white supremacists, proudly told Dean Acheson of the "letter" he received from "Mrs. Nora Acheson, a Canadian who married my mother's cousin, Patrick Acheson."[78] Evidently, Graham was related to the former U.S. Secretary of State.[79] The architect of "constructive engagement" with apartheid South Africa during the 1980s – Chester Crocker – also had intimate ties with Rhodesia. His wife and in-laws hailed from this country. Interestingly, when he visited Rhodesia in 1979 – as the war still raged – he pointed out that President Jimmy Carter was concerned about losing African-American votes if he were not sufficiently tough with Rhodesia; "but," reminded Dr. Crocker, "we are a white majority government . . . not a black

75   Ian Smith, *The Great Betrayal: The Memoirs of Ian Douglas Smith* (London, 1997), 24, 202.
76   Juanita Roberts to Kevin Lee, 24 April 1966, National Security File, Country File, Rhodesia, box 97, Lyndon Baines Johnson Papers, Johnson Library, Austin, Texas.
77   A. R. W. Stumbles, *Some Recollections of a Rhodesian Speaker* (Bulawayo, 1980), 171.
78   Angus Graham to Dean Acheson, 1 July 1968, Acheson Papers.
79   Dean Acheson to Angus Graham, 23 July 1968, Acheson Papers.

majority [government]."[80] The implication was that a Republican Party regime in Washington would seek to "constructively engage" the illegal minority regime rather than sanction it, in part because it was almost exclusively dependent on Euro-American – and not minority – voters.[81]

Crocker had a point. "Whiteness," if not "white supremacy," was rarely distant from the machinations of U.S. opinion-molders, even during a Cold War era when such racialist thinking was officially renounced. The United States had been founded as a bastion of "white supremacy" and this principle had not been eradicated totally in the twentieth century, despite enormous domestic and – particularly – global opposition. There were many reasons for this, not least being the perceived profits that seemed to flow from a special exploitation of Africans particularly. Still, it would be a mistake to neglect the point that there were blood ties, family relations that bonded influential forces in the United States to their brethren across the Atlantic; leaders of these minority regimes had a special call on the sentiments of Washington and this too helped to extend the operation of "white supremacy" as a principle of U.S. foreign policy. Similar to the beginning of the "American Century," Africa was continuing to reinforce and reinvigorate "white supremacy" as this epoch was winding down.

For a good deal of the American Century, "race" was seen as a global concern with Japan rarely far from calculations about this concept. Tokyo had proved to be a nettlesome foreign policy concern for Washington, as the Pacific War amply demonstrated. However, with the Cold War, Japan became an ally of the United States, and its ability to attract disgruntled African-Americans searching for leverage against their own government virtually disappeared. Correspondingly, "race" was reduced to a domestic concern – or at most, a concern that implicated Africans generally.

80 *Sunday Mail* [Rhodesia], 10 June 1979.
81 Kevin Phillips, *The Emerging Republican Majority* (New Rochelle, 1969); Dan T. Carter, *From George Wallace to Newt Gingrich: Race and the Conservative Counter-Revolution, 1963–1994* (Baton Rouge, 1996).

However, Washington's Cold War policy of anticommunism undercut the anti-racists of the left in Tokyo as it provided leverage to those Japanese who were the ideological descendants of the purveyors of prewar racialist thinking, particularly "anti-white" thinking.[82] When the Soviet Union collapsed, the adhesive that had bound many of the Japanese right – as well as many Chinese elites – to the United States eroded, and what emerged was a troubling eruption of racialist thinking.[83]

Mahatir Mohamad, prime minister of Malaysia, was a direct beneficiary of the protracted Cold War campaign – spearheaded by London and assisted by Washington – that routed the left in his country.[84] Shintaro Isihara, a leading Japanese conservative, was the kind of anti-Communist that the United States smiled on during the Cold War. Recently they produced a volume that raises intriguing questions about the future of "race" – and "white supremacy" – in the twenty-first century. They approvingly cite "Lenin who said that European prosperity was based on exploiting the cheap labor and abundant resources of the colonies. When that rapacious plunder became impossible, the sun began to set

82   Michael Schaller, *The American Occupaton of Japan: The Origins of the Cold War in Asia* (New York, 1985); Myles I.C. Robertson, *Soviet Policy Toward Japan: An Analysis of Trends in the 1970s and 1980s* (New York, 1988); Charles E. Zeigler, *Foreign Policy and East Asia: Learning and Adaptation in the Gorbachev Era* (New York, 1993).
83   Frank Dikotter, ed., *The Construction of Racial Identities in China and Japan* (Honolulu, 1997); Frank Dikotter, *The Discourse of Race in Modern China* (Stanford, 1992); Alf Hiltebeitel and Barbara Miller, eds., *Hair in Asian Cultures: Context and Change* (Albany, 1997); Benjamin Schwartz, *In Search of Wealth and Power: Yen Fu and the West* (Cambridge, 1964); Yoshino Kosaku, *Cultural Nationalism in Japan* (London, 1992); Cullen T. Hayashida, "Identity, Race and the Blood Ideology of Japan" (Ph.D. diss., University of Washington, 1976). Despite the paucity of Jewish people in Japan, there has been a persistent strain of anti-Semitism in this nation and, to an extent, in the region. See David G. Goodman and Masanori Miyazawa, *Jews in the Japanese Mind: The History and Uses of a Cultural Stereotype* (New York, 1995); David Kranzler, *Japanese, Nazis and Jews: The Jewish Refugee Community in Shanghai, 1938–1945* (New York, 1976); James R. Ross, *Escape to Shanghai: A Jewish Community in China* (New York, 1994); and Ernest G. Heppner, *Shanghai Refugee: A Memoir of the World War II Jewish Ghetto* (Lincoln, 1993).
84   Robert Jackson, *The Malayan Emergency: The Commonwealth's Wars, 1948–1966* (New York, 1991); Donald W. Hamilton, *The Art of Insurgency: American Military Policy and the Failure of Strategy in Southeast Asia* (New York, 1998); Edgar O'Ballance, *Malaya: The Communist Insurgent War, 1948–1960* (London, 1966); Richard Stubbs, *Hearts and Minds in Guerilla Warfare: The Malayan Emergency, 1948–1960* (New York, 1989); Robert Thompson, *Defeating Communist Insurgency: The Lessons of Malaya and Vietnam* (New York, 1966).

on Europe. . . . Europe 'surpassed' Asia through plunder and exploitation." "Western civilization" itself they state "was built on war." This broad assertion includes the United States ("Europeans and Americans are still dreaming of past glory") and they go on to warn that "Asians" – not just Japanese and Malaysians – "are fed up with the blustering and threats of American trade negotiators." "Asia," they warn, "presents a more serious threat to the West than even militaristic Japan did earlier this century." With bluntness, they charge that the Gulf War was no more than another expression of white supremacy: "If the United States can get away with this – peddling arms throughout the Middle East, intervening militarily to protect its supply of oil, and arm-twisting Japan to foot the bill – then the white race still rules the world"; "it is impossible to communicate with Americans as well as we do with Asians," they conclude. Why? "Color is one reason . . . the perception that white people are better than colored people." They pointedly observe that it may "take a cataclysmic event" to "shake the great majority of Americans out of their hubris and self-righteousness" and suggest that "we may have to form an Asian united front against Americanization." They raise the awesome specter of Genghis Khan, reminding how after he "extended the Mongol Empire to eastern Europe . . . Caucasians adopted Mongol-style haircuts and shaved eye-brows and even their bandy-legged gait." They even echo the Afro-centrists in averring that "Jesus was a person of color, a fact that discomforts Caucasians when it is brought to their attention."[85] Strikingly, this overt hostility to the United States – and particularly Euro-Americans – has not been abated by the financial crisis that has gripped Japan, Malaysia, and its neighbors, but instead has seemed to spread.[86]

Of course, unlike the pre-World War II era there is not – as of now – an identifiable constituency in the United States that would be willing to align with these Asian politicians, as the Black Nationalists of old once did. The Cold War took its toll on African-

85 Mahatir Mohamad and Shintaro Isihara, *The Voice of Asia: Two Leaders Discuss the Coming Century* (Tokyo, 1995), 22, 29, 53, 90, 98, 134.
86 *Far Eastern Economic Review*, 19 and 26 March, and 2 April 1998.

Americans, forcibly reducing internationalist thinking in this community.[87] However, this community is reeling, as it has come to recognize that the civil rights concessions it received – particularly affirmative action – were heavily dependent on a Cold War dispensation that has evaporated, while newly minted racialists posit ever more sophisticated versions of "white supremacy."[88] Thus, who is to say how U.S. minorities generally may react in the future to these more aggressive assertions of "white supremacy"? Perhaps U.S. minorities may feel compelled to align with "anti-white" Asians, just as some once aligned with Soviet Communists: the decline of the socialist project and the retreat of solidarity based on class makes such a prospect less far-fetched than it may appear at first glance. Once again, the moment could be near to contemplate a forced "race" from elements of the "power" that white supremacy was thought to provide.

The brusque reassertion of racial thinking in Asia has emerged just as the United States finds that relations with both China[89] and Japan are not the best; it is strategically impractical to maintain prickly relations with both of these Asian giants simultaneously, though the bluntness of "white supremacy" makes it difficult to forge subtle distinctions between and among "non-whites." Simultaneously, influential thinkers in this nation are warning of a "clash of civilizations" – warnings that bear an eery resemblance to the racial maunderings of Lothrop Stoddard and Madison Grant in the early part of this American Century.[90] As ever,

[handwritten margin note: They'r not that bad]

---

87 See generally Gerald Horne, *Fire This Time: The Watts Uprising and the 1960s* (Charlottesville, 1995).

88 Gerald Horne, *Reversing Discrimination: The Case for Affirmative Action* (New York, 1992); Joe L. Kincheloe, Shirley R. Steinberg, and Aaron D. Gresson III, eds., *Measured Lies: The Bell Curve Examined* (New York, 1996).

89 See, for example, Michael Pillsbury, ed., *Chinese Views of Future Warfare* (Washington, 1997); Richard Bernstein and Ross H. Munro, *The Coming Conflict with China* (New York, 1997); Ezra Vogel, *Living with China: U.S.-China Relations in the 21st Century* (New York, 1997); Daniel Burstein and Arne De Keijzer, *Big Dragon: China's Future: What it Means for Business, the Economy and the Global Order* (New York, 1998); Nicholas Kristof and Sheryl Wu Dunn, *China Wakes: The Struggle for the Soul of a Rising Power* (New York, 1995); Edward Gargan, *China's Fate: A People's Turbulent Struggle with Reform and Repression, 1980–1990* (New York, 1990); and Kenneth Lieberthal, *Governing China: From Revolution Through Reform* (New York, 1995).

90 Samuel P. Huntington, *The Clash of Civilizations and the Remaking of World Order* (New York, 1996).

the contours of race in this nation will be shaped by developments in the global arena and, it appears, U.S. foreign policy will continue to be shaped by racial considerations.

Nevertheless, it is difficult to predict where this uncertain situation may lead, but it is evident that we are experiencing the preliminary stages of a "general crisis of white supremacy" that may conclude with a fundamental reordering of concepts of "race" that – in a rudimentary sense – have been derived from "power."[91]

His problem: U.S. & Japan relations are good & U.S. have overlooked human rights abuses in China & supported most favored nation trade status.

Why doesn't he discuss U.S.'s failure to intervene in African civil wars?

→ Based on views of Japanese extremists, p. 334.

91 See generally Peter Ratcliffe, ed., *'Race', Ethnicity and Nation: International Perspectives on Social Conflict* (London, 1994); Robert Miles, *Racism after 'Race' Relations* (New York, 1993); Anthony Marx, *Making Race and Nation: A Comparison of the United States, South Africa and Brazil* (New York, 1998).

10

Immigrants and Frontiersmen: Two Traditions in American Foreign Policy

GODFREY HODGSON

It was Theodore Roosevelt and his circle who first put forward the idea that because the United States had grown to maturity as a power, it ought now to play a commensurate role in world affairs. By 1898 America's world role was no longer a theory, it was a fact. In that year American forces defeated Spain and annexed Cuba and the Philippines and also incorporated Hawaii as a territory. Over the next decade and a half the United States also became deeply embroiled in the affairs of Mexico, Latin America, and the Orient. Yet when the First World War broke out in 1914 a majority of Americans still did not see why the United States need become involved. It was three years before Woodrow Wilson, taking the nation to war against Germany, acknowledged that the United States was not only a world power but potentially the strongest of all the powers by virtue of population, resources, and industrial development.

It is the thesis of this essay that for a hundred years, ever since the Spanish-American War, the power of the United States and its involvement in the outside world have been growing rather steadily, while American attitudes toward that evolution have oscillated wildly. Seen from the outside, in other words, as a reality that other nations have had to confront, the growth of American power has been rather constant; seen from the inside, as an element of domestic politics and of national psychology, American involvement in the outside world has fluctuated in a process of action and reaction, systole and diastole.

The reasons for this conflict between the reality of steadily increasing American power and changing attitudes to it are not hard to discover. Two of the profound constants of American history, after all, have been the twin experiences of immigration and the frontier. Immigration peopled the United States with men and women whose attitude to the outside world, originally toward Europe but later toward other continents as well, was that of more or less resentful refugees, while the frontier built into the American psyche an expectation of steady expansion. Those two experiences, and the attitudes they engendered, set the templates for the development of American foreign policy: an alternation between the impulse to take advantage of America's growing economic, military, and political strength to export American ideas and values to the world, and the desire to avoid "entangling alliances" and other forms of involvement by which a corrupt outside world might soil the purity of American life. Throughout the American Century, as American power and influence steadily expanded, that dualism has continued to influence, and at times to hobble, American policy toward the outside world.

The very earliest settlers in colonial times, for ideological or economic reasons, had turned their backs on the British Isles and Europe. Bernard Bailyn's magisterial study of the emigrants who left the British Isles in the years immediately before the Revolution gives a snapshot of their motives, complex and down-to-earth, that is a healthy corrective to Fourth of July rhetoric.[1] And one of the most tantalizing statistics in all American history is that recorded without comment in Samuel Eliot Morison and Henry Steele Commager's great history: of the 37.7 million Europeans who emigrated to the United States between 1820 and 1930, 11.6 million returned home.[2] The initial emigrants, mostly from

---

1 Bernard Bailyn, *Voyages to the West: A Passage in the Peopling of America on the Eve of the Revolution* (New York, 1986).
2 Samuel Eliot Morison and Henry Steele Commager, *The Growth of the American Republic* (New York, 1942), 2:174.

the British Isles, were reinforced by Irish and German settlers whose experience of famine and revolution in 1848 had left them with no happy memories. And in the last quarter of the nineteenth century they were joined by others, from Ireland and Russia, Sicily and the Balkans, who had little desire to concern themselves with the continent where they had left behind hardship and unhappiness, when a new undeveloped continent, and a new and hopefully happier life, lay ahead.

In 1890, as every reader of Frederick Jackson Turner knows, the frontier of settlement was officially declared closed.[3] It was hardly an accident that, as the supply of new land in the continental United States came to an end, Americans began to turn their attention to new frontiers in the Caribbean, in Latin America, and in the Orient. It is no longer original to point out that to a considerable extent the political conflict over what came to be called "isolationism" was not one between those who wanted the United States to be involved abroad and those who wanted to remain in isolation, but was rather between those who wanted the nation to be involved with the politics of Europe, and those – the "isolationists" – who wanted no part of the quarrels of Europe, but were quite happy to see the United States expand in Cuba or Mexico, the Philippines or China.

It may be something of a simplification, then, but it is certainly not fanciful, to see the evolution of American attitudes to the outside world in terms of the play between these two principles: the immigration principle, motivating Americans to turn their backs on a world they had left behind, and the frontier principle impelling them forward to explore, as traders, investors, and missionaries, the new frontiers that were opening up in the early years of the twentieth century.

From the beginning, of course, the United States did not live in isolation. It was drawn into the gigantic convulsions of the Napoleonic wars, themselves the consequence of the ideological explosion touched off by the French Revolution. From time to time,

---

3 Frederick Jackson Turner, "The Significance of the Frontier in American History," originally read at the American Historical Association meeting in Chicago, 1893, republished in *The Frontier in American History* (New York, 1948).

it brushed up against the British Empire, in Canada, in the Caribbean, or on the high seas, and it was constantly entangled in the
filibusters, the debts, and the revolutions of Central America. But
it was not until the second decade of the twentieth century that,
under President Woodrow Wilson, the United States found itself
at once tempted and compelled to become a world power: tempted
because there was part of the American psyche, as well as those
ethnic elements in American domestic politics, that found it hard
to resist the idea of exporting to a world distracted by national
quarrels and imperialist policies the sovereign balm of American
democracy; compelled because the activities of imperial Germany
in Mexico, at the Black Tom plant in New Jersey,[4] and at sea
made it plain that mercantile America would not be left in peace
by the Central Powers if they were victorious. And that, too, has
been a continuing thread in the American Century: a Wilsonian
strand, sometimes repressed and concealed, sometimes boisterous and triumphalist, that has seen the world, in 1919 in Central
and Eastern Europe, in and after 1945 in Africa, Asia, and Latin
America, and since the fall of communism in the former Soviet
Union and elsewhere, as a field to be plowed and made fruitful by
American political example and economic precept.

Each of these waves of expansionist impetus was offset and
countered by an instinct of almost equal strength to leave a sorry
world to go to perdition in its own way. And so each of those
waves receded and was succeeded by periods – in the 1920s, in
the 1960s, and again in the 1990s – when the prevailing mood
was for Americans to rejoice and be exceeding glad that they did
not have to live in the rest of the world, and therefore to question
expansionist policies.

They did not, however, and they could not, avoid expansion itself. As early as the 1920s, American corporate enterprise became significantly interested in foreign markets and foreign raw
materials. (Even before that, American interests helped to de-

---

4   Thomas Alan Schwartz, *America's Germany: John J. McCloy and the Federal Republic of Germany* (Cambridge, MA, 1991), v.

velop oilfields in Mexico, Russia, and elsewhere, while American engineers, including future President Hoover, were active in discovering and exploiting minerals from Siberia to Chile.)[5] To be sure, the United States was until recently far less proportionately dependent on foreign trade than its rivals, the various other economic powers of successive periods, especially Britain, Germany, France, and Japan. Indeed it was not until the late 1960s and the 1970s that the United States became significantly dependent on imported oil and other raw materials, such as mineral ores from Canada, Africa, and Brazil. Until well after 1945, U.S. industry did not greatly depend on foreign markets, though in particular sectors these were from time to time important enough to generate noticeable pressure groups in Washington. By the 1970s, however, foreign markets had become crucial to the profitability of corporations in several key sectors: the Big Three automobile manufacturers, for example, began to depend heavily on their European subsidiaries for profit, and so did U.S. aircraft manufacturers. Again, it was not until after World War II that the U.S. share in the world economy, which had grown steadily since the 1870s, reaching a peak of close to 50 percent in the late 1940s, began to decline as a result of the explosive economic growth first of Europe, then of Japan, and finally of other nations in East Asia.

Three other characteristics of the U.S. economy should be mentioned at this point, because they have consistently pushed the United States in the direction of steadily expanding its role in the world, apparently unaffected by successive waves of domestic feeling about international involvement. The first is the role of technology in the U.S. economy and specifically in the expansion of U.S. exports. It is not the case – even if this is counterintuitive – that the United States has been unique in its capacity for technical innovation. The automobile, radio, movies, television, nuclear energy, and even the computer are all examples of technologies that were originally wholly or largely discovered elsewhere, but developed with much greater speed in the United States. U.S.

5 George H. Nash, *The Life of Herbert Hoover* (New York, 1983).

corporate business has been exceptionally good at finding and investing the resources to make techniques and technologies work.

The second is that U.S. business has been incomparably good at marketing, in the widest sense: successful, that is, not only at distributing ideas, machines, fashions, and techniques so that in the shortest possible time what is available in New York or Los Angeles is available, and is demanded, from Aroostook to San Diego and from Key West to Seattle, but also at organizing for this to be conveniently and profitably done. One essential element in the progressive involvement of the United States in the rest of the world, therefore, has come from the powerful mechanisms that have spread American fashions, American consumer goods, and American attitudes around the world, while another has been the steady appetite of non-Americans for American products.

Again, this should not be construed as a magical exceptionalism. There is little that is available in the United States now that is not available almost everywhere. Many of the goods and services that appear to be American are more truly Western. And it does not take long for even those innovations that are originally American to be available everywhere, and sometimes better made elsewhere. The point is simply that, while American attitudes to the world have fluctuated, American economic involvement has steadily increased, and is now far greater than it was in 1928 or even in 1958.

This has had interesting domestic consequences. Where once "internationalist" attitudes were identified with the East Coast and to a lesser degree with both coasts, now many metropolitan centers, notably but not only Atlanta, Houston, Miami, Minneapolis, and Seattle, not to mention Chicago, are deeply involved in, and therefore dependent on, international trade and investment in multiple ways. This has deprived those sections of the United States that traditionally suspected and resisted "internationalist" policies of leadership and influence. At the same time, the professionalization and a certain homogenization of the political elites has largely removed from national politics those strongly sectional political leaders who in the 1920s and again in the 1950s most effectively challenged internationalist orthodoxy. There are no William E. Borahs or Henry Cabot Lodges in Congress today, no H. R.Grosses and Bourke B. Hickenloopers; like their predecessors, Gingrich conservatives oppose government spending, unlike them, they do not oppose American involvement abroad. Protectionism survives, and has been espoused by such a major Democratic figures as Congressman Richard Gephardt. But it is now a philosophy held by the weaker, and rejected by the strongest, elements in American life, and this looks likely to continue.

Although the export success of certain U.S. high technology industries, especially those associated with computers and to a lesser extent aviation, has been a highly salient aspect of the pattern of U.S. international trade, the fact is that farm products and primary or semi-processed products like wheat, corn, rice, cotton, lumber, and construction materials account for a far larger proportion of U.S. exports than all high technology products put together. The pattern is complex, especially now that U.S. corporations have exported so much of their manufacturing operations, so that they receive their revenues in internal transfers, patent and license fees, and so on, rather than as straight export revenue. But these changes have also had effects on the domestic political map. Just as the South, heavily dependent on exports of cotton and other primary products, was traditionally internationalist even when its politics in other respects paralleled those of the more isolationist Midwest, so now it is hard to predict which regions or congressional districts will take more or less internationalist stances as far as these are determined by economic interest.

To some extent, of course, a progressively greater involvement in and therefore a greater dependency on, the world economically has been concealed from view by a series of massive crises in world politics, each of which led to deep transformations in the U.S. attitude to the rest of the world: World War I, the economic crisis of the 1930s, the rise of fascism, and the Cold War. It is noticeable, however, that one characteristic of these successive crises is that they have been perceived as demanding a progressively stronger and more lasting U.S. commitment to the outside world.

After World War I, U.S. withdrawal was clearly an option. Indeed, to some extent, at least in political terms, withdrawal is what took place in 1919, with the failure of Woodrow Wilson's campaign to get the United States to join the League of Nations. Partial withdrawal seemed to be an option in 1945–48, but then the threats implicit in the Cold War, essentially the prospect of military vulnerability to a nuclear-armed Soviet Union and of ideological and economic isolation, persuaded the American consensus to support the Truman-Acheson strategy of Cold War containment and international commitment.

After forty years and more of a Cold War that spread from central Europe to almost every corner of the globe, involving American political and military commitment of one sort or another in such remote and unlikely places as Afghanistan, Diego Garcia, Laos, and Thule, few now advocate withdrawal. The consensus is that the United States is now too deeply involved in the world even to contemplate any but what would once have been seen as an adventurously "internationalist" posture.

As the end of the century approaches, Americans contemplate with a blend of pride and reluctance the role of the United States as "the last superpower." It is easy to quibble with the term. Probably there never was any other nation to which the word "superpower" should have been seriously applied. It is plain that the profound weaknesses of the Soviet Union were concealed from sight for forty years by the coinciding interests of the Soviet elite, which didn't want its repressed populations to have any inkling of how weak it was, and of American elites with interests of various kinds in the nurturing of the national security state. As for China, it can still best be considered as a potential, rather than an actual, superpower, whose influence, though formidable, is still essentially regional. European powers, especially France and Britain, have a limited military capability, as they have shown from time to time in Africa, the Middle East, the Balkans, and elsewhere, and a considerable appetite for using it, inherited from their respective imperial pasts. But their geopolitical independence, already limited by resource constraints and to some extent by domestic politics, is also ultimately conditional on U.S. acquiescence, and has been so seen since the Suez crisis of 1956.

The United States is now, therefore, and has been at least since the Soviet withdrawal from Afghanistan, the only power capable of "projecting" military power (as the strategists say) virtually anywhere on earth; the only country whose economic resources make it, acting alone, decisive in the world economy both to promote and to protect development; the only civilization with an ideological appeal almost everywhere; and therefore the indispensable participant in any effective international enterprise.

Moreover, over the past two generations the United States has equipped itself with the institutional and human resources for hegemony. American government, as Professor Nelson Polsby has pointed out,[6] now trains a highly professional elite for diplomacy and international relations, instead of relying – as it did in the heyday of the "foreign policy Establishment" – on the amateur efforts of international lawyers, professors, and investment bankers. The government's own well-funded and well-staffed agencies are backed by an immense fund of expertise in universities, foundations, corporate business, and research institutions. And what is striking to a non-American observer is the extent to which, in spite of numerous and in some instances sharp divisions, these communities seem to share a sense of common purpose, almost an "American ideology" toward the rest of the world.

Certainly the United States has no competitor for the title of the world's last superpower. It is true that, taken collectively, the resources of Europe – economic, political, and even military – are not quite so insignificant as they sometimes seem from the United States, but Europeans have no appetite for contesting the superpower title with Americans. Possibly, the United States may one day be challenged or even outstripped by China, or—as Samuel P. Huntington seems to argue, surely implausibly[7] – by some unlikely coalition of China and Islam. But no such coalition has yet

6 N. W. Polsby, paper given at Oxford seminar, July 1998.
7 Samuel P. Huntington, *The Clash of Civilizations and the Emerging World Order* (New York, 1996).

appeared. There is no serious opposition to the prospect of the United States continuing to be accepted as the world's natural and necessary leader.

Indeed, if anything, other countries want the United States to get more involved in diplomatic mediation, to contribute more to the United Nations or to economic rescue packages, to be more willing to impose settlements in the Balkans or the Middle East, than the United States is keen to do. So much so that it is tempting to leave the proposition there, and to see the progression of American international relations through the twentieth century as leading, by a gradual but irresistible teleology, to unquestioned hegemony. History, if that view is accepted, could perhaps really be said to have ended.[8]

Unfortunately, the story is not as simple or as reassuring as that. For the United States remains profoundly divided in its attitude to involvement in international affairs, along the lines adumbrated above. The tradition of the frontier, which has impelled Americans toward expansion, still clashes with the memory of immigration, restraining them from involvement in a world that, if not always wicked, is at the very least entangling, frustrating, and potentially a damaging distraction from the essential American enterprise, which has been the realization of individual dreams of freedom and prosperity.

That conflict, in one form or another, has hampered foreign policy under every administration since World War II and still bedevils the efforts of the Clinton administration. When Bill Clinton took office in 1993, he and leading members of his administration outlined a diplomatic strategy that they themselves called "neo-Wilsonian."[9] The United States, Clinton and his colleagues promised, would be actively involved in spreading the

Handwritten marginalia: I don't see how the frontier is relevant now. — Some for immigration; people now aren't fleeing from the world. They're (fleeing) to go.

---

8 Francis Fukuyama's highly publicized essay, "The End of History," might more correctly have been called "The End of Historicism," since the collapse of the Soviet version of communism certainly did not bring the processes of historical evolution and competition to an end, but merely ended, at least for the time being, an era in which teleological systems, such as communism, fascism, and so on, sought universal domination. See Fukuyama, *The End of History and the Last Man* (New York, 1992).
9 Godfrey Hodgson, "American Ideals, Global Realities," *World Policy Journal* 10 (Winter 1993–94): 1–6.

core values of American civilization, which they summed up – perhaps, it is possible to see with hindsight, with dangerous over-simplification – as political democracy and free-market economics.

It didn't happen. In the aftermath of the collapse of communism, a positive policy to propagate American values had great appeal. Democracy was in the air, in Africa and Latin America as well as in Eastern Europe. It was easy, too, to assume that the enthusiastic adoption of capitalism in China and East Asia generally meant that it would only be a matter of time before capitalism's Siamese twin, democracy, took over in those countries too. For capitalism, in the 1990s, appeared to have triumphed, in both intellectual and financial marketplaces everywhere.

Six years later, the optimistic verities of Bill Clinton's first year in the White House have the sepia tint of an ancient photograph. Communists or former Communists have returned to power or are challenging for power everywhere in Eastern Europe and the former Soviet Union, because the crude version of Western democracy and capitalism that those unhappy countries had experienced turned out to mean widespread economic breakdown, gangsterism in politics, and war or the threat of war in international relations. No doubt that was not capitalism's fault. These were countries that had in most cases never experienced democracy, but had lurched from one form of autocracy to another for centuries, and had therefore never had a chance to develop the institutions and attitudes of the "public space" – churches, charities, newspapers, and voluntary associations of every kind – that the East German philosopher Jürgen Habermas pointed out were the necessary preconditions and accompaniments of political democracy.[10] Still, by the late 1990s, the record of democracy as it existed in the territories of the former Soviet Union was not encouraging, and one of the reasons was the perceived injustice of the form of "capitalism" that had appeared there.

In Western Europe, social democratic governments returned to power in France, Britain, and Germany as democratic electorates

---

10   Michael Pusey, *Jürgen Habermas* (London, 1993); Thomas McCarthy, *The Critical Theory of Jürgen Habermas* (Cambridge, MA, 1978).

demanded protection from uncontrolled capitalism and expressed their fury at the injustices of the "winner-take-all" society. In Italy a party descended from the more liberal wing of the old Italian Communist party even achieved power, though in a coalition. The hopes invested by American conservatives in the 1980s, based on the neo-liberal policies of governments in Britain, Australia, and New Zealand,[11] receded as those countries either elected governments that abandoned conservative "reforms" or quietly put the brake on liberalization. In Asia, governments in Japan, Indonesia, Korea, and Malaysia were reeling from the impact of an economic crisis seen as resulting from unregulated flows of speculative investment in globalized capital markets and widely, if irrationally, attributed to American influence. In the "developing" countries of Africa there was an uneasy awareness of the severe cost of the "Washington model" of reforms imposed by the International Monetary Fund and the U.S. government as preconditions for economic assistance.

It would be quite wrong to conclude, as some did, that these economic upheavals and political responses can be put down to the "failures" of "capitalism." Apart from anything else, capitalism can be regarded as the natural economic system, one interrupted by the Western export of socialism in its various forms between the 1880s and the 1960s, but one that historically predated socialism. What was being exported from the United States in the 1980s, on this theory, was not capitalism, but one particular form of capitalism. By this reckoning merchants and manufacturers in Russia, or Africa, or Indonesia did not have to adopt capitalism: they had always understood the fundamental relationships of capitalism, those of investment and return, and buyer and seller, and had only been prevented from acting on that understanding by the dictates of various Communist or Jacobin governments of one sort or another. But without getting bogged down in that argument, whose correctness or otherwise could only be verified by a whole new approach to economic history, it was

---

11   See the hopes expressed by Martin Anderson, *Revolution* (New York, 1988), 37: "The idea of capitalism, now sweeping across the face of the globe, is now stronger and more vibrant than it has ever been."

plain enough by the end of the American Century that there was more to economic success than cell phones and stock markets: profound changes in structures and attitudes would be necessary before the return, or the arrival, of capitalism could create wealth on the scale that was naively expected, let alone provide a steady impulse in the direction of political democracy.

As to the relationship between capitalism and democracy, it began to appear that this, too, had been oversimplified in the excitement generated by the collapse of the Soviet Union and the victory in the Gulf War. No doubt there was a relationship. But its exact nature appeared not to be as predictable or as causal as had been widely assumed. Pundits such as Dr. Henry Kissinger had been pronouncing since the 1970s that economic liberalization in China must lead to political freedom; but long after the brutal repression in Tienanmen Square in 1989, no matter how many bank buildings towered skyward in Shanghai, there was no sign of the Communist government in Beijing giving up autocratic control. Several Asian governments that had presided over the most spectacular growth, unleashing what looked a lot like capitalism to the naked eye, not only showed no enthusiasm for democracy but privately flouted and even openly derided such fundamental ideas as the rule of law or freedom of expression. Some East Asian intellectuals even argued that "Asian values," a term that appeared to embrace communism, Confucianism, Shinto, Buddhism, and half a dozen other philosophical or religious systems, previously supposed to be incompatible if not actually inimical, precluded democracy; to their shame, some Western intellectuals even agreed with them. Conversely, those countries that had most dramatically adopted political democracy, such as Russia and South Africa, seemed quite incapable of unleashing the wealth creation promised by the more triumphalist advocates of the American prescription.

At home, the Clinton administration was virtually immobilized, first by the Republican recapture of Congress, then by the president's self-inflicted (and Starr-inflicted) woes. The Clinton administration could claim one great success (and one that was a humiliating demonstration of Europe's inability to act effectively

in international affairs) in Bosnia. It sought to claim credit for
other "peace processes" too, in the Middle East, in Kosovo, and
in Northern Ireland, with varying, and contested, degrees of justification. Occasionally, in a somewhat random way, President
Clinton followed the precedents of several previous administrations by reacting boldly and dramatically to various perceived
provocations, mostly, it had to be said, from small and weak nations. But this by no means amounted to a reliable willingness to
commit American forces or resources in a political cause.

Just as Lyndon B. Johnson had invaded the Dominican Republic, Richard M. Nixon had bombed Laos (but not China), Gerald
R. Ford had intervened in Cambodia, Ronald W. Reagan had
shelled Lebanon, invaded Grenada, and bombed Libya, so George
H. W. Bush – in addition to his genuine triumph against Iraq –
invaded Panama and sent Marines to Somalia, so now President
Clinton invaded Haiti and sent cruise missiles to Sudan and Afghanistan.

Taken in conjunction with the use of U.S. (and European) air
forces in Bosnia, and with the threat of similar action in or around
Kosovo, here there would appear to be the outline of a tradition
here. The United States, on this evidence, would make itself available as the international policeman. Sometimes this would involve drawing a line in the sand, as with Saddam Hussein after
the invasion of Kuwait, and saying, "Thus far, and no farther."
Sometimes it would be a matter of intervening to allow indigenous forces to overthrow a tyrant, as President Bush did in the
Philippines; sometimes – if the dictator's country were small enough
or its forces sufficiently unthreatening – it might involve the use
of U.S. ground forces. Sometimes, again, it might involve nothing more than warnings or more or less minatory diplomatic intervention, as in the case of a number of démarches toward
North Korea, in which the erring leader was made to feel the lash
of Washington's disapproval, with dire, if unspecified, consequences being more or less tactfully invoked.

The snag to this "last superpower" policeman role is that a
convention seems to be growing up that it must not involve American casualties, or that if there were to be any American casualties

they must be minimal. It is already normal, in this connection, for ground troops from Britain, France, Ireland, Norway, or Fiji to be sent in, under the auspices of the United Nations, or NATO. But so far as possible American lives must not be put at risk. The episode in Somalia, when President Clinton was reportedly so upset by the sight of a dead American Marine's body being dragged through the streets that he pulled the Marines out, may have had more and less positive consequences than the president calculated at the time. No doubt this unwillingness of recent presidents to risk American lives is "the Vietnam syndrome," an understandable, even a healthy, reaction to the appalling waste of American and Vietnamese lives in the Vietnam War. Yet it contrasts rather sharply with the idea of the "last superpower" accepting responsibility for the peace of the world and its adhesion to at least minimum standards of international conduct.

If the last superpower is careful with the lives of its soldiers and sailors, it seems also to be sparing with its money. After an embarrassingly long period of doubt, it seems at the time of this writing that the Congress may finally authorize payment of the U.S. share of the money needed for the IMF to organize the salvage of the worst-hit East Asian economies. Everyone knows, however, that that money is far too little in relation to what might be needed in some future financial crisis, and indeed quite probably for later stages of the current crisis. There appears to be even less prospect of the United States paying its share of the United Nations' budget.

There could hardly be a clearer illustration of the problem. The United Nations was set up by the United States. Its goals reflect American ideals. If it was first frustrated by the Cold War and later corrupted by the willingness of the so-called Non-Aligned Nations to be manipulated and exploited by the Soviet Union, the collapse of the Soviet Union leaves the UN more likely to support than to obstruct the aims of American foreign policy. But because of the hostility of conservative Republicans to the whole idea of a supranational authority, itself exacerbated by responsible Republican conservatives' excessive deference to some truly irrational phobias on the far right, the United States is deprived

I'm not sure this is limited to the GOP.

of a potentially valuable device for recruiting international support for its policies.

The point does not need to be labored. As the American Century ends, the power of the United States, and the absence of any countervailing power, fully justifies the claim that it is the "last superpower." Powerful impulses in the American political tradition support the proposition that the United States should use its power to spread American values as well as American interests. Yet equally strong internal constraints hold the government of the United States back from the exercise of that power in behalf of those values. The isolationist and the interventionist traditions, so to speak, cancel one another out. What is more, on this analysis, stasis is even more likely in the future, as conservative politicians, responding to public attitudes, show greater reluctance to intervene abroad.

That is, however, an incomplete analysis. For one thing, as American economic interests overseas multiply, there are likely to be more cases where powerful domestic lobbies demand an effective response from presidents to threats overseas. Far more important is likely to be the way domestic politics work in the United States in relation to foreign affairs. Most of the time, over the past hundred years, foreign policy issues have not been particularly salient in American domestic politics. Even during the forty-odd years of the Cold War, except for brief periods, consensus reigned on foreign policy. Only during the anti-Communist scare and the Korean War, then during the Vietnam War, and in the late 1970s at the time of the Brezhnev offensive and the energy crisis did foreign policy feature prominently in domestic policy. Most of the time, foreign policy has been left to lobbies with special interests in particular foreign policy issues: economic lobbies like the sugar interests, the oil companies, or the farmers, but also ethical and political lobbies like the supporters of Israel, or Greece, or the "captive nations" groups, or the anti-apartheid movement. Only occasionally, as in the periods immediately preceding the two world wars, or for even briefer historical moments such as the months American hostages were being held by the mullahs in Tehran, or the duration of the Gulf War, did a normally indifferent general public focus sharply on a foreign issue. Then, large numbers of Americans joined what (on the analogy of legislative "committees of the whole") might be called "lobbies of the whole," for or against what was suddenly seen as an issue engaging the interests, the reputation, and the moral standing of the country.

If that pattern continues, and I cannot see any compelling reason why it should not, then the present stand-off between the neo-Wilsonian and the neo-isolationist traditions will not continue forever. Instead, in normal times, politicians, including presidents, will continue to see their interests as best served by flattering the electorate. So they will take advantage of every opportunity to present the United States as the arbiter of the world while taking great care to avoid being called on to take any risks to maintain that status. But from time to time, a dramatic event will get through to the general public, as distinct from the "foreign policy community" or the sundry lobby groups. Then presidents and other politicians will realize that they cannot avoid commitment. The risk of incurring casualties and massive expenditures will abruptly come to seem preferable to the risk of doing too little, too late. Indeed, if this analysis – all too briefly sketched – is correct, then the great test of a president's skill in foreign affairs will be to judge when the normal preference for caution has been replaced by a coalition for action.

Of course Republican presidents and Republican majorities in Congress will tend to be more reluctant than Democrats to engage the United States in foreign commitments. But Democrats, too, aware that they have been tagged as the "war party," will be leery of foreign commitments in normal times. Except in one of the comparatively rare periods when the general public is alerted to a foreign issue, the phrase "the last superpower" may become something of an honorific title.

It has been plain for a long time that the one instrumentality that can transform an issue into one that can engage American public opinion as a whole is the media. Over the last third of the century, that has meant essentially television, though newspapers play a vital part in suggesting and defining agendas for television news coverage. The pattern therefore is likely to be that most of the time, foreign policy issues will slip well down the list of political priorities. Then, often rather suddenly, an event or process, especially one that is caught by the graphic power of television news, will energize public opinion. It is possible to imagine events abroad – the detonation of an "Islamic bomb" in the wrong hands, a perceived dangerous threat to the integrity of Israel, a particularly horrifying act of terrorism – that could energize opinion at frightening speed. Woe betide a president who misreads or reacts too slowly to such a future Pearl Harbor or Korea, a Tehran or Kuwait!

Such a volatile prognosis for U.S. foreign policy may seem alarming. It is certainly not reassuring. For more than fifty years, the world has come to rely on the United States to respond to its crises, to arbitrate its quarrels, and to defend it against tyranny and aggression, too much, perhaps, for its own good as for that of the United States. Gratifying as it may be for Americans to think of themselves as inhabiting the last superpower, there would be small consolation if the cost were having to bear the burdens of that preeminence alone. It would be better for everyone if the United States more consistently followed what has been a wise instinct in the most impressive American statesmen of the past, namely, to seek multinational instruments for carrying out, under American leadership but not as part of American hegemony, the tasks that fall to what is, after all, only the most powerful single nation, and not one that will forever monopolize either military or economic power.

The Clinton administration has some creditable foreign policy successes to its credit, notably Richard Holbrooke's skillful mediation in the Bosnian crisis. But there have been too many failures as well. The Chechnya disaster, which eyewitnesses insist made the ordeal of Sarajevo look like a church picnic, must be attributed in part to the failure of the Clinton administration to diagnose correctly what the political situation in Russia was really like, and in particular to appraise Boris Yeltsin correctly and on time. There have been other, perhaps even more costly, failures, too. The Indian and Pakistani nuclear tests remind us that we do not live in a postnuclear world. NATO expansion may create more tension than it prevents. The calvary of North Korea may yet set off a catastrophic crisis in East Asia. All in all, the Bush and Clinton administrations both must be judged to have missed the historic opportunity presented by the collapse of the Soviet Union to put in place multinational mechanisms that could create a genuinely new world order, as opposed to a triumphalist and complacent hegemony that the American people may not be consistently willing to pay for.

For if the past century has taught any grand lesson, it has been that the world is indeed economically and politically, not to mention militarily, one world, interdependent. The United States can no more afford to turn its back on what the follies and the energies and unsatisfied ambitions of the rest of the world can do to it, than the rest of the world can afford to dispense with the strength, and the ideals, of the Americans. The great temptation for American leaders will be to fall back on preaching a pleasing but irrelevant exceptionalism; the great opportunity will be to persuade Americans of the long term advantages of sharing leadership as widely as possible.

11

Partisan Politics and Foreign Policy in the American Century

MICHAEL J. HOGAN

Reading Henry Luce's famous editorial today should remind us that the American Century was not inevitable. Remaking the world in America's image, which is what Luce had in mind, required a political will that Americans had yet to muster. They had to overcome their isolationist past and the old values that had supported it, including a deep-seated fear of the state and the conviction that global engagement, particularly war, would create "some form of dictatorship." They feared a garrison state, a "collectivism," as Luce put it, that would build on the "vast bureaucracy" growing out of the New Deal, sabotage the Constitution, run up the national debt, bankrupt the treasury, and socialize the economy. For Luce, the isolationist "virus" was especially strong among Republican politicians, who had to reform their ways if the American people were going to "accept wholeheartedly our duty and our opportunity as the most powerful and vital nation in the world" and thus "exert upon the world the full impact of our influence."

Luce's analysis of the struggle between isolationism and internationalism on the eve of Pearl Harbor, and of the ideological and partisan dimensions of that struggle, is right as far as it goes. But Luce was wrong to see the struggle as "peculiar" to that period, to argue, in effect, that Americans were only then coming to grips with the dangers that war and global engagement could pose to "constitutional democracy." On the contrary, the battle between isolationism and internationalism, between unilateralism and multilateralism, is as old as the nation itself. Grounded in ideological and political considerations, of the kind that Luce identified, the battle has had economic and regional dimensions as well and continues to reverberate in American politics today. The following essay reviews the history of this struggle in its various dimensions, with special emphasis on what Luce called the "American century."

Since the founding of the Republic, foreign policy and partisan politics have been linked inextricably. The first political parties emerged in part because of partisan differences over the direction of American diplomacy. The War of 1812 brought these differences to a head, at one point threatening the very survival of the Union, and there were similar differences during the war with Mexico in 1848 and the Spanish American War a half-century later. Woodrow Wilson's war to make the world safe for democracy also led to bitter partisan battles, especially over Senate ratification of the Versailles treaty. Indeed, so great were the differences, so intense the animosity, that Wilson's strongest opponents were know as the "irreconcilables," the "bitter-enders," and the "battalion of death."[1]

Nor did these partisan differences become less passionate as the American century unfolded. On the contrary, equally bitter battles erupted over military preparedness and intervention in the 1930s, as Luce's editorial makes clear; over the turn toward internationalism in the 1940s and 1950s; over the Vietnam war in the 1960s and 1970s; and over the American role in the post-Cold War world that began to emerge in the 1990s.

As this overview suggests, partisan conflicts have usually been party conflicts. Jeffersonian Republicans and Hamiltonian Federalists battled for control of the nation's foreign policy from the 1790s through the War of 1812. By the time of the Civil War, party labels had changed: The Democratic party had emerged as

---

1   Alexander De Conde, *A History of American Foreign Policy*, 2d ed. (New York, 1971), 470; Selig Adler, *The Isolationist Impulse: Its Twentieth-Century Reaction* (London, 1957), 102–5.

the champion of territorial expansion while the Whigs, and later the Republicans, were more likely to see this course as an aid to slavery and to support commercial expansion instead. In the twentieth century, as noted above, the partisan debate over foreign policy would become in large part a debate between nationalists and internationalists, with each group increasingly identified with a particular political party. During the struggle over the Treaty of Versailles, the Democrats under Wilson began to emerge as the champions of internationalism while the Republicans were more likely to be ardent nationalists, basically unilateralists, whose views on foreign policy made them vulnerable to charges of isolationism.

Although not always accurate in the case of particular politicians, these labels continued to cling to both political parties over the next several decades. As Luce's editorial suggests, some of Wilson's Republican critics reprised their roles in the 1930s, forming an isolationist vanguard in opposition to any attempt by the Roosevelt administration to embroil the United States in another world war. Similar critics took much the same position in the early Cold War. By that time the Republican party had split into nationalist and internationalist factions, with the nationalist wing, led by former President Herbert Hoover and Ohio Senator Robert A. Taft, pushing a strategic doctrine that would limit the country's commitments beyond the Atlantic and Pacific oceans, build a hemispheric system of defense, and rely heavily on air atomic power to safeguard the national interests. Guided by this doctrine, they raised the most serious reservations against the North Atlantic Treaty and other collective security arrangements; against military conscription, universal military training, burgeoning defense budgets, and the rising influence of the military establishment; against the British loan, the Marshall Plan, and the liberal design for a multilateral system of world trade. Nor did defeat on most of these issues silence the nationalists. Although their voice would be muffled within the anti-Communist consensus that stretched over the next forty years, much of what they had to say would resurface in the conservative politics of the late Cold War and the early years of the post-Cold War era.

If the battle over foreign policy has been drawn along party lines, other considerations also influenced the struggle and its outcome. This has been the case throughout American history. Historians, for example, have long been aware of a regional influence on foreign policy, dating back to the early years of the Republic. The split between the Jeffersonian Republicans and the Hamiltonian Federalists was in part a split between the south and the west, on the one hand, the northeast, on the other. In the era of Manifest Destiny, to cite another example, the debate over expansion became in large part a debate over slavery that followed sectional lines. The same point can be made about other debates in other times, including the struggle for the soul of American foreign policy on the eve of Pearl Harbor and in the early Cold War. In both cases, as historians have noted, internationalist sentiment was especially strong in the northeast, while nationalist or isolationist opinion was greatest in the midwest and west. Nor would this regional pattern change much in subsequent years. Throughout the Cold War and into the post-Cold War period, nationalist sentiment would remain particularly strong in the so-called Gunbelt, an area of the country, stretching from the western states across the new Republican party strongholds of the south, that has benefited most from military expenditures.[2]

As this reference to the Gunbelt suggests, the partisan struggle over foreign policy has long displayed economic as well as party and regional dimensions. I am not speaking here in strictly Marxist terms. While it would be a mistake to ignore social-class divisions entirely, the most interesting economic dimension has to do with function rather than class. The struggle between the Republicans and the Federalists in the early period was in part a struggle between the farmers and planters of the south and west and the commercial and mercantile interests of the northeast. The first group had a natural interest in territorial expansion across the continent and was largely hostile toward Great Britain; the second group gave the highest priority to commercial expansion,

2   The term "gunbelt" comes from Ann Markusen, Peter Hall, Scott Campbell, and Sabina Deitrick, *The Rise of the Gunbelt: The Military Remapping of Industrial America* (New York, 1991).

especially within the framework of the British Empire, and was generally pro-British. In the era of Manifest Destiny, as suggested earlier, the issue of expansion increasingly pitted southern planters, on the one hand, against western farmers and northern merchants, on the other. The imperial debate at the turn of the century had an economic dimension as well, with export-driven agriculture and its allies in the business and banking communities taking a prominent place among those groups supporting the outward thrust of the American empire.

Historians disagree over the part played by functional economic considerations in the modern shift toward internationalism and over when that shift occurred. Those who subscribe to an older, more conventional interpretation see the Cold War as the critical turning point on the road from isolationism to internationalism. They admit that Roosevelt had earlier brought the nation into World War II on the Allied side. But to their way of thinking the permanent transformation came in the postwar period, when the United States finally accepted the peacetime political and military responsibilities it had shunned in the 1920s. What is more, if the shift toward internationalism came with the Cold War, its causes, according to these historians, were almost wholly external to American politics and the American economy. They were rooted instead in the postwar international system, basically a bipolar system in which the Soviet Union menaced the security and well-being of the United States and its allies. Confronted with this menace, policymakers in Washington thought it prudent to expand American influence into the power vacuums created by the war and to bolster friends and allies with economic aid, military assistance, and defense commitments – all backed by a substantial arsenal of conventional and nuclear weapons.[3]

Another group of historians sees the shift toward internationalism beginning in the interwar period, and attributes this shift not

---

3   This argument is implicit in the works of postrevisionist scholars. See, for example, John Lewis Gaddis, *The United States and the Origins of the Cold War, 1941–1947* (New York, 1972); idem, *Strategies of Containment: A Critical Appraisal of Postwar American National Security Policy* (New York, 1982); and Melvyn P. Leffler, *A Preponderance of Power: National Security, the Truman Administration, and the Cold War* (Stanford, 1992).

only to changes in the international system but also to the changing structure of American politics and the American economy.[4] The economic changes, basically changes in the industrial structure, had to do with the emergence of a powerful bloc of large, capital-intensive firms with a growing stake in the global economy. These firms, and their backers on Wall Street, challenged the influence over public policy of a larger bloc of small, labor-intensive companies that were interested primarily in national rather than international markets. Their rivalry ruptured the Republican party, which increasingly became the party of small business, and created the New Deal coalition, which included organized labor, the large, capital-intensive firms, and their allies among investment bankers. Changes in the industrial structure thus led to a fundamental political realignment that made possible the New Deal at home and the turn toward internationalism abroad.

Under the New Deal, in other words, policymakers in Washington abandoned the economic nationalism that had marked American diplomacy in the early years of the Great Depression. They threw their weight behind the Reciprocal Trade Agreements Act of 1934, the tripartite currency accord that came later in the decade, and other measures of economic internationalism. To be sure, the road to internationalism was not smooth. The nationalist bloc, which remained strong in the Republican party, waged a determined defense of the home market, denounced the interventionist thrust of Roosevelt's foreign policy after 1939, and resisted the globalization of American commitments in the early years of the Cold War. Concessions to their point of view often resulted in an imperfect internationalism. Nevertheless, the shift toward internationalism was unmistakable, already in the 1930s, and was

4 I have developed this line of argument in *The Marshall Plan: America, Britain, and the Reconstruction of Western Europe, 1947–1952* (New York, 1987), and in *A Cross of Iron: Harry S. Truman and the Origins of the National Security State, 1945–1954* (New York, 1998). My argument borrows from Thomas Ferguson, "From Normalcy to New Deal: Industrial Structure, Party Competition, and American Public Policy in the Great Depression," *International Organization* 38 (Winter 1984): 41–94. For a similar argument see also Bruce Cumings, *The Origins of the Korean War*, vol. 2, *The Roaring of the Cataract, 1947–1950* (Princeton, 1990).

as much a response to changes in the country's industrial structure and party alignment as it was to external developments.

Although Hoover's vision of Fortress America was discarded for the global commitments undertaken by President Truman and his successors, a somewhat muted conflict between nationalists and internationalists, unilateralists and multilateralists, persisted throughout the Cold War before reaching a clamorous pitch again in the 1980s and 1990s. Once more, regional, economic, and party interests played a part. By 1980, the population of the southeast and southwest had surpassed that of the North and East, just as the economic power of the Rustbelt had given way to that of the Sunbelt. Under the weight of these demographic changes, American politics grew more conservative and American foreign policy became more nationalistic. The Republican party grew stronger as the Democratic party grew weaker and the Republicans began to reassert not only a virulent anticommunism but also a vigorous critique of liberal multilateralism and of the big banks and capital intensive firms, the Trilateral Commission and the Council on Foreign Relations, that had done so much to shape American policy in the postwar period.

Given the pressure of this conservative constituency, Washington abandoned the policy of detente for one of confrontation, escalated the nuclear arms race, and adopted a more unilateral diplomacy. It also faced a rising tide of opposition to liberal immigration policies, to such international stabilizing agencies as the IMF and the World Bank, and to such multilateral free-trade agreements as the North American Free Trade Agreement of 1993. Because the postwar trend toward multilateralism seemed to hurt workers and farmers as well as many corporations, neo-isolationist sentiment found expression in both major parties. But it was most evident in third-party candidates, from George Wallace to Ross Perot, and in areas of the country that had long been seedbeds of the kind of conservative populism primarily associated with the right wing of the Republican party.

The preceding summary notwithstanding, the partisan battles over foreign policy involved more than a clash of regional, economic,

What's the difference between party & ideology?

and party interests. As Luce understood, ideology played a part as well, especially fundamental ideological disagreements over the meaning of America and its global purpose. This was clearly the case with the bitter fighting between Republicans and Federalists during the early Republic—over the Jay Treaty, for example, or the War of 1812. Each side was driven by a different vision of America: The Federalists looked to a strong central government, commercial expansion, and rapprochement with England; the Republicans favored states' rights, territorial expansion, and friendly relations with revolutionary France. Other examples abound. The era of Manifest Destiny came to an end in part because southerners and northerners, slave holders and abolitionists, no longer shared the same vision of America. Southerners wanted to expand the empire of slavery; northerners envisioned an empire of free land, free labor, and free men. Ideology also colored the debate following the war with Spain in 1898, especially the debate over acquisition of the Philippines. In this case, the advocates of acquisition were often self-conscious imperialists who wanted to emulate the European system of colonialism, while anti-imperialists argued that a policy of military conquest and imperial grandeur would corrupt Republican virtue and depart from the simple principles of the Founding Fathers.

In the American century, the Cold War itself was as much an ideological battle at home as abroad, and the vocabulary of this battle often echoed the language of an earlier day. In the national security ideology of the Truman administration, peace and freedom were indivisible, so that American security and American liberty depended on the security and liberty of people everywhere. What is more, assuring security in an age of total war required a degree of military preparedness and international engagement that was out of step with the isolationist policies of the past and with the traditional opposition to military entanglements and a large standing army.

To justify their departures from tradition, however, Truman and his allies often drew on tradition itself, especially on a discursive tradition that dated from the era of Manifest Destiny and on a traditional cultural narrative that celebrated American exceptionalism and American destiny. To Truman and his allies, in other words, leadership of the free world was a sacred mission thrust upon the United States by the laws of both history and nature. "Providence," as George Kennan explained to the American people, had "made their entire security as a nation dependent on their pulling themselves together and accepting the responsibilities of moral and political leadership that history plainly intended them to bear."[5]

Taft, Hoover, and other nationalists also drew on tradition, especially on the traditional Republican ideology of the Founders, but they used their version of the past to defend a neo-isolationist alternative to Truman's policies. They denounced military training as a European device that would corrupt the institutions, especially the family and the school, on which American democracy rested. They worried that national security policies would accelerate the dangerous trend toward a centralization of power in Washington, a trend that had begun with the New Deal and would, unless stopped, destroy the balance of power between different branches of the federal establishment and between the federal government and the states. They also warned against a large standing army that could imperil civilian leadership, and they claimed that excessive defense spending was debasing the currency, bankrupting the treasury, and leading straight to a "garrison state" without private incentive and economic liberties. To avoid these dangers, as mentioned earlier, Taft and other nationalists wanted the United States to pursue a safer, more cost-effective foreign policy that relied heavily on air atomic power, rather than a large standing army, and limited the country's commitments beyond the Western Hemisphere.[6]

In a world where peace and freedom were indivisible, the United States, according to Truman and his allies, had no choice but to assume the role that history had thrust upon it – that of a great

5   X [George Kennan], "The Sources of Soviet Conduct," *Foreign Affairs* 25 (July 1947): 566–82.
6   Taft, "Constructive Criticism of Foreign Policy is Essential to the Safety of the Nation," 5 January 1951, *Congressional Record*, 97, pt.1:54–61. A full discussion of the conservative critique of U.S. national security policy in the early Cold War runs throughout my book, *A Cross of Iron.*

military power and defender of democracy globally. Doing so, they believed, would not repudiate the country's destiny but fulfill it, would not corrupt the nation's institutions but defend them, would not compromise liberty but spread its blessings to those threatened by Communist aggression. For nationalists like Taft, on the other hand, the uniqueness of America, its democratic traditions and capitalist economy, derived in part from its historic separateness. If the United States wanted to retain its democratic identity, they said, it could not become enmeshed in foreign intrigue, emulate old world imperialisms and militarisms, or play the game of power politics – all of which would corrupt the country's basic institutions and values. While Truman and the internationalists invoked the tradition of Manifest Destiny and wanted the country to be a missionary of freedom on a global scale, conservative nationalists like Taft invoked the tradition of nationalism, even isolationism, and wanted the country to lead by splendid example.

Taft's alternative did not prevail, as we know, but neo-isolationist sentiment did allow Republican nationalists to play a major role in shaping American politics and foreign policy after World War II – as they did after all the major wars of this century. The aftermath of each of these conflicts witnessed a great popular demand for relief from the burdens of war, especially the economic burdens, which led in part to the retrenchment or redesign of the country's commitments and strategy abroad. Following the First World War, industry and agriculture demanded an end to wartime controls and people everywhere wanted to reduce taxes and trim the budget. The Republican party gave voice to these expectations. Its victory at the polls in 1920 accelerated the pace of industrial demobilization and set the stage for budget cuts, especially cuts in the defense budget made possible in part through a large-scale program of naval disarmament. These cuts then paved the way to the peace dividend that Secretary of the Treasury Andrew Mellon distributed in the form of lower taxes, and this return to "normalcy," in Harding's phrase, robbed the American government of the resources it needed to deal with some of the major international problems of the day. It could not forgive the war debts that Allied countries owed the American treasury, which made it difficult for these countries to reduce their reparation demands on Germany. It also lacked the military power to enforce the terms of the peace treaty and the financial power to play a major role in reconstructing the European economy. Instead, the Republicans designed a foreign policy that relied on economic rather than military strategies to guarantee the peace and on private rather than public funds to rebuild Europe.

After the Second World War the Republican party again vented popular demands for rapid military and industrial demobilization. Although the Truman administration sympathized, these demands usually exceeded what policymakers had in mind. Economic controls were scaled back over Truman's opposition and despite inflationary pressures. The military establishment also shrank dramatically, notwithstanding complaints from the Army and the Navy. Liberals, mainly Democrats, and conservatives, mainly Republicans, squabbled again over how to spend the second peace dividend of the century, and the outcome in 1948 was another Republican tax cut that put a lid on domestic spending and forced even deeper reductions in a modest defense budget.

The Republican desire to cut taxes combined with Truman's hope for a balanced budget to shape a foreign policy that initially limited the scope of the country's commitments abroad, largely to Europe. This policy relied heavily on economic instruments to achieve its goals and on a military strategy that emphasized air atomic power rather than a large army and navy. The program of aid to Greece and Turkey, the Marshall Plan for Western Europe, and the North Atlantic Treaty encapsulated this policy, which remained the dominant policy until the outbreak of the Korean War in 1950, when Truman approved NSC–68, greatly increased defense spending in all categories, and turned toward military rather than economic instruments of containment.

In 1952 the Republican party gave voice once more to a widespread discontent with wartime economic controls, high wartime taxes, and mounting budget deficits. Dwight D. Eisenhower promised in his presidential campaign to cut federal spending by forty billion dollars over several years, and it was this promise, as much as his pledge to "go to Korea," that led to Eisenhower's victory at the polls. Once in office, moreover, the new president brought the Korean War to a conclusion and began to dismantle the wartime system of economic controls, burgeoning budgets, and high taxes. As in the first and second postwar periods, the Republicans delivered a peace dividend in the form of lower taxes made possible through budget reductions. For all practical purposes, these reductions came in the area of national security expenditures, which never returned to prewar levels, to be sure, but which shrank by about ten billion dollars between fiscal years 1953 and 1956.

Eisenhower's military strategy facilitated his budget and tax cuts, although it might be more accurate to argue that these reductions dictated the president's military strategy. As suggested earlier, something similar could be said of the Truman administration. The Republican tax cut of 1948, together with Truman's own plans for balancing the budget, had led to a military strategy prior to the Korean War that relied largely on atomic weapons to deter Soviet aggression. Eisenhower adopted a similar strategy to accommodate what were fundamentally economic rather than national security imperatives. The result was the New Look, basically a capital-intensive strategy of containment based on nuclear weapons, the B–52 bomber, and ballistic missiles. This strategy enabled Eisenhower to control the size of the Navy and drastically curtail the Army, which together accounted for most of the military savings.

The end of the Cold War, the last great war of the American century, brought similar results. Like the first and second postwar periods, the last years of the Cold War and its aftermath witnessed a revival of nativist sentiment and religious fundamentalism, an assault on labor and on liberal social legislation, a resurgence of antigovernment sentiment, and a vigorous defense of traditional values, including the value of a balanced budget. The conservative, nationalist wing of the Republican party was more dominant than it had been earlier. It again capitalized on popular concern with high taxes and mounting budget deficits, and it again delivered a peace dividend in the form of budget reductions and a tax cut. A fear of big government and of multilateral rather than unilateral foreign policies, both evident in Republican thinking in the first and second postwar periods, also resurfaced with the Republican resurgence that came in the 1980s and 1990s. This fear inspired conservative Republicans, mostly from the midwest, west, and south, in their neo-isolationist opposition to the United Nations, to international institutions like the World Bank and the IMF, to liberal trade and tariff policies, and to foreign aid and other "give-away" programs that contributed to high taxes, budget deficits, and big government.

The nationalist resurgence of recent years reminds us of the persistent challenge to internationalism that has marked the American century, and indeed all of American history. Luce delineated this challenge in his famous editorial, noting correctly that it was centered largely in the Republican party and driven in part by ideological considerations. He did not know that similar challenges had run through most of American history and would persist even after American entry into World War II, and even after the great outward thrust of American power in the half-century of Cold War. Nor did Luce give enough credit to the concerns of those who resisted internationalism and interventionism in the 1930s. Castigating them for denying the United States its right to remake the world in its own image, he did not pause to ask if war and global engagement ran the risk of unmaking America – of undermining the New Deal, as some liberals worried, or of busting the treasury and creating a garrison state, as some conservatives feared.

In the postwar period Truman and other policymakers would mimic Luce's rhetorical strategy: They would brand Hoover, Taft, and other critics as narrow isolationists and deride their opposition to military preparedness, to the centralization of authority in the Pentagon, and to the expansion of American power into every nook and cranny of the globe. To be sure, Republican nationalists were vulnerable to criticism. Their concern about the centralization of power in the Pentagon revealed a profound fear of big government that also inspired their opposition to progressive social policies. Their reservations about containing communism on a global scale belied their support for Senator Joseph McCarthy and his brand of red-baiting in the United States. Their reservations about the Marshall Plan and the North Atlantic Treaty revealed a reluctance to reinforce areas of the world that were vital to U.S. security. And their critique of collective security and wasteful defense spending could not conceal their willingness to invest heavily in certain forms of military power, especially air power and atomic weapons, and to use that power on a unilateral basis.

Nevertheless, much of what these critics had to say deserves a fuller hearing from historians of the American century, and especially from historians who want to assess what the last half of that century has cost the American people. To give them a fair hearing, moreover, it is useful to remember that liberals as well as conservatives shared some of the same reservations and to express these reservations in the words of Walter Lippmann, the distinguished journalist and persistent critic of American policy who is not as easily dismissed as Taft, Hoover, and their allies. Indeed, Lippmann's views not only summarize the most salient aspects of a powerful critique, they also suggest an alternative policy that might have been more effective and less costly than the one actually pursued.

Lippmann wanted the United States to maintain its military strength after the Second World War, and was not averse to confronting power with power, as he once put it. On the contrary, he saw balance-of-power diplomacy as the best way to safeguard the national interest and set the stage for productive negotiations with the Soviet Union. Guided by this kind of thinking, he supported the Greco-Turkish aid bill, the Marshall Plan, the military buildup that accompanied the war scare of 1948, and the deployment of American warships to the Formosa Strait in the early days of the Korean War.[7] It was this aspect of his thinking, particularly as applied to Europe, that distinguished Lippmann from Hoover and Taft and that allowed him to condemn both men as isolationists.

---

7   Ronald Steel, *Walter Lippmann and the American Century*, paperback ed. (New York, 1981), 486, 450–52.

What Lippmann opposed was a foreign policy without the limits and restraints he thought realistic. This opposition lay behind his devastating critique of the Truman Doctrine and George Kennan's famous article on "The Sources of Soviet Conduct," which inspired a series of newspaper columns that Lippmann later collected in a little book on the Cold War. Lippmann was critical of Kennan and Truman, as he would later be of John Foster Dulles and other policymakers who interpreted Soviet foreign policy in broad ideological rather than specific historical and geographical terms – who saw Soviet policy, in other words, as driven by the goal of world domination rather than the search for security along the Russian frontier. Such views, he was convinced, led the United States to support policies in Germany and elsewhere that only accentuated Soviet insecurities, and thus had the effect of actually escalating the Cold War rather than ending it.[8]

Lippmann also ridiculed the notion that God and history had assigned the United States a new role as leader of the free world. It was "not leadership," he said, "to adapt ourselves to the shifts and maneuvers of Soviet policy," which was the course that Kennan urged in his article on the sources of Soviet conduct. On the contrary, such a course actually surrendered leadership to the Soviet Union, whose actions then determined how the United States would react. Nor did Lippmann view the United States as the head of a coalition devoted to democratic principles. He might have been sympathetic with such a coalition, had it been limited in scope and restricted to real democracies. But he noted with some irony that America's free economy was not compatible with the kind of globalism envisioned in the Truman Doctrine or in Kennan's article, any more than American democracy was compatible with the weak and corrupt regimes that American leaders sometimes supported.[9]

Yet what most disturbed Lippmann was the notion that peace and freedom were indivisible, and that American security therefore depended upon the security of anti-Communist governments

8   Ibid., 426, 431, 433, 437, 443–45.
9   Walter Lippmann, *The Cold War: A Study in U.S. Foreign Policy* (New York, 1947), 13–14, 15–17.

Lippmann turned out to be right about that.

everywhere. This notion led Kennan to the conclusion that communism had to be contained through the "vigilant application of counter-force at a series of constantly shifting geographical and political points." According to Lippmann, however, such a policy had no boundaries and would therefore disperse American power too broadly, squander American resources, and weaken rather than strengthen the United States.[10]

Lippmann wanted American power concentrated in areas where the United States had a serious national interest, notably Western Europe, and where American leaders could work with their "natural allies" in the Atlantic community. Such a policy, Lippmann argued, would not be informed by the Truman Doctrine but by "an older American doctrine," which held that "we must not become entangled all over the world in disputes that we alone cannot settle." What is more, even in areas, such as Europe, where American interests were substantial and where power therefore had to be concentrated, Lippmann was reluctant to link the United States too tightly to countries with which it had little in common politically and whose economic and military weakness would diminish rather than increase American power.[11]

This same kind of thinking influenced Lippmann's view of the Korean War, which he considered a national disaster of monumental proportions. He had been pleased with Dean Acheson's famous speech at the National Press Club in January 1950, in which the secretary of state drew the American defense perimeter in the Pacific to include Japan but not Korea or Taiwan. American policymakers had never considered the national interests to be worth the risk of a major war on the Asian mainland, and he was convinced that Acheson's defense perimeter squared with this historic policy. Given this conviction, he was appalled when Truman sent American troops to Korea after the outbreak of fighting there. He considered the war a tragic waste of lives and re-

---

10   Ibid., 18–19. See also Steel, *Lippmann*, 438–39. The quote is from X [Kennan], "The Sources of Soviet Conduct," 566–82.
11   Lippmann, *The Cold War*, 24, 53–54. See also ibid., 25–28; and Steel, *Lippmann*, 458–60. For Lippmann's views on the Truman Doctrine and the policies leading up to it see his column, "Today and Tomorrow," in the *Washington Post*, 7 September 1946, and 6 March, 25 March, and 8 April 1947.

Gerald Horne
would call this
a racist.

sources in an area of marginal interest to the United States, and he was convinced that fighting in Korea would detract from the country's primary duties in Europe, dissipate its power, and disillusion its people. Given these views, Lippmann did not hesitate to say that American forces should be withdrawn as soon as the situation had stabilized, and to complain bitterly when General MacArthur's efforts to unify Korea provoked China's intervention, enlarged the war, and further eroded America's power and authority.[12]

Running through Lippmann's critique of American diplomacy, from the Truman Doctrine to the Korean War, was the conviction that the wrong kind of foreign policy could alter the American state at home. His thinking in this regard was more subtle than Taft's or Hoover's, but his concerns were similar, particularly his conviction that an open-ended anticommunism would cost more than the country could afford and more than the taxpayers would support. Lippmann called it "deficit diplomacy," whereby policymakers kept expanding the country's global commitments beyond the military resources available to meet them. Yet any attempt to match resources to commitments, he warned, would wreck the economy, lead to political and economic regimentation, and drive American taxpayers toward isolationism.[13]

Nor were these the only liabilities. Lippmann was also convinced that Truman's policies threatened the constitutional balance in the United States by inflating the authority of the executive branch, weakening that of Congress, and involving professional soldiers too deeply in American politics. His thinking in this regard again dovetailed to some extent with that of Taft and Hoover, as was apparent in his reaction to the North Atlantic Treaty, the program of arms aid that followed, and the dispatch of American troops to Europe. Much like Taft, he saw all of these initiatives as vastly expanding presidential powers, including the power to provide arms to any government on earth, to

---

12 Steel, *Lippmann*, 466–67, 474–76. See also Lippmann's column, "Today and Tomorrow," in the *Washington Post*, 11 December 1950 and 11 January 1951.
13 See Lippmann's column, "Today and Tomorrow," in the *Washington Post*, 25 July and 22 August 1950, and 26 February 1951. See also Steel, *Lippmann*, 460–61.

declare war without consulting Congress, and to send troops abroad without congressional consent. The same kind of thinking also influenced his critique of the Korean War, in which case he again faulted Truman for sending troops into battle without congressional approval and for thus bringing on a constitutional crisis over the conduct of American foreign relations. This crisis, in turn, had set the stage for the Truman-MacArthur controversy and for a congressional investigation of American military strategy, both of which, according to Lippmann, saw the "default of civil power" and the "rise of the generals to a place" they should not "hold in the Government of the Republic." The Truman-MacArthur controversy, said Lippmann, was "the culminating point" of the "most un-American and most unrepublican evolution of our affairs."[14]

Following Lippmann's critique, it is possible to extrapolate a foreign policy that went beyond the hemispheric system of defense favored by Hoover, Taft, and other nationalists in the Republican party but still stopped short of the globalism pursued by Truman and his successors. Under this policy, American commitments around the world would be more limited and American power would be more focused and less likely to be enchained in a network of debilitating alliances with weaker countries that had little in common with the United States. Under this policy, moreover, defense would cost less, taxes would be lower, fewer resources would be diverted from civilian to military investment, the military would be less powerful politically, and the constitutional balance would be protected against the dangers of an imperial presidency.

Lippmann's critique of American diplomacy, and his alternative recommendations, are similar in many ways to what Republican nationalists argued at the time. There is the same conviction that American resources were not inexhaustible, that American goals must therefore be limited, and that going beyond these limits would be counterproductive. Trying to reshape the world

---

14   See Lippmann's column, "Today and Tomorrow," *Washington Post*, 21 May 1951. See also ibid., 11 December 1950, and 9 January, 16 January, 13 February, and 5 April 1951; and Steel, *Lippmann*, 460–61.

in the image of American democracy and liberal capitalism, they both feared, would only weaken the economy, militarize the country, and destroy democracy.

And who can say that such fears were wholly unjustified? Although American democracy did not give way to a garrison state, as some had feared, the Cold War did witness a vast expansion of presidential powers. It also enlarged the role of the military in American life and altered the relationship between military leaders and civilian authorities. At a time when American foreign policy relied heavily on armed force to achieve its objectives, when the size of the permanent force was so large, and when the military establishment commanded such an enormous share of the nation's resources, it was inevitable, perhaps, that Pentagon policymakers would rival American diplomats in the field of foreign affairs, dominate the production of atomic energy, and otherwise assert an unprecedented degree of political authority and autonomy. Indeed, military leaders could no longer be counted on to bow before the principle of civilian supremacy. They demanded a greater voice in decision making, resisted decisions they did not like, and in some cases openly defied civilian authority, including the authority of the president.[15]

From its center in the Pentagon, moreover, military influence extended throughout the government, and from there to virtually every area of American life. Even before the Korean War, commentators had started to notice the increasingly visible presence of military leaders in American government and business. High-ranking military officials were playing important roles in the State Department, the White House, and other government agencies, and were also taking top positions in science and industry. Some commentators saw nothing wrong with this development, but others considered it a dangerous departure from American tradition, including Robert S. Allen, who worried that Pentagon officials

15   This story is told in Hogan, *A Cross of Iron*, but also see Arthur A. Ekirch, Jr., *The Civilian and the Military* (New York, 1956), esp. 271–77; Russell F. Weigley, "The American Military and the Principle of Civilian Control from McClellan to Powell," *Journal of Military History* 57 (October 1993): 27–58; and Richard H. Kohn, "Out of Control: The Crisis in Civil-Military Relations," *National Interest* 35 (Spring 1994): 3–17.

sought nothing less than to retain their wartime position as the "directing force in national policy, both domestic and foreign."[16]

Nor were these concerns without foundation. Besides an increasingly visible presence in government, military leaders began exerting an enormous influence over a large portion of American youth, and would continue to do so as long as conscription was on the books. They also started to negotiate helpful alliances with friends in the media, the trade unions, and the business communuity, and to use these alliances to safeguard their interests and add to their power. Along with the intelligence community, moreover, they forged a similar partnership with university administrators and faculty, especially scientists, and took advantage of this partnership, not to mention the Reserve Officer Training Corps, to establish a substantial presence on American campuses at a time when McCarthyites in government and their collaborators in the university were already creating a profoundly conservative academic environment.[17]

The partnership between science and the state, between university labs and Pentagon policymakers, was particularly important and especially helpful to a handful of elite universities. It helped MIT to sustain its leadership in government-sponsored research, enabled Stanford to break into the front ranks of American research universities, and brought similar gains to other institutions. In most cases, military research made it possible for universities to attract new faculty, build new facilities, and recruit good students, though often on terms, according to Stuart W. Leslie, that compromised the independence of university scientists, allowed the military to establish research priorities, and diverted scientific talent from more productive peacetime purposes.[18]

16   Allen, "The Big Brass Takes Over," *New Republic* 116 (10 February 1947): 19–21. See also "Yesterday, High Brass of Armed Forces . . . Today, High Brass of Industry," *Business Week* (5 April 1947): 20–21; "Toward Militarism," *New Republic* 117 (18 August 1947): 5–7; and Ernest K. Lindley, "The Military Mind," *Newsweek* 31 (2 February 1948): 30.
17   For McCarthyism on campus see especially Ellen W. Schrecker, *No Ivory Tower: McCarthyism and the Universities* (New York, 1986). For another view on the partnership between the universities and the national security state see Sigmund Diamond, *Compromised Campus: The Collaboration of Universities with the Intelligence Community, 1945–1955* (New York, 1992).
18   Leslie, *The Cold War and American Science: The Military-Industrial-Academic Com-*

The benefits of the partnership between science and the state spilled from the university into the private sector. It brought enormous gains to such firms as Raytheon, Sylvania, IBM, AT&T, and General Electric, to name a few, and to certain areas of the country, notably the western states. The federal government invested 62 percent of its budget in defense over the first twenty years of the Cold War, and the western states garnered the largest share of this investment. They received one fourth of all military prime contracts, not to mention a large share of indirect military expenditures by the Atomic Energy Commission, the Veterans Administration, and other agencies. According to James L. Clayton, California alone received more than $67 billion in defense contracts between 1951 and 1965, about 20 percent of the total. Defense spending of this scale raised the average income in the state, contributed to its population growth, and was the largest single factor in the rapid postwar expansion of its economy.[19]

At the same time, however, defense spending drained resources from productive investment in civilian technologies. Some industries in some areas of the country, notably the old industrial heartland, lost their competitive edge as defense expenditures migrated from states like Michigan and Ohio to the aviation, electronics, and other defense-based industries in the Gunbelt regions of the country. The social and political consequences of defense spending could be troubling as well, not the least because it provided more employment for white men than for women and minorities and because it increased the political power of areas that were more likely to be conservative than liberal, Republican than Democratic, unilateralist than multilateralist.[20]

In short, national security expenditures sustained employment in certain segments of the workforce in certain parts of the country, but they also distorted the landscape of American politics,

plex at MIT and Stanford (New York, 1993). See also Rebecca S. Lowen, *Creating the Cold War University: The Transformation of Stanford* (Berkeley, 1997), 95–146.

19   Clayton, "The Impact of the Cold War on the Economies of California and Utah, 1946–1965," *Pacific Historical Review* 36 (November 1967): 449–73. See also Markusen, et al., *Rise of the Gunbelt*, 3–25, 82–84, 230–34.

20   Markusen, et al., *Rise of the Gunbelt*, 3–25, 230–34.

Really?

drained resources from various states, kept taxes high, added to the national debt, and diverted a large share of the federal budget from welfare to warfare purposes. By the first year of the Eisenhower administration, the federal government was investing approximately three-fourths of its budget in national security programs, defense spending equaled 18 percent of the gross national product, and defense expenditures accounted for nearly one-third of the nation's business activity. The figures changed from year to year, but during the first two decades of the Cold War the federal government invested $776 billion in national defense, an amount equal to more than 60 percent of the federal budget, and more if indirect defense and war-related expenditures are included.[21]

And of this is bad?

As this brief summary indicates, American foreign policy since World War II has had an enormous impact on American life. To be sure, the cost could have been greater had policymakers like Eisenhower or agencies like the Budget Bureau not offset the influence of those who would pay any price for victory in the struggle against communism. But something similar could be said of Republican nationalists like Hoover and Taft, of their liberal allies, and of the realist critique mounted by Walter Lippmann. Maybe Lippmann's alternative would have brought results that were worse, not better, than those that actually occurred. But in some ways it compares favorably with the policy that Luce recommended and that American leaders followed through much of the Cold War. And with that war now behind us, is it not worth asking if the same gains could have been had at less than the price paid for them?

21   Clayton, "Impact of the Cold War on the Economies of California and Utah," 449; Paul G. Pierpaoli, Jr., "Corporatist and Voluntarist Approaches to Cold War Rearmament: The Private Side of Industrial and Economic Mobilization, 1950–1953," *Essays in Economic and Business History* 15 (1997): 263–75.

12

Philanthropy and Diplomacy in the "American Century"

VOLKER R. BERGHAHN

This essay is concerned with the role of the "big" foundations in the United States during the "American Century" and with the ways in which their activities related to the projection of the country's political, economic, and cultural power around the globe. In order to provide some fresh empirical backup for the more general arguments about the subject, central parts of what follows focus on the work of the Ford Foundation, which from 1948 onward grew to become the largest philanthropic organization in the world, spending millions of dollars every year on international projects.

Because the major expansion of American foundation activity did not occur until after the end of World War II, however, the topic also raises the question as to when the "American Century" in fact began if seen through the lens of the historian of corporate capitalism and of culture. Whatever the time frame of the political historian, certainly from the perspective of cultural and business history a very plausible case can be made that, broadly speaking, the year 1900 must be the starting point. It was at the turn of the century that Europe – then still the power center of the world – began to perceive the United States as the new world power of the future not merely in terms of political and military potential but also – and indeed most particularly so – in terms of industrial-technological and cultural power and influence. Historians

I would like to thank Oliver Schmidt for his comments and advice.

of international affairs, preoccupied as they tend to be with diplomacy and military (or naval) competition in the pre-1914 period of heightened nationalism and formal imperialism, have not been too interested in those latter aspects. Thanks to the work of the "new international historians," the picture may be more balanced for the interwar years and the period after 1945 when America's role in the reconstruction of war-torn Europe inevitably turned scholars' attention toward questions of finance and economics.[1]

Yet, much of this research was primarily concerned with quantifying the American impact on Europe in those two periods, and much less is known about the European-American relationship in terms of industrial technology, mentality, and culture.[2]

For the pre-1914 period the imbalance is particularly striking because it is precisely in those years that America's industrial and cultural development became a subject of intense debate among contemporaries in the wake of the Paris World Exhibition of 1900. At this forum, where the major nations of the world presented themselves, the American pavilion attracted much attention because of the modern machinery on display. If the European had hitherto perceived the United States as a wide-open country of settlers and trappers, of cowboys and "Indians," by the beginning of the new century America also came to be seen as a major technological power and as a highly modern society with an urban and industrial culture. European businessmen and engineers were particularly intrigued by the new methods of production and factory organization that were being developed across the Atlantic.

There were, to begin with, the novel ideas about rationalized manufacturing with ever more sophisticated machinery turning out inexpensive goods. Yet the vision of mass production became linked with concepts of more efficient organization of both the shop floor and various areas of management. Frederick Taylor had begun to advertise his methods of work organization and

---

1 For a discussion see Volker R. Berghahn and Charles S. Maier, "Modern Europe in American Historical Writing," in *Imagined Histories*, ed. Anthony Molho and Gordon Wood (Princeton, 1998), 393–414.
2 A good recent example of the latter approach focusing on the 1920s is Mary Nolan, *Visions of Modernity* (New York, 1994).

to conduct his time-and-motion studies with a truly missionary zeal.[3] But the influence of Taylorism and the Scientific Management movement more generally soon also spilled over into other parts of the modern manufacturing enterprise, such as finance and marketing. In short, when it came to the displays in the American Pavilion at Paris and their transferability to Europe, it was not just a question of the importation of machinery but also of whether and how far the new American ideas about factory and business organization could and should be adopted on the other side of the Atlantic. Ultimately, to be sure, this question was not about the wholesale "Americanization" of Europe – as the process has often been misinterpreted – but about a selective adaptation and blending of imported and indigenous industrial and social practices. Just as in other spheres of reality cultural transfer always involves negotiation, so it was with business.[4]

The debate was unleashed when some European companies began to experiment with Taylorism, while other firms were more skeptical about importing America's brave new industrial world. As the influential *Frankfurter Zeitung* editorialized in 1906, when it published an article on Taylorism by an engineering professor at Aachen Technical University, the adoption of American-style methods in industry had "cultural consequences" that were still difficult to fathom.[5] To begin with, there were the consequences of assembly-line manufacturing, which European critics argued would result in cheap, unreliable, and shoddy products. This concern probably found its neatest expression in the following statement by Daimler-Benz, the Stuttgart manufacturer of expensive cars and a paragon of *Qualitätsarbeit*: "Here [we do things] meticulously and thoroughly; over there [in America it is] skimping and rushing."[6]

---

3   On Taylorism see, for example, Richard Kanigel, *The One Best Way* (New York, 1997); and Samuel Haber, *Efficiency and Uplift* (Chicago, 1964).
4   See Volker R. Berghahn, *The Americanization of West German Industry, 1945–1973* (New York, 1986).
5   Quoted in Lothar Burchardt, "Technischer Fortschritt und sozialer Wandel" [Technological progress and social change], in *Deutsche Technikgeschichte*, ed. Wilhelm Treue (Göttingen, 1977), 74.
6   Quoted in Anita Kugler, "Von der Werkstatt zum Fliessband" [From workshop to assembly line], in *Geschichte und Gesellschaft*, 13 (1987): 315.

Yet it was not just the implications of mass production for European manufacturing practices, which – still steeped in a crafts tradition and mentality – upheld the idea of small-volume output of beautifully engineered, high-priced goods. European manufacturers understood, even if they did not say it so publicly, that mass production only made sense in a society that explicitly accepted and promoted the mass consumption of inexpensive products together with its democratic implications. But Europe's elites, with few exceptions, were wary of a dawning age of democracy. This elitism was expressed by Daimler-Benz in the following telling statement: "Over here we are still a long way from the American situation where every Mr. Jones owns a car. With us the automobile is for the most part a vehicle for the better-off classes."[7]

Worse, mass production brought with it not only mass consumption and the erosion of luxury production for the select few; it was also thought to undermine the high culture of Europe, leading down a slippery slope toward a "trashy," "vulgar," and "primitive" mass culture. And this threat was, in the eyes of many educated Europeans, in turn related to the dangers of an emergent mass society peopled by *Massenmenschen* over whom, in this age of a proliferating universal suffrage and pressure for democratic participation and socioeconomic equality, the elites might well lose control. Toward 1914 this came to be more than a serious possibility in light of the successful mass mobilization that the working-class parties and trade unions of Europe had undertaken. Millions of industrial and urban "proletarians" had joined these organizations in a new age of mass politics, making demands that sounded very radical to the middle and upper classes and seemingly destabilized the established political systems and oligarchies in charge of the centers of political and economic power.

Not surprisingly, Le Bon's *Psychologie des foules* became a best-seller in its time and was translated into other European languages.[8] Mass production, mass consumption, mass culture, mass society, and mass politics were thus seen by the elites of Europe to be

7 Ibid., 316.
8 Gustave Le Bon, *The Crowd: A Study of the Popular Mind* (London, 1910). The book was first translated into English in 1896. The seventh impression appeared in 1910.

dangerously interconnected, and developments in the United States provided a good example of this interconnection: if "you've seen one, you've seen the mall."[9] So while the Europeans developed a fascination with America as the embodiment of the new century, not all of them were pro-American. Fears of the consequences of mass production and mass consumption also generated anti-American feelings. If Taylor, the rationalizing engineer, was problematical, Henry Ford, the salesman of mass-produced cars to the mass consumer, was even more so. With the subsequent rise of the United States to world-power status and ultimately to hegemony in the Western world, these perceptions became intimately linked with attitudes toward the "American Century," as defined in Henry Luce's well-known article of 1941.[10]

Putting the above points together, a good case can therefore be made that this "American Century" began in 1900, if the problem is approached from the perspective of industrial organization and culture, and it is indeed within this time frame that research and debates about cultural and industrial "Americanization" have been conducted in the past and are now, at the end of our century, being conducted again.[11] The case is reinforced if we include in our analysis the cultural influence of the big American foundations, which began to leave their national confines during this same period. It is to this particular development that we shall turn in the first instance, and it will become clear only later how American international philanthropy relates to the new ideas of a culture of mass production, mass consumption, and mass politics. Suffice it to say at this point that the connection came about, at least in part, through an increasingly closer link between the foundations' activities and U.S. foreign policy – a link, that was still tenuous before 1914 but grew so strong after World War II

---

9   Rob Kroes, *If You've Seen One, You've Seen the Mall* (Amsterdam, 1996).
10   See Henry Luce, "The American Century," in this volume.
11   Among the more recent contributions see, for example, Richard F. Kuisel, *Seducing the French: The Dilemma of Americanization* (Berkeley, 1993); Richard Pells, *Not Like Us: How Europeans Have Loved, Hated, and Transformed American Culture since World War II* (New York, 1997); Rainer Pommerin, ed., *The American Impact on Postwar Germany* (Oxford, 1994); and David Ellwood, *Hollywood in Europe: Experiences of a Cultural Hegemony* (Amsterdam, 1994).

that it produced a temporary symbiosis. Philanthropy and diplomacy became close partners in the cold culture wars of the post-1945 era.

If in the nineteenth century philanthropy still kept its distance from diplomacy, it was to a considerable extent due to the separation of church and state, which meant that public relief agencies operated, if at all, side by side, but independently of religious charity, at this time the mainstay of private giving for good causes. While most of these philanthropic activities, private and public, were devoted to helping fellow-Americans in need, some aid also began to go overseas. Thus, American agencies got involved in the Irish Famine Relief effort during the Hungry Forties. The late nineteenth century then saw an expansion of benevolence to other continents, either, as previously, in the form of relief after natural catastrophes or in connection with missionary work in Africa and Asia, but it was accompanied by an increasing secularization.[12]

After the turn of the century, disaster relief was stepped up and Washington began to assume a larger role in it. In 1902, for example, President Theodore Roosevelt set aside some $500,000 for earthquake victims in Martinique and St. Vincent. In the same vein, U.S. diplomats overseas took a lead in the coordination of foreign relief work.[13] It was only in 1910, however, that the first of the major foundations with a strong and explicit international orientation was established, that is, the Carnegie Endowment for International Peace. Its creation must be seen in the context of growing worries about rising tensions between the European powers and the escalation of the arms race on land and at sea. The British businessman Norman Angell had just published his best-selling *The Great Illusion*, in which he tried to popularize the notion that the global expansion of liberal capitalism and free trade would make wars between nations superfluous.[14] To Angell,

12 See Merle Curti, *American Philanthropy Abroad* (New Brunswick, 1963), 41ff.; and Bernard Karl, "Philanthropy, Policy Planning, and the Bureaucratization of the Democratic Ideal," *Daedalus* 105 (Fall 1976): 106.
13 See Curti, *Philanthropy*, 219.
14 Norman Angell, *The Great Illusion* (London, 1910).

capitalism was in principle a peaceful and civilian system that made unnecessary the possession of formal empires based on military conquest and occupation, which in turn merely led to great-power rivalries and armed conflict. It was an argument that the economist Joseph Schumpeter later elaborated in his essay "The Sociology of Imperialisms," in which he interpreted nineteenth-century colonialism as an atavism perpetuated by a military caste that adhered to an outdated ethos of struggle and conquest and which would soon be permanently replaced by peaceful industrial and commercial capitalism.[15]

This is not the place to scrutinize the tenability of Angell's and Schumpeter's hypotheses. The crucial point to bear in mind is that their ideas were born from a concern that a catastrophic great war might engulf the nations of the world, cause horrendous, senseless losses, and ring in the end of the golden age of prosperity of the pre-1914 decades. It was such fears that also contributed to the founding of the Carnegie Endowment for International Peace, whose initial assets in U.S. Steel securities totaling $10 million were, ironically, boosted by the beginning of World War I.

As Merle Curti has emphasized, the Carnegie Endowment took a juridical approach to the question of war and peace and tried to promote the latter through research and international exchanges.[16] In line with Andrew Carnegie's broader ideas about friendship and personal relations, the new foundation was to enhance international understanding both at the level of prominent individuals in different countries and between nations. The other big foundation to be created at this time with an explicitly international program was the Rockefeller Foundation, set up in 1913. Its main focus at this time was on international health reform.

---

15 Translation of the German original in Joseph A. Schumpeter, *Imperialism* (Oxford, 1951).
16 See, for example, Katherine D. McCarthy, ed., *Philanthropy and Culture: The International Foundation Perspective* (Philadelphia, 1984); Robert A. Bremner, *American Philanthropy* (Chicago, 1988); Robert A. Fosdick, *The Story of the Rockefeller Foundation* (New York, 1952); and A. J. Zurcher, *The Management of American Foundations: Administration, Policies, and Social Role* (New York, 1972).

Although the United States did not enter World War I until 1917, the fighting and the massive casualties in Europe led to a further expansion of both public and private American benevolence abroad. The U.S. ambassador to France converted the American Hospital in Paris into a "military ambulance." Later government support was also given to Russia and to Jewish emigrants to Palestine. In February 1919, when faced with mass starvation in Bolshevik Russia during the civil war, the U.S. Congress ratified the American Relief Program, which subsequently and under the directorship of Herbert Hoover shipped food and clothes to the starving millions in that part of the world.

As in later years, however, there was also immediate criticism of Hoover's work. Some objected to the American Relief Administration's anti-Communist bias, while others came to believe that it used its charitable activities to influence European politics. There was also a more general feeling, particularly in the business community, that government should retreat from the wartime interventionism in the private sector. It seems that the political side effects of official philanthropic work resharpened earlier antigovernment feelings in the Carnegie Endowment, though it did not weaken the foundation's internationalism. Under the supervision of James T. Shotwell, an international lawyer at Columbia University, the endowment funded a major study, compiled by an international team of scholars, of the economic and social history of World War I that eventually ran to no fewer than 152 volumes.[17] Further studies on the subject were initiated by the endowment's Division of International Law.

Meanwhile, the Rockefeller Foundation had redoubled its support of international health programs, of scientific research, and fellowships for individual scholars. The universities of Oslo and Copenhagen received grants for nuclear research and astrophysics. Other funds went to Heidelberg and more generally for a reconstruction of German science after World War I to the Notgemeinschaft der Wissenschaft. In each of these cases giving was based on the assumption that support for educational institu-

---

17   See Curti, *Philanthropy*, 303ff.

tions would enhance international understanding. Programs such as these continued to be complemented by traditional disaster relief and aid to refugees, in the 1930s particularly to those who had escaped the clutches of Stalin and Hitler. It has been estimated that U.S. private giving to international causes and relief between 1919 and 1939 amounted to almost $1.3 billion, roughly one-third of which went to educational and scientific programs.[18]

Yet the interwar years were also a period when relations between the foundations and the American government underwent a marked change. Looking back on this development in 1984, Waldemar Nielsen, a thoughtful former Ford Foundation official, identified six postures that historically the big foundations had adopted toward Washington:[19] 1) They functioned as monitors and critics of government activities; 2) They developed their programs unconcerned about Washington and the complexities of American politics; 3) They acted as "pilot fish" to official policymaking; 4) Their programs became supplementary to government work; 5) They turned themselves into partners and collaborators of the politicians; and 6) They allowed themselves to be used as private instruments of public policy.

From what has been said so far, it should be clear that the first posture was rarely adopted. More common were postures two, three, and four. But with the approach of World War II, the big foundations increasingly saw themselves as collaborators and partners of Washington on the international stage. For both sides – philanthropy and diplomacy –this was in good part a response to the growing cultural activities of the Soviets and the National Socialists in the 1930s. Next to its more blatant propaganda aimed at the "proletarian masses" of the world, the Komintern had long tried to woo intellectuals, especially in Europe.[20] With

---

18 Ibid., 410.
19 Quoted in McCarthy, ed., *Philanthropy*, 65–81. See also Waldemar A. Nielsen, *The Big Foundations* (New York, 1972), esp. 379ff.; *Inside American Philanthropy* (Norman, 1996); and Edward H. Berman, *The Ideology of Philanthropy: The Influence of the Carnegie, Ford, and Rockefeller Foundations on American Foreign Policy* (Albany, 1983).
20 See, for example, Manès Sperber, *Bis man mir Scherben auf die Augen legt* [Until one puts shards of glass in my eyes] (Munich, 1982); Herbert R. Lottman, *The Left Bank* (San Francisco, 1991); and Tony Judt, *Past Imperfect* (Berkeley, 1992).

the rise of fascism and the political hothouse atmosphere of the Depression 1930s, Moscow had organized among other things a number of successful congresses designed either to rally support in the fight against fascism or to buttress pro-Soviet pacifist sentiments among European and American intellectuals. At the same time, the Hitler government had stepped up its efforts to spread its ideas about what, in its view, propelled international politics among both German-speaking minorities abroad and European intellectuals attracted by fascism.[21]

All these activities were, of course, anathema to the goals of the big American foundations which owed their existence to private enterprise and hence had no sympathy for a Bolshevik world revolution to overthrow capitalism and abolish philanthropy. Nor did they find the chauvinism and racism of the Nazis attractive. But with the rise of these two movements and their propaganda it became clear that larger issues were at stake. Almost inevitably this recognition made the big foundations more inclined to listen to the attitudes and positions of the State Department diplomats in Washington. Conversely, while the American population remained overwhelmingly isolationist, the Roosevelt administration had soon after 1933 begun to realize that the United States could not stand apart in the face of the mounting threat to world peace that European fascism was posing. On the contrary, Secretary of State Cordell Hull had never abandoned his internationalism and wanted the restoration of the Open Door as soon as the United States had overcome the worst of the Great Slump.[22] Given popular isolationism, however, he was forced to move cautiously and indirectly in his foreign policy, relying on commercial pressure and the threat of economic sanctions as he tried to nudge the fascist opponents of internationalism in Europe away from unilateral aggressive action and back into negotiation and cooperation within the community of nations.[23] For the same reason of

21   See, for example, Walter Laqueur, *Fascism* (Harmondsworth, 1979); and John V. Compton, *The Swastika and the Eagle: Hitler, the United States, and the Origins of the Second World War* (Boston, 1967).
22   See, for example, Cordell Hull, *The Memoirs of Cordell Hull* (New York 1948).
23   See, for example, Arnold A. Offner, *American Appeasement: United States Foreign Policy and Germany, 1933–1938* (Cambridge, MA, 1969); Callum A. Macdonald, *The United States,*

hoping to influence international politics indirectly Hull also came to see cultural contacts and internationalist propaganda as a vehicle for promoting understanding and compromise as a defining element of American national interest.

This latter trend reached a first climax in May 1938 when the State Department called a meeting of the major foundations, at which the diplomats unveiled the plan to establish in Washington a special division concerned with international cultural relations.[24] Yet, as the diplomats hastened to add, they had no desire to compete with private philanthropy. All they wanted was to achieve some coordination of American cultural efforts and to encourage increased giving for international causes within the larger framework of U.S. activities abroad. This restraint was partly born from the limitations that the Great Depression and congressional parsimony had imposed on public expenditure. In these circumstances, encouraging private institutions to commit themselves to larger international programs, with the State Department being the coordinating agency, seemed to offer the most promising approach. As this climate of financial austerity and diplomatic caution continued into the early 1940s, it is not surprising that it took until the middle of 1943 for the position of "cultural relations attaché" finally to be created within the organizational structure of the State Department.

In the meantime and even before Japan and Germany went to war with it, the United States had become involved in a massive program of military aid to its western Allies and, after June 1941, to the Soviet Union and, no less important in our context, the propaganda effort had also been strengthened. Funds were now available, and this also applied to the related efforts of intelligence and counterintelligence launched in Washington with the

Britain, and Appeasement, 1936–1939 (London, 1981); and Karl Rohe, ed., *Die Westmächte und das Dritte Reich* [The Western powers and the Third Reich] (Paderborn, 1982).

24   Frank Ninkovich, *The Diplomacy of Ideas: U.S. Foriegn Policy and Cultural Relations, 1938–1950* (Cambridge, 1981), 28. See also C. A. Thomson and W. H. C. Laves, *Cultural Relations and U.S. Foreign Policy* (Bloomington, 1963); Emily Rosenberg, *Spreading the American Dream: American Economic and Cultural Expansion, 1890–1945* (New York, 1982); and C. Frankel, *The Neglected Aspect of Foreign Affairs: American Educational and Cultural Policy Abroad* (Washington, 1965).

creation of the Office of Strategic Services (OSS). As a consequence of these wartime developments and with the end of the war in sight, differences of opinion began to develop over whether the United States should return to the prewar separation of philanthropy and diplomacy or whether cultural programming, public and private, should henceforth be integrated into the national policymaking machinery so that the international work of the foundations came to be closely linked to official activities in this field.[25]

The conflict within the Washington bureaucracy mirrored similar divisions among the foundation staffs and trustees. At the end of the war, there were those who wanted to preserve the traditional altruism and nonpolitical stance of philanthropy, while others, though not rejecting these notions as a matter of principle, wanted to add considerations of national defense to the equation. Fascism and National Socialism, they admitted, had been defeated, but ahead there was still the task of reconstructing the defeated countries not just in a material, but also in a moral-political sense. It was in pursuit of internationalism and of the national interest of the United States, so their argument continued, to foster a democratic political culture and a competitive industrial system, especially in Germany, which, despite carpet bombing and the dismantling of factories, potentially still commanded the most powerful economy in Western Europe.

Moreover, there was the threat of Soviet communism, which now, after the disintegration of the wartime alliance with Stalin, was increasingly viewed as the mirror image of fascist totalitarianism. As Carl J. Friedrich and Zbigniew Brzezinski later put it in their classic analysis of the totalitarianism paradigm that came to sweep the board in Western ideological discourse in the 1950s, Nazism and Stalinism were "basically alike" and represented very modern and brutally destructive versions of twentieth-century dictatorship.[26] Unless the West, led by the United States, so the argu-

25 Richard Harris Smith, *OSS: The Secret History of America's First Central Intelligence Agency* (New York, 1972).
26 Carl J. Friedrich and Zbigniew Brzezinski, *Totalitarian Dictatorship and Autocracy* (New York, 1956). See also Abbott Gleason, *Totalitarianism* (New York, 1995).

ment concluded, marshaled all its resources – military, economic, and sociocultural – in defense of its values of internationalism and popular participation in a free society, the struggle against Stalin, including the cultural one, would be lost.

There is no space further to dwell upon this American view, shared by many foundation people with the war experience behind them, of the "jobs" to be done in post-Nazi Germany and Western Europe. If the "division of the world"[27] into two camps along the Iron Curtain had by now become inevitable, the least that had to be done was to stabilize and reconstruct the Western half and to put up comprehensive defenses against the encroachments, physical and ideological, of the Soviet East. The central point to be remembered is therefore that powerful factions within a particular generation of decision makers and opinion shapers in the United States, in philanthropy and diplomacy, shared this interpretation of the postwar situation and its imperatives. They ultimately defeated those who, at the level of grand strategy, argued for a continuation of the wartime alliance with the Soviet Union and for a harsh treatment of Germany. Or to put it the other way around: the beginning of the Cold War saw the final ascendancy of men, inside and outside the foundations, who wanted to give priority to fighting communism and reconstructing Germany within a larger West European union.

This development provides the background to the realization of the Marshall Plan and of the North Atlantic Treaty Organization (NATO). It was also the orbit of discourse and activity into which American philanthropy was drawn. They became partners of official policymaking in Washington, and this applied to the food aid programs of the Quakers as well as to the funding by the large foundations of education in Europe and international exchanges. As far as this partnership is concerned, nothing probably moved them more irresistably into collaboration with the U.S. government than the expansion in 1948 of the Ford Foundation and the men who appeared at its helm at the height of the Cold War. This foundation had been in existence since 1936, but

---

27 Wilfried Loth, *The Division of the World* (New York, 1988).

its prewar endowment remained small. Following the death of Henry Ford in April 1947, however, its assets had grown by over three million shares of Class A nonvoting common stock in the Ford Motor Company valued at $417 million.[28]

Thanks to a booming stock market these assets had grown to $492 million by 31 December 1950, which included some $6.4 million in real estate "received from the Estates of Henry Ford and Edsel B. Ford or as other miscellaneous assets." After allowing for grants made prior to December 1950, the leadership had almost $69 million at its disposal for philanthropic ventures.

Although a reduction in income from its assets was expected in 1951 "and the foreseeable future" due to the Korean War, this figure was almost half of the total net income that the Ford Foundation had been able to draw upon in the previous fourteen years. Differently put, the foundation had become the largest philanthropic organization in the world. As Henry Ford II remarked, the years 1949–50 were "a turning point in the affairs of the Ford Foundation"[29] and, he might have added, in its relationship with Washington. If up to 1948 its modest income had been spent on "contributions largely focused on the Detroit area and its institutions," it had now become possible to go for large national projects and to appear on the international stage.

The people to undertake this had meanwhile also been found. Soon after his return from Europe, where he had been the administrator for the Marshall Plan (ECA), Paul Hoffman, a former president of the Studebaker Corporation and businessman-politician, was nominated president of the foundation. He took up his position on 1 January 1951. While in Europe, Hoffman had gained many deep insights into the problems and needs of Europe. He had also obtained a first-hand impression of the Cold War confrontation with the Soviet Union and the dangers of the East-West arms race that now, since Stalin also had nuclear weapons, might end in a war even more catastrophic than the last one. From his headquarters in Pasadena, California, he put together a team of

28 Ford Foundation, "Financial Statement," 31 December 1950, 1.
29 Ibid., 2.

aides to to help him with the implementation of his ideas. Among them was his former ECA deputy Milton Katz and, in a consulting role, Richard Bissell Jr., another high-ranking Marshall Plan official now at the Massachusetts Institute of Technology.

But before we examine how the new president's background and that of his advisers affected the foundation's international activities, it is important to remember two fundamental points about postwar American philanthropy. To begin with, the number of foundations and their assets had grown markedly in comparison with the interwar period. There were literally thousands of small foundations in the midst of a few giants. Before World War II the Rockefeller Foundation had occupied first place with assets of $18.4 million, followed by the Carnegie Foundation with assets of $16.4 million. After 1945, the Ford Foundation moved to the top of the league table.[30]

Second, like other charities, big and small, the Ford Foundation spent most of its budget on domestic programs. Thus, between 1951 and 1960 it gave $326.1 million for education initiatives at all levels; $67.5 million was spent on public affairs as well as on urban, regional, and youth development. Some $74.8 million went to economics and business and $294.7 million to hospitals and medical schools. International grants totaled $206.3 million, to which must be added a portion of the $97.9 million that was allocated to Arts, Science, and – as a major item and pet project – the Behavioral Sciences. Although the international grants did not rise as steeply as domestic ones, the increased largesse was made possible by further growth in the endowment, which by the end of 1951 reached $513 million.[31]

Six months after assuming office, Hoffman had pushed up spending on international affairs both at home and abroad to $13.8 million, almost half of what had been earmarked for domestic programs. Among the new international programs was a "Conditions of Peace" project designed to promote disarmament discussions and an agreement with the Soviets and to create a public

30 See Nielsen, *Big Foundations*, 31, 78.
31 Ford Foundation, "A Ten-Year Summary, 1951–1960," June 1960, passim.

climate back home that was favorable to this idea. In this era of strong McCarthyite anti-Communist sentiments in the United States, the project proceeded cautiously, trying to sound out expert opinion as a first step. The person who agreed to supervise the project, which was finally launched in the summer of 1952, was John J. McCloy, who had just returned from a three-year stint as the first U.S. high commissioner in the newly founded Federal Republic of Germany.[32] Joining the management of the Chase Bank in New York and being nominated a trustee of the Ford Foundation, McCloy brought with him Shepard Stone, his former public affairs director in Germany who was to look after the day-to-day operations of the Conditions of Peace initiative.

Hoffman's initial hope had been that the project would aid "wise planning and skillful operation by the U.S. Government" in general."[33] But by the summer of 1952, he had become even more ambitious. A supporter of Dwight D. Eisenhower's candidacy for the upcoming presidential elections, he also had Ike in mind as he began to draft an "address on 'steps to peace.'" From all we know, Eisenhower never heeded Hoffman's advice. McCarthyism caused him to move carefully in domestic politics when it came to relations with the Soviet Union. Once elected, he made John Foster Dulles his secretary of state, and the latter began to talk about rolling the Soviets back out of Eastern Europe and proclaimed the doctrine of massive retaliation. The Conditions of Peace initiative was not abandoned, but it remained relatively small-scale and was ultimately taken over, with continued Ford Foundation funding, by the Council on Foreign Relations.[34] It also yielded some useful information about the state of security studies and international relations as academic subjects at American universities. The basic idea experienced a revival in 1961

---

32 On McCloy see Thomas A. Schwartz, *America's Germany: John J. McCloy and the Federal Republic of Germany* (Cambridge, MA, 1991).

33 Hoffman to Eisenhower, 21 August 1952, Stone Papers, binder "Personal File, 1982." Shepard Stone's papers, comprising a larger number of boxes and filing cabinets are now in the Dartmouth College Library. They are not yet catalogued, however. The references given here are preliminary. I hope to publish a fuller study based on these and other materials in 1999.

34 On the CFR in general see Michael Wala, *The Council on Foreign Relations and American Foreign Policy in the Early Cold War* (Oxford, 1994).

after John F. Kennedy had succeeded Eisenhower as president. Interested in improving U.S.-Soviet relations, Kennedy asked McCloy and Stone to act as consultants in matters of arms reduction, and for a while the two traveled down to Washington to advise the new administration.[35]

Whatever the immediate fate of Hoffman's Conditions of Peace project, two larger issues emerged from it. It may be too far-fetched to say that the origins of détente go back to the early 1950s and came out of the experiences of a number of American officials in Europe who returned to the United States convinced that military tensions were too high along the Iron Curtain and that something had to be done to deescalate the nuclear arms competition. Still, at a time when sections of Congress and larger parts of the country were in a fiercely anti-Communist mood, calling for a vigorous fight against "Soviet aggression,"[36] there were some in the academic and business communities who, knowing about the dangers of war, looked for alternative strategies. The fact that Hoffman and his team were in the forefront of this movement also indicates that they took a view of the relationship between philanthropy and diplomacy that was quite different from those who had been arguing for a renewed distancing after World War II.

This is where, next to Hoffman, both McCloy and Stone enter the stage. Prior to 1945, McCloy had occupied leading positions in the War Department. Because he was much younger, Stone had never reached these heights; but he had been in the intelligence branch of the First Army as it advanced across France and Belgium into Germany in 1944–45. From surrender until the summer of 1946 he had worked as an occupation officer in the city of Marburg, trying to put the locals on the road to democratic government and politics. At the War Department McCloy had been closely involved with big business and trade unions during the war. The common cause against the Axis powers had

---

35 Some material on this mission is contained in the Stone Papers.
36 See, for example, David Caute, *The Great Fear: The Anti-Communist Purge under Truman and Eisenhower* (New York, 1978); and R. G. Powers, *Not without Honor: The History of American Anticommunism* (New York, 1995).

made it seem less important to his generation to uphold a strict separation of private and public. Stone had worked in a similar milieu at the grass-roots level. By ideological background and experience, he was an internationalist and liberal Democrat who after 1945 was open to the new ideas of a "Keynesian" management of economic and political affairs.[37]

This basic disposition became reinforced when McCloy and Stone arrived in Germany in 1949. They found that the U.S. Military Government under Gen. Lucius D. Clay had been deeply involved in the building of German democracy. Thus, Clay's office had financed all kinds of projects, including fledgling West German democratic newspapers. OMGUS put out its own German-language paper, *Die Neue Zeitung*, and kept intellectual journals, such as *Der Monat*, edited by the American Melvin Lasky, afloat.[38] The U.S. High Commission under McCloy and Stone continued most of these programs and forked out millions in subsidies for journalistic and cultural efforts to win over the Germans to the West. But there were also counter-pressures. Prodded by the McCarthyites, Congress began looking for cuts in occupation costs and soon the expenditures of Stone's Public Affairs division came under scrutiny. Having been exposed to these pressures in the High Commission, McCloy and Stone went back to the United States in 1952 convinced that other means had to be found to continue American cultural work in the broadest sense of the word. Could the Ford Foundation perhaps be brought in, if the U.S. government was getting out?

The Conditions of Peace project had been too tentative to achieve this and had involved Stone more in a consultative capacity. It was also clear that the project would sooner or later come to an end. Stone was therefore looking for a more permanent position and, after considering possible alternatives in journalism, the opportunity arose for him to become a full-time staff member of the

---

37   See Volker R. Berghahn, "Shepard Stone and the Ford Foundation," in *The Ford Foundation and Europe*, ed. Giuliana Gemelli (Brussels, 1998), 69–93.
38   For details see Pierre Grémion, *Intelligence de l'anticommunisme* (Paris, 1995), 15ff.; and Peter Coleman, *The Liberal Conspiracy: The Congress for Cultural Freedom and the Struggle for the Mind of Postwar Europe* (New York, 1989). The Rockefeller Foundation temporarily funded the German intellectual journal *Merkur*.

foundation. Quite early on into the Hoffman presidency the question had been raised whether Europe, next to U.S. relations with the Soviet Union, should be given greater attention. One indication of a shift of emphasis was the drastic reduction in 1953 of the foundation's Third World agricultural program. Meanwhile, although Western Europe had been making a satisfactory economic recovery from the ravages of World War II, domestic politics were far from stable. In Italy and France, precariously balanced coalition governments tried to cope with large Communist trade unions and parties. In Bonn, Chancellor Konrad Adenauer faced a vocal Social Democratic opposition, while having to work with a number of volatile right-wing splinter parties. The announcement of West German rearmament had generated heated debates everywhere in Europe about the desirability of creating German soldiers just a few years after the end of Wehrmacht occupation, while Washington was suspected of having pushed the idea in the first place.[39]

To the political suspicions of American economic and military influence in western Europe were added the old criticisms of American popular culture that went back to the interwar period and beyond. With the transition in Western Europe toward Fordist mass production, the idea of mass consumption and mass culture was reappearing from across the Atlantic. In the eyes of many European intellectuals on the right and the left, but also among the educated middle classes, the United States did not really have a culture at all. It seemed more like the end of civilization. What was coming out of America had no sense of quality. It was judged to be vulgar mass culture of the worst kind that could not possibly be compared with the high-cultural achievements of the Europeans.[40] These anti-American perceptions were fostered by the Soviet Union, which tried to play on the cultural superiority complex toward the United States, that Communist intellectuals shared

---

39   See, for example, Robert Wegs, *Europe since 1945: A Concise History* (New York, 1991).
40   See, for example, Kaspar Maase, *Grenzenloses Vergnügen: Der Aufstieg der Massenkultur* (Limitless pleasure: The rise of mass culture) (Frankfurt, 1997).

with fellow-travelers and neutralists in France, Italy, Britain, and West Germany.

Finally, although the administration in Washington held that the official financial support that had been given to a variety of pro-Western, Atlanticist organizations and journals must be continued, the situation in Congress had become more difficult. The Republicans wanted to cut government expenditures and if money was to be given covertly, the State Department and the CIA, the successor organization of the OSS, as the main channels constantly lived in fear of a scandal, should this secret support become public.

It is against this background that Hans Speier, a refugee from Nazism who knew Europe well and was soon to become a prominent figure at the RAND Corporation think tank (in part funded by the Ford Foundation), produced a statement on "administrative arrangements of the Foundation to support Foundation activities in Europe."[41] He began by stressing that granted "the support of organizations making valuable contributions to 'peacefare' in Europe etc., it becomes important for the Foundation to plan for the administrative arrangements which would permit the most effective pursuit of these interests abroad." He then illustrated his point by reference to "a number of organizations in Western Germany and in Berlin engaged in work that appears most valuable in supporting U.S. government policy in the cold war with the Soviet Union." Yet the State Department and the U.S. High Commission in Germany had come to find it "embarrassing to support some of these organizations in view of the constraints which the occupation statute places upon the U.S. authorities to lend open, overt support" to them.

For this reason, the two agencies were cooperating with the CIA "to channelize covert funds in such a way as to support worthy institutions and organizations." Speier added that "for un-

---

41 Speier to Gaither, 5 May 1951, Ford Foundation Archives, New York, Gaither Files, box 1, folder: 1. On the origins and development of the European program more generally see Francis X. Sutton, "The Ford Foundation and Europe: Ambitions and Ambivalances," in Gemelli, ed., *Ford Foundation*, 21–66.

derstandable reasons, the U.S. Government authorities would, in some of these cases, like to see private initiative play the role which overt government effort can no longer assume and which taxes the resources of overt help." Of course, "whenever the Foundation decides to come to the help of the U.S. Government in cases of this kind, it should be sure that its action will not only be useful to the U.S. Government but also unobjectionable in the light of Foundation objectives and reputation." Speier concluded by suggesting that "as the commitments of the Foundation to support projects located abroad increase in size, it will undoubtedly become desirable for the top officers of the Foundation to visit abroad" and to have highly qualified personnel available for this purpose.

The year 1952 saw further steps being taken in the direction of a fully fledged European program, after a number of individual programs had already been launched that harmonized with the foundation's larger aims in these Cold War years. Among them were a grant to the Free University in Berlin, start-up funds for an International Press Institute in Switzerland, support for *Perspectives*, a magazine devoted to European-American relations, and the creation for "continental Europe" of the equivalent of the Committee on Economic Development (CED), a caucus of prominent men drawn from big business, academe, and politics, founded during World War II to study the shaping of the postwar world economy.[42] Milton Katz, the author of these "Notes on Foundation Activities Concerning Free Europe," also listed potential candidates for an "advisory panel of Europeans to assist us," among them Jean Monnet, Sir Oliver Franks, Hugh Gaitskell, Robert Marjolin, Dirk Stikker, Dag Hammarskjold, and "a German, to be selected after discussion with McCloy, Mike Harris, Shep Stone, Schuster, Professor Friedrich of Harvard, and Karl Brandt."

Stone is mentioned here not only because he knew some of these Europeans from his days at the High Commission but also because he had meanwhile been traveling in Europe in connec-

---

42 Katz to Hoffman et al., 20 March 1952, Stone Papers, drawer "Old Chrons.," folder: European Program Paper (first draft).

tion with the Conditions of Peace project. Renewing his earlier personal contacts, he subsequently found himself being approached by prominent politicians who were hoping to visit the United States. Thus, he became involved in the preparations for trips by Konrad Adenauer and Ernst Reuter, the mayor of West Berlin, who had also requested more Ford Foundation funding for the Free University. Stone could not help immediately, but Berlin, where he had studied from 1929 to 1932 and had obtained a doctorate in history, was sufficiently dear to his heart to hold out to his friends there a reconsideration in 1953 of its unsuccessful application, referring as the reason to a change in leadership from Hoffman to Rowan Gaither that had meanwhile taken place.[43]

On the larger question of a more ambitious European program, however, the new president, in the face of much internal opposition, took much longer to make up his mind. When the decision finally came, it was based in part on a report that Stone had written in December 1953.[44] It began by asserting that "we are facing a long period of cold war." In these circumstances, "the United States will need wisdom and maturity to hold the free peoples together," and to this "the Ford Foundation can and should make a larger contribution in the international area." Indeed, the foundation – "as well as other private institutions – has an opportunity to take action which our Government is no longer in a position to initiate or carry through." One of these areas was Europe, where support was needed for the European Community and European-American joint ventures. As to "the cultural-political area," Stone proposed to "give aid to some of the activities now carried on by the Congress for Cultural Freedom in France, Italy, Germany, and the UK (and in Asia)," which included "conferences of politicians [and] intellectuals; meetings of scientists; [and the] publication of magazines."

Stone ended by suggesting the establishment of "a small European office headed by a man of wide experience." This office

43   Stone to Reuter, 12 August 1953, Stone Papers, drawer World War II, folder: Reuter.
44   Stone to Price, 3 December 1953, Stone Papers, drawer "Old Chrons.," folder: Area I (Organization).

was to keep in touch with European thinkers and thought, though it would not deal with specific projects. Pushed by McCloy, the president and the trustees slowly moved to expand the European program. The final step was taken in the summer of 1954 when Stone, together with two others, was appointed "Assistant Director of International Programs" and assigned to look after the European field.[45]

In an attempt to give his new job a clear focus, Stone went on another, longer trip to Europe. Knowing that a number of people at the foundation had opposed the creation of a European program, he began his twelve-page report by affirming the urgent need for such an initiative.[46] On the one hand, there was still the Soviet Union, "trying to advance its objectives with a new technique of reasonableness and good manners." Apart from "more civilized official contacts, Soviet representatives are coming out from behind the Curtain" to participate "in meetings and conferences," there were also "Soviet scientists, writers [and] diplomats . . . putting in friendly appearances and making friendly gestures." Such tactics, Stone continued, posed "new challenges to the free world." On the other hand, "the prestige of the United States" had fallen "to what is perhaps a postwar low," even if the Europeans recognized their "basic dependence" upon America's strength.

Worse, "American diplomatic representation, itself mixed in quality, is generally frustrated over its inability to act because it is confused over policies and trends in Washington." Although the foundation would not and could not replace official policy, it nevertheless had a role to play and, no less important, was "in a strategic position to act." Next to Rockefeller and Carnegie, the Ford Foundation was held in high regard in Europe, "even in the far Left circles of the British Labor Party, in the German SPD, and among many Leftist intellectuals in France." For these reasons, Stone concluded, "the Foundation, in the interests of the United

45 Price to International Programs Staff, 28 June 1954, Stone Papers, drawer "Old Chrons.," folder: Area I (Organization).
46 S. Stone, "Notes on European Trip, June 15–July 28, 1954," 1 August 1954, Stone Papers, drawer "Overseas Trips," folder: European Trip.

States and of carrying out its own program, should begin to make grants in France, England and other European countries, not excluding Yugoslavia." He spoke against developing a "master plan" but wanted to allow things "to emerge over the next two years." Having discussed the names of possible contacts in Europe and the situation in individual countries, he saw special potentialities in supporting Europe's youth movements and the Congress for Cultural Freedom. To him the latter was "the most effective organization in Europe working among political, intellectual, and cultural leaders." He added: "In the past the Congress has concentrated on combatting Communist efforts among the intellectuals of Europe and Asia. It now intends to emphasize the positive aspects of freedom and a free society."

This notable shift from East to West requires some further exploration, as it became a major plank of the foundation's European program for the next decade. In fact, leaders of the Congress for Cultural Freedom were not the only ones who had begun to feel that, in cultural and intellectual terms, the Cold War had been largely won. They were confirmed in this in 1956, when the uprisings in Poland and Hungary revealed the disaffection of many intellectuals with the existing Communist regimes and their Soviet watchdogs. Thereafter, the East European programs of both the Congress for Cultural Freedom and of the Ford Foundation tried to promote exchanges with academics and cultural producers across the iron curtain in the hope of accelerating thaw and reformist ferment in the Soviet Bloc. At the same time, more attention and money was given to cultural and scholarly causes in Western Europe to counter the persistent anti-Americanism there.

Stone knew what that meant. The son of poor Jewish immigrants from Lithuania who had become well-to-do department store owners in Nashua, New Hampshire, he had graduated from Dartmouth College in 1929 and then began his graduate studies in Berlin, where he obtained his doctorate just before the Nazis came to power. He loved the German capital and greatly enjoyed its sophisticated cultural life, going to concerts, plays, and the opera. But he also learned what Germans and the Europeans

more generally thought of American *Unkultur*. When he returned
to Europe after World War II, he experienced firsthand how little
these ideas had changed. On the contrary, they had become reinforced as the advent of mass production and the rising living standards of the 1950s in Europe opened the door to mass consumption and, in its wake, mass culture and entertainment. While
Elvis Presley and Bill Haley, James Dean and Marlon Brando,
Louis Armstrong and Benny Goodman became the heroes of a
younger generation, their properly bourgeois parents and intellectual commentators on contemporary society were appalled by
the "trash" that was coming to Europe from New York and Hollywood.[47]

In the meantime, Stone and likeminded people who had received their education at one of the Ivy League universities and
knew about the scholarly and artistic achievements of the urban
centers of America had also come to recognize how much these
European notions of American culture were based on prejudice
born of ignorance. In their different ways, they now set out to
demonstrate how unjustified European views of American culture were. Sociologists like Daniel Bell published influential books
that cast the democratic and diverse mass culture of the United
States into a positive light.[48] Michael Josselson and Nicholas
Nabokov at the Congress for Cultural Freedom did their bit by
supporting ambitious conferences and the publication of pro-
American intellectual journals like *Encounter, Preuves*, and *Der
Monat*.[49] And this is also where the Ford Foundation's new European program under its director, Stone, comes in. As he put it in
his memo of the summer of 1954: "In developing the Foundation's
overall program for Europe, special emphasis should be given to
the cultural area."[50] It should consider "the allocation of funds
for sending American plays, art, orchestras to Europe." The main

47   See, for example, Uta Poiger, "Rebels with a Cause: American Popular Culture, the 1956
Youth Riots, and New Conceptions of Masculinity in East and West Germany," in Pommerin,
ed., *American Impact*, 93–124; and David Strauss, *Menace in the West: The Rise of French
Antiamericanism in Modern Times* (Westport, CT, 1978).
48   See esp. Daniel Bell, *The End of Ideology* (Glencoe, 1960).
49   See Grémion, *L'Intelligence*, 53ff.; and Coleman, *Conspiracy*, 59ff.
50   As footnote 46 above.

problem, he believed, was "not to convince Europeans that we have a culture." In fact, the Europeans were "becoming bored with our insistence that we are a cultured people." Informed Europeans knew this all along. But "they want to see [it] for themselves. They read our books and periodicals, and they now want to see our art, our theatre, and to hear our music." One U.S. ambassador had urged him on his recent European trip to send *Porgy and Bess* and his colleague in Paris wanted the Ford Foundation to "support the American Art Festival which will take place in Paris next spring in the theatres, museums and halls being put at the disposal of the American people by the Government of France and by the City of Paris." Stone ended by pointing out that "cultural efforts of this type can have important effects politically."

When the Ford Foundation's European program therefore finally got under way in 1955–56, Stone initially still followed a dual-track policy of reaching out to Eastern Europe, on the one hand, and of furthering "Atlantic community relations,"[51] on the other. The former policy received a big boost in the fall of 1956 in the wake of the attempted revolutions in Poland and Hungary and the Soviet repression that followed. The foundation became deeply involved in aiding students, scholars, and intellectuals who fled to the West. Stone spent several months in Vienna trying to offer help wherever it was most needed, often in the form of scholarships to enable refugee students to complete their studies in Europe or the United States.[52]

Once the immediate refugee problem was over, he could begin to think about implementing the program that he had crafted in the years before the crisis in Poland and Hungary. The only major remnant left from the 1956 upheavals in East Central Europe was the Philharmonia Hungarica. This well-known orchestra, most of whose members had fled to the West, was subsidized by the foundation, and Stone also used his contacts in Western Eu-

---

51 W. A. Nielsen memorandum of conversation with president Gaither, (summer 1954), Stone Papers, drawer "Old Chrons," folder: European Program.
52 See the materials in Stone Papers, drawer "Countries," folder: SS[tone] – Europe, January–March 1957.

rope to secure the Philharmonia's survival. Because the orchestra presented such a splendid opportunity to illustrate how the West differed from the Soviet Bloc, the State Department, though unwilling to commit itself in public, also took an interest in the matter.

Thus, on 5 August 1958, no less a person than Christian Herter, at the time acting secretary of state, wrote to the president of the Ford Foundation praising the foundation for having been "instrumental in helping to establish in Europe the Philharmonica [sic] Hungarica."[53] However, he had been given to understand "that the Foundation has reached the conclusion that a further grant in support of the orchestra would not be consistent with Foundation policy." His letter was therefore to advise the president "of the importance the Department attaches to the orchestra, and our strong desire that it continue as a going concern" even though it was "not considered to be desirable that this be accomplished by official U.S. Government financial support." This is why Herter requested that the foundation "have another look at the matter."

It is possible that this high-level contact between philanthropy and diplomacy was touched off by exchanges of views that had meanwhile become well established between Stone and State Department officials. Although detailed records have yet to be found, the director of the International Affairs department, the position to which Stone had finally been nominated, traveled to Washington at fairly regular intervals to inform and to be informed. He saw high-ranking diplomats and dropped in on his friends at the CIA. Up to the late 1950s, the topics they discussed were frequently still concerned with Eastern Europe, where the big foundations concentrated on funding academic exchanges and research contacts. The largest of these programs was established with Poland and although the Polish authorities repeatedly put up bureaucratic obstacles and tried to interfere with the selection of scholars and the granting of visas, it was probably the most successful. Stone faced a more difficult task in Yugoslavia, surpassed only by the protracted negotiations with the Russians to establish

53   Herter to Heald, 5 August 1958, Ford Foundation Archives, New York, Heald Files, box 12, folder: 150.

closer academic relations. In the end the foundation's persistence paid off, and in December 1959 the Board of Trustees approved $300,000 "to support exchanges and other activities involving the Soviet Union, the United States, and Europe."[54] No less important, in the fall of 1958 the foundation began to look toward the other Communist Great Power, China, again after consultations with CIA director Allen Dulles and the State Department.[55]

These consultations revealed two further aspects of the proliferation of Ford's international activities. First, its operations now expanded increasingly into Third World regions. Second, the growing interest in contacts with the Communist world also opened up opportunities to strengthen Stone's West European program. A major element in this effort was to promote research on Eastern Europe at West European universities. A good example of this kind of foundation support is presented by St. Antony's College, Oxford. Founded in May 1950 and endowed by the French millionaire Antonin Besse of Aden and headed by William Deakin, the college was conceived as an international center for graduate training and research in history and the social sciences. As warden of one of the poorest colleges in Oxford, Deakin, a highly decorated liaison officer between Britain and Tito during World War II and author of an acclaimed study of *The Brutal Friendship* between Hitler and Mussolini, was constantly submitting projects to the big American and British foundations.[56]

Since the college had among its fellows and associates a number of well-known experts on the East,[57] it seemed logical for Stone to give money for the creation of an East European center there. And St. Antony's also looked like a good match when Stone, with the CIA's encouragement, had begun to work on a Ford Foundation program regarding the Chinese People's Republic. The fellows working in the Far Eastern field may not have been quite

---

54 Submission by International Affairs to Executive Committee meeting, 12 December 1959, Stone Papers, box 9, Loose Materials.
55 Stone to Central File, 24 October 1958, Stone Papers, box 2, file 7.
56 London 1962. A history of St. Antony's College is being written by Anthony J. and Christine Nicholls.
57 Among the people mentioned were David Footman, Max Hayward, Carew Hunt, George Katkov, Wolfgang Leonnard, Isaiah Berlin, and Max Beloff.

as well known as their counterparts at the East European Studies Center. But Deakin, like Stone, knew Dulles from their wartime intelligence work, and this no doubt also helped in the establishment of another center at the college. As Stone reported on 24 October 1958, "Mr. Dulles said that he was delighted to hear that the Foundation was considering the possibility of support for such programs. He indicated that there had been an improvement in the information recently about scientific and educational developments in Russia but that we were lagging in respect of Communist China. Mr. Dulles spoke with admiration about Mr. Deakin and expressed the hope that the Foundation would support this type of research and study."[58] Robert Murphy, the deputy under secretary at the State Department, similarly gave his "warm support for the project outlined" to him.

While St. Antony's College illustrates the cooperation between philanthropy and diplomacy in various Ford Foundation efforts in Europe to facilitate dialogue in the humanities and social sciences, the sciences were also seen as a potential bridge. At a time when Secretary of State John Foster Dulles and Pentagon strategists were talking about "massive retaliation" and all-out war against the Soviet Union as a viable doctrine of deterrence, other people in Washington and at the Ford Foundation, some of whom had been involved in the Hoffman-McCloy Conditions of Peace project, wondered whether it would be better to maintain contact between nuclear scientists in East and West who knew best of all what would be involved if this dangerous doctrine failed and World War III became inevitable. It was apparently for these reasons that the famous Danish physicist Niels Bohr, who had many academic acquaintances in the Soviet Union, was brought into the foundation's network. Bohr was, of course, also hoping to obtain a grant or two for his institute, and when he came to the United States in February 1958, Stone accompanied him to Washington, where they "had some fine talks with Allen Dulles and his boys, Senator Clinton Anderson, Senator Flanders, and other dignitaries."[59] According to Stone, Bohr believed "in open exchange

58 Stone to Central File, October 24, 1958, Stone Papers, box 2, file 7.
59 Stone to Nielsen, 13 February 1958, Stone Papers, box 2, file 2.

among the scientists of the world as the best security and best opportunity for the free world." The hope that such East-West contacts would contribute to the easing of tensions and build confidence between the two superpowers was apparently also behind the Ford Foundation's temporary support for the *Bulletin of Atomic Scientists*, in whose pages concerned scientists aired their views about the dangers of a nuclear holocaust.

Yet the foundation funded many other European projects whose connection with the Cold War was more tenuous. Indeed, it is probably better to see them in the context not of the ideological and intellectual struggle against communism, but of European cultural anti-Americanism. In other words, there was yet another cold culture war being conducted through the foundation's European program, and we have already had occasion to demonstrate that it was equally on the mind of men like Stone. It is against this background that another set of projects has to be seen designed either to help establish or strengthen certain European universities and research institutes or to promote international studies back in the United States. Apart from Britain (where old affinities and the nostalgia of the wartime "special relationship" were also factors) and Berlin (with which Stone felt a strong bond dating back to his days as a student there), France became a major beneficiary of American philanthropy.

One of the most important in a variety of ventures was a $1 million grant in 1959 to build up the Maison des sciences de l'homme in Paris.[60] Spearheaded by Gaston Berger, the director of the Higher Education department in the French Ministry of Education, the idea of a research and graduate training center for social scientists attracted the support of prominent academics, including the rector of the Sorbonne and the historian Fernand Braudel as head of the Sixth Section of the École Pratique des Hautes Études.[61] Similarly, the Ford Foundation helped Raymond Aron to launch his Institute of European Sociology in Paris.

60　Submission by International Affairs to Board of Trustees meeting, 11 December 1959, Stone Papers, box 9, Loose Materials.
61　On Braudel's American connections see Giuliana Gemelli, *Fernand Braudel* (Paris, 1995).

American philanthropic initiatives in individual European countries were complemented by support for the building of transnational institutions at the level of the European Community and for the fostering of trans-Atlantic ties. Jean Monnet, who knew America well and had worked hard, especially in connection with the construction of the European Coal and Steel Community (ECSC), to transcend national boundaries in Western Europe, and was now the elder statesman of European unification, was at the center of these initiatives.[62] While it would have been inappropriate for the Ford Foundation to try to influence the process of economic integration directly, its trustees agreed to provide collateral support, which would benefit both the Europeans and the Americans. The international conferences of the Bilderberg Group under the chairmanship of Prince Bernhard of the Netherlands represented one such enterprise in which both the Ford Foundation and the Carnegie Endowment invested.[63] The idea of creating an Atlantic Institute was perhaps the most emblematic of these efforts at the level of political research and discussion.

While the organization of this particular institute encountered many snags and never quite got off the ground, American philanthropic support for the reform and modernization of European industrial management practices yielded much more impressive results.[64] After the war it was clear that West European industry not only desperately needed to modernize its clapped-out machinery. Mass production of goods for a growing market in consumer durables required Fordist efficiency at the level of production as well as a change in the methods of leadership and administration in enterprises. American firms had turned their attention to management training before World War II and a number of universi-

---

62 See, for example, Jean Monnet, *Memoirs* (London, 1978); and John Gillingham, *Coal, Steel, and the Rebirth of Europe, 1945–1955: The Germans and French from Ruhr Conflict to Economic Community* (New York, 1991).
63 Submission by International Affairs to Executive Committee meeting, 24 September 1959, Stone Papers, box 9, Loose Materials.
64 See, for example, Giuliana Gemelli, "From Imitation to Competitive Cooperation: The Ford Foundation and Management Education in Western and Eastern Europe," in Gemelli, ed., *Ford Foundation*, 167–304.

ties had created business schools to educate people for white-collar supervisory careers in commerce and industry. The case-based curriculum of the Harvard Business School was deemed by many European businessmen to offer a suitable model, and by the early 1950s plans were being laid as far away as Greece and Turkey to found similar institutions. The Ford Foundation invested in American-style management education all over Western Europe, and by 1960 the European Association of Management Training, with Pierre Tabatoni as its president, acted as a roof organization for these schools, most of which, like INSEAD at Fontainebleau in France, were free-standing centers without attachment to a particular university.

The success of these business schools in the modernization of European management practices is reflected in a report which Waldemar Nielsen, a staff member in the Ford Foundation's International Affairs program, wrote in July 1959 after attending a conference of writers at Lourmarin, organized by the Congress for Cultural Freedom.[65] While touring Europe, the "principal impression this visit" had left on him was "the sense of self-confidence on the part of businessmen and government officials in all the countries" he had seen: "They have finally, thank God, given up the habit of whining and complaining and acting as if all of their troubles were somehow someone else's fault!" Unfortunately, so Nielsen continued, European intellectuals were learning rather more slowly. While the economic and political elites were abandoning their negative attitude toward America, he was "rather disheartened to say that the intellectuals . . . seem to be lagging behind in this healthy movement going on in other groups." This and indeed "the sickness of European intellectuals of the kind represented at this meeting, particularly [of] the French," had been sadly in evidence:

Perhaps thirty or forty percent of the people at the Lourmarin meeting were onetime Communists or fellow-travelers. And it was quite clear to

65 Nielsen to Stone, 19 July 1959, Stone Papers, drawer "Countries," folder: W. A. Nielsen.

me that even though all of them had now broken in a formal sense with the party and with much of Marxism, they have still not resolved in their own soul the intellectual and moral conflict. They simply did not talk about Russia and about Communism. On the other hand, they spent a lot of time worrying and stewing and griping about the United States, about American domination, about the inferiority of American values and so on.

European intellectual and cultural anti-Americanism of the kind that we have already discerned on a number of occasions above was, next to fighting the Cold War against the Soviet Bloc, the second major reason why American international philanthropy and diplomacy had come to join hands after 1945. Combating the Europeans' superiority complex toward American culture resulted in a symbiotic effort of the big private foundations and official Washington policy. While the foundations supported academic and cultural programs and exchanges that were designed to convince European intellectuals and the educated middle classes that "trashy" American mass culture was not all that America represented, that the country had a much richer cultural life, that it sustained great institutions of learning and produced a literature, music, and visual art that was equal to the best of European high culture, official Washington, though at reduced volume, continued its work in this field: the U.S. Information Agency distributed "facts and figures" that cast the superpower across the Atlantic in a positive light. Meanwhile the America Houses did their bit with film screenings and lectures. In Germany, for example, it was the jazz expert Joachim Ernst Behrendt who spoke in these places before audiences of young, usually middle-class Germans and explained to them that this American genre was not a "primitive *Negermusik*," as racist anti-Americanism maintained, but a highly sophisticated and deeply satisfying form of music.[66]
These ventures were ideologically intertwined, but organizationally separate; yet there was one major forum where the fund-

---

66   Joachim E. Behrendt, *Das Jazzbuch* [The book of jazz] (Frankfurt, 1953); Poiger, "Rebels"; and L. Bergreen, *Louis Armstrong* (New York, 1997).

ing of the big foundations and of the U.S. government merged: the Congress for Cultural Freedom, which, for its network of contacts of ultimately global dimensions, for its conferences, and for its many intellectual journals, relied on the Ford Foundation's public support and on the covert monies of the CIA. The congress was therefore the epitome of the cooperative relationship between philanthropy and diplomacy that had developed after 1945, but it was also its terminus. Significantly, the congress collapsed when, after years of rumors, its secret link with the CIA was finally unmasked. We have several good studies on the history of the congress and its collapse in scandal, and there is no space to repeat it here.[67]

To be sure, this scandal might never have happened had it not been for a major shift in American public attitudes toward Washington that set in during the early 1960s. It was a younger generation in particular that began to take a different and highly critical view of U.S. foreign policy during the Cold War period. "Revisionist" historians of the Williams School were among the more influential protagonists of this view, and the Vietnam War then led to a widespread disillusionment, especially in the colleges and universities, with American "imperialism" in the rest of the world.[68] Perhaps inevitably, the big foundations also came on the firing line.[69]

It must be said that as far as the link between private philanthropy and official diplomacy is concerned, the foundations, but also official Washington under the new Kennedy administration, had by the early 1960s become uneasy about the hybrid that the funding of the Congress for Cultural Freedom had evolved into. Knowing about the dangers to his entire enterprise, Josselson also pushed for a separation, and there were plans for the Ford Foundation together with other charities, including the newly emerging European philanthropic organizations, to take financial re-

---

67   Grémion, *L'Intelligence*, 429ff.; and Coleman, *Conspiracy*, 220ff.
68   See, for example, William A. Williams, *The Tragedy of American Diplomacy* (New York, 1959); and Gabriel and Joyce Kolko, *The Limits of Power: The World and United States Foreign Policy, 1945–1954* (New York 1972).
69   See, for example, R. F. Armore, ed., *Philanthropy and Cultural Imperialism* (Bloomington, 1982), with a number of very critical contributions on the big American foundations.

sponsibility for all of its worldwide operations.[70]   It is possible
that he was close to a deal in 1965–66 when the CIA story broke
resulting in the dissolution of the congress. Its successor, the International Association for Cultural Freedom, lived and increasingly lingered in the shadow of its influential predecessor; but in
one respect it achieved what Josselson had failed to engineer: it
was exclusively funded by the Ford Foundation. Its new president, Shepard Stone, soon realized that the association had no
future and that other foundations that he approached in Europe
were not prepared to contribute more than a temporary token.[71]

   Whatever his and Josselson's inklings in the early 1960s of the
rapids that lay ahead of American philanthropy and diplomacy,
they never quite understood the criticism of the younger generation that had not shared their experience of fascism, Stalinism,
and war. It was that experience and the close cooperation that
developed in the United States between all agencies, private and
public, involved in winning the war against the totalitarian Hitler
that made it seem natural for this cooperation to continue at a
time when the enemy was the – in their view – equally totalitarian "Uncle Joe." The rebellion against American foreign policy
and "imperialist cultural propaganda" abroad appeared to them
to be a reincarnation of the "romantic and irrational totalitarianism" that they had witnessed as students in Germany during the
early 1930s. But the clock could not be put back, and when the
upheavals in American society, which were of course also related
to major shifts on the domestic front, slowly came to an end in
the 1970s, the symbiotic relationship between the big foundations and U.S. foreign policy that the Cold War had fostered also
reverted to one of the looser postures on the above-mentioned
Nielsen scale.[72]

70   See, for example, Stone to McCloy, 8 June 1962, Stone Papers, drawer "Personal Files,"
folder: Organization—Undisclosed Funds": "During the past year there has been a discussion within the Foundation of the desirability and propriety of supporting institutions which
also receive funds from covert governmental sources. . . . This memorandum recommends
that in carefully selected situations which are considered to be of unusual significance, the
Foundation may make grants to institutions which are prepared to give up all financing from
and all connections with covert agencies."
71   Grémion, *L'Intelligence*, 460ff.
72   Nielsen, *Big Foundations*, 379ff., discusses "the endless, ambiguous interface," but his

What, in light of this conclusion, are we to make of the connection of philanthropy and diplomacy to the "American Century"? We began this article by arguing that that century may indeed be said to have begun in 1900, if examined from the perspective of American big business and culture making their first impact on the international stage. The activities of the Ford Foundation in the 1950s and 1960s, as we have interpreted them, were not just part of the Cold War battles against Soviet communism but also of a larger attempt by the U.S. elites to convince their West European counterparts that their impressions of America as lacking a high culture were false. Yet there was still another side to this equation, even if it was less visibly put into the foundation's European program: Among the American intellectuals who wrote about the dreaded American mass culture and who were sent on lecture tours to Western Europe were also some who, in their writing and oral contributions to the notion of an Atlantic cultural community, cast that mass culture into a positive light.

One of the most influential and articulate proponents of this position was Daniel Bell, whose volume of essays on *The End of Ideology* is, on closer inspection, not merely concerned with the notion that the Western industrialized nations had in principle solved all their major social problems and that the task of the future was merely slow improvement and reformist management of economy and society.[73] At the point of its publication and in later years too much emphasis has been laid on these technocratic aspects of this book written by a sociologist at a time when his discipline reigned supreme among the humanities. What has been overlooked is that the key essays in Bell's volume mount a spirited defense of a vibrant and rich popular American culture that was not at all conformist, cheap, and gray, as the cultural pessi-

book was published in 1972 and hence does not include later developments. It also seems that the other big philanthropic organizations never went as far as the Ford Foundation. On the other hand, there were a few smaller foundations that directly acted as conduits for covert government funds. The opening of the CIA files would presumably finally enable us to examine that end of the story. See also Richard M. Bissell, Jr., *Reflections of a Cold Warrior: From Yalta to the Bay of Pigs* (New Haven, 1996) and Cord Meyer, *Facing Reality: From World Federalism to the CIA* (New York, 1980).

73   See the discussion of Bell's work in this particular context in Berghahn, "Shepard Stone."

mists had been arguing. Above all, the spreading of this culture was not the end of Western civilization, but its democratization and evolution toward diversity.

If we take Bell's argument about American culture and follow its subsequent proliferation, a powerful argument can be mounted that the "American Century," which, viewed in industrial and cultural terms, began in 1900, is still unfolding. Stone would no doubt feel confirmed in his efforts if he witnessed how the American system of higher education has become a model – and in some European countries even *the* model – of excellence in research and training that creates opportunities both for upward social mobility in a democratic society and for the constant generation of intellectual and technical elites. After all, he himself was a typical product and beneficiary of this system, and this is what he and those involved in the networks within which he operated were hoping to proliferate.

But there is also the continued impact of American "mass" culture in the "American Century." While there is still some European criticism of this culture, often using well-worn arguments going back as far as the 1920s, the fear of it has largely disappeared. On the contrary, intellectuals and the educated bourgeoisie of Europe have long joined in its enjoyment. As the German anthropologist Kaspar Maase put it in a recent book: "Among the upper echelons of business, politics, science, and technology, among the academically trained professions, the right to enjoy the bliss of common culture is claimed extensively. Popular art and entertainment have become a culture of all."[74] During the Cold War neither the big foundations nor U.S. cultural foreign policy spent their money exactly to promote this development, but in countering European horror tales about popular culture and by appealing to a common Atlantic "community of spirit," they also helped the more general acceptance of Daniel Bell's propositions about the promises of American popular and commercial culture that is now no longer just affecting Europe but is

---

74 Maase, *Vergnügen*, 274f. See also Bernard Rosenberg and David M. White, *Mass Culture Revisited* (New York, 1972).

sweeping across the globe. And as before in Europe, it is creating positive as well as negative responses from the indigenous populations and cultural producers.[75]

75 See, for example Benjamin Barber, *Jihad vs. McWorld* (New York, 1995).

13

A Century of NGOs

AKIRA IRIYE

What is the connection between the twentieth century and the American Century? How is the history of the present century linked to the history of the United States? To establish the relationship between world history and U.S. history, it is, of course, crucial to identify themes in both world history and U.S. history in the twentieth century and explore whether there may have been a connection between the two. For instance, it is possible to point to such themes as total war, revolution, and totalitarianism as among the major features of twentieth-century history and to discuss what they have to do with developments in U.S. history. Michael Sherry's *In the Shadow of War* (1996), to take an example, suggests that there was a congruence between the theme of total war globally and the construction of a war-oriented American society.[1] Or, following Walter LaFeber and other historians, we may link American liberal capitalism to worldwide revolutionary movements in a dialectical relationship; in such a construction, the American Century would emerge as something of an antithesis to a major theme of twentieth-century world history.[2] A third and widely accepted perspective has been to stress the tremendous growth in the world's agricultural and industrial output and in cross-national trade and investment, and to see

1   Michael S. Sherry, *In the Shadow of War: The United States since the 1930s* (New Haven, 1995).
2   Walter LaFeber, *America, Russia, and the Cold War 1945–1990*, 6th ed. (New York, 1991); Robert Packenham, *Liberal America and the Third World: Political Development Ideas in Foreign Aid and Social Science* (Princeton, 1973).

these developments as linked to the growth of the U.S. economy.[3] Among the most popular interpretations of the linkages between world and U.S. history has been the postulation of an Americanized global culture in which American technology, food, fashions, popular entertainment (music, movies, television programs), and language have transformed the ways of life and consciousness of people throughout the globe. Reinhold Wagnleitner's *Coca-Colonization and the Cold War* (1996) is but one of many examples of this perspective.[4]

In this essay, I shall focus on another theme, the growth of non-governmental organizations (NGO), and argue that this phenomenon provides a plausible framework for linking one of the most impressive developments of twentieth-century world history to the history of the United States. By non-governmental organizations are usually meant voluntary and open (non-secret) associations of individuals outside of the formal state apparatus (central and local governments, police and armed forces, legislative and judicial bodies, and so on) that are neither for profit nor engage in political activities as their primary objective. Such a definition of an NGO would thus exclude a secret fraternity, a business enterprise, or a political party. NGOs, therefore, are generally interchangeable with, and sometime called, non-profit organizations (NPO) or private voluntary organizations (PVO). Whether religious organizations (churches, synagogues, cemeteries, and the like) are to be considered NGOs is a question about which there seems to exist no consensus among specialists, but in this essay I shall include religiously oriented organizations only where their primary purposes are not devotional or sectarian: for instance, the American Friends Service Committee and the Church World Service, both established by religious bodies for voluntary, humanitarian work.

---

3 Paul Kennedy, *The Rise and Fall of the Great Powers: Economic Change and Military Conflict from 1500 to 2000* (New York, 1987).
4 Reinhold Wagnleitner, *Coca-Colonization and the Cold War: The Cultural Mission of the United States in Austria after the Second World War* (Chapel Hill, 1994); Jacques Portes, *De la scène à l'écran: Naissance de la culture de masse aux États-Unis* [From the stage to the screen: Birth of mass culture in the United States] (Paris, 1997).

Alexis de Tocqueville noted in the 1830s that one of the principal characteristics of American democracy was the existence of "private associations" (*associations civiles*). As he wrote in *Democracy in America*, "Americans of all ages, all situations in life, and all types of disposition are forever forming associations." At the head of any new undertaking, "where in France you would find the government or in England some territorial magnate, in the United States you are sure to find an association." As is well known, Tocqueville saw voluntary associations as the key to the functioning of the American nation, as evidence that Americans were not so individualistic that they became self-centered and atomistic but rather were driven by a sentiment of reciprocity through which they helped one another. Even more fundamentally, private associations were at the heart of democratic civilization. "If the inhabitants of democratic countries had neither the right nor the taste for unity for political objects, their independence would run great risks, but they could keep both their wealth and their knowledge for a long time. But if they did not learn some habits of acting together in the affairs of daily life, civilization itself would be in peril."[5] Half a century later, James Bryce also noted the critical role associations played in American society. "In nothing," he wrote in *The American Commonwealth*, "does the executive talent of the [American] people better shine than in the promptitude wherewith the idea of an organization for a common object is taken up, in the instinctive discipline that makes every one who joins in starting it fall into his place, in the practical, business-like turns which the discussions forthwith take." Associations played an important role in the development of public opinion, "for they rouse attention, excite discussion, formulate principles, submit plans, embolden or stimulate their members, produce that impression of a spreading movement which goes so far towards success with a sympathetic and sensitive people."[6]

By the end of the nineteenth century, then, the United States had already become "a nation of joiners," as Arthur M. Schlesinger

5   Alexis de Tocqueville, *Democracy in America*, ed. J. P. Mayer (New York, 1969), 513–14.
6   James Bryce, *The American Commonwealth* (New York, 1895), 2:278.

was to write in 1944.[7] As the historian noted, however, many of the organizations the Americans joined in the nineteenth century were secret societies, political movements, and business associations – organizations outside our definition of NGOs. In the twentieth century, in contrast, there have been created numerous – a rough estimate today would be 1.1 million – private, voluntary, non-profit, and non-political organizations ranging from large philanthropic foundations to local Boys Clubs, from research institutions to civil rights organizations, from museum societies to old people's associations. What has been of particular significance has been the growth of those NGOs that are internationally oriented, or International NGOs (INGOs). These are organizations that are engaged in pursuing cross-national agendas, such as providing humanitarian relief to victims of earthquakes, famine, or war in some part of the world, establishing schools and orphanages abroad, engaging in educational and cultural exchanges with other countries, cooperating across national boundaries to cope with pollution and other instances of environmental degradation, or safeguarding the rights of women, children, and persecuted minorities. Sometimes INGOs originate in the United States, but quite often their world headquarters are somewhere else (such as the International Red Cross with its main offices in Geneva) though there are national branches in all parts of the globe. Counting such national branches as well as headquarters, the total number of INGOs in the United States has increased steadily throughout the twentieth century, reaching six hundred in 1960 and over fifteen hundred by the mid-1980s. The current number may well be double that.[8]

The growth of NGOs has been an important aspect of the history of the United States in the twentieth century. Quite apart from the nation's emergence as the military superpower or the economic hegemon, it has continued to exemplify what

7 Arthur M. Schlesinger, "Biography of a Nation of Joiners," *American Historical Review* 49 (October 1944): 1–25.
8 Statistical information in this essay is mostly derived from Union of International Associations, ed., *International Organizations: Abbreviations and Addresses, 1984–85* (Munich, [1985]).

de Tocqueville and Bryce noticed in the nineteenth century; it has been characterized by the networks of private associations linking different parts of the country in myriad ways.

Twentieth-century world history has also been characterized by the growth of NGOs. This is where U.S. history and world history intersect or converge, thus providing one supreme example of why this century may be called an American Century. The United States has led the way, and the rest of the world has followed, in the development of non-governmental, non-profit organizations. In the sphere of international affairs, the particularly impressive development has been the growth of INGOs, private, voluntary organizations that constitute part of the ever-expanding networks of cross-national associations. "The American Century" in this sense means the fantastic growth of such networks. It does not mean U.S. military or economic dominance; nor is it synonymous with cultural Americanization. Rather, this century has been an "American" century because a uniquely American experience in social organization has spread worldwide. In 1904, Frederick Jackson Turner noted, "the special contributions which students of American history are capable of making to the study of history in general are determined . . . by the peculiar importance of American history for understanding the processes of social development."[9] The process of social development in the United States in the nineteenth century had taken the form, among other things, of the organization of private associations. This was one of the nation's contributions to modern history. And in the twentieth century, U.S. history and world history have been joined together through the phenomenal growth of interlocking INGOs.

Kenneth Boulding has written, "The rise of international non-governmental organizations has been spectacular. . . . This is perhaps one of the most spectacular developments of the twentieth century, although it has happened so quickly that it is seldom noticed."[10] This essay is an attempt to "notice" this phenom-

---

9 Frederick Jackson Turner, "Problems in American History," in *Congress of Arts and Science: Universal Exposition, St. Louis, 1904*, ed. Howard J. Rogers (Boston, 1906), 2:184.
10 Kenneth Boulding, *Three Faces of Power* (Newbury Park, CA, 1989), 244.

enon. It must be pointed out, however, that political scientists and international relations scholars have long – at least since the 1970s – noticed the growth of INGOs and incorporated the development into their analyses of international affairs. Writers such as Paul Diehl, Johan Galtung, Harold Jacobson, and Robert Keohane have published important monographs.[11] But historians have been extremely slow to read this literature, let alone make use of it in their writings on twentieth-century history. Such standard histories of the century as Eric Hobsbawm, *The Age of Extremes* (1993), John Grenville, *A History of the World in the Twentieth Century* (1994), or William Keylor, *The Twentieth-Century World* (1995) are singularly lacking in any reference to NGOs, domestic or international.[12] But to ignore them is to misread the history of the twentieth-century world.

At the 1904 World Congress of Arts and Science held in conjunction with the St. Louis exposition commemorating the Louisiana Purchase, Woodrow Wilson remarked that "the deepest things are often those which never spring to light in events, and . . . the breeding ground of events themselves lies where the historian of the state seldom extends his explorations."[13] While state-focused historians of international relations have written volumes on "events" such as the wars (hot and cold) of the present century, they have seldom explored things that "never spring to light." Non-governmental organizations are one example. The remainder of this essay will explore how the history of the twentieth century looks if examined in the framework of NGOs,

11   Paul Diehl, ed., *The Politics of Global Governance* (Boulder, 1997); Johan Galtung, *The True World: A Transnational Perspective* (New York, 1980); Harold Jacobson, *The Networks of Interdependence* (New York, 1984); Robert D. Keohane and Josephe S. Nye, *Power and Interdependence*, 2d ed. (New York, 1989). To this list may be added some recent works in the new field of sociology of globalization, including Roland Robertson, *Globalization: Social Theory and Global Culture* (London, 1992); Mike Featherstone, *Undoing Culture: Globalization, Postmodernism, and Identity* (London, 1995); and Arjun Appadurai, *Modernity at Large: Cultural Dimensions of Globalization* (Minneapolis, 1998).

12   Eric Hobsbawm, *The Age of Extremes: A History of the World, 1914–1991* (New York, 1994); J. A. S. Grenville, *A History of the World in the Twentieth Century* (Cambridge, MA, 1994); William R. Keylor, *The Twentieth Century World: An International History*, 2d ed. (New York, 1992).

13   Woodrow Wilson, "The Variety and Unity of History," in Rogers, ed., *Congress of Arts and Science*, 6.

not of states, and how, in such a framework, the American Century may be better understood.

Although there was a small number of INGOs before the First World War – ranging from the well-developed International Red Cross to less formally structured associations of academics in various fields – it was not until after the war that many more of them sprang up. Quite clearly, this was in reaction against the traditional system of interstate relations that was considered to have brought about the unprecedented tragedy. Instead of sovereign states playing the game of power politics, men and women after 1919 were determined to develop new institutions on the basis of which a more durable and just international order would be constructed. It is true that among these institutions, intergovernmental organizations (IGO), of which the League of Nations was the most spectacular example, attracted the greatest attention. The growth of INGOs was no less impressive, however. According to one count, their number grew from 135 in 1910 to 375 by 1930.[14] The new INGOs included the International Research Council and various other organizations of scholars to facilitate their interchange, the national committees on intellectual cooperation established in forty or so countries, the International Educational Cinematographic Institute, the International Association for the Promotion of Child Welfare, and the International Council of Nurses. The United States was, of course, not the only country actively promoting such organizations. But because it did not join the League, its role in promoting the activities of INGOs was quite conspicuous. The newly established Social Science Research Council and the American Council of Learned Societies, for instance, were among the founding members of the International Research Council, and American doctors and nurses were deeply involved in the task of modernizing the work of the Red Cross to enable it to cope with peacetime health problems, not just wartime emergencies.[15] In a book published during the war, Mary

14   Saul A. Mendlovitz, *On the Creation of a Just World Order: Preferred Worlds for the 1990's* (New York, 1975), 161.
15   Paul Weindling, ed., *International Health Organisations and Movements, 1918–1939* (Cambridge, 1995), 19–23.

Follette, an American political scientist, wrote that since "association is the impulse at the core of our being," and since "the creative characteristic of war is doing things together," it was imperative to "begin to do things together in peace" through the efforts of "people united not by herd instinct but by group conviction." She may well have had in mind the American Friends Service Committee and other organizations established during the war when she noted that "the old-fashioned hero went out to conquer his enemy; the modern hero goes out to disarm his enemy through creating a mutual understanding."[16] The American Century was beginning to be defined in the postwar years not simply through the nation's mass culture, such as movies and music, as many observers noted then and since, but also through the spread of NGOs, both domestic and international.

Even the history of the 1930s, the "nightmare decade" as William Shirer called it, may be put in a new light, as very much part of the American Century if we take NGOs into consideration. The number of INGOs increased from 375 in 1930 to 427 in 1940, an amazing phenomenon when one considers that the decade was characterized by exclusionary nationalism and totalitarianism in many parts of the world. Part of the increase in the number of INGOs is explainable by the fact that international non-governmental (as well as governmental) efforts were needed for the rescue and relief of victims of war and persecution. The International Rescue Committee was established in 1933 and the Save the Children Foundation in 1938, both with major U.S. input. But there were other American initiatives as well. In 1933 the Experiment in International Living was launched in order to send American high school students to study and live abroad, and four years later the Ford Foundation was established. The Rockefeller Foundation, created just before the First World War, was active throughout the 1930s on behalf of efforts by individuals and educational institutions to promote exchange programs with countries of Latin America.

---

16 M. K. Follette, *The New State: Group Organization the Solution of Popular Government* (New York, 1918), 193–95.

It is impossible to know whether these organized activities were on Henry Luce's mind when he published his celebrated essay, "The American Century," in *Life* in February 1941. Its penultimate paragraph said, "Throughout the 17th Century and the 18th Century and the 19th Century, this continent teemed with manifold projects and magnificent purposes." Elsewhere Luce wrote of "democratic idealism" as "the faith of a huge majority of the people of the world." And he envisaged the twentieth century as one in which the United States would play the leading role "as the dynamic center of ever-widening spheres of enterprise . . . as the training center of the skillful servants of mankind . . . as the Good Samaritan . . . as the powerhouse of the ideals of Freedom and Justice."[17] If the article did not specifically refer to NGOs, at least these passages implied that the American Century would be built upon the "authentically American" experience of the past and establish networks of interdependence as the nation promoted the economic improvement of other countries, trained technical and scientific experts, engaged in humanitarian activities, and championed the cause of human rights.

In such a vision, the role of private, voluntary organizations would be of critical importance. In 1944, Schlesinger noted that "it is with calculated foresight that the Axis dictators insured their rise to power by repressing and abolishing political, religious, labor, and other voluntary groups."[18] Combining Luce's and Schlesinger's wartime assertions, we may have here a fairly accurate prognostication of the American Century that was to come into reality after the end of the Second World War. For that century, or more accurately that half-century (the 1950s through the 1990s), was to be characterized by a tremendous growth of NGOs both in the United States and throughout the world, and by their activities in humanitarian, developmental, human rights, and many other activities to such an extent that Luce's assertion in 1941 that "our world . . . is one world, fundamentally indivisible" has

17   See Henry R. Luce, "The American Century," in this volume.
18   Schlesinger, "Biography of a Nation," 25.

come to seem less and less hyperbolic and more and more realistic.

That, rather than the Cold War, is the meaning of the American half-century. The Cold War was essentially a geopolitical readjustment after a great war, just like other postwar readjustments in history. There was nothing uniquely "American" about it; it was probably more part of the Soviet than of the American Century. What made the half-century American was the efforts of the numerous individuals and organizations in the United States and elsewhere to develop an international community of interdependence, freedom, communication, and reciprocity. As I hope to argue in a book-length study of this phenomenon, "global community" as a vision and as a reality is a major theme of recent world history, a theme that is far more critical to our understanding of the contemporary world than the Cold War.[19]

In his magisterial study of European politics and diplomacy in the eighteenth and the early nineteenth centuries, Paul Schroeder has observed that the European statesmen who came together in Vienna in 1815 after more than twenty years of incessant fighting were determined to put an end to traditional geopolitics and develop a sense of community so that they would seek to cooperate with each other for the stability of the regional order. The "sense of inherent limits, acceptance of mutual rules and restraints, common responsibility to certain standards of conduct, and loyalty to something beyond the aims of one's own state distinguished early nineteenth-century politics from what had preceded and would follow it."[20] The architects of the post-1945 Cold War – the governments of the victorious powers – clearly failed to develop any

19 Some of my ideas about alternative perspectives on post-1945 are contained in *Cultural Internationalism and World Order* (Baltimore, 1997). It can be argued, of course, that the Cold War was waged by the United States precisely in order to create the kind of global community in which INGOs would prosper. But it may be questioned whether the Cold War was necessary and inevitable, logically or historically, to realize such a vision. The vision long antedated the Cold War, and unless we say that the idea of global community and the waging of the Cold War were two sides of the same coin, it seems better to view these two as distinguishable phenomena, each susceptible to analysis in its own terms, instead of submerging one into the other.
20 Paul W. Schroeder, *The Transformation of European Politics, 1763–1848* (Oxford, 1994), 802.

The world does not seem "as one" today by any stretch.

such system of interstate cooperation or to define a sense of community, regional or global. The task, then, had to be entrusted to IGOs and INGOs. But because the Cold War protagonists often extended their antagonism to the arenas of IGOs (most notably the United Nations), it fell upon the INGOs to assume a major responsibility for keeping the world "one, fundamentally indivisible." In that sense, the making of the American Century was in the hands of NGOs, both in the United States and elsewhere. It is a remarkable fact that the number of INGOs had grown from 427 in 1940 to 755 by 1950, and further to 1,321 by 1960 and 2,296 by 1970, a fivefold increase in those thirty years. While the Cold War rivalry was dividing the globe, the INGOs, old and new, were dedicating themselves to communication, understanding, and cooperation across national boundaries.

Power, Boulding has written, is of three kinds: destructive, productive, and integrative. Destructive power entails the use or the threat of use of force to achieve one's objectives. Productive power works through exchange, an economic activity. Integrative power is social and expressed in mutual affection. Institutions based on integrative power, according to Boulding, are "family, churches, religious and charitable organizations, the . . . international nongovernmental organizations, artistic and reformist organizations."[21] In reality, of course, some INGOs do engage in economic activities, albeit of a non-profit nature, such as helping rural people to develop domestic industry. That NGOs are not entirely free of the state, even including its military power, can be seen in instances where humanitarian relief workers must seek the protection of the host government, or when such programs fit into a government's foreign policy agenda and receive subsidies from the latter. Nonetheless, even in such cases the autonomy of an NGO is never questioned. To the extent that it works with the state, this should not be automatically viewed as an example of an NGO compromising its integrity, but rather as a case in which the state is altering its character, to turn to and accommodate NGO initiatives and expertise. In any event, NGOs as integra-

21   Boulding, *Three Faces of Power*, 31.

tive forces have contributed immensely to shaping the American Century.

In the immediate postwar years, it is true, the tasks of rehabilitation, reconstruction, and relief all over the world were so immense that only governmental agencies, both national and international, could cope with them. Private organizations' involvement in such work was rather modest. Even so, the establishment, in the United States, of such organizations as the Church World Service (1946) and Direct Relief International (1948) shows that NGOs were ready and willing to do their share in providing assistance to war-devastated areas abroad. That NGOs and governmental agencies cooperated in the task was demonstrated when CARE (Cooperative for American Remittances to Europe) was created in 1946. (Soon the "E" in CARE came to stand for "Everywhere.")

In the meantime, the vision of one world was kept alive by postwar international organizations, in particular the United Nations and its affiliates and committees such as UNESCO (United Nations Educational, Scientific, and Cultural Organization) and the Commission on Human Rights (a subcommittee of the UN Economic and Social Council). It is important to recognize, however, that many NGOs cooperated with these international bodies. At the San Francisco meeting of the allies in the spring of 1945 that led to the founding of the United Nations, 42 NGOs from the United States served as advisers to the official delegation, and another 240 NGOs sent observers.[22] The preamble of the United Nations charter, with its ringing declaration, "We, the peoples of the United Nations . . . have resolved to combine our efforts" to achieve a peaceful and just world, never mentioned nations or states, only peoples. And peoples would express themselves not simply through their governments – we should recall that there were only about seventy independent nations in 1945 and that the vast majority of Asians and Africans lived under colonial regimes – but through international agencies and NGOs.

---

22 Tadashi Yamamoto, ed., *Emerging Civil Society in the Asia Pacific Community* (Tokyo, 1995), 274.

The 1948 UN declaration on human rights, as forceful a statement of the unity of humankind as any, was a product of long deliberation not just by governmental representatives sitting on the drafting committee but also by many individuals and organizations who sought to provide their input. And UNESCO's creation in December 1945 immediately resulted in the establishment of national commissions throughout the world to support and carry out its objectives. Private citizens and groups actively participated in their work. And through UNESCO and other agencies, educational and cultural programs were resumed with renewed vigor. The Salzburg seminar, established in 1947 through Rockefeller Foundation support to bring American and European scholars and students together, was one of the earliest instances of an INGO working together with various governments to reestablish intellectual communication that had been severed by war.

Interestingly enough, it was during the 1950s, usually regarded as the decade when the Cold War provided the sole definition of both national and international affairs, that INGOs made impressive gains, both in number and in influence. Perhaps this reflected the fact that, while the U.S.-USSR confrontation divided the world, freezing the two alliance systems in a state of perpetual confrontation, and while national affairs, too, were driven by the overall preoccupation with "winning" the Cold War, INGOs, along with IGOs, stepped in to keep the globe together, to oppose the Cold War antagonists' destructive power with their integrative power. That can be seen most graphically in the cross-national endeavors to limit the arms race, in particular to stop the atmospheric testing of nuclear weapons. The antinuclear movement in the early postwar years had been dominated by pacifist groups or else by Communist organizations.[23] In the 1950s, however, citizens' movements sprang up in North America, Europe, and Japan to protest against atomic tests, and representatives of many of them began meeting in Hiroshima every August after 1955 to continue the movement. In the meantime, a group

---

23   Milton S. Katz, *Ban the Bomb: A History of SANE, the Committee for a Sane Nuclear Policy* (New York, 1983), 47.

of distinguished scientists and intellectuals led by Albert Einstein and Bertrand Russell organized a conference in Pugwash, Canada, in 1957 to call for a "nuclear weapons-free" world, and the conference was reconvened periodically. These movements were seeking to unite world opinion against the dangerous excesses of the Cold War, something only private individuals and groups could accomplish.

But to protest against the arms race was not the only function of INGOs in the 1950s. There were parts of the world that did not fit into the geopolitical equation of the Cold War, those that came to be called the Third World. Nearly twenty new states were created between 1945 and 1960, some with huge populations, such as India, Pakistan, and Indonesia. Others, like Egypt, established new systems of government. Not all of these countries chose to align themselves with one side or the other in the Cold War; indeed, India, Indonesia, and Egypt sought to stay out of the big-power rivalry, instead focusing on economic development, educational reform, population control, and other tasks of "modernization." For them the Cold War was of decisively less importance than these tasks, indeed than the simple task of feeding millions of people, a test of the legitimacy of the new states, and they preferred neutralism to siding with one side or the other in the global confrontation. In such circumstances, both IGOs and INGOs became critical for their well-being. They would do, or try to do, what the superpowers, with their preoccupation with the global geopolitics, were unwilling or incapable of performing.

INGOs that had earlier focused on humanitarian relief to refugees and other victims of the Second World War now reoriented themselves to help Third World countries with their demographic problems and developmental projects. Where necessary, new INGOs were created: for instance, the International Human Assistance Program (U.S.), the International Voluntary Service (U.S.), the World Rehabilitation Fund (U.S.), l'Association Mondiale de Lutte contre la Faim (France), and the Voluntary Service Overseas (Britain). Although incorporated in a particular country, these agencies had branches or offices in other parts of the world. Reliable budget and expenditure figures for these organizations are not always available, but there seems little doubt that in terms of voluntary personnel, far more were involved in developmental assistance programs than governmental officials. At a time when the United States, the Soviet Union, and their respective allies were augmenting their state apparatus and stockpiling arms, it was left to private individuals and organizations – admittedly, virtually all of them at this time were from the United States and its Western allies – to step in and go to Third World countries, there to meet their people and organizations as well as government officials in order to build up networks of people committed to nation-building.

Developmental assistance, however, was only one area of INGO activities in the 1950s. To cite one other area where INGOs grew increasingly active, a significant number of international women's organizations devoted themselves to peace and human rights issues. In addition to the venerable Women's International League for Peace and Freedom, whose history went back to the First World War years, several others became active during the 1950s, including the International Council of Women, the International Federation of University Women, the International Federation of Business and Professional Women, and the Liaison Committee of Women's International Organizations. The emergence of such organizations in the international arena, and their active participation in cross-national conferences, suggest one of the little-understood aspects of the history of the 1950s. They were important as part of the growing assertiveness of INGOs, and also as indicative of the rising concern with women's rights. The two phenomena were intimately related in that women were not represented in the usual status apparatus (governments, armed forces) in proportion to their numbers, so that, if they were to have their voices heard, the best strategy was to organize NGOs.

In 1952, at a meeting of the UN Human Rights Commission's subcommittee on the prevention of discrimination and protection of minorities, a delegate proposed that a conference of non-governmental organizations be convened to coordinate their work. As he said, "their zeal, independence, and, in some cases, very considerable resources [make] their assistance indispensable."[24] At another meeting, a representative of the World Jewish Congress asserted that non-governmental organizations represented "elements and aspirations in international public opinion which must play a significant role in the development and consolidation of a genuine world community."[25] These expressions, together with the activism of women's organizations, revealed an awareness of one of the significant developments of the 1950s. In retrospect, it seems possible to argue that these developments, rather than geopolitical vicissitudes, were defining the shape of the world to come.

That became even clearer in the decades following the 1950s. Space does not allow a detailed examination of INGOs during the 1960s through the 1990s, but certain salient characteristics of these recent decades may be noted. During the 1960s, for instance, in addition to a further growth in the number of organizations oriented toward developmental assistance – clearly in response to the decolonization and independence of many African states – INGOs were particularly active in peace movements. Going much beyond the modest beginnings of the 1950s, NGOs in many countries took to the street, organized demonstrations, and published advertisements in newspapers to demand a halt in nuclear testing and the arms race. "End the Arms Race – Not the Human Race" was the slogan of Women Strike for Peace, a group of American women (later joined by those elsewhere) concerned with the effects of nuclear tests on their children. "We join with women throughout the world," declared the American organizers of the movement, "to challenge the right of any nation or group of nations to hold the power of life and death over the world."[26] Such self-consciousness on the part of women was an important aspect of the history of the world and of INGOs in particular during the 1960s. Women were getting organized everywhere, and their national organizations were being linked

24 United Nations Human Rights Commission, subcommittee on prevention of discrimination and protection of minorities, 3 October, 1952, mimeographed.
25 Memo by World Jewish Congress, 5 October, 1951, mimeographed.
26 Harriet Hyman Alonso, *Peace as a Women's Issue: A History of the U.S. Movement for World Peace and Women's Rights* (Syracuse, 1993), 205.

through international bodies and conferences that brought their representatives together.

Another important development was in cultural exchange and communication. Going much beyond the level of activities achieved earlier, individuals and groups not just from North America and Western Europe but from other parts of the world increasingly interacted with one another. Some of the interactions, to be sure, were initiated or actively promoted by governments. Among examples of this would be the Olympic games and world's fairs. The Olympics in Tokyo (1964) and Mexico City (1968), and the world's fairs in Seattle (1962), New York (1964), Montreal (1967), and Osaka (1970) were public affairs, funded by national, regional, or municipal governments. But even these events drew on the support, both financial and in voluntary personnel, from non-governmental organizations. Indeed, it is difficult to draw a precise line between official and non-official roles in cultural exchange. Even when official sponsorship was indisputable, such as the programs promoted by the Soviet government, this should not always be dismissed as a case of Cold War propaganda. Philip H. Coombs, writing as early as 1964, was able to report that "only some" of Soviet objectives in promoting cultural and educational exchanges were "associated with the cold war," and that there was "heavier emphasis now on genuine intellectual, technical, and artistic exchange without immediate ideological connotations."[27] During the 1960s, the Bolshoi Ballet, the Leningrad Orchestra, and a number of other artistic organizations toured Western Europe, North America, and Asia, and NGOs in the host countries provided their hospitality and logistical support. And these countries in turn sent some of their best musicians, artists, and dancers on tours of the Soviet Union and its allies.

Cultural exchanges among the industrial democracies, and between developed and developing nations were even more impressive. Of the former category, it would suffice to note that in the United States alone a large number of NGOs were established

27 Philip H. Coombs, *The Cultural Dimension of Foreign Policy* (New York, 1964), 90–93.

during the 1960s with the primary objective of undertaking educational, intellectual, and professional exchanges. To cite but a few examples, the Academy for Educational Development was established in 1961, the Citizen Exchange Council in 1962, the International Agricultural Exchange Association in 1963, the American Institute for Foreign Study Foundation in 1964, the International Research Exchange Board (IREX) in 1968, and the American Secondary Schools for International Students and Teachers in 1969. The exchange programs these organizations undertook were no doubt facilitated by the increasing wealth of the United States and other industrial nations and by technological developments such as the jet aircraft for civilian travels and satellite television communication. (The Intelsat was established in 1964, and the games played at the Tokyo Olympics that year were instantaneously televised abroad through satellite transmission.)

NGOs were also active in promoting exchange and communication between advanced and developing nations. A large number of universities in the West organized area studies programs to understand non-Western civilizations better, and Western scholars and students, equipped with the newest theories and survey techniques provided by the social sciences, conducted their research in remote parts of the world. Liberal developmentalism, a key intellectual formulation of the 1960s in the United States, was not a tool of the Cold War, as is often alleged, but an essential part of the American Century agendas, something that preceded the Cold War. To be sure, the two could be conceptually blurred, at no time more so than during the 1960s when the geopolitics of international affairs heated up in Vietnam at the very moment that expanding cultural networks were tying different parts of the globe closer together. Thus, when in 1961 the U.S. Congress established the Center for Cultural and Technical Interchange between East and West (the so-called East-West Center) in Hawaii, it could be seen both as an official organ designed to influence Asian and Pacific opinion and as part of the forces bringing Americans and other people into communication with each other. Instead of viewing one as an aspect of the other, we should see the two – geopolitical and cultural – aspects of international affairs as developments with their respective momentums.

In 1975 the critic Susan Sontag wrote, referring to the world-wide movement against the war in Vietnam, that the "movement was never significantly political, its understanding was primarily moral, and it took considerable moral vanity to expect that one could defeat the considerations of 'Real-politik' mainly by appealing to considerations of 'right' and 'wrong.'"[28] That is an apt characterization of NGO activities and their relationship to the geopolitics of the 1960s. Sontag was correctly pointing to the dual structure of international affairs, power-political and moral. In the context of our discussion, the moral would include the cultural, the private, the non-governmental. Neither moral forces nor NGOs succeeded in determining the shape of geopolitics, but that does not mean they were not as real as the "realities" of power politics. To the extent that the state exemplifies the reality of power, and non-state actors the realities of morality and culture, there could have been no "American Century" without the latter.

The picture is even clearer for more recent decades. There has been a veritable explosion in the number of NGOs, both of domestic and international varieties. That there are today over one million NGOs in the United States alone is, perhaps, less surprising than the fact that in so many non-Western and formerly socialist states large numbers of them have emerged in the last couple of decades. And many of them seem to be inspired by the same forces that de Tocqueville and Bryce recognized in the early American republic: citizens' search for autonomy, their promotion of reciprocity, their diminishing trust in governmental authority, and, in short, their commitment to developing a civil society. Thus American voluntary associations have often served as a model, as have U.S. philanthropic foundations and research institutions. In the international realm, the total number of INGOs has reached some twenty thousand, with hundreds of thousands of local

---

28 Quoted in Katz, *Ban the Bomb*, 122.

branches all over the world. The whole globe is linked together by the networks established by INGOs.

Not all INGOs, to be sure, contribute to the making of one world. Terrorist organizations, drug trafficking syndicates, or exclusionary ethnic or religious bodies are antiglobalist and divisive. They oppose, often with force, the efforts of INGOs engaged in humanitarian and other activities. Moreover, the very fact that the vast majority of INGOs are committed to making the world more interdependent, more habitable, and more just impresses some – those on both sides of the ideological spectrum in all parts of the world – as subversive of local interests and loyalties. Some argue that because the phenomenal growth of INGOs is an aspect of the globalizing tendencies of our time, they in effect serve as agents of global processes that are fundamentally exploitative in nature; while others vehemently deny that NGOs of whatever variety, because their leaders are not chosen by the electorate, have any authority to speak on behalf of public opinion anywhere. These are valid arguments, and we shall need much more research into the workings of NGOs in order to develop a balanced perspective on the relationship between NGOs and governance, and in particular between INGOs and international order.

In the context of the American Century in relation to contemporary world history, however, it is clear that our understanding of that concept must incorporate the exponential growth of INGOs in the last decades. While, since the 1970s, they have continued to carry out tasks such as humanitarian relief, developmental assistance, and cultural exchange, the recent years have witnessed particular emphasis placed on more politically sensitive agendas, such as the preservation of wildlife, the protection of the natural environment, and the promotion of interracial justice and other human rights. Perhaps this fact suggests growing confidence on the part of INGOs. Certainly, their prestige has risen considerably, even as people's trust in their own government has declined. In 1977, Amnesty International (founded in 1961) received the Nobel Peace Prize, and twenty years later the same recognition was bestowed upon the International Campaign to Ban Landmines.

INGOs have played key roles in providing a semblance of order in such strife-riven countries as Somalia, Rwanda, and Bosnia. They have forced states to accept certain guidelines for the protection of the environment and strict rules against the export of ivory. Greenpeace, Amnesty International, and other INGOs have been more willing than governments, than even the United Nations, to speak out against violations of the rights of endangered species or of prison inmates.

What does such a phenomenon have to do with the American Century? The answer will have to be, everything. For the inspiration behind the organization of NGOs, their commitment to activism derived from a moral conception of the world, their humanitarianism, and their support of human (and animal) rights – they come close to defining American "core values," certainly far more than the pursuit of military power or economic wealth, about which there is nothing uniquely "American" or "twentieth century." The NGOs may not yet have created "the first great American Century," to borrow from the last words in Luce's article, but they are getting there faster than any other force in the world.

Do this implying Americans are the only nation with a moral conscience?

14

Consuming Women: Images of Americanization in the "American Century"

EMILY S. ROSENBERG

> Once we cease to distract ourselves with lifeless arguments about isolationism, we shall be amazed to discover that there is already an immense American internationalism. American jazz, Hollywood movies, American slang, American machines and patented products, are in fact the only things that every community in the world, from Zanzibar to Hamburg, recognizes in common. Blindly, unintentionally, accidentally and really in spite of ourselves, we are already a world power in all the trivial ways – in very human ways.
>
> Henry R. Luce, "The American Century"

Luce's famous essay "The American Century" called on Americans to accept their special "duty and opportunity" in the post-World War II era. They should, he wrote, exert "the full impact" of their influence on the world in four ways: through promoting systems of free enterprise, propagating training in practical, technical skills, becoming the Good Samaritan to the entire world in times of hunger and need, and spreading their ideals of freedom and justice. A central premise of Luce's essay was its identification of American power with the attractions of its culture. Luce's American Century was not articulated as a vision resting on arms buildups, nuclear capacity, covert intrigue, or other forms of realpolitik. It stemmed from the long tradition that identified

American influence (or Americanization) with an inevitable and presumably welcomed process of cultural and economic modernization. Luce's essay provides an embarkation point for considering the ways in which visions of modernity and Americanization interrelated with messages about gender roles, particularly changing roles for women. Representations of "modern" women provided powerful tropes within the discourse of "Americanization" and "modernization" that many Americans projected overseas.[1] As a consequence, controversies over "Americanization" in many countries interlaced in some measure with debates over what constituted proper gender orders and relationships. This gender dimension added considerable heat to foreign debates about American influence.[2] Presenting the projection and reception of Americanization as, in part, a process that involved messages about gender is not explicit in Luce's essay, but because women were so often symbolically identified with mass consumption, his vision of a new, consumer-driven Americanized international culture *implied* new gender orders.

Clearly, this brief essay cannot offer a comprehensive history of the significations of gender in the idea of an "American Century" throughout all of the globe. I seek not to trace out all of the possible contexts within which such investigations might be set but merely to *exemplify* the predominance of tropes about women

---

1   There is a substantial theoretical literature discussing the relationship between "Americanization" and "modernity." Is modernity a process that takes firmest root in America and thus becomes confused with a unique national culture? Is Americanization a process that becomes so globalized that it comes to be recognized simply as modernity? An introduction to some of the literature on these issues is John Tomlinson, *Cultural Imperialism: A Critical Introduction* (Baltimore, 1991). While I am mindful of the various objections to either term, and the ideological implications of linking them together, I am nonetheless using the terms "modernity" and "Americanization" to signify similar discourses that describe the culture (elaborated in America) that accompanies modes of mass-production/mass-consumption/mass-mediazation, a culture in which advertising and communications and transportation revolutions have led to greater physical and psychic mobility. It is this culture, I believe, that has marked both the American Century and the more globalized process that Arjun Appadurai describes as *Modernity at Large: Cultural Dimensions of Globalization* (Minneapolis, 1996).
2   Frank Costigliola, "'Unceasing Pressure for Penetration': Gender, Pathology, and Emotion in George Kennan's Formation of the Cold War," *Journal of American History* 83 (March 1997): 1309–40, argues that tropes related to gender can heighten the emotional content of structured images.

in certain larger discourses of Americanization and modernization and to suggest their relevance to histories of international
relationships.

"De Día en Día Aumenta el Número
de Damas que Manejan el Ford"

Even before the "American Century" there was a strong tradition
in Western, and American, culture in which representations of
women's roles served as emblematic markers for the degree of
"civilization" reached by society as a whole. William Cronon
points out, for example, that early English colonists saw American Indian women doing agricultural labor as a sign of a de-
graded gender inversion. In their eyes, tilling the soil was manly
work, and men who would command women to tend the fields
could only be uncivilized. (Indians, of course, correspondingly
looked down on Englishmen as feminized because they did the
kind of field work that native cultures took to be the domain of
women.)[3]

Western evolutionary science, gaining currency in the late nineteenth century, similarly helped cement an equation between the
evolutionary status of a particular "race" of people and the status
of women. In this evolutionary discourse, "civilized" societies
relieved women of the burdens of work and accorded them special respect. Reflecting these views, purity crusaders in the United
States linked the eradication of male oppression (whether from
drunkenness, domestic violence, polygamy, patriarchal economic
control, or harmful factory-labor conditions) to the advancement
of civilization. Reformers dedicated to Americanizing new immigrants often fought to eradicate what they saw as old-country
gender oppression in favor of heterosocial partnerships formed

---

3 William Cronon, *Changes in the Land: Indians, Colonists, and the Ecology of New England* (New York, 1983), 52. Acceptance of the idea that slave women should work in the
fields (denying them, in effect, status as "women") similarly confirmed and reinforced, among
white Southerners, the essential inequality of people of African descent that was the foundation of race-based slavery. See Jacqueline Jones, *Labor of Love, Labor of Sorrow: Black
Women, Work, and the Family from Slavery to the Present* (New York, 1985).

within the ideal of companionate marriages. Similarly, U.S. missionaries in China, India, and Africa (as well as among American Indians at home) often concentrated their efforts on women's uplift and on removing the visible signs of subordinated status: footbinding, sati, load-carrying. Spreading the gospel of Christianity and Americanism also often meant spreading the "gospel of gentility," in which women were accorded special physical protection because of their importance in reproduction. The identification between Americanization, at home or abroad, and the uplift of downtrodden women strengthened the discourses of American mission, helping to cast Americanization as a heroic enterprise. In short, the idea that the spread of American culture would improve the lives of foreign women comprised a consistent trope of American exceptionalism.[4]

The role that women's images played in representations of progress remained important to twentieth-century visions of modernization. Especially after World War I, as modernity increasingly came to mean the spread of systems of mass production and consumerism in the United States, the "new woman" became a preeminent symbol of the "new era." This "new woman," however, was hardly a stable signifier. It could be used to mean a professional woman who took on mannish characteristics by trying to enter a sphere of public activity; a "flapper" projecting a blatant sexuality; an urban working-class woman with some discretionary money and time; a wife who tried to manage the home according to new "scientific" principles. In almost all representations, however, the "new woman" symbolized the expansion of consumption, greater independence, and the power to command relatively unsupervised leisure time.

The consumer revolution, with its engines in advertising, mass merchandising, and media culture, fed on images designed to sell goods to women. Women's roles and identities increasingly shifted

---

4 These ideas are developed in Ian R. Tyrrell, *Woman's Work/Woman's Empire: The Woman's Christian Temperance Union in International Perspective, 1800–1930* (Chapel Hill, 1991) and Jane Hunter, *The Gospel of Gentility: American Women Missionaries in Turn-of-the-Century China* (New Haven, 1984). Leila Rupp, *Worlds of Women: The Making of an International Women's Movement* (Princeton, 1997), 75–81, discusses such views in the context of what she calls "feminist Orientalism."

away from an emphasis on production, with the home being a primary site for sewing, food preservation and preparation, and childrearing, to an emphasis on consumption, with the home being a base from which to stage family purchasing expeditions and a place in which to display and manage the new commodities that had been obtained. The "new woman" – who could be identified with the right to vote, greater equality before the law, more access to public realms, more sexual freedom and mobility – also remained circumscribed within a doctrine of separate gender spheres by the modern era's overriding emphasis on consumption as a particularly female activity.

Above all, the "modern" woman in America was constructed as the woman who consumed; who had the power, through purchasing, to change her image and, by so doing, possibly to change her life as well. A *McCall's* ad in 1937 expressed the new gender division: "Categorically . . . man is always the producer . . . woman, the consumer."[5] More athletic, more independent, more mobile, more outspoken than in the past, the slim "American woman" who sprang from the pages of mass circulation magazines and motion pictures, especially after World War I, presented both a contrast with earlier ideals of femininity and a continuation of separate gender roles. In all its complexities, however, her new image as a consumer often served as a symbolic marker of progress and modernity.[6]

Images of modern, mobile, consuming women became standard icons within American representations of modernity. These

5 Quoted in Roland Marchard, *Advertising the American Dream: Making Way for Modernity, 1920–1940* (Berkeley, 1985), 162.
6 Lois W. Banner, *American Beauty* (Chicago, 1983), 187–225, Kathy Peiss, *Hope in a Jar: The Making of America's Beauty Culture* (New York, 1998), and Janet Staiger, *Bad Women: Regulating Sexuality in Early American Cinema* (Minneapolis, 1995), 6 all discuss the meanings of the "new woman." Stuart Ewen, *All Consuming Images: The Politics of Style in Contemporary Culture* (New York, 1988) emphasizes the connection between projections of modernity and thin body images. It should be noted that throughout the foregoing discussion the emblem of the American "new woman" was clearly (at least into the late Cold War period) bound by race. Since the 1970s, with the "Madonna revolution" and the growing prominence of African-American models, a somewhat different international projection of the "American woman" may have emerged, but this essay will concentrate on the earlier periods when American nationality was almost exclusively represented abroad in terms of "whiteness."

images then traveled into foreign markets along with American products. The semiotic equation

America = modernity = consumption = modern women

is exemplified, for example, in images from early international advertising by U.S. automobile companies, Ford and General Motors. These ad campaigns during the late 1920s and early 1930s provide windows into the ways in which new roles for women often emblemized the processes of both modernization and Americanization, what Luce would later call the "immense American internationalism" that he believed had spread through the world even before World War II.

Domestically, automakers began to build their market appeal around the idea of women drivers during the 1920s. An automobile – a fairly complicated machine that stood for geographic movement – could easily have developed an image that was gendered male. Early critics of women as drivers had stressed the dangers of women being away from home and in "the streets," the potential problems with women's presumed emotionalism and frailty behind the wheel, and the simple bad taste of women driving too fast and having their hair blow in the wind. In the mid-1920s Henry Ford was reluctant to associate his car with fashion and obsolescence, which he considered frivolous and opposed to rational practicality. But as automobile makers began to struggle under surplus inventories, they astutely realized that an appeal to women would considerably broaden the potential market. By the late 1920s both General Motors and then, reluctantly, Ford embraced new marketing techniques of selling "style." (Henry Ford subsequently complained that he was now less in the automotive business than the millinery business.)

This new selling appeal overtly fostered the image of the "new woman." In a pamphlet titled *The Woman and the Ford*, for example, Ford Motor wrote that in the change toward the new woman "the automobile is playing no small part . . . It has broadened her horizon – increased her pleasures – given new vigor to her body – made neighbors of faraway friends – and multiplied tremendously her range of activity. It is a real weapon in the changing order. More than any other – the Ford is a woman's car." At the same time, many very different kinds of women eagerly appropriated automobiles to their own lives. Demonstrations on behalf of suffrage prominently featured cross-country automobile caravans; self-proclaimed "feminists" flaunted their automobiles as a symbol of their independent lifestyles; and even less "radical" women also came to emphasize their individuality and new mobility through use of an automobile.[7]

The cultural congeniality between automobile culture and the "new woman" did not stop at the water's edge. Powerful sets of images in the international advertisements of both Ford and General Motors from this era illuminate the equation between independent women, modern lives, and the purchase of U.S. automobiles.

A series of Ford ads for Latin America, from N. W. Ayer and Son, for example, featured glamorous women driving Ford automobiles and, quite overtly, promoted the idea of women driving.[8] In nearly all of the ads, slim young women occupy both the driver's and the passenger's seats and travel unescorted through an urban setting (Fig. 1). The headline on one, which was marked for distribution in Montevideo newspapers, reads (in translation): "The Number of Fords Driven by Women Increases Every Day." The text below it states that the day when autos were complicated and women were content to let men drive had passed. "Modern women throughout the world" now wish to drive their own autos and "the women of this country are no exception."

Taken together, the Ford advertising campaign provided a primer for how a "modern" woman might use an automobile: shopping, visiting, impressing her relatives. Most also suggested an independent, single lifestyle, showing the automobile and its passengers going or coming from leisure activities – tennis, the beach – with male heads turning in appreciation. In an ad designated

---

7 Virginia Scharff, *Taking the Wheel: Women and the Coming of the Motor Age* (New York, 1991), 53–54 (quote), 85–87, 115; Marchard, *Advertising the American Dream*, 158, 161.
8 N. W. Ayer Advertising Agency Records, Archives Center, National Museum of American History, Smithsonian Institution, Washington, DC.

Un Coche de Fácil Manejo para las Damas

EL NUEVO FORD merece especial estimación de la mujer que maneja tanto por la facilidad de su manejo, como por la seguridad en su funcionamiento. Particularmente en las secciones de intenso tráfico es donde mejor se aprecia por su rápida aceleración, admirable agilidad, eficaces frenos en las cuatro ruedas, facilidad en el cambio de velocidades y sencillez en las maniobras para estacionarse.

Otro factor que contribuye al aumento de su confianza y seguridad al manejar el nuevo FORD es el parabrisa de cristal inastillable TRIPLEX. Esta innovación disminuye el riesgo de resultar herido, como frecuentemente sucede en los choques de automóviles. La FORD MOTOR COMPANY ofrece esta mejora para contribuir así a la seguridad del automovilista en todos los caminos.

FORD MOTOR COMPANY, S. A.
MEXICO, D. F.

23843—7 1-4110 3-4   MEXICO BRANCH

Mexico - Tennis y Golf — 1 page - Nov.
El Hogar

FIG. 1 This Ford ad, part of a broader campaign to appeal to women drivers, suggests that Ford has made a car that appeals especially to women because of its ease of handling. Both the Ford and GM ad campaigns featured women as potential consumers and as emblems of modern lifestyles. N. W. Ayer Advertising Agency Records, National Museum of American History. Used with permission of Ford Motor Archives.

"Mexico Branch, Newspapers," one of the women was touching up her lipstick as she sat in the driver's seat, parked in front of a beach hotel. Another headline read "El Camarada de los Deportistas Jóvenes" ("the companion of young women drivers") and mentioned the car's "spirit of youth," its grace and agility. These ads consistently stressed qualities that would also presumably appeal to women. "BELLEZA que cautiva a la mujer," stated one headline. Security, easy handling, beautiful lines, varied colors, and quality with economy were mentioned repeatedly as being especially important to women. In these ads, "new women" were clearly positioned as consumers with discretion over how to use their leisure time in order to enhance their own pleasure.

The images from General Motors's international advertising, devised by J. Walter Thompson, had a similar tone to Ayer's ads for Ford. Although they did not directly mention women in their headlines (as nearly all the Ford ads did), most GM ads similarly featured slim, sporty, "modern" women in the cars, many driving. In one ad, as two smartly dressed women drive along, the driver speaks the ad's headline: "We changed to Chevrolet because we wanted a thoroughly modern car." Unlike auto ads in the domestic market, none of the ads showed children or depicted the women engaged in family responsibilities. GM's Oakland was especially marketed as a woman's car, both at home and abroad (Fig. 2). "Good taste with a sparkle – that's Personality. Any successful woman knows just how greatly it counts. . . . That's why the new Oakland V–8 interests smart women." The text of this particular ad, placed in Australia, goes on to explain that a man will examine the engine, the car's weight, the upkeep costs, "but a woman prefers to *feel* all this." Although ads for Egypt contained no women (or placed them only in the back seat), women were prominently featured in every other GM market – in Western and Eastern Europe, South America, South Africa, Greece, and Australia.[9]

Although the intervention of these ads into established gender norms sometimes appears (to me) to be jarring, J. Walter

9   J. Walter Thompson Archives, microfilm, reel 41, International Advertisements, Special Collections Library, Duke University, Durham, North Carolina.

Thompson's research on international markets stressed the importance of appealing to women. Ads were placed internationally in women's magazines as well as in general newspapers, as J.

FIG. 2 This ad for the GM Oakland emphasized the car's "personality" and "sparkle," qualities thought to appeal especially to "smart women." J. Walter Thompson Archives, Duke University. Copyright 1978 General Motors Corp. Used with permission of GM Media Archives.

Walter Thompson's market surveys showed that women had substantial, and growing, influence on purchasing decisions.[10]

The impact of these ads on automotive sales, however, is not my point here. (The mounting depression of the early 1930s would surely complicate any assessment of impact on sales, in any event.) It is, rather, to stress the iconography (taken into international markets) that equated modernity with American lifestyles, emphasizing leisure and consumption, and to illustrate the way in which "modern" women were constructed to exemplify this American style. J. Walter Thompson's other advertising campaigns, for Kodak cameras, Johnson and Johnson's Modess, and Johnson outboard motors, also featured "modern" women – mobile, slim, independent, and enjoying leisure.[11] These ads help reveal how the products of American mass culture – the movies, popular slang, machines, and patented products that Luce would come to celebrate as "common" to communities throughout the world in "trivial" but "human" ways – contained messages about gender roles that were hardly "trivial" at all. Whether it was called "modernization" or "Americanization," the products of American mass production/consumption and their cultural images clearly projected gender norms for women that could be potentially controversial.

Khrushchev: "Let's drink to the ladies!"
Nixon: "We can all drink to the ladies!"

If automobile advertisements may illustrate gendered images associated with Americanization in the interwar period, household consumer goods – especially the accoutrements of modern kitchens – provide a similarly suggestive icon for the Cold War period. Images from propaganda and advertising campaigns during World War II and the Cold War promoted America, above all, as a land

---

10 A discussion of the market research is in Jeffrey L. Merron, "American Culture Goes Abroad: J. Walter Thompson and the General Motors Export Account, 1927–1933" (Ph.D. diss., University of North Carolina, Chapel Hill, 1991), 142–51.

11 J. Walter Thompson Archives, microfilm, reel 41, International Advertisements.

of abundance and consumption, both of which were generally equated with freedom. Again, representations of American women continued to be a central icon in this equation:

America = modernity = consumption = freedom = modern women

Focusing on the famous "kitchen debate," it is possible, once again, to telescope the patterns of Cold War cultural themes, highlighting a gender analysis. In this celebrated conversation between Vice President Richard Nixon and Soviet Premier Nikita Khrushchev at the American National Exhibition at Sokolniki Park in Moscow in 1959, the two superpower leaders formulated their respective countries' claims to progress and goodness in representations about women's lives. They engaged in an our-women-are-better-off-than-your-women-no-they-aren't-yes-they-are kind of masculine display.

During this debate Nixon often used "freedom" and consumer choice as nearly synonymous. And the home, the special domain of women, became the exemplar of standards of living, of the abundance and leisure that the United States stressed in all of its informational campaigns during the period. Under Eisenhower, the United States Information Agency had refined its propaganda themes to focus on America's widespread prosperity – what it called "People's Capitalism." Though the term "people's capitalism" was subsequently dropped, the emphasis on consumer plenty remained.[12] During Nixon's radio-TV address to the Soviet people, he proclaimed that the United States had nearly achieved "freedom and abundance for all in a classless society."[13]

Even before the encounter in Moscow, kitchen appliances, ready-to-wear women's clothing, and cosmetics had become powerful American icons of freedom. Newly designed, so-called Freedom Kitchens were prominent in the advertisements of women's maga-

---

12   Walter Hixson, *Parting the Curtain: Propaganda, Culture and the Cold War, 1945–1961* (New York, 1997), 133–41.
13   Richard Nixon, "Russia as I Saw It," *National Geographic Magazine* 116 (December, 1959): 717.

zines at home. And in postwar Europe, these sleek American kitchens held special fascination for would-be foreign consumers. Historian Reinhold Wagnlcitner, whose work contains suggestive examples of the coming of the American Century as the consumer century, emphasizes the special attractions of the American kitchen to war-weary and impoverished audiences in Austria.[14]

A year before the kitchen debate, at the 1958 Brussels International Exhibition, the Soviets had featured Sputnik, the Bolshoi Ballet, and heavy machinery, while the United States had showed off such things as a pink built-in oven, a dishwasher, and frozen-food packages grouped in "islands" throughout the pavilion. Under the influence of Katherine Howard, a prominent Republican who was appointed second deputy commissioner, the exhibition had become a showcase for the diverse accomplishments of ordinary women in America – and for the household appliances and practical clothing styles that provided them with greater freedom. According to Howard, modern kitchens were one of the most important weapons in the "psychological battle to win the uncommitted nations to the free way of life. . . . It is one of the wonders of the world that Americans in every economic strata have kitchens with labor-saving devices which free the American woman from drudgery, which make the kitchen the heart of the home." The Sears, Roebuck catalog was especially popular at Brussels. And at the center of the circular American pavilion *Vogue* staged a daily women's fashion show emphasizing "the Young American look" – an array of clothing for various social roles, from jeans and plaid shirts, to tennis attire, to the functional and inexpensive "sack dresses," to evening gowns. Orchestrated by Lee Canfield (the sister of Jacqueline Bouvier Kennedy), the *Vogue* show underscored the "freedom" of ordinary, modern, American women to slip easily among a variety of social roles simply by changing clothes. Directed at a non-elite audience, this exhibit was the fourth international show that *Vogue*

---

14 Reinhold Wagnleitner, "The Irony of American Culture Abroad: Austria and the Cold War," in *Recasting America: Culture and Politics in the Age of Cold War*, ed. Lary May (Chicago, 1989), 285–301.

had arranged for the U.S. government's Cold War campaigns on behalf of people's capitalism. According to Robert Rydell, the entire American pavilion projected "a dream world premised on the freedom to consume and spend time in the pursuit of leisure."[15]

For the Moscow exhibition of 1959, U.S. planners again drew on themes that highlighted consumerism as an exemplification of freedom and emphasized consumer products directed toward women. *Three* model kitchens displayed an array of appliances, home gadgets, and convenience foods. Fashion shows again featured stylish clothing produced for a mass market. Leisure attire – for the beach, for golfing, and for other kinds of play – particularly surprised Russian visitors, who, according to Helena Rubenstein, considered such leisure activities for women unrealistic.[16] And U.S. planners, working with Coty cosmetics, readied $150,000-worth of free samples of make-up to be given away, a plan that Soviet officials forbade. Soviet women lined up so eagerly to get free beauty shop demonstrations by Helena Rubinstein that Soviet authorities banned this treatment as well.[17]

At the Moscow exhibition, the Cold War became refracted through images of the slender, youthful, colorful Pat Nixon versus the heavier, darkly clad wives of Soviet officials. U.S. magazines celebrated American labor-saving devices while showing disdain for the Soviet system in which women might do manual labor and other "men's" jobs.[18] The contrasts in women's images fed the gendered discourse of American exceptionalism about removing women from drudgery and became explicit the day that Nixon and Khrushchev had their celebrated "debate." The two

---

15 Karal Ann Marling, *As Seen on TV: The Visual Culture of Everyday Life in the 1950s* (Cambridge, MA, 1994), 43–49; Robert Rydell, *Worlds of Fairs: The Century of Progress Exhibitions* (Chicago, 1993), 193–211 (203, quote). Robert H. Haddow, *Pavilions of Plenty: Exhibiting American Culture abroad in the 1950s* (Washington, 1997), 104–68 (159 quote), discusses the roles of Katherine Howard and Lee Canfield.

16 Picture captions in Richard Nixon, "Russia as I Saw It," 718, 721.

17 Hixson, *Parting the Curtain*, 185–213.

18 Elaine Tyler May, *Homeward Bound: American Families in the Cold War* (New York, 1988), 18–19. See also Stephen J. Whitfield, *The Culture of the Cold War* (Baltimore, 1991), 73–75.

superpower leaders stood in the kitchen of the model six-room ranch-style home:

NIXON (pointing to a washing machine): "In America these are designed to make things easier on our women."
KHRUSHCHEV: "A capitalist attitude."
NIXON: "I think this attitude toward women is universal."
KHRUSHCHEV: "These are merely gadgets."[19]

Expressing Cold War rivalries in terms of the status and roles of women, Nixon had shifted the emphasis from political contests to the dynamics of the private home. More precisely said, he embedded the political contests within a tableaux of private life. As Karal Ann Marling suggests, "the model kitchen was also a model of appropriate gender roles" (a producing male; a wife who organized consumption at home). And it "provided a working demonstration of a culture that defined freedom as the capacity to change and to choose."[20] To Nixon, "our" modern, consuming women fulfilled a "universal" male aspiration to elevate women above the burden of hard work. America's roles for women continued to mark its civilization and progress.[21]

Early U.S. automobile ads and Cold War consumer pavilions, though providing only two sets of images, exemplified a common structure of metaphors that often accompanied the flow of American culture and products abroad. They aligned "modernity" with images of "modern women"; they made consuming women into icons of freedom and progress. But what Nixon had regarded as the universality of this American projection was by no means uncontested. In Moscow, Khrushchev tried to debunk America's path to modernity by suggesting that Russians were too serious about economic development to care about trivial "gadgets." Such

---

19   "Encounter," *Newsweek* (3 August 1959): 16–17 (and section-heading quote).
20   Marling, *As Seen on TV*, 281, 283.
21   On the display of the ideology of universalism in the Cold War international exhibit "Family of Man" see Eric J. Sandeen, *Picturing an Exhibition: The Family of Man and 1950s America* (Albuquerque, 1995).

counterpoints to American discourses about modernity and progress – and the role of the consuming "new woman" – had long been standard fare in all kinds of commentaries about America.

**"What better symbol of [the future] could there be
than this madly rushing machine, turned loose at
full speed between two pasteboard landscapes,
steered by a charming woman"**

After both World War I and World War II, debates over the consequences of "Americanization" became prominent among citizens in many countries. These debates often raised issues of political or strategic balance. They often involved issues of economic organization and financial muscle. As the examples of the interwar automobile ads and the Cold War exhibitions may suggest, however, they also derived much emotive power because they could be framed as cultural and even gender issues. Luce, like Nixon, may have believed that the world's peoples shared a kind of fundamental cultural universalism. But reception of the American Century was considerably more complicated.

Metaphors about America and the meanings of Americanization that have circulated outside the United States are, of course, complex and culture-specific. I would like here to focus only on Europe in both postwar periods, drawing on several excellent studies that help elaborate some of the complexities in this particular region.

Before discussing the diversity of European responses to the image of America's "new woman," one thing should be clarified. I am not referring here to European responses to the actual conditions and situations of American women, any more than the automobile ads or the Moscow exhibition represented actual American women. The lives of American women widely varied along lines of race, class, region, age, and temperament. Rather, as before, I am addressing persistently oversimplified tropes of "the American woman" that circulated widely as parts of larger metaphors about "America" and about the presumably desirable or undesirable consequences of "Americanization."

Europe's America had long been less a geographical place than a metaphor of otherness. European visions of America characterized the describer by counterpoint; America became the definition of what was, in Richard Pells's words, "not like us."[22] This complex metaphor of America could have both positive and negative elements. Opponents of the culture of capitalist mass production highlighted "Americanization" as a principal threat to alternative visions of national tradition or destiny. Others sought to learn from American techniques in order to transform their own economic and political systems or were simply attracted to American mass culture. In these debates, the American woman became, in some measure, emblematic of the supposed consequences of Americanization.

A number of historians have explored the metaphorical repertoire of European anti-Americanism. They generally agree that a diverse group of European intellectuals produced what J. P. Mathy has called a pervasive "intertext" about America – a collection of textual references, influencing each other and sharing similar features. This European intertext has had a distinct structure of meanings, a discursive formation that constructed America as restless, anti-intellectual, conformist, hedonist, technological, materialistic, consumerist, and beset by bad taste. Americans lacked a sense of history and led standardized, stupefied, and shallow lives.[23]

All of these attributes tended to be expressed as the product of feminization or, at least, of emasculation. Male pursuit of profits in America, in this discourse, left social direction and even

22 Richard Pells, *Not Like Us: How Europeans Have Loved, Hated, and Transformed American Culture since World War II* (New York, 1997).

23 This common description of America is discussed, for different countries, in many works, including Jean-Philippe Mathy, *Extrême Occident: French Intellectuals and America* (Chicago, 1993); Pells, *Not Like Us*; Mary Nolan, *Visions of Modernity: American Business and the Modernization of Germany* (New York, 1994), 108–27; Rob Kroes, *If You've Seen One You've Seen the Mall: Europeans and American Mass Culture* (Urbana, 1996), 1–42; Richard Kuisel, *Seducing the French: The Dilemma of Americanization* (Berkeley, 1993); and Reinhold Wagnleitner, *Coca-Colonization and the Cold War: The Cultural Mission of the United States in Austria after the Second World War* (Chapel Hill, 1994). The following paragraphs rely heavily on these works.

culture in the hands of women, often assumed to be by nature lessintellectually adept, more emotional, and more easily taken in by advertising. The resulting feminized society could not perpetuate any particularized *Kulture*; nor could it advance any worthwhile vision of *civilization*. American mass society itself was cast as feminine and contrasted with a Europe that was refined, aesthetic, spiritual, rooted, civilized, and appropriately masculine.[24] (It is interesting how both Americanizers and their critics structured metaphors to assign femininity to other cultures and masculinity to their own.[25])

This intertext about America emerged from influential European commentators who were positioned broadly across the political spectrum. During both postwar eras, the critique blurred lines between America/modernity/capitalism, and both left and right advanced a vision of America-as-social-devolution to combat the liberal capitalist culture that was transforming Western Europe. Both Marxists and right-wing nationalists used anti-American constructions to reinforce their own claims to cultural – and also political – authority. But even Social Democrats, labor, and those business groups who tended to admire America's productive capacities and its techniques of industrial organization feared the social and cultural consequences of a mass-production, "Americanized" economy. The creation of "America" as a metonym for whatever was advertiser-driven and "inauthentic" advantageously positioned the critic as the embodiment of cultural authenticity.

European images of "America" thus involved less the geographical place called America than domestic cultural fears and political contests. The notion of America, as Rob Kroes has written, was a "symbolic invention made in Europe . . . a metaphor made to serve in the context of essentially intra-European debates." Richard Pells points out that the cultural battle over "American-

---

24 Andreas Huyssen, "Mass Culture as Woman, Modernism's Other," in *Studies in Entertainment: Critical Approaches to Mass Culture*, ed. Tanya Modleski (Bloomington, 1986), 188–207.
25 Frank Costigliola, *France and the United States: The Cold Alliance since World War II* (New York, 1992).

ization" in Europe was not primarily one *between* the United States and Europe but one that inscribed generational, class, political, and cultural divisions within Europe itself. Mary Nolan argues that in post-World War I Germany, the debate about domestic "economic reform was conducted in the idioms of Americanism and Fordism." Reinhold Wagnleitner also discusses attitudes toward Americanization as marking a domestic cultural divide in Austria. And Richard Kuisel shows how alignments in French politics likewise often coalesced around claims about and fears of Americanization.[26]

American women often emerged, in these contests, as symbolic carriers of the consumerist, mass society that European commentators saw as quintessentially American. Foreign observers throughout the nineteenth century (and even before) had persistently commented on what they saw as an outspokenness, even brashness, among American women. The international spread of American mass production and mass culture in the post-World War I era, with the implicit or explicit tropes about consuming "new women," further highlighted such commentary and, for many observers, brought the consequences closer to home.

To many European intellectuals, from conservatives to Marxists, America's new woman became the exemplar of all the evils of mass society. The French commentator Georges Duhamel in his influential and controversial book, *America the Menace: Scenes from the Life of the Future* (1931), for example, recounts a sightseeing trip in which he "risked my life in the automobile of Mrs. Graziella Lytton":

My eyes, tired of the hoardings with their advertisements, turned to the interior of the car and I suddenly saw in it a symbol of the world of the future. What better symbol of it could there be than this madly rushing machine, turned loose at full speed between two pasteboard landscapes, steered by a charming woman with manicured nails and beautiful legs, who smoked a cigarette while traveling between fifty and sixty miles an

---

26 Kroes, *If You've Seen One You've Seen the Mall*, xiii; Nolan, *Visions of Modernity*, 5.

hour, while her husband, seated on the cushions of the rear seat, with a set jaw scribbled figures on the back of an envelope.[27]

The intertext of such critiques, which symbolized mass-modernity as a woman, clustered into two common tropes.

First, the American woman was a superficial, hollow product of mass-produced images. Many European commentators portrayed Americans in general as becoming undifferentiated and standardized by mass consumption, but often their critique pointed especially toward women. One American reporter in 1929, for example, wrote that the fear of Americanization in France had become a "national obsession" and that a major complaint was that "the modern woman tends even more [than Americans generally] toward uniformity: everywhere her hair and line of clothes are the same."[28] Shaped by advertising culture and driven by consumerism, according to this trope, she posed human relationships and independence but actually lacked both. Where the American idealization of the "new woman" exalted her freedom and independence, critical Europeans often suggested that such a pose was simply a false front for a shallow enslavement to material things and appearances – an unfree and insecure condition that the women were too superficial even to understand. Simone de Beauvoir, for example, visited the United States and quickly developed a disgust not only for America but especially for its "new woman." In her controversial travel account, *America Day by Day* (1948), de Beauvoir recounted how she was initially impressed with the appearance of health and independence among women at Vassar College but subsequently realized that they seldom dressed for themselves but for the gaze of men. Beset by feelings of inferiority and by a Puritanical inability to express physical love, she concluded, American women wished to attract men in order to dominate them, and relations between men and

27   Georges Duhamel, *America, the Menace: Scenes from the Life of the Future*, trans. Charles Miner Thompson (London, 1931), 70–71.
28   *Outlook and Independent* 153 (6 November 1929): 383.

women "consist in endless small vexations, disputes, and conquests."[29]

Second, American women were often cast as domineering, even frigid and castrating. European critics had long portrayed democracy as a feminized political order. The leveling of hierarchy, in this representation, had reduced the role of the father, and the penchant for the challenging of authority left the father with so little power in the family that the wife had become predominant. But modern mass consumption brought even darker visions of an American matriarchy. This view constructed a truly monstrous woman whose insatiable consumerism made her a parasite living on the production of males. Destructive of men, of families, ultimately of the very culture that was supposed to be her special domain, modern American women were "consuming," in every sense of the word. De Beauvoir, for example compared the American woman – in control of her husband's check book and dominating her children, especially her sons – to the "praying mantis that devours the male species."[30] De Beauvoir's characterizations, which echoed those of many male critics of the "new woman" both abroad and at home, portrayed America's "new woman" as both insecure and dominating.

Controversies over the social consequences of modernity, consumption, and "new women," of course, also circulated within U.S. culture throughout the twentieth century. People of various persuasions, from left and right, fiercely critiqued consumerism and warned about how "new women" threatened family, masculinity, and society in general.[31] Similar critiques in international settings, however, intertwined with debates over the consequences of the spread of American influence, sharpening contests over "national culture" and ultimately helping to shape rhetorical structures related to foreign affairs.

---

29   Simone de Beauvoir, *America Day by Day*, trans. Patrick Dudley (London, 1952), 254.
30   Ibid., 251; Mathy, *Extrême Occident*, 74–76.
31   The Cold War classic that popularized an influential critique of "momism" was Philip Wylie, *Generation of Vipers* (New York, 1942).

If certain groups of Europeans tended to denounce Americanization (mass production, consumption), the same was not necessarily true of all. In an intertext of more positive images that also circulated in Europe, Americans were portrayed as open, flexible, strong, self-made, productive, and prosperous (except during the Great Depression). American mass culture, particularly mass-mediated culture, could have enormous popular appeal.

The film scholar Jackie Stacey, in *Star Gazing*, has provided a detailed study of the popular attraction of the image of the American "new woman" that was projected overseas in American films of the 1940s and 1950s. After studying responses from female British moviegoers to the American stars who populated the Hollywood screens during the World War II and postwar eras, she concludes that the viewers had an overwhelmingly positive reaction to the film stars. Feminist film critics, Stacey argues, have tended to portray many women's film roles in terms of satisfying a "male gaze" and thus as reinforcing traditional roles of female subordination. She argues, however, that this interpretation pays too much attention to the critic's own reading of the plot narrative and too little to the reactions of viewers themselves. Survey data from viewers, she concludes, suggests that the impact of the movies came mainly from the aura of "celebrity" projected by the stars of the age. In this sense, the stars exemplified less whatever lessons might have been embedded in the plot narrative and more a series of attributes that the audiences admired and wished they could emulate. Stacey reports that these attributes included independence, leisure, consumer choice, and attractiveness to men. All of these were especially alluring to British women during the hardship of the war.[32]

The attractions mentioned by the women surveyed corresponded generally to the larger intertext about America as a land of abundance and opportunity. Just as the negative meanings of Americanization were projected onto women, so Stacey shows that the positive ones were likewise projected onto female images. J. Walter

---

32   Jackie Stacey, *Star-Gazing: Hollywood Cinema and Female Spectatorship* (London, 1994).

Thompson built on the celebrity image of America's female stars to build the appeal of Lux soap in Great Britain. Joan Crawford, the epitome of the glamorous, strong, and independent woman, for example, was a feature of Lux's advertising campaign in Great Britain during the same period covered by Stacey's study (Fig. 3).[33]

Stacey's research confirms what some cultural elites charged and feared: that images from American mass culture held tremendous popular appeal. Most women who admired the household consumer "gadgets" and the beauty parlors at the Cold War exhibitions, like Stacey's "star-gazers," probably saw not standardized, shallow, and devouring "new women," but affluent, healthy, independent ones who, as consumers, could make choices in their own lives.

The ways in which images of women figured in debates over Americanization in Europe fall into even sharper relief in those regions where cultural differences even are more pronounced. In discourses of Islamic fundamentalists such as the Taliban, for example, appropriate roles for women provide the principal staging ground for debates over mass culture, political democracy, and even the content of "modernity" itself. Various Islamic traditionalists, less extreme than the Taliban, also denounce the American modernity that, in their view, exploits women's bodies by the commercially driven emphasis on public display and suggestions of explicit sexuality. And Islamic advocates of women's equality have had to struggle to stake out an alternative view of a modern "new woman" that incorporates greater independence but avoids a consumerist emphasis on bodily exposure.[34] The trope that represents Americanization as a consuming-woman-out-of-control can, in many languages and cultures, be invoked as a defense of hierarchy, of patriarchy, of anticapitalist forms of economic organization, of traditional religions.

---

33 J. Walter Thompson Archives, International Advertisements, folder: England, Unilever-Lux.

34 See, for example, Deniz Kandiyoti, "Gendering the Modern: On Missing Dimensions in the Study of Turkish Modernity," in *Rethinking Modernity and National Identity in Turkey*, ed. Sibel Bozdogan and Reşat Kasaba (Seattle, 1997), 126–27.

FIG. 3 The J. Walter Thompson agency, by invoking the celebrity image of America's strong and independent stars – such as Joan Crawford – to build the appeal of products, spread images of Americanized modernity. J. Walter Thompson Archives, Duke University. Used with permission of Unilever Corp.

Conclusion

Implicit images of consumerism and mass production pervaded Luce's vision of the American Century as a global path toward modernity. In modern America, there was a strong identification between consumption (the ability to choose products, new images, new locations, new identifies) and freedom itself. Although women have often tended to be side players in the traditional political realms of diplomacy and realpolitik, images about women's roles have played a central role in the semiotics of Americanization. In this essay, I have not been examining the status of women in the "American Century" but have, rather, sought to explore how images of women have helped to construct the idea of and the responses to an "American Century."

The examples developed here have highlighted the ways in which gender imagery – particularly the iconography of "modern" women – has formed a part of the export of American mass culture and has interlaced with debates over Americanization and modernity. In U.S. culture, images of uplift and modernization were often encoded into representations of American women. Women became markers of civilization in such a way that "free" women, empowered by consumer choice and discretionary leisure time, signified advancement. Overseas, debates over modernization and Americanization and over alignments for or against the United States also often invoked images about gender. Anti-American critics, both from the traditionalist right and the anti-market left, often portrayed consuming women as signifiers for social disruption. Others, however, seem to have been often attracted to the representations of women-cum-modernity that came from American cultural products. American movie icons and international exhibitions featuring kitchens, fashions, and cosmetics clearly had popular appeal.

These cultural contests about Americanization underlay politics and diplomacy and provide critical background for even the most traditional of historical questions. Richard Kuisel's *Seducing the French*, for example, shows how the emotional debates over "Americanization" within French culture during the 1950s were intertwined with discussions surrounding a more independent French foreign policy. Walter Hixson's *Parting the Curtain* examines the relationship between the purveyance of American mass culture and the process that slowly undermined the authority of the Soviet state and helped bring an end to the Cold War. In these pathbreaking books, and many of the others cited in this essay, the interrelationships between culture and diplomacy are demonstrated. Pro- and anti-Americanism both consisted of a dense intertext of cultural symbols (including gender images) that could be easily invoked in a wide range of political, economic, international, and personal debates. Discourses about personal gender roles (such as views of appropriate roles for women) and discourses about public policy (such as debates over Americanization) often have dense symbolic interconnectedness. International relationships in the so-called American Century have thus been accompanied by cultural wars prompted by Americanization: a modern style marked by mass production and mass consumption. With women positioned as the special embodiment of consumer lifestyles, debates over capitalism and modernization – and ultimately over Americanization – often were staged within the highly personal and emotionally charged terrain of appropriate gender roles.

15

The Empire of the Fun,
or Talkin' Soviet Union Blues:
The Sound of Freedom and
U.S. Cultural Hegemony in Europe

REINHOLD WAGNLEITNER

Loosen up, don't be afraid, don't hold back! When he reaches
the end of his pitch he just goes wild, the other salesmen at his
side, hearty and true, their ringing voices making it plain that
what they're really selling is America, because in America the
fantasy of the country sells everything else and everything else
on sale sells the country: ALL YOU HAVE TO DO IS DREAM!

> Greil Marcus, *Invisible Republic,*
> *Bob Dylan's Basement Tapes*

OVERTURE

Once upon a time, the Spanish Habsburgs and their Austrian sib-
lings controlled the empire on which the sun never set. Looking
back at the demise of so many European empires after the First
World War, Edward G. Lowry laconically quipped in the *Satur-*

This essay is dedicated to Mary Johnson, Mildred Suppin, and Paula Wagnleitner, Elisabeth
Wagnleitner-Suppin, and Anna Wagnleitner: four generations of Austro-American
(mis)understanding.

day Evening Post in 1925: "The sun, it now appears, never sets
on the British Empire and the American motion picture industry." After the Second World War the sun finally set on all European empires as well as on the Japanese Empire of the Sun. They
were all replaced by a completely new kind of empire, Hollywood's
Empire of the Fun. This Celluloid Empire produced the metatext
of cultural power and hegemony of the American Century. The
visual and acoustic repositories of this global culture have more
and more been filled with messages from the imperial center to
the accompaniment of the soundtrack of the twentieth century,
the Sound of Freedom (jazz, and all its derivatives).

Who, after all, needed the Monroe Doctrine when the Marilyn
Monroe Doctrine seemed so much more desirable *and* much less
painful to boot? When the foreign policy spokesperson of Mikhail
Gorbachev, Gennadi Gerasimov, was asked about the validity of
the Brezhnev Doctrine in the light of the crumbling Soviet Empire
in 1990, *everybody* without *and* within the iron curtain under-
stood him when he said: "The Brezhnev Doctrine is dead. We
now have the Frank Sinatra Doctrine, I did it my way." The
noise of the celebrations of the putative U.S. victory of the Cold
War totally obliterated some thoughtful voices who, like Carlos
Fuentes, asked: "When, I would like to know, will the Frank Sinatra
Doctrine become applied to Latin America and the Caribbean?"
But this is not the only problem of the global hegemony of the
United States. In 1998, the question should be asked whether
anybody really won the Cold War – maybe not the most intelligent notion in the first place – when Russia just dramatically
exchanged two new prime ministers within the period of a few
months: Sergei Kirijenko, who had received his management training from the "church" of Scientology, for Yevgeni Primakov, who
had been the head of the Russian secret services not so long ago.

Act I: Europe as Fun Park

Exactly one hundred years after the beginning of the American
Century in the Caribbean (and Pacific) with the Spanish-American War, three stories in the 27 April 1998 issue of the Austrian

magazine *Profil* (itself a copy of the German magazine *Der Spiegel*, which, in turn, is a copy of *Time* magazine) are perfect examples of the complexities *and* ironies of American cultural hegemony. The leader, analyzing a purge within an Austrian right-wing party, is aptly alluding to Arnold Schwarzenegger, among the most famous (Austrian? American?) cultural exports of the twentieth century: "Die blauen Terminatoren (The Blue Terminators)." A story about the new Austrian Social Democrat party platform, which (following Tony Blair's New Labour, which in turn only had followed Bill Clinton's New Democrats) buried the concept of the classless society, is titled "Paradise Lost." (Remember, we are supposed to still speak German!) The third story, lapping up a positive report about the Vienna stock exchange by J. P. Morgan, is titled "Dagobert goes to Vienna."

This last headline is a beautiful example of the potentially grave misunderstandings embedded in the exportation of U.S. popular culture – because it is usually overlooked that cultural artifacts change their meanings, transform their messages, acquire local meanings, and become new significers as soon as they cross borders. So, Dagobert goes to Vienna! Most Americans will have no problem understanding the simple fact that the economic editor of a, supposedly, serious Austrian magazine resorted to (American) English in order to appear economically hip. But then, even American Disney fans will experience difficulties if they want to get behind the meaning of the completely bizarre mixture of the sex appeal of (American) business success with Disney's richest, world famous, *and* abstemious Duck – Dagobert Duck being nothing but the German pseudonym of Uncle Scrooge. But then, would the headline "Uncle Scrooge goes to Vienna" have worked at all?

The Social Democrat mayor and governor of Vienna ran into similar difficulties when he opened his election campaign with a much-publicized shaking of hands with an impersonator of Donald Duck in the autumn of 1996. Had he only known that he was shaking the hand of the biggest loser in the American pop pantheon, he might have been better prepared for the final election results. So petty politics and sound bites have become as much a European phenomenon of the 1990s as Happy Shoppers in One-

Dollar-Stores (10-Schilling-Laden in the Austrian version), who, of course, do not constitute the recently pauperized bottom third of society but (we are, remember, in the Empire of the Fun) *Intelligent Shoppers!* Anyhow, nothing should surprise us in the realm of cultural misunderstandings, when Europeans could (mis)read Elvis Presley as a left-wing working-class hero in the 1950s.

The history of mentalities is always a history of ambiguities,[1] and the history of the meaning of America in European discourse(s) especially so.[2] Since Columbus, the European reaction to America has been situated somewhere between condescension and fear, ignorance and fascination, superiority complexes and inferiority feelings, apprehension and (dis)information, appropriation and (mis)use. At best, it resembled a marriage of convenience where alienation (on both sides) was programmed, at worst a dangerous mixture of a love-hate relationship (in the German term *Hass-Liebe*, hate comes first) that hardly ever could overcome the worst clichés and stereotypes.

But even the area of the never changing, the *longue durée*, is under fire. For many a European Christmas (which is substituted by X-Mas as much as the Christ Child is substituted by Santa Claus, especially in advertisements), the favorite presents for girls and boys were Barbie dolls and Disney toys; the (German) computer games Stunt Race and Dr. Robotnik's Mean Beam Machine; the Grow Up *Kindertisch* as well as, *nomen est omen*, the Holy Sport Skateboard! The top five Austrian entertainment games were Activity, Yenga, Coco Crazy, Nobody is Perfect, and Trivial Pursuit. During the 1990s Toys 'R Us opened close to a hundred gigantic stores all over Europe – seven in Austria – and that company alone is dominating between one-fourth and one-third of the respective markets. Since 1995, in-line skating has been the

---

1   Jacques Le Goff, "Les mentalités: Une histoire ambigue" [Mentalities: an ambiguous history], in *Faire de l'histoire* [Making history], ed. Jacques Le Goff and Pierre Nora (Paris, 1974), vol. 3.
2   Rob Kroes, *If You've Seen One, You've Seen the Mall: Europeans and American Mass Culture* (Chicago, 1997), ix–xiv and 1–42; Reinhold Wagnleitner, *Coca-Colonization and the Cold War: The Cultural Mission of the United States in Austria after the Second World War* (Chapel Hill, 1994): ix–xiv and 1–45.

latest craze in Vienna, and Beach Ball has conquered Austrian lake sides and swimming pools since the summer of 1997.

Within one year, the image of basketball in Germany was transformed from an old-fashioned, unexciting, and relatively boring sport to absolutely hip entertainment. In 1992 all German TV stations together had transmitted a meager 4.3 hours of basketball. In the first seven months of 1993, ARD, ZDF, RTL, and SAT–1 alone showed 478 hours! Basketball had reached the third position in the top ten of German televised sports, behind tennis and soccer. The age group eleven to nineteen underwent a veritable basketball euphoria: 60.5 percent of young Germans chose basketball as their favorite sport-soccer (59.5) and tennis (46.9) came in second and third.[3]

What had happened? Had the German basketball team become world champions or triumphed in any other international competition? No. In 1992, the U.S. "Dream Team" had become Olympic gods in Barcelona, thereby adding a new meaning to the phrase "American Dream," and the explosion of cable and satellite television brought the breathtaking antics of U.S. NBA stars into more and more households. Of course, this is not an exclusively German phenomenon at all. *NBA-Entertainment* exports its shows already to more than one hundred countries in an ever growing market, and the global success of U.S. basketball is just one of the most recent examples of the striking worldwide attraction of many facets of American popular culture.

The sudden invasion of American sports fashions during the 1990s sounded the alarm bells for the major European sports accessory companies. Their strategy was exemplary for what countless European businesses have done for decades to revamp their sales. They counteracted by appropriating "typically American" images (and real U.S. sales strategies) for their products. Adidas, which battled the image of producing granddaddy's leisure outfit,

---

3 Lars Haider, "Das Fernsehen läßt die Riesen wachsen" [Television makes the giants grow], in *Kicker Sportmagazin* 96 (1993). See Wolfgang Braun, "Where have you gone, Joe DiMaggio? Die Geschichte der US-Teamsportarten und ihre Verbreitung in Europa" [Where have you gone, Joe DiMaggio? The history of U.S. team sports and their dissemination in Europe] (M.A. thesis, University of Salzburg, 1994).

successfully promoted Street Ball, a tough version of basketball. In the German Street-Ball-Challenge of 1993 alone, twenty-three thousand players participated in six thousand teams and the major games were watched by an audience of between forty and eighty thousand people. Accompanied by the soundtrack of HipHop and Rap, this "European" sales campaign succeeded (like many others before), in combining some modules of the "typically American" to sell their oversized (and overprized) products: the violence, aggressiveness, and smartness of the street, the global visibility and popularity of American stars – which, in the case of African-American sports stars beautifully amalgamates the image of the proverbial outsider and underdog with the achievement of the American Dream – and the overall immense attraction of U.S. popular culture.

Surely these ad campaigns are not lacking irony. In order to boost their sales, these companies veil their products with images of boisterous street gangs of the Bronx and Los Angeles whose macho violence most of their executives vehemently detest in public when connected with European youth (especially their own children). And while the world soccer association FIFA massively promotes soccer in the United States and European soccer managers and trainers, millionaires most of them, lachrymosely lament the fact that saturated, spoiled European kids stopped playing soccer in the streets (one of the major former recruitment centers), Adidas's major European competitor, Puma, has started a campaign for Street Soccer (32,000 participants in 150 German cities in 1994). Many youngsters now prefer individualist sports, like tennis and snowboarding, skateboarding, and even golf (with its highest approval rating in Germany in the age group *under* eighteen), and the image of the team sport soccer seems to be as old as daddy or, worse, socialism. Not so that of Street Soccer, which is the soccer for individualists who, of course, wear the Puma Street Soccer Collection.

"All of Germany Is Being Turned Into a Fun Park" mocked a *Spiegel* story on 15 September 1997. Despite (or because of) a dramatic explosion in unemployment, theme parks are mushrooming for the German *Erlebnis-Konsumenten* (in short *E-Mensch*, or adventure consumer) with the *Alpine Center Ruhr* and *Warner's Movie World* (both in Bottrop), the *Ocean Park* in Bremerhaven, the *Space Park* in Bremen, the *Fun-Temple* in Hannover, the *Holiday Park* in Hassloch, and countless *Urban Entertainment Centers* designed by *Imagineers* who all worship at the altar of Disney. The magic of the Empire of the Fun, it seems, even turns boring Old World countries into cool Adventure Lands.

And at the end of the twentieth century the fun frontier is not bound to planet earth any more. When the lunar module "Eagle" had descended from the command module "Columbia" to the moon's Mare Tranquillitatis in July 1969, the global audience could still watch a *classical* mixture of discovery and conquest deeply rooted in many hundreds of years of traditional European attempts to take over the world. After all, Neil Armstrong and Edwin A. Aldrin rammed the Stars and Stripes into the lunar barrenness exactly in the same manner as they had seen depicted in hundreds of pictures of European conquerors taking possession of the New World. Consequently, three craters of the moon were named after Armstrong, Aldrin, and Michael Collins, because naming has been synonymous with taking possession since antiquity. The lunar *mission* therefore was clearly anchored in the tradition of the occident (*das Abendland*). The quasireligious Christian blessing of Manifest Destiny was mixed (again) with scientific discovery and military conquest – after all, the three American astronauts shot through space on *Apollo 11*.

Thirty years later, the situation could not have been more different. No trace of *Apollo* (the god of rationality) any more, *Dionysus* (the god of fun) now also reigns supreme on other planets of the solar system. When the Mars Mobile received its orders from Houston in July 1997, it did not meet any classical gods, but exciting Martian Rock Stars. All analyzed rocks were named after popular American comic heroes – Yogi Bear and Barnacle Bill, Casper and Scoobie Doo and, what's more, the *whole world* understood! The Empire of the Fun had also conquered the Planet of War just as the awfully entertaining idea of virtual (comic) wars, with their tremendously euphemistic Newspeak vocabulary of *surgical strikes* and *collateral damage*, had hit home on planet earth.[4]

In 1992, 7.8 million Austrians bought more than 8 million pairs of jeans. In the same year, the business of McDonald's in Austria grew 21 percent. While 35 million Austrian customers were counted in 1992, more than 70 million ate at McDonald's in 1997, which means that, statistically, every Austrian visited a McDonald's restaurant ten times during that year. In 1994 the annual revenue of McDonald's Austria was 1.87 billion Austrian schillings, and in 1997, 3 billion schillings ($280 million). The doubling of guests in six and of revenue in three years marks a singular economic countertrend in a period when all other restaurants and Austrian tourism in general were experiencing the most extreme crisis since the Second World War. Pizza Hut (Pepsi Cola) and Submarine Sandwiches now complete the mix, and in company business reports McDonald's Austria now ranges as one of the three best markets worldwide (before Germany). Of course, very few Austrian critics of McDonald's will admit that their favorite *heisse Würstl* (frankfurters) are fast food par excellence and that mountain biking, a new sport that is plaguing wanderers and the environment alike, has very little to do with the United States – still how many would engage in a sport unfashionably called *Bergradfahren*?

European skinheads regularly beat their victims with American baseball bats, and the latest craze of proving one's daring for mega-bored European (and Latin American) youths has become air bagging, car hopping, and underground surfing (in German: *S-Bahn-Surfen*). What can the appropriate Austrian answer be but *Schluchting* or *Canyoning* (jumping up and down the ravines of the Alps, with the homo Alpinus hanging on ropes)? While *bodybuilding* is out, *bodystyling* is in, and the chic are interested not only in wellness but also in mindmapping. Advocates of globalization most certainly rejoiced when they heard that the profiteers of the dramatic changes in the former Soviet Union started

4 *Newsweek*, 13 April 1992, 14.

to call themselves, what else but: *businessmeni*. Yet, what kind of globalization is at work when prices in all good stores in Moscow are only given in U.S. dollars (where can I pay in rubles on Fifth Avenue?) or when four Russian gangsters demand $10 million as ransom for their kidnap victims at the end of 1993?

For many centuries the term *America* has been most ambivalently placed in the landscapes of most European minds: on the one hand, it has represented the prime example of (post)modernity and a laboratory for global social change, on the other, it has stood for a nostalgia for a pioneering past and simple freedom. Since Columbus, America has been seen as paradise or hell, as utopia or dystopia. The phantasmagorias that were provoked by America prove that the discovery of the New World was accompanied by a simultaneous *invention* of America. In the European cognitive maps America either became a part of Europe's illusionary past (under the heading of the paradisiacal second chance of the New Adam) or otherwise part of anticipatory dreams of America as Europe's future which, more often than not, quite fittingly turned into nightmares.

How else could we explain the fact that more than 1.5 million *Zippo* lighters are sold annually in France alone because, as the French film critic Eric Leguebe insists, their metallic click reminds French consumers of the sound of the *Peacemaker* (Colt)? Or why would the French company *Chevignon* make more than $100 million profit annually with a clothing line named "American Classic"? Can anyone in their wildest dreams imagine a clothing line successfully advertising itself as "Australian Classic"? Not without reason, *Newsweek* reminded its readers on the occasion of the opening of Euro-Disney in 1992 of one of the (not so hidden) secrets of contemporary European culture: "And perhaps the only notion shared by all is one no European will ever confess out loud: the cultural capital of the new Europe is not Paris or London. It's Hollywood."[5]

After initial difficulties, Euro-Disney has become a smashing success and a jewel in the crown of the Disney corporation. Be-

---

5 "Die Europaeer haben Mickey-Maus ins Herz geschlossen" [The Europeans have fallen in love with Mickey Mouse], *Die Presse*, 28 April 1998.

tween 1993 and 1997 visitor numbers grew from 9.7 to 12.7 million. Euro-Disney's fast food diners have become "France's biggest restaurant," selling 27 million portions in 1997 alone. Half of the 1997 revenue of a billion dollars remained as profit, and the first quarter of 1998 experienced a 16 percent growth in visitors. Since its opening no fewer than 60 million Europeans have visited Euro-Disney, 14 percent of them Germans, 20 percent from the Benelux countries, and 38 percent French.[6]

The list of the appropriation and rearrangement of various modules of "typical American" images, of their use and misuse by Europeans from all nations and walks of life, is nearly endless. For centuries, "America" (probably more as construct, invention, and simulation than as "reality") has functioned as a distorting mirror and as a screen on which European social, economic, political, and cultural changes were reflected and, often conveniently, misinterpreted. Even the archbishop of Bologna, Cardinal Giacomo Biffi, on 13 March 1994, had to resort to the worst bête noir of many a cultural critic to make one point clear: the introduction of female priests in the Catholic church would approximate the substitution of Coca-Cola for wine in holy mass.

Act II: The Cold War as Sporting Event: Real Consumption vs. Real Communism

So what has all that to do with the Cold War and the American Century? Quite a lot, if we consider not only the political, military, and economic character of that struggle but also its profound cultural implications – in the widest sense. If we understand the early Cold War years as a period of essential crises especially, but not exclusively, for traditional European cultures as a result of the immense human and material losses and moral depravity after the Second World War, then the seemingly endless flow of "American" goods and ideas into everyday European life and consciousness acquires a different dimension.

---

6   Howard Temperley and Malcolm Bradbury, eds., *Introduction to American Studies*, 2d ed. (London, 1989), 303; Geir Lundestad, *The American Empire* (New York, 1990), 40.

Of course, but what about the rest of Europe's population?

My central argument runs like this: however important the military power and political promise of the United States were for setting the foundation for American successes in Cold War Europe, it was the American economic and cultural attraction that really won over the hearts and minds of the majorities of young people for Western democracy. To be sure, abstract American freedoms and liberties had their attraction for quite a few. But how much greater was their appeal when they came in a new package – as Liberty Corn, Freedom Grain, and Equality Beans? However alien, especially for the older generation, some American practices seemed, however often American gadget mania was ridiculed, however much American naiveté and pragmatism were mocked, however strongly *American civilization* was despised – and the list is long – the century-old attraction the United States had held especially for the European poor was now bolstered by a variety of important factors: the presence of the incredibly powerful, rich, and wasteful U.S. Army, the generous assistance programs, and the ubiquitous presence of American wealth and good life in the products of American popular culture which had an unbeatable allure, especially for the young. *The Birth of Cool* (Miles Davis) in January 1949 made it clear that, despite the encroaching menace of McCarthyism, the cold of the Cold War was situated on the other side of the iron curtain.

In 1945, more than ever before, the United States signified the codes of modernity and promised the pursuit of happiness in its most updated version, as the pursuit of consumption. Whenever real consumption climbed into the ring, chances were high that real socialism had to be counted out. But a first caveat is necessary here: modernization and consumption are not particularly "American," and although they have taken on an increasingly American look in twentieth-century Europe, they are mostly of European origin. If terms connoting continents or nations make any sense at all in this context, which is rather doubtful, then we are not witnessing the *Americanization* of the world, but rather its Euro-Americanization.

The great majority of European women and men, the defeated as well as the victors, wanted nothing more than to go on with their lives, find family members, mourn the dead, overcome (or cultivate) their hatred(s), live in peace, get fed, make love, work, earn money, be left alone, and – after all those years of killing, running for shelter, fearing for loved ones, and scraping along – to have some fun again. But the devastation, both physical and moral, seemed too immense, the losses too great, economic improvement too slow, and fun much too far away.

In this crisis, the strong attraction of the materially (and thereby culturally) most powerful competitor, the United States, surely cannot come as too much of a surprise – especially as millions of American emissaries were not too far away at all. They were right there on the spot. And while some GIs did not always act like victors, they certainly looked the part. They were well fed, healthy, young, and sex- and fun-hungry, and they provided a daily demonstration of American abundance and wealth. They had everything Europeans were craving for and more: cigarettes, nylons, chocolate, and penicillin, which were probably more valuable than their dollars on the black market. In 1946, the starving and freezing people of Salzburg were quite impressed when they learned that the U.S. occupation army managed to feed its fifteen thousand troops sixty thousand portions of ice cream as dessert on a daily basis. Of course, the GIs' proverbial nonchalance and slackness – feet on the table and chewing gum seemed the utmost crimes – provoked never-ending parental admonitions and warnings. But that endeared them even more to large groups of the young who had had more than enough of senseless order and military marching music. Quite a few secretly suspected that an army advancing to the rhythm of Swing certainly *deserved* to win the war.

Never before had one nation been economically as overwhelmingly powerful as the United States in the years after 1945, not even Great Britain at the peak of its power in the middle of the nineteenth century. While the Second World War had left large parts of Europe and Asia in ruins, the United States emerged as the only undisputed economic superpower – and the propaganda drums of the United States made sure that this stunning success could not be ignored in Europe.

The American economic miracle was of unprecedented proportion as the gigantic leap in airplane construction exemplifies. In 1939 fewer than six thousand planes (civil and military) had been produced in the United States. When the war was over, more than three hundred thousand planes had left U.S. factories. In 1945, with roughly 6 percent of the world's population, the United States produced 46 percent of the world's electric power and consumed 40 percent of the world's energy. Its businesses controlled 59 percent of the world's oil reserves and 60 percent of the world's cars were driven on American roads. The United States produced one hundred times more cars than the Soviet Union and eight times as many as Germany, Britain, and France combined. In 1949, Americans used 70 percent of all telephones, 80 percent of all refrigerators, and close to 100 percent of all television sets. In the same year average Americans earned twice as much as Britons, three times as much as the French, five times as much as Germans, and seven times as much as Russians. By 1950, the United States possessed roughly 50 percent of the world's monetary gold, reserve currencies, and IMF reserves, and its per capita income was 44 percent above that of 1929.[7]

When the Second World War was over, the United States alone produced nearly as many goods as all other countries combined. While that lead slowly diminished, partially as a result of U.S. assistance and investments in former ally and enemy countries, to 40 percent of world GNP in 1950 and 30 percent in 1960, the impression of America as the land of milk and honey in the crucial first decades of the Cold War was never at stake, despite the ridicule and mockery of many critics. Even when the crisis signs could no longer be overlooked, the cultural parameters had been rooted too deeply in favor of the United States. In the symbolic war between the systems of symbols, the power of America was never rivaled. The Soviet Union may have been the first in space,

---

7 See David W. Ellwood and Rob Kroes, eds., *Hollywood in Europe: Experiences of a Cultural Hegemony* (Amsterdam, 1994); Mike-Frank G. Epitropoulos and Victor Roudometof, eds., *American Culture in Europe: Interdisciplinary Perspectives* (New York, 1998); Lary May, "Made for Export: Hollywood and the Creation of Cold War Americanism, 1940–1958," in *Empire: American Studies*, ed. John G. Blair and Reinhold Wagnleitner (Tuebingen, 1997), 91–121.

but it always came in last in the game of (material) cultures. The famous kitchen debate between Richard Nixon and Nikita Khrushchev may have been rather ludicrous, yet one point is surely undisputed: the *American* kitchen set the standards. The absurdity of the epithet "Evil Empire" surely remains supreme because the problem never really was whether the Soviet empire was evil but whether it was an *empire* at all, at least in cultural terms. Whoever, in Poland or Czechoslovakia, in Hungary or Romania, not to mention France and Italy, followed the fashions of Moscow? Where are the Muscovite cultural Cold War trend setters? Why did Nikita Khrushchev (just like Yves Montand) want to visit Hollywood (and Marilyn Monroe) while Richard Nixon enjoyed the (classical) pleasures of the Bolshoi Ballet?

These material advantages and disadvantages of the respective players in the field of transmitting their ideas, of conveying their mission, of interpreting their versions of the good life to far away peoples were decisive within the context of the cultural Cold War. Between 1940 and 1950 the United States not only controlled more than 80 percent of all major inventions, it also established a massive, long-lasting advantage in all those areas of technological innovations that are colloquially referred to as communication technology. For many years this, metaphorically speaking, technological lead in the sectors of transmitters, amplifiers, loudspeakers, and screens has made the United States the most visible and audible land of the world.[8] Quite often, though, the commu-

8   Most recently Kyoko Hirano, *Mr. Smith Goes to Tokyo: Japanese Cinema Under the American Occupation, 1945–1952* (Washington, 1992); Richard Kuisel, *Seducing the French: The Dilemma of Americanization* (Berkeley, 1993); Wagnleitner, *Coca-Colonization*; Ralph Willett, *The Americanization of Germany, 1945–1949* (London, 1989); Roger Rollin, ed., *The Americanization of the Global Village: Essays in Comparative Popular Culture* (Bowling Green, 1989); Timothy Ryback, *Rock Around the Bloc: A History of Rock Music in Eastern Europe and the Soviet Union* (New York, 1990); Steven F. White, *Progressive Renaissance: America and the Reconstruction of Italian Education, 1943–1962* (New York, 1991); Nicholas Haiducek, *Japanese Education: Made in the U.S.A.* (New York, 1991); Rob Kroes, Robert W. Rydell, and Doeko F. J. Bosscher, eds., *Cultural Transmissions and Receptions: American Mass Culture in Europe* (Amsterdam, 1993); Richard P. Horwitz, ed., *Exporting America: Essays on American Studies Abroad* (New York, 1993); David H. Flaherty and Frank E. Manning, eds., *The Beaver Bites Back? American Popular Culture in Canada* (Montreal, 1993); Scott Shane, *Dismantling the Iron Curtain: How Information Ended the Soviet Union* (Chicago, 1994); Philip H. Melling and Jon Roper, eds., *Americanization and the Transformation of World Cultures: Melting Pot or Cultural Chernobyl?* (New York, 1996); Walter L.

nication was rather one-sided, and while few doubted that the United States had the best loudspeakers, quite a few also wished that Uncle Sam would have better hearing and seeing aids.

Even when this technological lead eroded, when the hardware increasingly became Japanese or European, the cultural software still predominantly remained American, or at least had an American look. Although Columbia now belongs to Sony, what people really want to hear in their walkmen (also by Sony) is (mostly) American or, at least, American-inspired music. Even the unspeakable Austrian *volkstümliche* music, with its Alpine schmaltz and supposedly traditional *Gemütlichkeit*, uses modernized beats, instrumentation, and arrangements, which are clearly copied from U.S. pop. Lucio Dalla may be as Bolognese as can be, yet his music is not imaginable without American blues, jazz, funk, and rock. And Vladimir Vysotzky (until his untimely death in 1980) established himself as the most important pop star of the Soviet Union not only because of his dark Russian guitar poetry but exactly because he acted like an American pop star – excesses and scandals included – appropriating the image of the streetwise tough guy: a rather unusual but surprisingly effective combination of Charles Bronson and Bob Dylan!

This omnipresence of U.S. pop culture (the "real" thing) and the appropriated regional versions (Johnny Halliday was a *French* rock star and examples abound aplenty) represent one of the most important cultural developments of the twentieth century. Without this global attraction it would otherwise be completely impossible to explain the fact that the culture industries of the United States were able to maximize their profits like never before throughout the 1980s, a period when most other sectors of the U.S. economy experienced their deepest crisis since the Great Depression. It really seems that there's no business like show *business* – arms industries excepted, of course: but then it has become somewhat difficult to distinguish between the two. Most recent U.S.

Hixson, *Parting the Curtain: Propaganda, Culture, and the Cold War, 1954–1961* (New York, 1997); Richard F. Pells, *Not Like US: How Europeans Loved, Hated and Transformed American Culture Since World War II* (New York, 1997).

wars and invasions, under the seal of the United Nations, either resembled computer games (for the audiences, not for the victims), or seemed at least staged for prime time television.

ACT III: Washington and Hollywood:
Two Mighty Brothers in Arms

The central question here then quite obviously must be: was (and is) this global success of American pop culture only the result of the quality of its products? Or just a question of the economics of scale? Or the victory of the principles of free-market forces and the fair play of the respective players? Or was there an active, maybe even decisive role played by the American state in selling the products of U.S. (popular) culture to foreign audiences? Put the other way around: did the American state actively employ the messages of American (popular) culture for other (political and economic) ends? The answer to all these questions could be an unqualified yes – as long as we exclude the sacred principles of free-market forces and fair play.

All wars, especially all modern wars, are (also) propaganda wars, wars of words and pictures, wars of symbols and images, in short, wars over cultural hegemony – and the Cold War *especially* so. Never before had societies been able to draw on such a wide array of technologies and scientific achievements to persuade the losers and the winners of the Second World War alike of their (good) intentions and political, economic, and cultural promises. Immediately after the war, all four Allies tried everything to impress the population of their occupation zones with their cultural achievements. But while the British and French programs were usually balancing close to a financial abyss or, tactically even worse, were too elitist, the cultural initiatives of the Soviet Union hardly reached more than tiny minorities in most countries. Only one country had all the necessary ingredients as well as the energy and verve to win the (cultural) struggle for its version of modernity in the ruins of Europe, the United States: the political missionary zeal for the ensuing crusade for the American way of life, combined with enormous material resources, and a popular culture with mass appeal transcending many national and ethnic cultural tastes and differences: otherwise, it would never have had a chance to become popular within the United States in the first place.

Official U.S. cultural propaganda was strongest in the liberated and temporarily occupied former enemy territories, but certainly not restricted to them: American economic assistance, loans, investments, military installations, and the diffusion of popular culture guaranteed a strong American presence in all other European states under the U.S. umbrella. In Austria, Germany, and Italy these U.S. reeducation and reorientation programs initially had been predominantly designed to reestablish parliamentary democracies with capitalist free-market economies by fighting any remnants of fascism, National Socialism, and militarism. U.S. experts believed that fascist behavior patterns and autocratic attitudes, which had been diagnosed as a result of fascist brainwashing, could be eliminated only by democratic decontamination: just as DDT was applied for the disinfection of bodies, only sufficient doses of *the American way* would guarantee the decontamination of brains.

In the early period of occupation no field of culture escaped the scrutiny of controls: theaters and cinemas, operas and concerts, newspapers and journals, books, pamphlets, and advertisements, news agencies and radio stations, even circuses, balls, puppet theaters, street markets, and religious processions. In Austria, Germany, and Italy the U.S. Army established huge cultural public relations organizations that had four major objectives: to erase as many remnants of fascism as possible; to nip in the bud or discredit all Communist cultural activities; to guarantee the most positive presentation of all that was American; and to create the most efficient channels for the importation of U.S. (cultural) products, which had been cut off from these markets at least since the beginning of the war.

Soon the kid gloves in the cultural-ideological struggle against the former Soviet ally were taken off. While the initially strict denazification policies became sacrificed on the altar of the Cold War, the fight against communism dominated all American cultural activities. These efforts went far beyond the occupied territories and targeted all European countries, *including* those behind the iron curtain. These cultural agencies of the U.S. Army founded newspapers, news agencies, and radio stations. They promoted American arts and artists from literature to music, from theater to film, from painting to dance. They organized the translation of books and initiated the revision of school curricula. They assisted in the exchange-of-person programs and engaged in countless youth activities, from sports contests to Christmas parties, from soap-box derbies to youth camps. Understandably these youth activities constituted a central part of the whole strategy: in Austria alone 577 4–H Clubs were organized, 264 of them in the Soviet Zone of occupation!

These U.S. agencies not only cleared the road and restored the position of those U.S. businesses that had already controlled large parts of the European markets before the Second World War, like the U.S. film industry. They also managed to build the bridgeheads in many areas where American companies had been less successful, for example, in exporting American literature. The influence of this U.S. cultural offensive on the European media landscape was enormous. Thousands of journalists were trained on the spot and media experts also belonged to the top-priority group within the exchange programs. Such strategies familiarized many European opinion leaders in a variety of professions with the United States and guaranteed long-range goodwill.

All of a sudden, printed paper and airwaves, cinema and television screens, America Houses and Information Centers, theaters and concert halls, youth clubs and educational facilities (from kindergarten to university), trade union and business organizations were flooded by messages from America. U.S. cultural products seemed to appear everywhere: even in Vienna the operetta soon had to live in peaceful coexistence with the musical.

All groups of societies were targeted: from business to trade unions, from farmers to professionals, from artists to teachers, from children to youth groups. This direct intervention of the

American state in these cultures is well documented and analyzed.[9] Still, not all of the results were intended and some were quite surprising – for the European elites as well as for those within the United States. American planners of this massive cultural reorientation had been aware that they needed the cooperation of contemporary as well as future European elites for the creation of the "One World" of the American Century. But wherever these elites stood politically, one thing united most of them: their cultural anti-Americanism.

Ironically, most American cultural experts shared this aversion to most products of U.S. mass culture. They were convinced that the traditional prejudices against "American civilization" could only be broken by a constant demonstration of the quality of high culture in the United States, by constantly reminding their European audiences that the United States was not only the cultural equal of Europe but deserved the role of standard bearer of the culture of the occident (*das Abendland*) not only because of its military and economic might but even more so because of its cultural and moral achievements. But their parade of John Dos Passos and William Faulkner, Aaron Copland and Samuel Barber only reached a few. Most wanted Mickey Spillane and Mickey Mouse, Frank Sinatra and Elvis Presley.

It is quite telling that the enlistment of American popular culture in the service of the political goals of official U.S. cultural propaganda initially met strong resistance within the agencies concerned. Of course, they knew that jazz and Hollywood already had eroded the cultural hegemony of the WASPs within the United States, and they had little interest in repeating that experience in Europe, thereby strengthening European prejudices even more – like a self-fulfilling prophecy. But then, jazz, rock 'n' roll, and Hollywood did not need U.S. cultural propaganda as desperately

---

9 S. E. Siwek, "The Dimensions of the Export of American Mass Culture," in *The New Global Culture: Is It American? Is It Good for America? Is It Good for the World?* ed. Ben J. Wattenberg (Washington, 1992), 1–49; Annemoon van Hemel, Hans Mommaas and Cas Smithuijsen, eds., *Trading Culture: GATT, European Cultural Policies and the Transatlantic Market* (Amsterdam, 1996); David Puttnam, *The Undeclared War: The Struggle for Control of the World's Film Industry* (London, 1997).

as U.S. cultural propaganda needed jazz, rock 'n' roll, and Hollywood.

Film history is world history and nowhere else is U.S. cultural hegemony as nearly all-encompassing as in the area of movies. Nowhere else has the American Century become so much a "reality" as in the collective subconscious and communal dreams of the American movie empire, where *reel* history becomes *real* history. The global domination of the American film industry was never felt as strongly as in the last years of the twentieth century, not even immediately after 1945. While the share of foreign movies in the American market fell from 7 to hardly measurable 1 percent between 1970 and 1990, the profits of U.S. movies in foreign markets more than doubled between 1985 and 1990 alone – from $740 million to $1.65 billion. In 1995, Hollywood's foreign profits amounted to half of all its earnings, and the foreign side of the business continued to become increasingly important. While domestic profits had grown a mere 39 percent between 1985 and 1990, profits from foreign markets exploded by 124 percent in the same period. In these five years, profits of Hollywood companies grew by 741 percent in South Korea, 198 percent in Brazil, 188 percent in Spain, 187 percent in the United Kingdom and Ireland, 185 percent in Germany and Austria, 162 percent in Belgium, 149 percent in the Netherlands and Taiwan, 148 percent in Japan, 145 in Sweden, 144 percent in Switzerland, 133 percent in Italy, 109 percent in France, 107 percent in Australia, and 63 percent in Canada.[10]

During the 1990s, between 85 and 95 percent of all movies on Western European screens were of American origin, and Eastern Europe was so completely swamped by U.S. films that it is sometimes difficult to find a non-American movie in Moscow, Warsaw, or Budapest.[11] European film production has declined dramatically, and these trends have been aggravated by the explo-

10   During the weekend of 19–21 February 1993 only 6 Russian movies were shown in the cinemas of Moscow, as opposed to 111 U.S. films.
11   Reinhold Wagnleitner, "American Popular Culture on the Internet: A Further Step in Americanization or Globalization?" December 1997, http://www.salsem.ac.at/csal/progs/internet/intra.htm.

sion of European satellite and cable channels, the privatization of electronic media, and the increase of the economic importance of video sales and rentals. The already unhealthy European film industry was simply unable to produce anything on the economic scale necessary, and since 1990 the European markets, with their approximately ten-fold increase of time-slots, have been turned into an economic paradise for U.S. companies and their European subsidiaries, as well as for a few European media moguls.

The U.S. media industry therefore is the real heavy industry of the American Century, and Hollywood its most important center of education. In addition, about 80 percent of all information saved in computers is written in English, and the Internet still speaks a heavily accented American English.[12] Although all statistical data about the Internet, the hippest of hype's hype, are notoriously unreliable and usually out of date quicker than published, all surveys show that American users and companies dominate between 65 and 85 percent of cyberspace, while Europeans and Asians make up between 16 and 6 and 14 and 8 percent respectively.[13] The pending antitrust lawsuit against Microsoft at the end of the twentieth century may have the same (in)significance as the court action against Standard Oil at its beginning. While *Disneyfication* and *Microsoftization* have been added to *Coca-Colonization* and *McDonaldization* during the second half of the twentieth century, we may soon be facing a new virtual alternative as the trend of the new millenium: *Encartafication* vs. emancipation.

Although large groups of the conservative elites in postwar Europe hardly despised anything more than "American civilization," they were no longer in a position to go it alone. Many had discredited themselves as collaborators with or sympathizers of fascism and lacked the financial resources to reestablish a situation even remotely resembling the status quo ante without American help. Anticommunism and the fear of Soviet aggression united the majorities from conservatives to Social Democrats, from lib-

12 See http://www.nua.org/surveys/1996graphs/location.html; and http://www.cyberatlas.com/geographics.html.
13 David Porter, ed., *Internet Culture* (London, 1997).

erals to nationalist splinter groups, and despite the Communist contribution to the resistance movements and their long-lasting attraction for many intellectuals and artists, especially in France and Italy, they always remained more or less outside the cultural mainstream. Third Way advocates, finally, had no chance because the freezing political climate hardly allowed any neutral positions.

The conservatives (and Social Democrats) seemed to have no alternative to American assistance. But American aid meant modernization, rationalization, economic cooperation, and international integration on unprecedented levels. Richard F. Kuisel has demonstrated very well what it took to seduce the French to accept and adapt to these changes; how these transformations, the dilemma of Americanization, influenced all sectors of French society: from a seemingly impossible coalition between wine farmers and Communists who fought the supposedly poisonous Coca-Cola to grudging conservative entrepreneurs who refused to admit that their days of paternalistic business ways were finally over.[14]

The Marshall Plan, itself probably the most important propaganda victory of the United States, had many more implications than strictly economic ones. It not only profoundly changed the whole culture of business but also *the business of culture*. An important part of investments, for example, in electrification, contributed to the rapid establishment of a dense web of communication over all participating countries. Now the message of the nerve center of the world system could practically reach all households, even in the remotest rural areas. In its ideological essence, the Marshall Plan was the ideology to end all ideologies. It promised to abolish class conflict, not through redistribution, but through economic growth, the solution of social problems through supposedly ideology-free social engineering – in short, the metamorphosis of politics into economy.[15]

makes sense.

14   Kuisel, *Seducing the French*.
15   Charles S. Maier, "The Politics of Productivity: Foundations of American International Economic Policy After World War II," *International Organization* 31 (Autumn 1977): 607–33.

Ironically, while this participation in the economic miracle of Western Europe reestablished some of the economic and political power of the former elites, it also slowly weakened and finally eroded their cultural hegemony, their power as gatekeepers over the definition of what constitutes a desirable national culture. The defeat of fascism, which, first and foremost, had been a violent revolt against Western culture, "paved the way for the European states to accede to an American peace premised on free trade of goods and ideas and thereby relinquish a conception of nation-hood that presumed sovereignty over culture."[16]

Most European middle-aged and older conservatives (on the right and the left) experienced the cultural consequences of this dramatically accelerated modernization – which mostly meant an adaptation to U.S. models as cultural invasion of massive proportions, in short, as American cultural imperialism. Of course, few Europeans ever asked themselves what their cultures had done to the non-European world, and it could be argued that the greatest propaganda achievement of the Cold War was contained in the name itself: because it was a *Cold* War only when we consider Europe, but what about the many millions of casualties in Africa, Asia, and Latin America? In the face of fascist and National Socialist cultural imperialism the American version can certainly be interpreted as a necessary antidote. And, furthermore, the American cultural empire was, at least partially, an empire by invitation: it contained many characteristics of *self*-colonization.

Some aspects of modern mass cultures (not only those inspired by the United States), especially their mystification, idolization, and glorification of violence, give growing cause for concern. But American popular culture is not only a world in itself, it is a world culture providing its adepts with a myriad of choices. One of the secrets of the global success of American popular culture lies in the fact that "it has been able to absorb and assimilate forms and material from anywhere, and yet reproduce them as

---

16 Victoria deGrazia, "Mass Culture and Sovereignty. The American Challenge to European Cinemas, 1920–1960," *Journal of Modern History* 61 (1989): 53–87.

specifically 'American.'"[17] This "American" popular culture then, with strong support from the American state, managed to become a global semiculture, which, as Todd Gitlin has argued, "coexists with local cultures and sensibilities more than it replaces them."[18] It is no coincidence that the secret anthem of the European "youth rebellion" of the 1960s, which was supposedly anti-American, was "We Shall Overcome" and that most protesters wore jeans and T-shirts.

The fast adaptation of American popular culture by many Europeans after the Second World War certainly contributed positively to the democratization of these societies. It rejuvenated and revitalized European postwar cultures with its elementary connotations of freedom, casualness, vitality, liberality, modernity, and youthfulness.[19] It informalized societies, made them more elastic and differentiated, opened new ways of expression for upwardly mobile social groups (and the younger generation of the establishment alike). Soon the jeans pockets were full of money and, paradoxically, the market orientation of the consumption and culture industries, while strengthening the power of corporate capitalism, also weakened the position of the traditional gatekeepers and watchers of culture (the rich but even more so the educated) in favor of the younger generation and the lower classes. So the submission to the dictates of the market and business also contained an element of liberation from the straitjackets of traditional customs and mores.[20]

Gender relations and roles were influenced too, not only in Europe and Asia but also in the United States, where millions of women had to wait (some didn't) for their loved ones. While the

17   Richard Maltby, *Passing Parade: A History of Popular Culture in the Twentieth Century* (New York, 1989), 13.
18   Todd Gitlin, "The New Global Popular Culture: Is It American?" *The American Enterprise* (May/June 1992): 74; Reinhold Wagnleitner, "Sitting in the Jungle of the Global Market Place, Watching the American Tiger Prance: Some Fast Food for Thought on American Cultural Imperialism," in Wattenberg, ed., *New Global Culture*, 1–24.
19   Mel van Elteren, *Imagining America: Dutch Youth and Its Sense of Place* (Tilburg, 1994).
20   Kaspar Maase, *Bravo Amerika: Erkundungen zur Jugendkultur der Bundesrepublik in den fünfziger Jahren* [Bravo America: Observations on the youth culture of the Federal Republic of Germany in the 1950s] (Hamburg, 1992).

social and economic influences of fascism and National Socialism, the Second World War and the postwar reconstruction period on women's lives (for example, the German *Trümmerfrauen*)
have been thoroughly studied in their respective national contexts, the implications of "Americanization" for possible changes
of gender relations still needs further analysis.[21] More attention
has to be paid also to the tens of thousands of women driven into
prostitution, the war brides emigrating to the United States, and
the considerable number of women with short term relationships
with GIs. Many of these women were shunned by society – especially if these contacts resulted in children.[22] When the first year
of occupation was over, ninety thousand had already been born
in the American zone of Germany alone. Many men, already
defeated on the battlefields, now also experienced another defeat
closer to home. More often than not the Chocolate Girls were
reviled as *Ami-Huren* (Ami-whores) and their offspring as
Besatzungskinder (occupation-children). One does not need too
much fantasy to imagine what these women and their children
had to endure, especially when the father was a black GI.

Interestingly enough, the official cultural propaganda of the
United States actually reinforced traditional gender roles. The 4–
H clubs in Austria, for example, trained the rural youth how to
run a modern farm like a business. Boys learned everything from
the artificial insemination of cows and the use of chemical fertil-

---

21 See Cynthia Enloe, *Bananas, Beaches, and Bases: Making Feminist Sense of International Politics* (Berkeley, 1990); Sherma B. Gluck, *Rosie the Riveter Revisited: Woman, the
War, and Social Change* (Boston, 1987); Marc Hillel, *Die Invasion der Be-Freier* [The invasion of liberators and suitors] (Bergisch Gladbach, 1983); Elaine Tyler May, *Homeward Bound:
American Families in the Cold War Era* (New York, 1988); Sibylle Meyer and Eva Schulze,
Von Liebe sprach damals keiner: Familienalltag in der Nachkriegszeit [Nobody spoke about
love then: Everyday life of families in the postwar period] (Munich, 1985) and *Perlonzeit: Wie
Frauen ihr Wirtschaftswunder erlebten* [Plastic time: How women experienced the economic
miracle] (Berlin, 1986); Helke Sander and Barbara Johr, eds., *BeFreier und Befreite: Krieg,
Vergewaltigungen, Kinder* [Liberators, suitors and liberated: War, rapes, children] (Munich,
1992); and Elisabeth Wilson, *Only Halfway to Paradise: Women in Postwar Britain, 1945–
1948* (London, 1980).
22 Ingrid Bauer, "'Austria's Prestige Dragged Into the Dirt?' The GI-Brides and Postwar
Austrian Society (1945–1955)," *Contemporary Austrian Studies* 6 (1998): 41–55; Ingrid Bauer,
ed., *Welcome Ami Go Home: Die amerikanische Besatzung in Salzburg 1945–1955* [Wel-
come American go home: The American occupation of Salzburg, 1945–1955] (Salzburg, 1998).

izers to the electrification of production. Girls, however, were trained to knit and plant flowers, and in hygienic homemaking. Still, the general changes initiated (or restarted) by the United States opened different doors. The accelerated economic and social modernization and the spread of American popular culture – even some of those products that may have been read quite differently within the United States – strengthened trends toward further emancipation in the long run.[23]

The popular attraction of American mass culture and its European derivatives therefore also contained egalizing elements: while hardly changing the ratio of inequality between social groups, the participation of the lower classes in growing standards of living and (cultural) consumption certainly contributed to the defusing of class conflicts.[24] Of course, the democracy of goods is a democracy of appearances, and "the realities of the distribution of economic and political power could thus be disguised, to the satisfaction of capitalist and worker alike. Mass fashion allowed everyone to appear upwardly mobile."[25]

Immigrants to the United States had not only been the first owners and producers but also the first buyers of the products of American popular culture. After the Second World War many a dream had been lost in Europe or, worse, turned out disastrously, but at least now everybody could become a virtual immigrant into the land of plenty. American popular culture was even instrumental for the construction of new "national" identities. Austro-Pop, a (sometimes clever) mixture of rock music and the Austrian (dialect) version of the German language, for example, acted like a declaration of independence of Austrian artists from the schmaltz of German *Schlager*-music.[26]

---

23   Hermann-Josef Rupieper, "Bringing Democracy to the Frauleins: Frauen als Zielgruppe amerikanischer Demokratisierungspolitik in Deutschland 1945–1952" [Bringing democracy to the frauleins: Women as target group of American democratization policies in Germany, 1945–1952] *Geschichte und Gesellschaft* 17 (1991): 61–91.

24   Ulrich Beck, *Risikogesellschaft: Auf dem Weg in eine andere Moderne* [Society of risks: On the road to another kind of modernity] (Frankfurt, 1986).

25   Maltby, *Passing Parade*, 13.

26   Edward Larkey, *Pungent Sounds: Constructing Identity with Popular Music in Austria* (New York, 1993).

The culture of consumption as heralded by U.S. popular culture had an immense attraction for a growing proportion of European youth, with time gaps between various countries and urban and rural regions within these societies. Britain, the Netherlands, and Germany acted as forerunners, Greece, Portugal, and Spain carried the taillight. This new transitional youth culture symbolically traversed class differences but strengthened generational distinctions. Urban youth, especially industrial workers, acted as an avant-garde, but the cinema, radio, motorization, tourism, modernization of agriculture, and, especially, television soon covered most rural parts. American popular culture since then has become nearly everyone's second culture, "a global lingua franca, drawing especially the urban and urbane classes of most nations into a federated culture zone."[27]

ACT IV: The Cold War as Cool War

Hidden, and yet directly at the center of the attraction of U.S. pop culture, of course, also lies the eternal attraction of maximum power. Alison Lurie was correct when she pointed at the behavioral parallels between "primitive man" and his attempts to assume mythical powers by wearing bear skins and eagle feathers and European teenagers who seemed to hope that by wearing a pair of blue jeans some of America's power, myth, and essence might rub off.[28]   *Ridiculous*

However that may be, one major attraction of American popular culture for young people lay in the fact that it always contains an element of rebellion: a rebellion against the tastes of those in power, be they politicians, priests, the military, teachers – in short, the parental generation. The phenomenal global success of American popular music and jazz is intrinsically based on their expressiveness and vitality. And these qualities were mainly achieved

27 Gitlin, "The New Global Culture."
28 Alison Lurie quoted in Helmut Bausinger, ed., *Jeans: Beitraege zur Mode- und Jugendkultur* [Jeans: Contributions on fashion and youth culture] (Tuebingen, 1985), 90.

because, contrary to Europe, American popular music "was never swamped by the cultural standards of the upper class."[29]

And there may even exist another subtext, another layer behind and beneath it. As the composer Virgil Thomson noted in "America's Musical Autonomy," written in 1944, exactly at that moment when the United States established not only its *autonomy* but its *hegemony*,

One of the most fascinating stories in the world [is] that of the secret, or nonofficial, musical life of this country. It would seem that this is all bound up with religious dissent. It includes as much dissent from official America as from official Europe. It is based on the privilege of every man to praise God, as well as to court a damsel, with songs of his own choosing. For two hundred years it has refused institutional mediation in culture, as it has denied the necessity of institutional mediation for salvation. As a result, we have a body of British song that has survived the efforts of churches, of states, and of schools – for all have tried – to kill it.[30]

Still, American popular culture is much more than just a triumph of cultural or religious vulgarity. Some of its best products, like jazz, have incredibly enriched the cultures of the world precisely because they are brilliant expressions of the pain and joy of the suppressed. American popular culture therefore is a constant reminder of the mixture of African, European, North American (and more) (sub)cultures as a result of *European* imperialism and slavery as well as of the fact that the capitalist culture industries are brilliant and versatile enough to capitalize on, profit from, and cash in even on this chapter of inhumanity. And *that* is the main reason why every racist hates it with all his heart. Because in that particular discourse "American Popular Culture" is nothing but a code phrase, nothing but a cipher for "*race*" and *class*.

If, for a moment, we interpret the cultural Cold War as an old-fashioned band contest, and in many ways it resembled a loud

29 Francis Newton [E. J. Hobsbawm], *The Jazz Scene* (London, 1959), 43.
30 Virgil Thomson, "America's Musical Autonomy," in *A Virgil Thomson Reader*, ed. Thomson and John Rockwell (Boston, 1981), quoted in Greil Marcus, *Invisible Republic: Bob Dylan's Basement Tapes* (New York, 1997), 220.

drum battle, it becomes quite clear that the instruments of the Soviet orchestra were completely out of tune with the wishes of the majority of the European audiences, in the West as well as in the East. While tens of thousands of engineers had to be employed in the East to distort the electronic messages from the West, nothing like that was ever necessary on the other side – if we exclude the tens of thousands of Western secret service members whose listening in constituted about the same waste of taxpayers' money. The majorities of the audience deemed any message coming through Soviet amplifiers as distorted by definition if not cacophonic.

Of course, the Berlin Wall was not blown over by Western trumpets alone, like the biblical walls of Jericho by Joshua's, but the proximity of the famous KdW, the *Kaufhaus des Westens* (Shopping Temple of the West), to the Berlin Wall was more than symbolic. If we want to understand the allure of Western democracy (under the umbrella of the United States) in Europe, then the immense contribution of American popular culture for the establishment of a Pax Cultura Americana, which wasn't always very peaceful, must not be ignored. Any comprehensive list of important and immensely popular American artists of the twentieth century would fill many volumes. Substituting for them all, I would argue that U.S. artists, from Louis Armstrong to Frank Zappa, from Ray Charles to Marilyn Monroe (not to mention their animated compatriots, Mickey Mouse and Donald Duck), did more to win sympathies for "the American way of life" than any U.S. politician or military leader, probably with the exception of John F. Kennedy. But then, Jack and Jackie Kennedy, the rulers of Camelot, have become icons of popular culture, too.

Is it a complete coincidence that the Velvet Underground preceded the Velvet Revolution? All revolutions in Europe at the end of the twentieth century, Timothy Garton Ash reminds us, are tele-revolutions. And a long time before these political transformations occurred, many people behind the iron curtain had virtually overcome that obstruction by becoming electronic emigrants. Long before the iron curtain actually came down, multitudes of those who were forced to live behind it managed to tune in to the alluring messages of Western consumption capitalism and its chief propagandist (and sometimes critic, another secret of its success): American popular culture. "From Berlin to the Urals, to the sound of music," Christopher Hitchens summarized the revolutions of 1989, "the whole wall and edifice of brute power came crushing down, or rather evaporated, before the onslaught of blue-jeaned hordes accoutred with nothing but irony and optimism, and a good bit of sex and rock 'n' roll."[31]

The American Century was, without a doubt, at least as much the century of the global attraction of the *Sound of Freedom* – the *real* Sound of Music and Hollywood as that of Wall Street, Madison Avenue, and Pennsylvania Avenue. The real ambassadors of the United States of America in the Cold War were those artists who produced the soundtrack to the twentieth century, Louis Armstrong and Dizzy Gillespie, Ray Charles and Miles Davis. Again and again irritated diplomats had to report back to Washington that official attempts at proving the (high) cultural maturity of the United States only backfired, as was the case when the U.S. Air Force Band's symphonic recital in Bangkok was upstaged by a mediocre Thai jazz quintet that drew a much larger audience in 1956.[32] And the active participation of non-American youngsters in creating the success of black music, of re-anchoring it in mainstream U.S. society, must not be underestimated. After all, it was the British invasion of America by baby-faced British beat groups in the mid-sixties that brought the blues and rhythm 'n' blues back to "white" American teenagers *for the first time*. And, quite appropriately, the invasion started from Liverpool, which, together with Bristol, had been among the most notorious slave-trading harbors of the eighteenth century. When we think of America, it is an America made in Africa as much as it is an America made in England, the Netherlands, Germany, Ireland, Italy, China, and so on.

It is highly ironic (and telling) that most of the jazz musicians who created the "Sound of Freedom" and won so many sympa-

31 Christopher Hitchins, "The Children of '68," *Vanity Fair* (June 1998): 92–103.
32 Elliot Bratton, "The Sound of Freedom: Jazz and the Cold War. Part One: The Trick Bag," *Crisis* (February/March 1998): 14–19.

thies for the United States, were not only branded un-American at home but experienced a system of apartheid and repression for most of the American Century within their *own* society. Of course, postwar youth, inside and outside the United States, were also attacked as un-American when they opposed imperialist policies in Indochina and elsewhere. Again, it was ignored that European youngsters (outside *and* inside the iron curtain) had learned their lessons in democracy in part from the American civil rights movement. After all, sit-ins, teach-ins, and happenings became not only part of German but of most European languages. These young people did not sing the "International" but "We Shall Overcome," and, especially in West Germany, Austria, and Italy, their protest against the war in Indochina was directed predominantly against their own fathers' generation. The question most often asked was, "What did you do in World War II?" And that was a question quite necessary because it had been postponed far too long. It had become sacrificed on the altar of Cold War anticommunism – with disastrous consequences, until this moment.

This cultural paradox of the Cold War was as much repressed as it was ignored that the whole raison d'être for the existence of the United States was (and is?) anticolonialism.[33] After all, the American civil rights movement had parted the waters mostly by applying Mahatma Gandhi's strategy of peaceful protest. Because the whole world wasn't only watching Chicago, it was watching Little Rock and Memphis, Montgomery and Harlem, Selma and Detroit, Birmingham and Watts. As Americans could watch the mass killings in Vietnam on a daily basis, night by night the whole world became witness to armies safeguarding black students against amok-running white mobs and snarling police dogs, the clubbing and hosing down of peaceful demonstrators, the killing of freedom riders, and the burning of American city ghettos. "I have a dream" reverberated around the whole globe, and the extremely negative repercussions that the repression of American blacks had outside the United States (not only

33   Penny M. Von Eschen, *Race Against Empire: Black Americans and Anticolonialism, 1937–1957* (Ithaca, 1997); "Symposium on African Americans and U.S. Foreign Relations," *Diplomatic History* 20 (Fall 1996): 531–650.

in Africa) certainly played an immense role in finally enforcing policies to end (all open forms of) apartheid *within* America. Within all this violence, the immense attraction of the *Sound of Freedom* – gospel, spirituals, jazz, blues, rhythm and blues, soul, funk, rap, HipHop – for winning over the hearts and minds of the majorities of the youth for "Western democracy" remains largely overlooked and underresearched. The decisive contributions of American popular culture in general and African Americans in particular to the process of democratization of cultures outside and inside the boundaries of the United States are, at best, hardly understood and, at worst, kept silent.

The American Century was born a hundred years ago. It was born half a century before Henry Luce noted it in his celebrated article. The Spanish-American War marked its military birth in the Caribbean and Philippines (and, among others, in Hawaii and China). But at the beginning of the twentieth century, the dice not only of international power politics were cast anew, but also those of the worlds of economics, finance, and culture. Already on Christmas Day 1898, Santa Claus had good news for the readers of the *New York Times*, which ran the bold headline:

EUROPE FEARS AMERICA
This Country the Commanding Power in Finances and Commerce
MANUFACTURERS ARE ALARMED
American Steel Rails in Demand Everywhere
Russia Turns to US for a Loan [34]

Soon not only Russia was applying for loans in America but also Great Britain, which turned from senior to junior partner and was to become Little England in the process. Immediately after Great Britain's first application for a U.S. loan in 1900, the Brit-

---

34 *New York Times*, 25 December 1898, quoted in David Traxel, *The Birth of the American Century* (New York, 1998), 307; Emily Rosenberg, *Spreading the American Dream: American Economic and Cultural Expansion, 1890–1945* (New York, 1982); Donald W. White, *The American Century: The Rise and Decline of the United States as a World Power* (New Haven, 1996).

ish journalist W. T. Stead published a much-debated book, which was translated into German only a couple of months later: *The Americanization of the World: or, The Trend of the Twentieth Century*. Stead's charming analysis shows great foresight in many fields, yet he completely overlooked the area that produced the soundtrack of the American Century. Louis Armstrong was born in New Orleans in the summer of 1901, of course, but in addition to playing a mean trumpet Satchmo also knew, like all great artists, about the utmost significance of symbolic acts. He therefore altered his birth date to the 4th of July 1900, that date thereby forever transcending the birth of a little black boy on Independence Day to the birth of the *cultural independence* of the United States of America *as well as* of America's greatest contribution to twentieth-century world culture.

Whatever the social reality of millions in the United States may be, America first and foremost signifies wealth, power, youth, and success. It is not only the center of twentieth-century capitalist culture of consumption but, at the same time, itself its most successful product. Among our still well-to-do majorities, the general wealth acts as the great equalizer that is continuously demonstrated in the general conspicuous participation in mass consumption. The pursuit of success is the common philosophy, the transformation of success into consumption is the common practice. Malcolm Bradbury defined this phenomenon as the ten-minute revolution, which means that the brains are somewhat empty while the garbage cans are always full. I consume, therefore I am: Credit Card instead of Descartes.

In the culture of capitalism, in which the marketplace is promoted as the paramount, most cherished cultural value in itself, *the market* has become the supreme cultural good, the quasi-fetish of cultural globalization, which, in turn, has become nothing but a *fin-de-millenium* mantra disguising the ongoing Euro-Americanization of the world. It therefore is rather self-evident that the culture of capitalism must by definition be *popular* culture, and pop connotes the United States. Since the nineteenth century, European debates about popular (or, more revealing, *mass*) culture have been debates about *America*. In most cases, the development of modern mass culture has meant the adoption and application of American cultural practices and forms in all areas of culture. As many products of mass culture, especially movies and music, demonstrate, America *itself* has now become an object of consumption, the symbol of a new form of entertainment.[35]

But there is nothing inherently "American" about the *capitalist* culture of consumption. After all, most Europeans tend to forget that the United States is the result of the *Europeanization* of the world, which means that before America could consume Europe, Europe already had consumed America. Once we consider the fact that in the first 325 years after Columbus more than five times as many Africans were shipped in chains to the (not so) New World then the endlessly repeated question, whether American culture is really good for the world, should be dialectically put on its feet and rephrased. Because the question hardly ever asked, *at least in Euro-America*, is whether it wasn't European culture that constituted a much bigger global threat?

The introduction of street ball is a classic case for history being put on its head. The street, the only free space for impoverished city kids in Europe and America, its allure of vitality, machismo, and violence, is sold back to affluent youngsters as a mega-cool space of capitalist consumption. Of course, this is only one of the latest examples for what is at the bottom of the attraction of popular culture: where consumption becomes rebellion (vide the many "youth rebellions" since the 1950s), rebellion becomes consumption. Eventually this kind of revolt could even be welcomed by those in power. After all, in most cases it only represented a revolt into style and, even more important, it proved phenomenally profitable.

This revolution, then, did more than eat its children. It consumed them altogether – and they even paid for it.

---

35   Simon Frith, *Sound Effects: Youth, Leisure and the Politics of Rock 'n' Roll* (New York, 1978).

ACT V: Finale

It would soon be over. Actually, it really already was over for James C. Booker III, who had died on 8 November 1983 of a lethal dose of cocaine in New Orleans' Charity Hospital. James Booker had been born on 17 December 1939, and in his short lifetime he became the ultimate New Orleans pianist's pianist, a musician's musician. James Booker was the Ivory Emperor and the Maharaja of the Bayous in one person. If there ever was jazz royalty, Booker was a member. His grandfather had been the piano teacher of Jelly Roll Morton and he himself gave his licks away to Art Neville and Harry Connick, Jr.

But Booker's immense artistic talent, power, and grace were overshadowed by a darker side that many African-American artists experienced during much of the American Century: racism, bigotry, and artistic exploitation. Booker's slide into the hell of heroin addiction was not untypical among his peers, but even in desperation he stood out as the *ultimate rascal*, whose bouts of self-destruction on bad days would lead him to fight his audience verbally until he was alone – only to continue with the funkiest Beethoven or Chopin interpretations imaginable. He was a difficult character, indeed, and, what's worse, he didn't shut up. This exceptional producer of angelic piano music consequently did time in Angola Prison Farm. After his release, he was saved from complete obscurity only by a German (!) blues impresario who booked Booker for a European tour that included a concert at the Karl Marx University at Leipzig. Here, Booker not only found a congenial audience that really had the blues but also confronted a late socialist racism that was actually very reminiscent of home. As the East German comrade colonel of the artists agency had exclaimed: "*Muss et denn ausjerechnet n'Neja sein!*"[36]

36 A good introduction to James Booker's genius is the CD *Junco Partner*, Rykodisk, 1993, HNCD 1359. All quotes in italics are from the album *Let's Make a Better World!* by James C. Booker, Amiga, 001 91. The cover may be found at http://www.sbg.ac.at/gesc/people/eg/bookerr.gif, and http://www.sbg.ac.at/gesc/people/eg/bookerv.jpg.

But jazz actually could overcome the divide between the capitalist and socialist camps, as the Louis Armstrong tour of West Germany had shown in 1953. For the concert in West Berlin, Armstrong noted, "I couldn't count the Russians that came through the Iron Curtain to hear 'Our Louie.' Anybody who says that the Russians don't love good jazz, you send them to me."[37] Pretty strong words at the height of McCarthyism.

On 29 October 1977 it was James Booker's turn. He played in Leipzig, and he played for more than three hours. It was one of his best concerts and he received frenetic applause. When he was warned that his political comments and songs ("People Get Ready") offended the rather conspicuous gray people in the front rows, Booker pulled the stops *of the ambiguous humor of all suppressed* and addressed the members of the Leipzig nomenklatura as "Peoples from the CIA!" He left no doubt that his shout "Let's Make a Better World!" was directed at everybody outside as well as inside the iron curtain.

Twelve years after James Booker's sensational concert in Leipzig, it was all over. He had already been dead for eight years, and East Germany followed suit. What remained, in early 1991, was just some final clean up: some tearing down of flags, some destruction of documents (in the East), a lot of counting of cash (in the West and in the East), a lot of new wealth *as well as* a lot of new blues – and one more album. The final album ever issued in the German Democratic Republic. A live album of the Leipzig concert by James Booker, the legendary pianist from New Orleans. The last album of the DDR on the Amiga label, the final pressing before the machines were switched off at Potsdam/Babelsberg – and the workers thrown out, *abgewickelt* as unemployed. The final East German recording, *die Allerletzte* (001 91) with the classical comment *Sic transit gloria mundi* by James C. Booker, one-eyed pianist and singer from New Orleans, scarred by life but yet undefeated, weak but still cool, physically sick but mentally strong, insisting "Let's Make a Better World!"

---

37   Bratton, "Sound of Freedom," 16.

And, for anyone willing to listen, James Booker made one thing quite clear: that, despite the sleekly triumphant sound system of the American Century, there was still lots of room for desperately necessary improvements on *both* sides of the iron curtain, because the *Sound of Freedom*, however attractive and alluring, successful and enticing, had remained – mostly – sound.

16

American Empire and Cultural Imperialism: A View from the Receiving End

ROB KROES

Students of Americanization are in general agreement regarding the semantic transformations that attend the dissemination of American cultural messages across the world. Depending on their precise angle and perspective, some tend to emphasize the cultural strategies and auspices behind the transmission of American culture. Whether they study Buffalo Bill's Wild West Show when it traveled in Europe, Hollywood movies, or world's fairs, to name just a few carriers of American culture, their focus is on the motifs and organizing views that the producers were trying to convey, rather than on an analysis of what the spectators and visitors did with the messages to which they were exposed. All such cultural productions, taken as representations of organizing worldviews, tend to lead researchers to focus on the senders rather than the receivers of messages. Such a focus, in other words, hardly ever leads these researchers to look at the process of reception as more than one of passive imbibing. But whatever the words one uses to describe what happens at the point of reception – words such as hybridization or creolization – current views agree on a freedom of reception, a freedom to re-semanticize and re-contextualize meaningful messages reaching audiences across national and cultural borders. Much creativity and inventiveness goes into the process of reception, much joy and exhilaration springs from it. Yet making this the whole story would be as fallacious as a focus centered solely on the schemes and designs of the senders of messages. Whatever their precise angle, researchers agree on the need to preserve balance in their approach to problems of Americanization.

Furthermore, some researchers, such as Robert W. Rydell, in a contribution to the 1998 Lisbon conference of the European Association for American Studies,[1] tend to conceive of Americanization as tied initially to an American economic expansionism and then, more recently, to an emerging global economy structured by the organizing logic of corporate capitalism but still very much proceeding under American auspices. The main area in which Rydell sees Americanization at work – and I quote from his presentation – is in the "commodification of culture which colonizes the leisure time of people worldwide." World's fairs and other transmitters of America's commercial culture conjure up a "veritable 'dream world' of mass consumption, a simulation through spectacle of the good life afforded by the technological advances associated with modernization." Rydell goes on to contrast this simulacrum of the good life with the ravages wrought by corporate capitalism in many parts of the globe. He explicitly seeks to keep the concept of Americanization in our critical lexicon as a useful reminder of what American economic expansionism has meant in terms of advancing the interests of American corporate culture overseas.

I am not sure that this is the right tack. Rydell seems unduly to read the autonomous rise of global corporate capitalism as due to American agency. It is a common fallacy in much of the critique of Americanization to blame America for trends and developments that would have occurred anyway, even in the absence of America. From Marx, via Hobson and Lenin, all the way to the work of the Frankfurt School, there is a long line of critical analysis of capitalism and imperialism, highlighting its inner expansionist logic. Surely, in the twentieth century, much of this expansion has proceeded under American auspices, receiving an American imprint, in much the same way that a century ago the imprint

1 To be published in the forthcoming proceedings of that conference.

was British. The imprint has often confused critics, leading them to argue that the process of modernization, ranging from the impact of capitalism to processes of democratization of the political arena, was essentially a process of Americanization. From this perspective, however, the critique of Americanization exaggerates America's role in areas where in fact it was caught up in historic transformations much like other countries were.

From a different perspective, though, this view of Americanization is too narrow. It ignores those vast areas where America, as a construct, an image, a fantasma, did play a role in the intellectual and cultural life of people beyond the borders of the United States. There is a repertoire of fantasies about America that even predates its discovery. And ever since, the repertoire has been fed in numerous ways, through many media of transmission. Americans and non-Americans have all contributed to this collective endeavor, making sense of the new country and its evolving culture. Especially in our century America has become ever more present in the minds of non-Americans, as a point of reference, a yardstick, a counterpoint. In intellectual reflections on the course and destiny of their countries and cultures America became part of a process of triangulation, serving as a model for rejection or emulation, providing views of a future seen in either a negative or a positive light. America has become a *tertium comparationis* in culture wars elsewhere, centering on control of the discourse of national identity and national culture. When America was typically rejected by one party in such contests, the other party saw it as a liberating alternative. Writing the history of such receptions of America is as much American studies as it is an endeavor in the intellectual history of countries other than the United States. It also should form part of a larger reflection upon processes summarily described as Americanization.

Undeniably, though, in the course of this allegedly "American Century" America has assumed a centrality that one might rightly call imperial. Like Rome in the days of the Roman Empire, it has become the center of webs of control and communication that span the world. Its cultural products reach the far corners of the world, communicating American ways and views to people elsewhere, while America itself remains relatively unaware of cultural products originating outside its national borders. If for such reasons we might call America's reach imperial, and if it is still possible to use that word in a relatively neutral way, describing a factual configuration rather than the outcome of concerted effort and motive, then we might speak of an American economic imperialism, political imperialism, and cultural imperialism. Trying to accommodate themselves to their diminished role and place in the world, European countries have at times opted to resist these three forms of American imperialism. Thus, taking France as the most telling case, it chose to resist political imperialism by ordering NATO out of the country, it warned against America's economic imperialism through Jean Jacques Servan-Schreiber's *Le défi américain*, and it briefly considered trying to prevent *Jurassic Park* from being released in France, seeing the movie as a case of American cultural imperialism and as a threat to French cultural identity.

Yet, suggestive as the three forms of imperialism are of neat partition and distinction, they do in fact overlap to a large extent. Thus, America in its role as the new political hegemon in the Western world could restructure markets and patterns of trade through the Marshall Plan, which guaranteed access to the European markets for American products. Political imperialism could thus promote economic imperialism. Opening European markets for American commerce also meant preserving access for American cultural exports, such as Hollywood movies. Economic imperialism thus translated into cultural imperialism. Conversely, as carriers of an American version of the "good life," American products, from cars to movies, from clothing styles to kitchen apparel, all actively doubled as agents of American cultural diplomacy. Thus, trade translated into political imperialism, and so on, in endless feedback loops.

In my own recent work I have chosen to focus on the cultural dimension, evident in all these various forms of the American imperial presence. American culture, seen as a configuration of ways and means that Americans use for expressing their collective sense of themselves –their Americanness – is mediated through every form of American presence abroad. From the high rhetoric of its political ideals to the golden glow of McDonald's arches, from Bruce Springsteen to the Marlboro Man, American culture washes across the globe. It does so mostly in disentangled bits and pieces, for others to recognize, pick up, and rearrange into a setting expressive of their own individual identities, or identities they share with peer groups. Thus, teenagers may have adorned their bedrooms with the iconic faces of Hollywood or rock music stars in order to provide themselves with a most private place for reverie and games of identification, but they have also been engaged in the construction of private worlds they share with countless others. In the process they re-contextualize and re-semanticize American culture to make it function within expressive settings entirely of their own making.

In his contribution to the Lisbon conference Rydell referred to W. T. Stead, an early British observer who identified Americanization as "the trend of the Twentieth Century." As Rydell makes clear, Stead saw Americanization mostly as the worldwide dissemination of material goods, which in turn symbolized American technical and entrepreneurial prowess. It would be for later observers to look at these consumer goods as cultural signifiers as well, as carriers of an American way of life. An early example of an observer of the American scene with precisely this ability to read cultural significance into the products of a technical civilization was the Dutch historian Johan Huizinga. In his collection of travel observations, published after his only trip to the United States in 1926,[2] he showed an uncanny awareness of the recycling of the American Dream into strategies of commercial persuasion, linking a fictitious world of self-fulfillment – a world where every dream would come true – to goods sold in the market. Highminded aesthete though he was, forever longing for the lost world of late-medieval Europe, he could walk the streets of the great American cities with an open eye for the doubling of American

---

2   J. H. Huizinga, *Amerika levend en denkend: Losse opmerkingen* [America living and thinking: Assorted observations] (Haarlem, 1927).

reality into a seductive simulacrum. He was inquisitive enough to ask the right questions, questions that still echo in current research concerning the reception of mass culture in general, and of commercial exhortations in particular. He wondered what the effect would be on everyday people of the constant barrage of commercial constructions of the good life. "The public constantly sees a model of refinement far beyond their purse, ken and heart. Does it imitate this? Does it adapt itself to this?" Apposite questions indeed. Huizinga was aware of the problem of reception in a world of virtual realities spewed forth by a relentless commercial mass culture. More generally, he touched on the effect that film, advertising, and other media of cultural transmission would have on audiences not just in America but elsewhere as well. In these more general terms, the problem became one of the ways in which non-American audiences read the fantasy worlds that an American imagination produced and that showed all of the negative characteristics of an American culture so vehemently indicted by European critics.

In concluding this section, let me point out one cruel irony. If in his later writings Huizinga would dwell on the problem of contemporary history changing, if not actually losing, form, under the combined impact of mechanization, industrialization, and the advent of mass society, he may, in spite of his sophistication and open-mindedness, have missed one crucial way in which people's sense of history was also changing. Under the impact of precisely those media of mass communication that Huizinga had subtly explored, rather than ignoring or rejecting them out of hand, his contemporaries were beginning to furnish their historical imaginations with the ingredients of virtual fantasy worlds rather than the stuff that history used to be made of. What to Huizinga and other like-minded intellectuals may have been a mere epiphenomenon, hiding real historical forces from view, would become the markers of history to generations growing up in the second half of our century. In the following section I propose to explore how we might reflect on the intricate ways in which, in the post-World War II period, American mass culture, reaching a Europe that more than ever before had come within

America's imperial sway, may have affected the European sense of history. My focus will be on advertising, seen as a peculiar blend of economic and cultural imperialism.

A nation that stops representing itself in images stops being a nation. It is doomed to lead a life of derivation, vicariously enjoying worlds of imagery and imagination imported from abroad. Or so French President François Mitterrand was reported to have mused. In a mood of cultural protectionism, against the backdrop of a seemingly unstoppable conquest of Europe's cultural space by American images, Mitterrand's France called for – but failed to get – a clause exempting cultural goods from the free-trade logic of the General Agreement on Tariffs and Trade (GATT). The episode, in the final negotiating stages of the Uruguay Round, is reminiscent of earlier defensive ploys by France in the face of Americanization. There is the story, as told by more than one author,[3] of the fight that France chose to pick to keep Coca-Cola out of the country. Coca-Cola became the symbol of everything that a certain intellectual discourse in Europe had always rejected in America, as the country that had succeeded in mass-marketing bad taste. If there was much to be envied in America as a model of modernity, it was a model that France should follow selectively and on its own terms – under strict "parental guidance," so to speak. Yet the model was tempting precisely because it undercut parental authority and cultural guardianship, promising the instant gratification of desire rather than its sublimation, consumption rather than consummation. For the French, Coca-Cola became the symbol of the pernicious pleasure principle embedded in the global transmission of American mass culture. The soft drink, in this French campaign, was turned into an icon of an alleged American strategy of cultural imperialism. It even gave the strategy a name: Coca-Colonization.

More recently, another soft-drink commercial, for Seven-Up, illustrated the seductive semiotics that underlie so many of the

---

3   See Richard Kuisel, *Seducing the French: The Dilemma of Americanization* (Berkeley, 1993); and M. Pendergrast, *For God, Country, and Coca-Cola: The Unauthorized History of the Great American Soft Drink and the Company That Makes It* (London, 1993).

messages that reach us from across the Atlantic Ocean. It did this without drawing on the repertoire of American icons. There was no Marlboro Man roaming the open space of an American West, no Castle Rock, no Statue of Liberty. Instead it introduced a streetwise little brat, a cartoon character by the name of Fido Dido (If I do, they do?). Few among the European audience watching the commercial would have been aware of its American origins. As it happened, however, the cartoon character was American, and so was the commercial itself. Yet, to all intents and purposes, it could have been produced by advertising agencies anywhere. The only clearly American referent in the commercial was the product it tried to promote, a soft drink that saw its market share slipping and felt in need of a new image.

In the first installment of what turned out to be a little series of narrations centering on Fido Dido, we see him meeting the hand of his maker. Briefly it may seem like a lighter, cartoon version of the scene in the Sistine Chapel where a drowsy Adam, touching fingers with God, is brought to life. But Fido Dido's meeting is of a different kind. His confrontation is with parental authority, with the commanding hand of social propriety. The hand of the maker, "in living color," holds a pencil and gets ready to retouch Fido Dido. First his unkempt hair gets neatly combed and partitioned. Fido Dido indignantly shakes his hair back into its previous state. The pencil continues the attack and dresses Fido Dido in jacket and tie. It moves on to the object in Fido Dido's right hand, also in full color, as real as the hand and pencil: the can of Seven-Up. The pencil tries to erase the can, but it is beyond such manipulation. Fido Dido meanwhile has moved toward full rebellion. Jacket and tie have been thrown off; a well-aimed kick hits the pencil. Its tip breaks and hangs limply – a fitting symbol of parental impotence. Victoriously, Fido Dido walks off the screen. In final retaliation his yo-yo now hits the pencil. The broken point falls off. His victory prize is a taste of the elixir of freedom: cool, sparkling Seven-Up. The semiotics all merge into one message: a simple soft drink has been turned into a symbol of freedom. Much as the product, as well as the commercial and the cartoon character itself, may be American, the message is understood internationally.

We may see in this one example the end stage of a process of internationalization and generalization – decontextualization, if one wishes – of a sales pitch that was developed in America and, in its earlier stages, relied on much more explicit American iconography. I mentioned the Marlboro Man as a contemporary case of strong American symbolism – the West as open space, a realm of freedom – used to connect the sense of freedom, of being one's own man, to a simple item of merchandise like a cigarette. Yet the Marlboro Man is only a recent version of the commodification of American symbols of freedom that, as a process, has gone on for over a century. America as empty space, the epic America of the frontier, America as a mythical West, had been turned into a symbol of freedom long before the consumption revolution. The West as a beckoning yonder had kept alive the dream, in far-away corners of Europe, of a life lived in freedom and independence. As the promise of a new world and a new era, it could vie with contemporary utopian views offered by Marxism or similar emancipation movements. Posters produced for shipping lines, emigration societies, and land development agencies contributed their imagery to the continuing construction of America as the very site of freedom and space. To many, such imagery must have represented the promise of freedom and escape offered by America.

If such is the central appeal of "America" as an image, we need not be surprised at the craving for material that could visualize the image. Chromolithographs, photographs, and stereographs with their suggestion of three-dimensionality all tried to still this hunger. They allowed people to move beyond the limited horizons of their daily lives and to enter into an imaginary space, a fantasy world. They offered reality and illusion at the same time.

Nor need we be surprised that such pictures soon were turned into advertising tools. When images of the West, or rather of America as one huge space, could trigger fantasies of fulfillment and liberty, common merchandise might hope to benefit from an association with such images. Today everyone is familiar with the West as "Marlboro Country," with the successful marriage of a cigarette brand with the Marlboro Man. But as early as a century ago advertisements tried to bring about this union. A colorful 1860 poster advertises the Washoe Brand of the Christian and Lee Tobacco Company from Richmond, Virginia. No tobacco leaf, cigar, or pipe in sight. What we do see are images of the West – Western horsemen, distant horizons – grouped around a medallion that shows us a picture of the Goddess Columbia draped in the American flag, an eagle, a globe with the Western Hemisphere turned forward, and a pot brimming with gold coins. The West appears as a vision of plenty. Another poster, from the same period, advertises Westward Ho Smoking Tobacco. Its very name ties the tobacco to the beckoning call of the West. Yet the producer, G. W. Langhorne and Co., from Lynchburg, Virginia, did not leave it at that. The poster shows us an allegorical female figure, a version of Columbia with stark Indian features, feathers in her hair, her extended hand holding forth a calumet, her body, save her breasts, wrapped in the Stars and Stripes. This is not Europe abducted by Jupiter, this is America, impetuously galloping forth on elkback: "Westward Ho!"

Apparently, well before the decade of the "roaring twenties," commerce had appropriated the allegorical repertoire of the American dream. But with the 1920s the images that flooded across the country through techniques of mechanical reproduction could be endlessly rearranged to render new symbolic messages. The West as a realm for the imagination could connect with the world of trite consumption goods, such as tobacco or cigarettes. Advertising developed into an art of symbolic alchemy that has continued to retain its potency. The symbolic connection that advertisers sought to establish hinged on the concept of "freedom." This linking of evocative images of American freedom and space tended to work best with leisure time articles, such as cigarettes, beer, an automobile, a motorbike, or a pair of blue jeans. Consumption, leisure time, and "freedom" thus became inextricably interwoven. Even today "America" can be counted on to trigger an association with freedom. Indeed, the iconography of America has become international. Italian blue jeans manufacturers now advertise their wares in Germany on posters depicting Monument Valley. The German cigarette brand West mounted an international advertising campaign whose central metaphors revolved around the American West. The Dutch non-alcoholic beer Stender used the imaginary West of American road-movies for its television commercials, including brief encounters at gas stations in an empty West, an exchange of glances between the sexes, the half-inviting, half-ironic sizing up, the beginning of erotic tension. The release of tension occurs, surprisingly, when he or she, in gleaming black leather, in the true macho style of the West, flips the top of a bottle of Stender and takes off on a shiny motorbike into the empty distance.

America's national symbols and myths have been translated into an international iconographic language, a visual lingua franca. They have been turned into free-floating signifiers, internationally understood, free for everyone to use. Yet it is only a replay, on an international scale, of what had previously occurred in the United States. Given the characteristic American bent for disassembling whatever presents itself as an organically coherent whole, only to reassemble it differently, this American leadership need not surprise us. In their production of commercial messages this same cultural bent has been at work, removing symbols from their historical context and rearranging them into novel configurations. The appropriate metaphor may be that of Lego-construction, which uses the individual pieces as just so many "empty signifiers," combining them into ever-changing meaningful structures. Commerce and advertising are but one area where we can see these rituals of cultural transformation at work. For indeed, consumption goods as well can freely change their meaning, appearing in ever-changing configurations, furnishing a realm of virtual reality, turning into simulacra at the hands of the wizards of advertising. They become true phantasmas set free by the human imagination.

No bastion of conventional order is immune to this erosive freedom. In the area of advertising as well as in other areas of cultural production we can discern a moving American frontier, affecting an ever-increasing number of social conventions with its "deconstructing" logic. Recent shifts in this frontier have affected the established constructions of gender, rearranging at will reigning views of what constitutes the typically male and female, the masculine and feminine. "Genderbending" is the word that American English has invented for describing this process. Pop culture heroes like Michael Jackson, Grace Jones, or Madonna project invented personae that are strangely androgynous. Hollywood is busy bending gender in films like *Alien II*, where the enemy computer is called *Mother* and the heroine copes as if she were a man. Commercials like those for Stender also play on the repertoire of accepted gender definitions. The best recent example is a television commercial for Levi's 501. A young, chocolate-skinned woman, invitingly dressed, her midriff bare, is shown taking a New York cab. While the driver is ogling her in his rear-view mirror, his lips moving a toothpick back and forth, suggestively, as if engaged in a mating ritual, she coolly adds a few final touches to her makeup. But then the tables are turned. What gives the driver a start and brings his cab to a full stop is the sound of an electric razor and the sight of his passenger shaving. The last shot is of the passenger walking away, the victor in another battle of the sexes, the Levi's as snug and inviting as ever. As the text reminds us, in case we didn't know already: "Cut for Men Since 1850." Thus, in all these cases, an entire new area has opened up for fantasies of freedom to roam.

There may be a cultural "deep structure" underlying such developments that is characteristically American, yet my point is that the appeal of such cultural *bricolage* is international. Even in the absence of clearly "American" markers, as in the case of the Fido Dido commercial, the underlying logic of recombination, tying "freedom" to a soft drink, is American, yet the appeal is worldwide. In that sense we have all become Americanized. We have grown accustomed to a specific American mode of cultural production, or rather to the ways in which American culture reproduces itself, through endless variation and recombination. Not only have we cracked American cultural codes and can read them flawlessly, we have also appropriated these codes. They have become part of our collective imaginary repertoire.

One illustration will make an additional point. In the spring of 1994, on walls all over Italy, there were magnificent posters displaying a scene taken from the history of the conquest of the West. We see a covered wagon in what is clearly a Western landscape, dry and desolate. A few men gather together in front of the wagon. The scene is one of relative relaxation. Clearly, the day's work is done. The poster's color is sepia, suggesting a reprint of an old photograph. The legend informs us that *Vendiamo un'autentica leggenda* – We sell an authentic legend. Clearly a variation on Coca-Cola's claim of being "the real thing," the viewer is left wondering what the authentic legend is. Is it Levi's blue jeans? The answer is yes. Is it the American West? Again, the answer is yes. A commodity, a piece of merchandise as down to earth as a pair of workingman's trousers, has become a myth, while the West as a myth has become commodified. And Levi's, as the poster honestly tells us, sells it. Yet there is still more to this poster. There is an ironic *sous-entendu*, an implied wink to the audience. After all, the audience has long since got the message. They *know* that Levi's is a myth and they *know* what the myth represents. It represents more than the West, it represents their own collective memory of growing up in a Europe filled with American ingredients. Generation upon generation of Europeans, growing up after the war, can all tell their own story of a mythical America as they constructed it, drawing on American advertisements, songs, films, and so on. Ironically, these collective memories – these imagined Americas where people actually spent part of their past growing up – are now being commodified: to those who, on the basis of Jack Kerouac and a pop song, remember *Route 66* but have never crossed the Atlantic, a Dutch travel agency now offers nostalgic trips down that artery. The road may no longer exist, but it reoccurs as a replica of itself, a simulacrum in the great Disney tradition.

The point is clear: generation upon generation of Europeans have grown up constructing meaningful worlds that they shared with their peers and that drew on American ingredients. Mythical "Americas" have become part and parcel of the collective memory of Europeans. This takes us back to Mitterrand's musings, and his apparent misreading of the way the collective memory of Europeans was built in the postwar period. Why must a nation's collective memory be grounded, as Mitterrand would have it, in its own national images? Why not admit that the collective memory of national populations is crucially a matter of the appropriation and digestion of foreign influences? One could counter such intrusion only by centrally imposing definitions of what constitutes the nation. And in fact many of the arguments in favor of the cultural exemption clause, so as to protect national cultural identities, seem to take such a narrow paternalist view of the nation and its identity.

Commercial messages have been only one of the transmission belts of American culture in the course of the twentieth century. The modern media of mass reproduction and mass distribution, like film, photography, the press, radio, television, and sound recordings, have filled the semiotic space of people everywhere with messages made in America. Americans themselves, through their physical presence abroad, in the form of expatriate colonies, of armies, of business men, have equally contributed to the worldwide dissemination of their culture. Yet commercial messages, in the way they transmit American culture, form a particular case. They are not simply neutral carriers, conveying American culture for others to consume and enjoy, but give a particular twist to whatever ingredients of the American imagination they use. A recent illustration of this process can be seen in a commercial message broadcast by CNN, the worldwide cable news network, and paid for by the "Advertising Council" in London. In what is basically an advertisement for advertising, the point is made that without advertising we would get less information through the media, whether the press or the electronic media, and would be worse off. Advertising is presented as a necessary prop for the continued existence of a well-informed public in a functioning democracy. The little civics lesson, offered by this commercial, ends with the slogan: "Advertising – The Right to Choose."

This blending of the rationale of capitalism and democratic theory is not new. It is reminiscent of what happened in the early

1940s in America. Then, on the eve of America's participation in World War II, President Franklin D. Roosevelt made a powerful contribution to American public discourse in his "Four Freedoms Speech," a rallying cry in which he called on his countrymen to fulfill an American world mission as he saw it. In all likelihood he had picked up the Four Freedoms as a rhetorical device in the public domain. The Four Freedoms, as a group of four statues erected along the main concourse of the New York World's Fair of 1939–40, had already left their imprint on millions of visitors to the fair. Working on his final draft of the State of the Union Address, Roosevelt briefly toyed with the idea of Five Freedoms, but clearly did not want to move away from the popular foursome at the fair. If he wished his words to reverberate among the larger public, he needed to draw on a popular repertoire that was already established. The link with political views among the larger public was further reinforced through Norman Rockwell's series of four oil paintings, made after Roosevelt's speech, each representing one of the four freedoms. Using his appeal as an artist who had succeeded in rendering a romantic, small-town view of life cherished by millions of Americans, he managed to give the same endearing touch to Roosevelt's message. Through the mass distribution of reproductions, Rockwell's paintings of the Four Freedoms facilitated the translation and transfer of Roosevelt's high-minded call to a mass audience.

If this is an illustration of American political culture as an element of American mass culture, of political rhetoric as it emanates from the public domain and returns to it, it was unaffected by the rationale of business. If anything had to be sold at all, it was a matter of political ideas; if a sales pitch was needed, it was a matter of public suasion, of explaining the world to the larger democratic public and calling upon it to take appropriate action. Yet it was not long before Roosevelt's Four Freedoms would be joined by a Fifth, in an advertisement by the Hoover Vacuum Cleaner Company in a 1944 issue of the *Saturday Evening Post*. It was an illustrated ad in the style of Norman Rockwell. We recognize the setting, the faces are familiar. An old woman, a middle-aged man, and a young girl – "people from the neighborhood." They look upward toward a beam of light; providence, if not the good provider, is smiling upon them. In their arms they hold an abundance of packages, all of them gift wrapped. This is Norman Rockwell country, but with a difference. Rockwell's mythical small-town people, carriers of democratic virtue, now appear in the guise of Americans as consumers. Three years after Roosevelt decided that there were four, not five, freedoms, the Hoover advertisement reminded Americans that "the Fifth Freedom is Freedom of Choice." If America had joined the struggle to safeguard democratic values, this implied safeguarding the freedom of choice. By a simple semantic sleight of hand, the (con)text of the advertisement shifted the meaning of freedom of choice: the "signified" was no longer the realm of politics, but the freedom of choice of the citizen in his role as consumer. Thus, spheres of freedom smoothly shaded into one another.

And they still do. The Hoover Company may have chosen to use language popular at the time, and to speak of a Freedom. The CNN message is cast in the language of rights, reminding us of our Right to Choose. In either case what we see is the commodification of political discourse. The language of political ideals, of rights and freedoms, is being highjacked in order to dress purposeful commercial action in stolen clothes. Whether dressed as a freedom or a right, a commodifying logic appears in pure form, unconnected to any particular product. Yet it is a logic we met before in particular cases, which tied the promise of freedom to cigarettes or soft drinks. It is a logic that commodifies, and pedestrianizes, political ideals by putting them in the service of commercial salesmanship. In that sense, we seem to have struck upon just another instance of the vulgarizing impact of American culture, corroborating a point made by so many European critics of American mass culture.

Yet this is not the whole story. The very slogans chosen by sales departments, affirming our "Freedom of Choice," or our "Right to Choose," are semantically unstable and may well convey a message different from that the salesmen had in mind. A word like choice, when left unspecified, sits uneasily astride the divide between the political and the economic spheres. "Free-

/ 0 0 2 ᵥ β . ϟ .

dom of Choice" in particular may well read as the "Choice of Freedom," a simple inversion that may well put political ideas into the heads of an audience that is addressed in its role as consumers. Paradoxically, then, advertising stratagems cooked up by commercial sponsors may well have the effect of a civics lesson, if not of a subversive and anti-authoritarian call. Precisely there, it seems, lie the secrets of the appeal that so many American commercial messages have had, domestically as well as abroad. Exploring frontiers of freedom, of children rebelling against parental authority, of sexual freedom, of freedom in matters of taste and in styles of behavior, American consumer goods have been instruments of political and cultural education, if not of emancipation. Generation upon generation of youngsters, growing up in a variety of European settings, West *and* East of the iron curtain, have vicariously enjoyed the pleasures of cultural alternatives conjured up in commercial vignettes. Simple items like a pair of blue jeans, Coca-Cola, or a cigarette brand, thus acquired an added value that helped these younger generations to give expression to an identity all their own. They have been using American cultural language and have made American cultural codes their own, and to that extent they have become Americanized. To the extent, though, that they have "done their own thing" while drawing on American cultural repertoires, Americanization is no longer the proper word for describing what has gone on. If anything, those at the receiving end of American mass culture have adapted it to their own ends. They have woven it into a cultural language whose grammar, syntax, and semantics – metaphorically speaking – would still recognizably be French, Italian, or Czech. All that the recipients have done is make new statements in such a language. And the point is ?.

There are more instances of such recontextualization. Surrounded as we are by jingles, posters, neon signs, and billboards, all trying to convey their commercial exhortations, we all at one point or another ironically recycle their repertoires; we quote slogans while bending their meaning; we mimic voices and faces familiar from radio and television. We weave them into our conversations, precisely because they are shared repertoires. Used in this way, two things happen. First, international repertoires become national, in the sense that they are given a particular twist in conversations, acquiring their new meanings only in particular national and linguistic settings. Second, commercial messages stop being commercial. A decommodification takes place in the sense that the point of the conversation is no longer a piece of merchandise or a specific economic transaction. In this ironic recycling of our commercial culture we become its masters rather than its slaves.

Many things have happened along the way since American mass culture started traveling abroad. American icons may have become the staple of a visual *lingua franca* that is understood anywhere in the world, yet their use can no longer be dictated solely from America.

For one thing, as I mentioned earlier, it is clear that European commercials made for European products may draw on semiotic repertoires initially developed in and transmitted from America. Yet, in a creolizing freedom not unlike America's modularizing cast of mind, Europeans in their turn now freely rearrange and recombine the bits and pieces of American culture. They care little about authenticity. T-shirts produced in Europe are as likely to say "New York Lions" as they are "New York Giants."[4] What is more, American brand names, as free-floating signifiers, may even be decommodified and turned into carriers of a message that is no longer commercial at all. Admittedly, the T-shirts, leather jackets, and baseball caps, sporting the hallowed names of Harley Davidson, Nike, or Coca-Cola, still have to be bought. Yet what one pays is the price of admission into a world of symbols shared by an international youth culture. Boys or girls with the word Coca-Cola on their T-shirts are not the unpaid peddlers of American merchandise. Quite the contrary. They have transcended such trite connotations and restored American icons to their pure semiotic state of messages of pleasure and freedom. Within this

4   As pointed out in a piece on U.S. pop culture in Europe, by Elizabeth Neuffer, in the *Boston Sunday Globe*, 9 October 1994.

global youth culture, the icons youngsters carry are like the symbol of the fish that early Christians drew in the sand as a code of recognition. They are the members of a new International, geared to a postmodern world of consumerism rather than an early modern world centered on values of production.

There are many ironies here. What is often held against the emerging international mass, or pop culture, is precisely its international, if not cosmopolitan, character. Clearly, this is a case of double standards. At the level of high culture, most clearly in its modernist phase, there has always been the dream of transcending the local, the provincial, the national, or, in social terms, to transgress the narrow bounds of the bourgeois world and enter a realm that was nothing if not international: the transcendence lay in being truly "European," or "cosmopolitan." But clearly what is good at the level of high culture is seen as a threat when a similar process of internationalization occurs at the level of mass culture. Then, all of a sudden, the defense is not in terms of high versus low, as one might have expected, but in terms of national cultures and national identities imperiled by an emerging international mass culture. There is a further irony in this construction of the conflict, contrasting an emerging global culture seen as homogenizing to national cultures seen as havens of cultural diversity. In the real world, of course, things are different. There may be a hierarchy of taste cultures, yet it is not a matter of higher taste cultures being the more national in orientation. It seems to be the case that this hierarchy of taste cultures is itself transnational, that indeed there are international audiences who at the high end all appreciate Beethoven and Bartok, or at the low end all fancy Madonna or Prince. Yet in a replay of much older elitist tirades against low culture, advocates of high art see only endless diversity where their own taste is concerned, and sheer vulgar homogeneity at the level of mass culture. They have no sense of the variety of tastes and styles, of endless change and renewal in mass culture, simply because it all occurs far beyond their ken.

Allow me a final observation. From the point of view of American mass culture traveling abroad, in many cases the exploration

of cultural frontiers is taken to more radical lengths than anything one might see in America. Whereas sexual joy and freedom
are merely hinted at in American commercials, where Coca-Cola
at best holds the promise of more intimate intercourse in its vignettes of rapturous boys and girls on the beach, in boats, floating down rivers, European posters and TV commercials often are
more explicit. There is an erotic Italian wallposter of a macho
guy, bare-chested, with a scantily clad, sexually aroused young
woman crouched between his legs. She wears a crown reminiscent of the Statue of Liberty. There is also an American flag. The
commercial is for the one piece of clothing on the man's body, his
pair of blue jeans. Similarly, in the Netherlands, in a poster and
TV campaign sponsored by the government, inviting (in small
print) people to become organ donors and to wear a donor codi-
cil, we see a young couple making love, both naked, she sitting
on his lap, curving backward in rapture. The text, in large print,
reads: "Give your heart a new lease on life." Pasted across the
country, on railway platforms, on bus stops, the poster must have
made visiting Americans bashfully turn their heads away. To
them the campaign would not appear as the outcome of a process
of Americanization taken a few daring steps further. Nor for that
matter would another poster campaign, again sponsored by the
Dutch government, on behalf of safe sex. Graphically, for everyone to see, couples are shown, taking showers or engaged in similar forms of foreplay. Shocking stuff indeed, and that is not all.
The posters also expose, if they do not cross, another frontier: in
addition to hetero couples, they also display gay couples.

Admittedly, these poster campaigns no longer convey commercial messages, although in fact the Dutch government, in order to
get its messages across, has adopted advertising techniques and in
fact uses advertising billboards, rented, one assumes, at the going
market rate. In a sense we have come full circle. Where the
Hoover Company advertisement drew on republican language to
claim the freedom of the advertiser, we now see advertising space
being reclaimed for statements *pro bono publico*. If democracy is
a marketplace, it has become inseparable from the economic
market. It is in fact one indivisible and noisy place with cries and

calls vying for the public's attention, echoing back and forth. The perfect illustration of this was pasted all across the Netherlands. A huge poster advertised Levi's 508, yet playfully drew on American political language for its commercial message. What viewers saw was the lower part of a half-nude male torso, covered from the waist down by a pair of jeans. Playing on the classic version of the Four Freedoms the poster rephrased them as follows: freedom of expression, freedom of thought, freedom of choice, and – Levi's 508 – freedom of movement. The third freedom, as we have seen, already makes the transition from the political to the commercial; the fourth, political though it may sound, is meant to convey the greater room of movement provided by the baggier cut of the 508. The picture illustrated the point by showing the unmistakable bulge of a male member in full erection, casually touched by the hand of its owner. Clearly, the semiotics of American commercial strategies have been taken to lengths, so to speak, that are inconceivable in America. America may have been less embarrassed in exploring the continuities between the political and the commercial, Europe later on may have been more daring in its pursuit of happiness, graphically advertising it all across Europe's public space.[5]

For indeed, as European examples from the political and the economic market place serve to illustrate, the logic of a choice of freedom knows no bounds, once set free from controlling American standards of taste and decency. As is a lingua franca's wont, it moves in a realm of free creolization, where the controlling authority of a mother culture no longer holds. In this allegedly "American Century," then, Americanization should be seen as the story of an American cultural language traveling and of other people acquiring that language. What they actually said with it is a different story altogether.

---

5   In this connection it is of interest to point out that the campaign for Levi's 508 was produced by a Dutch advertising agency solely for the Dutch market. The video for the 501s that I referred to earlier was made by a British agency for the European market.

Index